THE ESSENTIAL ARTICLES SERIES

Bernard N. Schilling

General Editor

Essential Articles

for the study of John Donne's Poetry

Edited by **John R. Roberts**
University of Missouri
Columbia

Archon Books   Hamden, Connecticut   **1975**

Library of Congress Cataloging in Publication Data
Main entry under title:

Essential articles for the study of John Donne's
    poetry.

    (The Essential article series)
    Bibliography: p.
    1. Donne, John, 1572-1631—Criticism and interpretation—Addresses, essays,
lectures. I. Roberts, John Richard.
PR2248.E8   821'.3   75-20059
ISBN 0-208-01447-0

First published 1975 as an Archon Book, an imprint of The Shoe String Press, Inc.
Hamden, Connecticut 06514

Printed in the United States of America

CONTENTS

IV. PROSODY AND RHETORICAL TRADITION

V. LOVE POETRY

CONTENTS

VI. RELIGIOUS POETRY

VII. THE ANNIVERSARIES

VIII. MISCELLANEOUS POEMS

FOREWORD

Immense resources are now available for literary study in England and America. The contributions to scholarship and criticism are so numerous and often so valuable that the student preparing himself for a career in literary teaching and study may be embarrassed, not to say overwhelmed. Yet from this mass of commentary certain titles have emerged which seem to compel attention. If one offers a seminar in one of the standard areas or periods of English literature, the syllabus will show year after year some items which cannot be omitted, some pieces every serious student should know. And with each new offering of the course, one must face the task of compiling a list of these selections for the seminar's reserve shelf, of searching out and culling the library's holdings, and reserving space for the twenty or thirty or forty volumes the list may demand. As if this were not enough, one must also attempt to repair or replace the volumes whose popularity has had the unfortunate side effects of frequent circulation and the concomitant wear, abuse, and general deterioration.

We propose an alternative to this procedure. We propose to select from the many learned journals, scholarly studies, and critical books the best selections available, the selections which consistently reappear on graduate seminar shelves and on undergraduate honors program reading lists. Let us choose from those articles which time has sanctioned, those too from the best of more recent performances, and let us draw them into a single volume of convenient size. This offers a clear gain in simplicity and usefulness. The articles chosen make up a body of knowledge that cannot fail to be valuable, and they act as models of the kind of contributions to learning which we are training our students to make themselves. And if we can have at hand a concentration of such articles for each of the standard areas, and several individual authors, we may conduct the study of these subjects with greater confidence, knowing more fully the extent and kind of reading we can take for granted. And, while we benefit our classes and students, we can also allow the library to keep the original editions of the articles on its shelves and so fulfill its proper and usual function.

The preceding paragraphs, written some 15 years ago, are still valid. We have reason to believe that our series has fulfilled its declared purposes: that the volumes have been useful to teachers, librarians and graduate students, that they have made a contribution to professional literary study.

From the beginning it was our aim to provide materials at a reasonable cost so that all those interested could afford to purchase them. Many factors including increased costs of permissions (for which special funds must often be secured) and the recent inflationary spiral, have required increased prices. However the editors and publishers have continued to make every effort to keep costs at a minimum.

We hope this collection of essays will become truly "essential" for the study of Donne's poetic achievement.

Rochester, N.Y.
June 17, 1975   B.N.S.

PREFACE

During the past three centuries various critics have announced John Donne's demise as a poet. In his own day, Ben Jonson predicted "that Done for not being understood would perish" (*Conversations with Drummond*). In 1912, the date of the publication of H. J. C. Grierson's monumental two-volume edition of Donne's poetry, Edward Bliss Reed wrote: "Today Donne's poems are never imitated; they are not even widely read, for though he has his circle of devoted admirers, their number is small" (*Elizabethan Lyrical Poetry from Its Origins to the Present Time* [New Haven: Yale University Press; London: Humphrey Milford and Oxford University Press], p. 233). As late as 1917, George Jackson dismissed Donne by saying: "It must be freely admitted that neither as poet, preacher, nor letter-writer is Donne ever likely to gain the suffrage of more than the few" (*Expository Times*, 28: 216-20). In 1931, the tercentenary anniversary of Donne's death, T. S. Eliot announced, in what then seemed like a prophetic voice, that "Donne's poetry is a concern of the present and the recent past, rather than of the future" ("Donne in Our Time," in *A Garland for John Donne 1631-1931*, ed. Theodore Spencer [Cambridge, Mass.: Harvard University Press], p. 5). Both Lloyd E. Berry's *A Bibliography of Studies in Metaphysical Poetry 1939-1960* (Madison: University of Wisconsin Press, 1964) and my own *John Donne: An Annotated Bibliography of Modern Criticism, 1912-1967* (Columbia: University of Missouri Press, 1973) prove that Eliot and the others were rather seriously mistaken in their predictions. Since 1931, more than one thousand books and articles on Donne have been published, and the most recent *PMLA Bibliography* (1972) lists for one year alone more than forty entries. Although some of the studies written during the past half century are clearly minor efforts, most of them suggest that Donne engaged and continues to engage some of the best minds of the scholarly world. They confirm perhaps Donne's own punning comment, "When thou hast done, thou hast not done, / For, I have more." Not only has Donne continued to intrigue the scholars and critics, but, unlike many of his contemporaries, Donne has also remained interesting and vital to many poets of the twentieth century. Today nearly all serious students of English literature recognize that Donne occupies a permanent and central position in the development of English poetry.

Since there is such a plethora of good criticism on Donne, it was clear to me from the start of this project that certain severe, even arbitrary limitations had to be imposed on my selections. First of all, in a volume of this size it seemed impractical to include criticism on both Donne's poetry and prose. I decided, therefore, to include articles on Donne's poetry only or on his thought as related to the poetry. Although some of the most distinguished criticism of this century concerns itself with the prose, Donne the poet has always received more critical attention and has had more influence than Donne the prose stylist. Also much of the significant criticism of the prose is contained in book-length studies, and many of the better essays have been incorporated into book-length studies.

The editors of this series suggested that only articles in learned journals or complete essays in volumes by various hands be included; thus I have excluded possible selections from book-length studies. Since one of the primary purposes of this series is to make available critical essays that are not readily accessible to many students, I have also excluded all articles which have been reprinted in modern collections of Donne criticism (see Selective Bibliography, essays readily available in paperback books, and articles contained in books which have been frequently reprinted. The recently published collections of original essays edited by A. J. Smith (*John Donne: Essays in Celebration*, 1972) and by Peter A. Fiore (*Just So Much Honor: Essays Commemorating the Four-Hundredth Anniversary of the Birth of John Donne*, 1972) contain many worthwhile and critically important essays on Donne's poetry, but since both are readily available, I have excluded all items from them. I have, then, tried to select articles beyond those familiar pieces that the reader usually expects to find in a collection of Donne criticism. T. S. Eliot, one of the critics most responsible for Donne's enormous popularity in this century, is not represented; nor are H. J. C. Grierson, C. S. Lewis, Joan Bennett, J. B. Leishman and others closely associated with the modern Donne revival.

In order to be completely accurate, I should have liked to entitle this volume "additional important articles" on Donne's poetry, for this volume is intended to complement rather than supplant the now almost established canon of Donne criticism. From the remaining abundance of riches, I have chosen thirty-nine items (reprinted here without editorial changes) which seem to me to be both critically interesting in and for themselves and which also reflect in some way several of the major concerns of modern Donne scholarship. For example, I have included several essays which effectively challenge the concept of the dissociation of sensibility, a concept, first presented by T. S. Eliot in 1921, that for several decades not only dominated and shaped critical evaluation of Donne and the seventeenth century, but was also used as a touchstone for judging much modern poetry. The attempts of some of the so-called "new critics" to claim Donne as a precursor of modern poetry, as a man born out of his time, is challenged by such a selection as Merritt Y. Hughes's "Kidnapping Donne." Likewise, the items in Part III, on Donne's uses of tradition, show that Donne's poetry was fully informed by the thinking and sensibility of his own day, that Donne was, after all, a Renaissance poet, in spite of many earlier attempts to view him in some way as a maverick genius. In Part IV, I have included several articles that deal with Donne's uses of rhetoric, one of the major concerns of modern criticism. A. J. Smith's sometimes overlooked article on Ramism, for instance

puts into proper perspective some of the exaggerated claims made about
Donne's connection with that particular school of rhetoric and logic. Since
most of Louis L. Martz's work has been extensively reprinted, the short
item by him is intended simply to whet the reader's curiosity about the so-
called "meditative tradition" in seventeenth-century verse so that he will be
encouraged to read Martz's book-length study, *The Poetry of Meditation:
A Study in English Religious Literature of the Seventeenth Century* (see
Selective Bibliography). In like manner, Donald Guss's article on Donne's
uses of Petrarchism is included so that the reader will want to follow up by
reading *John Donne, Petrarchist: Italianate Conceits and Love Theory in
the Songs and Sonets* (see Selective Bibliography).

In selecting the articles that should or could be included in a volume such
as this, no two editors could possibly agree on all points. One is confronted
with so much good criticism that all limitations or guidelines in the end seem
curiously subjective or perhaps even quixotic. My overriding purpose has
been to provide students of Donne with the opportunity of reading more of
the excellent criticism on Donne that will complement the more familiar
items contained in the collections of Gardner, Kermode, Clements, Keast,
and others.

I wish to thank the Research Council of the University of Missouri for
a generous grant which made this book possible. I should also like to thank
Professors A. J. Smith, Laurence Stapleton, Barbara Lewalski, and David
Novarr, each of whom gave me useful suggestions and much encouragement.
And finally, I want to thank Douglas Collins, my research assistant, whose
expert help and dedication are so very much appreciated.

John R. Roberts
Columbia, Missouri

I. DONNE'S REPUTATION

THE CRITICAL IMPORTANCE OF THE REVIVED INTEREST IN SEVENTEENTH-CENTURY METAPHYSICAL POETRY

Mario Praz

The bewilderment of the public in face of *avant-garde* literature, art, and music of today is a fact of common experience. An Italian art critic, Matteo Marangoni in 1933[1] went so far as to say, apropos of painting, that 'contemporary art has so succeeded in breaking off from tradition, that the visual categories so far used for the art of the past do not seem to apply any longer; perhaps it will be necessary to find new ones'. Indeed anyone who happens to cross from the rooms of ancient painting to those of modern and contemporary art in a gallery like that of Basel, might actually imagine himself transferred to another planet, where a different visual language is employed; that same cleavage which once would have been noticed between rooms of Western and Eastern art in a museum, may strike us nowadays within the compass of the European development. Ortega y Gasset, in *The Dehumanization of Art* (Princeton University Press, 1948), maintains that modern art—he is thinking chiefly of painting—is one of the periodical recurrences of iconoclasm, of hatred for the forms of living bodies, of return to geometry, such as took place for instance in very ancient times, when the snake and the sun became stylized in the meander and the swastika: modern art is therefore in opposition to the Greek tradition, which can be said to have dominated Europe until recently with its deep love for living forms. It would of course be absurd to maintain that all connexions with the past have been broken off; but it has become increasingly difficult to establish such connexions. Who, without being previously warned, would ever think of Poussin in front of Cézanne's canvases? Do we not find it rather surprising to hear of Cézanne's avowed intention 'vivifier Poussin au contact de la nature'? Who would think of Homer's *Odyssey* while reading Joyce's *Ulysses*? Who would notice a likeness between Vico's idea of history and *Finnegan's Wake*? Still, in the author's intentions, *Ulysses* was meant to be a modern unheroic transposition of the *Odyssey*, a sort of *ricorso* (in Vico's sense of the word) of the Homeric poem as it has been interpreted by Victor Bérard in his famous work *Les Phéniciens et l'Odyssée*.

Reprinted from *English Studies Today*, ed. C. L. Wrenn and G. Bullough, pp. 158–66. London: Oxford University Press, 1951. By permission of the author and The Clarendon Press, Oxford.

A poem like Eliot's *Waste Land*, with its complex cultural allusions, within
a frame which does not seem to be linked up with any tradition, is perhaps
the best instance of a fact now of everyday occurrence in modern art,
namely that the relation of the artist to the past is no longer based on imitation but rather on allusion, it has a polemical character, it is filtered
through the medium of irony. Let us again quote Ortega y Gasset:

> The new art ridicules art itself. Art has never shown more clearly its
> magic gift than in thus flouting itself. Thanks to this suicidal gesture art
> continues to be art, its self-negation miraculously bringing about its
> preservation and triumph. I doubt much whether any young person of
> our time can be impressed by a poem, a painting, or a piece of music
> that is not flavoured with a dash of irony.

Ortega y Gasset goes on to say that this is no new phenomenon; something
like it took place with the German romantics, under the leadership of the
two brothers Schlegel who pronounced irony the foremost aesthetic category.

> Art [he writes] has no right to exist if, content to reproduce reality, it
> uselessly duplicates it. Its mission is to conjure up imaginary worlds.
> That can be done only if the artist repudiates reality and by this act
> places himself above it. Being an artist means ceasing to take seriously
> that very serious person we are when we are not an artist. This inevitable
> dash of irony, it is true, imparts to modern art a monotony which must
> exasperate patience herself. But be that as it may, the contradiction be-
> tween surfeit and enthusiasm now appears resolved. The first is aroused
> by art as a serious affair, the second is felt for art that triumphs as a
> farce, laughing off everything—itself included—much as in a system of
> mirrors which indefinitely reflect one another no shape is ultimate, all
> are eventually ridiculed and revealed as pure images.

For romantic irony we may quote the brothers Schlegel; the irony of
modern poetry (limiting our remarks now to this) has also a critical precedent. For, as is well known, critical thought, guiding taste, is the habitual
forerunner of creative activity. I have chosen poetry as the subject of this
paper because, of literary genres, poetry is the one which displays a more
decided cleavage with the past. This term, literary genres, may sound out
of date after Benedetto Croce's devastating criticism of it, but the fact that
nevertheless genres continue to exist, springing up in different, but still
recognizable shapes, is witnessed to by the different development of poetry
and prose in contemporary literature. Obscure prose, notwithstanding
Joyce's model, is rare, not to say non-existent, in modern fiction; whereas
any poetry worth the name is abstruse, written in what a candid reader may
take as a conventional language, a cipher. There are not only commercial
reasons for clarity in prose composition. It is indeed a well-known fact
that the volumes of even the best contemporary English poets sell very badly,
and that publishers continue to print them only for reasons of prestige and
enlightened patronage; but no publisher is likely to print novels which fail

to appeal to a comparatively wide public. But if novelists have not all and sundry followed suit after Joyce, in the same way as all poets, more or less, have learned from the example of T. S. Eliot, the chief reason is not commercial, but rather one of a general character, namely that poetry by tradition has always been a form of divine madness, bearing to madness the same relation as sleep bears to death, so that rare and abstruse language seems to be demanded by the very condition of singing; a commonplace passage, a snatch of *sermo pedestris*, may indeed occur in poetry with a view to deliberate artistic effect (as happens with Eliot and his followers), but is not the natural way of expression, as it is in the novel. But, beside this general reason, there is a special one which has suggested the theme of this paper, that is: a revolution of taste, a breaking off from the nineteenth-century tradition, has taken place in poetry first of all, because modern poetry is closely linked up with the rediscovery of the metaphysical poetry of the seventeenth century, and with the poetic theory which underlies that output of verse. It is well known how Eliot rediscovered John Donne, whose poems had been critically edited in 1912 by Grierson; Eliot had been predisposed and almost put in the way of this discovery by his admiration and imitation of Laforgue. We may note that Laforgue's irony, which distinguishes him from the other *poètes maudits*, descends directly from Heine's irony: thus, in a roundabout way, the irony of the modern poets is also linked up with the romantic tradition.

Of course Donne and his school had not been altogether blotted out from the memory of later generations, but if we take up, for instance Palgrave's *Golden Treasury,* we shall vainly seek there for Marvell's masterpiece, *To his Coy Mistress.* Anthologies codify current taste. *To his Coy Mistress,* one of the greatest poems of the seventeenth century, had been excluded in consequence of the rationalist reaction against metaphysical poetry which set in at the end of the century. Dryden's condemnation of Donne and his school in his *Essay on Satyre* is too well known to bear quotation; behind a poet there is usually, as I have said, a critic and a philosopher: behind Dryden there is Hobbes. The modern interpretaiton of Hobbes's influence could be no better summed up than in the words of John Crowe Ransom:

> What Bacon with is disparagement of poetry had begun, in the cause of science and protestantism, Hobbes completed. . . . The name [of Hobbes] stood for common sense and naturalism, and the monopoly of the scientific spirit over the mind.

—and in the remarks which Cleanth Brooks has added to this quotation.[2]

The weakening of the metaphor, the development of a specifically 'poetic' subject matter and diction, the emphasis on simplicity and clarity, the simplification of the poet's attitude, the segregation of the witty and the ironical from the serious, the stricter separation of the various genres—all these items testify to the monopoly of the scientific spirit. This process of clarification involved the *exclusion* of certain elements from poetry—the prosaic, the unrefined, and the obscure. The imagination was weakened from a 'magic and synthetic' power to Hobbes's conception of it as the file-clerk of the memory.

The metaphysicals—and here lies Eliot's critical contribution, stimulated by suggestions from such disparate personalities as Ezra Pound and Sir Herbert Grierson—had suceeded in giving a peculiar blend of passion and thought, of feeling and intellect: in a word 'sensuous apprehension of thought'. This happy formula is the keystone not only of the modern interpretation of the metaphysicals, but also of contemporary poetic theory. How far does it actually fit seventeenth-century poetry? Miss Rosemond Tuve[3] has warned us against misreading earlier imagery, and has insisted on the necessity of interpreting the poets in the light of the poetic theory of their age; she would have us close our Eliot and open our Puttenham:

> Would Donne, or any Metaphysical poet, have understood T. S. Eliot's attribution to him of a 'direct sensuous apprehension of thought', or have recognized himself in that intellectual poet who 'feels his thought as immediately as the odour of a rose'?

And still apropos of the formula 'direct sensuous apprehension of thought':

> This famous phrase of Eliot's has come to be used by modern criticism almost as an explanation of the peculiar nature of Metaphysical poetry. I think that any Elizabethan or Jacobean would have found it obscure and psychologically untenable; their own orthodox explanations of the operation of metaphor and its variants illuminate Metaphysical tropes more simply and clearly.

And again:

> It is clear that 'varying' through metaphor would make for 'delightful' images not primarily sensuous in function, though plentiful in the mention of particulars. Donne's style, for example, highly tropical rather than schematic, is jammed with concretions, but no one could call it sensuous. Such a fact would cause nobody in the Renaissance any embarrassment, for that era did not share the modern antirational bias which has led us to seize with relief upon phrases like Eliot's 'sensuous apprehension of thought'.

The importance of historical correctness needs no emphasizing, but the vitality of poetry depends in a large measure on what later generations see in it: the two elements must concur in a critical estimate. For the present discussion, however, what interests us is not so much how far Donne and his contemporaries were aware of their own type of inspiration, but what we feel when surveying their poetry from the point of view of our present taste. Even if Eliot's interpretation should prove biased from a strictly historical standpoint (and William Empson has justly remarked that Miss Tuve's strictures do not dispose of it)[4], we have to take that interpretation as a positive starting point in order to appreciate the effect of the rediscovery of the metaphysicals on modern poetry.

Accepting therefore the modern interpretation of Hobbes's influence, we see how 'the tendency towards order and simplification, taken over into a sphere in which it was inappropriate, succeeded in destroying metaphysical poetry'.[5] Once poetry had been reduced to poetic diction and to certain categories of poetic themes, like a water-tight compartment, a poem like *To his Coy Mistress,* which blended wit and paradox with passion, would as a matter of course be judged a hybrid and fail to satisfy the critical test. Dr. Johnson's strictures on the metaphysicals have been frequently quoted: 'Their attempts were always analytic; they broke every image into fragments; and could no more represent, by their slender conceits and laboured particularities, the prospects of nature or the scenes of life, than he who dissects a sun-beam with a prism, can exhibit the wide effulgence of a summer noon.' Sainte-Beuve did not express himself in a very different way when bent on advising Baudelaire: 'Vous vous défiez trop de la passion—de la passion naturelle. . . . Vous accordez trop à l'esprit, à la combinaison. Laissez-vous faire, ne craignez pas de sentir comme les autres, n'ayez jamais peur d'être commun. . . .' And Croce's criticism of Dante, his distinction between the elements of the *Divine Comedy,* his separation of the theological framework (non-poetry) from the actual poetry, are inspired by similar criteria to those of Dr. Johnson and Sainte-Beuve. Now the moderns, with Eliot in the lead, have tried to react against this idea of poetry as a poetry of exclusion, they have attempted to revive the poetry of inclusion which belongs to metaphysical periods, of which, according to Eliot, there are three in the history of European poetry: a medieval one, with Guinicelli, Cavalcanti, Dante (a field revealed to Eliot by Ezra Pound), a Baroque period, with Donne and his school, and a modern one with Baudelaire and Laforgue as its chief representatives. What has attracted the moderns to Donne is the sinuous, contrasted progress of his songs, one would almost say their *linea serpentinata,* to use a term introduced by the Cinquecento mannerists; their mixture of prosaic, refractory materials, that tangle of intellect and emotion which to the critical judgement of the eighteenth and nineteenth centuries appeared a clear sign of impure inspiration, has been interpreted by the moderns as a symptom of imaginative power: no longer non-poetry, but rather poetry inclusive of all reality. The discovery of the metaphysicals has been more than a literary fashion, has resulted not only in the adoption of certain images, in the cult of certain conceits and imaginative processes; it has rather amounted to the awareness of a similar disposition of the spirit, of the same perplexity in facing life, of the same ironical reaction.

It appears likely that poets in our civilization, as it exists at present, must be *difficult* [Eliot said in his essay on *The Metaphysical Poets*]. Our civilization comprehends great variety and complexity, and this variety and complexity, playing upon a refined sensibility, must produce various and complex results. The poet must become more and more comprehensive, more allusive, more indirect, in order to force, to dislocate if necessary, language into his meaning.

Besides there has intervened in many poets whose formation dates from around 1930 a political and social preoccupation, or rather anxiety, which was subtly analysed by Virginia Woolf in her essay on *The Leaning Tower*. Donne's was an age of anxiety, an anxiety before the spectacle of the collapse of the old medieval world under the blows of the new science; our modern epoch is also an age of anxiety, which has found its affinities in the seventeenth century. Auden, in *The Age of Anxiety* (1947), has chosen an appropriate title to define a climate common to all the poets for whose sense of insecurity, and dizziness, Virginia Woolf had found the image of the leaning tower. The feeling of frustration which is common to much intellectual English poetry of today finds a counterpart in Donne's bewilderment at the new discoveries in astronomy (Copernicus, Ticho, Galileo) and philosophy (Bacon). In the *Anniversaries* Donne surveys that medieval conception of the world which he has learned from the books so that it has become part and parcel of his thought, and he is dismayed at perceiving how all its supports have been shaken by the recent revolution in the scientific field. The perplexity of the seventeenth-century thinker who sees the very foundations of his thought undermined, and the perplexity of the twentieth-century poet who foresees 'another long day of servitude to wilful authority and blind accident', represent a link of sympathy much deeper than the mere revival of a fashion after a leap of centuries.

Irony, as it has been pointed out, is a customary attitude with modern poets. Their poetry of inclusion has brought about also the revaluation of another great poet in whom the romantics had seen the very opposite of the poetic disposition, Alexander Pope. The utmost the romantics were willing to grant him was an 'artificial' inspiration, inferior to the 'natural' inspiration of the true poets. The objection was substantially the same as the one made to metaphysical poetry by Dryden and Johnson, with their rationalist standards. In the antithetical wit, in the allusions to persons and events of the narrow circle of his contemporaries, in such abiding features of Pope's verse, the romantic critics saw the antithesis of that solemn, nostalgic world, the more poetical as it was more vague, which their poets had sung, from Coleridge and Keats to Poe and Tennyson. Indeed the romantic revolution seems to us nowadays much less revolutionary, since, as it has been remarked by Cleanth Brooks,[6] in attacking the neo-classic conception of the poetic, they tended to offer new poetic objects rather than to discard altogether the conception of a special poetic material; and that is why many eighteenth-century features reappear today in Coleridge and Wordsworth, let alone the more obvious case of Byron, now that time has toned down and worn the specious glitter of their varnishing-day. It may at first sight seem incongruous that the revaluation of the metaphysicals should have had among its consequences also a revaluation of the chief poet of that Age of Reason which actually reacted against the metaphysicals. But Pope's poetry, like Donne's, shows also, though in a different way, the interpenetration of intellect and emotion. Whoever is capable of overcoming the prejudice that satire cannot be a subject of poetry, sees that warmth of feeling is not absent from Pope's great satirical poem, *The Dunciad.*

Another echo of Eliot's formula of 'sensuous thought' devised for the interpretation of metaphysical poetry, can be noticed in Herbert Read's appreciation of Wordsworth.[7]

> Wordsworth's poetry at its best [says Read] is philosophical poetry, and belongs to that rare species of poetry in which *thought is felt.* . . . If I were asked: how can thought be felt? I should reply: not in pure ecstatic contemplation of its own processes, but by being conceived in some analogy which blends it vicariously with the passions and volitions of our vital frame. . . . The abstractions are as it were vitalized by contact with phenomena: they are no sooner thought of than they suggest an object lesson. The objects in the object lesson are so real in Wordsworth's case that they have the force of direct sensational experience.

The formulas of sensuous thought, of the objective correlative, of the poetry of inclusion, which date from the redintegration of metaphysical poetry into the main English tradition, are found by Read applicable also to Wordsworth.

The revaluation of the metaphysicals has been an earthquake in the English Parnassus, reshaping the outline of its summit as if it were a volcano. Donne's influence had been stemmed by the Age of Reason, ignored by the romantics; yet not long ago Professor Merritt Y. Hughes, wrote:[8] 'In the history of English literature the only forces comparable to it [Donne's power over modern poetry] are Shakespeare's influence, or Milton's in the eighteenth century.' An age capable of enjoying Donne was not calculated to be moved by the traditional music of Milton; T. S. Eliot voiced the new point of view on Milton in a famous essay whose assertions he has qualified since; an age trained to appreciate the intelligent poetry of Donne and Pope has found fault, through Eliot, with the pseudo-philosophical background of Shelley, and has defined Tennyson, in the words of W. H. Auden, 'the stupidest' of all the English poets: 'there was little about melancholia that he didn't know; there was little else that he did'. Of the nineteenth-century English poets the moderns have exalted the one who, born in an uncongenial period, has received only a posthumous recognition, Gerard Manley Hopkins. Hopkins, says Cecil Day Lewis,[9] has produced an effect opposite to that of Wordsworth: while Wordsworth tried to bring the language of poetry closer to everyday language, Hopkins, in his aversion to the commonplace, has done everything to remove the language of poetry as far as possible from ordinary speech. Language becomes with him incantation again; his prosody, on the other hand, has swung to the other extreme, for it is based on the rhythm of common speech (sprung rhythm). Such characteristics do we find, to a greater or lesser degree, in most contemporary poets. To quote again from Lewis: 'We find in post-war poetry [i.e. in the poetry written after the

First World War] a tendency to combine these two results, to use common speech rhythms together with a mixture of simplified, superficially unpoetical language and highly poetical incantatory language.' These two languages, admirably blended in Hopkins as they had been in Donne, are used side by side and often contrasted in the poems of Pound, Eliot, and his followers, in order to produce effects of dissonance and surprise apt to convey the confusion of the modern world.

Thus the revaluation of Donne has not only resulted in a change of perspective in literary criticism, but has also furthered the reaction against the critical standards and the poetic theory of romanticism: Donne, we may say without fear of exaggeration, has had in the last thirty years a catalytic function.

JOHNSON'S CRITICISM OF THE METAPHYSICAL POETS[1]

William R. Keast

In perhaps none of Johnson's critical writings so much as in the *Life of Cowley* is the modern reader likely to feel that mingling of critical sagacity and wrongheadedness that has always been the burden and despair of Johnson's commentators. It is widely acknowledged that modern criticism of the seventeenth-century poets is heavily indebted to his analysis of metaphysical wit—even if modern critics spurn the inferences which Johnson draws from that analysis; but it is even more widely felt that in dealing with these writers, Johnson's sensitivity failed to keep pace with his analytic powers—that only a man disabled by nature, tradition, or doctrine could be as unperceptive as Johnson seems to be of the beauties of Donne—if not of those of Cowley and Cleveland.

While the *Life of Cowley* has come to be a symbol of the imperviousness of Johnson—and with him, of the eighteenth century—to a state of feeling, a condition of language, and a mode of writing which we now, for whatever reasons, tend to value, certain others of his works, signs of a like incapacity to earlier generations, no longer attract much interest. I do not imagine that a proposal to base this afternoon's discussion on the *Life of Milton* or the *Life of Gray* would have met with much enthusiasm. Yet it was once Johnson's supposed sins against taste and judgment in these, rather than in the *Life of Cowley*, that made his critics storm and his defenders seek cover. The history of Johnson's reputation has yet to be written, but when it is, it will do more than progressively reveal the thought and character of its subject; it will be a miniature history of literary taste and critical theory, recording the vicissitudes of poetic reputations and the fluctuations of critical doctrine and method. Lacking such a history, we may ask ourselves how far our disappointment with Johnson's treatment of the metaphysical poets reflects genuine deficiencies in Johnson and how far it reflects merely our present conviction that Donne is a greater poet than, say, Gray or even Milton, and our preference for a critical theory that specializes in detailed accounts of metaphorical structure to one that emphasizes the general conditions of literary pleasure.

Our choice of the *Life of Cowley* as the basis for a discussion of Johnson as critic thus implies a judgment, which may not be free of the influence of

Reprinted from *English Literary History*, 17 (1950), 59-70, by permission of the author and The Johns Hopkins University Press.

11

prejudice and fashion: Johnson thought it the best of the *Lives*; we do not. Our selection of the *Life of Cowley* also seems to express a hope—a hope that we shall be able to give a comprehensive account of Johnson's failure here, a full assemblage of the causes that led him to pronounce as he did upon the metaphysical poets. If we cherish such a hope, I think we are bound to be disappointed—certainly what I am about to say, which is not at all so ambitious as this, will be disappointing. Of the multitude of causes which combine to produce a complex literary judgment, many are buried beyond recovery and many more are but hazardously recoverable, through speculation and conjecture. We can be sure that taste, temperament, education, admired models, ear, habit of mind, and linguistic experience—to mention only a few of the more obvious influences—must have helped to shape Johnson's preferences, as they do our own. But how much? and in what ways? We may speculate about two modes in the use of language, the Augustan and the dramatic-Shakespearean, and about the inhibiting effect of the former on Johnson; but this will not really help us, since Johnson admires and condemns works composed in both these modes, if indeed they are genuine modes. We may conjecture about the temper of the age and its reflection in Johnson's criticism, but this will get us into as many difficulties as it delivers us from, since, among other things, our knowledge of the temper of the age is derived in no small measure from our knowledge of what Johnson wrote.

These and similar questions I shall avoid, although I hope you will not take my silence on them to imply that I do not think them important, or at least entertaining. I should like instead to deal with the more explicit causes of Johnson's judgment on the metaphysical poets: namely, with the assumptions about criticism and poetry which underlie his arguments and control his discussion. Even in so limited an attempt there is a crucial difficulty. Johnson is notably not a literary theorist, by which I mean not that he has no theory of literature but that he never sets it all forth in theoretical fashion in one place. With a few minor exceptions, his criticism is entirely practical— the statement and adjudication of particular cases. His theoretical views are introduced only when needed, and only in such quantity as is needed, for the problem immediately in hand; his general views must often be inferred from the particular lines of argument he devises, or expanded from all too brief assertions. The necessity imposed by this feature of his criticism is that of being careful, as we consider one of his essays, that we do not take the theory which seems to underlie it for the whole of his critical position, or suppose, on the other hand, since the subjects of different essays differ as widely as Cowley from Collins, that the theory fluctuates at random from one to another, or that the assumptions used in the criticism of one species of literary work are uniquely adapted to it and not transferable to works of other kinds. We must read the *Life of Cowley* in relation to the *Rambler*, the *Preface to Shakespeare* and the other *Lives*. Despite this difficulty, however, by centering our attention for a moment on the rational bases for Johnson's judgments in the *Life of Cowley,* and on their relation to the

larger body of his criticism, we may be able to recover some of the force
which he thought his arguments carried, and perhaps to raise some questions
of general interest for literary study.

Johnson's examination of the metaphysical poets, like his criticism in
general, is marked by the prominence in it of questions which, if they have
not entirely disappeared from modern critical discussion, have been relegated
to a position so subordinate as to amount effectively to disappearance. At
the same time Johnson fails to give any serious or extended consideration to
those questions with which modern critics have been chiefly occupied. Johnson is not much interested in the development and cross-fertilization of metaphor, the structural employment of ambiguity, or the formative use of irony
and paradox. His primary concern is with the pleasure which literature is
capable of producing. He wants to know chiefly whether poems interest
readers, engage their attention, and move them emotionally. The brilliance
of his discussion of wit is widely acknowledged, but analysis and discrimination of literary devices are not for him the central business of criticism.
Criticism is above all a matter of judgment and evaluation. The true task of
the critic is to determine the value of a work on the basis of its permanent
power to please and to fix the position in the scale of human ability which
the powers of the author merit.

Judgment and taste, Johnson is well aware, are fallible, and the critic
deals with an object whose essential character derives from the imagination,
a faculty that is limitless in its potentialities for discovery and combination.[2]
If he is to render a valid judgment, the critic cannot depend merely on the
critical reputation or popular success of a work. He must discover the causes
which underlie literary effects.[3] But an adequate explanation of these cannot be found in the rules of art or the examples of past performance: "the
performances of art," he says, are "too inconstant and uncertain, to be reduced to any determinate idea"; "there is therefore scarcely any species of
writing, of which we can tell what is its essence, and what are its constitu-
ents; every new genius produces some innovation, which, when invented and
approved, subverts the rule which the practice of foregoing authors had
established."[4] Johnson's fundamental conviction—to which his spirited defense of Shakespeare's violation of the unities most eloquently testifies—
is that no valid poetic criteria can be derived from a consideration of linguistic
or technical devices, apart from their function in achieving poetic effects. The
only secure basis for critical judgment is not art but nature, for art proceeds
from natural powers, uses natural materials, represents natural objects, and
appeals to natural desires—and nature, unlike art, is everywhere the same.

Since literature is ordered to the reader—and the prominence of the
common reader, not the élite, is a notable feature of Johnson's criticism—
it is these natural desires to which the poet must write and from which the
critic must reason in estimating the poet's success. Johnson does not think
of the reader as one who submits himself to a work in order, after patient
_____ of its verbal structure, to gain understanding; the end of poetry is not
_____ perfection of an object, nor is the end of criticism the disclosure of its

inner nature. The work of the poet and the labor of the critic are subordinated to the natural appetite for pleasure from which literature derives its distinctive features and in the satisfaction of which it has its true value. And he insists that the conditions of literary pleasure are twofold. The mind, he says, "can be captivated only by recollection or by curiosity; by reviving natural sentiments or impressing new appearances of things."[5] All readers demand, if they are to be attracted and pleased, two qualities in literary works: truth—the ideas that slumber in the heart and the sentiments to which every bosom returns an echo—and novelty—the pleasures of sudden wonder. The two most engaging powers of an author satisfy these demands together—making new things familiar and familiar things new. As one or the other of these qualities is emphasized, the two great poetical effects on which Johnson rests his assessment of the metaphysical poets are produced. The pathetic, the movement of the passions, arises fundamentally from the representation of what is uniform in human experience; the sublime, the stimulation of wonder and admiration, arises basically from the presentation of what is new and hence striking. Johnson does not introduce this division of poetic effects into his discussion of the seventeenth-century poets because they seem to him the effects at which these poets were probably aiming; rather they are for him an exhaustive enumeration of poetic effects—the only fundamental ways in which poets can please—and if the metaphysicals are to be regarded as poets, their success in achieving one or the other of these effects must be the basis of judgment.

Both truth and novelty have their root in human passion. Our emotions are engaged only when we are struck by something new or out of the ordinary —"The pleasures of the mind," he says, "imply something sudden and unexpected";[6] "nothing can strongly strike or affect us, but what is rare or sudden."[7] And equally our feelings are moved only by what is recognizably human, like ourselves: "we are affected only as we believe"; "What I cannot for a moment believe, I cannot for a moment behold with interest or anxiety."[8] The poet who—unlike the metaphysicals—traces intellectual pleasure to its natural sources in the mind of man, discovers that the passions are so constituted in nature as to permit him to achieve both truth and novelty. The passions are on the one hand few, permanent, and regular in their operations: "their influence is uniform, and their effects nearly the same in every human breast: a man loves and hates, desires and avoids, exactly like his neighbour; resentment and ambition, avarice and indolence, discover themselves by the same symptoms in minds distant a thousand years from one another."[9] But the passions, if few, are susceptible of infinite modification: the careful observer sees that the regularity and varied complexity of human life can be brought together, as Johnson joins them in one of the scientific metaphors of which he was so fond: "It has been discovered by Sir Isaac Newton," he says,

> that the distinct and primogenial colours are seen only seven; but every
> eye can witness, that from various mixtures, in various proportions, in-

finite diversifications, of tints may be produced. In like manner, the passions of the mind, which put the world in motion, . . . from whence arise all the pleasures and pains that we see and hear of, if we analyze the mind of man, are very few; but those few agitated and combined, as external causes shall happen to operate, and modified by prevailing opinions and accidental caprices, make such frequent alterations on the surface of life, that the show, while we are busied in delineating it, vanishes from the view, and a new set of objects succeed, doomed to the same shortness of duration with the former . . . the mutability of mankind will always furnish writers with new images.[10]

Johnson's criticism of the metaphysical poets is based on these premises—these poets do not move the passions, because they deal with the remoter feelings and with peripheral situations; they do not evoke wonder, which is akin to surprise, because they are not content to rest in the presentation of striking juxtapositions but must pursue them to the last detail. Johnson develops these general views in the *Life of Cowley* with a high degree of sophistication. His analysis of wit, for example, is conducted with an analytic subtlety not always recognized. Johnson discriminates three meanings of wit, corresponding to the three sources from which poetic effects arise—the language of a poem, its thoughts, and the objects which it represents. The first gives Pope's definition of wit, the second yields the conception of wit as thoughts at once natural and new, and the third gives the famous conception of wit as *discordia concors*. The effect of each kind of wit depends on that which follows it, and the last—the *discordia concors*—is a definition not of metaphysical wit merely, but of all wit, valuable in general, the seventeenth-century poets having merely "*more* than enough," and yoking the "*most* heterogenous" ideas together "by *violence.*" And similarly the other premises Johnson uses to criticize the metaphysical poets are not limited in their applicability merely to writers marked by metaphysical wit. The same principles underlie his discussions of poets who are quite un-metaphysical. It is thus not a peculiarity of the metaphysical style that it led Cowley and Donne to miss the sublime by paying too much attention to details; Johnson criticizes Shakespeare's description of Dover Cliff in *King Lear* in precisely the same terms, and he finds Young's poem *The Last Day* languid and unaffecting because a succession of images divides and weakens the general conception.[11] And again, if the metaphysical poets miss the pathetic through their disregard of the uniformity of sentiment which enables us to conceive and excite the pains and pleasures of other minds, so too do many others, among them poets whose language at least has been thought to bring them within the range of Johnson's taste. Like Cowley's, the amorous effusions of Prior are not happy: dictated neither by nature nor by passion and having neither gallantry nor tenderness, they are the work of a man trying to be amorous by dint of study; *Hudibras* is a poem of inexhaustible wit, but most of its effect is now lost, for it is founded not on standing relations and general passions but on those modifications of life and peculiarities of practice which, being the progeny of error and perverseness, must perish with their parents.[12] If the common reader cannot feel the effects of metaphysical poems based on esoteric lore, neither can the reader of Pope's *Imitations of Horace* or West's *Imitations of Spenser*: "An imitation of Spenser is nothing to a reader, however acute, by whom Spenser has never been perused. . . . The noblest beauties of art are those of which the effect is co-extended with rational nature, or at least with the whole circle of polished life; what is less than this can be only pretty, the plaything of fashion and the amusement of a day."[13]

And so it is with the other items in Johnson's bill against the seventeenth-century poets—each rests on a premise that is brought into play many times elsewhere in Johnson's work, applied with the same result to works superficially very different from the poems of the metaphysicals. But if we cannot find anything peculiar to the metaphysicals in the grounds on which he criticizes them, neither can we arrive at Johnson's conception of poetic excellence by simply taking the contraries of their faults as poetic virtues. Johnson, it is true, seems occasionally to talk as if literary pleasure is to be achieved through the grandeur of generality or the uniform simplicity of primitve qualities; but bear in mind the practical orientation of his criticism that I mentioned earlier. Only so much theory emerges as Johnson needs to decide the case in hand; if he is dealing with a witty or allusive writer like Cowley or Butler, deficiencies can be adequately defined by emphasizing the lack of attention to general passions and large appearances evident in their work. But his criticism is filled with cases of the opposite sort, where the writer, aiming only at general truth, contents himself with the large appearance and the common passions. With these writers Johnson is no less severe, for they too fail to command interest or provide pleasure, and his criticism of them sounds often as if he were recommending a liberal dose of metaphysical subtlety and surprise.

Thus the plays of Nicholas Rowe seldom pierce the breast with pity or terror because they contain no deep search into nature, no accurate discrimination of kindred qualities or nice display of passion in its progress: in them "all is general and undefined."[14] Of Young's *Universal Passion*, Johnson says that the poet "plays, indeed, only on the surface of life; he never penetrates the recesses of the mind, and therefore the whole power of his poetry is exhausted by a single perusal: his conceits please only when they surprise."[15] And the defeat of Dryden's *Eleanora* is that Dryden wrote without exact knowledge: "the praise being therefore inevitably general fixes no impression on the reader nor excites any tendency to love, nor much desire of imitation."[16]

From an opposite direction we come at precisely the defect of Cowley— *The Mistress* has no power of seduction; she plays round the head but reaches not the heart; her beauty and absence, her kindness and cruelty, her disdain and inconstancy, produce no correspondence of emotion.[17] The effect is the same; the causes are contrary—Cowley is too learned and particular, Dryden and Young too vulgar and general. Lasting excellence in poetry—the power to please many and please long—arises neither from wit nor sublimity merely, neither from the merely particular nor the merely general. The irregular combinations of fanciful invention may delight awhile, by that novelty of which the common satiety of life sends us all in quest, but uniformity too must tire at last, even though it be uniformity of excellence, for the pleasures of the mind imply something sudden and unexpected; that which elevates must always surprise. A great poem is a composite of qualities which taken alone are evanescent or unaffecting. It must represent the permanent and enduring emotions such as any man, merely because he is a man, has felt and must feel again; it must figure forth an object in which the human imagination can recognize itself. But at the same time it must plumb deeply enough the recesses of the heart and the complexities of human life to seize the attention and hold the interest of the reader with unexpected combinations of the ordinary.

These general principles are not less true for being occasionally employed in the examination or praise of writers and works which it is not the modern fashion to enjoy, nor are they less necessary, in some form of statement, to a comprehensive esthetics, even though their generality—which is in one sense a guarantee against rigidity and dogmatism—makes them difficult to apply in particular cases. But the question remains of the validity of Johnson's judgment on the metaphysical poets themselves, and at the risk of seeming heretical, or of appearing to attempt what Johnson accused Sprat of trying to do—propagate a wonder—I should like to contend briefly for the essential correctness of Johnson's censure of the metaphysical poets. First we must notice that his criticism is by no means unqualified, for if these poets usually fail to please, it is not because they do not have great abilities: "To write on their plan it was at least necessary to read and think. No man could be born a metaphysical poet."[18] They have a quality which Johnson prizes beyond most others—originality; and when they err it is not through lack of ability or pains but through a failure of intention—whatever in their work is improper or vicious "is produced by a voluntary deviation from nature in pursuit of something new and strange, . . . the writers fail to give delight by their desire of exciting admiration."[19] Nor, again, is Johnson's general criticism of the metaphysical style equivalent to a condemnation of the individual poems of Donne, Cowley and the rest. We do not know what he would have written about those of Donne, but when later in the *Life* he comes to examine Cowley's works individually he gives several of them great praise: the ode on Wit, for example, "is almost without a rival"; *The Chronicle* is "a composition unrivalled and alone"; and even of the Pindarics he says that "those verses are not without a just claim to praise, of which it may be said with truth, that no one but Cowley could have written them."[20] What Johnson criticizes is the characteristic manner of a school—of "a race of writers"—which in individual poems may not predominate or may be assimilated to a compelling effect. And who will say that he has not hit off accurately the distinguishing aims and characteristics of this school? There can be little doubt, if we examine the work of Cleve-

land, Cowley, and the numerous minor imitators of Donne, that it is the
manner in which the special distinction of the metaphysical style was
thought by them to reside. One must search hard, in these writers, for poems
in which genuinely complex states of feeling demand and control a witty or
ironic structure. For every *Valediction: Forbidding Mourning* there are a
dozen poems like *Fuscara: or the Bee Errant.*

It does not seem likely that anyone not fanatic in his devotion to Cleveland or Cowley will disagree with Johnson's verdict that their poetry is on
the whole without any genuine power to interest or move, that it is remarkable chiefly for the extravagance of fancy displayed on every occasion and
always in the same way. But can Donne himself be exempted from this
charge? Johnson's knowledge of Donne's poetry was curious and extensive;
he ranges over the whole corpus of Donne's work except the divine poems,
drawing examples of the metaphysical manner from poems rarely read today save by the biographer, the professional critic, and the historian of
ideas. And great tracts of Donne's poetry can be read only with difficulty;
it is precisely from these much more often than from the smaller body of
Donne's work which modern taste has fixed upon as providing the true
measure of his talent that Johnson quotes—from the epithalamions, the
epicedes, the verse letters, and the Anniversaries; only four of his sixteen
quotations, indeed, are from the *Songs and Sonnets.*[21] If we leave aside all
consideration of Donne's influence on the development of the language,
of his contribution to the sophistication of the lyric, and of his fascinating
personal history, how many great poems did he write?—how many that the
intelligent common reader, uninstructed by precept and unprejudiced by
authority, is likely to read with passion or wonder? I venture to think that
they are but few, that they are not to be found primarily among those
Johnson quotes, and that the pleasure we take in them does not depend
chiefly on the heterogeneity of the elements joined in their metaphors or
the distance which naturally separates them.

As a critic Johnson is not without important defects, of which the most
serious is not his taste but the absence in his theory of any save a rather
general account of literary effects, such as are common alike to all forms
of the art. He has no method for isolating the peculiar effects of different
species of poetry and for analyzing and judging the means for their production. But this lack—which even modern criticism has made no real progress
in supplying—should not obscure the central value of Johnson's example.
For he forces upon our attention a concern for the ultimate effects and
values of literature—its power to interest and move our emotions—without
which the utmost refinement of wit and technique in the poet or of analysis in the critic must prove illusory. He insists, thus, upon a high standard
of excellence, and it is no wonder if under it so few works and so few
writers win unqualified praise.

"It is not by comparing line with line that the merit of great works is to
be estimated," he says in the *Life of Dryden,*

but by their general effects and ultimate result. It is easy to note a weak line, and write one more vigorous in its place . . . but what is given to the parts may be subducted from the whole, and the reader may be weary though the critick may commend. Works of imagination excel by their allurement and delight; by their power of attracting and detaining the attention. That book is good in vain which the reader throws away. He only is the master who keeps the mind in pleasing captivity; whose pages are perused with eagerness, and in hope of new pleasure are perused again; and whose conclusion is perceived with an eye of sorrow, such as the traveller casts upon departing day.[22]

DONNE'S POETRY IN THE NINETEENTH CENTURY (1800-72)[1]

Kathleen Tillotson

No serious student is deceived by statements frequently encountered in literary journals that Donne's poetry was 'discovered' forty or fifty years ago; such statements generally signify no more than the writer's emotionally possessive attitude to Donne, with perhaps a vague recollection of the dates of Mr Eliot's essays of 1921, or Grierson's edition of 1912. But the latter, indeed a landmark in Donne scholarship, was a culmination as well as an initiator of interest in his poetry; publishers cannot afford to be philanthropists, and the edition would not have been undertaken without some assurance of existing demand. The period really notable for a rapid quickening and extension of interest in Donne is the 1890's; the evidence has been well assembled by Joseph E. Duncan in 'The Revival of Metaphysical Poetry, 1872-1912',[2] and some of it will be readily remembered by those who grew up in days when Saintsbury, Dowden, and Gosse were still obvious critics to consult.

Mr Duncan chose 1872 as the date of the Rev. Alexander Grosart's edition, from which existing demand is not a necessary inference as it was printed for private circulation and Grosart's choice of poets was nearly as undiscriminating as his editorial methods. Nevertheless the interest was there,[3] and it is a mistake to dismiss the forty years before Grosart as a period of neglect or misunderstanding, and to regard Browning's known admiration as merely another instance of his oddity and independence in his time. No doubt what has blocked inquiry is the notorious omission of any poem of Donne's from the most popular and influential of Victorian anthologies, Palgrave's *Golden Treasury of Songs and Lyrics* (1861); but Palgrave, as I hope to show, had some excuse, and is not in this respect representative of nineteenth-century anthologists. The forty years before Grosart have their own contribution to the establishment of Donne's poetic reputation, and the true picture is rather one of a gradual (though not steady) recovery than of a revolutionary discovery; so gradual that any starting-point much later than Johnson's *Lives of the Poets* would be

Reprinted from *Mid-Victorian Studies*, ed. Geoffrey and Kathleen Tillotson (Athlone Press, 1965), pp. 278-300. First appeared in *Elizabethan and Jacobean Studies* (Oxford: The Clarendon Press, 1959), pp. 307-26, by permission of the author and The Clarendon Press, Oxford.

arbitrary, and it has seemed best to include the early nineteenth century[4]
in this inquiry, although this means recalling some familiar material.

2

There is some apparent set-back after that first and best-known phase
associated with the 'romantics'. This is understandable; while to the modern
reader the evidence of appreciation and insight in Lamb, Coleridge, Hazlitt,
Landor, and De Quincey is clear enough to constitute a body of enlightened
opinion, their references to Donne are in fact mostly casual, fugitive, or
oblique. Lamb seems to have been the first of them to record his appreciation in print and was probably the instigator of Coleridge's interest,[5] certainly of Hazlitt's; but all he has left us is in the long note to *Philaster* in his
Specimens of English Dramatic Poets (1808), where he quotes the whole of
Elegy xvi and commends its sense, wit, and pathos, and a 'fragment of criticism' countering the common antithesis of wit and feeling and defending
Donne and Cowley: 'in the very thickest of their conceits,—in the bewildering mazes of tropes and figures,—a warmth of soul and generous feeling
shines through'. Most of the other evidence of Lamb's reading of Donne
comes from Hazlitt, who in 1820 remembered from twelve years before his
reading of that same Elegy 'with suffused features and a faltering tongue'
and the 'gusto' with which he quoted Donne's 'most crabbed passages'.[6]
Hazlitt, whose remarks on Donne are the nearest approach to formal criticism in the period, never really assimilated his poetry, which he seems not
to have read until 1818. Early in that year, in his *Lectures on the English
Poets,* he says he 'know[s] nothing' except Lamb's favourite Elegy and
'some quaint riddles in verse which the sphinx could not unravel'. Some
months later, in the third of the lectures on *English Comic Writers,* he
quotes from three of the *Song and Sonets,* with comments emphasizing
Donne's unevenness: the second verse of 'The Blossom', for example, is
'but a lame and impotent conclusion from so delightful a beginning'.[7]
Coleridge, who had already in 1811 begun annotating volumes borrowed
from Lamb, referred to Donne in the *Biographia Literaria* (chs. i and xviii),
and in 1818 projected a lecture on 'Dante, Donne, and Milton' ('the middle
name will perhaps puzzle you', he wrote to Cary);[8] but no report survives,
and Crabb Robinson's diary records it simply as a lecture on Dante and
Milton. Some of Coleridge's comments and marginalia were published in
Table Talk and *Literary Remains,* but the best of his criticism—the marginalia in Lamb's copy of the *Poems*—not until 1853, in *Notes Theological,
Literary, and Miscellaneous,* and (more completely) in the American *Literary
World.* De Quincey's reading of Donne is known only from a few penetrating sentences on the 'metaphysical' poets (whom he prefers to call 'Rhetorical') in a review of Whately's *Rhetoric* in *Blackwood's* (1828): 'Few writers
have shown a more extraordinary compass of powers than Donne; for he
combined—what no other man has ever done—the last sublimation of
dialectical subtlety and address with the most impassioned majesty'; and
Landor's reading, probably extensive, is known only from the 'Imaginary

Conversation'[9] of Walton, Cotton, and Oldways (1829) where the several
imaginary quotations indicate what struck him most in Donne; these lines
are a comment in themselves:

> She was so beautiful, had God but died
>   For her, and none beside,
> Reeling with holy joy from east to west
> Earth would have sunk down blest;
> And, burning with bright zeal, the buoyant Sun
> Cried thro' his worlds *well done*!

Leigh Hunt shows some knowledge of Donne in his later writings, and in a
review of Tennyson's 1830 poems[10] notes, of 'Love and Sorrow', that 'the
author must have been reading Donne. . . . This is the very Analogical Doctor come back again.' The poem is one of those that Tennyson never reprinted; it exemplifies an interest which was evidently current among his
undergraduate contemporaries, and which we shall meet again, with a difference, in Henry Alford. Hartley Coleridge has some verses on Donne which
quote and expand his father's line on iron pokers; and two more sympathetic notes, buried among his marginalia on Carew in Anderson's *British
Poets*:

> Men may joke or quibble till they cannot do otherwise, and yet not
> have joked away all feeling. . . . Is there any difference in style between
> Donne's Sacred Poems and his wildest love riddles?
> Carew is far smoother [than Donne]; but where is the strength, the
> boundless wealth of thought, the heart beating beneath its twisted mail?[11]

An unexpected enthusiast from an older generation was William Godwin,
who in *Thoughts on Man*, 1831, a volume of essays published in his old age,[12]
calls Donne 'one of the most deep-thinking and philosophical poets', and
praises his 'originality, energy, and vigour . . . every sentence . . . whether
in verse or prose, is exclusively his own . . . his thoughts are often in the
noblest sense of the word poetical; and passages may be quoted from him
that no English poet may attempt to rival, unless it be Milton and Shakespeare'; the present neglect of Donne is attributed to his obscurity (Jonson's
'Donne, for not being understood, would perish' is quoted as 'prophetic')
and his 'crabbed and repulsive' phraseology and versification.

Thomas Phillips in a lecture at the Royal Academy in 1827 (published
1833) compares Giotto with Donne; the student of art should forget his
'gothic imperfections' which resemble Donne's 'uncouth phraseology' in
being nevertheless 'full of sentiment'—a stock distinction, but an unexpected
application. The extent of Wordsworth's knowledge is doubtful; the sermons
and poems were in his library, and in the winter of 1830 he was reading the
sermons aloud to his wife, but he refers only once to any poem, when urging
Dyce to include 'Death be not proud' in his *Specimens of English Sonnets*;
Dyce did so, and recorded Wordsworth's plea in his copy of the 1633 poems.[13]
Scott's references in the 'Life of John Dryden' in his edition of 1808 are per-

functory, and unfavourable. Southey was unconverted in 1807, when he collected his *Specimens of the later English Poets*: 'Nothing indeed could have made Donne a Poet, unless as great a change had been worked in the structure of his ears, as was wrought in elongating those of Midas';[14] which possibly provoked Coleridge to his masterly defence of Donne's verse.

Coleridge's notes, our most valued legacy of Donne criticism from this period, seem not to have been well known save for the line 'wreathes iron pokers into true-love knots'. Nothing came of Barron Field's project of a Percy Society edition incorporating these marginalia[15]—though their publication in the *Literary World* may have stimulated Lowell's interest and his encouragement of the Boston edition of Donne in 1855,[16] the only near-complete and separate collection of Donne's poetry between Tonson's and Grosart's. But American interest goes farther back and Emerson's, as shown in his letters and journals, has a more obvious source. A letter written in 1815, at the age of fifteen, shows him reading Johnson's life of Cowley, and struck (like Ayrton at the evening party of 1808, in 'Of Persons one would Wish to have Seen') by the stanza beginning 'Here lies a he-sun and a she-moon here'. His comment is 'I should like to see the poem it was taken from.'[17]

For many readers meeting Donne for the first time in Johnson's dozen or so of ample quotations, this would be a natural response. We need not go to Johnson to account for Lamb, who had his own 'midnight darlings, [his] folios'; but there is other evidence, some of it on lower levels,[18] that Donne was increasingly read after about 1790, and this almost certainly reflects the popularity of the life of Cowley.[19] Boswell thought it the best of the *Lives*, because Johnson had 'exhibited' the metaphysical poets 'at large, with such happy illustrations from their writings, and in so luminous a manner, that indeed he may be allowed the full merit of novelty, and to have discovered to us, as it were, a new planet in the poetical hemisphere'. This is a tribute often overlooked.

The curious could not pursue their interest in Johnson's edition, which started with Cowley; but Donne's poems were available in Bell's edition (1781), and after 1793 in Robert Anderson's *British Poets,* which adds a 'life' based on Granger's in his *Biographical History,* and quotes Johnson. Any Victorian gentleman's library would be likely to include Bell or Anderson or Chalmers (1810), and though the text of Donne is unsatisfactory the collection is reasonably complete,[20] and the lack of any further edition in England until Grosart's is not necessarily an indication of neglect. After the turn of the century, Donne also begins to be represented in anthologies and selections: George Ellis's *Specimens* (1801)[21] has 'Go and catch a falling star' and the first stanza of 'Negative Love', and Capel Lofft's *Laura; or an Anthology of Sonnets* (1814) has three sonnets. Thomas Campbell's *Specimens* (1819) has four poems (two incomplete), Ezekiel Sanford's *Works of the British Poets* (Philadelphia, 1819) has fourteen of the *Songs and Sonets* and twenty-three other poems or parts of poems, James Montgomery's *The*

Christian Poet (1827)[22] has two Holy Sonnets and the 'Hymn to Christ',
Southey's *Select Works of the British Poets* (1831) has five *Songs and Sonets,*
all the Holy Sonnets, and sixteen others, Robert F. Housman's *Collection
of English Sonnets* [1835] has two sonnets, Richard Cattermole's *Sacred
Poetry of the Seventeenth Century* (1836) has seven Holy Sonnets, the First
Anniversary, 'Hymn to Christ', and a few others, and Samuel C. Hall's *Book
of Gems* (1836) has ten *Songs and Sonets.* The choices rarely coincide; each
editor has read Donne for himself, and made his own selection. In the same
period, casual quotations from Donne turn up in odd places; the 'Biographical Notice' of Jane Austen by her brother Henry (1818) says that 'her
eloquent blood spoke through her modest cheek' (this is in all periods the
most frequently quoted passage); Scott quotes from Carew's elegy on Donne
in his introduction to *The Black Dwarf,* and has a chapter-motto wrongly
attributed to Donne in ch. iii of *The Legend of Montrose*; Julius and Augustus Hare, *Guesses at Truth* (1827), quote from the third satire (and in the
1838 edition also from a sermon); Hood quotes both the 'he-sun' lines (perhaps caught from Hazlitt or Lamb) and another favourite pun from 'old
Donne';[23] Edmund H. Barker, the ill-starred classical scholar, quotes two
'Specimens' from *Paradoxes and Problems* (1652) in the *Constitutional
Magazine* of September 1835 (p. 156); two lines (53-4) of Elegy xvi appear
as motto to a story in the annual *Friendship's Offering* (1835); and No. 76
(by Newman) of *Tracts for the Times* (1836) quotes a passage from Sermon
xxxi. A different kind of knowledge is suggested by Anna Jameson's *The
Loves of the Poets* (1829), who quotes 'The Message' as 'long popular, and
I can remember when a child, hearing it sung to very beautiful music'.

Most of the selections mentioned also include some criticism, some but
not all in stock phrases about harsh versification, obscurity, and cold conceits. 'His ruggedness and whim', says Campbell, 'are almost proverbially
known'—testimony at least to common knowledge; 'yet there is a beauty
of thought which at intervals rises from his chaotic imagination, like Venus
smiling on the waters'. Cattermole thinks that modern readers find Donne
obscure only because they prefer 'voluptuous sweetness' to 'depth of sentiment and originality of thought'. S. C. Hall, while taking the usual line about
'beauties and deformities', tilts the balance decisively; his specimens, he says,
show that Donne was often 'smooth even to elegance'.

> He was absolutely saturated with learning—his intellect was large and
> searching . . . his wit playful yet caustic. At times he is full of tenderness;
> and in spite of himself submits to the mastery of nature.

He believes that Donne's 'name as a poet is largely known and esteemed'—
in contrast both to Anna Jameson seven years earlier, who had thought him
'little read, except by those who make our old poetry their study', and
probably chiefly known 'from the lines at the bottom of the page in Pope's
version'; and also to the egregious Nathan Drake, who in 1817 writes that

'A more refined age, and a more chastized taste, have very justly consigned
his poetical labours to the shelf of the philologer.'

'Those who make our old poetry their study' are best represented by an
unknown, independent, and at times strikingly perceptive writer in the *Retrospective Review* of 1823.[24] Here indeed are the accents of discovery; if the
progress of Donne's reputation is ever to be fully charted, 1823 should be as
important a date as 1921.

This essay I propose to describe in some detail. Though headed with the
title of the 1669 *Poems,* it is almost entirely concerned with the *Songs and
Sonets,* seventeen of which are quoted, either whole or in part. It begins by
mocking at Theobald's phrase 'nothing but a continued heap of riddles' but
makes no other reference to earlier criticism, and never uses the term 'metaphysical'. At the outset Donne is placed 'at the head of the minor poets of
his day', for his learning, his

> active and piercing intellect . . . imagination, if not grasping and compre-
> hensive, most subtle and far-darting—a fancy rich, vivid, and picturesque,
> and at the same time, highly *fantastical* . . . a mode of expression singu-
> larly terse, simple, and condensed . . . a wit, admirable as well for its
> caustic severity as its playful quickness.[25]

Far from objecting to his verse, the critic finds in Donne 'an exquisite ear';
his only deficiencies are in 'sensibility and taste', and the former is interestingly qualified:

> His sensibility was by nature strong, but sluggish and deep-seated. It
> required to be roused and awakened by the imagination, before it would
> act; and this process seldom failed to communicate to the action which
> it created an appearance of affectation (for it was nothing more than the
> appearance).

His 'scholastic habits . . . without weakening his sensibility', contributed
greatly 'to deform and denaturalize its outward manifestations; feeling and
thoughts were heightened and illustrated by a 'host of images and associations',
supplied by 'quick-eyed wit' and 'subtle ingenuity'. This is seen as a fault,
but a fault of his age and school, springing from a disregard of the principle
'that an idea or a sentiment may be poetical *per se*':

> They considered that *man* was the creator of poetry, not Nature; and
> that any thing might be made poetical, by connecting it, in a certain
> manner, with something else. A thought or a feeling was, to them, not a
> thing *to express,* but a theme to write *variations* upon—a nucleus, about
> which other thoughts and feelings were to be made to crystallize.

Donne's 'school' is then compared with, but distinguished from, the Della
Cruscans: superior, because the latter 'tried to make things poetical, by
means of words alone', the former, by 'a vast fund of thoughts and images'.

Having thus cleared the ground, the critic announces his main intention:
'to bring to light some of the exquisite beauties which have hitherto lain

concealed from the present age'—beauties of every kind, though unaccount-
ably mixed with 'deformities', which perhaps explains the 'total neglect',
remarkable in 'an age which boasts that it has revived a knowledge of, and
a love for its great predecessor'. The reader of Donne should not judge
hastily from transient irritation; he will soon find 'great exercise for his
thinking faculties (if nothing else) even in the objectionable parts of Donne'.
Some pieces are entirely free from this 'mixed character': notably the 'Valediction: forbidding mourning' (quoted complete), which 'for clearness and
smoothness of construction, and a passionate sweetness and softness in the
music of the versification, might have been written in the present day'—if
indeed any modern poet is capable of it. 'The simile of the compasses, notwithstanding its quaintness, is more perfect in its kind, and more beautiful,
than anything we are acquainted with.' On other poems, the critic is often
felicitous, finding in 'The Good-Morrow' 'an air of serious gaiety . . . as if
composed in the very bosom of bliss', and in 'The Message' 'a certain wayward simplicity of thought peculiarly appropriate to such compositions';
in 'The Prohibition' Donne 'bandies a thought about (like a shuttlecock)
from one hand to the other, only to let it fall to the ground at last'. No
other poet could have made the comparison of the nerves and the braid of
hair in 'The Funeral' *tell* as he had done; 'The Will'[26] illustrates 'his infinite
fullness of meaning . . . almost every line would furnish matter for a whole
treatise in modern times'; 'Negative Love' shows 'a love for the passion
excited, rather than the object exciting it . . . that lives by "*chewing the cud
of sweet and bitter fancy*" . . . that broods, like the stock-dove, over its own
voice, and listens for no other'. Later, this comparison with Wordsworth is
made explicit, and his style is called a return to that of the first stanza of
'The Blossom'. Many more poems and passages are quoted and praised, and
the divergence from traditional views is evident in the repudiation of Pope's
'brilliant and refined' version of the satires: nearly a hundred lines from the
fourth Satire[27] (from 'Towards me did run') are quoted, with the simple
comment, 'It strikes us as being nearly the perfection of this kind of writing.'
And althought the essay concludes with some concessions to the common
view of Donne's faults, this enthusiasm is the note of the whole; indeed, the
specific comments seem slightly at variance with the general framework, as
if the writer were captivated in the act of quoting. His judicious assessment
of faults and beauties crumbles before the conviction of Donne's uniqueness—
his poems 'bear a mark that we cannot very well expound, even to ourselves,
but which we know no one could have placed on them but him'.

3

In the Victorian period, 'official' opinion, as represented in histories of
literature, encyclopedias, and biographical collections,[28] represents a harden-
ing and simplification of the views of Johnson and of Hazlitt; the term
'metaphysical' is generally objected to,[29] but Donne is associated with his
'school', and the same phrases recur parrot-wise—'remote analogies', 'far-
fetched images'—and usually with emphasis on his inequalities—'He mixed

up with what was beautiful and true much that was fantastical and false'.
But the merely contemptuous tone of Henry Hallam in his *Introduction
to the Literature of Europe*[30] is exceptional:

> Donne is the most inharmonious of our versifiers, if he can be said
> to have deserved such a name by lines too rugged to seem metre. Of his
> earlier poems many are very licentious. The later are chiefly devout. Few
> are good for much; the conceits have not even the merit of being intel-
> ligible, and it would perhaps be difficult to select three passages that we
> should care to read again.

To parallel that we must go back to Southey or Theobald. But in the same
year, 1839, Henry Alford allows Donne 'a fine musical ear' (with three examples cited in a footnote) and attributes his harshness to that 'laborious
condensation' typical of the juvenile poems of great men. The anonymous
editor of the *Book of the Poets* (1841?), who includes 'His Picture', part of
'The Dissolution', and one sonnet, finds, despite harshness and pedantry,
'an innate vigour and freshness which will always ensure [his poems] a high
rank in English poetry'. The writer of the article on Donne in *Chambers's
Cyclopædia of English Literature* (1844) trims his course; this poet's reputation has 'latterly in some degree revived', and whereas earlier critics spoke
of his 'harsh and rugged versification, and his leaving nature for conceit', it
is now acknowledged that 'amidst much rubbish, there is much real poetry,
and that of a high order'. To show his merits four quotations are given, including the first verse of the 'Valentine' *Epithalamion*,[31] a passage from the
fourth satire, the 'Valediction: forbidding mourning', and 'The Will'. (The
later fortunes of this entry are not without interest; the 1858 edition
merely added a little more information on editions and manuscripts, but
the 1876 edition was revised, and 'rubbish' was altered to 'bad taste'.)[32]
G. L. Craik in his *Sketches of the History of Literature* (1845) quotes
'Sweetest Love' to illustrate Donne's ear for melody, and thinks the verse
of the satires was 'adopted by choice and on system' and is 'not without
a deep and subtle music'.

'Why are Donne's sermons not reprinted at Oxford?' Coleridge had asked,
and the question was repeated by his nephew, the editor of *Table Talk,* and
by the *Quarterly*'s reviewer of *Literary Remains* in July 1837. The result
was the six-volume edition by the Rev. Henry Alford[33] in 1839, miscalled
Works of Dr John Donne; the new interest in Donne's prose was also reflected in *Selections from the Works of John Donne D.D.* (Talboys, 1840),
two editions of the *Devotions* (Talboys and Pickering, both 1840), Richard
Cattermole, *Literature of the Church of England* (2 vols., 1849), James
Brogden, *Illustrations of Liturgy and Ritual* (3 vols., 1842), and Robert
Aris Willmott, *Precious Stones, Aids to Reflection* (1850). All this helped
to draw further attention to the divine poems. Alford included them all,
the 1840 selection had several, and so did another Oxford collection, *Gems
of Sacred Poetry* (2 vols., 1841), with an introductory essay which notes
'a great, though gradual revolution' in the taste of the last thirty years, for

both the poetry and the theology of Elizabethan and Jacobean writers.
Cambridge followed in 1847 with *Select Poetry Chiefly Sacred of the Reign
of James the First,* edited by Edward Farr, which has a fuller selection.
There are similar later examples (including a very Gothic-looking volume,
W. H. Rogers's *Spiritual Conceits, extracted from the Writings of the Fathers,
the old English Poets, etc.,* 1862), and one interesting omission; Leigh Hunt's
posthumous *Book of the Sonnet* (1867), though praising 'La Corona', refrains from including it because 'Donne's piety, though sincere, was un-
healthy'. No extended criticism of the divine poems is found until 1868
when George Macdonald, recently Professor of English Literature at Bedford
College, included a chapter on them in *England's Antiphon,* a popular account of English religious poetry. He is perplexed by their 'incongruities',
on which he at least is specific, commenting in some detail on 'Hymn to
God in my Sickness', which he regards as typical of Donne's 'best and worst'.
The 'best' is contained in the first and in the last two stanzas: he explains,
and praises, the music image:

> To recognize its beauty . . . we must recall the custom of those days
> to send out for 'a noise of musicians'. Hence he imagines that he has been
> summoned as one of a band already gone in to play before the king of
> 'The High Countries': he is now at the door, where he is listening to
> catch the tone, that he may have his instrument tuned and ready before
> he enters. But with what a jar the next stanza breaks on heart, mind, and
> ear!

The sudden shift of comparison of himself from map to navigator is
thought 'grotesque and absurd'; still worse is the next stanza, where 'he is
alternately a map and a man sailing on the map of himself'. These strictures
must have influenced Emerson, who gives only Macdonald's three preferred
stanzas, without notice of omission, in his anthology *Parnassus* (1875). In
the same year as Macdonald's book, the Archbishop of Dublin (R. C. Trench)
brought out his *Household Book of English Poetry,* which included the 'Lecture on the Shadow' and two Holy Sonnets, 'Death, be not proud' and 'As
due by many titles', the last of which he describes as 'rough and rugged' but
'the genuine cry of one engaged in that most terrible of all struggles'; he goes
on to compare Donne with St. Augustine, 'the same tumultuous youth . . .
and then the same passionate and personal grasp of the central truths of'
Christianity'.

But sometimes the new interest in Donne as divine encouraged the playing-
down of his secular poems. Alford apologized for having 'pruned' so 'unsparingly' from them, but 'it seemed to me that the character of this work being
theological, the Poems which were to be inserted should be of the same
stamp'. He accordingly gave no satires, only three of the *Songs and Sonnets,*
one elegy, and one epithalamion. The Rev. Augustus Jessopp in his edition
of *Essays in Divinity* (1855) regarded Donne as 'the greatest preacher England has ever produced' but thought his powers 'comparatively trifled away'
up to 1613—a remark which prepares one for his article on Donne in the

Dictionary of National Biography (1888), twenty columns long but with only a cursory reference to the poems. To accept Donne whole has been difficult for critics ever since Walton.

That is one reason why there are few attempts at comprehensive criticism, though it is not quite fair to call Donne 'yet unappreciated', as De Quincy did in 1851.[34] In 1838 the youthful G. H. Lewes[35] apostrophizes the poet as 'Honest John Donne—rough—hearty—pointed and sincere' and observes in 'The Good-Morrow' 'the true language of passion, which will appear unnatural only to those who never felt *une grande passion*'. There is true appreciation in an essay in *Lowe's Edinburgh Magazine* of February 1846, the first of a series of three including Herbert and Herrick. Grosart quoted it as 'by Dr. Samuel Brown of Edinburgh, I believe'; it has since been attributed to Coventry Patmore.[36] Whoever the author, his approach is independent and unusual (though there are signs that he has read the *Retrospective* essay), and he has strongly marked views on poetry in general. Some of his preferences in Donne are surprising at that date. The satires are ranked highest, 'the best in the language', and Pope's sophistications exposed by parallel quotations from the fourth satire (this passage is quoted by Grosart). Donne's verse may be rough, 'But who . . . would not . . . prefer climbing, with Donne, these crags where all the air is fresh and wholesome, to gliding, with Thomas Moore, over flats, from beneath the rank verdure of which arises malaria and invisible disease?' Those who submit his poems to 'affectionate reflection' will pardon his worst versification: 'since no sacrifice of meaning is ever made to it,—it thus being so much more palatable to the truly cultivated taste than the expensive melody of some modern versifiers'. The unfavourable contrast with modern poetry is pursued in a rather obscure statement that in Donne's day poets acted unconsciously on their 'instinctive immediate perception . . . without limits imposed by the logical faculty, or the hyperbole-hating decencies of flat conventionality', whereas 'our modern carpet-poets tread their way upon hyperbole, as nicely as they would do over ice of an uncertain strength, dreading every moment to be drowned in ridicule'. Donne was also fortunate in living in an age 'when English intellect was at its height' and when religion had 'enhanced poetic liberty' and 'extinguished that false shame which Romanism had attached to the contemplation of the sexual relations'. But his poetry is never likely to be popular, because of its ruggedness and its difficulty; the meaning demands constant attention, and only to the 'most faithful and disciplined lovers of the muse' will he be 'a peculiar favourite'. This aristocratic, rather truculent tone is certainly not unlike that of Patmore's later criticism.

He has not much to say of particular poems. The love-poems show 'the love of love' rather than the passion for its object, and their conceits make them inferior to the satires; but the 'Valediction' is an exception, a 'noble poem', 'exquisite' in versification. It is quoted entire, and there are also short quotations from 'The Ecstasy', 'The Good-Morrow', 'The Blossom', and the first Epithalamion, but the quality of the last is impossible to show in extracts —it has an 'inexpicable, incommunicable aura'. There are quotations from the First Anniversary, but the divine poems as a whole are slighted.

His next essay, on Herbert, contrasts Donne's rough strength with Herbert's smooth sweetness, and reveals the writer as an admirer of Tennyson, who is compared with Herbert in his combination of 'activity of thought' with 'native sweetness of feeling and . . . expression'. But he adds, disputing Coleridge's view, that the highest genius is 'masculine', and Herbert's and Tennyson's 'feminine'; which again is reminiscent of Patmore. If he is the writer, we may guess that this early interest was stimulated by Coleridge, and by his father P. G. Patmore, the friend of Lamb and Hazlitt. It may have affected his poetry. Mario Praz (who is unaware of the essay in *Lowe's*) makes a case for Donne's influence,[37] citing similar images ('as turning spirals draw the eyes'), verbal echoes ('some say, "It lightens", some say "No"'), and the movement of the quatrains. Dowden had noted this too, with more moderation: 'The metre of the *Extasie* is the same as that of the *Angel in the House,* and the manner in which meaning and metre move together closely resembles that of Mr Patmore's *Preludes.*'[38] But if Patmore really was inspired by Donne, the effect is counteracted by his firm narrative line and the deliberate surface simplicity of his style; his contemporaries were not so obtuse as Praz thinks in emphasizing the influence of Tennyson.

Tennyson's only known comment on Donne is on the 'Valediction: forbidding mourning'. But as this poem is quoted in full in Walton's *Life*[39] — which, as the *Lowe's* essay says, had 'a hundred readers' for every one of Donne's poetry—this is not necessarily evidence of wider knowledge of Donne. Such wider knowledge is, however, shown by some of Tennyson's friends and contemporaries, besides Browning: for example, Sir Henry Taylor, who quotes not only the 'Valediction' but twice from the *Elegies* in his *Autobiography*;[40] by Edward FitzGerald;[41] John Forster, who praised Landor for catching the style of the poet so happily, 'not only its extravagance, but its genius',[42] and George Eliot, who quotes 'The Undertaking' and 'The Good-Morrow' in two chapter-mottoes[43] of *Middlemarch*—chosen, significantly, for chapters concerning Ladislaw and Dorothea, and the latter (ll. 8-11) touchingly forecasting Dorothea's admission of her love.

Palgrave's knowledge of Donne is not in doubt. He quotes him in *The Passionate Pilgrim* (1858); in preparation for the *Golden Treasury* (1861) he went through Chalmers's *English Poets* twice; and he shows his knowledge and his opinion of Donne in a review[44] published in the same year, where he contrasts the 'imaginative conceits' of Ralegh's 'Come live with me' with the 'frostwork ingenuities of the intellect' in 'The Bait', and notes that 'farsought conceits and allusions' and 'strange contorted phraseology' are not peculiar to Donne and Cowley 'but more or less mark English poetry from Surrey to Herbert and Crashaw'. In his *Treasury of Sacred Song* (1889) he included three Holy Sonnets and one hymn, noting in Donne's poetry generally a 'strange originality almost equally fascinating and repellent', and a 'strange solemn passionate earnestness' underlying the 'fanciful conceits'.

It was Palgrave who recorded Tennyson's moving recitation of the last four stanzas of the 'Valediction' and his praise of their 'wonderful ingenuity'.[45] We do not know whether this was before or after 1860, or whether 'all that stood near admission' to the *Golden Treasury* and was submitted to Tennyson for final decision included any of Donne. The manuscript, Tennyson's notes, and several marked volumes, survive, but provide no answer, Chalmers's *Poets* unfortunately not being among them. But it is interesting to see from notes on the manuscript that Tennyson, who was an enthusiast for Marvell and introduced the 'Horatian Ode' to Palgrave, not only approved for inclusion 'The Garden' and 'The Emigrants' Song' but 'greatly pleaded for the *Lover*' ['To his Coy Mistress']—'but', adds Palgrave, 'I thought one or two lines too *strong* for this age'. We know too that Palgrave omitted Spenser's *Epithalamion* 'with great reluctance as not in harmony with modern manners', and other love-poems which he privately described as 'too high-kilted', and that he thought of a separate collection of the more 'decidedly amorous'. The original standard for inclusion was evidently strict; one of the advisers wrote 'too coarse' against 'It was a lover and his Lass,'[46] which was, however, included. This fear of the 'young person' is one possible reason for omitting many of the *Songs and Sonets;*[47] as Grosart says, 'it needs courage to print the poetry of Dr. John Donne in our day', and even he hesitated long over Elegy xix. But a nearly contemporary anthologist, J. C. M. Bellew, who says in the Preface to his *Poets' Corner* (1868) that he had a 'black list' of authors 'whose works it would be impossible to put into the hands of a youth or a schoolgirl', nevertheless managed to find seven poems which could safely represent Donne, mostly divine poems, but one of them 'The Anniversary' from *Songs and Sonets*. Palgrave, however, had narrowed his choice at the outset by explicitly excluding religious lyrics; and some of the other criteria given in his notes and Preface would tend, on his view, to keep Donne out:

> a comparative absence of extreme or temporary phases in style . . . will be found throughout.
>
> That a poem shall . . . reach a perfection commensurate with its aim— that we should require finish in proportion to brevity—that passion, colour and originality cannot atone for serious imperfections in clearness, unity or truth . . . above all, that excellence should be looked for in the whole rather than in the parts,—such and other such canons have been always strictly regarded.
>
> If no verses by certain writers who show . . . more thought than mastery of expression are printed in this volume, it should not be imagined that they have been excluded without much hesitation and regret.

Palgrave made many later additions to Books I and II,[48] but he did not take the opportunity to add any of Donne; by 1891, the last revised edition, there could be not doubt of Donne's recovery of fame, and his continued exclusion shows rather Palgrave's firmness in holding to his original principles. But I have found some interesting new evidence of a momentary wavering. He acquired Grosart's edition, and his copy is in the British Museum, with a few markings.[49] He used this for his *Treasury of Sacred Song,* marking with

approval five Holy Sonnets (two more than he finally included) and also
writing 'fine and pathetic' against the 'Hymn to Christ' and 'spoiled by its
own cleverness' against 'The Cross'; but he was evidently also thinking of
the revised *Golden Treasury*, for he set a mark of approval on 'Sweetest
Love', and also on the first verse of 'The Anniversary', with the words 'Si sic
omnia!' That might be taken as his final word on the love-lyrics.

'More *thought* than mastery of expression' was a disqualification for the
Golden Treasury. But Grosart dedicated his edition of Donne 'to Robert
Browning, the poet of the century for *thinkers* . . . knowing how much his
poetry, with every abatement, is valued and assimilated by him'. As Browning's poetry gained in fame and influence in the last quarter of the century,
the way was prepared for a wider and truer appreciation of Donne. The
extent of the 'assimilation' is less important than the increasing notice taken
of the likeness between them, not only by Grosart but by Dowden, Gosse,
Schelling, and many others;[50] it is clear from these critics that the movement
of their reputation was partly interdependent, like Tennyson's and Keat's in
the 1840's, or Mr Eliot's and Donne's in the 1920's.

At the date of Grosart's dedication, Browning had known Donne's work
for over forty years. He was reading it in 1826-8 (fired, perhaps, by the
Retrospective Review?) and is said by Griffin to have set 'Go and catch a
falling star' to music. When writing *Paracelsus,* as he afterwards recalled, he
was once lightheaded and fancied he had to go through a complete version
of the Psalms by Donne. In 1844 he and Miss Barrett, as yet unknown to
each other, were applied to by R. H. Horne for mottoes to suit individual
writers in *A New Spirit of the Age,* and one for Henry Taylor was an aptly-
chosen quotation from Elegy iv.[51] The quotations in his letters to Elizabeth
Barrett in 1845-6 show a close familiarity with Donne, and are lightly inter-
woven with his courtship; he quotes (from memory and inaccurately, but
very aptly in the context) from the third stanza of the 'Valentine' *Epithalamion*; in another letter he asks her why she should 'lean and hearken' after
Italy. The line 'as an amber drop enwraps the bee', from 'Honour is so sublime perfection', is applied to Carlyle's view of poetry. (It has not previously
been noticed, however, that another quotation, from 'Donne's pretty lines
about seals', is really from Herbert's 'In Sacram Anchoram Piscatoris'.)[52]
Elizabeth Barrett quotes in her turn from 'The Will' and the second satire,
calling the author 'your Donne'. When Browning writes 'Soule-hydroptique
with a sacred thirst' in 'The Grammarian's Funeral' he is again virtually
quoting Donne; not, as Mr Duncan suggests, the Second Anniversary, but
'an hydroptique immoderate desire of human learning and languages', in the
well-known letter given by Walton. In 1869 William Rossetti[53] recorded
Browning's enthusiasm for 'a poem by Donne named *Metempsychosis*'; by
then he had written the poem in which he quotes it, *The Two Poets of
Croisic:*

> He's greatest now and to de-struct-i-on
> *Nearest.* Attend the solemn word I quote,

>O Paul! *There's no pause at perfect-i-on*
>   Thus knolls thy knell the Doctor's bronzed throat!
>*Greatness a period hath, no sta-ti-on!*
>   Better and truer verse none ever wrote
>
>(Despite the antique outstretched *a-i-on*)
>Than thou, revered and magisterial Donne!

Finally, in a late uncollected poem, 'Epps', he called Donne 'brave' and 'rare', and drew on the supposed sixth satire and Grosart's note on it.

Whether Browning did more than read, quote, and praise is impossible to establish. Readers of both poets—fewer now than fifty years ago—must often be haunted by a fleeting sense of likeness, especially in Donne's satires and *Metempsychosis,* but it is doubtful whether this amounts to influence. Mr Duncan has collected possible parallels, and also considers the 'kinship' of the two poets under the four general headings of philosophical ideas; casuistical logic, metaphor, and wit; development of the dramatic mono- logue; and experiments with a conversational metric and idiom. The first seems to me the weakest, the last the strongest part of his case. But, as he justly says in conclusion, the influence was such as 'to supplement and re- inforce . . . natural talents and predilections'; and therefore, we might add, virtually impossible to distinguish from them. Both poets were eccentrically learned, restless in thought and fancy, proud, reserved, and independent; free of 'all the four corners' of 'grammar'; and both sometimes harsh and unconciliating in their attitude to readers—'this sullen writ Which just as much courts thee as thou dost it'. But the danger of emphasizing the 'kin- ship' is that it may blind us to some of the special virtues of each poet: on the one hand, to Donne's control and scrupulosity, the habitual leanness of his style, as opposed to Browning's comparatively slapdash and sprawling exuberance; and on the other, to Browning's dramatic power of penetrating into a great variety of other characters and situations, where Donne is almost wholly confined to his own various but single self. Consider each at his best: though the verse and style of 'My Last Duchess' carry echoes for the reader of Donne, the character and situation lie outside his range; and Browning could never have attained the intensity and formality of the *Holy Sonnets.* It might be hazarded that no later poet has come nearer to Donne than Browning, though the nearness is the measure of an impassable distance.

But this is doubtful ground, and what I have wished to establish is rather the nature of the whole nineteenth-century context of Browning's interest in his 'revered and magisterial Donne'. Unenlightened as many Victorian critics and readers of Donne may appear to our own far more fortunate age, they were not so benighted as it has been the fashion to suppose.

II. DONNE AND THE DEVELOPMENT OF ENGLISH POETRY

KIDNAPPING DONNE

Merritt Y. Hughes

"It is as much one's life is worth nowadays among young people," Mr. Edmund Wilson remarked not long ago, "to say an approving word for Shelley or a dubious one about Donne."[1] He made the remark in passing, as one who accepts a "cult" of Donne because he knows that all lovely and life-giving religions have their esoterics. When a poet becomes a touchstone his adepts begin to practice strange sorceries, and in current discussion of poetry Donne is often a touchstone. A casual example is the observation made in a review of Mr. Alan Porter's *Signature of Pain, and Other Poems*,[2] that Mr. Porter's work has been compared "without embarrassment . . . to all but the very greatest passages of even the greatest of the seventeenth-century masters, of Donne himself"; the reviewer then going on to deplore the fashion of comparing modern poetasters to Donne, and finally proceeding himself to make the comparison in Mr. Porter's favor. Without in the least doubting that *The Signature of Pain* bears proof by the touchstone which its title challenges, Donne's jealous friends may question whether it is altogether fair to him to make him the measure of modern work.

It is the critical self-consciousness in our admiration for Donne that is dubious. There can be no doubt of his power over modern poetry. In the history of English literature the only forces comparable to it are Shakespeare's influence, or Milton's in the eighteenth century. Today, however, Dr. Johnson's rationalization of the hold of Shakespeare upon his contemporaries is interesting only for what it betrays to us of him, and of them. Is it possible that Donne's hold upon our imaginations has given us an illusion that we understand him better than we really do? We pick up Mr. John Crowe Ransom's *Greeting to a Lady on Her Birthday* and find the serene recklessness of Donne's pathetic fallacies in the great *Elegies*:

> Too quick the annual sun returns,
> Mounts to the ledge and scans the pillowed face
> Whereon four seasons hardly have writ the trace,
> Though ever he on his timeless circuit mourns
> That faintlier his fire burns.

Reprinted from *Essays in Criticism* (Second Series) University of California Press Publications in English, 4 (1934), 61-89, by permission of the author's widow and the publisher.

We watch the theme of Donne's *Good-morrow* flowering inexhaustibly in Miss Millay's *Fatal Interview* and in the rival sonnets of Miss Wylie. Even in such fiction as Mrs. Muir's *Imagined Corners* we see the divine spark, although no nook or cranny in that story would have been imaginable to Donne. Above all, in Mr. T. S. Eliot's *poetry* we feel the justification of his recent assertion[3] that it is the special glory of our time to have understood Donne. Perhaps it is to the by no means accidental fact that Mr. Eliot has both responded to Donne as an artist and devoted much critical attention to him and to his contemporaries that we should attribute the confident possessiveness of recent criticism. Our comprehension of poetry has become involved in our analysis of Donne. He has become the key, or one of the principal keys, to the great mystery.

Critical rationalization of our passion for Donne has two aspects which are at bottom one. We kidnap him from the past and make him a "philosopher" and "poet-hero," as Mr. Sitwell calls him in *Doctor Donne and Gargantua,* by insisting on (*a*) his intellectuality, which is our term for his wit, and on (*b*) his skepticism, which is our term for his attitude toward the natural sciences and metaphysics. This study will raise some objection to both these critical rationalizations, and especially to the second of them. To the first, so far as it is a strictly technical canon of criticism, no objection can be raised. Although in 1912 Professor Grierson did justice to the technical importance of what he called "the blend of passion and thought" in the *Song and Sonets,* we owe our present appreciation of the fusion of mind and sensation in Donne largely to Mr. T. S. Eliot. His response to Donne both as artist and as critic has resulted from his perception that metaphysical poetry is—as he said in his Clark Lectures—"that in which what is ordinarily apprehensible by thought is brought within the grasp of feeling." To this fundamental insight he must owe many of the technical qualities which he shares with Donne, even to the metrical dexterity which Mrs. Rachel Annand Taylor attributes to his sophistication by "the bitter breaks and pauses, the deep-sought and far-carrying music of Donne."[4] In more than one context Mr. Eliot has restated his belief, and his definitions of metaphysical poetry are likely to rank historically with Dr. Johnson's, or even to outrank Johnson's by their power to arouse poetic purpose. His disciple, Mr. George Williamson, has recently phrased his principles in one clear formula: "Metaphysical poetry springs from the effort to resolve an emotional tension by means of intellectual equivalents which terminate in the senses, or possess the quality of sensation."[5] How far and fast we have moved under Mr. Eliot's guidance can be measured by comparison of this definition with that of Professor Alden in 1917. Mr. Alden defined Metaphysical "wit" as making such considerable use of intellectual processes as to "take precedence, at least for the moment, of the normal poetic process."[6] Here there is still a trace of Dr. Johnson's distrust of metaphysical "wit," and in Professor Grierson's Introduction to his edition of the *Poetical Works* in 1912 the entire essay—which is still the best complete appraisal of Donne—is moderated by the authority of Johnson and Dryden.

In the end it may prove that Professor Grierson was right in placing a
certain discount upon Donne's wit—in insisting that there is bad taste in some
of Donne's work. No poet can polarize his faculties in all that he writes, and
no amount of faith in the value of mind in poetry can justify the unassimi-
lated elements in Donne's verse. Even so excellent a principle as Mr. Eliot's
doctrine of the fusion of thought with feeling as the basis of his poetry can
be overstated. Mr. Eliot himself is responsible for the dubious turn which
has been given to it in.interpreting the metaphysical poets. Writing of their
"wit" generally in his essay on Marvell, he says:

> We can say that wit is not erudition; it is something stifled by erudition,
> as in much of Milton. It is not cynicism, though it has a kind of tough-
> ness which may be confused with cynicism by the tender-minded. It is
> confused with erudition because it belongs to an educated mind, rich in
> generations of experience; and it is confused with cynicism because it
> implies a constant inspection and criticism of experience. It involves,
> probably, a recognition, implicit in the expression of every experience,
> of other kinds of experience which are possible.[7]

This is silencing Dr. Johnson with a vengeance. For Mr. Eliot, metaphysical
wit has become a symbol for the artist's intelligence working in a complex
civilization with full poetic control of all the factors which are active in
the minds of his contemporaries. We may be pardoned for suspecting that
his judgment in this matter does more violence to Donne and his congeners
historically than Dr. Johnson's opinions have done, and that it perilously
disregards history. Let us look for a moment at its effect upon Mr. Williamson.

In a book published in 1931, to which Mr. Eliot has given his general
assent[8] and praise within the past few months, Mr. Williamson founds his
study of "The Donne Tradition" upon the challenge that:

> Great as Milton was in learning, Donne was probably greater. In know-
> ledge of the world they cannot be compared. Of all the explorers of the
> soul who come within the seventeenth century, Donne, and not Milton,
> deserves to stand next to Shakespeare.[9]

As a whole, Mr. Williamson's book pivots upon his challenge to the reputations of Milton and Spenser. The nature of the Donne tradition is defined
"concisely . . . as complex, sensuous and intellectual as opposed to the
simple, sensuous and passionate tradition."[10] By appealing to doctors of
every critical school the defense of complex, sensuous, and intellectual
poetry is shrewdly consolidated. Beginning with Johnson's definition of
metaphysical wit, as a *discordia concors,* Mr. Williamson descends the years,
gathering support for Johnson's analysis of Donne's talent and at the same
time discrediting Johnson's disvaluation of that talent. Man after man is
quoted to warrant the use of Donne's astringent fusion of mind and sensation as a poetical touchstone; and the whole modern critical host deploys
—with Professor Courthope alone playing the part of Abdiel—to agree with

Mr. F. L. Lucas that:

> It is in fact toward more brain that poetry must continue to travel, as
> it has travelled since it began. There is no going back. If the reason has
> taken too much, it has given other things; if it destroyed the ballad, it
> brought us Donne; we need more of it, not less.[11]

Armed with his touchstone, Mr. Williamson attacks the poetical reputations of both the Renaissance and the nineteenth century. After sacrificing
Milton and Spenser, he laments that "the nineteenth-century poets lost this
quality [of sensuousness suffused with intellect], that they think and feel
by starts, that their images are not the very body of their thought."[12] Then
with equal boldness he assumes that Donne's influence has been the dominant
creative stimulus in English poetry since his death. "The influences which
moulded the Cavalier school," we are told, "were no doubt three; Donne,
Jonson, the Latin and Greek lyrists; and of these the chief was Donne."[13]
Man by man the seventeenth-century poets go into Mr. Williamson's crucible,
and when the dross has been refined away the gold is stamped as pure
Donnean metal. The elixir is present not only in Marvell's *Coy Mistress* and
Crashaw's *Saint Theresa,* but even in Dryden's *Hind and the Panther.* And
the nineteenth century is partly redeemed by the stream of power that
flows from Donne, reflection of whose imagination Mr. Williamson finds it
"difficult not to see . . . in the images of Browning, Meredith, Rossetti,
Coventry Patmore and Francis Thompson."[14]

Tennyson and Spenser will probably survive the raid upon their reputations, and critical scholarship should be grateful for any reminder that the
stars differ in glory. The objection to Mr. Williamson's theory is not its on-
slaught upon the immortals but the claims that it makes for Donne's influence.
Let us take a crucial application. Mr. Williamson illustrates his assertion that
Donne was the greatest poetic stimulus among his later contemporaries by
focussing a chapter upon the tension imparted to his poetry by his treatment
of death. Hence comes a quality to which he refers several times as the
"metaphysical shudder." The mood of death-consciousness—of awareness
of ultimate contrasts and of amazement like Pascal's in the infinite presence
—seems to him to be a stamp set upon the work of Donne's followers by the
master. He catches it in many an allusion to death in the *Songs and Sonets,*
such as

> A bracelet of bright haire about the bone,

and in Walton's story of the portrait taken in the shroud, and in all that
fascination by death which is represented for us by Webster's plays and by
the religious poetry which culminates in Crashaw. In George Herbert's poems
he identifies it particularly in the following lines from *Vertue:*

> Only a sweet and vertuous soul,
> Like season'd timber, never gives;

> But though the whole world turn to coal,
> Then chiefly lives.[15]

The shock of the image of the world turned to a coal evokes the authentic shudder. It is a capital application of the touchstone. But to at least one reader the thrill given by Herbert's image is that of St. Paul's "O death, where is thy sting?" And Herbert's passage, instead of stirring a sympathetic tremor in Donne's lute, moves a vibration in an iron string of the least metaphysical of poets:

> Iustum et tenacem propositi virum,
>
> . . . . . .
>
> Si fractus inlabitur orbis,
> Impavidum ferient ruinae.

The real basis of Herbert's thought is neither Horace nor Donne, but the meditation which was the climax of most of the books of devotion in the sixteenth and seventeenth centuries. "Nullum est genus mortis, quod nocere potest iusto," is the caption of the final chapter of John Conway's *Meditations and Praiers* (1570), which, "like all the writings of its kind ends up with death, a subject of alchemic potency for the imagination of the time."[16]

Whatever ground there may be for making Donne's wit a touchstone for contemporary poetry, there is none for making it a master key to literary history. The more absolute we make our estimate of Donne's wit, and of metaphysical wit in general, the less historically revealing becomes our appreciation of Donne.

II

Because skepticism rather than faith is the basis of modern thought, Donne's singularly intellectual imagination seems to us skeptical. It is in the character of a skeptic, indeed, that he is most familiar in current criticism. Mrs. Simpson thinks that it is the "sense of questioning and adventure which keeps much of Donne's work alive today."[17] Mr. Williamson names skepticism, flanked by sex, as the axis of Donne's poetic personality.[18] Mr. Theodore Spencer devotes several pages of his essay on *Donne and His Age* to proof that Donne was in harmony with both his own age and ours through his skepticism. An extensive parallel is drawn between Hamlet's cosmic doubts as they are expressed in the doctrine that "there's nothing good nor bad but thinking makes it so" and Donne's challenge that

> There's nothing simply good, nor ill alone,
> Of every quality comparison,
> The onely measure is, and judge, opinion. . . .

"Donne's melancholy," says Mr. Spencer, "is the result of inaction; he cannot choose; his will is in a state of paralysis. And it is just this lack of fusion between action and will which makes *Hamlet* so interesting to us and so significant of its time."[19] The parallel with *Hamlet* may be even more significant than Mr. Spencer suggests. To realistic students of Shakespeare his whole discussion will seem scandalous; and if his meaning is that by some fineness of nature or some doubtful inner struggle of purpose against weakness Hamlet is inhibited from acting, he deserves the scorn which Mr. Stoll has poured upon "the dark and cryptic ways of psychological exegesis."[20] If—transcending the realists with another commentator—he means that *Hamlet,* the play and not the man, is, as Mr. Masefield describes it, "a questioning of vision," he must follow Mr. Knight in regarding Hamlet, the man, as embodying some of Shakespeare's "dark, death forces."[21] Then Donne also must become a sinister type of skeptic and a man headed for tragedy. It is not quite in this way that current opinion regards the "sense of questioning and adventure" in his poetry, but we may find more reason to think that his skepticism had a genuine strand of this kind than that it was germinal and revolutionary, as we are taught to regard it. There are two distinct skepticisms in the Donne who exists for us in the *Paradoxes and Problems* and in the profane poems. One of them is hesitation between the old religion and the new. That, of course, is antithetical to all modern skepticism, and even in the seventeenth century it won respect as the deepest expression of religious faith. The other was a genuine "questioning of vision," which is a different matter—as will appear later—from modern philosophical relativism. It seemed to Donne a kind of sin against the light; and even to us it can hardly appear other than sinister—a "death force," as Mr. Knight uses the term in his discussion of Shakespeare's imaginative world.

The skepticism which makes Donne seem modern to moderns is of a quite different order. They discover in him what seems to them an open-minded dubiety about cosmic matters, and a Baconian enthusiasm for natural science coupled with a more than Baconian prescience in things astronomical. The promptness of his perusal of the books of Tycho Brahe and Kepler is regarded as proving his sympathy with the outcome of their speculation, which was still on the knees of the gods. Indeed, his interest in scientific subjects generally is sometimes made to seem rather like that which is attributed now to M. Paul Valéry, and his poetry is regarded as a precipitate from his reading in natural philosophy. When he wrote that the "new philosophy" (i.e., the Copernican astronomy) called all in doubt, he is thought to have been looking down the future with some grand, Baconian surmise. Among laymen, respect for his poetry sometimes proves to be founded upon the illusion that he was a pioneer of the Copernican astronomy in England. Even scholars are not entirely immune to the temptation. Mrs. Simpson yields to it in some degree by her italicization of Ignatius Loyola's words, in *Ignatius his Conclave,* that Copernicus' theory may well be true.[22] On the other hand, Miss Ramsay counters with the positive statement that Donne was never shaken in his belief in the Ptolemaic system.

In Donne's Sermons there are several passages which may be quoted against Miss Ramsay, but opinions about their real significance will differ.

Thus, for example, Mr. Bredvold prints the following passage from the sermon at the funeral of Sir William Cokayne:

> . . . What one thing doe we know perfectly? Whether wee consider Arts, or Sciences, the servant knows but according to the proportion of his Masters knowledge in that Art, and the Scholar knows but according to the proportion to his Masters knowledge in that Science; Young men mend not their sight by using old mens Spectacles; and yet we looke upon Nature, but with *Aristotles* Spectacles, and upon the body of man, but with *Galens,* and upon the frame of the world, but with Ptolomies spectatacles.[23]

To Mr. Bredvold and also to Mrs. Simpson this passage seems to show that Donne in his later years was impatient of the conservatism of his contemporaries. To other readers, the passage, if account be taken of its context, may indicate that he doubted the possibility of scientific knowledge in every field, and despised the doctors of all schools because they deluded the laity. After a short break, Donne continued on the same page:

> And if there by any addition to knowledge, it is rather a new knowledge, than a greater knowledge; rather a singularity in a desire of proposing something that was not knowne at all before, than an emproving, an advancing, a multiplying of former inceptions; . . ."[24]

In the famous passages in *Ignatius his Conclave* where Donne introduces Copernicus with Paracelsus, Pietro Aretino, and a host of charlatans all competing with Boniface III and Mahomet for the highest place in hell's penetralium, he is not maintaining a skeptical impartiality between the old philosophy and the new. Only in the light of subsequent events does he seem to have been skeptically suspicious of ancient falsehood and receptive to dawning truth. Much may be surmised from the rather spoofing speech of Ignatius to Copernicus, which contains an aside observing that the astronomer's theory may be true. Just as much has been surmised— quite without justification—from the random note of Nicholas of Cusa, made in 1444, suggesting a triple motion for the earth. In spite of the reputation which Nicholas of Cusa has enjoyed as a precursor of Copernicus, it seems that he has been misjudged, and that he never deviated from the mystical skepticism toward natural philosophy which he embodied in the *De Docta Ignorantia.*[25] Probably Donne's attitude in *Ignatius his Conclave* can be much better understood in the light of the *De Docta Ignorantia* than it can in that of Copernicus' *De Revolutionibus Orbium Coelestium.*

Yet Donne was no mystic and no obscurantist. When Kepler proved that the Ptolemaic catalogue of the stars fell short of the number actually visible, he accepted the evidence; and in *Biathanatos* we find him scoring the "pertinacy" which "is imputed"—by others, as he is careful to imply, although he evidently sympathized with them—

to *Aristoteles* followers, who defending the Heavens to be inalterable, because in so many ages nothing had been observed to have been altered, his Schollers stubbornly maintain his Proposition still, though by many experiences of new Stars, the reason which moved *Aristotle* seems now to be utterly defeated.[26]

Here again it would be easy in the twentieth century to mistake Donne's meaning. The superlunar immutability which had been one of Aristotle's capital legacies to the Middle Ages was a theory quite independent of the Ptolemaic geocentric universe, although the two had been complementary. The changelessness and perfection of the heavenly bodies was a bulwark of human security which had long ago fallen. By general acknowledgement Mutability had climbed to heaven, but God in some strange way still governed a Ptolemaic cosmos.

Setting aside for the moment Donne's intellectual curiosity about the new science, we can make sure that in the depths of his imagination he was unmoved by Copernicus. In the Sermons there is good evidence that the new theory never disturbed the bottoms of his mind and that his emotions were deeply involved in the old cosmic scheme. Thus, for example, at St. Paul's on Easter Day in 1627 he said:

> . . . Nay, the ordinary things in Nature, would be greater miracles, than the extraordinary, which we admire most, if they were done but once; The standing still of the Sun, for *Josuahs* use, was not, in it selfe, so wonderfull a thing, as that so vast and immense a body as the Sun, should run so many miles, in a minute; The motion of the Sun were a greater wonder than the standing still, if all were to begine againe; . . .[27]

Similar passages might be multiplied, all indicating that, like King John and the Archbishop's brother in the ballad, Donne believed that,

> In twenty-four houres, with-out any doubt,
> Your Grace may the world goe round about;
> The world round about, euen as I doe say,
> If with the sun you can goe the next way.

His repetition of his wonder at the sun's terrific motion betrays the unbroken set of his imagination from youth. In his Songs his Ptolemaic notions were even more dogmatic than Hamlet's in the appeal to Ophelia to

> Doubt that the sun doth move.

Donne invoked the movement of the *primum mobile* itself:

> Nay, if I wax but cold in my desire,
> Think, heaven hath motion lost, . . .[28]

We may be sure also that if Donne had any inclination to accept the Copernican theory he was unenthusiastic. At the close of the sixteenth century the old astronomy and the new were respectively in positions resembling those of the Newtonian and the "new" physics today. The strength of the new astronomy was partly the weakness of the old, and the old was weak not only technically but also in its appeal to men's imaginations. By recent evidence and speculation the Ptolemaic system had been made to seem not only decadent in itself but also to involve the decadence of the universe. The conception is embodied in Spenser's Prologue to the Fifth Book of *The Faerie Queene,* where he refers to the disturbing precession of the equinoxes and introduces the then current delusion that the sun was receding from the temperate zone:

> Ne is that same great glorious lampe of light,
> That doth enlumine all these lesser fyres,
> In better case, ne keepes his course more right,
> But is miscaried with the other spheres.
> For since the terme of fourteene hundred yeres,
> That learned Ptolomaee his hight did take,
> He is declyned from that marke of theirs
> Nigh thirtie minutes to the southerne lake;
> That makes me feare in time he will us quite forsake.[29]

Reflections like those in this stanza represent a kind of sixteenth-century version of the modern physical law of entropy. They proved that the universe was running down. An inevitable corollary was belief in the decay of the biological and moral universe; and to that belief Spenser gave expression in the following stanzas, where he contrasted the perfection and stability of the Golden Age with the unquiet misery of his own. When the Copernican cosmos broke upon men's minds—coming as it did after bitter struggles against several other novel theories which were at war with it as well as with the obsolescent Ptolemaic doctrine—it brought no emotional relief and little imaginative stimulus with its bolder and clearer vision of the skies. To most men it brought the final evidence of the mutability of all things, and on that account Donne showed himself unfriendly to it in his sermon at the funeral of Sir William Cokayne:

> I need not call in new Philosophy, that denies a settlednesse, an acquiescence in the very body of the Earth, but makes the Earth to move in that place, where we thought the Sunne had moved; I need not that helpe, that the Earth it selfe is in Motion, to prove this, That nothing upon Earth is permanent; . . .[30]

In all his allusions to the "new philosophy" in the sermons and equally in the profane poems Donne showed himself conscious of it as a portent of evil. The *Second Anniversarie* is built upon the idea that the universe is at the end of a degenerative process which began with the fall of Lucifer, and its climax is the exclamation that the "new philosophy calls all in doubt," which is sometimes quoted as an example of Donne's sympathy with the new theories. His real feeling about them was perhaps not unlike Tennyson's, in *In Memoriam,* toward the new biology, except that Donne in his heart felt himself so secure in God's earth-centered universe that the core of his

religious faith never suffered. Certainly he never rose to the challenge of
Copernicus. That way, for him, lay madness, as one of his figures in a verse
letter to the Countess of Bedford indicates:

> As new Philosophy arrests the Sunne,
>   And bids the passive earth about it runne,
> So wee have dull'd our minde, it hath no ends; . . .[31]

We have seen reason to suppose that Donne was as conservative as his
contemporaries in his very limited recognition of the depredation of mutability in those eternal, quintessential heavens which St. Thomas Aquinas took
from Aristotle and the Neo-Platonists and handed on to Dante. For many
of his contemporaries the "new philosophy" had consquences in the biological realm which threw open the doors to genuine skepticism about man
and his destiny. In the *Paradoxes, Songs,* and *Elegies,* where—as we shall
see—Donne was enamored of a traditional form of moral skepticism which
made "Nature" its shibboleth, we might expect to find some trace of this
more dangerous, contemporary skeptical naturalism that was abroad in the
world. In 1623 Donne might have read a polemic (the *Doctrine curieuse des
beaux esprit de ce temps* of the Père Garasse[32]) replying to Pomponazzi's
denial of immortality and to the very much more subversive doctrines which
Cardan and Vanini drew from the prevalent belief that lower forms of life
were spontaneously engendered from the slime. Such ideas may have been
the basis of Sir Walter Raleigh's mooted "atheism" and they had their
adepts in England, perhaps as early as Marlowe, but we look in vain for any
sign of interest in them in Donne. If they reached him at all it was by way
of his theological studies. We find him in his salad days, in the *Problemes,*[33]
making sport of "the *disputation* of the *Schoolemen,* why the *Divell* could
not make *lice* in *Egypt,*" and arguing on the eve of entering the Church, in
the *Essays in Divinity,*[34] that it "is a kind of treason and clipping of God's
coin" to deny that, "either then the creature [i.e., the "cyniphs" or lice]
being entirely new, the devil understood not of what it was composed; or
God changed the form of dust into another form, which the devil could
never do." The recurrence of this interest appears to have been the result
of his early reading of the Catholic writer, Pererius, whose commentary on
Exodus gave it currency in minds that were absorbed in theology and in-
trigued by black magic. Donne's interest in the matter began by being
satirical and ended by becoming serious, but he was blind to the skeptical
affinities of the topic. To his mind the spontaneous generation of life from
the slime was significant of the end of the world rather than of its beginnings.
In his Whitsunday sermon in 1625 he remarked that:

> The seasons of the yeare[were] irregular and distempered; the Sun fainter,
> and languishing; men lesse in stature, and shorter-lived. No addition, but
> only every yeare, new sorts, new species of wormes, and flies, and sick-
> nesses, which argue more and more putrefaction of which they are en-
> gendred.[35]

All the evidence shows that from his first literary experiments until he wrote *Death's Duell,* Donne thought of the universe as the Ptolemaic machine pictured by St. Thomas and Dante, and that for him time began and ended with creation. In the *Paradoxes* we find him arguing that death is the perfection of all things and that, barring the miracle of God's activity, "the frame of the whole *World,* . . . because it *began,* must *dye.*"[36] In the *Essays in Divinity* he prepared himself for Holy Orders by recollecting that:

> Another instrument and engine of Thine [St. Thomas], whom thou hadst so enabled that nothing was too mineral nor centric for the search and reach of his wit, hath remembered me: That it is an article of our belief that the world began.[37]

In the *Sermons* he is often fascinated by God's eternity and by the brevity of created time. Those themes went down to the lowest levels of his consciousness, and they emerged in countless forms.

> Clocks and Sun-dials were but a late invention upon earth; but the Sun it self, and the earth it self, was but a late invention in heaven: God had been an infinite, a super-infinite, an unimaginable space, millions of millions of unimaginable spaces in heaven, before the Creation. And our afternoon shall be as long as Gods forenoon; . . .[38]

A curious indication of the deep roots struck into Donne's consciousness by the conception of the noon of time dividing the morning from the afternoon of eternity is his attitude toward the doctrine of transmigration. He was prone to deny the idea, and his attacks upon it always involved his dislike of its implication of a backward, earthly eternity. His belief was always that of divine infusion of the soul into the human embryo, which he recognized incidentally in the *Paradoxes.*[39] To his essentially Catholic mind transmigration seemed monstrous. The monstrousness of that doctrine as it seemed to him is the basis of his "blasphemous" *Progresse of the Soule.* In that "sullen writ" the wanton invention mocks the enemies rather than the friends of orthodoxy.

The break in Donne's thinking made by his entry into holy orders is easy to overstress. The old Donne never quite disappeared and, sincerely devotional though he tried to be in his later years, Mrs. Taylor is right in saying that "there lingers about him something unexorcized, as if pagan incense were burning in a Christian crypt."[40] But his paganism was the paganism of the Renaissance, and it is misleading to build a biographical study upon the intellectual gulf between Donne the pagan and Donne the preacher, as Mr. Hugh I'A. Fausset has done, bridging it only by the survival of the dynamic passions of the first stage in the last; or to follow Mr. Sitwell in his fancy that Donne's whole experience was a drift toward submergence in the passion of the Poseidonia. In *Doctor Donne and Gargantua,* Mr. Sitwell writes as a good contemporary of D. H. Lawrence. He puts his personal problems, and the problem of us all, essentially as it is put and answered in *The Plumed Serpent.* Like Mrs. Mary Austin, watching the aboriginal dances in New Mexico with robust enthusiasm, and like the hero of Mr. Walpole's *Portrait of a Man with Red Hair,* who resolves his stresses by intoxicating himself with a primitive Welsh festival, Mr. Sitwell makes a sympathetic glimpse of a Dionysiac ceremony the final insight of Donne's life. For that reason he believes that Donne and Gargantua patterned

> . . . past and future with the moment's mark;
> They are the walls between these times,
> That move, but not with either,
> For their bulk is our fine watershed
> And watching through the window
> Time has its arbiter in their two shapes,
> That march where they please, but carry fate
>   with them.[41]

By confusing Donne's paganism with our contemporary brand, Mr. Sitwell furnishes us with a fine example of the kidnapping in which current criticism is setting the fashion for scholarship.

Donne's paganism, like that of Nature's devotee, Edmund in *Lear,* was a revolt against the divine laws which was a kind of homage to the divinity which it defied. It was a revolt of the body rather than of the brain. The *Songs* and *Elegies* show no trace of the scientific and metaphysical skepticism which was penetrating England from Italy at the close of the sixteenth century, but, as Mr. Louis I. Bredvold has shown in an admirable application of the results of research to criticism,[42] they are full of the Pyrrhonism and naturalism which for Donne's contemporaries were associated with the names of Lucretius, Jean de Meung, and Montaigne. One of Mr. Bredvold's capital points is his observation that the insolence and perverse wit of the *Songs* and *Elegies,* their bold defiance of the *ius naturale,* which "had been the fundamental doctrine of political thought and social ethics in Europe from the Stoics and Cicero through the Renaissance," was a form of moral revolt which had been traditional for centuries. Its cardinal doctrine of ethical relativity, which underlies Donne's secular poems in large measure and which he declared in the lines,

> There's nothing simply good, nor ill alone,
> Of every quality comparison,
>   The onely measure is, and judge, opinion. . . .

was a challenge to the Stoic law of nature in the name of that sinister power which Edmund invoked when he asked "Nature" to be his goddess. Challenges to the *ius naturale* left as a legacy to posterity by Cicero's *De Legibus* had been a part of western literature for sixteen centuries or longer. The *Elegies* and *Songs* of Donne preserve its stigmata of thought and even of language as they are recorded as far back as Lactantius' record of the sophistries to which Cicero's argument in the *De Legibus* was addressed. Perhaps it goes back to the Greek distinction between φύσις and νόμος. In the Renaissance the challenge was renewed and reinterpreted by Machiavelli and Mon-

taigne. Ethical relativism became almost, but not quite, respectable. Superficially it was related to the current ideas of the mutability of the universe
to which the "new philosophy" gave rise. In one of the *Paradoxes,* where
Donne is talking about the changeability of women, we can see the curiously self-conscious and external union of the two relativisms:

> They cannot [wrote Donne] be immutable like stockes, like stones, like
> the Earths dull Center; Gold that lyeth still, rusteth; Water, corrupteth;
> Aire that moveth not, poysoneth; then why should that which is the
> perfection of other things, be imputed to Women as greatest imperfec-
> tion? . . . *Inconstancy* is a most commendable and cleanly quality, and
> Women in this quality are farre more absolute than the Heavens, than
> the Starres, Moone, or any thing beneath it: for long observation hath
> pickt certainety out of their mutability.[43]

The spirit of this passage is like that of Queen Elizabeth's motto, *Per
molto variare la natura è bella.* It falls just short of Montaigne's understanding that man is "divers et ondoyant." In Donne's passage there is a suggestion
of recklessness, as if with schoolboy glee he were playing with fire. The
themes with which he was playing are the same as those which were imaginatively felt in many of Shakespeare's tragedies, such as *Troilus and Cressida*
and *Hamlet,* as "death forces." From Donne's language it is plain that he
regarded his defense of changeability in women from mutability in nature
as sophistical. Like Nash, he took delight in upsetting the polite world by
means of its own principles and its own logic, but even in the *Paradoxes* he
was fully conscious of his pose. We may be wrong to discount his positive
assertion in 1608 that they were written as whetstones for other men's wits.
The inversion of old ideas to find new meanings was the essence of Donne's
"wit," but in the best of his poetry the new meanings were never mere in-
versions of the old. In his youth his conception of nature was hardly that
which in later life he was fond of stating in St. Augustine's words, "Dei
voluntas rerum natura est"; but the man who spent a part of his twentieth
year in comparing the Protestant with the Roman Catholic apologists is not
likely ever to have been altogether emancipated from the sanctions which
he recognized in 1608 in *Biathanatos,* by appealing first to Nature, then to
Reason, and finally to God.

A passage in the *Second Anniversarie,* although it was written in 1612,
when Donne was "within the pale of Thy Church, and not in the wild
forest, and enlightened by some glimmerings of natural knowledge,"[44]
displays what was always his attitude toward natural science—an attitude
of contempt seasoned with restless curiosity:

> Have not all soules thought
> For many ages, that our body'is wrought
> Of Ayre, and Fire, and other Elements?
> And now they thinke of new ingredients,
> And one Soule thinkes one, and another way

Another thinkes, and 'tis an even lay.
Knowst thou but how the stone doth enter in
The bladders cave, and never breake the skinne?
Knowst thou how blood, which to the heart doth flow,
Doth from one ventricle to th'other goe?
And for the putrid stuffe, which thou dost spit,
Know's thou how thy lungs have attracted it?
There are no passages, so that there is
(For ought thou know'st) piercing of substances.
And of those many opinions which men raise
Of Nailes and Haires, dost thou know which to praise?
What hope have wee to know our selves, when wee
Know not the least things, which for our use be?
We see in Authors, too stiffe to recant,
A hundred controversies of an Ant;
And yet one watches, starves, freeses, and sweats,
To know but Catechismes and Alphabets
Of unconcerning things, matters of fact; . . .[45]

Here the felling about science may be explained as a mystic's obscurantism
or as a kind of Socratic skepticism. Neither explanation hits the mark, for
Donne was neither Socratic nor mystic. In his passages of most impassioned
Christian profession in the *Sermons* he does not reach St. Augustine's desire
to know nothing but God and the soul, although he may have sympathized
with St. Thomas' condemnation of all physical science as irreligious, if not
sacrilegious.

So much has been written about Donne's scientific curiosity and his
skepticism that we wrap him up in our modern scientific consciousness.
Throughout his poems the number of allusions to all the sciences is not
large and their points of focus are not far apart. The most typical of them
is recognized in the figure of the spreading and closing compass in *A Valediction: forbidding mourning.* The theme is the division and reunion of lovers,
and that matter, or else the value of love, the ever fixed mark whose worth's
unknown although its height be taken, is the theme of them all. The figure
of the compasses was not original with Donne. It stared up at him from the
title-page of his copy of Justus Lipsius' *De Constantia* and from the title-page
of every book from the Plantin Press which fell into his hands. The figures
of a man with a spade, symbolizing labor, and of a woman are separated in
the Plantin insignia by a pair of compasses manipulated on a sheet of paper.
Labore et Constantia is the motto. The application to lovers who are separated by the man's response to the challenge of labor may not have been the
accepted meaning of the insignia, but it is on the surface. Donne simply
translated it into a passionate, realistic poem. The sensuous power of his
lines, which some critics have described as an almost tactile apprehension of
his thought or a veritable grasp upon it by several of his senses together, may
be a result of repeated glimpses of his idea made visible and almost tangible

in a drawing. It would be rash to suggest that some of his great conceits
might prove to be unconventional translations into poetry of fancies which
were already dear to his contemporaries in pictures. Certainly, in his youth,
he can have had little sympathy with the writers of Emblem poetry, although
in age Walton reports him as susceptible to their taste for allegorical pictures.
How much of his sensuous enjoyment and expression of his thoughts in his
poetry was a part of his common inheritance with Spenser and Ben Jonson
of the habit of twisting ideas into vivid, fanciful, symbolic images in Emblems
and Masques, who can tell? There is a catastrophic Ph.D. thesis in the question.

In *A Valediction: of the booke,* although the closing simile is hardly
more "scientific" than that of the compasses, it is more elaborate and
strange:

> Thus vent thy thoughts; abroad I'll studie thee,
>   As he removes farre off, that great heights takes;
>   How great love is, presence best tryall makes,
> But absence tryes how long this love will bee;
>   To take a latitude
>   Sun, or starres, are fitliest view'd
>   At their brightest, but to conclude
>   Of longitudes, what other way have wee,
> But to marke when, and where the darke eclipses bee?[46]

Such use of scientific imagery as this only faintly adumbrates that "unifying
of his sensibility by the integration of his reading in anthropology, biology,
psychology and philosophy" which Mr. Blackmur regards as vitally relating
Mr. T. S. Eliot's work to that of Donne.[47] In spite of his consistent interest
Donne never took natural science seriously; from first to last his attitude
resembled that of Nicholas of Cusa in the *De Docta Ignorantia.* His contempt for adepts of natural philosophy can hardly be distinguished from
contempt for natural philosophy itself. In the *Problemes* he despised
"Physitians contemplating Nature [who], finding many abstruse things subject to the search of Reason, thinks [sic] therefore that all is so."[48] His candid mind recognized the validity of those scientific discoveries which, like
the increase in the number of stars beyond Ptolemy's catalogue, could be
attested by the senses, but it balked at the theories—and that is tantamount
to the significance—of the "new philosophy." In contrast to Bacon, Donne
never looked forward to a discovery of truth which would give him mastery
and the enjoyment of it symbolized by Bacon's figure of the mind turning
on the poles of truth. His nearest approach to the modern attitude was his
playful contention in the third Paradox that "Discord increases Religion."
On the surface this seems amazingly modern, if it be contrasted with the
timidity of Donne's contemporary, Samuel Daniel, in the face of the skepticism which warring creeds together with new philosophies had brought upon
Europe. In *The Civile Wars* Daniel made Nemesis charge Pandora to empty
her box over Christendom:

Goe therefore thou, with all thy stirring traine
Of swelling Sciences, the gifts of griefe:
Go loose the links of that soule-binding chaine;
Inlarge the vninquisitiue Beliefe:
Call-up mens spirits, that simplenes retaine:
Enter their hearts, & Knowledge make the thiefe
To open all the doores, to let in light;
That all may all things see, but what is right.

Opinion Arme against Opinion growne:
Make new-borne Contradiction still to rise;
As if *Thebes*-founder, *Cadmus,* tongues had sowne,
Instead of teeth, for greater mutinies.
Bring new-defended Faith, against Faith known:
Weary the Soule with contrarieties:
Till all Religion become retrograde,
And that faire tire, the maske of sinne be made.[49]

In Donne's *Satyre III* we have an expression of his attitude toward truth, in the widest meaning of the word, which must have been carefully expressed and deeply felt. His defense of liberty of conscience against the principle *cuius regio eius religio* deserves to be even better known than it is, and his assertion that truth is a spirit to be wooed by hard *ascesis* of the flesh and brain is familiar:

On a huge hill,
Cragged, and steep, Truth stands, and hee that will
Reach her, about must, and about must goe; . . .[50]

The essential matter in the satire, however, for the investigator of his thought, is the assertion that

. . . though truth and falsehood bee
Neare twins, yet truth a little elder is;[51]

and the opening assertion that his "Mistresse" is "faire Religion." Like Milton in the *Areopagitica,* Donne thought of truth as a power in the realms of both knowledge and behavior, of which men had been in possession in the past and to which they must win their way back. He made the relation of natural science to truth humbly, if not negligibly, ancillary. There was an element of primitivism in his thought, as there was in Milton's; and each did its part to break the ground for the primitivism which Professor Lovejoy has studied in the deism of the seventeenth century.[52] Of the two men Donne was immeasurably the more conservative, the more appreciative of tradition. His faith in the possibility of finding truth was radical, but it did not lie in the way of founding new commonwealths or preaching the advancement of learning.

III

Here the discussion of Donne's "skepticism" might be left, yet it may be of interest to examine a recent attempt to read a modern meaning into one of his best known poems, *The Extasie*. The poem has been variously interpreted as a frank plea for the flesh—a plea springing from the poet's deepest "philosophy"—and as a revolt against "Platonism," a revolt carried, in the judgment of one critic, to the point of treating *The Extasie* as a purely objective study in seduction. The most extreme statement of the former point of view is Mr. Sencourt's comparison of the poem to Rodin's *Baiser suprème*.[53] The latter is adopted by M. Pierre Legouis,[54] to whom the poem appears to represent a seduction studied with a technique like that of Browning in *Men and Women*. M. Legouis' attitude resembles that of a recent writer who pities the nineteenth-century public for "not being able to understand that one may follow with a great deal of intellectual interest the growth of a passion . . . out of purely intellectual curiosity."[55] Repudiating Professor Grierson's notes on the poem, which compare it with the Plotinian conception of mystical ecstasy and with Donne's own definition of letter-writing as a kind of ecstasy which mystically unites friends, he sees it as a dramatic analysis of the degradation of a liaison which has begun by being "Platonic."

Two treatments of the situation in *The Extasie* were familiar to Donne. They may be called the Puritanical and the Metaphysical. Both were parts of the "Platonic" tradition. One of the songs in George Withers' *Fair Virtue* exemplifies the Puritanic handling of the theme. Two lovers in a garden with "their souls infus'd into each other," after hours of innocent communion, felt lust enkindled. Deadly sin would have been the consequence, if the lady had not inquired:

> What goodly thing do we obtain
>   If I consent to thee?
> Rare joys we lose, and what we gain,
>   But common pleasures be:
> Yea, those (some say) who are to lust inclined,
>   Drive love out of the mind;
>   And so much reason miss,
>   That they admire,
>   What kind of fire
> A chaste affection is.[56]

After seven such stanzas as this all danger is past and the lover is no less delighted than the lady to have escaped unscathed. "Go wantons, now," he exults,

> and flout at this

> My coldness, if you list;
> Vain fools, you never knew the bliss,
> That doth in love consist.[57]

The best "Platonists" themselves had reacted against this kind of thing, but modern readers and even modern scholars are inclined to submerge the Metaphysical under the Puritanical strain in the Platonism of the Renaissance.

We can meet the idea that *The Extasie* was a realist's reaction against the Neo-Platonic love poetry of the Renaissance by comparing it to another treatment of its theme which was traditional in that poetry. Once we perceive its relation to that tradition, M. Legouis' conception of it as a study of seduction can hardly be entertained. Elsewhere[58] I have traced the theme of the poem in Continental literature; here it is sufficient, in order to realize the traditional background, to quote from one of the most famous of the now forgotten poems of the sixteenth century in France, *La Parfaicte Amie* of Antoine Héroët. I translate from Héroët's third book, where he is treating the formal question in the casuistry of love which he derived from the adepts of Neo-Platonic passion in Italy (a casuistry which Donne in his turn was treating in *The Extasie*):

> Impute no ill if sometimes Cupid's saints—
> Rapt by the god beyond our world's restraints,
> Their souls united while their bodies lie
> Dead and forgotten in their ecstasy—
> Yield them naïvely to that hour's bliss,
> Exchange a hand-clasp, come even to a kiss.
> The heart's instinctive bounty is the source
> Of kind caresses bringing no remorse.
> And when the masters take a noble pleasure,
> The slaves, the bodies, must enjoy their treasure,
> Minting their wealth to images of joy
> Which the swift moments instantly destroy.
> The spirits in their absence take no keep
> Of what the bodies do in their dead sleep;
> Nor can the body's imbecility
> Know or tell aught of the soul's deity.

Evidently in Héroët's lines there is something more than a mere defense of the rights of the flesh. Here is something like what is symbolized by the "Prince," liberated from prison in *The Extasie*, and also like that other Prince of the lovers in *The Anniversarie,*

> Who Prince enough in one another bee.

We might regard the "Prince" as an emblem of sensual liberation with an overtone of the sympathy that it engenders between lovers, or perhaps see in it the spirit of the half-cynical "*kissing,* that strange and mysticall union of soules," of the second Paradox,[59] if we did not chance upon occurrences of the same theme with similar imagery elsewhere, not only in Donne's poems but also in those of a contemporary. Chapman, in *The Tears of Peace,* was certainly approximating to the theme of *The Extasie* when he spoke of the sun's rays penetrating the earth's atmosphere and soil to create gems, and added that so our "souls'. . . beams" must "dig in Bodies' mines"

> To find them rich discourses through their senses.[60]

The resemblance of Chapman's thought to Donne's cannot be mere coincidence. It forbids us to regard Donne's image of the Prince as the crowning irony in a drama of seduction. In the style of *The Extasie* there is revolt, but the whole poem is best read in the light of tradition. One final element in the tradition of which it was the heir, we may observe in the ambiguity of the term which is its title. The connotations of the word were both technical and emotional. Jean Bodin used it again and again in his *Theatre of Nature* as a part of his proof of the immortality of the soul. He triumphantly affirmed that "the phenomenon of *extasis* is certain; its positive assertion is possible."[61] Dreams and visions he regarded as forms of the phenomenon and its highest variety he thought was the beatific vision of God. Bodin was no mystic and he did not seriously reckon with Plotinus' conception of ecstasy as the final step in perception of Truth and of union with God—the supreme step where the ministry of the senses and of Beauty itself is transcended. Not many even of the religiously inclined poets of the Seventeenth Century shared the suspicion of raptures and transports which was felt by St. John of the Cross. The distinction was never really clear to Donne himself. His religious as well as his love poetry justifies the remark which Signor Mario Praz puts into the mouth of Mr. Narrowgate, in an essay on "Mysticism" in *The Criterion*: "No wonder ecstasy was popular during the Seventeenth Century, the century in which, more than in any other age, intellect, as an English critic has said, was on the tip of the senses."[62]

*　　　*　　　*　　　*　　　*

An attempt to rescue Donne from admirers who suppose that his intellect had a skeptical cast which disposed him to sympathy with modern psychology and with modern science generally, can hardly avoid the appearance of aspersing both him and them. To try to see him as he was, is like removing the fourteenth-century gilding from a Russian icon of the tenth century. Every audience makes its own experience of an artist's work, and when the artist is removed from his public by three hundred years, and when the modern conception of him has been interlaced with original and fructifying theories of poetry by at least one great poet, the recovery of the historic reality is an ungrateful task. Perhaps that may be why in recent years interpretation of Donne has been inclined to decry the scholarly approach. Donne, we are told, was more learned than Milton, yet the study of him by Miss Ramsay in terms of the medieval writers whom he passionately examined seems to Mr. T. S. Eliot to have been "outgrown,"[63] while Mr. Bredvold condemns it unsparingly:

> It is a great error to represent Donne's mind as always preoccupied with
> the subtleties of medieval thought. He was really preoccupied with the
> subtleties of his own soul.

In *Les doctrines medievales chez Donne* Miss Ramsay does overstate her
case, and Mr. Bredvold has fully earned the right to criticize her by his investigation of a stream of medieval influence on Donne's work of which she
took no account. Mr. Bredvold, by using the equipment of a modern literary
critic under the control of scholarship, indicates a *via media*; and in the
field indicated by the title, *Secentismo e marinismo in Inghilterra,* Signor
Mario Praz has traveled far by that route.[64] A poem such as *The Dreame,* for
example, gains as a work of art when it is placed in its historical setting so
that the elements of convention and revolt which went to its creation can be
felt by a modern reader.[65]

Unfortunately, Donne did not leave a word of literary criticism behind
him, and we know nothing about his theories of poetry, if he had any. Conceits he seems to have taken for a part of the universe in general rather than
as a property peculiar to literature. At least, in his *Devotions* he told the
Deity, "Thou art a metaphysical God," and he added, "full of comparisons."[66]
Our only information about his conception of the wit for which he was famous is his judgment that Duns Scotus, the *Doctor Subtilis,* was the wittiest
of the School Divines," and that the Kabbalist Zorgi was a "transcendent
wit." We discount this hint because the Subtle Doctor represents a world
which we think insignificant for us, while Donne's world—especially his
world of imagination—seems to us significantly like our own. We fancy
Donne's spirit as drifting passionately among the data of a world distant
but real. We think of his spirit as a *parvula animula vagula,* which Hadrian
or Mr. Joseph Wood Krutch would understand, but which would be incomprehensible to St. Thomas Aquinas. Because we are out of sight of Kabbalism
and Scholasticism, and because Donne is a fiery beacon on our horizon, we
cannot imagine that his sky was constellated differently from ours. Since
we have entered the southern hemisphere, we deny that he could see the
North Star.

As a matter of historical probability, we might surmise that Donne's
outlook would be closer to that of Duns Scotus than to ours. In spite of
the discovery of America and of the impact of the "new philosophy," the
march of ideas between 1300 and 1600 was hardly more rapid than it has
been during the centuries since Donne's death. However we may discount
the influence of medieval thought upon him, we cannot deny that almost
all his prose was dominated by the thought of God as the supreme ontological reality, or that his religious poems express "Nature's nothing" and
God's absoluteness. Even the unregenerate poems could not do without
the divinity which was all "love and wonder." Such uncritical divinity was
the legacy of Neo-Platonism to the Renaissance quite as much as to the
Middle Ages.[67] Even by such seemingly revolutionary thinkers as Giordano

Bruno and Spinoza the gulf between *natura naturans* and *natura naturata* was never bridged, and the resultant paradoxes were sometimes veiled and sometimes boldly enunciated. For them and for Donne alike, God was more actual than his world, and the mists of illusion hung around all created things. Dependence upon that idea was the source of the subtleties of the Kabbalists and Scholastics; it gave unity and direction to philosophy until the decline of Descartes' influence. It reached from Plotinus' conception of the ineffably immanent One—which because it is nowhere is everywhere—to Leibnitz's attempt to explain divine transcendence immanent in the cosmic harmony on the ground that God is universal because, having all points of view, he has none. The inner contradiction of the thought is betrayed by the unimaginable spatial image by which it was illustrated. By thinker after thinker—from Plotinus to Spinoza—its unintelligibility and inconsistency were spirited away by abrupt transitions from metaphysics to geometry, like that which we see in the doctrine that "minimum must coincide with maximum, and the centre of the universe with its circumference; for its centre and circumference are God."[68] The words belong to Nicholas of Cusa and they were the foundation of the *De Docta Ignorantia*. Donne was fascinated by this false image, by which his contemporaries exorcized their fear of the infinity that terrified Pascal. At the Spital on April 23, 1622, we find him saying:

> . . . past, and present, and future, distinguish not his *Quando*; all is one time to him: Mountains and Vallies, Sea and Land, distinguish not his *Ubi*; all is one place to him: . . .[69]

When Donne thought of the *parvula animula vagula*, he addressed it as, "Poore intricated soule! Riddling, perplexed, labyrinthicall soule!" And then abruptly he nerved it with the ontological assertion of God's supreme reality in its starkest form.[70]

So we may leave him within sight of the road on which Plotinus and Leibnitz are termini. To insist on his vital relation to them is not to make him "medieval-minded." It makes him a man of his own time. His Mistress (except when, in the character of "rebell and atheist too," he deviated into the primrose path) was fair Religion. And he never entirely lost hope of finding Falsehood's elder sister, Truth.

CONTRIBUTIONS TO A DICTIONARY OF CRITICAL TERMS

II. Dissociation of Sensibility

F. W. Bateson

Hazlitt has described, in the fourth of his *Lectures on the English Poets*, how a critical term sometimes becomes 'a kind of watchword, the shibboleth of a critical party'. The two examples Hazlitt gave of this process were the word *wit* in Pope's time and the word *genius* in 'the present day', i.e. 1818. But the list could, of course, easily be extended. The word *sensibility* is a particularly instructive example of this critical cant, as Hazlitt called it, because it has been the shibboleth of two separate and very different critical parties. It is not proposed to discuss here, however, that eighteenth-century ability to feel 'the *Misery* of others with *Inward Pain*', which was then 'deservedly named *Sensibility*'.[1] The sensibility that is dissociated in the critical writings of Mr. T. S. Eliot and his followers seems to have no connection with its sentimental predecessor. The modern term is almost certainly French in origin. Though the sense is not recognized by the *Oxford Dictionary* (S-Sh, 1908-14), or its Supplement (1933), the indications are that the term was borrowed by Mr. Eliot—who was soon imitated by Mr. Middleton Murry and Mr. Herbert Read—in or about 1919 from Remy de Gourmont's *Problème du Style* (1902), a refreshing but irresponsible work, in which *la sensibilité* makes frequent appearances. Mr. Eliot certainly had Gourmont's book open on the table before him when writing several of the essays and reviews collected in *The Sacred Wood* (1920). The word *dissociation* may also derive from Gourmont, with whom it was a favourite, though I have noticed only one example in his writings of the two words in combination. This is in the essay called 'La Sensibilité de Jules Laforgue' in the first series of the *Promenades Littéraires* (1904). Laforgue's intelligence, Gourmont says in this essay, was closely connected (*liée étroitement*) with his sensibility; he adds that Laforgue died before he had acquired the scepticism which would have enabled him to dissociate his intelligence from his sensibility (*dissocier son intelligence de sa sensibilité*). It is at least possible that this passage may have been at the back of Mr. Eliot's mind when he coined his phrase.

That phrase enters English critical terminology in the course of a discursive

Reprinted from *Essays in Criticism* (Oxford), 1 (1951), 302-12, by permission of the author and the editors of *Essays in Criticism*.

review of Sir Herbert Grierson's *Metaphysical Lyrics and Poems of the Seventeenth Century,* which appeared anonymously in *The Times Literary Supplement* of October 20th, 1921, under the heading 'The Metaphysical Poets'. (The article was reprinted by Mr. Eliot in 1924 in *Homage to John Dryden.*) The words occur in a passage in which Mr. Eliot outlined a new 'theory' of the evolution of English poetry in the seventeenth century. The gist of this theory was that the poetry of the first half of that century was characterized by 'unification of sensibility', but in the second half 'a dissociation of sensibility set in', as a result of which the eighteenth- and nineteenth-century poets 'thought and felt by fits'.

The theory, as Mr. Eliot has recently told us, has had 'a success in the world astonishing to [its] author'.[2] 'The Metaphysical Poets' is certainly—in spite of several brilliant passages—one of Mr. Eliot's less finished performances. At one point, for example, in the discussion of Chapman, the grammar breaks down completely. And it is odd, to say the least of it, to be told that Lord Herbert of Cherbury's very Platonic 'Ode upon a Question moved' is concerned with 'the perpetuation of love by offspring'. No doubt it would be pedantic to expect precise definitions of the concepts *thinking* and *feeling* in a review that may well have been written against time. Nevertheless the imprecision has resulted in unfortunate misconceptions. Thus it has often been assumed that by *feeling* Mr. Eliot meant emotion. This is unmistakably implied in the gloss that Professor Basil Willey provides of *dissociation of sensibility* in *The Seventeenth Century Background* (p. 87):

> The cleavage then began to appear, which has become so troublesomely familiar to us since, between 'values' and 'facts'; between what you *felt* as a human being or as a poet, and what you *thought* as a man of sense, judgment and enlightenment. Instead of being able, like Donne or Browne, to think and feel simultaneously either in verse or in prose, you were now expected to think prosaically and to feel poetically.

By 'to feel poetically' Professor Willey must mean 'to respond emotionally'. This amounts to ascribing to Mr. Eliot the conventional nineteenth-century view that the Restoration saw the end of 'a poetry in which emotion always accompanied thought'.[3] Emotion, however, does not come into Mr. Eliot's 'theory'. His exemplars of the unified sensibility were able to 'feel their thought as immediately as the odour of a rose'—a sensuous, not an emotional response. It is clear that here—as elsewhere in Mr. Eliot's early critical writings[4]—*feeling* means sensation. And the *sensibility* is the faculty which registers sensations. In practice the two words are interchangeable, as is demonstrated by another passage in 'The Metaphysical Poets':

> But while the language became more refined, the feeling became more crude. The feeling, the sensibility, expressed in the 'Country Churchyard' (to say nothing of Tennyson and Browning) is cruder than that in the 'Coy Mistress'.

The word 'sensibility' is obviously being used here to *define* the word 'feeling'; the former is something that can be equated with the latter. And there is another example earlier in the essay of the virtual synonymity of the two words. Jonson and Chapman are commended because they 'incorporated their erudition into their *sensibility*: their mode of *feeling* was directly and freshly altered by their reading and thought' (my italics). (The sentence which follows makes it clear once again that 'feeling' is used in the sense of 'sensation': 'In Chapman especially there is a direct sensuous apprehension of thought, or a recreation of thought into feeling, which is exactly what we find in Donne.')

A paradox, therefore, emerges. Sensibility is feeling, i.e. sensation, but it is also *a synthesis of feeling and thinking* (the two elements that are unified in the undissociated sensibility). This is puzzling. If sensibility is sensation, or the faculty of registering sense-impressions, how can one of the products of its dissociation be 'thought'? On the other hand, if the unified sensibility is an intellectual as well as a sensuous faculty, how can it be equated with 'feeling'? But it is not Mr. Eliot's habit to use words loosely. The apparent ambiguity of the term in his early writings derives from a doctrine to which he subscribed at that period about the nature of the ratiocinative process. The paradox, if there is a paradox, lies one stage further back. For its elucidation we must return to Remy de Gourmont.

That Gourmont is the *fons et origo* of Mr. Eliot's 'sensuous apprehension of thought'—and so of its modern descendant 'thinking in images'—is demonstrated by the Massinger essay in *The Sacred Wood*. This essay, written only some eighteen months earlier, covers much the same ground as 'The Metaphysical Poets'. What is essentially the same theory about the seventeenth century is presented at greater length and in more plausible terms:

> . . . with the end of Chapman, Middleton, Webster, Tourneur, Donne we end a period when the intellect was immediately at the tips of the senses. Sensation became word and the word was sensation. The next period is the period of Milton (though still with a Marvell in it); and this period is initiated by Massinger.

A passage follows on the lucidity of Massinger's style ('the decay of the senses is not inconsistent with a greater sophistication of language') that exactly parallels the eulogy of Collins, Gray, Johnson and Goldsmith in 'The Metaphysical Poets'. But, whereas in that essay the echoes of Gourmont are few and remote, here they are numerous and explicit. For example, the dictum that 'Immature poets imitate' is clearly a condensation of Gourmont's *Pour un adolescent—et il y a des adolescences prolongées—admirer, c'est imiter* (*Le Problème du Style*, p. 109). And towards the end of the Massinger essay there are two actual quotations from 'the fine pages' that 'the great critic' devoted to Flaubert in *Le Problème du Style*. The second quotation is particularly significant because it is from a passage where Gourmont defines the sense that *la sensibilité* bears in his writings, though

Mr. Eliot has omitted the definition in his quotation. What Gourmont wrote was (p. 107):

> Flaubert incorporait toute sa sensibilité à ses œuvres; *et, par sensibilité, j'entends, ici comme partout, le pouvoir général de sentir tel qu'il est inégalement développé en chaque être humain. La sensibilité comprend la raison elle-même, qui n'est que de la sensibilité cristallisée.* Hors de ses livres, où il se transvasait goutte à goutte, jusqu'à la lie, Flaubert est fort peu intéressant.

I have italicized the sentences omitted by Mr. Eliot. In the special context of his argument in the Massinger essay there was, of course, no reason why he should have quoted these sentences, but for an understanding of the general critical position that he takes up in *The Sacred Wood* they are of the greatest interest. For here, it is clear, is the clue to the paradox of sensibility. Like Mr. Eliot's, Gourmont's *sensibilité* does and does not include the element of thought. This is because for Gourmont thinking was only a kind of sensation. The reduction of thinking to a crystallized sensibility had, as a matter of fact, been effected earlier on in *Le Problème du Style*. According to Gourmont, who quotes Hobbes here and refers to Locke, the cycle of our mental activities can be divided into three separate segments or stages. The first stage is from sensations to images (*mots-images*). The second stage is from images to ideas (*mots-idées*). The third stage is from ideas to emotions (*mots-sentiments*). The cycle then closes in action. The literary sensibility, therefore, straddles the first two of Gourmont's stages. Not only does it build up the sensation into an image, but it at least begins the process by which the image is crystallized into the idea. It is at this transitional point, according to Gourmont, that the best thinking is done (p. 70):

> Le raisonnement au moyen d'images sensorielles est beaucoup plus facile et beaucoup plus sûr que le raisonnement par idées. La sensation est utiliseé dans toute sa verdeur, l'image dans toute sa vivacité. La logique de l'oeil et la logique de chacun des autres sens suffisent à guider l'esprit; le sentiment inutile est rejeté comme une cause de trouble et l'on obtient ces merveilleuses constructions qui semblent de pures œuvres intellectu- elles et qui, en réalité, sont l'œuvre materielle des sens et de leurs organes comme les cellules des abeilles avec leur cire et leur miel.

As examples of the superiority of the logic of the senses Gourmont pro- duces the works of Schopenhauer, Taine and Nietzsche. Their thinking is apparently 'surer' than that of such abstract philosophers as Aristotle, Hume or Hegel! Gourmont was never afraid to follow a bright idea to a nonsensical conclusion.

Mr. Eliot's 'theory' can now be seen in perspective. What he has done, essentially, in 'The Metaphysical Poets' and the Massinger essay, has been to transfer to the nation Gourmont's analysis of the mental processes of the individual. The unified sensibility that Gourmont found in Laforgue Mr. Eliot

finds in the England of the early seventeenth century. The scepticism that
would have led, if Laforgue had lived longer, to a dissociation between his
sensibility and his intelligence receives its national parallel in Mr. Eliot's
'something which . . . happened to the mind of England between the time
of Donne or Lord Herbert of Cherbury and the time of Tennyson and
Browning'. In Gourmont's terminology, English poetry proceeded from
a period of *mots-images* (Donne, Lord Herbert, Marvell) to one of *mots-idées* (Milton and Dryden). And with the coming of 'the sentimental age'—
the second effect, according to Mr. Eliot, of the seventeenth-century dissoci-
ation of sensibility—it reached the period of *mots-sentiments* (Collins to
Tennyson). Mr. Eliot does not use Gourmont's terms, but a general debt is
sufficiently clear. *Le Problème du Style* did not, I think, make Mr. Eliot a
better or a worse critic than he would have been if he had never come across
it. What it did, in several of these early essays, was to provide him with a
framework to which his own critical ideas and intuitions—even then incom-
parably profounder and more original than Gourmont's—were able to attach
themselves. But Gourmont's psychology is a ramshackle affair, and as a
metaphor from it *dissociation of sensibility* suffers from the weakness of
its 'vehicle'.

It is not unlikely that Mr. Eliot soon came to some such conclusion himself. Echoes of the dissociation of sensibility can, it is true, be heard in some
of the reviews that Mr. Eliot contributed to *The Times Literary Supplement*
and the *Nation & the Athenaeum* between 1922 and 1926. On June 9th,
1923, for example, writing on a new selection from Donne in the *Nation &
the Athenaeum,* Mr. Eliot praised the *unity* of Donne's feeling:

> The range of his feeling was great, but no more remarkable than its unity.
> He was altogether present in every thought and in every feeling. It is the
> same kind of unity as pervades the work of Chapman, for whom thought
> is an intense feeling which is one with every other feeling.

And the anonymous notice of a volume of the English Association's *Essays
and Studies* in *The Times Literary Supplement* of December 31st, 1925,
emphasizes the importance of 'the "sensibility" of thought' to Chapman in
a way that recalls the 'direct sensuous apprehension of thought' attributed
to that dramatist in 'The Metaphysical Poets'.

But these are only passing references. In 1926 Mr. Eliot gave some lectures
on Donne. (They have not been printed.) In the preliminary reading for
them, as he tells us in 'Shakespeare and the Stoicism of Seneca' (1927), he
came to the conclusion that Donne did not really do any thinking at all: 'I
could not find either any "mediaevalism" or any thinking, but only a vast
jumble of incoherent erudition on which he drew for purely poetic effects.'
This is a long way from the intellect at the tips of the senses! Even further
from it is the statement in the essay Mr. Eliot contributed to *A Garland for
John Donne* (1931) that 'In Donne, there is a manifest fissure between
thought and sensibility.' In 'The Metaphysical Poets' we had been told that
'A thought to Donne was an experience; it modified his sensibility'! Was

Mr. Eliot's later comment intended as a specific repudiation of the unified sensibility? It reads rather like it.

Mr. Eliot's last words on the dissociation of sensibility are in the lecture on Milton that he gave to the British Academy in 1947:

> I believe that the general affirmation represented by the phrase 'dissoci-
> ation of sensibility' . . . retains some validity; but I now incline to agree
> with Dr. Tillyard that to lay the burden on the shoulders of Milton and
> Dryden was a mistake. If such a dissociation did take place, I suspect
> that the causes are too complex and too profound to justify our account-
> ing for the change in terms of literary criticism. All we can say is, that
> something like this did happen; that it had something to do with the
> Civil War; that it would even be unwise to say it was caused by the
> Civil War, but that it is a consequence of the same causes which brought
> about the Civil War; that we must seek the causes in Europe, not in
> England alone; and for what these causes were, we may dig and dig until
> we get to a depth at which words and concepts fail us.

If this is not repudiation, neither is it endorsement. The change of emphasis is particularly significant. Mr. Eliot is less interested now in the nature of the change that English poetry underwent in the seventeenth century than in its origins. As a critical watchword, a propagandist device to exalt the kind of poetry he and Pound were writing and to depreciate those of Milton and the Romantics, the phrase had presumably done its work.

Of course, something like this *did* happen. The relationship between the sensuous and the intellectual elements in poetry did change in or about 1650. And the trend towards their coalescence or confusion in Metaphysical poetry can be called 'unification', though some of the poets themselves, as a matter of fact, preferred to emphasize the 'double sense and meaning' of their style.[5] Dissociation, however, is a misleading term to apply either to Augustan poetry or to its social sources. The poetry of Dryden and Pope is characterized by the *tension* between its constituent elements. If from one aspect the image and the concept can be said to be dissociated, from another they appear almost to collide. *The Dunciad,* for example, is vivid *and* ab-stract. It is surely these opposite 'pulls' of centrifugal and centripetal forces that is the crucial fact about the Augustan poet.

With the exception of Mr. Eliot himself *dissociation of sensibility* and its attendant 'theory' have had few critics until recently. The first even faintly hostile comment of which I am aware is on the first page of Sir Herbert Grierson's *Milton & Wordsworth* (1937):

> The favourite phrase is 'unified sensibility'. We are told, a little pon-
> tifically, that this unified sensibility was disturbed by the great influ-
> ence of Milton, so that the natural medium for the expression of our
> thought has become exclusively prose, while poetry, I suppose it is
> contended, became the expression of feeling, of thought only in so
> far as this had become crystallized as the representative of some

mood of feeling . . . I am stating the contention as I understand it, not
ratifying it.

The imputed identification of thought with crystallized feeling is interesting;
it suggests an acquaintance with the definition of *sensibilité* in *Le Problème
du Style*. A more explicit criticism is to be found in the short *Studies in
Metaphysical Poetry* (1939) of Theodore Spencer and Mark Van Doren.
Mr. Van Doren doubted, for example, whether Mr. Eliot had 'thoroughly
examined the value in his mind of the words "sensibility" and "experience"'
(p. 22), when he wrote 'The Metaphysical Poets'. Professor Bonamy Dobrée's
'The Claims of Sensibility', a review of L. C. Knights's *Explorations* in
Humanitas (Autumn 1946, pp. 55-8), was apparently the first outright
attack upon the new doctrine (which had, of course, been swallowed whole
by Professor Knights). The key passage runs as follows:

> The theory is that in the good old days before the Great Rebellion, before
> Bacon, before the Renaissance (the evil spreads its roots ever further
> down), man was whole. Everything was thought of together by a process
> in which thought and emotion danced together, when 'imagination' and
> 'reason' were one, so that man lived more fully and completely . . . Are we
> quite sure, however, that the old 'integration' was not really just being muddle-
> headed? And is it not possible that this new analysis may be simply part of the
> Anglo-Catholic movement seeking arguments to justify its attitude, or merely
> seeing the course of history through its own spectacles? And was not the
> change in language far more the answer to purely social demands and the
> growth of a large new reading public than to an incipient schizophrenia? And
> finally, is it really better to write like Sir Thomas Browne than to write like
> Swift? or to write like Nashe than to write like Defoe?

Professor Dobrée's questions have not, to my knowledge, been answered.
Some of them at any rate would seem to be unanswerable.

The associated concept 'thinking in images' has not been challenged
hitherto. It is doubtful, however, if this is not also essentially a metaphor.
There is an obvious analogy between the poetic statement and the statements of philosophers and scientists. Both involve the use of words; both
are meaningful; both require the intervention of the intelligence for their
appropriate effects to be attained. It is natural, therefore, to applaud the
'beauty' of a philosophical argument, or the 'logic' of a poem's structure.
But such flowers of speech must not be taken too seriously. If we do, we
are likely to find ourselves talking the same sort of nonsense as Gourmont,
when he finds a greater certainty in Taine's reasoning than in Hegel's, because Taine's diction is more concrete. The fact is, surely, that propositional
thinking is *different* from poetic thinking, and it only causes confusion to
use the same word for both processes. In so far as there *is* thinking in images
in poetry, it is not 'thinking' in the ordinary sense. And if there was more
'thinking in images' in the first half of the seventeenth century than in the

second half, perhaps it was not because people like Dryden did less think-ing than people like Donne, but because they used fewer images.

For *sensibility* divorced from *dissociation,* unless it is restricted to the faculty of sensation (Mr. Eliot's 'feeling'), there is little to be said. In the 1920s the word was the shibboleth of a vigorous critical party. At that time its imprecision was useful because *sensibility* appeared to unite the whole of the Anglo-American *avant-garde*—those for whom the senses stood for the concrete objective fact (the Imagists) and those for whom they meant the instincts (like Joyce and D. H. Lawrence). Its use today as a loose honorific synonym for 'taste' or 'personality' can only be deprecated.

DISSOCIATION OF SENSIBILITY

Frank Kermode

The "dissociation of sensibility" has lately been wilting under well-directed criticism, and it may seem gratuitous at this stage to examine the concept in so much detail. But although it is "going out," like Donne, there are two good reasons for paying it this attention. The first is that, though it may soon be bad form for anybody to use the term, a whole generation has grown up believing in a pattern, applicable not only to poetry but to general intellectual history, formed and codified by the expression "dissociation of sensibility"; in other words we are still likely to have the effects of the doctrine though the doctrine itself is démondé. There are plenty of signs that critics whose "line" is heavily committed to the "dissociation of sensibility" are burning the flag without abandoning the position; the new, extraordinarily bad, volume in the Pelican Guide to English Literature (a publication dominated by such critics) contains amusing evidence of this. Now if it is, in its historical aspect, a fallacious doctrine, some effort should be made to say so definitely, otherwise a mere change of title will perpetuate the error. The second good reason is that we don't, by proving it wrong, find out how and why the doctrine has been such a success; and the fact that it is apparently in decline itself suggests the present as a good moment for doing this job; an important job, I think, because the doctrine *was* so influential, and we ought to know why it seemed so satisfactory.

Nobody reading this will need to be told about the origin of the expression, nor of how it has come to be used, but it will be convenient to have set down here a few lines from the essay on "The Metaphysical Poets" (1921) in which Mr. Eliot first used it, and a much later passage from his Lecture on Milton, in which he qualified what he had said in the light of a quarter-century's thinking about it. The first passage, as printed in *Selected Essays,* and in the heart of every undergraduate, runs like this. Mr. Eliot has been saying that the dramatic verse of the late Elizabethans and early Jacobeans "expresses a degree of development of sensibility" which is not found in any of the prose. . . . In Chapman especially there is "a direct sensuous apprehension of thought, or a recreation of thought into feeling, which is exactly what we find in Donne. . . ." He then compares a passage of Chapman's and one by Lord Herbert of Cherbury with bits of Tennyson and Browning, and comments:

Reprinted from *Kenyon Review,* 19 (1957), 169-94, by permission of the author.

The difference is not a simple difference of degree between poets. It is something which had happened to the mind of England between the time of Donne or Lord Herbert of Cherbury, and the time of Tennyson and Browning; it is the difference between the intellectual poet and the reflective poet. Tennyson and Browning are poets, and they think; but they do not feel their thought as immediately as the odor of a rose. A thought to Donne was an experience; it modified his sensibility. When a poet's mind is perfectly equipped for its work, it is constantly amalgamating disparate experience; the ordinary man's experience is chaotic, irregular, fragmentary. The latter falls in love, or reads Spinoza, and these two experiences have nothing to do with each other, or with the noise of the typewriter or the smell of cooking; in the mind of the poet these experiences are always forming new wholes.

We may express the difference by the following theory: The poets of the seventeenth century, the successors of the dramatists of the sixteenth, possessed a mechanism of sensibility which could devour any kind of experience. They are simple, artificial, difficult, or fantastic, as their predecessors were; no less nor more than Dante, Guido Cavalcanti, Guinicelli, or Cino. In the seventeenth century a dissociation of sensibility set in, from which we have never recovered; and this dissociation, as is natural, was aggravated by the influence of the two most powerful poets of the century, Milton and Dryden.

Of course there are other loci in Mr. Eliot's earlier criticism that amplify this, but we will content ourselves with his last pronouncement on the subject:

> I believe that the general affirmation represented by the phrase "dissociation of sensibility" . . . retains some validity; but . . . to lay the burden on the shoulders of Milton and Dryden was a mistake. If such a dissociation did take place, I suspect that the causes are too complex and profound to justify our accounting for the change in terms of literary criticism. All we can say is, that something like this did happen; that it had something to do with the Civil War; that it would be unwise to say it was caused by the Civil War, but that it is a consequence of the same cause which brought about the Civil War; that we must seek the causes in Europe, not in England alone; and for what these causes were, we may dig and dig until we get to a depth at which words and concepts fail us.

In this passage Mr. Eliot seems to be recommending, as a desideratum, what had in fact already been done; for by 1947 supplementary enquiries into the dissociation had long ceased to be conducted entirely in terms of literary criticism. Almost every conceivable aspect of 17th Century life had been examined by scholars anxious to validate the concept, and much historical investigation that had been conducted from quite different and unrelated points of view was dragooned into service. Admittedly the scholars involved nearly all belonged to English Faculties, sometimes venturing outside their own disciplines to find support in Weber and Tawney, for instance, or in the

medievalism of modern Catholic theology; sometimes seeking it nearer
home, in the precise investigations of such scholars as R. F. Jones. But who,
after all, is in a better position to spread such a doctrine than professors of
English? It is certainly to them that the doctrine owes its success. Yet they
are not alone in their love for simplicity and design in history; many others
are equally attracted to the notion of a pregnant historical crisis, of great
importance in every conceivable sphere of human activity. And there was a
predisposition to locate this crisis in the 17th Century. So there was an at-
tentive audience for G. Williamson when he gave a full account of it from
the point of view of the historian of poetry; for F. R. Leavis when he developed the extremely influential theory of the Line of Wit, evaluating all
later poetry in terms of the criteria declared appropriate for that of the
early 17th Century; for L. C. Knights when he invoked and interpreted the
economic history of the period in support of the doctrine; and for Basil
Willey when he provided, in a book which has had an enormous influence
in England, formulations of the theory to fit almost every aspect of the
thought of the whole period. And of course one could mention many more
contributions. A period which frankly confessed that it thought and felt
by turns did homage to a period when men did these things simultaneously:
a double-minded period measured itself by a serenely single-minded one.
Intellect deferred to imagination; the slaves of second to the devotees of
first causes: men habituated to asking *how* longed for a period when the
proper question was *why*? Poets tried once more to be concrete, to banish
ratiocination, to be "physical" rather than "platonic," to charge their thinking with passion and their passion with thought; to restore to poetry a truth
independent of the presumptuous intellect. They looked admiringly toward
those early years of the 17th Century when this was normal; and the scholars
attended them with explanations of why it was so, and why it ceased to be
so. There was an implicit parallel with the Fall; man's soul, since 1650, had
been divided against itself, and it would never be the same again, though
correct education might acieve something.

It is indeed a measure of Mr. Eliot's extraordinary persuasiveness that
thinkers in this tradition have accepted the 17th Century as the period in
which the disaster occurred. As we see from his second pronouncement, he
himself has stuck to this position, although he advises us to look back into
earlier history for fuller explanations. Nor is his attitude difficult to understand; it is animated by a rich nostalgia for the great period of Anglican
divinity, the period when the Church of England, beset on all sides by determined recusancy, confidently proposed itself as truly Catholic and
apostolic—looking back, itself, to a vague past when the folly and arrogance
of human intellect had not yet begun the process of dissociating Christianity.
This period ended with the Civil War; and the end of the first Anglo-Catholi-
cism coincided with the end of an admired poetry and a great drama, both
affected, to some extent, by ecclesiatically-determined literary attitudes,
the drama remembering (but how faintly!) its devout origins, "metaphysical
poetry" the *concetto predicabile*. In the view that the Civil War was histori-

cally and culturally decisive he had the support of Marvell and Dryden, as well as of those historians who explain the particular evils of the modern world as stemming from the dissidence of the early dissenters. Yet it must be confessed that, if we look to Europe and not to England alone, there was never a reasonable chance that the claims of the Church of England would be universally recognized, and that "something" had presumably "happened" long before to predispose people against their acceptance. And when one considers the position of those who say everything was all right before Bacon, or before Descartes, one is forced to a very similar conclusion, namely that the kind of wrongness these philosophers represent, for scholars anxious to show how the modern mind got split, is observable in earlier thought.

In itself, this is an old story, but it has to be told when someone makes a case for the absolutely decisive historical importance of a particular event or idea. Even Milton's Adam had to allow passion to get the better of reason before he ate the fruit, and so fall before the Fall. But in fact there is a great deal more to be said against the theory than that its supporters simply got the date wrong; though for the moment we are simply looking at the particular period that has been regarded as crucial, and asking whether it was so, in any of the ways proposed. (At present I am leaving poetry out of account.) One often hears the term "dissociation of sensibility" used as if it stood for a real historical event, like, say, Pride's Purge; after it, feeling disappeared from certain mental transactions, leaving a rump of intellect, with which we are still conducting our business. (It is this last inference that will survive the nominal death of the doctrine.) A lot of the blame naturally falls on the Royal Society, because of its interest in the accurate notation of observation and experiment without constant recourse to that First Cause which, they felt, often invalidated earlier philosophical argument. Certainly they took, quite early in their career, a great beating from Swift and his friends, who interpreted the modern fixation of interest on "nature" as a wanton violation of what seemed to them the proper order of human studies, in which ethics, economics and politics, theology and poetry, all ranked above anything that Wotton's intellect, unaided by earlier accumulations of wisdom, could produce. And there is no doubt that Swift and Pope (even in his assault on Bentley and Theobald) were protesting against an abuse of human learning and tradition which is somewhat like a "dissociation of sensibility," though they would hardly have understood the expression. So were Blake and Coleridge and Wordsworth and Lamb and Keats. . . . But there is no point, as yet, in looking forward; the theory itself says that the lamented condition was never cured. The truth is that it is difficult to find a time when a roughly similar situation did not exist. In other words, the chronological placing of the "dissociation" is suspect.

This becomes clear when one considers such aspects of the doctrine as the dissociative force of science and the un-dissociated condition of pre-Baconian and pre-Cartesian philosophy and theology, basic antipositivist positions and always, by the dissociator, connected with a specifically 17th Century collapse.

The achievements of pre-Baconian science in England had been consistently undervalued until less than twenty years ago, but it is now quite clear that experiment and observation, notably in optics and astronomy, had proceeded very effectively on a basis of mathematics and with an influsion of Platonic mysticism. There was no automatic ecclesiastical objection to this; God the geometer was acceptable to churchmen as well as to scientists, and astronomy was a way of understanding the heavens' declaration of the glory of God. Most scientists were ready enough to emphasize that their discipline was ancillary to theology and in fact they rejoiced that mathematics could illuminate the doctrine of the Trinity and glorify the God who made the world in number, weight and measure. Everybody knows of Kepler's devoutness; and his was a scientific type that lived on into the 18th Century. The 16th Century in England was perfectly familiar with this type, which never proposed to set the human reason against faith, any more than Bacon did ("as we are to obey his law, though we find a reluctation in our will, so we are to believe his word, though we find a reluctation in our reason. For if we believe only that which is agreeable unto our sense, we give consent to the matter, and not to the author; which is no more than we would do towards a suspected and discredited witness"). So long as the scientist labored for the greater glory of God he would not incur the condemnation of the Church for impiety of intellect—a sure symptom of "dissociation." But there were two ways in which he might be held to be working against God; he might develop his Platonism to the point of heresy, like Dee, or he might carry on with his work without sufficiently indicating that he had the proper end in view which was "atheism"; and there was a growing number of such men. "The quiet indifference" of such scientists, as Mr. P. Kocher has said, "was to work worse mischief to religion in the long run than the conjuring of a Dee or the blaspheming of a Marlowe." Both types, in their different ways, were guilty of the sin of *curiositas,* of "seeking knowledge merely to be known," as Greville said, or of seeking it in order to gain power by forbidden knowledge, a sort of witchcraft. (Incidentally, the Royal Society's supposedly indiscriminate thirst for, and allowance of, human learning, might be supposed to have liberalized the views of members on the black arts; but in fact the attitude of Glanville, for example, was superstitious and fearful—whereas Reginald Scot, living in the old pre-dissociation days, was a healthy rationalist.) The Church did not on the whole feel obliged to condemn new knowledge unless acquired for improper ends. So Copernicus evaded condemnation for decades. But when another authority was preferred to that of the Scriptures and the Church, or when the human intellect grew so self-centered as to omit its duty to God, there followed all that obscure disturbance which characterizes the intellectual life of the later part of Elizabeth's reign; charges of scientific "atheism" invade literary life, where other "naturalisms," like the political naturalism of Machiavelli and the ethical naturalism of Montaigne, were already setting in. All this, of course, was going on before Donne, whose importance to the theory of dissociation I shall discuss later, was fully mature; and when the political strength of Puritanism was still half a century short of war (this has to be mentioned because, fundamentally, the dissociator's emphasis on the Civil War implies an allegory with Parliament as Pride of Intellect and Charles as Spiritual Unity—that is why Mr. Eliot says it "has never been concluded"). In Elizabethan science there were men guilty of precisely the sins of the Royal Society; and in every other department of life there were plain indications of a conflict between "naturalism" and "custom," which last word was already used to mean irrational authoritarianism in any sphere. Perhaps the "split" should be placed earlier, in the last quarter of the 16th Century?

But the merest glance backwards—and here I come to my second point—makes it clear that this won't do. Sixteenth century science owed much, we are told, to the intellectual traditions of the University of Padua; and dominant in these was a variety of Aristotelianism. It is indeed obvious that, in some sense, the rediscovery of Aristotle, which was the cause of what we understand as medieval philosophy, necessarily involved a dissociation in Christian thought. Aquinas did present a whole and consistent view, but even that was admittedly a laborious synthesis with little promise of stability; the decade of his death was marked by ecclesiastical condemnations, notably that of 1277, of a philosophic tendency to exalt reason independently of faith, and from these condemnations St. Thomas himself was not completely exempted. It was not merely that there were necessarily points of doctrine upon which Aristotle and the Scripture were incompatible, as in their pronouncements on the creation and the nature of the soul; such difficulties dissolve in Aquinas because Aristotle can always be called wrong, as he worked by the light of nature. The real problem arises when philosophers (differentiated from theologians but not, we may remember from scientists) flatly declare that the intellect of a Christian, guided by the rules of reason, can determine certain matters in a manner totally contradictory to revealed religion, and let the issue rest there; that is, on the suggestion that there are two kinds of truth. Now the controversy about "double-truth," habitually associated with a 17th Century "dissociation," is endemic throughout the supposedly un-dissociated Middle Ages. There is a hint of it much earlier in Christian thought, notoriously indeed in Tertullian; but at the height of the scholastic period it is always likely to crop up when philosophers are trying to cope with the Aristotelian tradition as Averroes and his followers represented it.

The theologians of the period were on the whole unwilling to explain the difference in the findings of philosophy and revelation by arguing that human reason had been hopelessly obscured by the Fall, or to restate the old argument that there was more merit in believing what was apparently untrue; both these answers as a matter of fact were offered in 17th Century apologetics when the same sort of problem arose, and it is surely not without interest that the Middle Ages were more reluctant to surrender the intellect than their successors and admirers. First Bonaventure and then the Bishop of Paris condemned all those points of Averroistic philosophy that would have been flat heresy had they not been protected by the doctrine of the

double-truth; but Bonaventure also sought the root of these errors in the
thought of Aristotle; that is, attempted an intellectual refutation, in addition to abusing the philosophers for vain learning (the usual reaction right
up to the end of the 17th Century from those who would not entirely give
up human learning) and for the *specialized* pursuit of philosophy in *isolation
from* theology. The situation is much the same as in the late 16th Century.
Finally in 1277 there was a wholesale Papal condemnation of the Averroist
positions, which M. Gilson calls a critical date in the history of philosophy
because henceforth "a spirit of suspicion towards the 'philosophers' began
to replace . . . the spirit of friendly and confident collaboration with philosophy which had generally prevailed, from the beginning of the century,
in the minds of the theologians." The fact that the condemnation of 1277
was not confined to Averroism, but treated that body of doctrine as an
aspect of what M. Gilson calls "a sort of polymorphic naturalism stressing
the rights of pagan nature" (Andreas Capellanus came in for some hostile
comment) is perhaps proof that the dissociation is not merely a matter
of philosophy and theology, but affects the whole emotional and intellectual
life of the 13th Century. Certainly the distinction between *scientia* and
sapientia is not unknown outside the field of scholastic philosophy, and
the condemnation of *curiositas* was to develop into a literary convention.
From this time on, right up to Pomponazzi, who invoked the double-truth
clause in his opposition to both Neo-Platonic and Christian thought, denying
on philosophical grounds the immortality of the soul, and to Cremonini,
that very influential friend of Mr. Eliot's un-dissociated Lord Herbert,
Padua continued to produce its rationalist Averroists, and, as we now know,
to lay the foundations of modern science. Having split the truth, it was possible to ignore, for all practical purposes, revelation; and theologians, suspicious of philosophy, devoted their attention, as M. Gilson says, to the
elimination of the naturalism of Greek thought, and the necessitarianism
of Graeco-Arabic divinity. Is this not the historical locus of the great dissociation?

Alas, it is clearly not so; for example, Averroes takes us back to Aristotle
and Athens, where we find similar conflicts. Perhaps a philologist would
suggest that unless we are looking for a very primitive society we shall
never find a state of culture in which language refuses to admit thinking
that is not numinous; in which there is no possibility of a naturalist assault
on the society's beliefs. The Christian "West" has never wanted to be as
primitive even as the Song of Solomon, and its whole immense allegorical
tradition is the result of applying intellectual instruments to the dissection
of writings in which thought and feeling are, if anywhere, inseparable.

I have taken the liberty of discussing, doubtless in an over-elementary
way, these two matters, Elizabethan "atheism" and that "naturalism"
we associate with Averroes and Padua, simply to show that the theory of
dissociation has difficulty, outside poetry, in choosing its period. The fact
seems to be that it is normal for what we may loosely call "naturalism" to
threaten an establishment which claims supernatural sanction. And however

this threat is countered—by denunciations *ex cathedra* that reason cannot possibly conflict with faith, or that the intellect is a fallacious instrument—it cannot be suppressed. I have drawn attention to its occurrence in the 13th and 16th Centuries. Of course it happened in the 17th also; and the success of the doctrine of "dissociation of sensibility" is testimony that it is still happening in the 20th. And it would not be difficult to provide many more examples from other periods. The 17th Century conflict is well-documented and easily to hand, but it was not the peculiar catastrophe that supporters of the doctrine argue for.

But of course poetry is the heart of the theory, and I have been wasting my time showing that the "dissociation of sensibility" doesn't belong to the 17th Century if I can't do for poetry what I have tried to do for these purely secondary matters. In point of fact this is far easier to do, because the poets and critics responsible for the development of the theory have themselves not always agreed about where and when the great split occurred; and for that reason I propose to vary the method followed so far, and instead of taking historical samples, to consider this question of the genesis of the theory.

Full consideration would fill a book, in which the "dissociation of sensibility" would be merely one chapter; but the short answer is that the "dissociation of sensibility"—it has not always gone under that name—is an attempt to project upon the history of poetry a modern theory of the image. This theory owes something to Blake, and something to Coleridge; through the French Symbolists it owes something to Schopenhauer, and through Hulme something to Bergson. Before Mr. Eliot made his particular projection of it, it was familiar to Yeats (who got it directly from Blake and indirectly through Symons) and to Pound, who got it from Symons and de Gourmont and the French poets themselves. Ultimately this image is the product of over a century of continuous anti-positivist poetic speculation, defining and defending the poet's distinct and special way of knowing truth. It involves a theory of form which excludes or strictly subordinates all intellectual speculation, and which finds in music, and better still in the dance, an idea of what art should be: entirely free of discursive content, thinking in quite a different way from the scientists; as Donne said of Elizabeth Drury, in a passage much favored by writers in the tradition, "Her body thought." Form and meaning are coessential, and the image belongs not to the mechanical world of intellect, but to the vital world of intuition; it is the aesthetic monad of the Symbolists, the Image of the Imagists, the Vortex of the Vorticists, and finally the ideogram of Pound. It is antipositivist above all; for Symons and Yeats it was even frankly magical, having a function very similar to that of the magician's seal; that is, a complete representation, with occult powers over the otherwise unimaginable matters represented. All the emphasis is on the inseparability of formal, intellectual and emotional aspects of the image or symbol, and this is as true of Pound and Eliot as it is of Blake and Mallarmé. The image is the philosopher's stone of the whole movement of poetry from Blake and the early German Romantics to the present day. It has been described in many different ways, but it is recognizably the same thing, and occasionally even men wild with excitement about their discovery of it will perceive a resemblance to an earlier formula, as Hulme grudgingly quotes Coleridge, and Wyndham Lewis quotes Pater. The full story of this Image cannot be told here; it is enough to say that its in-dissociability is its prime quality—much as for Aristotle form and matter could not be separated except by intellectual abstraction—so that one now speaks of the "heresy" of paraphrase: that is, the wickedness of separating out the intellectual content of a poem. This in-dissociability is, in the end, proposed as the poet's only but infallible defence in a world of naturalists, his only hope in what is otherwise a universe of death. The price he pays is that nothing binds him to society but a mutual hatred.

It is reasonable to recall Coleridge's part in the early stages of the development of this theory, because apart from Blake he was the first Englishman to see the importance of a complete break with empiricist aesthetics. But mention of him may also remind us that in the movement we call Romantic there is another well-recognized characteristic relevant to this argument, and that is its medievalism. And it is hardly surprising that an anti-intellectual view of poetry, which insists upon special ends and values for the art, seeks in the past some epoch, some golden age, when the prevalent mode of knowing was not positivist and anti-imaginative; some age when the Image, the intuited, creative reality, was habitually known and respected; when art was not permanently on the defensive against mechanical and systematic modes of enquiry; when the truth of poetry, which resides in the Image, was a truth of self-evident importance. As the order of reality postulated as the proper study of the poet tends, in one way or another, to be granted supernatural attributes, the ideal epoch is usually a religious one. Hence the medievalism or Byzantinism of Hulme and the Decadents, of Yeats and Henry Adams. On such a view the extraordinary unease of Cowley, his shifty concern about what you can say in poetry and expect people to believe, is a direct consequence of a certain Renaissance development which culminates catastrophically in Hobbes; the later religious poetry of Dryden exhibits the new, defensive fideism; the strange confusions of the *Essay on Man* indicate that a point has been reached at which the poet, out of mere ignorance of his birthright, sells himself to the enemy—a Catholic poet writing rational theology. The revolt of Coleridge against Hartley saves poetry because even in the hands of its most skilful apologists the aesthetics of empiricism could not restore the autonomy of the Image; Coleridge himself tried in the old way, but soon discovered that he must make a clean break; and on his own showing his mentors (who were to speak in the ear of all Romantic thought) were the mystics of Renaissance hermeticism, proclaiming in an age of reason the magical oneness of the world and the powerlessness of the discursive intellect to understand it. One has to go back to a point earlier than the moment when philosophy developed an exclusive interest in second causes.

Somewhere in the past, then, there must have been a time when the poet's way of knowing, by images in the full Symbolist sense, was the normal human way, when the full play of the whole mind—not merely of the reason —in knowing, was taken for granted. The only question for the historiographers of the Image is when this golden age really was. There is a passage in Pound's *Make It New* that illuminates the problem.

> When the late T. E. Hulme was trying to be a philosopher . . . and fussing about Sorel and Bergson . . . I spoke to him one day of the difference between Guido's precise interpretative metaphor, and the Petrarchian fustian and ornament, pointing out that Guido thought in accurate terms; that the phrases correspond to definite sensations undergone. . . . Hulme took some time over it in silence, and then finally said; "That is very interesting"; and after a pause: "That is more interesting than anything anyone ever said to me. It is more interesting than anything I ever read in a book."

The only aspects of this odd interchange that I wish to discuss are those which are relevant to what I am trying to say about the historiography of modern Symbolist aesthetics. One is that Pound is describing Cavalcanti as a poet of the integral image, and contrasting him with Petrarch, a poet of the ornamental image, the image appended to discourse, the flower stuck in sand. In the one there is (to use the well-known formula) a unification of thought and feeling; in the other, a dissociation of them. Another is concerned with Hulme's reaction to what Pound said. The general idea could not have been unfamiliar to him; after all, it was the reason why he was fussing about Bergson. But a man is never more impressed by an argument than when it seems to provide unexpected support for opinions he already holds; and Hulme could not have been other than charmed to discover that Petrarch of all people—the First Man of that Renaissance he blamed so strenuously—already exhibited the symptoms of error which characterized the whole period, whereas Cavalcanti, an older contemporary of Dante, habituated to the hallowed concept of discontinuity, brought up on Original Sin, had precisely those Imagist qualities, that reluctance to glide away into abstraction, which for Hulme was the index of true art. Somewhere between Cavalcanti and Petrarch a dissociation of sensibility, it would seem, had set in; and from it, Hulme was doubtless willing to add, we have never recovered.

But we have now to remind ourselves that Mr. Eliot claimed for the poets of the 17th Century the very qualities of Dante, Cavalcanti, and Cino; and that after *them* this dissociation set in. It is not in the nature of the concept of dissociation, any more than it is of the Fall, that it should occur more than once—only Yeats with his cyclic theory of history imagines that it can. What are we to conclude from this confusion?

The fact is that Mr. Eliot's argument for a historical dissociation that can be detected in art is meant to satisfy precisely the same need as Hulme's. Hulme, powerfully influenced by Worringer's historical projection of the doctrine of empathy, and by the desire to justify a new abstract art, looked back into the past for a period of "life-alien" art, produced by a "life-denying" society; such art will be quasi-geometrical, emancipated "from all the contingency and temporality of the world-picture," non-organic, inhuman. For Hulme this was the society that existed before the Renaissance destroyed the belief in Original Sin. After that, art was empathy; it was anti-religious, anthropocentric, organic, preferring life to the truth that exists discontinuously from it, accessible only to a special intuitive act that Renaissance attitudes discouraged. The right kind of art is Egyptian and Byzantine; the wrong kind Greek and Renaissance. In the right kind, Hulme found his Image, free of the meddling human intellectual pride; in the wrong, a characteristic irreligious formlessness, the sloppiness and sentiment of the modern denial of limit. For him the Renaissance (though he is vague about when this was), is the critical moment since when nothing has been the same. Romanticism is just the new disease at the stage of mania; hence Hulme's utterly misleading description of himself as a classicist, when all his thinking is complepletely in the Romantic tradition. With Yeats, the case is not radically different. For him, there was a great moment in history (celebrated in some of his most splendid prose) when soul and body were one—nobody more explicitly relates the aesthetic and the historical than he does. His date is 1550: for a century before that there was a tense perfection; but after that everything changed. Of course he did believe it had all happened before, and found a similar dissociation in the history of ancient art. Yeats, indeed, wrote his history in terms of this doctrine, and wrote it in a world that offended him socially and imaginatively, a world of "shopkeeping logicians," the very existence of which he had to explain by exhaustive glosses on every conceivable aspect of the idea of dissociation. My own belief is that Yeats's expression of the whole aesthetic-historical complex is by far the most satisfactory and, in terms of poetry, by far the most fruitful. But my immediate point is that all these writers search history for a critical moment after which everything went wrong; and because they share, to a large extent, the same poetic heritage, they are looking for much the same kinds of rightness and wrongness. They seek, in short, a historical period possessing the qualities they postulate for the image of art—unity, indissociability; qualities, which though passionately desired are, as they say, uniquely hard to come by in the modern world.

Two consequences are to be noted, I think, if it is conceded that Eliot's "dissociation" differs from the others only in that it has gained wide currency. The first is that the formula is absolutely useless historically. It will not do to say that it is partly true, or true in a slightly different way, as people are now claiming. A once-for-all event cannot happen every few years; there cannot be, if the term is to retain the significance it has acquired, dissociations between the archaic Greeks and Phidias, between Catullus and Virgil, between Guido and Petrarch, between Donne and Milton. "Dissociated in sensibility" some might still find a possible, though very nasty, *stylistic* description; but as a way of speaking about "periods" it is much less useful than even "baroque." At its worst it is merely a way of saying which poets one likes—as the Symbolists, with more justification because

they were professedly using aesthetic and not historical criteria, held that
all the great poetry of the past was Symbolist. At its best, the doctrine is an
interesting primitivism, looking for an unmodern virtue not as the noble
savage was sought in the impossibly remote past or in Tahiti, but in Christian
Europe right up to some moment in, or shortly after, what is vaguely called
the Renaissance.

The second consequence is that the period or the poets chosen to illustrate
the pre- and post-dissociated conditions are bound to be perversely treated;
you must misrepresent them if you propose to make them illustrate a false
doctrine. And this is precisely what has happened in recent years to Donne
and Milton.

It is common knowledge that these two poets somehow got involved in
an unhappy relationship existing only in the minds of historians, the long
and short of which was that one of them—Milton, in fact—had to be occulted
to enable Donne to light up (and we note that Mr. Eliot's change of opinion
on Donne was followed by an upward revision of his estimate of Milton).
At the very time when Donne was being admired for thinking freely, Milton
was being despised for writing monuments to dead ideas in a dead language.
Milton, self-conscious post-lapsarian that he was, obstinately thought and
discoursed about feeling, divorcing the body and soul, the form and matter,
of the image. Donne, writing before the same Fall, had his intellect at the
tips of his senses.

Or so it proved possible, for a considerable length of time, to argue.
Superficially, the argument was attractive because it gave major status to an
obscure poet whose diction was inartificial, even colloquial; and because he
was a poet who lived in times supposed to be very like modern times, in
that the established order was already being threatened by those "naturalist"
forces which eventually dissociated sensibility.

There is, of course, a contradiction here somewhere. Donne is admired
because he was deeply troubled, or so they say, by the new philosophy, and
also because he was lucky enough to live just before it became really trouble-
some. There is also an error of fact; Donne alludes frequently enough to the
"new philosophy," but nobody who has cooly examined these allusions
in their context can seriously believe he was much put out by it, and considering his religious views it would indeed be surprising if he had been. It
might have been useful for the dissociationist argument if somebody had
been prepared to capitalize this point, by way of emphasizing Donne's pre-
dissociation status; but there seems to have been a heavy commitment to
the view that Donne was important to modern poets because of the ways
in which his world resembled theirs, as well as because it was completely
different from theirs. As usual, the history is feeble. But pure criticism has
had very similar difficulties: Miss Tuve's famous demonstration that Donne's
images have a logical, or at any rate a pseudo-logical function, was a direct
affront to the basis of the theory that he was a poet of the modern image;
but it can scarcely have surprised anybody who had read Donne open-eyed

and seen how much he depends on dialectical conjuring of various kinds, arriving at the point of wit by subtle syllogistic misdirections, inviting admiration by slight though totally destructive perversities of analogue, which re-route every argument to paradox. Some of this Mr. Eliot perhaps felt when he prematurely prophesied the demise of Donne during the tercentenary celebration of 1931, and showed how far he had gone towards excluding Donne from the category of unified sensibility, saying outright that in him "there is a manifest fissure of thought and sensibility." And to say the least, Donne is a doubtful ally. The ambiguous quality of his contribution can be seen at a glance; consider a poem where most people would be inclined to say he is near his best, "Batter my heart, three-person'd God. . . ." It is certainly unusual at such a moment of sensibility to qualify the vocative with a reference to the Trinity, and it may be that this is the measure of Donne's ability to marry his incessant intellectual activity to powerful feeling. On the other hand, it is hard to answer the charge—a charge Herbert might have supported—that this is indecorous, a mere grotesquerie, with no point unless it be that three Persons can batter better than One. Mr. Eliot, one feels, had come down on this side by 1931. On the whole, although the doctrine of "dissociation of sensibility" is inextricably involved with the Donne revival, one might be excused for wondering how he ever got mixed up with it.

In attempting a partial explanation of this, I also come to the point where I can wind up this essay. Mr. Bateson has noticed in passing how little separates Mr. Eliot's formula from the conventional 19th Century view, which he exemplifies by Stopford Brooke's teaching that the Restoration saw the end "of a poetry in which emotion always accompanied thought." After Grosart's edition of 1872 some people were already remarking that in Donne the note of passion, the true voice of feeling, was audible in love poems unpromisingly couched in terms of alchemy, astronomy and law. And it was this discovery of the true voice of feeling in such surroundings that led to what was in effect a late Romantic glorification of Donne. This was contemporary with the Blake revival, the teaching of Pater, and finally with the assimilation of the parallel but more important phenomenon of French Symbolism—in short, with the emergence of the modern poetic image as it was understood by Symons (a great champion of Donne and the Jacobean Drama), and those who came under his influence: Yeats, and later Pound and Eliot. One can watch the older thought-and-feeling formula developing from a Romantic into a characteristically Symbolist hypothesis. George Eliot, who knew Donne by the time she wrote *Middlemarch*, assumes like her master Wordsworth that the true voice comes from artists of higher organic sensibility than other men, but can say in that novel—doubtless unconscious of her role as critical pioneer—that the poet is "quick to discern," but also "quick to feel" because he possesses "a soul in which knowledge passes instantaneously into feeling, and feeling flashes back as a new organ of knowledge."

A paper recently published by Mr. J. E. Duncan in the *Journal of English and Germanic Philology* is relevant here. Any one who has used the Victorian

editions upon which so much of our reading in 17th Century poetry still
depends must have occasionally felt, if obscurely, that there was some hal-
lucinatory resemblance between certain observations made by these enthusiastic clerical editors and those of Mr. Eliot. Mr. Duncan has collected a great
deal of evidence to show, not only that Donne was well and truly revived
long before Eliot's essays, and indeed Grierson's edition, but that even
seventy years ago people were talking about the poet in what we recognize
as the modern way. Grosart's edition of 1872 launched the revival, and by
1911 Courthope, in his *History,* was already complaining that it had probably gone too far. Grierson's great edition of the following year was accepted
as merely setting the seal on Donne's reputation. But what is more interesting than this mere setting back of the starting post is the terminology which
the Victorian critics, pleased with their rediscovery of the conceit and of
hard-thinking poetry, devised in order to praise the Metaphysical poets.
They speak of its intellectual cunning *and* its power of "sensibility" and
then, quite early, we find ourselves approaching, with a sort of unconscious
inevitability, the modern formula which combines these two qualities as
two sides of a coin. Grosart says that Crashaw's thinking "was so emotional
as almost always to tremble into feeling"; Cowley's thought is "made to
pulsate with feeling." Symons finds that Donne's "senses speak with un-
paralleled directness"; Schelling that Donne's contribution to the English
lyric was "intellectualized emotion." Poets began to find Donne-like qualities
in their own work; in so doing, Francis Thompson spoke of his own "sen-
soriness instinct with mind," and the parallel was supported by Symons and
by Mrs. Meynell. The familiar comparison between the 17th and 20th
Centuries began as early as 1900; after that it was easy to play the game
of parallel poets, and both Brooke and Bridges were credited with resem-
blances to Donne. Gosse and Grierson alike saw the similarities between
Donne and Baudelaire, and briefly hinted at the parallel between English-
Jacobean and French-Symbolist which Mr. Eliot was to find so fertile.
Arthur Symons in fact developed the parallel to a considerable extent; he
is, as I have suggested, a crucial figure, combining as he does in a speculative
synthesis all that Pater had taught, all he himself had learned from Blake
and Coleridge, with the fullest information of anybody in England about
French Symbolism; he was not only indispensable to Yeats, but the admitted, though somewhat despised, mentor of both Eliot and Pound on
this last subject. He is the link between 19th and 20th Century orthodoxies
of the Image or Symbol, and Donne and the 17th Century.

Long before the great edition of Grierson, which made Donne relatively
easy to read, and long before Mr. Eliot's phrase had its remarkable success
in the world, powerful aesthetic interests were being satisfied by a process
of converting an almost unknown poet into an early English Laforgue; and
the same interests demanded a catastrophic start to the modern world
shortly after the death of Donne, and before *Paradise Lost,* that great dissociated poem which you must, said Mr. Eliot, read once for the meaning
and once for the verse, and which is therefore of no use either to poetry or

to that illiterate audience he desiderates for his unified Symbolist poetry nor
for the next best thing, a highly cultivated audience that also likes its art
undissociated. The strangest irony in all this—and it is all I have to say about
the other perverted poet—is that Milton, rather exceptionally, actually believed in and argued for the unity of the soul (a continuum of mind and
sensibility); allowed his insistence on the inseparability of form and matter
to lead him into heresy; and believed that poetry took precedence over
other activities of the soul because it was simple (undissociated by intellect),
sensuous and passionate. But unfortunately he wrote long poems; this alone
disqualifies him as, on the Symbolist view, long poems are impossible.

In fact, the history of these distortions is the history of 19th and early
20th Century aesthetic, the projection onto an historical scale of a developed
Romantic-Symbolist view of the Image.

It is necessary, now, for the sake of whatever completeness this paper can
pretend to, to allude a little more fully to Mr. Bateson's attack on the doctrine, which was delivered from another quarter altogether. I don't think he
goes as far as I do in denying absolutely the value of the hypothesis; but he
does, as I have consequently refrained from doing, analyse the idea itself—
what, if you look closely at it, does the phrase "dissociation of sensibility"
mean? I have tried to show that it is only a way of rewriting history to emphasize the importance of poets you happen to like—a very extravagant way;
that it is a way of talking about poems and poets which satisfy certain
aesthetic criteria (notably that discourse should be purged from poems so
that the poet doesn't appear merely to be thinking about something he felt,
or worse still feeling about something he thought; the whole thing has to
happen at once). But, as several critics have said, it is not very helpful to
talk about *thought* and *feeling* here—these are the terms used for those elements which add up to a *sensibility* capable of receiving the Image. Yet the
reason for the choice of the words is clear enough; they are used in a Romantic way as being not only opposed to each other, but subject to combination
only under unusual circumstances and in a most exceptional person. There
is even a kind of primitivism involved; just as Mill argued that Shelley was,
virtually, in a blessedly backward state of intellectual development, getting
sensations straight into words without any intervening intellection, so Gourmont, as Mr. Bateson has brilliantly reminded us, was speaking of a sort of
happy immaturity in Laforgue when he wrote the essay upon which Mr.
Eliot drew. "Laforgue's intelligence, Gourmont says, . . . was closely connected with his sensibility; he adds that Laforgue died before he acquired
the scepticism which would have enabled him to dissociate his intelligence
from his sensibility (*dissocier son intelligence de sa sensibilité*)." (I quote
Mr. Bateson). In other words, Laforgue could still *feel* his thought as immediately as the odor of a rose. Laforgue was a poet Mr. Eliot admired, and
here he found a way of talking about him as the older critics had talked
about Donne; but Mr. Bateson shows that he draws more from Gourmont

than this. For Gourmont "thinking was only a kind of sensation," and he held that

> our mental activities can be divided into three separate segments or stages. The first stage is from sensations to images (*mots-images*). The second stage is from images to ideas (*mots-idées*). The third stage is from ideas to emotions (*mots-sentiments*). The cycle then closes in action. The literary sensibility, therefore, straddles the first two of Gourmont's stages. Not only does it build up the sensation into an image, but it at least begins the process by which the image is crystallized into the idea. It is at this transitional point, according to Gourmont, that the best thinking is done.

After this explanation, says Mr. Bateson, we can see Mr. Eliot's theory in perspective. "What he has done . . . has been to transfer to the nation de Gourmont's analysis of the mental processes of the individual"; a remark which chimes well with my earlier observation. Mr. Bateson was ably challenged by Mr. Eric Thompson, who showed how much F. H. Bradley must have been in Mr. Eliot's mind when he used this terminology; but Mr. Bateson is right in replying that one would never guess it. All we can see is an attempt (very sophisticated and of course highly qualified) to block out poetry between 1650 and the critic's own time; Blake and Wordsworth had made roughly similar attempts in the interest of their own kind of poetry.

The age of pre-dissociated sensibility is, then, the Golden Age of Romantic-Symbolist thought, the time before somebody ruined England. For many of the prophets, the moment in which they themselves live is the point at which a series of new times begin; it was so for Blake and, up to a point, Wordsworth; the young Yeats thought so; so did Hulme; and there is a hint of it in Pound. The Astraea of the Image is to return, with all manner of beneficial results upon life at large; out of the Image will come, perhaps, many other benefits appropriate to an age of unified sensibility—Catholicism, the abolition of usury and so on.

So we look back nostalgically to archaic Greece, to the early epoch of Ravenna, to Guido and to Donne; and such is the power of this primitivist urge that it succeeds, for a moment, in representing Milton as a kind of magnificent disaster. There can be no doubt that the success of Mr. Eliot's formula, which happens not to be a very good way of putting something that had been put many times, is due in part to the fact that he was the first Symbolist poet in English to achieve wide recognition as distinctively "modern," and in part to the respect rightly accorded to the criticism of distinguished poets. Also his version, if not in its formulation then in its application, has the air of being more moderate and reasonable than Hulme's or Pound's, and he was directing attention to Donne and the Jacobean drama at a moment when they were easily available, and when the work of his contemporaries, as well as his own, had removed some of the extra-literary ob-

jections to such reading. But it is important to remember also the great
accumulated flood of Romantic thinking that swept into the channel of
Symbolism. Symons, for instance, was a poet who announced himself as
deriving from the French Symbolists and from the Jacobean Drama; but
the time was not ripe. When it was, the flood that fertilized the land in
which Mr. Eliot as poet sowed his seed, came from sources in Coleridge and
Blake and Pater, in German Romantic thought and its French developments;
and the sluice gate through which it poured happened to be labelled "dissociation of sensibility." The landscape of English poetry was for a while
curiously changed; now the waters are subsiding. Fine crops grow, though
some crocodiles were generated. Now we may wonder about the form of
the next catastrophe, and hope it won't be drought.

There is no good reason why the history of poetry should not be rewritten from time to time in terms of a powerful new historical myth. If
we think of "dissociation of sensibility" as that, it will seem that the vague-
ness of the expression itself was part of its strength. It gave plenty of scope
to the team of laboring historians who sought to establish it where Mr. Eliot
had simply made a sketch. But now it is clear that it has done its work, and
in so far as people continue to behave as though it constituted a valid way
of talking about history, it is a nuisance. So it is worth trying to show
that it really is untenable as a way of talking about the 17th Century, and
to show where its importance lies. It does not refer to a moment when Bacon
or somebody else ruined England, but to a necessary attempt on the part of
Symbolists to find an historical justification for their poetics.

III. DONNE'S USES OF TRADITION

CLASSICAL ALLUSIONS IN THE POETRY OF DONNE

Beatrice Johnson

A recent critic declares of John Donne: "He had none of that enthusiasm for Greek culture which distinguished More, Colet, and Ascham. He appears to have studied certain Greek authors in Latin translations. . . . His learning was chiefly of the Mediaeval type."[1] No evidence, it is true, comes forward to establish Donne's acquaintance at first hand with Greek authors. At the same time, an examination of the allusions to Greek mythology in the poetry of Donne makes it clear that he had part in the all-but-universal interest of the Elizabethans in classical material, and that he uses this material with characteristic independence and originality.

The theogony which was for the Greeks a fixed and formal system became for the Elizabethan writers material for the fancy and imagination to work upon. Mythological characters interested them not only in themselves but as offering points of departure for innumerable flights of fantasy.

Allusions to the figures of Greek mythology are most common in the sonnet cycles.[2] Among these, the highest number of individual references is eighty-seven, found in Watson. The nearest approach to this is forty-two, in Donne's songs and sonnets. The median is approximately twenty-six, but only Drayton, Barnes, and Smith, besides Watson and Donne, exceed it.[3] Classical divinities mentioned by Donne are The Fates, Jove, Venus, Cupid, Sybil, Prometheus, Mercury, Cynthia, Proserpine,[4] Chaos, Orcus, Boreas,[5] Orithyia, Pluto, Helicon,[6] Morpheus,[7] Circe, Phoebus,[8] Phaeton, and he handles each of them with remarkable spontaneity of wit.

As is to be expected in poetry of this type, the mythological figure which assumes special importance is the God of Love. The sonneteers refer repeatedly to Cupid, with his traditional associations; he shoots arrows from eyes, dances in eyes, lights fires at them. Sidney constructs an extravagant scheme of military symbolism to represent the warfare of love.[9] Mediæval imagery occurs also in

> When Cupid, having me, his slave, descried
> In Mars' livery, prancing in the press,
> What now, Sir Fool? said he.[10]

There is a suggestion of mediæval alchemy in Drayton's reference to the

Reprinted by permission of the Modern Language Association of America from *PMLA*, 43 (1928), 1098-1109.

power of Love to refine the spirit in his fires.[11] But Sidney becomes almost
modern in his psychological analysis here:

> It must be true, what we call Cupid's dart
> An image is, which for ourselves we carve.

Shakespeare's Cupid is alluringly human in this passage:

> Love's eye is not so true as all men's: no,
> How can it? O how can Love's eye be true
> That is so vex'd with watching and with tears? . . .
> O cunning Love! with tears thou keepst me blind
> Lest eyes well-seeing thy foul faults should find.[12]

However, on another occasion Shakespeare calls Cupid a fool[13]; and in truth
Cupid does seem very stupid, for he often relaxes his vigil by falling asleep
and allows his flame to be extinguished.[14] He replenishes it, however, at the
mistress's eyes—a conceit which grows out of all proportion in the legend
accounting for hot springs.[15] Some other vagaries in treatment may be noted
in Barnes' comparison of Cupid to Medusa, Tofte's conceit of the snake, and
Constable's painting of a picture on the heart. The last brings to mind vividly
Donne's *The Damp*:

> When they will find your picture in my heart.

    The traditional figure of Cupid is accepted by Donne, but his allusions
invariably have an individual note. He declares, indeed, against the conventional treatment of the God of Love by the Court poets:

> Our little Cupid hath sued livery,
> And is no more in his minority.[16]

and

> Yet am I not so blind as some men be,
> Who vow and swear they little Cupid see
> In their fair mistress' eyes.[17]

In even stronger terms he indicts convention as opposed to the "golden laws
of nature"—

> We are made servants of Opinion . . .
> Here love received immedicable harms . . .
> Only some few, strong in themselves and free . . .
> Yet make a throne for him within their breast.[18]

    With Shakespeare and all the Elizabethans, Donne agrees that Love is pur-
blind for he "fits actives to passives,"[19] yet his inherent bent for paradox and
contrast determines his expression:

> I must love her that loves not me[20]

and

> Falsehood is worse than hate; and that must be,
> If she whom I love, should love me.[21]

Finally, Donne is unique in placing Cupid among the infernal gods, for although he prays to Love:

> Give me thy weakness, make me blind
> Both ways, as thou and thine, in eyes and mind.[22]

he asserts that Love's dwelling-place is with Pluto,[23] and calls him a devil:

> Love, any devil else but you
> Would for a given soul give something too.
> At court your fellows every day
> Give th' art of rhyming, huntsmanship, or play.[24]

Perhaps the most stereotyped of Elizabethan poetic conventions is the address to the Muse. Wholly conventional, too, is the reference in the address to Elizabeth Drury:

> Immortal maid, who though thou wouldst refuse
> The name of mother, be unto my Muse
> A father, since her chaste ambition is
> Yearly to bring forth a child as this.[25]

and to Lord Harrington:

> Do not, fair soul, this sacrifice refuse
> That in thy grave I do inter my Muse.[26]

In this connection once more we may note both conformity and independence on the part of Donne. He refers to the Muse seventeen times—the frequency of the allusion establishing it as native to his thought. In some instances he voices a traditional opinion, as when he vouches for the divinity of the Muse in calling her "heaven's high holy Muse."[27] Again the traditional attitude of complaint—found in Barnfield, Watson, R. L., Tofte, Sidney,[28] Drayton,[29] Fletcher, Smith, Barnes, and Shakespeare[30]—is to be noted in his complaint of the ineffectiveness of his Muse, who inspires him to inconsequential love-songs when he would be writing more ambitious and more artistic poetry.[31]

All the writers of sonnet cycles[32] refer to their lady as their muse, Shakespeare calling her the tenth muse.[33] Certain references to the Muse, however, appear to reflect something of the actual attitude of the poet toward his own work—the term Muse being interpreted as the state of mind conducive to creating. Perhaps calling upon some power outside himself for the energy to perform tasks or duties, establishes for Donne, as for other poets the very state of mind necessary to the act of creating, the contemplative mind being thereby freed from all disturbing elements, and produces a silent psychology of effectiveness. Donne adopts toward his Muse the critical attitude of the familiar friend. At one point he speaks of her as "undiscerning,"[34] at another, he pleads for a proper reward for "his Muse's white sincerity."[35] He accuses her of infidelity, of being to another what she should be to him; but, in turn, he accuses himself of being the cause, indicating that he is not doing justice to his powers of writing nor to his own aspirations.[36] In his fifth satire Donne is self-critical, he evidently has done some piece of work which he considers unworthy of his inspiration; but in spite of this he exhibits considerable self-confidence:

> Thou shalt not laugh at this leaf, Muse.[37]

Like Drayton, he holds his gift of poesy as noble and lofty. There is nothing trivial in the nature of his muse; yet there is nothing audacious or patronizing as in Sidney,[38] Smith, Brooke, Lodge, Breton, and Drayton.[39]

An author's attitude toward his own genius is always of intense interest: Dante seemed most assured of his rank when he placed himself with Homer and other famous writers as "sixth amid so learn'd a band."[40] This self-assurance is especially true of John Donne; he is always frank with his readers in regard to his reasons for writing, or in criticizing his skill in composition.

One of Donne's references which permitted of varied treatment was the spheres. His idea that heaven is made up of many spheres[41] may be an echo of the general belief in the Ptolemaic system of astronomy in the sixteenth century, although in several of his works he indicates that he has investigated and is familiar with the Copernican theory of the universe.[42] Since Donne says, "we look upon Nature, but with Aristotle's Spectacles, and upon the body of man, but with Galens, and upon the frame of the world, but with Ptolemies' spectacles," he must wish to speak in a language that will be generally understood when he refers frequently to the "earth's frame" and the older cosmic scheme of things. Although the Ptolemaic system has lent itself to poetic treatment in such poems as Milton's *Paradise Lost* and Rosetti's *Blessed Damosel,* Donne must have used it because it was the natural course for thought to run. Beyond all question, however, his keen intellect had grasped the significance of the "New Philosophy."

Donne hears "the music of the spheres" in spite of "that day's rude hoarse minstelsy,"[43] and wishes to "behold those hands which span the poles and tune all spheres at once,"[44] in which we seem to have a confusion of the Greek goddess Necessity and the Hebrew Jehovah. Again, Donne compares the prayer of a sinner with the musical praises of the spheres.[45] The passage which follows is reminiscent of both Greek and Jewish thought[46]:

> Make all this all three choirs, heaven earth and spheres,
> The first, Heaven, hath a song, but no man hears;
> The spheres have music, but they have no tongue,
> Their harmony is rather danced than sung.

Donne's references to the spheres as the framework of this universe are more numerous in his sermons[47] than are his references to the "New Philosophy."

No writer interested in the idea of the music of the spheres could over-look the possibilities in the idea of the Fates, the three daughters of Necessity. Donne assumes the duties of Clotho toward himself when he says:

> I have a sin of fear, that when I have spun,
> My last thread I shall perish on the shore.[48]

But this fear is defied much as Browning defies death:

> Come, Fates, I fear you not! All whom I owe
> Are paid but you; then rest me ere I go
> But Chance from you all sovereignty hath got.[49]

He says to death:

> Thou'rt slave to Fate, chance, kings and desperate men.[50]

His bitterness toward Fate is revealed in:

> and with us, methinks, Fate deals so
> As with the Jews' guide, God did; He did show
> Him the rich land but barr'd his entry in";[51]

and he finds Fate modernized in the Law of the Land:

> Oh! ne'er may
> Fair law's white reverend name be strumpeted
> To warrant thefts; she is established
> Recorder to Destiny on earth, and she
> Speaks Fate's words.[52]

Then again, he mentions Fate in the conventional way as having a book of record,[53] much as Shakespeare does in *Henry IV*:

> That one might read the book of Fate,[54]

and in

> Hapless Aegeon, whom the Fates have marked,
> To bear the extremity of mishap,[55]

and

> O Fates! Come, come; Cut thread and thrum,[56]

and

> What Fates impose, that men must needs abide.[57]

The references to Jove which Shakespeare introduces are quite according to the traditional manner: "Jove sometimes went disguised,"[58] "Supreme Jove,"[59] and "your emperor continues still a Jove."[60] Donne, on the other hand, speaks of the invasions of Jove's[61] prerogatives by every modern god,[62] and he affords an insight into his mental attitude toward religion in such passages as

Here Peter, Jove's; there Paul hath Dian's fane.
So whether my hymns you admit or choose,
In me you've hallowed a pagan muse.[63]

The praises of inconstancy in love are common in the followers of Donne,
but this attitude was singular among the Elizabethans, who reproached love
for inconstancy. Shakespeare mentions the inconstancy of Venus in her intrigue with Mars,[64] which accounts for the being of Cupid, called "That
wicked bastard of Venus."[65] The same note is sounded by Watson:

Here lyeth Love, of Mars the bastard Sonne.

In Donne's philosophy of love, Venus takes on the character of the light,
buoyant evanescence of the foam of ocean waves and in this phase she
visualizes for Donne a much more attractive love than the constant love
often idealized by poets of the conventional type:

Venus hear me sigh this song;
And by love's sweetest part, variety, she swore.[66]

Other creatures of Greek Mythology which are used by Donne are the
following: Sirens,[67] Mermaids, Argus,[68] Furies,[69] Chimera, Vengeance, and
Python.[70] The songs of the sirens[71] and mermaids[72] interested him as they
do all poets. He bequeaths his eyes to Argus, the hundred-eyed monster
charm'd by "sweet Mercury," in his satiric poem, "The Will." The Furies
are the spirit of the storm in his vivid description in the letter to Christopher
Brooke. His use of Chimera as "this she-Chimera with eyes of fire,"[73] indicates
familiarity with the myth itself, for Chimera was the fire-breathing monster,
the son of Echidna, and is not found in Elizabethan literature commonly.
Vengeance[74] and Opinion [75] are personified much as are Mischief in *Julius
Caesar* and Rumor in the *AEneid*. Opinion is "a monster in no certain shape
attired . . . formless at first but growing on its fashions" much as in Book IV
of the *AEneid,* "Rumor sped . . . small at first, because afraid, she soon
exalts her stature skyward, stalking through the lands . . . born of Earth,
the last of the Titans."

Donne speaks of Earth as the mother of all, "our mother which these
things doth bear,"[76] and of the heavens as begetting all things here, reminding us of the myth concerning Gaea and Uranus, the parents of the Titans,
among whose children were Mnemosyne, mother of the Muses, and Phoibe,
goddess of the moon before Diana. His reference to "Darkness, Light's
brother, his birthright claims o'er the world,"[77] belongs to this myth, although his genealogy is not quite precise since Erebus was the father of
Aether. However, both were children of Nyx, the proverbial mother of
every divinity whose origin was shrouded in the darkness of uncertainty.
Chaos, father of Erebus, is mentioned several times in his poems: "Like to
the first Chaos,"[78] and "view old Chaos in the pains we feel,"[79] are the most
significant. The latter bespeaks a careful study and understanding of the
Greek idea of the origin of the universe, for this elegy is called "His Parting

from Her," and the idea of the great general disturbance at the parting of the elements from each other as they dwelt in Chaos, in order to form the universe, suggests most acute pangs of severance. This conceit bears out the idea that all of Donne's conceits are really figures of speech which are the natural product of a keen intellect.

Always, Donne uses terms of Greek Mythology with a skill or adeptness which is amazing. His use shows both an analysis of the meaning of the myth and a synthetic conclusion as to its significance, in his application of it to the particular matter in hand. For instance, "was more than for Acteon not to look"[80] and "Could Promethean art either unto the northern pole impart the fire of these inflaming eyes,"[81] both show the ability to assimilate a thought and to present it again in a new and surprising form essentially his own. Again,

> I more amazed than Circe's prisoners, when
> They felt themselves turn beasts, felt myself then
> Becoming traitor, . . .[82]

implies that he not only knew the myth,[83] but that it had become real to his own experience. The myth does not say that Odysseus' men were "amazed," nor does it imply the idea connotative with that word in the sixteenth century. They were chagrined and repentant after they found what they had made of themselves through their eating. Donne, by power of his vivid imagination, knew that they must have felt mystified or bewildered while the change from man to beast was taking place.

In regard to Homer, Donne says something that arrests the attention of a reader of the Greek Epics:

> And her, whose book (they say) Homer did find and name.[84]

Evidently, Donne had been reading about a possible authoress of some work ascribed to Homer. There is no hint as to who the author might be. Samuel Butler would probably say the work was "The Odyssey."

Both Homer and Virgil were extremely fond of the use of altars and sacrifices in their literature. Donne, also, uses them frequently and they are pagan altars:

> Gods, when ye fumed on altars, were well-pleased
> Because you were burnt, not that they liked the smell.[85]

In these poets, Pluto's realm figures strongly; Pluto is a term common among poets, including Donne,[86] but he uses the term "Orcus,"[87] an unusual name for the god of death. His acquaintance with the infernal regions of Greek Mythology is shown in "Elysian bliss,"[88] and Lethe.[89] Donne speaks of his tears as a "heavenly Lethan flood to drown his sins' black memory,"[90] and in his extravagant verses about Elizabeth Drury, he says they are all "drown'd in Lethe and have forgotten all good"[91] because they are forgetful of her.

Donne's references to Sibyl are unique, for he refers to the Sibyllin Books, those prophetic documents revealing the fate of Rome and sold by Sibyl to Tarquin, in wishing for the lasting fame of his own book[92] and also in connection with the mystical quality of the book of a friend.[93]

Other terms of classical literature used by him are Pygmalion,[94] Vestal, Colossus, golden fruit, the torch, the holy plough, the Heliconian spring, the Greek philosopher Heracleitus, and the circle in its philosophical sense:

> O soul, O circle, why so quickly be
> Thy ends, thy birth and death closed up in thee.[95]

Here again he has grasped the whole idea of the Greek figure of speech and fitted it to his own conception with his usual nicety. His precision suggests the skill of a juggler.

> Would not Heracleitus laugh to see[96]

is a clever expression to measure degree, especially when used in a satire, surely ridiculous enough if it would cause the "weeping philosopher" to laugh.

A very amusing epigram illustrates the fact that Donne had a broad knowledge of classical terms and ideas:

> Thou art like Mercury in stealing, but liest like a Greek.

This brings to mind the many fictitious stories which Odysseus fitted to his needs, the false Sinon of the Trojan horse, and the long-drawn-out story of the Guardian of Sophocles' Electra.

A continuous comparison of how the Elizabethans handle each classical allusion would grow monotonous; hence only enough of those allusions have been used here to show that there is a certain degree of similarity between them, as well as to show which of the sonneteers have initiative and originality. The study has made evident the fact that John Donne reflects to a considerable degree his own age.

JOHN DONNE'S KNOWLEDGE OF RENAISSANCE MEDICINE

Don Cameron Allen

I

Were all biographical evidence wanting and the corpus of Donne's work reduced to just the poetry and sermons, we should not hesitate to label him as a valetudinarian. Medical data, anatomical terminology, physiological theory, apothecary's "drug tongue," and physician's jargon elbow from the pages of his poetry and sermons the classical allusions so popular with his contemporaries. Some of the poems have titles drawn from the *ars medica*; and in the sermons, where Donne is unhampered by the requirements of rhyme and meter, he unwinds his medical knowledge to the delight of the hypochondriacs of his parish. We have, however, other evidence. The *Devotions Upon Emergent Occasions* is a fine clinical account of the progress of an illness; the *Letters to Severall Persons of Honour* contain many reports of Donne's maladies; and all of this is substantiated by the tesimony of Walton. We could almost establish a dictionary of medical terms based on Donne's writings because they are studded with words like *ague, anatomy, antidote, apoplexy, balm, chirurgery, disease, dissect, fever, gangrene, gout, hydropsy, lethargy, palsy, physic, plaster, purge,* and others that are most sparingly used by even the sicklier poets of Donne's age. Since Donne's medical lore is an intrinsic part of his egocentric self, and since the meaning of his verse sometimes depends on an understanding of this material, an explanation of this matter is certainly required. Donne, in many ways, was more interested in medicine than he was in those problems of cosmology and astronomy about which scholars have been so agitated in their attempt to prove that Donne was well-read in the "quantum theories" of his day. He was certainly interested in the extrinsic problems of the universe, but he was much more interested in the intrinsic agonies of his own viscera.

II

When Donne was a young man, he seems to have been very skeptical about the progress of medicine, for he says in the *Paradoxes and Problems* that physicians "climb no higher" because having found many things in nature obstruse, they think "that all is so."[1] He revised this opinion later in life, for we find him including a history of the progress of medicine in a letter to Sir

Reprinted from *Journal of English and Germanic Philology*, 42 (1943), 322-42, by permission of the University of Illinois Press.

Thomas Lucey. Men, he states, were first satisfied with hit-or-miss cures; then they demanded rules and Hippocrates supplied this demand. In due time, men wanted to know why certain simples produced certain effects, and Galen answered this question.

> And after (not much before our time), men perceiving that all effects in Physick could not be derived from these beggerly and impotent properties, of the Elements, and that therefore they were driven often to that miserable refuge of specifique form, and of antipathy and sympathy, we see the world hath turned upon new principles which are attributed to *Paracelsus,* but (indeed) to much to his honour.[2]

A discussion of the evolution of medicine can be found in most medical books of Donne's age,[3] but the praise of Paracelsus, grudging though it be, is quite unusual, for the great Bombastus was considered a charlatan by Donne's literary contemporaries[4] and was either passed over in silence or attacked with vigor by men of medicine.[5] Under these circumstances can we call Donne a Paracelsian?

There is no doubt that Donne had read certain works of Paracelsus and knew something about the general Paracelsian philosophy. In a poetical letter to Sir Henry Wotton, Donne compares the purgation theories of Galen and Paracelsus to the advantage of the latter.[6] In the *Biathanaios* there are three allusions to Paracelsus with marginal references; there is also an annotated reference to Paracelsus in the *Paradoxes and Problems* and in the *L Sermons.* In the whole of Donne's works, there are two references each to Galen and Hippocrates, and only in the case of one of the latter allusions do we find a direct bibliographical notation. No other medical authorities are mentioned by Donne, and were we to take the assertion of "The Will" literally, we should have to say that "my physic books" were treatises by Paracelsus and Hippocrates. Before we agree to this conclusion, we should consider Donne as a maker of footnotes and the exact nature of his Paracelsian knowledge.

One of the characteristics of Donne as a quoter of authorities is that he either quotes incorrectly or sets down the reference inaccurately. His single direct citation of Hippocrates is given as *"Hippocrat. Aphor. 1.* 2.38,"[7] but in every Renaissance edition of the *Aphorisms,* the source of Donne's allusion is *Liber* IV. 57. The same type of inaccuracy is observable in some of his references to the writings of Paracelsus. He recommends, for example, Paracelsus' theory of amulets, and refers his reader to *"Paracelsus Chyrug. Mag. tract. 2. Cap. 8 et de trans. cap. 10."*[8] The first footnote is correct, but there is nothing pertinent in any chapter of the *De Transplantatione.* In another place, Donne says that venereal diseases were sent by God as a scourge for sin, and when the disease was not enough, "he sent a second worse affliction, which was ignorant, and torturing Physitians."[9] The marginal reference is *"Chyrurgia mag. de ulcer."* Now this is either a summary of the whole of Paracelsus' treatise or it is a rendering of one of Paracelsus' repetitious asides.[10] Other statements attributed by Donne to

Paracelsus are more evasive. Paracelsus is alleged to have said, "It is all one whether God or the Devill cure, so the Patient be well," and the reference is given as "*1. de morb. cad.*"[11] Such a statement is not to be found in the *Liber de Caducis*; it is, in fact, quite out of keeping with Paracelsus' pious manner and definitely out of harmony with the early section of the treatise in which we are supposed to find it.[12] We see then that Donne was acquainted with two of Paracelsus' tractates, but his knowledge of them seems most casual.

One finds, however, in Donne's writings certain ideas that have the backing of Paracelsus, and in these instances we can probably say that Donne accepted them on the authority of the master. Paracelsus was a great believer in "experientia" and a great opponent of "experimentum." Phrases like "Scientia enium est experientia" are forever in his mouth, and often he writes little essays on this theme.[13] This notion pleased Donne, who caught it up and expounded it to the credit of Paracelsus in a sermon preached at Lincoln's Inn.[14] The experience of Paracelsus led him to base his medical philosophy on the popular doctrine of the sympathies and antipathies existing between the microcosm and the macrocosm, a theory with which Donne was also infatuated. Paracelsus compares the pest to an earthquake,[15] apoplexy to lightning,[16] thunder to epilepsy,[17] and eclipses to fainting-spells;[18] consequently when Donne writes, "these *earthquakes* in him selfe, sodaine shakings; these *lightnings*, sodaine flashes; . . . these *Eclypses*, sodaine offuscations, and darknings of his senses . . . ,"[19] we know where he got his similes. The debt to Paracelsus does not end here; in another instance—the doctrine of the intrinsic balsum—Donne is a complete disciple.

Paracelsus believed that every living body—even the earth itself—contained its antidote for all poisons. When this balsum was exhausted, the man, animal, or plant was dead, but until that time, all could be cured if they would observe certain rules that permitted the balsum to work.[20] Donne was charmed by this idea. He refers to it in the second epistle to Lady Bedford and in the *First Anniversary* and at various places in the sermons. Two of the sermons[21] contain accounts of the value of the "Balsamum naturale" in the healing of wounds, which are little more than translations of Paracelsus' disquisition on this subject in the *Chirurgia Magna*,[22] a work that we are sure Donne knew. All of this suggests that Donne had looked over some of Paracelsus' writings and been attracted by some of his ideas. This is more than we can say for Donne's literary contemporaries, but it does not make Donne a paracelsian. Ninety per cent of Donne's medical allusions belong to traditional medicine and have no paracelsian flavor about them. In a few cases, the doctrine of Paracelsus may have encouraged Donne to take one side or the other of a medical controversy, but of this we cannot be sure.

III

Before we consider Donne's knowledge of anatomy, physiology, pathology, and *methodus medendi,* we may pause on some of his general medical concepts that may be glossed by the writings of practising physicians. He believed, like most men of his age, that there was a geographical distribution of diseases[23] and that this fact depended in part on the quality of the native air,[24] a theory that Burton elaborated so genially. He felt that in the case of leprosy, at least, contagion was effected by the breath, for he writes in "Elegie IV,"

> By thee the seely Amorous sucks his death
> By drawing in a leprous harlots breath.

Pareus insists that lepers be separated from the healthy, "et que l'air ambiant ou environnant, lequel nous inspirons et attirons en nos corps, peut estre infecte de leur haleine."[25] But there are other ideas more interesting than these.

In the *First Anniversary* we read,

> There is no health; Physitians say that wee,
> At best, enjoy but a neutalitie.

Donne provides his own commentary on these lines in one of the sermons preached before his old colleagues at Lincoln's Inn. "*Non sanitas,* there is no health in *any,* so universall is sickness; nor at *any time* in any so universall; and so universall too, as that *not in any part* of any man, at any time.[26] Although the great French physician Gui Patin was later to take his doctorate with a thesis on exactly this subject, the physicians who wrote books during Donne's time are singularly silent; they thought, perhaps, that such a heterodox opinion would be bad for business. There is, however, a brief discussion of this question in Fernelius, the favorite medical authority of George Herbert.

> Inter has (health and sickness) media quaedam interiecta est utrinque obscura: quae idcirco nec sanitas, nec morbus, sed neutra est constitutio. Neutrius enim est particeps & neutrum corpus reddit nec sanum nec aegrum, sed inter utrumque quodammodo medium. Argutas quidem & multiplices huius verbi potestates nonnulli percensent, sed profecto rei medicae parum utiles, & & quae interpretes in varios sophismatum labyrinthos praecipitarunt. Neutra haec constitutio latitudine circumscribitur in tres ordines distincta, in neutram obscure sanam, neutram obscure aegram & neutram quae inter has vere media intervenit.[27]

The sixteenth century physicians recognized certain diseases as of hereditary origin; these diseases, Donne writes, "last more generations in families, then the inheritance it self does," and when the lands and manors are gone, the son still inherits the gout or the stone.[28] Pareus discusses the hereditary nature of the gout and tells us how diseases are transmitted in a family;[29] Fernelius[30] writes on the stone as an inherited ailment, for he thinks that diseases like nephritis, arthritis, and epilepsy are contained in the father's seed. He concludes his discussion of this question with a statement that is almost parallel with Donne's remarks: "qua tandem in morbos similes, haereditarios idcirco nuncupatos, incurrant, ut parentibus liberi succedant, non minus morborum, quam possessionum haeredes."[31] Now none of these statements of Donne show special learning; he knows exactly what any man of his age might garner by reading a medical work or by talking to a physician. He goes into none of the minutiae of medical philosophy, but he does know the general theory. In this, or perhaps in expressing it, he is different from his contemporaries.

IV

The medical science of the sixteenth century was based on a more thorough knowledge of anatomy and physiology than that of any previous age. Galen, Hippocrates, and the Arabs are still cited with reverence, but where experience or investigation showed these ancients to be in error, they were quickly corrected. The *methodus medendi* still depended to a large degree on the teachings of Galen save in those cases where Paracelsus and "the chimiques" had made their stand, but in anatomy and physiology, thanks to the efforts of the guild of barber-surgeons, progress was immense. The reason for this advance resides in the new emphasis placed on the dissection of cadavers, which taught men more about their bodies than they could learn from mediaeval diagrams. Then too, vivisection, which had been approved by Galen, was again in vogue, and every year—if we can believe the medical books—a large number of apes, bears, dogs, and swine were carved up alive for the glory of medicine. This new departure in medical studies was undoubtedly of great interest for Donne, who never tires of using the words *anatomy* and *dissection* in both his verse and prose. If we select from his works those allusions that seem to have some scientific basis to them, we discover again that he is following the trend of contemporary surgery.

In the *LXXX Sermons*, Donne talks of the importance of "Dissections and Anatomies" for the understanding of man's body and "consequently health;"[32] his remarks on this occasion are quite conventional and can be found in the preface to the "anatomy" of almost any work on general medicine. But Donne is more specific than this. "Criminals," he writes, "do publike good, cut in Anatomies";[33] and we learn from Columbus that anatomists got their supply of cadavers from the gallows.

> Profecto hodie cum ob cummunem vivorum utilitatem Pontifices, Reges, atque Imperatores, ut in publicis Academiis quatannis Anatomici reorum cadaveribus secandis Anatomen profiteantur, facile est controversias istas diiudicare.[34]

In spite of the relative scarcity of cadavers, the anatomist of the sixteenth century selected his bodies with great care. Fernelius urges the physician to select the body of a man who was hanged, strangled, or drowned; in no case should he choose one who had died of wounds or a disease.[35] Sylvius is even more careful. He avoids the carcasses of men who died of wounds, illnesses, hanging, torturing, and beheading; the best body for dissection is that of one dead by drowning.[36] Donne assuredly had cautions of this nature in mind when he wrote,

Rack't carcasses make ill anatomies.[37]

Since the embalming methods of the sixteenth century were still very
primitive, the anatomist had to comment upon the specimens in the order
of their durability. De Vigo, an Italian surgeon famous enough to be translated into English before the middle of the sixteenth century, describes the
method.

And when the body is layed upon the table, they make foure elections
or chosynges therof. The fyrst is of membres nutritive, for they ben more
apte to receyve putrefactions or rottynges then other. The second election is of membres spirituall, as of the hart, of the pannicles or thynne
skynnes, of the longes. The thyrde election is, of the membres animale,
that is to say of the heade, and hys partes. The fourth of the extremities
of the bodye, as of the armes, the legges, and theyr partes.[38]

This account gives us a gloss on some lines in the *First Anniversary*.

But as in cutting up a man, that's dead,
The body will not last out, to have read
On every part, and therefore men direct
Their speech to parts, that are of most effect.

From these accounts of anatomical practice, we may turn to consider
Donne's knowledge of anatomy.

V

The physicians of Donne's age knew a great deal about the brain and the
nervous system although they were not yet agreed on the exact functions
of the nerves themselves. Donne was in possession of some of the basic facts.
In "The cross," a poem that is prophetic of Sir Thomas Brown's pursuit of
the quincunx, he says that the brains vents itself through sutures "which a
Crosses forme present." To this idea no sixteenth century physician whom
I have read subscribes. The anatomists say that the skull contains three true
and either two of five false sutures. The three true sutures are the coronal or
stephanic, the sagittal or obelaea, and the lambdoide, so named because of
its resemblance to the lambda.[39] None of these sutures is cruciform. Donne's
statement probably goes back to Hippocrates, whose observations, as the
Latin translation of the age records them, read: "Ut H cum utraque
eminentia servatur: X vero cum utraque perit."[40] Donne's description of
the nervous sytem as "the sinewie thread my braine lets fall"[41] or "those
snowie strings which do our bodies tie"[42] is in keeping with the accounts of
the medical writers, who all find the nerves descending from the brain as
white strings that give motion and sensation to the limbs.[43] Equally correct
is Donne's reference to the spinal pith or cartilage which "strings fast the
little bones of necke, and backe."[44] Fernelius[45] writes: "Quorum beneficio
interiores vertebrarum nodi cohaerescunt, utpote quae inter nodos fusa nexu
illos firmissimo colligant." Whether or not bones were sensitive was one of

the problems that the surgeons of the sixteenth and seventeenth century liked to discuss. Columbus, the discoverer of pulmonary circulation, considers all aspects of this question in a lengthy essay,[46] but for our purposes, the conclusions of Pareus are more succinct.

> Ce que ie confesse: mais ie respons aussi, que la membrane qui les couvre, & les arteres & nerfs qui entrent en leurs cavitez, ont un exquis sentiment: & que quand lesdites arteres se meuvent, estans eschauffees de l'os malade, elles causent douleur à la membrane qui l'enveloppe: tellement que les patiens disent sentir une douleur pulsative au profond des os.[47]

This observation throws light on a remark made by Donne in his second sermon of the penitential psalms. The bones, says Donne, feel no pain, "but *membranae dolent*; those little membrans, those filmes, those thin skins, that cover, and that line some bones, are very sensible of pain."[48]

To some medical authorities of the Renaissance, the brain was the noblest member of the body, but others still clung to the older notion that the heart as the seat of the soul was most to be honored. *Heart* is an important word in Donne's vocabulary, and he knew something about its structure and functions. In the *Second Anniversary* he touches on one of the great medical controversies of the age.

> Know'st thou how blood, which to the heart doth flow,
> Doth from one ventricle to th'other goe?[49]

On this question Vesalius writes quite frankly:

> Adeo ut ignorem (quicquid etiam de foveis hac in sede commenter, & venae portae ex ventriculo, & intestinis suctionis non sim immemor) qui per septi illius substantiam ex dextro ventriculo in sinistrum vel minimum quid sanguinis assumi possit: praecipue quum tam patentibus orificiis vasa cordis in suorum ventriculorum amplitudinem dehiscant: ut modo taceam verum ve ne cave ex corde progressum.[50]

Columbus, on the other hand, thought that his discovery that the blood poured from the right ventricle into the lungs, whence, after it was mixed with air, it passed through the venal artery to the left ventricle solved the problem. "Quod nemo hactenus aut animadvertendum, aut scriptum reliquit: licet maxime sit omnibus animadvertendum."[51] Pareus admits that the answer to this problem is yet to be learned; he thinks, however, that the hypothesis of Columbus is more probable than Botallus' theory of the "vena arteriarum nutrix."[52]

At various places in his writings, Donne speaks of the spirits of the blood, a doctrine that stood fast in medicine until Harvey's discovery of the mechanics of circulation shattered it. We read, for example, in "The Extasie":

> As our blood labours to beget
> Spirits, as like soules as it can,

> Because such fingers need to knit
> That subtile knot, which makes us man.

According to Renaissance medical philosophy, the spirits were subtile substances of an aerial nature made of the lightest part of the blood, which
governed the body and all its parts. There were three types of spirits. The
animal spirits were made in the veins and arteries of the brain and distributed
through the nervous system. They were responsible for sensations; and when
their passage was blocked sensation was lost. One's hands became numb in
winter because the cold interrupted the course of the spirits. If the interrup-
tion was permanent, apoplexy resulted. The vital spirits were produced in
the left ventricle of the heart and were a compound of blood and air. They
preserved the innate heat, without which nothing could live, for when it
was wasted, the man died. Donne is thinking about this spirit when he
writes in "The Paradox," "Death kills with too much cold."[53] The vital
spirits were exhausted by a corruption of the humours, by excessive evacu-
ation, and by frequent breathing or sighing. The notion that sighing shortened
life was commonly used by Donne and his fellow men of letters. In "The
Computation," we read of the many years that have elapsed since Donne
saw the beloved, "Tears drown'd one hundred, and sighes blew out two."[54]
The third spirit of the blood, the natural spirit, was produced in the liver
and circulated through the veins. This was a cruder spirit than the other
two, and its task was to nutrify the various parts of the body.[55] All of this
lore was undoubtedly known to Donne.

   Donne has very little to say about the digestive tract beyond the fact
that the capacity of the stomach, veins, and "all the other conduits and
cisterns of the body"[56] is known to physicians. This statement is probably
incorrect, because the medical authorities admit that the exact capacities
of these organs vary with the individual;[57] he is closer to the textbooks
in his remarks about the spleen. According to Donne the spleen is the
"sewar of the body,"[58] and can "suffocate the heart."[59] All of the medical
authorities talk of the cloacal labors of the spleen,[60] and Fernelius reports
how its malevolent action destroys the heart.[61] A final anatomical question
as widely discussed in Donne's age as the passage of the blood from the
right to left ventricle of the heart will conclude this study of Donne's knowledge of anatomy and physiology.

   In the "limits of knowledge" section of the *Second Anniversary*, we find
the following couplet.

> And of those many opinions which men raise
> Of Nailes and Haires, dost thou know which to praise?[62]

Physicians were then arguing whether or not the nails and hair were true
parts of the body. They did not resemble either organs or skin; they did not
grow like bones or plants; they had no internal vessels of nutrition; and
they did not seem to draw nutritives from without. Finally, unlike anything

else in nature, they grew in length but not in width and thickness. Some of the authorities think that the nails are a type of ligament; others say that they are produced by the excrements of the tendons. Vicary thinks that hair is produced by "the grosse fume or smoke passing out of the viscous matter"; Pareus says that it develops from the thickest part of the superfluity of the third concoction; Columbus says that it is nourished by the fatty layers under the skin. Vesalius, after reviewing the whole controversy, says that all one can do is define what they are.[63]

VI

The study of the mechanics of conception, gestation, and delivery are a part of physiology, but Donne's knowledge of matters is so broad that an exposition of it requires a separate section. In the *Metempsychosis,* we find a poetical account.

> Adam and Eve had mingled bloods, and now
> Like Chimiques equall fires, her temperate wombe
> Had stew'd and form'd it: and part did become
> A spungie liver, that did richly allow
> Like a free conduit, on a high hils brow,
> Life-keeping moisture unto every part;
> Part hardned it selfe to a thicker heart,
> Whose busie furnaces lifes spirits do impart.
>
> Another part became the well of sense,
> The tender well-arm'd feeling braine, from whence,
> Those snowie strings which do our bodies tie
> Are raveld out. . . .

A prose account, which is a partial commentary on these verses, appears in the *Parodoxes and Problems.*

As in the naturall generation and formation made of the seed in the womb of a woman, the body is joynted and organized about the 28 day, and so it begins to be no more an *Embrion,* but capable as a matter prepared to its form to receive the soule, which faileth not to insinuate and innest it selfe into the body about the fortieth day; about the third month it hath motion and sense.[64]

The theory of conception at this time was very simple. The male and female sperms were drawn from the purest blood in the sanguinary mass. Riolanus[65] writes, "Semen fit ex pinguiore & puriore sanguinis"; Vicary[66] states, "this sparme that commeth both of man and woman, is made & gathered of the most best and purest drops of blood in all the body." This information not only provides a gloss for these passages but is the explanation of the whole point of "The Flea." After the blood of the parents is mingled concoction takes place in the womb. "And as the Renet and mylke make the cheese, so doth the sparme of man and woman make the generation of the Embreon."[67] This remark of Vicary gives point to Donne's line, "This curded milke, this poor unlittered whelpe my body."[68] After concoction took place, the foetus began to develop according to the schedule mentioned by Donne in the *Metempsychosis* passage. Pareus' account provides a convenient annotation.

> Le quatrieme iour apres que la veine umbilicale est faicte, elle succe par les cotyledons, le sang plus gros, & de plus grand nourrissement, lequel à cause de sa grossesse se coagule aisement au lieu où se doit engendrer le foye. . . . l'artere umbilicale succe pareillement le sang arterial des arteres cotyledoines, qui est tres-chaud, & fort spirituel: duquel en cette seconde ampoulle se forme le coeur, qui est de substance charneuse, solide & espesse, ainsi qu'il appartient au membre le plus chaud de tous les autres. . . . Apres la production des parties devant dictes la plus grande partie de la semence est poussée en la troisieme ampoulle, de laquelle le cerveau est fait. . . . Or du cerveau & de la moüelle de l'eschine procedent les nerfs, qui sont distribuez par toute les parties du corps, qui ont besoin de mouvement & sentiment.[69]

The chronology of Donne's prose account may also be checked against the authorities. The body, says Donne, is joined in twenty-eight days, the soul enters on the fortieth day, and the foetus has motion and sense after the third month. Fernelius states that the body is joined on the twenty-seventh day, but that it is not perfected in the case of the male until the thirtieth day and of the female until the thirty-sixth day.[70] Pareus[71] writes that the soul enters on the fortieth day, but Vicary says that "there is xlvi dayes from the day of conception unto the day of . . . receyving of the soule."[72] The occurrence of motion and sense vary, according to Fernelius, in moment. "Aliae praegnantes semper die quadragesimosecundo, aliae mense tertio, aliae non nisi medio praegnationis cursu eum loco dimoveri sentiunt."[73] In due time, the child is born, and according to Donne,

> children come not right, nor orderly;
> Except they headlong come . . .[74]

In this view the physicians concur.[75]

VII

Donne's knowledge of morbid nomenclature provides the best introduction to his knowledge of pathology. We find in the *Devotions*—that treatise on the futility of medicine—a discussion of medical terminology that recalls Petrarch's outbursts against the doctors.

> The names will not serve them which are given from the *place affected,* the *Plurisie* is so; nor from the *effect* which it works, the *falling sicknes* is so; they cannot have names ynow, from *what it does,* nor *where it is,* but they must extort names from what *it is like,* what it *resembles,* and but in some one thing or else they would lack names; for the *Wolf,* and

the *Canker,* and the *Polypus* are so; and that question, *whether there be more names or things,* is as perplexed in sicknesses, as in any thing else; except it be easily resolvd upon that side, that there are more *sicknesses* then *names.* . . .[76]

This may seem like the considered remark of a layman who had his fill of physician's jargon, but we find just such a statement in the *Opera* of Fernelius.

Sed quum ipsi rudem adhuc & incultam rerum cognitionem haberent, nomina morbis confinxerunt, non ex rei essentia cui primum & maxime medemur, sed ex eo quod sorte primum occurreret, quemadmodum & lui venereae haec aetas maxime varia aptavit nomina. Itaque morbi alii a parte cui insident nuncupati sunt, ut pleuritis, nephritis, peripneumonia: alii ab ingenti quodam symptomate, ut epilepsia, apoplexia, paralysis, tremor: alii ab externarum rerum similitudine, ut elephas, cancer, polypus, satyriasis.[77]

Now Donne's knowledge of disease is seldom as exact or as specific as his knowledge of anatomy and physiology. He mentions a large number of ailments, but he says little that can be glossed. We hear about the morphew, jaundice, and the tympany, and all the fevers—the tertian, quartane, hectic, and pestilential,—but we hear little or nothing of cures or symptoms, save that the morphew is black or the dropsy causes thirst. Full accounts of all these diseases appear in medical works, but it seems pointless to gloss them. On two occasions,[78] however, Donne mentions the calenture, a disease rarely enough mentioned in his age to require glossing. De Vigo describes it as a sailor's fever, a tertian, that comes from eating salt meat, wormy bread, from drinking "wyne eger, & mengled manytymes wyth roten water." The patient feels no heat in the outward part of his body, "But wythin, and chieflye about the harte . . . he burneth."[79] Donne also mentions the false symptoms produced by the spleen[80] about which Pareus tells us more.[81] He knows the causes of foul breath,[82] and one of the accepted causes of gangrene.

If a man doe but prick a finger, and binde it above that part, so that the Spirits, or that which they call the *Balsamum* of the body, cannot descend, by reason of that ligature, to that part, it will gangrene.[83]

With the phrase "the Spirits, or . . . the Balsamum," Donne tips his cap to both the paracelsians and the orthodox; both schools, however, recognized a tight ligature as one of the causes of gangrene. Pareus says, for example, "Par trop lier une partie on est cause de gangrene."[84]

The paracelsian coloring of Donne's account of gangrene leads us to believe that Paracelsus may have had something to do with Donne's remarks about the natural objects that are found unnaturally in man. He writes to the Countess of Bedford:

First seeds of every creature are in us,

What ere the world hath bad, or pretious,
Mans body can produce, hence it hath beene
That stones, wormes, frogges, and snakes in man are seene.[85]

The general theme of these lines could have been drawn straight from the
writings of Paracelsus;[86] on the other hand, the orthodox physicians had
more lurid accounts of the creatures found in man than Paracelsus furnished
in his nebulous records. Pareus, who is charmed by the microcosmic-macro-
cosmic notion, goes into picturesque detail to establish engaging parallels.

Exemple des pierres: on les voit a ceux ausquels on en extrait de la
vessie, & autres parties du corps . . . Exemples des animaux qui se procreent
en nos corps, à sçavoir, pouls, punaises, & morphions, & autres.

Houlier, he says, extracted a scorpion from the brain of an Italian; Fernel,
probing in a soldier, brought forth two hairy worms with horns; and Guille-
meau having discovered a serpent in a patient brought it to Pareus in a glass
vial. Other physicians have found other creatures "comme grenouilles,
crapaux, serpens, lezars, harpies" in the bodies of men.[87]

In addition to these more important pathological accounts, Donne was
possessed of a large hoard of information that might either come from
reading, from conversing with physicians, or from the common knowledge
of his age. In "Elegie VIII" he used the unpleasant image of a maggot
"sucking an envenomed sore"; now this figure was probably part of his
experience, but it can also be glossed in medical books.[88] The same may be
said of his statement that melancholy is the most difficult humour to
purge[89] or his remark that one may break a vein while vomiting.[90]

VIII

We come finally to estimate the extent of Donne's knowledge of the
modus medendi, and here we must confess that his information is far behind that of the modern hypochondriac. He knows the mechanics of a
purge,[91] but he errs when he supports Hippocrates' thesis that an induced
fever is a cure for convulsions or tetanus, for physicians were abandoning
this remedy as early as the thirteenth century.[92] On the question of the
value of the nutritive clyster, Donne took a pessimistic view, for he writes
in "Elegie XVIII,"

his error is as great,
As who by clyster gave the stomach meat.

Riolanus[93] supports Donne, but Pareus,[94] who prints some recipes, does
not. The contents of Donne's medicine chest may be classified as simples,
chemical drugs, and that popular Renaissance anodyne, "mummy."

In spite of Donne's seeming preference for the "chimiques," who sometimes glorify their pregnant pots by finding remedies instead of the elixir,
he is as confident in the power of herbs as Galen or George Herbert. It is
true that Donne being of a more explosive temperament advocates the use

of more potent herbs than Herbert; syrup of rhubarb is a favorite of Donne, whereas Herbert likes the more gentle effects of a distillation of white or damask roses. Donne, however, was no gardener—the residence at Mitcham might have been pleasanter had he been so—, and so while Herbert might raise his own pharmaceuticals, Donne undoubtedly got his at the chemists. When he wished to purge choler, Donne took rhubarb,[95] an approved remedy; to purge phlegm he advised agaric;[96] and to cleanse the lungs, he suggests hyssop.[97] He knows the general properties of opium[98] and aloes,[99] and he talks about methods of infusion[100] and distillation.[101] Perhaps his most unusual information is contained in the following lines from the *First Anniversary*.

> Since herbes, and roots, by dying lose not all,
> But they, yea Ashes too, are medicinall.[102]

Various medical writers prescribe the ashes of certain herbs for specific diseases, but Fernelius provides the best gloss.

> Cinis omnis ustione igneas partes conquirit: ficulneus valide extenuat & absumit, acrimoniae urentisque facultatibus plurimum sortitus. Huic proximus est sarmentitius & qui ex ilice aut brassica sumitur. Omnes cum axungia vel oleo illiti oedemata discutiunt, articulorum doloribus, nervorum nodis & contusionibus mire prosunt.[103]

The other medicines that Donne mentions are gold, mummy, and bezoar,[104] and we may believe that it was the authority of Paracelsus that caused him to mention the two first seriously. In "Elegie XI" Donne uses the so-called restorative properties of gold as the foundation of a pun, but since *gold* like *heart* was one of his favorite words, we find the allusion frequently. A few of the physicians of the time advised the use of gold medicines, and Gesner[105] devotes a whole chapter to them, but there seem to have been doubts about the efficacy of gold as a restorative. Pareus attacks the givers of potable gold, which, he says, has no place in nutrition. The doctors say that after they have made gold-water, the pieces of bullion weigh less; hence something of value has passed into the liquid. Undoubtedly, says Pareus, that is the filth "qu'auront accueilly les pieces d'or, pour avoir este longtemps maniees ou portees du peuple, voire de verolez, ladres, & vieilles harangeres, pourra estre demeure dans less restaurans."[106] In the writings of Paracelsus, we find gold celebrated as one of the master drugs. It is, writes Paracelsus, the perfect medicine for "nec solum hominem, verum etiam omnes pecudes, fructus, herbas & arbores."[107]

One of the mysterious forces of the universe discovered by Paracelsus is "Mumia," which contains all the properties and powers of herb and tree, the salt of the earth, the virtues of water, metals, gems, and the "Marchasite;" in fact, "omnia in homine inveniuntur: omnia nec minus, nec inefficacius reperiuntur in mumia."[108] We do not know how carefully Donne read Paracelsus, but if he ran across one of the discussions of "mumia" without fully comprehending the whole philosophy of Paracelsus, it may have

seemed to him to be an endorsement of the more mundane remedy, which
was known in the Renaissance as "mummy." This latter substance is described by Donne in the *Devotions*[109] as the only help man has for man; he
writes Goodyere[110] that mummy may be used when "our naturall inborn
preservative is corrupted or wasted." We find this drug mentioned by most
of the medical authorities, but none of them share Donne's enthusiasm for
its curative properties, and some of them disapprove of it entirely. Fernelius
tells his readers what it is and indicates that it may be useful as an astringent;[111]
and Sylvius[112] in defining it calls it "nomen et res barbara." Pareus, the
symbol of sane French reason, makes sport of it. Some readers, he says, will
be surprised that he does not prescribe it "comme font la plus part des
Medecins & Chirurgiens," but he knows better than to do that. In 1564,
Fontaine visited a mummy factory in Alexandria and talked with the owner.
The Alexandrian admitted that mummies for the European trade were manu-
factured on the spot from the bodies of beggars and people who died of
plague; he was surprised that Christians were "tant friands de manger les
corps des morts." I have used the drug, Pareus writes, on a few occasions,
but it always made my patients sicker than they were before.[113]

IX

It seems curious that Donne, who was less of a sick man than Herbert and
less of a physician than Vaughan, should be a more habitual employer of
medical allusions than they. We feel that Herbert as the student of Fernelius
and as the translator of Cornarus certainly knew more about this subject
than Donne, but the medical allusions in his work are very limited and even
in *A Priest to the Temple,* where the occasion was fitting and space was un-
limited, the discussion of medicine is short and guarded. The difference
resides perhaps in a contrary set of attitudes. Donne is never hesitant about
displaying his knowledge; it is a form of personal vanity that he never gave
up. He is as guilty of it in his sermons as he was in his earliest verse. Herbert,
on the other hand, seems as tired as God of worldly wisdom. But Donne is
something better than a culture-bore. While he exhibits his learning, he
sometimes seems to scorn it, to talk like a learned cynic in a circle of eager
savants. We feel this as we study his medical references, just as we feel it
when we consider his remarks about astronomy, optics, or geography.
"Here it is," he seems to say, "and the professionals think it has absolute
reality." It is for this reason that it is often impossible to pin him down, to
decide on what side of a controversy he stands. He varies in his medical
beliefs as much as he varies in his search for orthodoxy or in his search for
a satisfactory planetary system. And while he varies he laughs. He laughs
at Dr. Butler, whom he mentions with a sort of respect in his *Letters,* by
making him the author of the *De Pessario Animato, et omni morbo foeminis
dando,* the twenty-sixth title in the fabulous *Courtier's Library.* There is
none of this wavering in Herbert and none of the laughter; hence, there is
no exhibitionism and no display. For this reason he remains less interesting
as a man than Donne, but a poet greater by far.

JOHN DONNE AND THE EMBLEMATIC PRACTICE

Josef Lederer

I

'Since every poetical image contains a potential emblem, one can understand why emblems were the characteristic of that century in which the tendency to images reached its climax, the seventeenth century', says Professor M. Praz,[1] the only critic who treats this 'literary bypath' of the Renaissance and the Baroque as something more than a mere collector's curiosity.

In their purest form, then, emblems[2] are illustrations of conceits. Samuel Daniel, in the introductory essay to his translation of an Italian treatise on imprese, betrays a rudimentary appreciation of this aesthetic function of emblematic symbolism: '. . . besides the figuring of things corporall and of visible forme, men have also represented things incorporal, which they could not doe more fitly then by colours . . .'[3] Emblematists themselves always insisted on a perfect balance between the 'body' of an emblem (the picture) and its 'soul' (the motto and the accompanying verse) as a requirement of an ideal emblem.

The seventeenth-century man had all the sensuality of the Renaissance man with a much greater longing for the spiritual. He was, in Herbert's phrase, 'a nothing between two Dishes',[4] suspended between reality and the impalpable, between intellect and emotions. The Baroque attempted the fusion of arts while the gap between the symbol and the thing signified was constantly widening. Emblems became a field for the play of intellectual fancy springing from a powerful source of emotion. In their small way they are the only instance of a successful *Gesamtkunstwerk*.

Though English Protestantism was not a very fertile ground for the extravagancies of emblem writers, the taste for emblems and devices seems to have been fairly widespread in England. Puritan writers were frequently influenced by Jesuit authors, which is not as paradoxical as it may sound, since they had more than one thing in common: a militant spirit, fanaticism, and a passion for edification.[5]

Before the death of Donne several emblem books or works discussing the practice were published or written in England.[6] Donne was, of course, not limited to English works. His library, as we know, was well stocked

Reprinted from *Review of English Studies*, 22 (1946), 182-200, by permission of The Clarendon Press, Oxford.

with foreign books and it is highly probable that some emblem books were among them. Well over seven hundred emblem books appeared before the death of Shakespeare,[7] and the rather ruthless plagiarism of the writers makes it often quite impossible to trace an emblem to its original source.

In the seventeenth century the medieval conception of poetry as a branch of rhetoric still lingered in the minds of poets, and a poet's idea of what was admissible to draw upon for his imagery vastly differed from the stricter notion of later poetical codes. The much-praised modernity of Donne's technique may well be exaggerated, as many of his recent critics are only too apt to rejoice over Donne's originality, looking eagerly for points of contact with the modern English school, and overlooking the fact that much of Donne's vaunted modernism was quite common in the style of his contemporaries, if not in England at least on the Continent. The late Lord Alfred Douglas was quick enough to recognize this fallacy and did not hesitate to condemn in Donne what had offended his conservative taste in 'modern heretical verse', as he called it.[8]

The emblem writers did not regard their work as a trifling pastime. They were mostly men of science, humanists, many of them Italian academicians full of disputative passion and seriousness. As for the poets of the seventeenth century, wit was for them anything but flippancy; it was rather a brilliant result of long study, a quintessence of deep learning. For their compositions they drew on the vast stock of Renaissance, medieval and ancient knowledge: poetry, science, real or otherwise, ancient historians, theological works, fanciful natural history, animal lore of the bestiaries, proverbs in current use—in other words, the same sources which the poets could and did exploit quite independently. Therefore many instances of a seeming connection between emblematic works and literary passages often turn out to be mere illusions.[9]

Many English poets and playwrights were, however, directly influenced by emblem writers.[10] Richard Crashaw happened to be the most devoted to this Baroque symbolism. He was thoroughly versed in Jesuit emblem books and his imagery is richly decorated with devotional emblems and imprese.[11]

There can be no doubt that Donne knew and appreciated this witty foreign invention.[12] His innovations of style were the result of a conscious effort. He was anxious to part company with the accepted contemporary fashion. For a poet striving to say what is seldom said and, moreover, to say it in a new way, witty but at the same time scholarly, which was often one and the same thing for him, emblems must have been a welcome addition to the body of his bookish knowledge. As he seemed to belong to the passionate and dramatic but also sober, earnest and even coarse side of the Baroque, he cannot be expected to have had Crashaw's predilection for the meltingly sensual emblems of the Jesuits which were so completely in accord with their external semi-mysticism.

Yet the emblematic practice may sometimes be consonant with his method of expressing deeply personal conflicts in terms of the most abstruse sciences, of externalizing and objectifying subjective states of mind by novel and startling images. The greater the confusion in his mind, the more tangible and exact were these metaphors; and the more abstract the matter discussed, the more realistic was his imagery.

How far some of his images were really drawn from actual emblem books remains, of course, impossible to demonstrate incontrovertibly. But critical sifting of Donne's imagery will show that there are several possibilities of establishing a correspondence with the emblematic practice without unduly stressing direct influences; for the purpose of the collected evidence is to illustrate Donne's participation in the general style-currents of his age and the effect it had on his creative process. First of all, Donne may be using an image in a way which has a decidedly emblematic cast, without necessarily having had recourse to one of the emblem books; or he may lift an image straight from one of these works or from a poet who had done so before him; or again he writes a clearly emblematic poem or prose passage having in mind an existing device.

The word 'embleme' occurs altogether seven times in his poetry,[13] always carrying its orthodox meaning, and allusions to 'emblemes', 'hieroglyphs', and 'types' are equally frequent in his prose works, especially in his sermons.

II

Donne, it is truly said, cleansed English love poetry of the Petrarchan mood, and so it is almost paradoxical to find one of his favourite images clearly Petrarchan in origin, if not in spirit. Some images have a kind of immortality throughout the ages of verse-making. Many of Petrarch's metaphors were inspired by the late Greek anthologists and then were developed and repeated *ad nauseam* by scores of Petrarchists. They became one of the chief sources of emblem writers, and from their pictorial representation in a changed, but still recognizable form, they found their way back into poetry. In the second and third decades of the seventeenth century emblematists, mostly Jesuits, began to convert amatory emblems to devotional purposes with the mixture of crude realism and ecstatic mysticism so typical of the Baroque. A single passage will suffice to illustrate this point; the image of his love comes to Petrarch to torment him:

> E'n sul cor, quasi fiero leon, rugge
> La notte, allor quand'io posar devrei![14]

This note of heart imagery, with all its subtle naïvety of sentiment, is heightened in Donne to a provocative and, at times, crude literalness. Donne's employment of the image of the heart reminds us of the tension arising between the 'body' and the 'soul' of an emblem; he takes a metaphor and treats it as a real, palpable object to produce a new, superimposed metaphor. Having 'ripp'd' his chest 'and searched where hearts did lye', he could not find his heart:

> Yet I found something like a heart,
> But colours it, and corners had . . .[15]

The 'broken heart' of the common saw becomes a solid object, a piece of
china or glass; the splinters:

> . . . as broken glasses show
> A hundred lesser faces, so
> My ragges of heart can like, wish and adore, . . .[16]

It is possible to dismiss the various cardiomorphoses of the post-Tridentine
emblem books[17] as excessive Baroque licence; the heart is weighed in scales,
tied with cords, split open and showing hieroglyphs, a maiden with closed
eyes holds a huge heart with a large wide-open eye to symbolize the motto
EGO DORMIO ET COR MEVM VIGILAT,[18] Jesus sweeps with a broom
the human heart of snakes and toads.[19] The heart suffers sundry changes:
MOLLESCO, CRESCO, ALTA PETO, AMO, LATEO, &c.[20] Yet none of
them has surpassed the blankly visual progress of Donne's heart bordering on
the grotesque:

> . . . poore heart
> That labour'st yet to nestle thee,
> And think'st by hovering here to get a part
> In a forbidden or forbidding tree . . .[21]

Religious writers did not scruple to take profane imagery and apply it to
the new cults of the Infant Jesus and the Sacred Heart. The little Cupids
and amoretti which people the pictures of Vænius[22] and other Dutchmen,
are transformed into animæ and Infants, the Anadyomene becomes the
Virgin and the Petrarchan antics of the lover's heart continue in the guise
of a holier figure. Nor is there a cleavage between profane and sacred imagery
in Donne. The heart of the deceased lady in the elegy 'Death' grows into the
flaming bush of the Old Testament, a favourite emblematic device:[23]

> Her heart was that strange bush, where, sacred fire,
> Religion, did not consume, but'inspire
> . . . piety, . . .[24]

Neat, almost quaint, is the clearly emblematic image from the 'Holy Sonnet
I' where he addresses God as he did his mistress: '. . . thou [may] like Ada-
mant draw mine iron heart'.[25] God's love is a ram which opens the gates of
the sinner's heart:

> Batter my heart, three person'd God; for, you
> As yet but knocks, breathe, shine, and seeke to mend . . .[26]

The very anatomical and physiological properties of the human heart hide
a hieroglyphic significance:

> And crosse thy heart: for that in man alone
> Points downewards, and hath palpitation.[27]
> My heart is by dejection, clay,
> And by selfe-murder, red.[28]

All these metaphors show an analogy with contemporary or slightly later emblems. By a strong visualization the image acquires an extraordinary hardness and correspondingly a certain brittleness; there is always the danger that it will snap and become ridiculous, though Donne, unlike the more extravagant and looser Marini, manages to hold it in balance wonderfully well.

Too often unable to grasp the supernatural, to touch the impalpable, to introduce some order into the tormenting turmoil of his mind, Donne attempts sometimes to fix and rationalize the irrational by means of comparison with a precise object. The clock pleased Donne by its mechanical ingenuity and exactness. In his day it still was a technical miracle. 'Questa nobil macchina, progidio raro dell'arte', exclaims Filippo Picinelli in his Dictionary.[29] He recommends the clock as emblematic of a just prince, quoting Bargagli's[30] picture of the clock with the Sun in the Zodiac and the motto ÆQVE IMPARTITVR. It may also symbolize human life (VARIANDO CONSTAT).

As a symbol of man's life and its brevity, and of the soul, the clock occurs several times in Donne's verse:

> Alas, we scarce live long enough to try
> Whether a true made clocke run right, or lie,[31]

Elizabeth Drury may not be dead, but only

> . . . as a sundred clocke is peecemeale laid,
> Not to be lost, but by the makers hand
> Repollish'd, without errour then to stand . . .[32]

and in his prose:

> But will *God* pretend to make a *Watch,* and leave out the *springe?* to make so many various wheels in the faculties of the Soule, and in the organs of the body, and leave out *Grace,* that should move them? or wil *God* make a *springe,* and not *wind* it up?[33]

Donne addresses his dead patron in a generous hyperbole:

> Why wouldst not thou then, which hadst such a soule,
> A clock so true, as might the Sunne controule,
> And daily hadst from him, who gave it thee,
> Instructions, such as it could never be
> Disordered, stay here, as a generall
> And great Sun-dyall, to have set us All?[34]

As, in the emblematic practice, the moon stands for mundane and transitory causes and the sun for God, Picinelli says that "l'horologio da sole, segnato co'l titolo; ME PHOEBVS, NON PHOEBE, servirà per tipo d'huomo giusto, che non dal mondo, mà da Dio prende la direttione, e la luce,'[35] the very words of Donne's adulation of Lady Lucy's brother.

The magnetic properties of the lodestone in the compass fascinated Donne

because they supplied comparison with the theotropic tendency in human
beings:

> And though the faithfullest heart is not ever directly & constantly
> upon God, but that it sometimes descends also to Reason; yet it is there-
> by so departed from him, but that it still looks towards him, though not
> fully to him: as the Compass is ever Northward, though it decline, and
> have often variations towards East, and West.[36]
> Neither is that starre which we call the North-pole, or by which we
> know the North-pole, the very Pole it selfe; but we call it so, . . . because
> it is the neerest starre to that Pole. He that comes as neere uprightnesse,
> as infirmities admit, is an upright man, though he have some obliquities.
> To God himself we may alwayes go in a direct line, a straight, a perpen-
> dicular line; For God is verticall to me, over my head now, . . .[37]

The lodestar was originally an erotic emblem. Vænius has a picture of Cupid
gazing at the face of a woman. He holds a quadrant in his hand; a compass
with the needle pointing to the lodestar completes the emblem. The motto
declares: ERO NAVIS AMORIS, HABENS TE ASTRVM LUCIDVM.[38]
Vaenius's emblem descends from Giovio, who uses the motto ASPICIT
VNAM.[39] With a great ease the Catholic emblematist H.A. turned it in his
English emblem book into two Marian devices with the mottoes IN ITINERE
PHARUS; RESPICE STELLAM, INVOCA MARIAM, spiritual emblems
similar to that in Donne's prose.[40]

Two other religious emblems are the cedar and the sun. In 'The Annuti-
ation and Passion' Donne's soul sees

> . . . a Cedar plant it selfe, and fall,
> Her Maker put to making, and the head
> Of life, at once, not yet alive, yet dead.[41]

On 25 March 160$\frac{8}{9}$ both great feasts fell on the same day, a rare occurrence
which inspired Donne to a poem full of mystical and emblematic allusions.[42]
The Cedar of Lebanon, as an emblem of high birth,[43] is, of course, symbolical
of the Virgin and Christ. Thus Picinelli mentions the Marian device of Mon-
signor Aresio, a cedar bearing flower and fruit at the same time, with the
motto NOVA, ET VETERA SERVAVI TIBI, and a similar emblem with the
motto NEL FIORE IL FRVTTO.[44]

Evidently emblematic is the frequently employed image of the sun of
which Donne was fond because it gave him occasion for the pun on 'sun-son'.
Though condemned by stricter emblematic decorum which required that an
emblem should be noble, rebuses and pictorial representations of puns were
by no means rejected by authors of the sixteenth and seventeenth centuries.[45]
Like Hamlet's puns, Donne's quibbling is not frivolous; it usually marks a
state of a profound emotion or spiritual anxiety. If used in conjunction with
an emblematic image the pun contributes to the clarity of the conceit and
renders a prayer more penetrating:

> *Salute the last and everlasting day,*
> Joy at the uprising of this Sunne, and Sonne . . .[46]

The 'sacred Academie' of Church Fathers may be likened to smaller lumi-
naries: '. . . call them stars, but not the Sunne'.[47] In apprehension of death
and Judgment, under the oppression of Original Sin, Donne exclaims to God:

> But sweare by thy selfe, that at my death, thy sonne
> Shall shine as he shines now, and heretofore . . . ;[48]

and in the hymn 'To Christ':

> Sweare by thy self that at my Death, thy Sunn
> Shall shine as it shines nowe, & heretofore . . .[49]

The sun is a symbol of Christ's Passion and Resurrection, the one-in-two
miracle of setting and rising, expressed, as often, by a fervent paradox:

> There [in the East] I should see a Sunne, by rising set,
> And by that setting endlesse day beget;
> But that Christ on this Crosse, did rise and fall,
> Sinne had eternally benighted all.[50]

It may also symbolize the Scriptures:

> . . . we have . . . the Sunne, which is the Fountaine and Treasure of all
> created light, for an Embleme of that third best light of our understand-
> ing, which is the Word of God.

Donne suggests himself a suitable motto from the *Proverbes: 'Mandatum
lucerna, & Lex lux'.*[51]

Picinelli speaks of Bargagli's device of Christ the Judge, the sun and the
motto VNIVS SPLENDOR, INCENDIVM ALTERIVS; 'tale Cristo sole
eterno, nel finale giudicio ripartirà gli splendori di gloria à i giusti, e gl'incen-
dij tormentosi à gli scelerati'.[52] With the motto OCCIDIT ORITVRVS it may
serve for the impresa of Christ, 'mistico Sole'.[53] Donne's monument in the
crypt of St. Paul's Cathedral was designed by himself on emblematic principles: the statue shows his dead body shrouded, with closed eyes but standing in an upright position facing the East; the last two lines of the epitaph,
also composed by the Dean, allude to an erroneous Vulgate reading of the
Hebrew:

> HIC LICET IN OCCIDVO CINERE ASPICIT EVM
> CVJVS NOMEN EST ORIENS.[54]

III

The Renaissance and later the Baroque period took an even more pom-
pous delight in magnificent pageantry. Solemn entries of princes into towns,
canonizations of saints of the Tridentine Church, court masques, wedding

ceremonies, and funeral processions achieved an unequalled splendour in the first half of the seventeenth century. Petrarch's *Trionfi* furnished innumerable ideas for the architects and decorators whose task it was to contribute to the sumptuousness of ceremony. Even great masters like Mantegna and Dürer painted triumphs and triumphal arches studded with emblematic insignia.[55] It is sufficient to look at Inigo Jones's designs for court masques to see how far, under the influence of poetry, he abandoned his otherwise very guarded Vitruvian principles. The wedding of the Princess Elizabeth to the Prince Palatine in 1613 had, as Camden says in his *Annales,* 'all the Pomp and Glory that so much grandeur could express'. She wore white vestments, 'the Emblem of Innocency; her hair dishevel'd hanging down her Back at length, an Ornament of Virginity; a Crown of pure God upon her Head, the Cognizance of Majesty'.[56] Donne's 'Epithalamion' written for the occasion, though an adroit piece, full of clever and apt conceits, lacks the usual magnificent disregard for his theme which was more in place in his funeral elegies with their long-drawn, brooding hyperboles, and remains brilliantly on the surface, hardly more than a part of the general *décor,* which probably was just what the patrons expected from an epithalamion. It is, therefore, not surprising to find in it the image of the phoenix, threadbare enough in poetry, but used with a typically emblematic twist, one more impresa to add to those which probably adorned the hall. One can imagine that the miraculous bird was much to the taste of emblem writers. Of the many fabulous properties, the most popular with the later emblematists was the uniqueness of the phoenix. In a time of splendid absolutism it was selected as the most fitting emblem of princes. C. Paradin, whose book of heroical devices was printed twelve times between 1551 and 1600, prints the emblem with the motto VNICA SEMPER AVIS, because 'Phoenix semper unica, sic optima quaeque, & pretiosissima sunt inventu difficilima.'[57] In his complimentary ardour Donne perverts the miracle, calling the Prince and Princess a couple of phoenixes:

> Two Phœnixes, whose joyned breasts
> Are unto one another mutuall nests,
> Where motion kindles such fires, as shall give
> Yong Phœnixes, and yet the old shall live.[58]

Though prophetic of the many children of the future Winter Queen, this *tour de force* is somewhat shallow, constituting, as it does, the mainstay of the poem. The consummation of the marriage restores the emblem to its former significance:

> For since these two are two no more,
> Ther's but one Phenix still, as was before.[59]

It is a pertinent illustration of the mutual interdependence of profane and sacred poetry in the seventeenth century that, in a conceit worthy of Donne, the author of *Partheneia Sacra* applies the emblem of the phoenix with

'joyned breasts', or, as he says, 'with a twin-like heart', to the Union of
Mother and Son: EADEM INTER SE *dash*, SVNT EADEM VNI TERTIO.[60]

The well-known love emblem of the sunflower or the chicory following
the sun (EN TOVS LIEVX IE TE SVIS),[61] slightly changed, figures in
Donne, with unusual prettiness:

> The Marrigold opens to the Sunne, though it have no tongue to say
> so, the Atheist does see God, though he have not grace to confesse it.[62]

In the mournful litany in the opening lines of 'The second Anniversarie'
where Donne describes the misery and decay of the world after the death
of Elizabeth Drury, there is a simile which is the theme of several emblems:

> Or as a Lute, which in moist weather, rings
> Her knell alone, by cracking of her strings . . .[63]

Picinelli cites the emblem of Alcibiade Lucarini who 'per dinotare che le
disgratie succedono anco nel mezzo alle felicità, figurò un liuto, con una
corda spezzata, ed il motto; MEDIIS ETIAM IOCIS'.[64] It has the same painful abruptness as Donne's conceit; with the death of the girl all joys came
to a sudden end.

Another musical instrument, the organ, is employed in emblem literature
as a symbol of man's harmony with God. A preacher, says *Mondo Sim-*
bolico, is an organ into which the Holy Ghost is blowing, AFFLATVM
RESONAT; the Apostles are a choir of divine harmony filled with the
breath of the Spirit, INFLAT DVM INFLVIT.[65] Donne's metaphors of the
organ bear a very close resemblance to this symbolism. The world is an
organ,

> . . . those fine spirits which do tune, and set
> This Organ, are those peeces which beget
> Wonder and love; . . .[66]

Elizabeth Drury shares this metaphor with Lord Harrington:

> Faire soule, which wast, not onely, as all soules bee,
> Then when thou wast infused, harmony,
> But did'st continue so; and now dost beare
> A part in Gods great organ, this whole Spheare . . .[67]

As Picinelli's Apostles, God's 'Eagle-sighted Prophets' in Donne

> . . . were thy Churches Organs, and did sound
> That harmony, which made of two
> One law, . . .[68]

and Sir Philip Sidney and his sister, the Countess of Pembroke, are

> Two, by their bloods, and by thy Spirit one;
> A Brother and a Sister, made by thee
> The Organ, where thou art the Harmony.[69]

It may be seen by now how very anxious Donne was to enrich his
imagery by novel, sometimes emblematic, metaphors, or to give the old
ones a provocatively new import. He had little patience with the obsolete
moralized emblems of the Renaissance; he condemns the contemporary
London theatres, because

> . . . these mimicke antiques jeast,
> Whose deepest projects, and egregious gests
> Are but dull Moralls of a game at Chests. [70]

Such still quite medieval moralizations can be found in Gilles Corrozet's
emblem book and other works of the early sixteenth century: at the end
of a game the victorious player is putting the checkmated King into a bag.
The motto declares: LA FIN NOVS FAICT TOVS EGAVLX, and the verse
expounds the 'dull' moral:

> La terre est eguale à chascun,
> Par tous les pays & provinces,
> Aussi tost faict pourrir les princes,
> Que les corps du pauvre commun. [71]

Donne consciously avoids conventional images which abound in the verse
of greater poets than himself. The word 'rose', for instance, occurs only
once in the whole body of his poetry, and in an uncommonly naturalistic
comparison at that: 'sweat drops' on the breast of his mistress are 'As the
sweet sweat of Roses in a Still . . .'[72] More meaning should, therefore, be
read into the curious passage in 'The Canonization' with its cluster of more
or less commonplace images:

> Call us what you will, wee are made such by love;
> Call her one, mee another flye,
> We'are Tapers too, and at our owne cost die,
> And wee in us finde the 'Eagle and the Dove.
> The Phœnix ridle hath more wit
> By us, we two being one, are it.
> So to one neutrall thing both sexes fit,
> Wee dye and rise the same, and prove
> Mysterious by this love. [73]

If these images appeared singly, one would not dare suspect their emblematic origin and significance; but here it looks as if Donne was running
quickly through the pages of an emblem book. There is also the conspicuous
use of the words 'ridle' (often only another word for emblem) and 'mysterious' (emblem writers always emphasized the esoteric character of their art).
The conceit of the phoenix is the same as that in the epithalamion. The
uniqueness of the bird is likened to the unifying embrace of lovers.
    The self-destructive infatuation of the moth for the flame of the candle
is one of the most hackneyed metaphors of poetry, which the emblematists
rescued from its staleness by pictorial representation. It is included in many

of the emblem books, frequently with the mottoes COSÌ DE BEN AMAR
PORTO TORMENTO,[74] taken from Petrarch's canzone 'Ben mi credea',
COSÌ VIVO PIACER CONDVCE A MORTE,[75] BREVIS ET DAMNOSA
VOLVPTAS,[76] or some other well-meant warning. As with the phoenix,
Donne gives the faded figure a new lease of life by uniting its polarity in
his conception of passion, which, while abolishing the original sense of the
emblem, establishes it as a fresh and vigorous image. In the metaphor of the
eagle and the dove Donne's mysticism of the flesh is expressed with the
same technical cunning. Hadrianus Iunius has a picture of a caged dove
upon which an eagle swoops down. The motto, also taken from Petrarch,
on a scroll round the cage, reads: IL MAL MI PREME E MI SPAVENTA
IL PEGGIO.[77]

The episode of the elephant killed by a mouse in that obscure satire
'The Progresse of the Soule' has, like most others in the poem, some concealed meaning which has now become hard to decipher. If, as Sir Herbert
Grierson asserts, 'the great soule which here amongst us now doth dwell'[78]
is Queen Elizabeth, whose body is the receptacle of archheretics' universal
soul, and if the poem was written in the widespread bitterness following
the fall and death of Essex,[79] and there is no reason to doubt it, it may not
be quite so fantastic to conjecture that the elephant may be an allegory of
the executed earl, the great and generous gentleman, the victim of slander,
as he must have seemed in the eyes of his partisans:

> Natures great master-peece, an Elephant,
> The onely harmlesse great thing; the giant
> Of beasts; who thought, no more had gone, to make one wise
> But to be just, and thankfull, loth to offend,
> (Yet nature hath given him no knees to bend) . . .[80]

In the emblematic practice the elephant stood always for grandeur wedded
to meekness. In hieroglyphics an elephant shepherding a flock of sheep
reads MANSVETUDO.[81] In Whitney there is under the motto NVSQVAM
TVTA FIDES an emblem[82] whose picture depicts hunters preparing to kill
an elephant whom they had trapped; the verse bears some resemblance to
Donne's passage:

> The Olephant so huge, and stronge to see,
> No perill fear'd: but thought a sleepe to gaine
> But foes before had undermin'de the tree,
> And downe he falles; and so by them was slaine . . .

Another emblem in Whitney's collection has for its subject an elephant who
met with a different end (VICTORIA CRVENTA).[83] Stung by a snake,

> . . . doune he sinkes, and on the serpente falles:
> Which creature huge, did fall uppon him soe,
> That by his deathe, he also kill'd his foe.

The death of Donne's elephant is equally Samsonic:

> . . . Like a whole towne
> Cleane undermin'd, the slaine beast tumbled downe;
> With him the murtherer dies, . . .
> And thus he made his foe, his prey, and tombe . . .[84]

Donne refers to the fable once more in the *Devotions*: '. . . how great an
Elephant, how small a *Mouse* destroyes?'[85] The hunters and the snake in
Whitney, just as the mouse in Donne, symbolize base and envious treachery
capable of undermining a great and powerful prince.

IV

The best example of an indirect influence of emblematism is the well-
known and much-eulogized metaphor of the compass from 'A Valediction:
forbidding mourning'. If lovers' souls are two at all, Donne says,

> . . . they are two so
> As stiffe twin compasses are two,
> Thy soule the fixt foot, makes no show
> To move, but doth, if the'other doe.
>
> And though it in the center sit,
> Yet when the other far doth rome,
> It leanes, and hearkens after it,
> And growes erect, as that comes home.
>
> Such wilt thou be to mee, who must
> Like th'other foot, obliquely runne;
> Thy firmnes makes my circle just,
> And makes me end, where I begunne.[86]

One could hardly desire a metaphor which would better fulfil all the strictest
requirements of emblem writing. An almost mechanical precision in juxtaposition with the sentiment underlines the unwonted tenderness of the poem.
The metaphor is entirely visual and immediately evokes a single and simple
image which stands for a moral quality: constancy. The last couplet serves,
as it were, as motto to the emblem. Professor Grierson says on this subject,
not without irony: 'Donne's famous simile has a close parallel in Omar Khay-
yam. Whether Donne's "hydroptic immoderate thirst of human learning and
languages" extended to Persian I do not know.'[87] We need not, however, go
quite as far. Already in the early sixteenth century the compass can be
found as a symbol of prudence and constancy.[88] Picinelli recommends the
compass as a symbol of active and contemplative life with the motto VNO
IMMOTO,[89] and refers to a madrigal of the Cavaliere Giambattista Guarini
which, under the title 'Risposta dell'amante', contains the reassuring answer
of a lover departing for foreign countries to his mistress's fears that he might
forsake her, expressed in the preceding madrigal:

> Con voi sempre son io

> Agitato ma fermo;
> E se'l meno v'involo, il più vi lasso.
> Son simile al compasso,
> Ch'un piede in voi quasi mio centro i' fermo,
> L'altro patisce di . . . i giri,
> Ma non può far, ch'ntorno à voi non giri.[90]

Donne' simile is perhaps better poetry: it has more feeling and is less formal; but the theme, the farewell of a parting lover, is identical, even the same words are used. Though, of course, a case of independent parallelism cannot be entirely ruled out, all circumstances seem to point to the fact that Donne knew the passage and that all he did was slightly to enlarge Guarini's madrigal.[91]

Guarini's simile of the compass is only one of the emblematic images in which his poetry abounds. It is impossible to say by which emblem book he was inspired, but it is highly probable that he took it from the typographic ensign of the Antwerp printer Christopher Plantin, who printed nearly thirty emblem books in his lifetime, and whose shop, the Officina Plantiana, continued to be the chief source of emblematic literature well into the seventeenth century. His emblem, known to all scholars of the time, depicts a hand striking a circle with a compass, with the motto LABORE ET CONSTANTIA. It occurs in Picinelli immediately after the quotation from Guarini.

Donne must have been aware of the neat effect of the simile, for he repeats it several times:

> O Soule, O circle, why so quickly bee,
> Thy ends, thy birth and death, clos'd up in thee?
> Since one foot of thy compasse still was plac'd
> In heav'n, the other might securely'have pac'd
> In the most large extent, through every path,
> Which the whole world, or man the abridgment hath.[92]

The distance between profane and spiritual poetry is very small indeed in Donne and there is no difference of poetical technique. Any amatory image may be promoted into the realm of abstract notions. The compass recurs in Donne's prose, a further development of the image from his poetry:

> As hee that would describe a *circle* in paper, if hee have brought that *circle* within one *inch* of finishing, yet if he remove his *compasse,* he cannot make it up a perfit circle, except he fall to worke againe, to finde out the same *center*; so, though setting that *foot* of my *compasse* upon *thee,* I have gone so farre, as to the *consideration* of my selfe, yet if I depart from *thee,* my *center,* all is unperfit.[93]

As in the 'Obsequies to the Lord Harrington', God is the centre of human life; only from it can be described a perfect circle of human actions from

birth to death. Donne has journeyed far from the self-centredness of the
Renaissance man to the renewed God-centredness akin to the heliocentric
system of Copernicus, which, though regarded by contemporaries as revolutionary and sacrilegious, was well in accordance with the general absolutist
and deterministic tendencies of the age:

> The *Body* of Man was the first point that the foot of Gods Compasse
> was upon: First, he created the body of *Adam*: and then he carries his
> Compasse round, and shuts up where he began, he ends with *Body of
> man* againe in the glorification thereof in the Resurrection.[94]

As every diameter must pass through the centre, so all human deeds should
tend towards God, who alone can wield the compass.

How emblematic an image it is, and how congenial Baroque imagery
may be, are exemplified by another instance of its use. G. Hesius, a Belgian
Jesuit, undoubtedly without any knowledge of Donne's writings, following
probably Guarini's amatory poem, converted it into an edifying spiritual
emblem according to the favourite practice of his order: a cherub with
butterfly's winglets, exuberantly Baroque like one of Rubens's angels, a
sanctified Cupid, is striking a circle with a huge compass. The motto declares: STANS VNO CAPIT OMNIA PVNCTO. Two Latin poems and a
piece of prose attached to the picture expound at great length the same
truth as Donne:

> Ut capiat, quidquid circùm iacet; ambulet uno,
> Uno sed constans hæreat ille pede.
> Stet summo pede, stet puncto defixus in uno,
> Nec dubium, pavidè torqueat inde latus.
> Sic constans stabilisque suum se flectet in orbem,
> Consimilem cælo, consimilemque Deo.
> Tanti est in medio fixum consistere puncto,
> Tanti est immotum tenere pedem, &c.

The Latin prose reads almost as a free translation from Donne:

> Hominis animum stabili suâ voluntate fideliter fixum debere con-
> sistere in Deo puncto illo rerum omnium medio, individuo & immenso,
> ut intellectu tandem suo, omnia in orbem etiam longissimè à se posita
> sine varietate vel errore concludat.[95]

The metaphor of the compass is often connected with the image of the
circle which it naturally evokes. Judging by the extraordinary frequency and
persistence of its application, it can perhaps be called Donne's most typical
image, which becomes, at times, a veritable obsession. In his later writings
the emblem of the circle, 'one of the most convenient Hieroglyphicks of
God',[96] gave him inspiration for a typically Baroque pseudophilosophy.

The preceding evidence of Donne's emblematic bias will put into the
right perspective the well-known fact that he designed his own impresa and

wrote an explanatory Latin poem to accompany the seal sent to George Herbert.[97] We have his own translation of the 'soul' of the emblem.

The emblematic practice played an important part in the creative process of Donne's mind, and, as should be seen, it made a not negligible contribution to his imagery.

DONNE AND PARACELSUS:
AN ESSAY IN INTERPRETATION

W. A. Murray

It has long been realized that Donne was familiar with the alchemical and medical writings of Paracelsus,[1] and a number of isolated conceits and allusions have in the past been referred to this source.[2] The initial stage of a more comprehensive comparison between these works, especially the less well-known medical books, and the *Songs and Sonnets,* has already shown some interesting new parallels, and has established a closer connexion than was previously suspected between Donne's poetry and the speculative theories of Paracelsus. The concepts and terms of Paracelsian medicine provide a 'matrix' from which grow the basic ideas and images of certain poems, a matrix which Donne knew to be already familiar to his intimate audience. It is, therefore, often difficult to understand the intricacies of Donne's thought without starting from his starting-point, that is, with the original context of term or idea. This process can best be demonstrated by a detailed examination of two of the *Songs and Sonnets,* 'Love's Alchymie' and 'A nocturnall upon S *Lucies* day'.

The essential idea of 'Love's Alchymie' appears in the following passages of Paracelsus:

1. For it is on account of this vessel [i.e. the womb, which Paracelsus compares to a *vas*], that woman is provided, and not on account of our need of any other member or part.[3]

2. The element of water [elsewhere used as a figure of woman] is the field, the human imagination is the seed.[4]

3. Man [or the male quality] exists in woman like a fish in the water, in which he lives and grows, and without which he cannot live. Now the fish is of the water indeed, that is, has the nature of water, but on account of this is by no means at all the same as water. Just as, then, fish and water are different, yet joined in one, so is man in woman. Woman does possess the male reason. [For] it is the element in which the complete man like the fish [in water] has its being, although the complete man is divided in birth [i.e. into male and female] . . . it is therefore suitable for a doctor to regard this likeness and learn it, that *man* is the seed, and the *woman* the field.[5]

Reprinted from *Review of English Studies,* 25 (1949), 115-23, by permission of the author and The Clarendon Press, Oxford.

These, and other similar passages, may be summarized as follows: Woman, as a class, represents the animal instinctive will, the blind instrument of nature; man represents the intellect and imagination. As Donne himself puts it, 'Hope not for mind in women'.

While this parallel is suggestive, it is far from conclusive; other sources for such a view are obviously possible, as the idea was a common one at the time. There is, however, other evidence of a connexion with Paracelsus. Although it might be argued that the main conceits of this poem were commonplaces of alchemy, they are expressed in a terminology which is, in fact, that of Paracelsus, and have an atmosphere very reminiscent of his speculative writings. Love's 'centrique happinesss' is seen as the perfect metal hidden in 'Love's Myne': the lover is the Alchemist searching for the Elixir which will heal him and transmute all his longings and sorrows into the perfect metal. The first of these conceits suggests that close connexion with mines and metals for which Paracelsus was famous; the second is a natural extension of that application of alchemy to medicine which distinguished him as the first great iatrochemist. Thus Donne's poem shows associated with each other the two chief characteristics of Paracelsian alchemy.[6]

What is true of these comparisons is equally true of their vocabulary. The word 'chymique' in 'And as no chymique yet th' Elixar got' would have suggested to Donne's contemporaries the alchemical medicine of the Paracelsians, as opposed to the traditional medicine of Galen. That Donne himself used it thus may be seen from the following reference in a verse epistle to Sir H. Wotton, assigned by Sir H. J. C. Grierson, probably 1597-8:[7]

> Onely' in this one thing, be no Galenist: To make
> Courts hot ambitions wholesome, do not take
> A dramme of Countries dulnesse; do not adde
> Correctives, but as *chymiques,* purge the bad.

These lines show clearly that Donne was by this date familiar with some of the main differences between the two schools of medicine.

The great controversy with the Galenists, begun by Paracelsus, interpenetrated the whole medical world for more than a century after his death, and had various periods of quiescence and activity. If vernacular translations of pamphlets in this debate may be taken as indicating peaks of activity in England, the first occurred in 1570[8] before Donne's birth, the second c. 1600. By this date the controversy was sufficiently topical to produce the famous reference in *All's Well that Ends Well* (c. 1600) which couples Galen and Paracelsus in the same line as of equal importance.[9] In 1603 the first general edition of Paracelsus began to be published at Frankfurt, and was completed, in eleven volumes, by 1605.

In 1605 J. Quercetanus appeared again in English with *The Practise of Chymicall and Hermeticall Physike* translated by Thomas Tymme, minister, and dedicated to Charles Blount, Lord Mountjoy. The translator gives it as his view that medical knowledge, like knowledge of scripture, should be as widely diffused as possible, *even amongst laymen.* The dedication is particularly interesting, both for this opinion and because it connects this controversy directly with the aristocratic and intellectual circle on the fringes of which Donne moved.[10]

The pamphlet itself is important for the understanding of the poem 'Love's Alchymie', as it shows that the word 'Mumie' in English was about this date undergoing changes and extensions of meaning due to its use by Paracelsus as a technical term of his medical theory.[11] Thus the point of the final couplet:

> Hope not for mind in women; at their best
> Sweetnesse and wit, they are but Mumie, posses't.

is almost wholly lost or perverted if we do not start from the meanings of 'Mumia' in Paracelsus.

The term had strictly two interconnected senses, which may be arrived at by collating the principal references in the works[12] and which are both involved here: (i) Mumia—an ethereal invisible essence or life-force of all nature; (ii) Mumia—visualized as an actual sweet balsam or healing fluid of the body. Paracelsus had observed that open wounds grew new flesh from the inside outwards, and he attributed this process to the operation of 'mumia', which he visualized as a sweet, penetrating combining form of 'quicksilver'.[13]

From these meanings it is possible to interpret or expand Donne's couplet thus: Do not expect to find mind (the male factor) inherent in woman. At her best, that is, when actually possessed by man, a woman is a compound of sweetness (Balsam or mumia in sense (ii) above), and wit, or the male principle; she is merely the brute life-force of all nature, possessed by the rational soul, or wit.

Although the use of 'mumia' in this couplet seems to imply several layers of association, the Paracelsian explanation gives the poet a deeper, though no less bitter, meaning than that conveyed by the older connotation, which was probably also in Donne's mind.

As Paracelsus said, 'This chain of Venus, indeed, is nothing other than a constancy of human balsam, which brings it about that the human body will not decay',[14] and woman may be said to have exactly that function, in the dual sense that she both satisfies or heals a destructive appetite in the lover, and ensures the continuation of humanity in the physical world. She is thus exactly, and Donne claims, no more than, the mumia of the alchemist, and it must therefore follow that the mind, 'which he in her Angelique[15] findes', is only the reflection of the lover's own divine, male *ratio* or wit.

'Love's Alchymie' is something more than a mere cynical *jeu d'esprit*. It embodies, in images which are charged with scorn and impatience of imposture, a mood which is often found to be part of the experience of marriage and which may easily have been felt by Donne in the course of his love for Ann More. Certainly no more ample fulfilment of the couplet:

> Our ease, our thrift, our honor, and our day
> Shall we, for this vaine Bubles shadow pay,

could be imagined than the first few married years of John Donne—illness, poverty, uncertainty, a struggle of conscience, an increasing family, and deep depression culminating in the despair reflected in *Biathanatos*.[16]

Whatever the circumstances may have been which inspired 'Love's Alchymie', my second example, 'A nocturnall upon S *Lucies* day', does seem to be closely connected with the inner history of Donne's love for Ann More. The 'Nocturnall' has always been regarded as a difficult poem. Commentators have felt compelled by certain literal interpretations of phrase, which I shall discuss later, to conclude that the beloved was not dead, and that the poem was either addressed to an earlier love than Ann or to Lucy, Countess of Bedford. Yet Sir H. J. C. Grierson felt the sincerity of the poem to be inconsistent with such assumptions and indicated the possibility that it *might* be for Ann More's death.[17]

If we place this poem in its Paracelsian matrix and interpret it image by image, almost word by word, the difficulties which stand in the way of its acceptance in this last sense will one by one disappear.

First, here are some ideas and phrases from Paracelsus which suggest the general concepts of the 'Nocturnall'.

1. 'For there are spirits celestial and infernal, of human beings and of metals, of plants, stones, etc., etc. . . . Wherefore you may know that the spirit is in very truth the life and *balsam* of all corporeal things.'[18]

2. 'The life of man is an astral effluvium, an expression of balsam in form, a heavenly invisible fire, an enclosed essence or spirit; . . . the death of man . . . is the taking away of the aerial element, *the disappearance of the balsam,* an extinction of natural light, the great separation of body, soul and spirit. [It is] a return into the matrix of the mother. Natural earthly man is from the earth, and earth will be his mother into whom he must return.'[19]

3. Paracelsus occupies an important position in the development of the theory of Macrocosm and Microcosm, which he made a central point of his speculative writings.[20] He may even have been the first user of the term 'Macrocosm'. His numerous references may be represented by the following selection: 'This, therefore, is the condition of the Microcosm, or lesser world, that he contains within his own body all the minerals of the world.' 'You have learned from my other writings that the Macrocosm is the parent of the Microcosm.' 'God thus arranged it, that Man has within himself one Magnet from the elements whence he himself attracts these very elements, and one from the stars, by the force of which he has his Microcosmic sense from the stars.' 'Thus, then, man is a quintessence, the Microcosm, the child of the whole universe.'

4. It is plain from numerous references that Paracelsus visualized, as other speculative writers had done, a series or order in the modes of Universal life, somewhat as follows: (*a*) Intellect, reason, the Angelic portion; (*b*) the 'Sapientia Brutalis' or instinctive will, which causes, for example, man and animals to herd together, or choose some way of self-protection; (*c*) the sidereal body, which is like a reflection in a mirror, and though

normally invisible may sometimes be seen after a man's death 'haunting those places for which he thirsted'; (d) the life of plants, stones, and metals. As a pendant to this, I add an interesting idea about the shadow, since it concerns the 'Nocturnall': 'Wherever the *whole human being* goes, there as his comrade goes his shadow, and whatever can be elicited from his shadow can be elicited from his sidereal spirit.'[21]

5. The continual insistence of Paracelsus on the mutual necessity of man for woman is well shown by the following: 'Man and woman are one body. Just as the farmer is useless without his field, and the field in turn without its farmer, but together both are one unit, such is the whole human being, not man alone, or woman alone, but both together constitute one unit, from which is generated a whole human being.'[22] *'Vir sine foemina integer non est.'*[23] Paracelsus, like other alchemists, took the sun as the male symbol and the moon as the female.[24] In the 'Nocturnall', Donne appears to develop and change such ideas in a characteristic fashion when he makes his beloved the sun of their microcosm.

This list, though incomplete, is sufficient to provide a background for my interpretation. The 'Nocturnall' shows a very complete absorption of Paracelsian material. The terminology is that of Paracelsus, and the association of ideas in the poem sometimes closely parallel with his; and although some of the concepts are not peculiar to Paracelsus, he is the only single source in which all the main ideas are found together.

The general subject of the 'Nocturnall' is the annihilation of spirit, the death-in-life which follows supreme loss. Within that framework the poem first sums up the history of a passionate, complete and deeply personal love, and then in an elaboration and outgrowth of Paracelsian metaphysical terms shows Donne grappling with the task of self-analysis in his moments of deepest grief.

'Nocturnall' should be read in the sense of 'midnight hymn', at one time a portion of the divine service of matins.[25] This gives an initial hint of solemnity and sincerity and of the death of the beloved. St. Lucie, who has caused the reference of this poem to Lucy, Countess of Bedford, here appears as the saint of light (*lux*), and hence associated quite normally with the shortest day (death or martyrdom of light) and possibly also with *lux* as a symbol of the soul, a common metaphor of speculative medicine.[26]

The first line, and refrain, of the poem—'Tis the yeares midnight, and it is the dayes'—sets the tone for the initial images and refers by analogy to the sympathy between the Macrocosm and Microcosm. Donne lies upon his bed, a four-poster of the period, perhaps with carved pillars and canopy (floral emblems, trees), a bed strangely reminiscent of a tomb. The sun has sunk, remembered, perhaps, as seen at sunset through leaded panes, a broken sun, a series of flask shapes, which pour forth ever-lessening gouts[27] of fluid light.[28]

The general balm[29] of the Macrocosm (see Extract 1 above) is regressing into the earth; the day and the year are dying. The Microcosm, Donne, in sympathy and sharing the same vital principle finds his life receding, like a tree's sap, down the tree-pillars of his bed into the matrix of the mother, earth (cf. Extract 2 above).

Left on the bed, now become a tomb, is the last remnant of man, the sidereal body, *prima materia,* which has lost all other manifestation of the life-force save form. Donne's figure is like a sepulchral marble laid on his tomb, an actual 'Epitaph' in the radical sense of the word.[30]

But the year's death is not a final one; the Macrocosm will see its sun again—'Yet all these seeme to laugh, Compar'd with mee'. The year's death, the loss of its sun, seems but a bitter jest of Nature, compared with the loss which Donne must endure, who will never again see *his* sun, the beloved. Study him, then, you who walk past this tomb. Here is his history.

He is a type of, and one with, every dead thing. He is the residue of the final distillation process of love, the death of the beloved; and yet, contrary to logic and expectation, in the last act of distillation there is something left, the quintessence, it must be, of nothingness, which has yet a life of its own, a life in death. This is indeed a new alchemy, a new experience.

Love distilled him in a similar way before, yet not so completely, in the turmoil and sorrow inevitable to a passionate relationship, in years of privation, in separation; but now the process is complete; as the macrocosm will have its rebirth, he has had his, which is at once his death, rebirth into nothingness.

This new state is in violent contrast with that of the normal throng of man—'All others, from all things, draw all that's good'. To those who have their loves, everything in the universe is real and positive, a source of life. (This is an extension of a fundamental doctrine of Paracelsian medicine: see above, Extract 3.) But to Donne everything else in the universe merely emphasizes the absolute negation which he has become. Thus he is 'the grave of all', the exact antithesis of life, and that through this final distillation of the alembick of love,[31] the alchemist. Paradox indeed! Yet in time past temporary nothingness had come upon him and his beloved—in quarrel and tears,[32] when the perfect union was broken and two microcosms, which were one, separated into two Chaoses. (The association, tears—ocean—chaos, recalls the chapter of Paracelsus in which, discussing the waters above the firmament, he uses the actual phrase, '*Ideo chaos duo sunt.*')[33] Sometimes thoughts of selfish aims, sometimes forced absences, broke this unified whole human being, and left two carcasses, two bodies dead, but real.

But by *her* death—No! she is not, she cannot be dead, she is no animal soul whose regression into earth ends her for ever! This parenthesis—'But I am by her death, (which word wrongs her)'—is, one supposes, the origin of the theory that the beloved was not dead.[34] Yet placed thus in its context, it seems the very stuff of which grief is made, sprung from the strong reality of death itself, thus for the first time mentioned in the poem with an immediate personal emphasis—'her death'—and followed by the strongest expression and rhythm of this new state of being—'Of the first nothing, the Elixar grown'. This is the climax, this the distillation, this the final agony of Love's alembic.

Then follows that search for reconciliation which is at least implicit in every tragedy. With Donne, not unnaturally, it is the intellectual process that revives first:

> Were I a man, that I were one,
> I needs must *know*.

We begin with this to descend through the Paracelsian order of life. (Cf. Extract 4 above.) No! he is not a whole being, his angelic portion is lost. Nor has this residual existence even an animal or instinctive soul, a preference for means and ends, a brute choice of actions. Not even the slow but true life of plant or stone is his. And back Donne comes full circle to the intrusive normality of the beginning of the stanza—'All, all some properties invest'.

Then the endless round of baffled questioning of his new state begins again on an even lower level of vital activities. Not even an ordinary nothing is he, as shadow is, shadow which goes with the whole man, and exists at least in having a cause, which the first Nothing did not require. A shadow needs a light (the beloved, the sun) and a body (that is a complete body, the beloved's and his) to exist at all. He is no longer even the Shadow of his love, his sun is for ever set. You lovers who see that sun of the Macrocosm, which is so much the less than his, which has moved to the tropic of Capricorn, the wanton Goat, make of your suns what you can.

He himself, John Donne, will prepare[35] towards the festival of his beloved's long night of death, prepare in the vestments of this their bed, their tomb, and to this midnight prayer, their epitaph.

The 'Nocturnall' is indeed a poem 'elemented of sadness'.[36]

It is apparent from the examples given that the act of relating Donne's Paracelsian borrowings to their original context performs two main functions: it illuminates the actual meaning of the poetry, and it provides a unified basis from which one can reasonably imagine a true lyric intensity taking its rise. Thus one fundamental conception of metaphysical wit, as Dryden's 'ranging spaniel' of poetic ingenuity, may undergo a sudden transformation, when we find, for example, that the famous conceit of the compasses has a close parallel in the 'First Step in Medicine' of Paracelsus, and thus shares a common origin with a number of other images in the same poem.[37]

DONNE, MONTAIGNE, AND NATURAL LAW

Robert Ornstein

Few scholarly monographs have been so widely read and admired as Professor Louis I. Bredvold's "The Naturalism of Donne in Relation to Some Renaissance Traditions."[1] Long established as a reference work on Donne's early poetry, it has directly stimulated further research into the libertine ideas and backgrounds of early seventeenth-century literature.[2] And yet, curiously enough, one of its most provocative suggestions has been completely ignored: namely, that Donne's early poems were influenced by the ethical thought of Montaigne's *Essays*. According to Professor Bredvold, "Montaigne had, before Donne, brought together the two philosophies, Scepticism and Naturalism, which characterized the 'Libertine' tradition. To this tradition or school, John Donne for a time belonged, and Montaigne seems to me most likely to have been his master."[3] Since there are no obvious references to, or borrowings from, the *Essays* in the *Songs and Sonnets,* however, Professor Bredvold supports his contention by pointing out general similarities of idea in the two works.[4]

It would not be difficult to buttress Professor Bredvold's argument with additional material from the *Essays*. One could even find passages more directly libertine in spirit than those which he uses as illustrations. Such evidence, however, would be inconclusive, for the *Essays* are rich in incidental observation, ironic comment, and candid self-confession. Since they are not the systematic exposition of a philosophical view of life, the determined researcher can find in them diverse and contradictory attitudes—perhaps diverse and contradictory "Montaignes." But though it is easy to portray Montaigne according to one's likes (or dislikes), it is difficult to equate his ironic dissection of hypocritical sexual mores with the witty sensuality of the *Songs and Sonnets,* or to reduce the subtle reasoning of "An Apologie of *Raymond Sebond*" to the poetic exaltation of physical appetite in "Elegie XVII." If Donne's early poems were significantly influenced by the *Essays,* we would, I think, discover in them some reflection of Montaigne's momentous attack on the concept of natural law. Yet Donne never singles out natural law as his target. Like other Renaissance Libertine poets, he condemns *all* moral restraints on appetite as the artificial chains of custom. And without specific reference to "Law Rational" he upholds unrestricted pleasure as the only true commandment of nature.

Reprinted from *Journal of English and Germanic Philology,* 55 (1956), 213–29, by permission of the author and the University of Illinois Press.

Actually there is no immediate evidence in Donne's poetry which leads us back unerringly to Montaigne's writings. But such evidence seems to exist in *Biathanatos*. In this later[5] prose work we do find speculation about moral values comparable to that in the *Essays*. More important, we find a critical analysis of natural law remarkably similar to arguments in the "Apologie." I do not intend, however, to demonstrate that Montaigne was Donne's Libertine "master." On the contrary, my purpose is to show that Donne and Montaigne criticized natural law independently from the Libertine tradition and from each other. Like the Renaissance Libertines, they denied that nature establishes immutable and categorical imperatives. But unlike the Libertines, they reaffirmed in unmistakable terms, the rule of reason in human life.

Now an ethic based on reason but opposed to absolute precepts is not strange in the history of ideas. If it seems strange in sixteenth-century thought, it is because we have fallen victims to our own generalizations about the community of Renaissance beliefs. Professor Bredvold's study of Donne's naturalism, for example, implicitly divides the sixteenth-century intellectual world into a vast majority of right thinking men, who believe in natural law, and a small minority of moral and political subversives, who deny its authority.[6] But it is dangerous to equate Renaissance skepticism about natural law with a denial of moral principle when the "skeptics" included such defenders of Christian doctrine as Cornelius Agrippa.[7] Moreover, the "universal" acknowledgment of right reason in the sixteenth century did not mean universal agreement about the nature or meaning of natural law. For during its long history the Stoic concept suffered many revisions and reinterpretations, which, by the early seventeenth century, had transformed an ethic based originally on individual conscience into one of inflexible dogma variously and often confusedly expounded. Indeed, it is this very dogmatism and confusion which Montaigne and Donne attack, in attempts to return to a more primary definition of right reason. Thus, instead of trying to place Donne and Montaigne in one or another Renaissance traditions, we will study their thought, perhaps more fruitfully, in relation to the historical development of natural law and the continuing process of intellectual change that characterized the Renaissance.

Turning back from the encyclopedic and eclectic moral speculations of the sixteenth century to the philosophy of antiquity, one is struck anew by the simplicity of the original Stoic ethic. According to Zeno, the natural and the virtuous life are one, because man follows nature when he uses reason to discover moral law and attain virtue.[8] Actually, the original Stoic equation of reason and nature is twofold: First, man, because of his superior attribute of reason, is committed to moral goals by the law of his own rational nature. Second, he is governed by the commandments of reason because he is part of universal nature, whose law is rational; i.e., he shares in the divine fire of Reason which informs all parts of the universe. But whether the law of nature is considered in respect to the universal nature of men, or more largely in respect to the natural order of the universe, that law is rational, immutable, and everlasting. "True law," says Cicero, reformulating Stoic ideas, "is right reason in agreement with nature; it is of universal application, unchanging and everlasting; it summons to duty by its commands, and averts from wrong doing by its prohibitions. And it does not lay its commands or pro- hibitions upon good men in vain, though neither have any effect on the wicked. It is a sin to try to alter this law, nor is it allowable to attempt to repeal any part of it, and it is impossible to abolish it entirely. We cannot be freed from its obligations by senate or people, and we need not look out- side ourselves for an expounder or interpreter of it. And there will not be different laws at Rome and at Athens, or different laws now and in the future, but one eternal and unchangeable law will be valid for all nations and all times, and there will be one master and ruler, that is, God, over us all, for he is the author of this law, its promulgator, and its enforcing judge."[9]

The distinguishing characteristic of the Stoic ethic in antiquity, however, was not its simplicity but its "inwardness."[10] The Stoic philosopher speaks of the necessity of joining oneself to the universal order of nature, but he addresses himself to individual man, who independently controls his own moral destiny. Indifferent to all outward accidents and circumstances, the true Stoic is supremely self-sufficient. He follows the rule of reason—of his own reason—in making ethical decisions and despises the voice of Opinion, which rules the majority of men. To be sure, the Stoic philosopher recog- nizes the community of all men under reason and he stresses the duty of humanitarianism and altruism. But the universal community of men is a philosophical, not a political or social reality. To the Stoic, virtue is an in- ward state of rational control expressed in such outward actions as altruism; it is a consonance between a man's actions and the dictates of his reason rather than a conformity to set religious, political, or communal laws.[11]

The inwardness of the Stoic ethic persisted in the Roman era in the fiercely asserted individualism of Seneca[12] and in the melancholy reflections of Marcus Aurelius. But with the Roman jurists and Cicero, the major trans- mitters of Stoic ideas to Christian thinkers, the "externalization" of natural law had already begun. The Roman jurists, men of pragmatic rather than speculative bents, were not concerned with the metaphysical bases of the Stoic ethic or with right reason as a personal, moral discipline. They were primarily interested in natural law as a normative legal concept; i.e., they conceived of natural law as one which corresponds to "the nature of things, to a concrete situation of fact and of life."[13] In the *Corpus Juris*, natural law took its place as merely one of the categories into which all existing and proposed laws can be placed. And even among the Roman lawyers these categories were not uniformly distinguished. Some interpreters established three main categories of law, some two. Some identified *ius naturale* with *ius gentium* while others opposed them.[14] When the Roman legal tradition passed into Church law, the Canonists unequivocally "re- stored" the ideality of natural law. Announcing its divine origin, its absoluteness and eternality, they set it up as the highest moral standard against which all positive human codes must be measured. But in Canon law the Stoic concept of right reason was once again externalized, for it was now dogmatically identified with one particular group of moral precepts—those revealed in Scripture.[15]

From Cicero, the medieval philosophers inherited a more speculative idea of natural law, one which links true moral precept with individual right reason and with the universal order of nature. But Cicero's interests are closer to those of Plato and Aristotle than of Zeno. He is concerned primarily with man as a political and civic animal, not with man as a creature of reason per se. He does not, like Marcus Aurelius, exalt right reason as a refuge from an evil world; rather he envisions an ideal state whose laws are consonant with nature and therefore just.[16] The ideal secular state governed by "externalized" natural laws was not the main concern of the medieval theologian, however. He looked beyond Cicero and the Stoics to the divinely created universe, in which Eternal law (the exemplar of Divine wisdom and government) rather than natural law is supreme.[17] Indeed, St. Thomas makes it clear that natural law, as it operates in man, is but the instrument of Eternal law since human reason shares in the eternal reason of God (Ques. 91, art. 2).[18] Because God's universe naturally inclines towards the good, the first precept of the law of nature is that all things naturally seek the good; and since man's ultimate good is the beatific vision of God, his law of nature is to seek God. That is to say, when man obeys natural law, he uses reason not only to determine and adhere to moral law but also to ascertain those theological truths of his existence which can be apprehended by reason (Ques. 94, art. 2). Thus in the *Summa Contra Gentiles*, St. Thomas appeals to non-Christians to use "natural reason" and discover for themselves the truths of Revelation and of Christian doctrine.[19]

Within the framework of Thomistic theology there is, of course, a place for a modified Stoic idea of natural law as the "light" of natural reason that leads men to worldly virtue and happiness. St. Thomas notes that "human virtue, directed to the good which is defined according to the rule of human reason, can be caused by human acts; for such acts proceed from reason, by whose power and rule the good in question is established" (Ques. 63, art. 2). But this good is very imperfect, transient, and beset by evils. In actuality man has only one "end," one perfect good—the vision of the Divine Essence, which can be achieved only through grace. To the medieval Thomist, the careful Renaissance distinctions of moral laws ascertainable by reason *alone* would have seemed not only irrelevant but, in a literal sense, misleading, since reason alone would not suffice to make a man virtuous or enable him to fulfil all the precepts of divine law. Without grace, St. Thomas announces, man cannot attain to charity (Ques. 109, art. 5), nor can he avoid all sins (Ques. 109, art. 8). Thus in the dominant medieval Christian view, morality could not be reduced to a secular science or divorced from the ultimate theological problem of salvation.[20]

The humanistic scholarship of the Renaissance, however, loosened and even, in some instances, severed the intrinsic medieval knot of morality and theology. The sixteenth-century moral philosopher[21] inherited the Scholastic concept of natural law, but he also discovered in the newly reprinted works of Cicero, Seneca, and Epictetus, the classical ideal of right reason, which was outside of, and independent from, the previously all-embracing theological framework—an ethical ideal rooted entirely in this world and based solely on the laws of reason. The Renaissance didacticist humbled himself before the eloquence, the wisdom, and the sententiousness of the Greek and Roman philosophers. He marveled (somewhat naïvely) at the identity of Christian and classical ethics. But he was most profoundly impressed by the fact that the great pagan systems of morality had been established *without* the aid of Revelation.

An actual return to a classical ideal of virtue was, of course, rare in the sixteenth century. Only in such works as Pomponazzi's *De Immortalitate Animae*,[22] was a humanistic ethic based on a philosophical denial of the supernatural bases of morality. Much more common was the unconscious rationalism of the moral philosopher who insisted that natural laws are innate ideas implanted by God in the human breast, but whose concept of right reason was essentially more Stoic than Thomistic. Where the medieval theologian, intent on assimilating pagan truths, stressed the contingency of human reason on the divine, the moral philosopher stressed the independence of natural reason from Revelation. He customarily defined natural law as that light of reason which governs purely "humane" affairs, not as that which leads men to a knowledge of God. In theory the moral philosopher recognized the "incompleteness" of his ethical system based only on reason; he announced in his prefaces that Revelation and grace are necessary to lead men to their eternal good. But in practice he severed this theoretical link between natural law and theology by reducing morality to a purely humane discipline based on the ideas of antiquity. Indeed, even so Christian a gentleman as Sir Thomas Elyot announces that for pedagogical purposes the *Nichomachean Ethics* contains "the definitions and propre significations of every vertue."[23] In short, the sixteenth-century moral philosophers established an ideal of right reason that was, in relation to medieval thought, more secular than religious, and more classical than Christian, because (as Léontine Zanta remarks) they were incapable "d'aller au bout d'une doctrine et de voir les dangers qui la guettent; ils sont encore chrétiens; mais pensent en païens."[24]

It would be foolish, however, to overemphasize the secularization of natural law in the Renaissance. For, in glorifying human reason, the sixteenth-century moral philosopher did not divorce natural law from the divinely established universe of the medieval theologian. He merely focused his attention on the world of man and allowed that world to fill his horizon. In fact, his exposition of natural laws was usually based on the explicit premise of a cosmos governed by ascending hierarchies of law. But disdainful of Scholastic superstitions and speculations, he ascertained the universal laws of nature by supposedly objective, rational criteria. In practice, however, he

was not far removed from the medieval didacticists. The ancient custom of
obedience to authority was too deeply engrained to change; what changed
were the authorities themselves. Instead of appealing to the Church fathers,
the moral philosopher quoted the *sententiae* of antiquity; or, more usually,
he combined his Christian and classical learning with no sense of incongruity.
He did not find philosophical method and discipline in antiquity; he found
rather a great body of accumulated wisdom which seemed to him authoritative precept. He systematized "natural laws" by turning the classical ethical
theories into a body of absolute imperatives.[25]

Not all sixteenth-century "natural laws" derived from classical Greece
and Rome, however. As in preceding centuries, men in the Renaissance
attempted to validate their particular beliefs by asserting their naturalness
or universality. And with the humanistic emphasis on the achievements of
human reason, natural law was enthroned as the arbiter of even minute
details of social, political, economic, familial, and moral life. Inevitably,
many of the natural laws supposedly universal among men were simply
rationalizations of the existing political and social hierarchies (or of the desire to overthrow them). Here was the final step in the long continuing externalization of natural law: a vast and often uncritical accumulation of
"natural" laws, rights, prerogatives, and prohibitions in encyclopedic tomes
and treatises.

But unreason masquerading as universal law could not forever remain
unchallenged, especially when the very forces of intellectual change which
enthroned natural law in the Renaissance (the increasing secularistic and
naturalistic interest in man and society) made it vulnerable to skeptical
analysis. For even while political idealists expounded the natural obligations
of royal authority, Machiavelli was describing political realities. Even while
the moral philosopher delineated the moral order of nature, the Paduans
were formulating a scientific materialism which presaged Galileo's quantita-
tive theories. And even while the humanists elaborated their ideal of reason,
more empirical researchers were announcing that passion, appetite, and
desire are as natural to man as reason and moral prohibitions. Exploration
and scholarly research brought to the relatively unified society of western
Europe knowledge of the diversity of moral laws throughout the world and
throughout the centuries. What did this diversity suggest? Not that moral
law is universal and "natural," but that it is the variable product of custom.
By the close of the sixteenth century, the time was growing ripe for analysis
of traditional assumptions. All that was needed were minds as independent as
Donne's and Montaigne's—minds schooled in dialectic argument or the meth-
odology of ancient skepticism; and the results were *Biathanatos* and such
essays as "The Apologie of *Raymond Sebond.*"

For obvious reasons, Donne and Montaigne make the inconsistency of
interpretations of natural law a crucial issue. Donne comments:

This terme the Law of Nature, is so variously and unconstantly deliver'd,
as I confesse·I read it a hundred times before I understand it once, or

can conclude it to signifie that which the author should at that time meane.[26]

In the "Apologie" Montaigne notes such inconsistencies with less tongue in cheek perplexity and more ironical satisfaction:

> What goodnesse is that, which but yesterday I saw in credit and esteeme, and to morrow, to have lost all reputation, and that the crossing of a River, is made a crime? What truth is that, which these Mountaines bound, and is a lie in the World beyond them? But they are pleasant, when to allow the Laws some certainetie, they say, that there be some firme, perpetuall and immoveable, which they call naturall, and by the condition of their proper essence, are imprinted in mankind: of which some make three in number, some foure, some more, some lesse: an evident token, that it is a marke as doubtfull as the rest.[27]

Donne and Montaigne do not much exaggerate the diversity of opinion over the nature of natural law, which began, as we have seen, among the Roman jurists. By the close of the sixteenth century one could choose among a wide variety of interpretations and interpreters. Pomponazzi (a Paduan rationalist), Charron (a disciple of Montaigne), Suárez (a Jesuit neo-Thomist), and Du Vair (a "Christian Stoic"), all believed in natural law, but their ideas of right reason were hardly identical or even compatible. Actually, in noting the diversity of interpretations of natural law, Donne and Montaigne were making fairly commonplace statements. In *De Legibus* (1612) Francisco Suárez remarks:

> However, with respect to "natural law," it should be noted that this term is variously understood by the philosophers, the jurisconsults and the theologians. For Plato, in the works above cited, apparently understands "natural law" as referring to every natural inclination implanted in things by their Creator, whereby they severally tend towards the acts and ends proper to them. . . . St. Thomas (I-II, qu. 91, art. 2) has even said that all things ruled by divine providence partake in some fashion of the eternal law, to the degree that they derive from its efficacy, propensities toward their proper acts and ends. But the jurisconsults, while they hold that natural law is common to other living beings as well as to men, apparently exclude inanimate things from participation in this law, . . .[28]

Such disagreements of interpretation, however, do not perturb Suárez, who proceeds to define natural law "in the proper sense of the term."[29] Donne and Montaigne, more detached analysts, see the essential irony of centuries of disagreement over the universal and immutable law of reason. They see also the vulnerability of the criterion of universality in regard to natural law. In the *Summa Theologica,* St. Thomas insists that natural laws must be validated ultimately by speculative reason. But Donne and Montaigne's humanistic contemporaries preferred to emphasize a more "empirical" criterion: Cicero's equation of natural law with the *consensus gentium*. Thus we find even in Hooker's Thomistic exposition of natural law:

> Laws of Reason have these marks to be known by. Such as keep them resemble most lively in their voluntary actions that very manner of working which Nature herself doth necessarily observe in the course of the whole world. The works of Nature are all behoveful, beautiful, without superfluity or defect; even so theirs, if they be framed according to that which the Law of Reason teacheth. Secondly, those Laws are investigable by Reason, without the help of Revelation supernatural and divine. Finally, in such sort are they investigable that the knowledge of them is general, the world hath always been acquainted with them . . .[30]

Donne accepts such "empirical" criteria only to demonstrate the conclusions which must be reached by applying them (p. 39):

> Now this law of nature as it is onely in man and in him directed upon Piety, Religion, Sociablenesse; (and such for as it reacheth to the preservation both of Species and individualls, there are lively prints of it in beasts) is with most authors confounded and made the same with *jus gentium*.

But he points out that if universality is the mark of natural laws, then we must number among the "natural" customs of men idolatry, "which like a deluge overflowed the whole world, and only *Canaan,* was a little Ark swimming upon it," and "immolation of men," which was so ordinary that "almost every nation, though not barbarous, had received it" (p. 40). Like Donne, Montaigne accepts universality as the most important criterion of natural law:

> Now is the generalitie of approbation, the onely likely ensigne, by which they may argue some lawes to [be] naturall: For, what nature had indeed ordained us, that should we doubtlesse follow with one common consent; and not one onely nation, but every man in particular, should have a feeling of the force and violence, which he should urge him with, that would incite him to contrarie and resist that law (II. xii. 297-298).

Montaigne finds, however, that there are no laws universally followed by men. On the contrary, change, diversity, and contradictions characterize the morals and mores of the world, so much so in fact, that no action is "so extreame and horrible, but is found to be received and allowed by the custome of some nation" (II xii. 298).'

As before, Donne and Montaigne are not actually making radical observations or assertions. In the *Ecclesiastical Polity* Hooker acknowledges that moral codes do vary throughout the world even though he insists that natural laws are universal. But he reminds the reader that the Fall darkened the light of human reason in varying degrees. "The first principles of the Law of Nature are easy," he comments; "hard it were to find men ignorant of them. But concerning the duty which Nature's law doth require at the hands of men in a number of things particular, so far hath the natural understanding even of sundry whole nations been darkened, that they have not discerned no not gross iniquity to be sin."[31] In short, Christian ethics are natural to man and would be universally accepted were it not for human perversity and error. In Hooker's explanation the fundamental difference between his thought and that of Donne and Montaigne becomes clear. Despite his presumably empirical criteria for the distinction of natural laws, Hooker begins with an a priori theological concept of natural order to which he makes the world of fact conform by explaining all disparities as deviations from the divinely ordained norm—from the natural course of the universe. Donne and Montaigne, on the other hand, directly measure the ideal of natural law against the reality of human moral codes; they demand some empirical validation of the speculative ideal itself.

So far we have traced in *Biathanatos* and the *Essays* parallels of idea which seem far more significant out of context than they actually are. For Donne's criticism of conventional concepts of natural law, like Montaigne's, is not an end in itself but is subordinate to the larger controlling purpose of his work. And when we examine this controlling purpose, we begin to see more clearly the independence and individuality of Donne's thought. Knowing the prejudices of his contemporaries, he opens his defense of suicide by pointing out the irrationality of the conventional reactions to such "unnatural" sins. Why, Donne asks (pp. 40-41), is an "unnatural" sin more heinous or abhorrent than any other, when all sins are committed against reason (and nature) and are therefore "unnatural"? The answer, Donne suggests, is that the horror with which any action is regarded and the severity of the laws that forbid it do not necessarily argue its intrinsic "unnaturalness," but rather "a propensnesse of that people, at that time, to that fault" (p. 93).

In such passages, and when he notes the diversity of laws and their utilitarian purposes, Donne seems to imply that moral law is more often than not simply the product of custom. But he does not conclude that there are no objective moral standards. He merely insists that objective moral standards can only be deduced in each particular instance by reason itself, not by the unthinking application of immutable rules. It is supposedly unnatural, Donne says, to kill (p. 35), and most unnatural for son to kill father. Yet there are times (in wars, for example) when it is good rather than evil to kill and when we praise a son for killing his enemy father. Donne points out, moreover, that God can command or condone a killing, but He cannot sin or act unnaturally (p. 37). And although the desire for death is supposedly unnatural, Donne points out many instances in which that desire is not culpable—instances which suggest that "there is no externall act naturally evill; and that circumstances condition them, and give them their nature; as scandall makes an indifferent thing hainous at that time; which, if some person go out of the roome, or winke, is not so" (pp. 173-74).

The illustration which Donne appends to his generalization is particularly
unfortunate, smacking as it does of the ethic of Restoration comedy. But
he wittily attacks moral dogmatism in *Biathanatos* only to return to a more
primary concept of right reason (pp. 45-46):

> Our safest assurance, that we be not mislead with the ambiguity of the
> word *Naturall Law,* and the perplex'd variety thereof in Authors, will be
> this, That [all the precepts of Naturall Law, result in these, *Fly evill,*
> *seek good*;] That is, doe according to Reason.
>
> For these, as they are indispensable by any authority, so they cannot
> be abolished nor obscur'd, but that our hearts shall ever not onely re-
> taine, but acknowledge this Law. From these are deduced by consequence,
> other precepts which are not necessary alwaies; as *Redde depositum,* For
> although this seeme to follow of the first, *Doe according to reason,* yet
> it is not alwaies just. And as *Aquinas* saies, The lower you goe towards
> particulars, the more you depart from the necessitie of being bound to it.
> So *Acacius* illustrates it clearly, [It is naturall, and bindes all alwaies,
> to know there is a God. From this is deduced by necessary consequence,
> that God (if he be) must be worshipped; and after this, by likely conse-
> quence, that he must be worshipped in this or this manner.] And so every
> Sect will a little corruptly and adulterately call their discipline *Naturall*
> *Law,* and enjoyn a necessary obedience to it. But though our substance
> of nature, (which is best understood of the foundations and principles,
> and first grounds of Naturall Law,) may not be changed, yet *functio*
> *natura,* (which is the exercise and application thereof,) and deduction
> from thence may, and must.

Donne accepts a Thomistic definition of natural law, not for the sake of
argument, but because it represents a return to first principles. Nature, he
believes, establishes only one categorical imperative, only one immutable
law: that is to follow the dictates of reason. And though circumstances may
"condition" actions and custom influence our opinions, neither circum-
stance nor custom can prevail over true discursive reason: "This primary
reason therefore, against which none can plead lycense, law, custome, or
pardon, hath in us a soveraigne, and masculine force; and by it, through our
Discourse, which doth the motherly office of shaping them, and bringing
them forth and up, it produces conclusions and resolutions" (p. 76). And
no set of commandments absolutely asserted can replace the "primary and
originall Reason, which is the light of Nature"; "No law is so primary and
simple, but it foreimagines a reason upon which it was founded: and scarce
any reason is so constant, but that circumstances alter it" (p. 47).

By comparison to Montaigne's, Donne's heterodoxy is limited, indeed,
intramural. He argues for a liberal but fundamentally Christian definition
of natural law, one which relies upon and expands the traditional idea
(stated by Suárez) that natural law "discerns the mutability in the subject-
matter itself, and adapts its own precepts to this mutability, prescribing in
regard to such subject-matter a certain sort of conduct for one condition,

and another sort of conduct for another condition; so that the law in itself remains at all times unchanged, although, according to our manner of speaking and by an extrinsic attribution, it would seem, after a fashion, to undergo change" (*De Legibus*, p. 264). Indeed, Suárez seems almost to paraphrase Donne when he announces that in certain cases natural law "does not lay down an absolute command . . . rather does it command that the act in question must be preformed, assuming that the proper circumstances exist . . ." (p. 264).

But even such pragmatic reasonableness would not appease Montaigne, who challenges the whole attempt of the Christian moralist to validate his ethic as natural to man. The conclusion which Donne skirts but never draws is explicit in the *Essays*: namely, that "The lawes of conscience, which we say to proceed from nature, rise and proceed of custome: every man holding in special regard, and inward veneration the opinions approved, and customes received about him, cannot, without remorse leave them, nor without applause applie himselfe to them . . ." (I.xii.114). This conclusion, however, does not commit Montaigne to either a naïve philosophy of ethical relativism or of "individualism based on 'Nature'."[32] Though modern scholars attempt to place Montaigne in the libertine tradition, an Elizabethan or Jacobean reader of the *Essays* could not have failed to discover in them a humanistic ideal of virtue, whose goal was tranquillity and happiness in this life.[33] Wary of speculative truths, Montaigne nevertheless believes that through reason man can learn about himself—his individual bent, limitations, etc.—and order his life accordingly. Indeed, if Montaigne candidly endorses the sensual pleasures of life, he would not have man enslaved by physical appetites:

> Since it hath pleased God to endow us with some capacitie of discourse, that as beasts we should not servily be subjected to common lawes, but rather with judgement and voluntary liberty apply our selves unto them; we ought somewhat to yeeld unto the simple auctoritie of Nature: but not suffer her tyrannically to carry us away: only reason ought to have the conduct of our inclinations. (II.viii.67-68)

Unlike Donne, Montaigne asserts the complete autonomy of the rational moral judgment from supernatural sanction or religious precept:

> Shall I say this, by the way, that I see, in greater esteem that 'tis worth, and in use solely among ourselves, a certain image of scholastical probity, a slave to precepts, and fettered with hope and fear. I would have it [probity] such as that laws and religions should not make, but perfect and authorize it; that finds it has wherewithal to support itself without help, born and rooted in us from the seed of universal reason, imprinted in every man by nature.[34]

Scorning a "captive" religious virtue, Montaigne seems to return to a more Stoical idea of right reason, but he openly rejects the severe rationalistic discipline of the Stoics as well as their metaphysical premises. To Montaigne, the seed of universal reason (cf. Donne's "primary and originall Reason") is not a speculative but an empirical faculty that enables man to apprehend his world through direct and vicarious experience. Montaigne's attack on the conventional idea of natural law is, in fact, merely part of his greater attack on the metaphysical "universe" of the Renaissance theologian and moral philosopher. In the "Apologie" he ridicules the human pride which seeks to establish the nature of God and of His universe:

> Notwithstanding we prescribe him [God] limits, we lay continuall siege unto his power by our reasons . . . we will subject him to the vaine and weake apparences of our understanding: him who hath made both us and our knowledge. Because nothing is made of nothing: God was not able to frame the world without matter. What? hath God delivered into our hands the keyes, and the strongest wards of his infinit puissance? Hath he obliged himselfe not to exceed the bounds of our knowledge? Suppose, oh man, that herein thou hast beene able to marke some signes of his effects: Thinkest thou, he hath therein employed all he was able to doe, and that he hath placed all his formes and *Ideas* in this peece of worke? (II.xii.229)

It is this distrust of metaphysics which leads Montaigne to prefer the empirical reality rather than the speculative ideal of nature, and to oppose the nature-that-is to the nature-that-should-be. But the nature-that-is does not justify the "si libet, licet" of the Libertine poets. It is true, of course, that Montaigne says, "Follow nature," when he seems to equate the natural with the instinctive behavior of animals. In the "Apologie," for example, he comments: "It is credible that there are naturall lawes; as may be seene in other creatures, but in us they are lost: this goodly humane reason engrafting itselfe among all men, to sway and command, confounding and topsi-turving the visage of all things, according to her inconstant vanitie and vaine inconstancy" (II.xii.298). But Montaigne does not conclude that reason is "unnatural"[35] or that man must disregard reason if he is to act naturally. Montaigne knows, however, that virtue is difficult to achieve precisely because it is a restraint imposed by reason on impulses and desires which are (despite the arguments of Stoics and moral philosophers) natural to man. He knows too that man's unique possession of reason irrevocably divorces him from the rest of the nonrational natural world. Because man reflects upon his experiences, he cannot live naturally (i.e. intuitively) as do the animals, for he does not and cannot possess purely instinctive appetites and needs. Man lost his earthly paradise in gaining reason, which creates unnecessary luxuries and sophisticates his necessities. But however imperfect and delusory reason may be, man must live by it and hope through it to achieve happiness and the tranquillity of moderation. Unlike many of his humanistic contemporaries, Montaigne perceived that reason is a source of man's tragedy as well as his greatness—a divine attribute, but one purchased at an exceedingly heavy price.[36]

It is quite possible, one may conclude, that Donne found in the *Essays*

the stimulus and seminal ideas for his own analysis of natural law. But such
indebtedness is not very likely. For though *Biathanatos* is larded with quotations from, and references to, sources and authorities, Montaigne's name
and works are conspicuously lacking. And though *Biathanatos* and the
Essays express analogous skepticisms about moral absolutes, they are, I
think, distinctly independent responses of two Renaissance "free thinkers"
to the same contemporary issue. Indeed, we leave these works with the
strong conviction that Donne and Montaigne actually lived in widely separated intellectual worlds. In the *Essays,* Montaigne approaches modern
naturalistic and empirical interests in the individual and in the world of man.
In *Biathanatos,* Donne looks back upon a medieval Christian heritage out
of which he fashions a satisfactory moral framework. Shocking as his defense of suicide may have been in his age, its fundamental arguments extend
from traditional and quite respectable ethical theories.

A true skeptic, Montaigne was radical in his philosophical speculations
but conservative in his acceptance of established mores—in his profession
of orthodox Catholicism. Donne's attitudes toward his world, though more
complex and many-faceted, were perhaps more of a piece. In the final
analysis, it is not really amazing that the author of *Biathanatos* (and of the
Songs and Sonnets, for that matter) became the Dean of St. Paul's.[37]

DONNE AND THE MEDITATIVE TRADITION

Louis L. Martz

It has now been hearly forty years since that memorable date, October 20, 1921, when T. S. Eliot publicly observed that Donne and his fellow poets could "feel their thought as immediately as the odour of a rose."[1] It is a date worthy of some ceremony, since no critical remark of our century has had a more profound effect upon the study of English poetry, and, more important, upon the writing of English poetry. Eliot's essay on "The Metaphysical Poets" came, Mr. Duncan has shown, as a culmination and a focusing of blurred and flickering insights that had been developing throughout the late Victorian and the Edwardian eras: Arthur Symons as far back as 1899 had found in Donne's poetry a "rapture in which the mind is supreme, a reasonable rapture." "This lover loves with his whole nature, and so collectedly because reason, in him, is not in conflict with passion, but passion's ally."[2] Issuing, then, as the major voice of this long-developing view, Eliot's twin theories of the "unification of sensibility" and its subsequent "dissociation" were bound to have "a success in the world astonishing to their author," as Eliot observed in 1947, when he permitted us to read John Milton once again.[3] But these theories about the "fusion of thought and feeling" have now clearly run their course. Within the past few years Mr. Kermode has assured us that the whole hypothesis was only a fallacious effort to find historical justification for the Symbolist aesthetic of the Image. Mr. Unger has argued that "there was no unique fusion" in Donne's poetry, no evidence of "unified sensibility," but only "an urgent search for unity." And Mr. Hunt, who deeply admires Donne, nevertheless has told us that for true unification we ought to look toward Spenser and Milton, for Donne was a poet of extraordinary limitations: "an ear relatively dull to the sonorities of language; a limited sensory response and an insensitivity to many subtleties of emotion; a lack of pleasure in the beauties of the natural world and an inability to invest its physical facts with the aura of the romantic imagination; an absence of any strong feeling for the cultural traditions of his own civilization, or of any strong sense of personal community with the rest of mankind; and a certain deficiency in human sympathy."[4] Yes, there are signs, clearly, that before long a new exemplar of true poetic unification will be found in Percy Bysshe Shelley, and that Donne will prove most lamentably dissociated—if not utterly dismembered.

Reprinted from *Thought*, 34 (1959), 269-78, by permission of the author and the publisher.

It seems that the "naked thinking heart" of Donne's poetry can offer little to those who seek again that old embroidered coat that Yeats and Donne both cast away. Perhaps it is time, then, to pronounce a Valediction, in Donne's own kind, admitting mutability in the world, but affirming the immortality of certain true relationships—in particular, the deep and valid relation between Donne and the later age that loved him: an age that might have applied to Donne's poetry these lines from Donne's own "Valediction: of the book":

> When this booke is made thus,
> Should againe the ravenous
> Vandals and Goths inundate us,
>
> Learning were safe; in this our Universe
> Schooles might learne Sciences, Spheares Musick, Angels Verse.

The timing of Eliot's famous essay indicates the basis of this liaison. The essay came, in 1921, just as William Butler Yeats was deep within the composition of his private guide to "Unity of Being," *A Vision*, which appeared in 1925; in composing the *Vision*, Yeats tells us, he learned from his mysterious teachers that he must, in effect, feel his thought, or, in his own words, "give concrete expression to their abstract thought." ". . . and if my mind returned too soon to their unmixed abstraction they [his 'communicators'] would say, 'We are starved.'"[5] The essay came, too, as I. A. Richards was conceiving his *Principles of Literary Criticism*, which appeared in 1924, offering us the poetry of "inclusion," as represented in Donne's "Nocturnall upon S. Lucies day"; such poetry, for Richards, offered a way by which modern man might achieve the "resolution of a welter of disconnected impulses into a single ordered response"—with the resultant consciousness of "completed being" that for Richards comes from participation in the greatest art.[6]

That Donne seemed to answer this general quest for unity of being is made especially plain by Eliot in a note on Donne that he wrote for *The Nation and the Athenaeum* in 1923, by way of "inquiry into the reasons for Donne's present popularity." Casting aside all matters of mere fashion, all accidental relationships, he asserts the one basic cause: Donne's "mind has unity and order." "The range of his feeling was great, but no more remarkable than its unity. He was altogether present in every thought and in every feeling." Our age, he says, "objects to the simplification and separation of the mental faculties." "Ethics having been eclipsed by psychology, we accept the belief that any state of mind is extremely complex, and chiefly composed of odds and ends in constant flux manipulated by desire and fear. When, therefore, we find a poet who neither suppresses nor falsifies, and who expresses complicated states of mind, we give him welcome."[7] The last sentence might almost have been written by Richards.

What Eliot and Richards, and Yeats all admired in Donne has been brilliantly summed up by Wallace Stevens when he wrote that modern poetry must give "The poem of the mind in the act of finding/What will suffice." We must emphasize the *act of finding*. For Donne presents the very process by which unity of mind is discovered: he does indeed, as Mr. Unger says, present the search for unity, in all the agony of its exploration, but in the end of every great poem that he wrote, his speaker has discovered "what will suffice":

> If our two loves be one, or, thou and I
> Love so alike, that none doe slacken, none can die.

> But wee will have a way more liberall,
> Then changing hearts, to joyne them, so wee shall
>   Be one, and one anothers All.

> Let us love nobly, and live, and adde againe
> Yeares and yeares unto yeares, till we attaine
> To write threescore: this is the second of our raigne.

> But wonder at a greater wonder, for to us
> Created nature doth these things subdue,
> But their Creator, whom sin, nor nature tyed,
> For us, his Creatures, and his foes, hath dyed.

> And, having done that, Thou has done,
>   I feare no more.

After so many decades of talk about Donne's "anguish of the marrow" and the contraries that met to vex him, it is perhaps too easy to forget the noble serenity of these conclusions; yet the movement from anguish and vexation to the finding of what will suffice is the essential action of Donne's poetry and of his entire life. Whether it is the early "Satire 3," or the late "Anniversaries," or the even later (I think) "Nocturnall upon S. Lucies day," the essential action of the mind is the same. The typical Donneian poem opens with a searing vision of the follies and foibles and infidelities of the world, sometimes given in a comic tone, as in "The Sunne Rising," where that "pedantique wretch," the sun, insists on arising punctually, only to reveal the sorry world of time-servers:

>   goe chide
> Late schoole boyes, and sowre prentices,
> Goe tell Court-huntsmen, that the King will ride,
> Call countrey ants to harvest offices;
> Love, all alike, no season knowes, nor clyme,
> Nor houres, dayes, moneths, which are the rags of time.

Or it may be the fierce and bitter opening of a Holy Sonnet:

> If poysonous mineralls, and if that tree,
> Whose fruit threw death on else immortall us,
> If lecherous goats, if serpents envious
> Cannot be damn'd; Alas; why should I bee?

Or it may be the sombre vision of universal decay in the "Nocturnall":

> The Sunne is spent, and now his flasks
> Send forth light squibs, no constant rayes;
> The worlds whole sap is sunke:
> The generall balme th' hydroptique earth hath drunk. . . .

But whatever the mood and tone, whatever the vision of time and decay, whatever the era of Donne's life, "the poem of the act of the mind," as Stevens would call it, moves steadily onward to the finding of what will suffice. Sometimes it is found in carnal love:

> This bed thy center is, these walls, thy sphaere.

Sometimes in the operation of Grace:

> That thou remember them, some claime as debt,
> I thinke it mercy, if thou wilt forget.

Sometimes in death and the after-life:

> Since shee enjoys her long nights festivall,
> Let mee prepare towards her, and let mee call
> This houre her Vigill, and her Eve, since this
> Both the yeares, and the dayes deep midnight is.

Why should we find, nowadays, a tendency to deny unity to the mind that could execute so perfect a movement? For two reasons, I believe. First, because Eliot's theory of unification and dissociation was grossly unfair to Milton and other poets: in an effort to defend Milton, or Dryden, or Shelley, critics have been led to counterattack. More important, however, is a serious fallacy in the assumption that underlies most criticism based on the doctrine of the unified sensibility. The assumption is implicit in Eliot's phrase "mechanism of sensibility"; in Williamson's view that the fusion of learning and passion in Donne was "spontaneous and natural"; in Ransom's early contention that the term "metaphysical" ought to be equated with "miraculous," since the unity in metaphysical poetry was achieved by a "miracle" of metaphor.[8] All these views assume that Donne's alleged power of unification was something given, native, inherent in the fortunate man and the more fortunate age; something inexplicable and magical that Donne and his age possessed, and we do not. This attitude is not very far from Matthew Arnold's weary cry in "The Scholar Gipsy": "O Life unlike to ours!" "Thou hadst *one* aim, *one* business, *one* desire" "And we imagine thee exempt from age . . . Because thou hadst—what we, alas, have not!"

But such a view will not describe the action of Donne's poetry. The unity enacted within his poetry was not a gift: it was a unity achieved in much the same way that Eliot and Yeats and Hopkins and Paul Claudel were later to follow—the way of arduous and disciplined meditation. It is ironical that Eliot, around 1930, should have lost his early confidence in Donne, just as

he himself was beginning to follow a mode of inner life that Donne had
known from his childhood; yet Eliot almost predicted this result in his note
of 1923, when he concluded: "We cannot have any order but our own, but
from Donne and his contemporaries we can draw instruction and encouragement." The encouragement, we may say, came from Donne and his fellow
poets; the *instruction,* toward a unified meditative poetry, came primarily,
it seems, from a Spanish contemporary of Donne's who died in 1591:
St. John of the Cross. Eliot's debt to the spiritual writings of St. John of
the Cross has been widely recognized by the commentators on *Ash Wednes-*
day, Murder in the Cathedral, and the *Quartets;* the debt extends even to
the essential organization and inner process of the *Quartets,* which enact a
spiritual progress from meditation to contemplation, after the manner prescribed by St. John of the Cross in his subtle treatises of self-analysis.

If this is so, then the total careers of Donne and Eliot bear the most profound analogy; both, we may say, spent their lives in an arduous effort to
achieve the state of mind described by Paul Claudel in his prose meditation,
A Poet before the Cross, where Claudel envisions a state of mind which is
"both infinitely multiple and intensely one." "From the north to the south,
from alpha to omega, from the east to the west, all is one with us, we are
clothed with it, we instigate it, we are both revealed and humbled in this
orchestral operation. . . . Our brief blind impulses are wedded, revived, interpreted and developed in immense stellar movements. Outside of us, at
astronomical distances, we decipher the text microscopically inscribed in
the bottom of our hearts." "With all our senses we shall contemplate the
first cause." We shall work "with an intelligence so clear and informed that
it will become as immediate as sensation is in us, with a fidelity of all our
being, with a will as prompt and subtle as the flame of a fire."[9] Those words
of Claudel, written between 1933 and 1935, at the height of the vogue for
Donne, describe the central action of all meditative poetry, the central action of Donne, Herbert, Crashaw, Vaughan and Marvell, the central action
of Hopkins, Dickinson, Yeats, Eliot and Claudel.

If I seem to be exaggerating the importance of the act of meditation for
the poetry of Donne, we may turn to Donne's own testimony in a verse
letter to Rowland Woodward, written, it seems while Donne was in his
early thirties. It is a poem that displays the typical Donneian movement.
It opens with the usual satire against the infidelities of the world (including
himself):

> Like one who'in her third widdowhood doth professe
> Her selfe a Nunne, tyed to retirednesse,
> So'affects my muse now, a chast fallownesse;
>
> Since shee to few, yet to too many'hath showne
> How love-song weeds, and Satyrique thornes are growne
> Where seeds of better Arts, were early sown.

Where seeds of better Arts, were early sown. What were these better Arts
that came before the love-songs and the satires? The rest of the poem seems

to tell us. They are the arts by which, "If our Soules have stain'd their first white, yet wee/May cloth them with faith, and deare honestie." And the method?

> Seeke wee then our selves in our selves; for as
> Men force the Sunne with much more force to passe,
> By gathering his beames with a christall glasse;

> So wee, If wee into our selves will turne,
> Blowing our sparkes of vertue, may outburne
> The straw, which doth about our hearts sojourne. . . .

> Wee are but farmers of our selves, yet may
> If we can stocke our selves, and thrive, uplay
> Much, much deare treasure for the great rent day.

It seems fair to say, then that John Donne's literary career, like that of Eliot, or Yeats, or Claudel, or Hopkins, represents a record of the farming of the self, the stocking of the self, the gathering of the beams of the self into one intense and burning focus. And if such ways of meditation, as Donne seems to say, were learned by Donne *before* the writing of his love-song weeds and satiric thorns, it will not be illegitimate to expect some impact of this meditative discipline upon the writing of those songs and satires. This is not to argue that the "Songs and Sonets" are really religious meditations in rake's clothing; though I believe that the "Nocturnall" is a deeply religious poem, that it deals with the death of Donne's wife, and that it was therefore written *after* most of the Holy Sonnets. But for most of Donne's love-poetry and satires, one should say no more than this: that it is the inward farming of the self which gives these poems their distinctive structure, direction, and inclusiveness.

It is upon this inward base that most of Donne's poems organize themselves: the strong satirical texture that runs throughout his poetry forms an essential part of the inward quest. The universe cannot be reorganized about an inward center unless the outward straw "which doth about our hearts sojourne" is first burned away. The "naked thinking heart" will not reveal itself without this burning. One is reminded of Eliot's strong satirical vein, and of Claudel, who in the midst of a meditation on the words, "My God, My God, why hast thou forsaken me?" is able to give us the following satirical disquisition:

What? What is he saying? . . . *Eli* . . . *Eli*. . . . Did you hear what he just said? No, but did you hear it? Allow me, gentlemen and dear colleagues, to call your attention to the decisive confession which the inexorable torture of scientific investigation has just snatched from ignorance and superstition and imposture. . . . I am sure that the root *El* we find on Sumerian inscriptions and Arabic tombs will intrigue the old campaigners of Semitic philology. Whether you see in it a Mesopotamian totem, or a Hittite allusion, or a Moon lover, it is undeniable in any case that in this syllable which has so curiously reached our ears you find the origin of that *Elohim* which in opposition to *Jahveh*, has generously stained in blue the pages of our polychrome Bible.

. . . I consider the form *Sabachthani* doubtful and even shocking, and I am almost ready to agree with delightful Professor Pumpernickel who finds in it a Galilean deformation. *Eli, Eli,* or *Eloi* (another form of the vocative) *why have you abandoned me?* Why did he abandon our attractive subject? I see, gentlemen and dear colleagues, and you, ladies who grace this meeting, by the smiles on your faces, I see that no one of you would be embarrassed to answer this naive question. (*op. cit.,* pp. 124-5).

The colloquialism, the range of the learning, the bitter ironies are akin to Donne; and if this tirade furthermore reminds us of the speeches of Eliot's Knights in *Murder in the Cathedral,* the reminiscence may be more than coincidental. Such racy outbursts are likely to play an important part in any meditative vision of the world.

So then, one might use the word "meditative," rather than "metaphysical," in discussing these poets, for "meditative" seems to point directly toward the inner organizing principle of this poetry, and thus to provide a term of greater discrimination. It might be said, for example, that Ransom and Tate, or Auden and MacNeice, are modern metaphysicals, just as Sam Johnson could find "the metaphysick style" in Donne, Ben Jonson, Suckling, Waller, Denham, Cowley, or Cleveland. But of all these poets only Donne and Tate could truly be called *meditative* poets. The term "meditative," as I see it, does not serve to replace the term "metaphysical"; it rather intersects the term "metaphysical," and serves a different purpose by associating Donne with a particular tradition in European culture. Reading Donne in the context of European meditative literature may help us to see more clearly the nature of his greatness, and to grasp his firm centrality in the life of his age and our own. It may even help to preserve Donne's poetry against the encroaching shadow of myths and archetypes.

But can we ever give a satisfying and precise definition of meditative poetry? We might begin by saying that meditative poetry displays an actor who, first of all, seeks himself in himself; but not because he is self-centered in our sense of that term—no, he seeks himself in himself in order to discover or to construct a firm position from which he can include the universe. If we go on to seek for a more detailed definition, we may find it in the following words of Paul Claudel, who may be found speaking here with the voice of all meditative poetry:

Thus we understand that the soul is not . . . a kind of fluid fabricated somehow or other which the body yields like a gas-generator. On the contrary, everything takes place as if there were a motor-directive principle governing our organized matter, and as if there were in us someone who is master and who knows what he has to do with everything. It is not our body which makes us, it is we at each second who make our body and who compose it in that attitude adapted to every situation which we call sensation and perception. It is not movement which drags us along in an irresistible flow. Movement is at our disposal. We can exploit it. We who are able to oppose and stop it, and, by using a free and limitless choice, impose on our perceptions the firm pattern of a concept, of a figure, of a will (*op. cit.*, pp. 196-7).

It is, at least, exactly what the last generation found remarkable in Donne: that he could impose on his perceptions "the firm pattern of a concept, of a figure, of a will."

DONNE'S PETRARCHISM

Donald L. Guss

In the *Songs and Sonets,* Donne sometimes expresses dramatic emotions through the gallant conceits of the Petrarchans. For example, in "The Dreame"—which Mario Praz considers a variation on a Petrarchan theme[1] — Donne says that his lady's knowledge of his thoughts proves that she is divine. This bit of amorous theology is an extension of the Petrarchan lady-goddess figure; it has many Petrarchan analogues, among them Desportes' *Hippolyte* iv:

> Madame, helas! monstrez que vous estes divine,
> Lisez dedans les cœurs ainsi que font les dieux.

In the same poem, Donne compares himself to an extinguished torch. His prosaic simile is an elaboration of the Petrarchan love-fire metaphor; many conventional poets anticipate it, Desportes, in *Hipp.* vii, quite closely:

> ainsi qu'un flambeau qu'on ne fait que d'étaindre,
> Si le feu s'en approche est aussi-tost repris:
> Dans mon cœur chaud encor un brasier s'est épris.[2]

In "The Dreame" the lover's enthusiasm is evoked by a scenically conceived situation; it is expressed through Petrarchan hyperboles.

In "A Valediction: of weeping" and "Witchcraft by a picture," Donne realizes drama in Petrarchan minuteness. Serafino's Sonnet xxxvi, "Mentre che amore in me non abitava," complains that his lady, who used to enjoy seeing her picture in his eyes, has ignored him since his amorous tears began to distort her reflection. Donne uses the particularity of a similar image to reflect the intimacy and tender sorrow with which his lovers regard each other. Once more he dramatizes a Petrarchan conceit.

Such instances suggest that Petrarchism may have been important to Donne. For Donne could hardly have been unaware of English and French Petrarchism; he was acquainted with the Italian language and literature, regularly inscribing in his books a line, in Italian, from one of Petrarch's love poems; and he imitated Petrarchan ideas in "The Extasie," and a Petrarchan conceit in "A Valediction: forbidding mourning."[3] Donne must, then, have been acquainted with Petrarchism; and Petrarchism—traditionally introspective, dialectical, and conceited—offered him a clear alternative to

Reprinted from *Journal of English and Germanic Philology,* 64 (1965), 17-28, by permission of the author and the University of Illinois Press.

Elizabethan neoclassicism. It is therefore significant that in two of his most
characteristic poems, "The Apparition" and "The Canonization," Donne
submits Petrarchan conceits to a dramatic imagination.

It is drama and Petrarchism—and not the Counter-Reformation, the
metaphysical shudder, or Anglo-Saxon melancholy—that explain "The
Apparition":

> When by thy scorne, O murdresse, I am dead,
>   And that thou thinkst thee free
> From all solicitation from mee,
> Then shall my ghost come to thy bed,
> And thee, fain'd vestall, in worse armes shall see;
> Then thy sicke taper will begin to winke,
> And he, whose thou art then, being tyr'd before,
> Will, if thou stirre, or pinch to wake him, thinke
>   Thou call'st for more,
> And in false sleepe will from thee shrinke,
> And then poore Aspen wretch, neglected thou
> Bath'd in a cold quicksilver sweat wilt lye
>   A veryer ghost then I;
> What I will say, I will not tell thee now,
> Lest that preserve thee'; and since my love is spent,
> I'had rather thou shouldst painfully repent,
> Then by my threatnings rest still innocent.

"The Apparition" considers the lover's afterlife in terms of his present
amorous situation. Its remote origin is the courtly-love cliché that the poet
will continue to worship his lady after death. Jacopo da Lentini, for example,
says that if his lady were not in heaven, he would refuse to go there, but
that, since she will be blessed, he will shun damnation. This sort of amorous
eschatology—which is employed by Guido Guinizelli, among others[4]—approaches "The Apparition" more closely in Neapolitan lyrics of the mid-
fifteenth century. These lyrics treat the lover's death for unfulfilled love
as though it were a prosaic murder, warning the lady, for example, that she
will have trouble disposing of her lover's corpse. By thus establishing the
lady's guilt, they fit the theme of amorous death to the theory that hard-
hearted ladies are punished after death, saying, for example, that when the
poet has died for love, should he go to hell he will have the consolation of
seeing his lady suffer there.[5] Thus the Neapolitans anticipate Donne in ex-
pecting that justice will be done on the lady-murderess. In "Voi, Donna, e io
per segni manifesti"—a sonnet imitated throughout Europe, and admired by
the Marinisti—Chariteo treats the theme with magniloquence, sentimental
refinement, and logical elaboration. He asserts that when he and his lady are
sent to hell—she for her cruelty to him, and he for his presumption in loving
her—she will suffer from the sight of him, but he will consider himself

blessed so long as he sees her. Interestingly, Chariteo's sonnet has, like
Donne's lyrics, been mistakenly likened to Baudelaire.[6] In its fusion of love,
death, and justice, it develops a conventional motive and anticipates "The
Apparition."

Unlike Donne, neither Chariteo nor his predecessors threatens that he
himself will punish his lady. But in "S' io per te moro e calo nell' inferno,"
Serafino adapts the conceit to a scorned lover's desire for revenge:

> If I die for you and go to hell,
> All my sufferings will cry for vengeance;
> I shall compose a legal brief of accusations against you,
> And give it to the infernal furies.
> You will be condemned to eternal fire
> And thrown down beside me;
> And should you live a while in song and holiday,
> My ghost will always stand before you.

Thus Donne's amorous eschatology is often paralleled by Petrarchan
poems which do not elaborate a ghostly vengeance. The vengeance is
suggested at the close of "S' io per te moro," and also in the *Aeneid,* IV,
384-87, where Dido bids Aeneas go (in C. Day Lewis' translation, Oxford,
1952):

> I'll dog you, from far, with the death-fires;
> And when cold death has parted my soul from my body, my spectre
> Will be wherever you are. You shall pay for the evil you've done me.
> The tale of your punishment will come to me down in the shades.

In *Epistola V,* "Tu sei disposto pur, crudel, lassarmi," ll. 97-112, where a
Dido-figure writes to her departing lover, Serafino assimilates the Virgilian
theme to the manner of Chariteo:

> But you cannot go so quickly
> As to escape my ghost, which will track you down
> And remain beside you forever, visible
> And bleeding, exactly as I was
> When, with cruel hand, I killed myself.
> It will be next to you whether you sleep or wake,
> Not to harm you—for I couldn't—
> But so that you may regret your errors one day,
> And understand my sufferings one day,
> Hearing me howl wildly,
> Lamenting repeatedly on your account,
> And all my outcries reproaching you.
>
> And, although my simple, foolish soul
> May be out of its weary, worn body,
> Do not hope that it will be untied from you on that account:
> For a true love is not weakened even by death.

These lines would be very much like "The Apparition" were it not that
they depart from the Petrarchan clichés by portraying a deserted lady and
considering a suicide rather than an amorous wasting-away. In Strambotti
103 and 104, "E se gli é ver che l'alma tormentare" and "E se glie é'l ver
che 'l spirto vada atorno," Serafino adapts the theme of the haunting to the
Petrarchan situation of an extraordinarily cruel lady and her suffering lover.
He thereby very precisely anticipates "The Apparition":

> And if it is true that the soul must be tormented
> In the very place in which it sinned,
> I hope to abide within your body,
> Since through your cruelty I die damned.
> And with my own hand I want to tear apart
> That false heart that has been so hard to me,
> Until I kill you, for my revengeı
> For every sin meets its just reward at last.
>
> And if it is true that one's ghost wanders about
> When his soul is untied from his body,
> Know that I will always be about you,
> And never weary of warring upon you—
> So much so that you will always curse the day
> That you refused to content me upon earth.
> And thus I hope to possess you some time,
> And, alive or dead, to have you in my hand.

These analogues place "The Apparition" squarely in the Petrarchan tradition. Donne is not here more realistic, more baroque, more manly, or, indeed,
more rebellious than his Petrarchan predecessors: his complaint against his
lady and his conjunction of love with death are rooted in Petrarchan clichés;[7]
and his picture of the afterlife follows Chariteo and Serafino. "The Apparition" is original; but its originality is the result of a dramatic imagination.
Donne, more than any of his predecessors, visualizes the scene of the haunting and comprehends the feelings of the lady as, unprepared and unsup-
ported, she suffers a horrible visitation. And, more clearly than the Petrarchans, he develops the emotional turmoil, the exacerbation and the jealous
anguish, of a lover who hopes to avenge himself on his beloved after death.

For the fifteenth-century Petrarchans, the conceit of the lover's death
and revenge was a means of refining the popular theme which appears in
Antonio da S. Croce da Valdamo's "Venir tipossa el diavolo allo letto":

> May the devil go to bed with you,
>   Since I'm not welcome there,
>   And may he break two ribs of your chest,
>   And the other members that God made for you,
>   And drag you across mountains and valleys
>   And chop your head off your shoulders.

Donne abandons the aristocratic tone, the emotional simplification, and the persuasive intent of the Petrarchans. But it is Petrarchism which separates him from such naïve statement and gross sentiments as Antonio's— which permits him his conceit and his self-awareness. And thus "The Apparition," in many ways a crucial example of Donne's style, is a dramatic elaboration of a Petrarchan conceit.

Donne's Petrarchism appears again in the third stanza of "The Canonization." In the 1633 text, this stanza reads:

> Call us what you will, wee are made such by love;
>   Call you one, mee another flye,
>   We'are Tapers too, and at our owne cost die,
>   And wee in us finde the'Eagle and the Dove,
>   The Phoenix ridle hath more wit
>   By us, we two being one, are it.
>   So, to one neutrall thing both sexes fit.
>   Wee dye and rise the same, and prove
>   Mysterious by this love.

The conceits in this stanza, like many others in *The Songs and Sonets,* are related to emblem literature. The moth in the flame, the eagle, the dove, and the phoenix all appear in emblem books, as Lederer notes; and Donne uses them as the lovers' imprese, and perhaps intends them to retain some traditional emblematic significations—perhaps his eagle means virtue tired by wandering, for example, or his dove true love.[8] But, because most amorous emblems are derived from Petrarch,[9] where there is an emblematic parallel there is usually a Petrarchan parallel as well. For example, Lederer refers Donne's line 4 to an emblem in which an eagle swooping down on a caged dove signifies future ill-fortune; but this emblem—whose motto is drawn from Petrarch—is merely a pictorial representation of the conceit of Tansillo's "Come augellin, ch' umane note finge." Since, as shown by Miss Rosemary Freeman, the form of Donne's conceit is not emblematic,[10] and since the emblem itself is a manifestation of Petrarchism, it seems wisest to consider the stanza within a Petrarchan context. And in fact Petrarchism provides a clearer interpretation of line 4 than does emblem literature. For if one interprets the line emblematically it is impossible to know what the line means—the dove, for example, might be anything from Christian resurrection to marital fidelity, anything from contemplation to an alchemical reaction.[11] But in Petrarchan poetry the lover is conventionally an eagle gazing at the sun of his lady's beauty;[12] and since a beloved lady is traditionally a dove, the convention provides a clear sense in which the lovers are noble birds, and not mere moths.

The stanza's Petrarchan background is particularly useful in elucidating the lovers' death and resurrection, whose obscurity has led to a textual difficulty. Grierson, though he maintains that the 1633 text is to be followed wherever possible, substitutes a comma for the period after "fit" in line 7: he considers the 1633 reading to make no sense. Later editors—Hebel and

Hudson, Shaaber, Hayward, and Bennett—follow Grierson. But Grierson's
reading is itself intelligible only if the lovers' death is sexual consummation;
and if it is, Donne's exalted confidence in his "mysterious" love seems mis-
placed. Thus the editors have departed from the best text in order to get
an infelicitous reading. And George Williamson's attempt to defend the
1633 punctuation without reinterpreting amorous death, is unconvincing:
for Williamson says that line 7 is a challenge to the lovers which lines 8-9
answer; but line 7—unlike line 1, which Williamson considers analogous—
contains no syntactical indication that the belief it expresses is not the
lover's.[13] The 1633 text can be vindicated, however, and Donne's enthusiasm
explained, by a consideration of the stanza in its Petrarchan context.

That lovers "dye and rise the same" is a conceit which, as Mario Equicola
notes, appears in classical poetry, where it expresses the extremities of amorous desire.[14] It is a commonplace among the Provençal poets, who, with
characteristic wit, assert that the lover dies in his lady's radiance like a
moth in a flame, and that he dies and is reborn a hundred times a day (see
Equicola, fols. 183[v]-84[r], 185[r]). Provençal poets and their imitators, with
their taste for peregrine comparisons, associated this conceit with the
phoenix. Giovanni d'Arezzo, for example, says in "L' uscel fenice quando
ven' al morire" that, like the phoenix, he dies and is re-created in the fire of
his unfulfilled love. And in "Sicomo il parpaglion, ch' a tal natura," Jacopo
da Lentini says that, foolishly ignoring the dangers of his lady's radiance,
he draws near her like a moth to a flame; and that, being burnt in the sweet
flame, he, like a phoenix, is brought back to life by his lady's beauty.[15] In
135, "Qual piú diversa e nova," Petrarch uses the traditional conceit to
describe one of the many miraculous metamorphoses which he claims to
have undergone for love:

> Whatever most strange and unheard-of thing
>   Ever existed in even the most uncanny regions,
>   That thing, if one judges rightly,
>   Is most like me: to such a state have I come, Love.
>   There where the day comes forth
>   There flies a bird that, unique and without consort,
>   From a willing death
>   Is reborn, and recreated, entirely alive.
>   Similarly alone is my desire,
>   And similarly on the summit
>   Of its high thoughts it turns to the sun,
>   And similarly crumbles,
>   And similarly returns to its original condition;
>   It burns and dies, and retakes its body,
>   And then lives, a rival of the phoenix.

The love tracts, which seek truth in literature, interpret the lover's death
and resurrection philosophically. Marsilio Ficino, whose influence was vast,
uses it for a central statement of his belief that a lover dies in himself and is

reborn in his beloved.[16] After the conceit had been used by Petrarch, explained by Ficino, and recognized by Equicola, it became, of course a Renaissance commonplace. It is frequent in sixteenth-century French Neoplatonic poetry; in English, it is a special favorite of Thomas Watson, who uses it as a symbol of the torments of unfulfilled love.[17] Among the most interesting of the lyrics which anticipate Donne's stanza is Serafino's Stram. 106, "O morte: o la: soccorri: ecco che arrivo" (cf. Watson, *Hec.* 22):

> *Lover*: Oh Death! *Death*: Yes? *L*: Help! *D*: Lo, I am here; Why do you
> call? *L*: I burn. *D*: Who burns you? *L*: Love.
> *D*: What can I do? *L*: Take my life.
> *D*: Why, I kill you continually. *L*: Not me. *D*: Just ask your heart.
> *L*: Heart! *Heart*: What is it? *L*: Are you dead? *H*: Sometimes dead, sometimes alive.
> *L*: But what can you mean? *H*: Alas! *L*: Was a dead man ever reborn?
> *H*: Only I. *L*: Then, Death, what can I do? Bit by bit,
> Like a phoenix I renew myself in the fire.

Perhaps the most precise analogue of Donne's stanza is an elegantly sentimental bit of Neoplatonizing, Guarino's Madrigal 37, "Una farfalla cupida, e vagante":

> My loving heart has been made
> A wandering moth, filled with desire,
> That goes, as though in play,
> Dancing around the fire
> Of two lovely eyes, and so many, many times
> Does it fly away and back, and flee and return, and circle,
> That in the beloved light
> It will at last leave both its life and its wings.
> But who sighs at that,
> Sighs wrongly. Dear, fortunate ardor [both "flame" and
>   "passion"],
> It will die a moth, and rise a phoenix.

The Petrarchan background elucidates Donne's stanza. First, the lyrics of Jacopo and Guarino indicate that Donne's stanza is based on the contrast between moth and phoenix. Williamson, treating the stanza as a series of emblems, obscures this contrast. He finds in line 3 a reference to the emblem of the burning taper—which, like the moth, is an independent symbol of self-destruction. But Williamson's interpretation ignores the emphatic contrast between "Call her" (l. 2) and "We're" (l. 3), and obfuscates the meaning of "And" in line 4—a word which clearly implies that line 3, like line 4, supports the lovers' case. In fact, lines 2-3 are both about the moth in the flame. They say that if the lover is conventionally a moth, it is his beloved who is conventionally the candle which lures him—and that therefore Donne's counsellor need not fear that the fire will be at his expense. These lines, then, mock Donne's friend's materialism—much like stanza one, which recommends that he contemplate money, and stanza two, which insinuates that he dislikes love only because he fears it may interfere with trade.[18] Then, having revealed the baseness of the world at large through his ironical use of the moth and candle, Donne proceeds to celebrate the lovers through the phoenix. And so his stanza, like its Petrarchan analogues, is primarily an opposition of phoenix to moth.

Furthermore, the Petrarchan background shows how Donne could have employed the conceit of the lover's death and resurrection with an exalted tone and a metaphysical intent; and thus it justifies the period after line 6. For Donne probably follows Ficino in arguing that the resurrection of the lovers is caused by their union (see l. 6)—he certainly uses the Neoplatonic, and therefore exalted, implications of the theory—and, since the strange immortality of lovers was generally acknowledged, it did not need the particular explanation that a comma after line 6 might afford. Donne's general intention in lines 5-9 is to prove that the lovers are the phoenix, and thereby both repudiate the accusation that they are moths in the flame, and reveal that, being "mysterious," they are superior to the counsels of reason. Donne cites three essential similarities between lovers and phoenix: their unity; the sexlessness of their joint being; and their revivification (cf. Petrarch, who cites his desire's uniqueness, exalted dwelling place, and repeated rebirth). Each of these similarities involves a paradox, and thus elevates love through the conventional theme of "loves magique" (cf. "A Valediction: of my name, in the window," st. II)—much like Petrarch's claim that his transformation into the phoenix is marvellous, and Ficino's demonstration that the lovers' rebirth, being double where their death is single, is miraculous. Line 7, then, is not an explanation of lines 8-9, nor a challenge to the lovers. It is an independent and miraculous parallel between lovers and phoenix: it may echo Sperone Speroni's assertion, in the *Dialogo d'amore,* that the joint being of united lovers is hermaphroditic,[19] and it certainly parallels Donne's own statement, in "The Extasie" (ll. 33-48), of the differences between an amorous union and the individuals who compose it. Thus the stanza is elucidated and the 1633 reading of it justified by a consideration of its Petrarchan analogues.

The third stanza of "The Canonization" is, like "The Apparition," a dramatic interpretation of a Petrarchan conceit. If Donne imitates Guarino's Mad. 37 here, he treats Guarino's langorous conjunction of two conventional sentiments as a vibrant quarrel between two uncongenial men. If not, his stanza still reveals three dramatic elements that are not found in its Petrarchan analogues. First, through a casuistic argument Donne adapts the phoenix image to a defense of mutual love—a relationship much more susceptible of dramatic development than is the introspective solitude of Petrarchism. Second, Donne brings the lover out of Arcadia and makes him aware of various non-amorous elements of ordinary life. And, third, Donne bases his mysticism on common sense. Petrarch uses the phoenix as a mystic symbol that elevates his story and distinguishes him from common men. Serafino uses it as an authoritative emblem that supports his paradoxical demonstration and his absurdly prosaic gallantry. And Guarino uses it as a catalyst to heroic and elegant folly, a Neoplatonic reminder that causes him to rededicate himself to his torment with fatuous ardor. Unlike the Petrarchans, Donne grounds the lovers' miraculousness—which the phoenix-conceit expresses—on a close and satirical observation of men as they are: he explains it as the gap between the serene lovers and base, busy worldlings. Donne thereby completes his adaptation of Petrarchan conceits to his dramatic concerns. With great originality but not unconventionality, he employs Petrarchan language to express amorous fervor and Petrarchan logic to defend love. And so "The Canonization," like "The Apparition," is a dramatic realization of a Petrarchan conceit.

IV. PROSODY AND RHETORICAL TRADITION

METER AND MEANING IN DONNE'S VERSE

Arnold Stein

All Donne's poems are equally metrical (misprints allowed for)
though smoothness (i.e., the metre necessitating the proper reading)
be deemed appropriate to songs; but in poems where the writer thinks,
and expects the reader to do so, the sense must be understood in order
to ascertain the metre.

—COLERIDGE.

What is the ultimate test of the prosody of a line of verse? It is possible to compile a system of metrical variations which will explain nearly all of Donne's lines that strongly depart from the norm. Yet one may easily seem to be underestimating the influence of this norm, which is really considerable. Many readers of poetry have so powerful an impression of this ideal pattern that it enables them to defy stress-shift by giving more mental stress to the syllable which everyday pronunciation would make light. One prosodist, Chard P. Smith, even maintains that "there is no shift of the accent [i.e., metrical stress] . . . no substitution of a trochee for an iamb. The accent [stress] remains where it falls and there is, *in addition,* a prose stress [prose accent] on the unaccented [unstressed] syllable." Thus the ten syllables of the heroic line, according to this theory, correspond one by one with the ten of the base, and a syllable may be accented though not stressed.

This opinion is held by many readers of poetry, though few would carry it to such an extreme, or admit it if they did. And it will work out fairly well in lines where the base is strongly asserted and makes a deep, tenacious impression on the reader. But this approach loses its validity when one is dealing with verse the meaning of which is more important than the music. Coleridge's distinction, quoted at the head of this essay, is useful in emphasizing the difference between these two kinds of verse. A similar, more explicit, distinction between "song-verse" and thoughtful "speech-verse" has been made by Egerton Smith. Song-verse, "nearer to music, tends to conceive of verse as dominated by the metrical sound-scheme and the melodic effect. The other kind, nearer to prose-speech, is dominated by the sense or thought-scheme."

In considering Donne's *Satires* we need have no more concern than did the author for "melodic effect." That is one compelling reason why we

Reprinted from *The Sewanee Review*, 52 (1944), 288-301, by permission of the author and the publisher.

cannot accept a theory like the one offered by Légouis in *Donne the Crafts-man,* that Donne was really writing the old four-stress verse lamented as lost by Gascoigne. It would mean that Donne was more intent on melody than meaning, and was trying to decorate these satires with lilting rhythms. This proposal is a symbol of the despair with which Donne may inspire proso-dists—and there have been many—who believe that only the "normal" foot is "correct." To read Donne as if every foot were an ideal iambic is impos-sible; that is, except by such esoteric methods as reading with "hovering accent," "level stress," or "veiled rhythm:" and these consist in refusing to commit oneself audibly, while enjoying infinitely delicate rhythms within the private recesses of one's own ear. Another symbol of despair is the as-sertion that Donne's only metrical concern was to write ten syllables. But this is to attribute most of his dramatic and rhetorical emphasis to accident rather than to art—a proposition which can hardly be maintained.

The trend of recent criticism has been to emphasize the importance of meaning in determining the metrical structure of Donne's verse. In this respect contemporaries are anticipated by Coleridge and De Quincey. The remarks of Coleridge are better known: that to read Donne you must read "as the sense and passion demand," "with all the force and meaning which are involved in the words;" "you must measure *time,* and discover the time of each word by the sense of passion;" "the sense must be understood in order to ascertain the metre." De Quincey's criticism, also far in advance of his age, has been mentioned less often than it deserves:

> The very first eminent rhetorician in English literature is Donne. Dr. Johnson inconsiderately classes him in company with Cowley & c., under tht title of *Metaphysical* Poets; but Rhetorical would be a more accurate designation. In saying that, however, we must remind our readers that we revert to the original use of the word *rhetoric,* as laying the principal stress upon the management of the thoughts, (the *dispositio*), and only a secondary one upon the ornaments of style, (the *elocutio*).

This emphasis on the rhetoric, on the sense which ascertains the meter, is of course the correct approach, but even here critics have gone astray. George Williamson, in many ways a sensitive critic of Donne, speaks of the intruding "rhythm of prose, accenting the sense and not the sound, to the wrenching of the metrical rhythm." Evidently he regards the prose rhythm as a sort of enemy to the metrical rhythm, "wrenching" it; and he confuses the metrical rhythm with the metrical pattern—a different thing entirely. He has high respect for the sense, especially when it coincides with the sound—by which he means, when the modulation is confined to the slight adjustments within each syllable, and no adjustment is heavy enough to cause a stress-shift. He can even be pleased "when sound is sacrificed a little to sense." But this is the limit of his confidence in the "sense"; for "when, as in the satires, sound is sacrificed almost altogether to sense, he gives us the jarring mon-strosities which even his admirers cannot condone.

Almost all of the modern critics have said eloquent things about the suit-
ability of Donne's rhythm to his state of mind—however, without committing
themselves as to the state of his rhythm, though they have not hesitated to
intrude themselves into the innermost recesses of his mind. His versification
has often been glibly compared with the versification of Jacobean drama,
though no one has evidently thought it worth-while to do more than make
the analogy. Perhaps C. S. Lewis is right when he says that "most modern
readers of poetry do not know how to scan," that "Donne may be metrically
good or bad, in fact; but it is obvious that he might be bad to any degree
without offending the great body of his modern admirers."

Certainly one may find fault with those who in print admire Donne's
poetry, and even his versification, yet think it beneath the dignity of
criticism to indicate, except in the vaguest terms, how a line should read.
Even relatively clear statements concerning Donne's metrical practise
are marred by a critical cautiousness. Take for instance Grierson's remarks—
among the clearest one can find—on the relation between meter and meaning in Donne:

> The wrenching of accent [i.e., metrical stress] which Jonson complained
> of is not entirely due to carelessness or indifference. It has often both a
> rhetorical and a harmonious justification. Donne plays with rhythmical
> effects as with conceits and words.

This is not far from the truth, but how much more convincing it would be
with a few illustrations of stress-shift rhetorically and harmoniously justified! Or take a statement by another good critic of Donne's poetry, Miss Joan
Bennett:

> Often the rhythm is as intricate as the thought and only reveals itself
> when the emphasis has been carefully distributed according to the sense.

Does this mean that Miss Bennett would read Donne's verse solely according
to the sense, as if it were prose? It would seem not, though one may suspect
that this is the practise of many contemporary enthusiasts. Miss Bennett,
however, does not appear to understand or recognize stress-shift by attraction,[1] or otherwise she would never say that the following line is "defective"
and "demands slower reading"—an evasion familiar to temporal prosodists:

> Nor *long* / *beare* this *tor*turing *wrong*
> *A Feaver*, I, 21, 18.

And if she does not understand Donne's use of stress-shift, especially by attraction, how can she—except by concealing her stresses with extra slow
reading—pretend to understand Donne's metrical emphasis?

Poetry is not to be read as prose, solely according to sense; nor as verse,
solely according to meter, regardless of sense. Meter is an important part of
the musical element in poetry, but still this is only one element; and whenever it comes into conflict with sense it is forced to submit, or what is more
accurate, to compromise. The modification of meter to suit the sense actually

improves the rhythmical beauty by furnishing variety and welcome modula-
tions. On the other hand, the meter certainly aids the expression of the
sense, by affording beauty of form, and in the case of a poet like Donne,
added point and emphasis.

Only one conscientious attempt has been made to study the emphasis
which Donne secures by his metrical technique. It is W. F. Melton's *The
Rhetoric of John Donne's Verse*, dedicated to the principle of secondary
accent and the theory of arsis-thesis variation. This is another version of
C. P. Smith's theory by which metrical stress is unvaried—though subtle,
and therefore unrecordable, changes in pitch are allegedly maintained. Melton's ideas may best be illustrated by quoting an example of his scansion:

> Wit*ty* now *wise*, now *tem*pe*rate* now *just*.
> In *good* short *lives*, vir*tues* are *fain* to *trust*
>
> My Muse—for I had one—because I'm cold
> Divorced herself, the cause being in me.

Thus "witty" and "virtues" may receive a stress on the second syllable,
and "herself" and "the" are pronounced according to their place in the
metrical pattern. If it had not been for his theory and "accurate instruction
in regard to the scansion of verse"—Melton's own words—he too "might
have 'hung' Donne, and passed on." Instead, it is plain, he lingers to torture him.

Any theory dependent on the evidence of scansion like this can hardly
be acceptable. And in this respect Melton does much to obscure the real
importance of his arsis-thesis theory, according to which Donne is supposed
to emphasize words and sounds by putting them first in a stressed and then
in an unstressed position. It is truly painful to see all this enthusiastic spend-
thrift labor, and Melton's jubilant exultation is a depressing caution as he
marches after his theory, as if it were a banner, eyes front. His observation
is correct to the extent that Donne often uses the same word or phrase or
sound in what is—according to the basic pattern—now arsis, now thesis. And
the close proximity of these repetitions will naturally cause a sort of reinforcement that produces increased rhetorical emphasis. It is not especially
significant whether the repetitions are in stressed or unstressed places (and
Donne is by no means consistent, even according to the pattern), for internal adjustments of weight, from syllable to syllable, will provide more
variety and subtle emphasis than Melton on his see-saw.

Even Puttenham, who would train young Pegasus to plod foot for foot
in harness with the heavy-paced iamb, recognizes that an exception must
sometimes be made for the sake of emphasis. The remarks that he makes on
this subject are particularly significant, and innocently reveal the shortcom-
ings of his and his contemporaries' prosodic theories. A word "inferring a
subtilitie or wittie implication, ought not to have the same accent as when
he hath no such respect." To illustrate this he provides an example:

> Geve me mine owne and when I do desire,

> Geve others theirs, and nothing that is mine,
> Nor give me that wherto all men aspire.

The unusual emphasis given the first "me," according to Puttenham, is due to its relation with "others." In another illustration,

> *Prove* me (Madame) ere ye *re*prove;
> Meeke minds should *ex*cuse not *ac*cuse

he says that, because of the "extraordinary sence," "it behoveth to remove the sharpe accents from whence they are most naturall, to place them where the nicke may be more expresly discovered."

This is what poets often do, especially those who, like Donne, love fine distinctions. In this respect one may compare another Elizabethan equally fond of quibbles, Shakespeare. A line like the following is by no means unusual:

> Love bade me swear, and Love bids me forswear
> *The Two Gentlemen of Verona*, II, vi, 6.

His sonnets are full of the insistent repetitions Melton has observed in Donne, but these are certainly not ordered into any scheme of arsis-thesis variation. On one occasion Shakespeare has a character repeat the word "legitimate" five times within the space of six lines, always with a different rhythm, squeezing every last drop of implication out of the word. But this serves a special dramatic purpose, for it is the bastard Edmund (*King Lear*, I, ii, 16-21) contemplating his brother Edgar.

This kind of repetition is of course an old rhetorical device. Quintilian discusses it, and quotes Cicero's remark that repetition can produce either grace or strength. Donne's use very seldom resembles that of the lyric poets who so beautifully echo and reecho, yet he can combine both grace and force in a striking repetition:

> If thou stay here. O stay here, for, for thee
> Elegy XVI, I, 112, 43.

More often, however, his repetitions are not so harmonious, nor are they meant to be. One cannot forget his taste for mental dissection, and for turning ideas over and over again, to see them from all aspects. He plays with words, and with sounds, in the same way, afraid to let them go until every slightest implication has been realized. Sometimes the results warrant this insistence on subtlety; at other times he is little short of ridiculous; but the style is a true reflection of his taste and his mind, and if we do not like it we do not like what is characteristic of Donne. Occasionally in his repetitions he may be following rhetorican methods, as in the line,

> All his cloathes, Copes;/Bookes,/Primers; and all[2]
> I, 170, 66.

where he begins and ends with the same word. Or he may repeat a word for greater emphasis:

> Like a Kings favourite, yea like a King
>   I, 152, 70
>   where these
> Meet in one, that one must, as perfect please
>   Elegy II, 1, 80, 10.

Or he may repeat words slightly altered, or used in a different sense:

> All things are *one,* and that *one none* can *be,*
> Since all *formes,* uni*forme* de*formity*
> Doth cover, so that *wee,* except God say
> Another Fiat, shall have no more day.
> So violent, and long th*ese* fur*ies bee,*
> That though thine absence sterve *me,* 'I wish not *thee.*
>   *The Storme,* I, 177, 69-74.

In this passage we may observe the repetition of sounds as well as words.
This too is a characteristic—often an unpleasant one—of Donne's taste, for
he seems to love these jingles and cultivates them with assiduous delight.
But he can nevertheless employ assonance for a deliberate artistic effect,
as in the admirable passage from Elegy XIV:

> But oh her minde, that Orc*us,* which includes
> Leg*ions* of mischiefs, countlesse multitudes
> Of formlesse curses, projects *un*made *up,*
> *A*buses yet *un*fashio*n'*d, thoughts corr*up*t,
> Mishapen Cavils, palp*able un*troths.
> Inevit*a*ble err*ou*rs, self-*a*ccusing oaths;
> These, like those At*om*s swarming in th*e* Su*n*ne,
> Throng in her bos*ome* for creati*on.*
> I bl*u*sh to give her halfe her' due; yet say,
> No poys*on*'s halfe so bad as Iuli*a.*
>   I, 105, 23-32.

But repetition of word, syllable, or sound can become a tiresome device
that defeats its own end and produces monotony rather than emphasis.
Fortunately, Donne does not rely on this technique so much as Melton thinks;
nor does he depend particularly on rhetorical figures, though he uses them
with great skill and aptness. He is most often emphatic by means of a highly
developed metrical technique.

One kind of emphasis may be seen in the famous lines,

> I Wonder by my troth, what thou, and I
> Did, till we lov'd
>   *The good-morrow,* I, 7, 1-2
> For Godsake hold your tongue, and let me love
>   *The Canonization,* I, 14, 1.

Here there are no stress-shifts, though each line uses the iambic form only

as a base for its own rhythms, the while making subtle variations, impossible
to record exactly, within each syllable. Yet the iambic pattern which is implicit in these lines gives them a beauty and a force beyond the reach of
mere prose. It is true that we pronounce these words with their prose accent,
but we nevertheless have the iambic pattern in our heads, and though we
delight in varying it, we will not violate it. And so, we give extra emphasis
to the first syllable of "wonder" and "Godsake," to "hold" and even to
"by"[3]—not distorting our prose accent, but reinforcing it a little with the
metrical stress that happily coincides with the rhetorical emphasis of the
line.

This kind of reinforcement becomes particularly emphatic when one or
two words which are highly important in the context also receive the full
weight of the metrical stress:

> Natures lay Ideot, *I* taught *thee* to love
> > Elegy VII, I, 89, 1
> Richly cloth'd Apes, are *called* Apes, and as soone
> > Elegy XVI, I, 112, 31
> That neither *would,* nor *needs* forbeare, nor stay;
> Neither desires to *be* spar'd, nor to *spare.*
> > *Epithalamion on the Lady Elizabeth,* I, 130, 91-92.
> Whither, why, when, or *with* whom thou wouldst go
> > I, 147, 64
> So to the *most* brave, stoops hee *nigh'st* the ground
> > I, 148, 78
> I bid kill *some* beasts, but no Hecatombs
> > I, 154, 108
> By giving others their soars, *I* might growe
> Guilty, and *he* free
> > I, 163, 135-36.

Nor is this technique limited to a single line or two, for often Donne manipu-
lates the rhythms of a sustained passage in order to increase the emphasis of
certain key-words:

> Are not heavens *joyes* as valiant to asswage
> Lusts, as earths *honour* was to them? Alas,
> As wee do them in *meanes,* shall they surpasse
> Us in the *end,* and shall thy fathers *spirit*
> Meete blinde Philosophers in heaven, whose merit
> Of strict life may be imputed *faith,* and heare
> *Thee,* whom hee taught so easie wayes and neare
> To follow, *damn'd*?
> > I, 154, 8-15.

We now come to the most important part of Donne's metrical rhetoric,
the use of variations, particularly stress-shifts, not for the sake of variety,
but for emphasis. Single stress-shifts have always provided a method of at-

tracting attention, and nothing illustrates so aptly the mutual relationship between meter and meaning. For a stress-shift is determined by the prose accent, which, to prevent distorting either a customary pronunciation or the meaning, refuses to stress a syllable merely because it falls in a stressed position of the ideal pattern. Then this stress-shift, that was determined by the prose accent, assumes the natural emphasis of metrical language, plus the added emphasis of a very distinguished place in the rhythm.[4] Furthermore, the effort required to reverse—in active movement—the flow of a rhythm, necessitates a brief pause to collect energy. This, in physical terms, may be advanced as the explanation of a phenomenon which is both physical and psychological. Naturally such a pause and expression of energy will place added emphasis where it occurs. If, through the strength of the established rhythm, or the resistance of the consonants at the shifting-place, more energy is required, then the longer will the pause be, and the greater the emphasis. And therefore people who read Donne as if he were prose miss almost as much of his point and emphasis as those who try to read him as if each line were composed of five model iambs. Examples in Donne are numerous, from all the periods of his poetry. Here are a few selected at random from the *Satires*:

> And so imprisoned, *and hem'd* in by mee
> > I, 147, 69
>
> But these *pun*ish themselves; the insolence
> > I, 151, 39
>
> Are like the Sunne, *daz*ling, yet plaine to all eyes
> > I, 157, 88
>
> Nor are they Vicars, but *hang*men to Fate
> > I, 157, 92
>
> Goe through the great *cham*ber (why is it hung
> > I, 167, 231
>
> Enough to cloath all the great Carricks Pepper
> > I, 171, 85.

Any other decisive variation from the basic pattern will also call attention to itself, and therefore be emphatic—unless, of course, the reader has grown accustomed to it; and then it will merely provide a refreshing movement in the rhythm. This appears to be partly true of Donne's use of the extra syllable, but not of the pyrrhic followed by a spondee, or of stress-shift by attraction.

This unit of two unstressed syllables followed by two stressed syllables has rhetorical capabilities which are easily apparent. The hammer-blows of two stressed syllables coming together are perfect for strong effects:

> But cor*rupt wormes,* the worthyest men
> > *A Feaver,* I, 21, 12.

They are also useful to drive home an idea:

> Poore *cousened cous*enor, *that* she, and *that thou*
> > *The Second Anniversary,* I, 262, 391.

The contrast between light and heavy syllables provides emphasis:

> I must pay mine, and my forefathers sinne
> To the *last fa*rthing
> > > I, 164, 139
> That *thou* mayest *righ*tly *obey* power, her *bounds know*
> > > I, 158, 100.

But the chief use of this unit in Donne is for cumulative emphasis, in which
the third syllable is stressed more than either of the first two, and the fourth
more than the third:

> > > > nor blesse nor curse
> Openly loves force, nor in *bed fright* thy Nurse
> > > > Elegy XVI, I, 112, 50
> The *men board* them; and *praise,* as they *thinke, well,*
> Their *beau*ties; *they* the mens *wits; Both* are *bought*
> > > > I, 165, 190-1.
> To sleepe, or runne *wrong, is.*   On a huge hill
> > > > I, 157, 79

Unusual though the prosody is, we must certainly admit that it is effective;
and if we do not understand it we cannot hope to appreciate all of Donne's
dramatic emphasis.

In conclusion, we come to Donne's most frequent metrical variation,
and the one by which he secures his most important emphasis—stress-shift
by attraction. If we ignore his use of this device a large number of lines,
including some of his best verse, will make little or no metrical sense. Take
for instance the famous line,

> > > *at* their *best*
> *Sweet*nesse and *wit/, they*'are but *Mum*my, poss*est*
> > > *Loves Alchymie,* I, 40, 24.

Melton would accord full stress to the second syllable of "mummy," making
the line indescribably jingly, and causing the rhythm to rise, like the gallop
of a merry-go-round Pegasus, to exactly the same height. Or what metrical
sense can one make of this line, without recognizing the stress-shifts?—

> *Love* might *make* me leave *lov*ing, *or* might *trie*
> A deeper plague
> > > *Loves Deitie,* I, 54, 24.

The rhythm which is strong enough to attract more than one stress-shift
brings dramatic emphasis, not to a word or two, but to the whole line. And
this is the sort of emphasis particularly well adapted to convey the determined athletic reasoning of Donne's intellect, and the pleasure which it takes

in the exertion of its own strength. In lines like these we recognize the authentic voice of Donne, and once they are scanned they speak for themselves:

> *Wilt* thou *grin* or *fawne* on him, *or* pre*pare*
>   I, 146, 23
> *Sat*an *will* not *joy* at their *sinnes,* as *hee*
>   I, 152, 80
> *Soon*er *may* one *guess*e, who shall *beare* a*way*
>   I, 147, 57
> *Are* they *not* like *sing*ers at *doores* for *meat*
>   I, 150, 22
> *Like* a *wedge* in a *blocke, wring* to the *barre,*
> Bearing-like Asses; and more shamelesse farre
>   I, 152, 71-72.
> *Where* are *those* spred *woods* which *cloth'd* heretofore
> *Those* bought *lands?* not *built,* nor *burnt* within *dore.*
> *Where's* the'old *land*lords *troops,* and *almes?* In great *hals*
>   I, 153, 103-05.

This is the real rhetoric of Donne's verse, requiring no formula or key to understand it, but requiring that the sense guide the prosody, and that the prosody guide the sense.

DONNE'S METRICAL PRACTICE

Michael F. Moloney

Of commentaries upon Donne's prosody there would seem to be no end and of final agreement upon the details of his metrics there would seem to be no hope. Nevertheless, in still another attempt to prove Donne's technical mystery, it may be useful to recall the rather large area of agreement in principle which can now be assumed as undebatable. As opposed to Dryden's implication of a lack of metrical skill the modern student may be certain with Gosse that "what there was to know about prosody was . . . perfectly known to Donne." Most careful readers, too, will accept the essential rightness of Saintsbury's generalization that Donne's poetic manner is not of one piece. Fletcher Melton's thesis-arsis variation principle remains significantly valid despite the injudicious lengths to which it was pushed. Mario Praz has stressed the contrast between the "traditionally poetical and the normally prosiac" in Donne's poetry, and Sir Herbert Grierson has pointed out that historically the "poetic rhetoric" of Donne was continued with characteristic originality by Dryden. Arnold Stein, the most recent contributor to the literature of Donncan prosody, has written with graphic illumination of Donne's use of stress-shift and of his matching of feminine with masculine rime.[1] Concerning elision in Donne's poetry Stein has commented at some length:

> . . . we cannot in a poet like Donne ignore the problem of elision; for from his practice we may conclude that some elidable [sic] combinations are very lightly articulated—these we may leave to the analyst of rhythm— whereas some receive enough stress to be considered extra syllables. Because of the admitted difficulty in scanning many of Donne's lines, it is imperative to distinguish between the elisions that must be taken account of in the prosodic scheme, and those which may be left to the individual reader as part of the rhythmical subtleties which he must ultimately experience for himself.

But, finally, he rejects elision as a major element in Donne's art:

> But, actually, the problem of possible exceptions to elision is not very important so far as the *Satires* are concerned. [Stein bases his study of Donne's prosody primarily on the *Satyres*—"Donne's Prosody," p. 376,

Reprinted by permission of the Modern Language Association of America from *PMLA*, 65 (1950), 232-39.

n. 16.] In almost every case the extra syllables are not combinations subject to elision. And in this respect the *Satires* furnish useful evidence
that Donne did not intend that extra syllables should be elided, no matter
what the damage to rhythm of emphasis.[2]

Contrary to Stein's view, this paper will attempt to show that elision is
one of the most important elements in Donne's prosody and that it cannot
be disregarded without serious damage to a rightful technical understanding
of his poetry. Ultimately the approach here taken has its inception in Robert Bridges' *Milton's Prosody,* and more immediately in Appendix A of
Pierre Legouis'*Donne the Craftsman.* But behind the theories of Bridges
and Legouis lie those curiously challenging pronouncements of Ben Jonson,
Samuel Johnson, and Thomas Gray which must give the student of Donne's
prosody pause. Why should Jonson have said that Donne, "for not keeping
of accent, deserved hanging"? If the commonly accepted scansion of
Donne's poetry is correct, was not the dogmatic Ben straining at the
wrenched accent and swallowing, without demurrer, the violated numbers?
Why should Samuel Johnson have observed that the metaphysical poets
"only wrote verses, and very often such verses as stood the trial of the
finger better than of the ear" when clearly in the commonly accepted scansion they do not stand the "trial of the finger," that is, they are not regularly syllabic? And why should Gray have noted that ". . . Dr. Donne (in his
satires) observes no regularity in the pause, or in the feet of his verse, only
the number of syllables is equal throughout"?
    Obviously, it is not necessary to prove here the Elizabethan and Jacobean
awareness of elision. The heavy weighting of public school and university
curricula with classical studies inevitably brought Englishmen of the sixteenth and seventeenth centuries an intimate knowledge of Greek and Roman
theory and practice. Apart from the classroom there was the formal justification of Campion's *Observations in the Art of English Poesie* and Gabriel
Harvey's *Fourth Letter* as well as Gascoigne's earlier comment on the wide
ranging of "poeticall licence."[3] But perhaps even more important for Donne,
who had been "a great frequenter of plays" in his youth, was the example
of the popular playwrights, notably Shakespeare. All in all, the use of elision
in English poetry was an ancient thing in Donne's time; it had come in with
Chaucer.[4] The problem, then, is to set forth Donne's specific practice and
whatever variations may exist within that practice.[5]
    Close analysis would seem to force the student of Donne's metrics to one
of two conclusions. Either he must view Donne as a poet who, accepting
the basic metrical practice of his age, sought within its framework to achieve
a characteristic freedom and spontaneity; or he must frankly judge him to
have been an uncompromising revolutionary who, rejecting the conventions
of his time, boldly sought to create a new system designed to outrage contemporary sensibilities. Aside from the fact that thoroughgoing revolutions
are much more likely to be led by a Whitman who stood on the cultural

periphery of his epoch than by a Donne who, from his earliest youth, was established in the center of Elizabethan learning, there is convincing evidence that Donne's innovations derive from the first attitude rather than the second. Whether or not he agrees completely with Legouis, the careful reader of the *Songs and Sonets* will soon be convinced that what seems like anarchy on first reading, particularly when approached from the vantage point of Elizabethan song, is not anarchy at all but an effect consciously planned. The reader is jolted to attention by an artful rudeness, the most important element of which is stress-shift in the opening lines of a poem or of a stanza:

> I wonder by my troth, what thou, and I . . .
> Now thou hast lov'd me one whole day . . .
> Blasted with sighs, and surrounded with teares . . .

Yet nearly allied to stress-shift in a rightful understanding of Donne's versification, and contributing largely to the exhilarating shock of stress-shift is, I am convinced, elision. For the effect of stress-shift would be dissipated quickly and certainly were the line length not controlled. And on the other hand, if the line were too mechanically measured, artificiality would result. This is not to say that stress-shift and elision necessarily occur in the same line. Very often they do not. But just as stress-shift breaks up the unvaried beat of the strict iambic line, so elision protests against, while still observing, the unvaried line length of the fixed stanzaic pattern. Both are movements toward freedom, but freedom that is still governed by law.

If the interpretation of Donne's metrics set forth here be correct, Donne not only used elision but he used it variously in different poems, the elisions in the *Songs and Sonets* being quite different in number and character from those in the decasyllabic couplets. It must be insisted that to stress the importance of elision in Donne's prosody is not to reduce the movement of his lines to the "piston-like rise and fall" which Stein fears.[6] Donne's prosody, no more than Milton's, determined the reading of his line.[7] It is an elaborate fiction which gave the poet wide freedom while preventing his verses from falling into chaos. "The prosody is only the means for the great rhythmical effects and is not exposed but rather disguised in the reading."[8]

My scansion of the 1,616 lines of the *Songs and Sonets* identifies 159 unquestionable elisions or 1 to every 10.2 lines. These elisions are distributed as follows:

The good morrow, 3; Song, 1; The undertaking, 2; The Sonne Rising, 3; The Indifferent, 1; Lovers Usury, 3; The Canonization, 4; The triple foole, 1; Lovers infinitenesse, 2; Song, 2; The Legacie, 3; A Feaver, 3; Aire and Angels, 2; Breake of day, 2; The Anniversarie, 3; A Valediction: of my name in the window, 8; Twicknam garden, 2; A Valediction: of the booke, 6; Loves growth, 4; Loves exchange, 7; Confined Love, 1; A Valediction: of weeping, 1; Love's Alchymie, 4; The Curse, 5; A Nocturnall upon S. Lucies day, 4; The Baite, 5; The Apparition, 3; A Valediction: forbidding mourning, 6; *The Extasie*, 10; *Loves-Deitie*, 3; *Loves diet*, 4; *The Will*, 6; *The Funerall*, 7; *The Blossome*, 9; *The Primrose, being at Montgomery Castle*, 8; *The Relique*, 2; *The Dampe*, 2; *The Dissolution*, 2; *A Ieat Ring sent*, 2; *Negative love*, 2; *The Prohibition*, 2; *The Expiration*, 2; *The Computation*, 3; *Farewell to love*, 3; *Sonnet. The Token*, 1.

But in addition to elisions there are 124 speech contractions. Although some of these are true elisions, I have thought it advisable to consider them separately. They are, for the most part, verbal contractions ('twas, I'am, we'are, thou'art), contractions of the solemn forms occurring frequently (thoughtst, lovest, savest, knew'st, goest). (Donne never, I believe, gives syllabic quantity to the solemn endings, although there is no consistency in his spelling, the vowel sometimes being supplied, perhaps more often omitted.) The effect of the speech contractions is very nearly that of the elisions. They contribute as do true elisions to the shattering of the metronomic line beat, but with this important distinction. Whereas the true elisions actually violate the metrical norm, which can then be saved only by an elaborate and often laborious effort on the part of the reader, the speech contractions, for the most part, add weight to the line and impede its facile flow without actually destroying its character. Their overall effect is to rescue Donne's lyric, even when it is most Elizabethan, from the artificial atmosphere of courtly song, and to give it the less rarified music of speech.

The conclusion which I reach after a systematic application to the *Songs and Sonets* of the rules of elision, known and applied by Donne's contemporaries in various degrees and unquestionably practiced by Donne himself to some extent, as the text of his poems indicates, is that the number of metrically irregular lines is actually somewhat fewer than twenty.[9] Surely then the explanation for the characteristic effect of Donne's verse must be sought elsewhere than in a supposed deliberate disregard for metrical law.

The system of elisions utilized in the *Songs and Sonets* was put to even more daring use in the decasyllabic couplets. The following table shows the frequency of occurrence of elisions and speech contractions in the *Satyres*.

	Lines	Elisions	Contractions
Satyre I	112	24	4
Satyre II	112	36	5
Satyre III	110	25	3
Satyre IV	244	55	5
Satyre V	91	27	8
	669	167	25

By comparison with the *Songs and Sonets* several interesting facts emerge. In the *Songs and Sonets* the ratio of elisions to total number of lines was 1 to 10.2; of elisions plus contractions to total number of lines, 1 to 5.73. In the *Satyres* the ratio of elisions to total lines is 1 to 4.00; of elisions plus contractions, 1 to 3.48. Thus Donne uses proportionately two and one-half times as many elisions in the *Satyres*. Although he uses far fewer speech contractions, the number of lines whose metrical regularity is disturbed remains significantly greater in the *Satyres*. But that is not all. The relatively large number of contractions in the *Songs and Sonets* would seem to indicate that Donne in them was rejecting the facility of Elizabethan song but in a manner which would not too greatly perturb his cultivated readers. Even the true elisions in the *Songs and Sonets* are frequently justified by contemporary speech practice: *seaven, heaven, dangerous, being, reverena, business, etc.* Trying elisions such as that in line 17 of *The Primrose* are very rare. But in the *Satyres* Donne's practice approaches license. The multiple and sometimes strained elisions of lines 28, 33, 140, and 144 of *Satyre IV* rob the decasyllabic line of all but a faint and shadowy reality.

From the evidence here set forth, the following conclusions seem justifiable:

1. That elision is a major and continuous practice in Donne's versification.

2. That it is employed in the *Songs and Sonets* deliberately to weight the lines with extra syllables which, being technically elidible, succeed in ballasting the rhythm without destroying it. The elisions of the *Songs and Sonets* are reenforced by closely allied speech contractions. This device enables Donne to maintain the fiction of regular line length, which is essential to his complicated stanzaic patterns, with surprising success.

3. That the elision practiced in the *Satyres* is an accentuation of that utilized in the *Songs and Sonets*. The elisions of the *Satyres* are used more frequently and more daringly. Double and triple elisions in the same line, plus fantastically far-fetched elisions, frequently leave regularity of the line length fictional indeed.

4. That Donne indicated the fictional nature of his metrical regularity in the *Satyres* by deliberately violating the decasyllabic norm on frequent occasions.[10] Such frequent violation was possible in the *Satyres*, where the couplet pattern could not escape the reader's ear, to an extent which would have resulted only in chaos in the multiple stanzaic patterns of the *Songs and Sonets*. Here, too, Donne had the example of Juvenal and Persius, or at least of the renaissance conception of the versification of Juvenal and Persius.

Yet it must be frankly admitted that elision is not the answer to all the problems of Donne's metrical practice. No careful reader can fail to see that some of Donne's most characteristic rhythmic effects are obtained in lines where he does not employ elisions at all. In addition to the lines already quoted consider the following:

> Twice or thrice had I loved thee . . .
> Love, any devil else but you . . .
> Before I sigh my last gaspe, let me breath . . .
> Some man unworthy to be possessor . . .
> Of old or new love himselfe being false or weake . . .

> Are Sunne, Moone or Starres by law forbidden . . .
> Comforted with these few bookes let me lye . . .
> Bright parcell gilt with forty dead mens pay . . .
> Sir; though (I thanke God for it) I do hate . . .

There is no question here of elision, yet the effect seems curiously parallel
to that of elision. What is sought by the poet is greater ease and naturalness,
not by disregarding the linear norm through the introduction of extra
syllables (real or fictional), but by imposing the clear and sometimes conflicting rhythms of prose meaning upon the conventional rhythms of verse.[11]
Donne assuredly knew this device and I have no doubt that dramatic practice had impressed him with its utility.

Here I hazard a provocative suggestion. T. S. Eliot twenty-odd years ago
expressed the then startling opinion that Donne belongs in the main stream
of English poetic tradition.[12] Whether at the time he made that acute critical
judgment Eliot was aware of a possible critical reconciliation of Donne and
Milton I do not know, although his most recent pronouncement on Milton
serves to restore that poet to a position of honor he had formerly denied
him. But that Donne may have been one of Milton's prosodic mentors,
that he may have served as an intermediary between the Elizabethan
dramatists and Milton, seem to me highly possible. I know of only one
direct echo of Donne in Milton.[13] Nevertheless, despite Milton's contemptuous reference to "our late fantastics" there is more than a hint of metaphysical imagery in Milton's early poems.[14] But more significant is the "centroidal grouping"[15] of rhythms which is common to both Donne and Milton.
It is obvious that such lines as the following by Donne do not conform to
an iambic pattern:

> Some man unworthy to be possessor . . .
> O desperate coward, wilt thou seeme bold and . . .
> Even our Ordinance plac'd for our defence . . .
> T'have written than, when you writ seem'd to mee . . .
> All whom warre, dearth, age, agues, tyrannies
> Despaire, law, chance, hath slaine, and you whose eyes . . .
> Thou art slave to Fate, Chance, kings and desperate men . . .
> Father, part of his double interest . . .

The rhythmic effect of these lines is very bold, yet granting, when necessary, the fiction of elision (for elision is frequently an inescapable factor in
the "centroidal grouping"), the lines all submit to decasyllabic limitation.
Still the abruptness here achieved is scarcely more emphatic than that
familiar in Milton. For example, from *Paradise Lost:*

> Thick swarm'd, both on the ground and in the air, [I, 767]
> Powers and Dominions, Deities of Heav'n, [II, 11]
> Alone th' Antagonist of Heav'n, nor less [II, 509]
> Days, months, and years, towards his all-chearing Lamp [III, 581]
> Your military obedience, to dissolve [IV, 955]

> Accompani'd then with his own compleat [V, 352]
> This our high place, our Sanctuarie, our Hill [V, 732]
> Burnt after them to the bottomless pit. [VI, 866]
> Imbu'd, bring to thir sweetness no satietie [VIII, 216]
> Sin opening, who thus now to Death began [X, 234],

The characteristic effect of the lines of both poets may be assigned to stress-shift. But the origins of stress-shift in the cases of both Donne and Milton may not be too far to seek. Early in the English Renaissance Gascoigne had lamented that "our Poemes may justly be called Rithmes, and cannot by any right challenge the name of a Verse,"[16] very likely basing his regret upon Quintilian's distinction between *metrum* and *numerus*. And certain it is that English poetry, from its beginning, with all of its borrowings and indebtedness to other literatures, classical and vernacular, displayed a sturdy independence in matters of form. The August eclogue of the *Shepherd's Calendar*, as Legouis has noted, was a significant foreshadowing. It was inevitable by the nature of the medium in which they worked that the dramatists should take the lead in accommodating poetry to the rhythms of speech, and the progress of dramatic blank verse from the stiff sonority of Marlowe's early plays through the superb flexibility of Shakespeare's late period to the anarchy of Fletcher is a commonplace. Donne, too, was concerned with the same problem, and much that is puzzling in his rhythms is best understood when approached from the vantage-point of contemporary drama. The metrical practice in the lines of Donne (and of Milton) which we have been considering is not basically different from that of such lines as these of the early Shakespeare:

> Lord of the wide world and wild watery seas [*C. of E.*, II, i, 21]
> And little mouse, every unworthy thing. [*R. & J.*, III, iii, 31]
> That shall she, marry; I remember it well. [*R. & J.*, I, iii, 22]
> One half of me is yours, the other half yours, [*M. of V.*, III, ii, 16]
> His tedious measures with the unbated fire, [*M. of V.*, II, vi, 11]

Donne did not follow Shakespeare into the late hypermetrical vagaries which, magnificently as Shakespeare marshalled them, point to rhythmic dissolution. The innovations to be found in his poetry are doubtless there by deliberate intention, but the revolution was achieved by most unrevolutionary means. The most significant technical features of Donne's verse are the consistent employment of elision and the consistent rejection of a fixed iambic rhythm through the utilization of stress-shift. With regard to the first he was no more revolutionary than Milton, if the greatest critic of Miltonic prosody be correct. With regard to the second, he had ample lyric and dramatic precedent. Indeed, unless Shakespeare and Milton are revolutionary, Donne was of the centre not eccentric.

AN EXAMINATION OF SOME CLAIMS FOR RAMISM

A. J. Smith

It was perhaps with a sense—certainly justified—that the old clever nostrums of 'Metaphysical' criticism had had their day, that scholars welcomed in 1947 the revolutionary evidence concerning the effects of sixteenth-century rhetoric massively presented by Professor Tuve in her *Elizabethan and Metaphysical Imagery*. Other American voices, of great authority, had then been urging for some time the general literary importance of this or that aspect of the contemporary academic disciplines. In these writings one name recurs as likely to be of prime moment, that of the inaugurator of certain reforms in the organization of the disciplines, Peter Ramus. The Bartholomew martyr Ramus, thus resurrected with his disciple Talaeus and his devoted English following from his centuries of obscurity, is provided with a mighty progeny, if a posthumous one. We are told that we may hail him as a father of science, as the dispeller of frothy rhetoric, as the very matrix of the Metaphysical style. Ramus, declares Professor Hardin Craig, turned what had been in great part a theoretical science into a practical art; and his logic was a general force in the direction of the advancement of science.[1] Professor Perry Miller finds that it was the 'inescapable tendency' of Ramism towards the divorce of thought from expression, content from style, which brought on the plain, toughly logical manner of preaching and the Puritan contempt for rhetoric, compelling poets to replace ornamental figures with knotty dialectical manœuvrings.[2] For Miss Tuve, most detailed and, to the literary student, most important of these commentators, Ramism provides a satisfactory explanation not only of certain major elements in so-called 'Metaphysical' poetry, but even of the very thought processes of the greatest 'Metaphysical' poet, Donne.[3] Yet, to turn to the work of the writers for whom these tremendous claims are made is to be disappointed, almost shocked. The cause they so fiercely championed seems, to the ordinary eye at least, much as it has seemed to the intervening centuries, puny, and dead.

Miss Tuve's chief arguments are briefly these:

> (i) The Ramists brought logic and poetry into a peculiarly close relationship; so close, in fact, that for their disciples no distinction was possible between poetry and dialectic. After Ramus, the poet was to be

Reprinted from *Review of English Studies*, n. s. 7 (1956), 348-59, by permission of the author and The Clarendon Press, Oxford.

dialectician; and his imagery was to be dialectically functional as argument—'Decorative images would not be a desideratum, they would scarcely by a possibility'. These doctrines were powerfully urged by the Ramist method of illustrating the places and functions of logic from all the various types of writing, including poetry.

(ii) As a result of Ramus's readjustment of the traditional relationship of logic and rhetoric, whereby *Invention* and *Disposition* were to be taught by the logician alone, and only *Eloquence* by the rhetorician, the 'rhetor', or the poet, would be a logician *'in the first stages of composition'*.

(iii) 'The old separation between demonstrative and deliberative "orations"' had gone 'into the discard, and with it the conception it preserved of different structures and ornament for differing purposes, in lyrics.' These old demonstrative and deliberative intentions 'pretty well cover the lyrical output of earlier years'; but after Ramus all pieces were to have, alike, 'a dialectical base'.

(iv) The omission of the discussion of special types of oration from the bare Ramist handbooks amounts to a denial that there could be differing functions of oratory needing differing methods. The orator or other writer is now impelled to 'declare reasons and causes, to examine the nature of something, to consider from various sides, to figure out, look into, mull over'. This is 'precisely what most Metaphysical poems do', and the process is bound to be accompanied by the 'deliberate use of intellectually acute and strong images'. One 'comes out with the description of a Metaphysical poem' if one adds to this two more Ramist concepts: (*a*) dialectically sound statements 'prove', that is, 'argue the truth or advisability of something': (*b*) 'images (tropes, concretions, metaphorical epithets, descriptions, definitions) are "arguments"'.

(v) The result of the notion that images are 'arguments' was that 'The nature of their terms might range from the most subtle of abstractions to the most ordinary of daily objects', and that their chief characteristics would include subtlety, logical power, ingenious or startingly precise relationships or parallels, 'a certain "obscurity" due to logical complexity or tenuous attachment—but an obscurity capable of becoming sharp "clarity" upon thoughtful reading'.

One would be happy to augment with such weighty authority one's own conviction that Donne's processes of thought are better explained by the intellectual conditions of his own day than by 'any of the current popular phrases about "feeling his thought"'. But the traditional teaching explains much; and even preliminary scrutiny in the light of that teaching indicates that these large claims for Ramism are not all justified.

Ramism. One has to search hard in sixteenth-century English literature to find any considerable mention of Ramus and Ramism.[4] Ascham, in his *Scholemaster,* curtly dismissed Ramus and his henchman Talaeus. The proselytizing Ramist Abraham Fraunce claimed that he had interested Sid-

ney in the movement.[5] In 1576 de Banos dedicated his life of Ramus to
Sidney, remarking that Sidney 'not only loved Ramus as a father when
alive, but esteemed and reverenced him after death'.[6] That Sidney's interest
in Ramus continued is suggested by William Temple's dedication to him in
1584 of his *P. Rami Dialecticae Libri duo.* Temple afterwards became Sidney's secretary. Marlowe gave Ramus, notable victim, and Talaeus, a brief
scene in *The Massacre at Paris*: that is, in an event which took place when
Talaeus had been dead for twenty years. A number of obscure Puritans,
forerunners of one less obscure, John Milton, produced translations or
expositions of Ramus—Dudley Fenner, 'M.R.M. Scotum', 'R.F.', Alexander
Richardson. Cambridge, indeed, is assumed to have welcomed the Ramist
reorganization of rhetoric and logic; and this seems possible by reason
both of the Cambridge connexions of several of the names quoted and of
the undoubted fact that Gabriel Harvey was publicly advocating the reform
there in the mid fifteen-seventies.[7] But if, as is said, Ramist innovations had
so far ousted traditional teaching by the beginning of the new century that
they could be certainly counted as influences on later writers, how curiously
anomalous was the experience of that Ramist writer who in 1632 spoke of
the suppression of a first volume of translation from Ramus, and of the
'storms of reproch and ignomie' that he expected for his new one![8]

The typical Ramist logic or rhetoric might have a good deal of disputatious matter on the nature of an Art, and the imperfections of its assailants,
but the characteristic of its didactic section was brevity. Only a skeleton
system was given. In the logics *Invention* and *Disposition* were ruthlessly
abridged, and explained with little more than a few illustrations from popular classical authors, or from the Scriptures. The Rhetorics of Talaeus and
Fraunce, shorn by Ramus's decree of *Invention* and *Disposition,* treat only
the schemes and tropes, and their authors proceed in the same stark fashion
as the logicians, merely giving the figure with the briefest of descriptions
and illustrations. The removal of the first two parts of traditional rhetoric
was another economy, recognized as artificial. *Invention* and *Disposition*
were to belong 'not to Rhetorike for doctrine, but onely for use' as Alexander Richardson revealingly put it.[9]

These peculiarities of the Ramist system are explained by two circumstances. Firstly, there is Ramus's notion of what constitutes an Art—it is
simply a body of precepts properly organized and systematized in good
teaching order, 'a Methodicall disposition of true and coherent precepts,
for the more easie perceiving and better remembring of the same'.[10] This
notion issued in three fundamental axioms or *Documents.* I quote them
from the translation of 'M.R.M. Scotum':

> . . . three generall documentes to be observed in all artes and sciences.
> The first is that all the preceptes and rules should be generall and of
> necessitie true: and this is called a documente of veritie: The seconde
> that every arte be contained within his owne boundes, and witholde
> nothing appartaining to other artes, and is named a documente of

iustice. The third, that every thing be taught according to his nature, that is: generall thinges generally: and particuler, particulerly: and this is called a documente of wysdome.[11]

The consistent application of these principles throughout the teaching of any Art was what the Ramists meant by a second canon, *Method*—the reduction of all Arts to their bare and proper essentials for convenient teaching and the treatment of general matters before particular, in the orderly disposing of the single discourse as much as in the whole educational system.

Logic and rhetoric were thus general Arts. Logic, indeed, gave *Method* to all the others, as 'the Art of Arts, the instrument of instrumentes, the hand of Philosophie'.[12] Hence it would have been improper—an offence against the Document of Wisdom—for logic and rhetoric to pursue the aim of any one particular art, while on the other hand they were necessarily manifested in all particular arts. Despite occasional definitions of logic as *ars bene disserere*, the traditionalist bias towards the teaching of practical polemics was on the whole absent from Ramist systems, not because Ramists did not favour polemics but because teachers of general Arts had no business with them: 'Disserere, docere, disputare, are rather particular functions of Methode, than general operations of the whole art.'[13] This, and not any theory about the methods of writing, or wish to reform writing, was the reason for the frequent protestations that logic was the property of all reasoning men, disputants and non-disputants alike. It was the reason, too, for the choice of illustrative material from popular literature which was obviously not written for the purpose of demonstration—'Now Logicke is a general Art, *ergo* it is best to fetch examples out of Poetry, &c which belongs to Rhetoricke a generall art.'[14]

As with logic, so with rhetoric: 'for Rhetorick is a generall arte, *ergo* it may be everie where'.[15] Particular Arts, such as oratory and writing, could not be a peculiar concern of rhetoric, and that great discipline was reduced to a trivial art of titivation, its task merely the making of any discourse eloquent. The features of oratory formerly taught by rhetoricians under *Invention* and *Disposition* were necessarily excluded. No account was given now of devices of persuasion, or of the use of the places of logic in the various kinds of oration. But these were purely formal changes. Ramists did not question the traditional notion that the orator is a popular persuader, who needs his own less stringent types of proof 'to leade the people, viz. the beast like heads of the multitude'.[16] 'The Orators attribute all to victory. Therefore this seemeth to be placed chiefly by them not so much to teach as to persuade'.[17] And although logical *Disposition* could not treat of the types of the oration, as did the *Disposition* of traditional rhetoric, the Ramists manifestly continued to think of oratorical functions in terms of these traditional types and the methods and places associated with them. 'Explications, illustrations, amplifications, and extenuations are set from this place', says Fraunce of *Subject*:[18] and of *Adjunct* even more significant-ly:

Here are also set prayses and disprayses, deliberations and consulta-
tions. Herein are contained also all those Rhetoricall places concerning
the giftes and qualities of body and soul, as also externall and those of
fortune.[19]

Ramus himself had pointed out in an aside on *Etimologie* that 'the use then
of this place is, to prove or disprove, prayse or disprayse any thing by the
Etimologie of it'.[20] These, the special functions of the traditional oratorical
types, had obviously not gone 'into the discard' for him.

What the Ramists did say under *Disposition* was very general. They
plainly relied, as in other places, on a knowledge of the traditional systems,
cavilling only because traditionalist rhetoricians taught them as their own
—'it doth not follow, that because the Rhetorician useth disposition, *ergo*
it belongs to Rhetorike'.[21] The principle of rhetorical decorum is admitted—
'As brevity is commended in a perfect definition, so copious amplification
is fitted for a description: yet so as swelling superfluitie bee alwayes
avoyded.'[22] And the reader may be incidentally referred, though in very
general terms, to kinds of oratory taught only in traditional rhetoric:

> It shall be sufficient for us to follow a more easie and elegant kinde
> of disputation [than a speech to formal rules of axioms, syllogisms, and
> the rest] joyning Rhetorike with Logike, and referring that precise
> straitnesse unto Philosophical exercises.[23]

There was no hint of any intention of replacing the traditional types of discourse with some one form, or of teaching a detailed method of discourse
at all.

The figures of rhetoric, no longer devices of persuasion, were useful only
as general helps in any kind of discourse, that is, as embellishment and
garnishment, 'a certeine decking of speech, whereby the usual and simple
fashion thereof is altered and changed to that which is more elegant and con-
ceipted'.[24] Rhetoric lost at once the many figures which had been quite
explicitly tactics of disputation, and the traditional notion that style is an
important article of persuasion. 'Now whatsoever hath affection to argue,
that belongs to Logike.'[25] The probatory use of the similitude and its
fellows went therefore to logic alone. But the few mentions of them that
the Ramist reader would have found there were most unpractical compared
with the instructions for the use of all the techniques of comparison in, say,
The Rule of Reason, or *The Art of Reason, rightly termed Witcraft,* bare
statements of the traditional view that things could be compared 'from the
less, the aequall, and the more', with a number of quite unargumentative
similies from *The Shepheardes Calender,* or some such, forced in as illustration. This really conveyed no notion at all of the use of analogy and simile
in persuasion and proof, any more than it indicated the necessary traditionalist distinction between these popular arguments 'by example' and the
strict syllogistic argument 'by rule'. So little were the Ramists concerned
with particular practice.

The Ramists, then, had no new notion of style to put forward. All that was now remarkable was that the orator was to receive no special instruction from the rhetorician; that his methods were admitted, but never described in detail; and that if the 'proofs' formerly held to be popular, and proper to the orator's art, were treated at all, their impropriety for any other form of discourse was never indicated, nor were they distinguished practically from the more legitimate forms of proof. Practical interests were rigidly subordinated to strict theoretical consistency.

Ramus and verse. The Ramists had little to say of verse. They used poetic fragments, with other popular writings, to illustrate logical relations and arguments. Occasionally, though always incidentally, they revealed their views in direct comment. Miss Tuve has attempted to infer Ramus's intention concerning poetry from the Ramist habit of illustration. Explicit avowal and open show of opinion would surely be a more reliable guide, particularly since the views inferred are said to have been startlingly new.

The Ramists used verse and other writings as illustrative material because, as Richardson tells us,

> Logicke being a general Art, it is therefore best to fetch his examples out of the most common and general writers, as out of Poets and Historians, which the Gentiles and Turkes may receive, these being more generally knowne to the worlde, then are the Scriptures.[26]

Poetry was to be taken in preference to anything else because it is 'more generally knowne to the world'. The aim professed was not, as Miss Tuve asserts, to establish an especially close relationship between verse and dialectic, but merely to illustrate in the most persuasive manner the dictum that Logic is a general Art. It was the strength of the Ramists' case that they could show all the logical relationships in the writing not of logicians or metaphysicians, but of non-technical reasonable men—writing which was not produced for the purpose but already existing and popular, such as the *Metamorphoses* and *The Shepheardes Calender* and the *Arcadia*. With Rhetoric, too, their aim was to prove that it was a general and not specifically a persuasive art; and accordingly all illustrations of the Schemes and Tropes were drawn from the most popular literature.

When Miss Tuve claims that the stream of Ramist illustration is sufficient to convince 'even the twentieth-century reader' that poetry and logic cannot 'be kept in separate compartments', she appears to have failed to distinguish between senses of the word 'logic'. It is not too much to say that this claim, with as much of her argument as depends upon it, is the product of linguistic confusion. 'Traditional' logic as it is now commonly understood, and as Miss Tuve plainly understands it, is the art of dialectics. As it was taught in the sixteenth century, however, logic was primarily analytic, the art whose concern was first and foremost the classification of matter according to the traditional Aristotelian categories, and only after that the disposition of the classified matter in mode of proof. When Ramists said that all reasonable discourse is necessarily logical, they meant simply that all writing must be about things—must refer to matter and its interrelationships: that all good writing will be well ordered; and that when, occasionally, discourse involves inference, the forms of inference will be found to be reducible to syllogistic moods. They certainly did not mean that all discourse must be argumentative, or full of tough reasoning processes and techniques of proof. On the contrary, embellishments and ornaments of style, without any argumentative function at all, would on this broad view of logic be thoroughly logical, since they all refer to matter and the relationships of matter.

Miss Tuve's claim for Ramist illustration is in fact merely a truism. Not only Donne, but all the world's poets, have filled their verse with logic, in the sixteenth-century sense of that word. The verse illustration themselves are insignificant; and in Ramus, indeed, only a small part of a body of quotation taken from a variety of sources, including the Scriptures and classical prose-writers. Here are a few such from Fraunce's *Lawiers Logike,* a work in which *The Shepheardes Calender* is used to demonstrate the features of logic:

(*Cause . . . Procreant*). Pan may bee proud that ever he begot such a bellibone. April.

(*Material*). So in August *Willy* sheweth what matter his cup was made of, thus

> Then lo, *Perigot,* the plege which I plight,
> A mazer ywrought of the maple warre.

(*Of the whole, part, generall, speciall*). *Morell* in July, to enforce the general commendation of hils, bringeth in special examples, as Saint Michaels mount . . . &c.

(*Of the Adiunct*). In August Perigot describeth his bouncing Bellibone by hir attire.

(*Disparates*).   Bring here the Pincke and purple Cullambine
> With Gelliflowres
> Bring Coronations, and sops in wine,
> Worne of paramours:
> Strow me the ground with Daffadowndillyes
> And Cowslyps, and Kingcups, and loved Lillyes
> The pretty Paunce
> And the Chevisaunce,
> Shall match with the fair Flowredelice.

All which herbes bee equally differing one from another, and are therefore Disparates.

(*Axioms.* Compound; congregative; copulative). *Thomalyn* in July.
> But shepheard mought be meeke and milde,
> well eyed, as *Argus* was.

(Segregative, hypothetical disjunctive). In September.

> *Diggon Davy* I bid her good day,
> Or *Diggon* her is, or I missay.

(*Syllogisme* . . . Second kinde. Proper affirmative).

> Ferio. O blessed sheepe, O shepheard great,
>   that bought his flocke so deare
> And them did save with bloody sweat,
>   from wolves that would them teare.

> Fe The great God Pan saved his flock with bloody sweat,
> ri Christ is the great God Pan.
> o   Therefore Christ saved his flocke with bloody sweate.[27]

'Surelie', says Stupido, pointedly named, in the St. John's play *The Pilgrimage to Parnassus*, 'Surelie in my . . . simple opinion, Mr. Peter maketh all things verie plaine and easie.'[28] This is plainly not writing for men already trained in the academic disciplines. It is beginners' stuff, and its purpose is at once to show the unschooled that logic is, simply, a necessity of all coherent discourse, and to display the categories and forms of logic in the form most easily remembered by them. In these crude Ramist illustrations the only form that the contemporary poet is not likely to have used habitually all his mature life is the one piece of pure logic, that Aristotelian quiddity, the syllogism. One need not ascribe to him a belief that syllogism is not proper to poetry. Fraunce's painful attempts to scrape examples of the syllogistic modes from quite unargumentative lines sufficiently demonstrate its intractability. But it has to be remembered, in fairness to the Ramists, that their system was not intended to revolutionize poetry, only to reform teaching—their concern was the best method of teaching their twin subjects, and to that end alone they reorganized them. Their writings seem naïve almost beyond belief if they are read in expectation of the revolutionary designs and reforms Miss Tuve attributes to Ramists at large, designs they never had and 'reforms' which were commonplaces. Yet without doubt such specimens as those quoted answered admirably the humbler purpose proposed.

Ramists did not concern themselves to parade their views about verse, but occasional side-references indicate only acceptance of traditional teaching and current notions. Poetry was still an offshoot of Rhetoric—'Poetry . . . which belongs to Rhetorike';[29] and poets, like Orators, were allowed still a laxity improper in more learned Arts, being 'not bound so strictly to observe the perfection of the first methode'.[30] They were feigners, teaching 'notable truths' by such Allegories as the story of Dido and Aeneas, and the fables of Aesop:

> Now the Poets fall into many figments, but they meane thereby things, and so they belong to some speciall Arts: and all *Esops* Fables, and other fables, are but Allegories belonging to natural Philosophy, or to morall Philosophy.[31]

They were makers of sweet sounds, fine writers rather than sober and grave ones, by some patronized, by others held in contempt:

> . . . and thus much of garnishings of speache by the measure of soundes, rather to give some taste of the same to the Readers, then to drawe any to the curious and unnecessarie practise of it.[32]

Even in Fraunce, the admirer of Spenser, one can detect the common note—verse is pleasant, but trivial:

> Mary, quoth hee, thease fine University men have beene trained up in such easie, elegant, conceipted, nice, and delicate learning, that they can better make new-found verses of Amyntas death, and popular discourses of Ensignes, Armory Emblems, Hieroglyphikes, and Italian Impreses, than apply their heads to the study of the Law, which is hard, harsh, unpleasant, unsavoury, rude and barbarous.[33]

Fraunce concludes his *Lawiers Logike* with the usual formal demonstration that the best authors in prose and verse have always observed strict method, on this occasion a tabular analysis of Virgil's Second Eclogue. His inconsistency would be monumental if he had been advocating revolutionary courses, for he carries into it all the notions about the aims and methods of oratory which had been current at any rate in the previous sixty years.

Like so much else in sixteenth-century writing, Ramist logic is too easily praised for innovations not its own, common notions and the traditional doctrines of rhetoricians. Mr. Miller's account of the effects of Ramism fatally ignores traditionalist teaching. The 'inescapable tendency' he detects to 'divorce thought from expression, to dissever content from style' was inescapable only because it was the common assumption throughout the sixteenth century. Unless Mr. Miller means to imply that all non-Ramist writers subscribed to a Bradleian theory of the unity of thought and expression, he is surely saying no more than that the Ramist writer could control the number and quality of figures used in discourse, as others could not—'he was committed to working out his sermon structure in terms of logic, and only thereafter going over his work to punctuate it with tropes or to cast sentences into schemes'. But the traditional system of the three styles depended largely upon this very ability, more figures to be added for one purpose, most to be taken away for another:

> . . . thei be not partes of the matter, but eyther may be taken out, or quite left of:[34]

Careful analyses of bare structures, and continual reminders that 'arguments' were to be drawn from the places of logic, were in fact characteristic of non-Ramist works. In any event, it is difficult to see why it should be expected that a concentration on the handling of schemes and tropes would produce a total excision of all figurative embellishment. The opposite seems as likely, stylistic aberrations deriving from an excessive use of figures.

Miss Tuve's great claims, so powerfully urged, have no more substance.

Ramus and the Ramists were not arguing or intending to argue that poetry and dialectic are the same, and their ends the same; indeed, to have maintained such a position would have been a denial of their fundamental tenets. The 'Ramist idea of a Unity of Arts of thought', which helps Miss Tuve to the discovery of the identity, is not readily discoverable in Ramus or the Ramists, unless it be revealed in such commonplace references as this:

Q. *Shew the force of this example.*
A. Art is the genus, Poesie and eloquence the species.[35]

It was, moreover, no innovation of Ramus's that the rhetorician was to be a logician 'in the first stage of composition'. This was the merest commonplace of traditional rhetoric:

Therefore, I wishe that every manne should desire and seke to have his Logique perfect, before he looke to profite in Rhetorique, considering the grounde and confirmation of causes, is for the moste part gathered out of Logique.[36]

The Ramists did not put the *Demonstrative* and *Deliberative* types of oration 'into the discard', any more than they put the important *Judicial* type (which Miss Tuve has been obliged to ignore) 'into the discard'. They simply held that it was not the business of the logician or rhetorician to teach particular functions.

The particular functions of discussion of philosophical and ontological problems, 'figuring out', looking into, and mulling over, were not mentioned by the Ramists, let alone taught. The writer would have needed to go to traditional accounts of the *Judicial* oration for general instruction in such procedures. As for the claim that the Ramists sought to make these the methods of poetry, it is doubly untenable, for the reason stated, and because Ramists were quite unconcerned with the writing of verse, tamely acquiescing in traditionalist unwillingness to allow it any more than popular status. Miss Tuve has here overlaid and distorted the slight truth that Ramus tended to free logic and rhetoric from thraldom to the particular functions of polemics and persuasion.

The 'image' (presumably 'figure' is meant) was not rendered 'dialectically functional' by Ramism, if this phrase means 'having a function in proof, argument, or persuasion', and not just 'being locally classifiable as a meaning in a context'. The figure was actually less likely to be so in Ramist writers than in traditionalist, for readers of Ramus would have learned only incidentally and fragmentarily—or from other sources—of the use of figures as devices of persuasion or argument. Correspondingly, it cannot be true that with Ramists 'Decorative images would not be a desideratum; they would indeed scarcely be a possibility', or that 'Images would be many, and oftener tropical than schematic'. Decoration for delight was the only function specifically assigned to figures in Ramist manuals, and in so far as the Ramist writer's occasions of stylistic delight were likely to be less frequent than the traditionalist's occasions of persuasion or proof, Ramism must have issued in a somewhat less frequent use of figures among its devotees, not more.

The conclusion is inescapable that altogether too much has been made of the attempt at reform in teaching method called Ramism, in itself and as an influence. But this does not mean that Donne criticism would do well to fall back on its old formulas, those empty catchwords Miss Tuve herself has so ably scouted, the 'emotional apprehension of thought', 'discordia concors', 'passionate thought and thoughtful passion', 'radical image', and the rest. It does mean that for the true explanation of 'Metaphysical' qualities and techniques one need seek no farther than the great sixteenth-century tradition of which Ramism was but a backwater—that of *wit* as it was developed in conventional rhetoric.

THE RHETORIC IN THE POETRY OF JOHN DONNE

Thomas O. Sloan

The terms which the New Critics have applied to Donne's poetry would gladden the heart of any rhetorician in search of literary sanction: "discursive," "argumentative," "disputatious," "dialectical," "having the look of logic." But the New Critics rarely, if ever, lose sight of the fact that the subject of their analysis is literary rather than oratorical in nature and that consequently it contains a range of potential experience beyond its rhetorical foundations. However, by focussing solely on the rhetoric in poetry, this discussion seeks to discover what value there may be in analyzing Donne's poems by means of a specific Renaissance rhetorical theory.

In New Criticism there are as many different approaches to literary analysis as there are schools of New Critics, so that it is easier to characterize New Criticism in terms of its attitude toward literature than it is to describe it in terms of its methods of analysis. And this attitude is that what is analyzable in a poem is its rhetoric: the analytical concern of New Criticism is a concern with the persuasion-situation, or dramatic situation, of a poem and with the poem's modes of expression, its form.[1] This search for the more-or-less objective principles of communication in a poem we would call a rhetorical concern if we permit rhetoric to have its traditional meaning, as the art of giving public form to private convictions. Although throughout its history rhetoric has at times absorbed the art of poetry and at other times vigorously excluded it, rhetoric nonetheless has an ancient claim on the process whereby ideas are made *intelligible* and *attractive* to experts and laymen alike.[2]

Furthermore, there is historical justification for a rhetorical analysis of Donne's poetry. The popularity and the pervasiveness of rhetoric in the English Renaissance are well known. There is no need to review the history of Renaissance rhetoric or to explore in detail its close connection with logic.[3] But it is necessary to note that the most important rhetorical system during Donne's formative and productive years was little more than a reorganization of traditional theories of logic and rhetoric. Renaissance logic consisted of two procedures, *invention* and *judgment* (or, as it was sometimes called, *disposition*), which closely resembled the first two of the five traditional divisions of rhetoric (*invention,* finding the thought; *disposition,*

Reprinted from *Studies in English Literature*, 3 (1963), 31–44, by permission of the author and the publisher.

arranging material in a discourse; *elocution,* style; *memory*; and *pronunci-ation,* oral delivery). It was partly a concern with the overlapping and dupli-cation of precepts in logic and rhetoric that caused Peter Ramus to attempt to separate the two disciplines, but Ramus and his followers separated them in a way that made logic and rhetoric inseparable: they merely took inven-tion and disposition away from rhetoric and told poets and orators that they would henceforth find these two procedures in logic only; this left rhetoric with only elocution and pronunciation, since in the Ramist system memory was not seen as a distinct division. Ramist logic (invention and disposition) was meant to be useful alike to poets, orators, historiographers, and philosophers, for to the Ramists the modes of proof were always actual, regardless of the type of discourse in which they were employed.[4] When Ramist rhetoric (elocution and pronunciation) is added to the logic, one has a systematized treatment of four of the traditional five divisions of rhetoric. In their textbooks and in their treatises on pedagogical theory, the Ramists indicated that their newly reorganized system of invention, disposi-tion, elocution, and pronunciation was intended for the "genesis" as well as for the "analysis" of all types of discourse.[5] The system was designed to serve the functions both of a complete logic and of a complete rhetoric. Because of its emphasis on the "logical" part of the creative process (inven-tion and disposition), the Ramist system accorded well with the late six-teenth-century anti-euphuistic spirit in England, which decried excesses of style and mannered speech, and with the growing humanist exaltation of "natural reason."[6] Moreover, because Ramist analysis tends to regard the poem or speech or treatise as an artifact independent of the sensibilities of either its creator or its hearer, concentrates on its form, and seeks to show forth its principles of composition, it is similar to much modern literary analysis.

In short, the analysis of Donne's poetry by means of Ramist invention, disposition, and elocution has historical justification and it could have modern meaningfulness. But what is involved in such an analysis? And what should one see when he uses these points of view?

Rosemond Tuve has observed that in his poetry Donne makes use of many "places" of invention.[7] But analyzing with the places of invention is very difficult, and after the analysis one would find he could do little more than observe that Donne uses many places of invention. However, the theory of invention does shed an interesting light on Donne's poetry by bringing into account a seldom-discussed aspect of Donne's mode of argumentation.

Invention, according to Abraham Fraunce, is that art which "helpeth to inuent argumentes."[8] Noting that "'Argument' is a special, technical word in Ramist writings," Rosemond Tuve states, "The best I can do with it is to say that it seems to indicate the relatable*ness* of a word or thing; that as-pect by which we conceive of it as relatable to another word or thing."[9] This meaning of "argument" is, of course, not peculiarly Ramist; it is typical of a period in which the concepts of man as microcosm and of the great chain of being provided a pattern within which "natural reason" could evolve true relationships and correspondences. It is certainly the meaning of "Argument" in the following passage from Donne: In describing the illness which inspired his *Devotions* Donne wrote,

> I am *up*, and I seem to *stand*, and I goe *round*; and I am a new *Argument* of the new *Philosophie*, That the Earth moves round; why may I not beleeve, that the *whole earth* moves in a *round motion*, though that seeme to me to *stand*, when as I seeme to *stand* to my *Company* and yet am carried, in a giddy, and *circular motion*, as I *stand*?[10]

Invention was a means of systematic investigation by which arguments could be produced. Reason guided by the places of arguments could rapidly invent all the matters which each word or thing argues. For example, to form concepts of man one may consider that his *efficient cause* is God, his *material cause* is his body, his *formal cause* is his soul, his *final cause* is God's glory, his *effects* are his actions, and so on.[11] Man argues all these, and all these are part of his true relationships within a known and knowable order.

One may go *almost* so far as to state that Donne believed a proposition was established if it could be proved by means of similitudes—that is, if its existence could be tested or experienced by drawing conclusions from demonstrable relationships. If one thing is true or exists, a similar thing could be true or could exist; the construction of the demonstration requires axioms which relate the two things—the known with the unknown, or the familiar with the unfamiliar—in terms of their causes, effects, subjects, or adjuncts. But one may go only *almost* so far as to say that this process is true of Donne's argumentation, for to state this categorically would be to assign to Donne's argumentation the sort of cogency the modern reader would find in the following demonstration from Francesco Sizzi's *Dianoia Astronomica* (Venice, 1611):

> There are seven windows given to animals in the domicile of the head ... two nostrils, two eyes, two ears, and a mouth. So in the heavens ... there are two favourable stars, two unpropitious, two luminaries, and Mercury undecided and indifferent. From this and many other similarities in nature ... we gather that the number of planets is necessarily seven.[12]

Even though we may not expect poetry to meet strict rational requirements, we know that Donne's argumentation is deeper, more complex, and usually more convincing than this. But the habits of thought underlying his argumentation and Sizzi's are not at all dissimilar. Perhaps it was in jest that Donne made the following statement; perhaps at the same time it was also a justification for the logical seizures which he makes upon the mind with the armament of comparatives:

> If all things be in all,
> As I thinke, since all, which were, are, and shall
> Bee, be made of the same elements:

Each thing, each thing implyes or represents.

(Satyre V. 9–12)

Thus, in *The Dissolution* one dissolution implies another, for the dead and the seeming dead are alike in *material causes*; the *effect* of one death and dissolution implies the *effect* of the other. Or the procedure may be employed for amusingly bitter purposes, as in *Communitie*, where because we may neither hate nor love all women, they therefore belong to the class "indifferent," and a similitude between them and fruit is merely an exhibition of class characteristics. Or the procedure may be reversed, as in *A Nocturnall Upon S. Lucies Day,* where the denial of the comparison between his "properties" and those of "all" (man, beast, plants, stones), and even between his properties and those of "an ordinary nothing," proves his being "Of the first nothing, the Elixer grown."

As a concept underlying the use Donne makes of invention, relatability shares importance with a second concept: visibility. Actually, the belief in the persuasive efficacy of helping the mind apperceive thought by means of visual imagery united the factors of visibility and relatability, giving each determinant roles in the process of finding the thought. The importance of visual imagery in Renaissance argumentation and dialectic cannot be overestimated. As Ong has shown, the background in which Ramist invention and disposition appeared was one in which "the spatialized world apprehended by vision came to be more and more exploited to aid thinking."[13] In Donne's poetry a proposition is frequently established by starkly visual means: vision brings an image of the proposition within the light of reason with sharp clarity, and reason agrees not only that the proposition implies the image but also that the image demonstrates the existence of those things stated in the proposition. Let us look at one striking example from *The Second Anniversary* (ll. 207–213), where Donne describes the ascent of the soul from earth to heaven:

> And as these starres were but so many beads
> Strung on one string, speed undistinguish'd leads
> Her through those Spheares, as though the beads, a
> string,
> Whose quick succession makes it still one thing:
> As doth the pith, which, lest our bodies slacke,
> Strings fast the little bones of necke, and backe;
> So by the Soule doth death string Heaven and Earth;

In these lines Donne uses two images as arguments of his proposition that death unites heaven and earth by means of the soul's "quick succession" through the spheres. The mind's assent to the truth of the proposition is won in two ways: first, vision presents to the mind two images which serve to make the ideas clear; and second, the mind will agree that the passage of something through many things does not distinguish those things and can make those things one, as the images show. It is not simply the clarity of these arguments which makes them persuasive; it is also the fact that they indicate by means of similitude that there is such a thing as an undistinguishing passage which makes one thing of many little things. Relatability and visibility form the essence of the persuasiveness in these lines. But here, as usual, Donne's argumentation is complex. The visually conceivable relationships between a string of beads and the backbone and the soul's ascent through spheres, or those between beads and bones and spheres, or even those between the string and the pith and the soul, should not be ignored, for they heighten the demonstration to reason that the proposition lends itself to a proving view from any angle of vision. Furthermore, the fact that one of the comparing subjects is from the world of artifice (beads) and the other from the natural world (backbone), their parallelism enhanced by the use of the words "string" and "Strings," gives the quality of completeness to the demonstration: if the phenomenon exists both artificially and naturally, there would be little cause to doubt that it could exist metaphysically as well. Thus, like those emblematic, often grotesque pictures in old logic books, the starkest, most visible realities can serve as simple spatial models of the most abstract propositions whenever some aspects of one argue some aspects of the other. Reason is reached, and memory served, through the mind's eye.[14]

Visibility and relatability may have been important factors in Donne's arrangement of material within his poems—a feature rhetoricians would study with the precepts of disposition. The epitome of visibility and relatability in arrangement is that device which the Ramists used for teaching and for analysis: the diagram, which by means of brackets could indicate the structure of an entire discourse. The diagram provides a pattern of relationships that can be seen by the mind—the mind of the poet, the reader, the listener, or the critic. To the Ramists, that discourse was most persuasive in which the thought was clear because it could be visually apperceived and in which the arrangement of the material was easy to follow, or even to memorize, because it could be reconstructed by means of a visible pattern.

Because it progressively divides material into two parts, the bracketed diagram is in many ways a visual representation of "method," the most famous part of the Ramist doctrine of disposition. In its strictest terms, "method" demands that the discourse move from the general to the specific, or from the simple to the complex, by means of dichotomies or twofold divisions, although the Ramists allowed poets and orators to make certain prudential variations in order to please their audiences.[15] Something like the "method" can be seen in many of Donne's poems. At least, he most frequently organizes his material on the basis of dichotomies or twofold divisions and carries his arguments to the point where further division is superfluous or impossible—as in *The second Anniversary*, where the discussion of "essentiall" and "accidentall" joys comprises the last indivisible stage in the contemplation of (1) the incommodities of the soul in the body and (2) the exaltation of the soul in heaven.[16]

Employing the principles of "method," or using the diagram, in analyzing
a poem by Donne serves functions similar to those served by using the
syllogism to examine a dialectical discourse: "method," Fraunce states, is
"the onely iudge of order or confusion" and "the chiefest helpe of memory."[17]
For example, when the arrangement of material in *The Undertaking* is reconstructed on the basis of principles similar to those of "method," as in
the following discussion, the intricate lines of argument become clear and
easy to follow.[18]

The Undertaking is in two parts. The first part speaks in general terms
and consists of the first four stanzas; this first part has two sub-parts: statement and proof. Donne states (first stanza) that (1) he has done something
braver than all the Worthies did and (2) by keeping that something hid, he
thereby did something even braver than doing something braver than all the
Worthies did. The proof takes two courses, the first of which is contained
in the second and third stanzas, and the second of which is contained in
the fourth stanza. In the first course of the proof, he examines the fact that
he is keeping this something hid, and he makes this examination by means
of similitude: uttering this would be as useful as teaching someone how to
cut the specular stone. Although the full meaning of this argument depends
on the second part of the poem, it will be useful here to examine the correspondences of the terms. "Prophane men" believe that it is just as impossible to find "vertue" or "lovelinesse" in women as it is to find the
specular stone. Thus, teaching a man to love only "lovelinesse within" is
just as useless, so most men believe, as imparting the skill of cutting the
specular stone. Therefore, even if the poet "should utter this," men "would
love but as before." Donne's use of the word "love" moves toward the
specific argument involved in the second course of proving. The second
course (the fourth stanza) relates to the first part of the statement (the one
braver thing than all the Worthies did). The second course of proving has
a double argument: the first is an implied contrast between the men who
"love but as before" and the man "who lovelinesse within/ Hath found"; the
second is a contrast between finding loveliness within and without. The
diagram so far is the following:

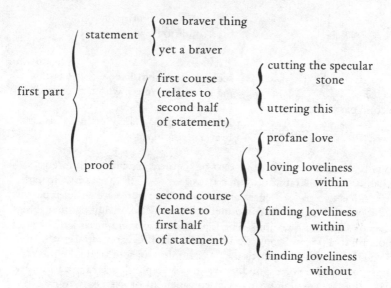

As the poem moves toward the specific, the smoothness of the movement is aided by the subtle shift from "he who" to "you." The second part of the poem (the last three stanzas) is expressed in one sentence of the syntactic structure the Ramists called "connective axiom." All connective axioms have two parts: condition and consequent. In this case, the condition (fifth and sixth stanzas) is in two parts: I. if you (a) see virtue attired in women (the metaphor "attir'd" is related to the metaphor "oldest clothes"—seeing virtue in women is related to finding the specular stone) and (b) dare love that (related to the skill of cutting the specular stone) by (1) admitting it to yourself and (2) forgetting the "Hee" and "Shee" (related to finding loveliness within and loathing "all outward"); and II. if you hide this from profane men, who (a) would not believe you (for, to them, "no more/ Such stuffe to worke upon, there is"), or (b) if they do believe you, would place no value on what you've done and are doing (for they love "colour" and skinne").

The consequent has two parts. You will then have done (1) a braver thing than the Worthies did, and (2) by keeping it hid, a braver thing than that—for you will be doing something the Worthies didn't do (keeping their bravery hid). This last stanza has the effect of revealing the complete argument of the poem; its structural correspondence to the vague first stanza increases this effect.

The diagram of the second part, without the subtle connections with the first part, follows:

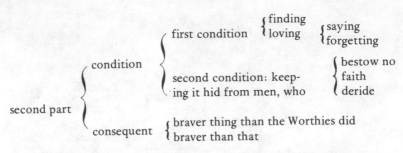

Finally, Donne used the third part of rhetoric, elocution, to intensify the visibility and relatability of all parts of a poem. In the Ramist scheme, elocution has two parts: figures and tropes. The figures are either repetitive, including such things as rime and meter, or dramatic, including such things as exclamations and questions. The figures give both emphasis and artistic proportion to a poem. Proportion in a poem can be very important to the Ramists; the figures of repetition, for example, can serve to make the various parts of a poem correspond, and such correspondence can in turn serve to make the arrangement of material conspicuous or even easy to cast in the form of a dichotomized diagram, particularly when the poem is being read aloud—like the repetition of "Shee, shee is dead; shee's dead" in *The first Anniversary,* or of "so" and "goe" in *The Expiration,* or of "Little think'st thou" in *The Blossome.*

The trope which the Ramists called *allegory* is most characteristic of Donne's style. Unlike metaphor, which was "a similitude contracted into one word,"[19] allegory was a similitude expanded through several words or even several sentences. Actually, both metaphor and allegory are concepts through which the analyst may view the relating and visualizing process integral to Ramist invention. In developing an allegory, Donne frequently does not hesitate to name, often by simile, the points of contact between a thought and its allegory, and in so doing he heightens the analogizing process to the point where a few sharply defined things which may be said concerning the allegory may also be said concerning the thought. In this process there is the real blending of "reasoning" and "ornamentation"—even on the theoretical level, for to the Ramists the simile is part of a logical mode of proof, while the allegory belongs to rhetorical embellishment.

For example, Donne's compass image, his most famous "Metaphysical Conceit," is a fusion of similes and allegory. In creating the image at the end of the poem, Donne states that if the union of his soul and his mistress's soul has two parts, they are like the two parts of a compass. Then the simile shifts to allegory. Her soul is the fixed foot, which makes no move until the other foot does. And the motion that the fixed foot makes is a leaning and hearkening after the other and growing erect when the other comes "home." Returning to simile, Donne states that he must "Like th'other foot, obliquely runne." Then shifting again to allegory, he states that the "firmnes" of her soul makes his motion true and makes him end where he began. Again, the argument is the similitude; the thought expressed in terms of the compass becomes a virtual demonstration in which the points of contact are so carefully drawn by simile that any truth about the compass can become a truth about his relationship with his mistress.[20]

Donne employed the tropes *catachresis* and *hyperbole* also as means of intensifying his arguments. To paraphrase Hoskins's statements regarding hyperbole, both catachresis and hyperbole extend the comparison far beyond rational bounds so that the mind may on its own discover the truth or the "unspeakableness" of the relation.[21] The dead virgin who is father to the offspring produced by his muse, the heart that shivered like glass, the carcasses the lovers became when absences removed their souls—all these shock reason, and it is the reader himself who ultimately creates the true comparison by establishing a framework of relationships just this side of the logical distention marked by hyperbole and catachresis.

What value is there in using rhetoric as a critical tool in analyzing Donne's poetry? In the first place, the use of a specific rhetorical system—particularly the Ramist system—gives an historical insight into the modes of proof and indicates the rhetorical efficacy of visibility and relatability. Second, rhetoric offers a method for studying that most important and most difficult aspect of Donne's artistry: his arrangement of material. Finally, the nature of rhetoric lends a valuable perspective in which all critical problems may be ranged, for the objective of a full rhetorical analysis is to find out how well the proposition is stated and proved. The importance of all parts of the poem—arguments, arrangements, tropes, and figures—depends upon their role in demonstrating the truth of the proposition.

Rosemond Tuve's enthusiastic appraisal of the causal connections between Ramism and metaphysical poetry, particularly Donne's, has become a matter of controversy.[22] Though the aim of the present discussion is the construction of a critical view from the position of Renaissance rhetoric, the "new Petromachia" cannot be sidestepped. The analysis of Donne's poetry suggested in this discussion need not be seen as an attempt to assign Ramism an influential role in the creation of that poetry.[23] The basic reason the Ramist theory is useful in analyzing Donne's poetry is that Ramism accords with important intellectual developments in the sixteenth century and perhaps embodies a critical view held by the poet's audience. But considering the poet's complex personality, Ramism could at best only reflect some of the undoubtedly many factors that gave his poetry those distinguishing features we recognize as peculiarly Donnesque. Moreover, it is also true that most of the Ramist theories were merely epitomes of traditional rhetorical theories; but when Ramism is defined solely in terms of those few characteristics which distinguish it from other rhetorical systems of the time Donne cannot be called a Ramist—for example, his complex, ambiguous procedures differ greatly from the "plain style" the Ramists considered important. But for that matter, any attempt to argue strong connections between Ramism and poetry is weakened by the Ramists' notorious indifference toward poetry as a unique type of discourse.[24] However, Ramism in both its innovative and its traditional features is unquestionably representative of Donne's milieu, and it is therefore serviceable for the analytical operations involved in studying the *rhetorical* foundations of Donne's poetry. Consequently, the question most relevant to the present discussion is not whether Ramism caused this or that characteristic in Donne's poetry, but whether employing Ramism in a *rhetorical analysis* of his poetry is meaningful.

On the other hand, one cannot deny the validity of William Empson's argument that analyzing Donne's poetry by means of Renaissance rhetoric is at best partial, for rhetoric sets definite limits beyond which the reader's experience of the poem is not allowed to go.[25] But at the same time one cannot deny the historical fact that in the Renaissance poetry was analyzed by means of rhetoric. With the rhetorical analysis the modern reader may see some of those things which were probably important both to Donne and to his readers—without having to rely solely upon the variable results of modern verbal analyses, which too often stress ambiguity at the expense of the cohesiveness of the poem's argument. With the rhetorical analysis the modern reader may see the rhetoric which Renaissance theorists, poets, and readers knew was *in* poetry.

THE RHETORIC OF TRANSCENDENCE

R. L. Colie

I

TRADITIONS OF PARADOX IN RENAISSANCE VERSE-EPISTE-MOLOGIES

The period in European thought from 1550 to 1650, just before the great schematic reformulations of the Enlightenment, displayed a prodigal enthusiasm for speculation into the nature of things. The nature of man, the nature of God and of His Son, the nature of nature itself—all were primary subjects for investigation during that century. Montaigne is properly the secular patron of the investigation, with his catholic interests, his intelligent if transient commitment to a variety of philosophical positions, his talent for combination, for paradox and surprise, as well as his remarkable concern both for himself and for his society. The work of the generation after Montaigne bore his stamp (and in England, Florio's)[1] not only upon the subject and style of its speculations, but in the lack of prescribed system, the flexibility, the toleration, and the nonchalance with which Montaigne faced the implications of the philosophical materials he assayed. Most of all, the generation after Montaigne followed his lead in self-conscious speculation about the processes of the mind, about, in short, human understanding.

In his inconstancy and his eclecticism, Montaigne conveniently reflects both the philosophical openness of the period (that amateurishness of which more traditional logicians complained so bitterly) and the practice of the Christian tradition itself. In spite of a reputation for doctrinal intolerance, Christianity has throughout its history proved remarkably adaptable to different philosophical systems, or parts of them; in many ways, distorted though they have been within Christianity, western philosophies have been preserved within Christian orthodoxy. Platonism, Neoplatonism, Aristotelianism, Stoicism, and Skepticism all found their way into the Christian tradition. Once the great renaissance shift away from orthodoxy had taken place, in religion, in political theory and practice, in geography and cosmology, in economics, there was opportunity for intellectual recombination, deliberate and random: Montaigne's stout corpus of essays is not only the record of one man's inner life but also a convex mirror-reflection of the intellectual universe in which he lived. No stock adjective

Reprinted from *Philological Quarterly*, 43 (1964), 145-70, by permission of the publisher.

can characterize the speculative activity of Montaigne, or of the Renaissance:
no scheme reduces to a single formulation their irregular, independent, and
arbitrary activities.

For various reasons, some of which I hope to discuss in this paper, the
kinds of speculation current in the Renaissance resulted in a rich variety of
formally stated paradoxes—paradoxes in faith and doctrine, in philosophy,
in the natural sciences, and in the literary and visual arts. This paper describes
the natural coincidence of several traditions of paradox in epistemological
thought. It attempts to show how the "epistemological paradox" became
one of the poetic themes of the late Renaissance, as well as how, once that
paradox entered poetry, poetry by its own operation enriched the traditional
paradoxes of content by an appropriate rhetoric.[2]

Most ideas in the western tradition are to be traced back to the dialogues
of Plato: certainly this route can be taken by paradox. One might defend
the whimsical thesis that the *Parmenides* is the ultimate source for all the
paradoxes in the western tradition. That dialogue is a rhetorical paradox,
since it deliberately cheats the reader's expectations; it is a paradox in that
it provides no fixed solution to the problem it raises. The *Parmenides* is
about the speculative paradoxes always ambushed at the limits of knowledge
and of discourse. It is, literally, the *locus classicus* for the statement of
problems about the one and the many, about appearance and reality. It
contains one of the most ironic self-references in literature, that of Socrates
continually abashed by his opponents' arguments, perhaps worsted by them;
and it is itself an infinite regression. The *Parmenides* is a riddle that manages
to express, in both its matter and its form, the paradoxes of self-conscious
speculation and reflection. The words themselves, "speculation" and "reflection," are metaphors for the ultimately paradoxical nature of all epistemology: epistemology, is, after all, the fundamental tautology, the inevitable
self-reference, that of the mind reflecting on its own operation by means
of its own operation. Reflection and speculation, those mirror-words, are
theoretically limitless; or, to put it another way, their limitations are simply
those of the speculative instrument.

In Plato's dialogue, Parmenides and his pupil Zeno demonstrate, negative-
ly and positively, the logical fallacies inherent in their opponents' view of
reality. Their monism disregards all variant manifestations of things as mere
"appearances," and their brilliant logic is designed to bring their opponents
—in this case, Socrates—to admit the unique legitimacy of the monist thesis.
In other words, their legacy to their followers, the Stoics, was the paradoxical dialectic persuasive to the monism to which both Eleatics and Stoics
were sworn—to the view that, despite all appearances, the many are in fact
one.[3]

The enemy of Eleatic and Platonist alike, the Sophist of antiquity played
with the same contradictions exploited by the Eleatics, but to quite different
ends. Sophists, like Skeptics, were unwilling to admit the supremacy of any
single system among the multitudinous, tumultuous competition for ideas
in the late antique world. In Sophist hands the paradox became a standard

rhetorical category, an argument contrary to common opinion and expectation, often contrary to truth, designed to display the power of argument. Uncommitted to any philosophical program or idea, the Sophist came to the market place displaying, not an ethical or metaphysical system, but his forensic art.[4]

Though the Sophists contributed to the Skeptical tradition, they cannot be counted as serious Skeptics, since they did not so much doubt truth as dismiss truth altogether. The Sophist had, like Prufrock, "known them all already, known them all," until all "truths" came to seem to him merely the commodities of relative and expediential value. The Skeptic, on the other hand, was more philosophical: he attempted the exhausting intellectual task of doubting his way through all the hypotheses presented to him. Skepticism is not for the insecure man, for radical doubt does not lead to certain conclusions: it is, like the Sophists' *techne,* more a method than a system of philosophy.

To make his relativist point, the Skeptic exploits the appearances of truth, develops the inconsistencies, contradictions, and problems of philosophical systems, whether singly or together, and thus naturally expresses himself in paradox. When Skeptical doubt and Stoical monism collide or coincide, as they habitually did in renaissance speculation, the paradox involved is often double and triple—double, because both Stoic and Skeptical methods employed formal and rhetorical paradoxes, often very traditional ones; triple, because there was inevitable "paradox," or contradiction, in the coincidence of attitudes so strikingly opposed.

The elements of the two systems concurred very often. Montaigne himself, that constant reader of Plutarch and Seneca, with whose maxims he decorated his study, took the Pyrrhonist part in his greatest and most sustained essay, *The Apologie of Raymond Sebond.* Among his other tortures, Hamlet was stretched on the rack of a Stoicism appropriate to the king's son of Denmark and the Horatian Skepticism of modernist Wittenberg. For all sorts of reasons, Stoicism and Skepticism provided methods for dealing with the excitements, confusions, and disruptions of late renaissance thought. The first offered against a too pressing world the traditional bulwark of ethical single-mindedness; the second permitted indefinite postponement of commitment to any idea or set of ideas. Montaigne and Hamlet, like many a lesser man, balanced the two philosophies against each other.[5]

Stoicism and Skepticism not only concurred, they also conjoined with Christianity. With its assertion of a single truth absolute against a bewildering confusion of accidentals, of a single natural law, of a philanthropic morality nonetheless capable of detachment from ordinary mortal concerns, Stoicism was an obvious support to Christianity, as the list of renaissance Christian Stoics shows.[6]

The Stoic's chief duty, like that of the Christian, was to know himself. Detachment from the world, for which the Stoic had at hand instruction in a hundred books of morality and a thousand ready maxims, necessarily in-

volved him in detaching himself also from the sciences that interpreted the
world. All the same, the Stoic could not take hasty refuge in a blank anti-
intellectualism. Before he was allowed to reject either the physical world
or its intellectual counterpart, he was obliged to understand them. For the
Stoic, to know himself meant to know the world of which he was a part.
To know what he was, he had to know exactly what he was giving up, what
he was subtracting himself from—or, he had to know what he was not.

This is, of course, a paradox, one result of which is, for example, the
spectacle of an extraordinarily learned man, Erasmus, learnedly doubting
in *The Praise of Folly* (perhaps even denying) all that he had come to
know, as well as the methods by which he had come to know what he
knew. Another result is the sight of another learned man, Henry Cornelius
Agrippa, rejecting the supernatural learning he had been at such pains to
gather. After he had written his huge defense and compendium of occult
philosophy, Agrippa denied out of hand the worth of that study, and
published a systematic derogation of all the arts and sciences of the
learned world. His *Vanity of Learning* owed its being, though, to his
thirst for knowledge; his invention sprang from his own passions:

> . . . the name of Cornelius in his vanity of Learning was famous, not
> only among the *Germanes,* but also other Nations; for Momus himself
> carpeth at all amongst the gods; amongst the Heroes, *Hercules* hunteth
> after Monsters; amongst the divels *Pluto* the King of hell is angry with
> all the ghosts; amongst the Philosophers *Democritus* laugheth at all
> things, on the contrary, *Heraclitus* weepeth at all things; *Pirrhias* is
> ignorant of all things; *Aristotle* thinketh he knoweth all things;
> *Diogenes* contemneth all things; this *Agrippa* spareth none, he con-
> temneth, knows, is ignorant, weeps, laughs, is angry, pursueth, carps
> at all things, being himself a Philosopher, a Demon, an Heroes [sic],
> a god, and all things.[7]

He "knows, is ignorant, weeps, laughs": the tone of Agrippa's work tells us
that it denies itself. The critic dare not assign Agrippa the role he seems to
demand, for in demanding to be believed, he presents us also with the evidence for disbelieving him. Even his retractions do not leave Agrippa's
ultimate view of knowledge very clear.[8]

Most Stoical writing is less ticklish than Agrippa's, or Erasmus'—less
Skeptical, one might say; Stoical writing is habitually plain to the point
of boredom. Three very influential Stoical works, however, were far from
boring, and were thus widely read and calmly plundered: Philippe du
Plessis Mornay's two books, one on religion, the other on self-knowledge,[9]
and Pierre de la Primaudaye's compendium of all knowledge, *The French
Academie.*[10] For both authors, a strong Christian Stoicism dominates their
doctrine and their view of the world. Both were men of the real world and
knew that knowledge of one's self involved above all things knowledge
of the world, as well as sufficient judgment to reject the world and a will
ready to receive true revelation. With Erasmus, Agrippa, and the Stoic

moralist Du Vair,[11] Du Plessis Mornay and La Primaudaye counsel ultimate attention to spiritual matters, through the gradual mastery and rejection of the things of this world.

Like the Skeptics, the Stoics recognized the importance of the senses in transmitting, however inadequately, information about the external world to the human mind. Inviolable right reason dwelt, for them, among the extremely transitory data of human lives. So Du Vair could say, "Silence is the father of discourse and the fountaine of reason,"[12] an axiom which could be explicated into sense (called reason) only after considerable reflection. The Stoic system of ethics was full of such ambiguities, dependent for their formulation upon the inward life of a reflective man. After all, when the world is reduced to a "thing indifferent," when a man's senses and reason must measure the whole world, when values are turned into value judgments, paradoxes like Du Vair's are inevitable. The world becomes a set of indeterminate circumstances, as Stoical meditation attests. In spite of natural law, each Stoic makes his own interpretations of the world, invests the world with the qualities he judges it to have. As Du Vair said,

> For by this meanes wee shall come to know, that griefe and pleasure are drawne both of them out of the same well, if a man have but the skill to turne his bucket when he would fill it with either: for the use is all in a thing, and every thing as it is used [is] good or bad.[13]

When even Stoics view the external world so subjectively, paradoxes can be counted upon to appear.

One fundamental tenet of Stoicism, however, tended to counteract the subjectivism to which the system sometimes led: the belief in an external, objective natural law, by which all things from the beginning had been providentially organized by the deity. Belief in natural law runs parallel to belief in innate right reason, with which every man is endowed; and exploits the notion that all knowledge, however partial or partially apprehended, ultimately derives, both externally by natural law and internally by right reason, from the word and work of God. The theory implies, though it does not insist, that all knowledge is good. The natural law theory was extremely useful in renaissance thought, since it provided a ready-made justification for the study of external nature. God had created an orderly nature, both in the world and in the mind of man; one way to know Him was to know His works.

Since one knows by the senses before one can know by right reason, the Stoic was not lightly anti-sensationalist. Du Plessis Mornay included among atheists not only those whose wit denied God, but also those whose senses denied Him, those who refused to read God's word from "natural law," from the "book" of His steady and orderly creation.[14] Morally, too, the senses held the balance of salvation, for only by the proper regulation on earth of his senses might a man's reason bring him into the salvation promised by faith.

By the same theory, another way to know God was to know the workings of one's own mind.[15] For the antique Stoic and his Christian descen-
dent, epistemology was a problem in morality, that of the relation of the
reason to the soul, or of the intelligence to the will. In Stoic philosophy
and free-will Christianity, that relation is crucial, since his choosing reason
relates a man's multiple behavior to the single truth of God. Though
Christian Stoics were committed to the orthodox view that ultimate truth
is beyond the reach both of reason and the senses, they put their faith in
common human reason to lead man to the point where faith takes on the
burden of truth and makes revelation credible. As Du Plessis Mornay put
it,

> so farre off is Reason from abasing fayth, to make us attaine therto,
> that contrariwise shee lifteth us up as it were upon her shoulders, to
> make us to see it, and to take it for our guide, as the only thing that
> can bring us to God; and the onely schoolemistresse of whom we
> ought to learn our salvation.[16]

Neo-stoic defenders of religious truth insisted on the value of knowledge
in general, on the value of sense-evidence derived from a world created good,
and on the conviction that knowledge is possible and the attainment of
knowledge part of man's obligation.[17] The Skeptic punctured such conventional securities. Montaigne's "Que sçay-je?" provoked, not a resolute
justification of things as they had been considered to be, but a relativist
consideration of man's variability, fragility, and waywardness in a world
fluid, variable, and broken.[18] Like the Stoics on whom he modelled so
much of his style of life and letters, Montaigne was forced back into himself for his intellectual and moral definitions. Unlike the Stoics, though,
Montaigne could never fully acquiesce either in the idea of a right reason
common to all mankind or in the idea of a universal law of nature. His
Apologie is the classic renaissance statement of the dilemmas of knowledge,
with all their intricate interrelatedness. Montaigne's disciple, Pierre Charron,
affords by his simplicity more economical Skeptical truisms than his
master does (like John Donne's work, Montaigne's is excerpted at the
critic's peril. Charron is less complex). Charron began with the classical
and Christian maxim, to know one's self; and he knew from Montaigne
the difficulty of this riddling and lifelong task. Unlike Montaigne, who
moved in and out of paradox without warning and without preparation,[19]
Charron codified the antinomies, contradictions, and paradoxes of skepticism in his handbook. At the end of Charron's *Of Wisdome,* the reader
finds real difficulty in distinguishing his message from the stoical one, for,
like Du Plessis Mornay, like La Primaudaye, Charron laid his command
ultimately upon the human will, to choose well among the bewildering
data presented to the human mind.[20] The greater part of his teaching simply
counsels the proper control and direction of the passions. In an ultimate ·
anomaly, then, the teachings of the two schools of thought traditionally
opposed, Stoicism and Skepticism, turn out to be identical.

The connection of Stoicism and Skepticism in renaissance thought is not simply complementary. Renaissance thinkers did not typically go through a Skeptical, then a Stoical phase,[21] or *vice versa*; it is that their subject-matter was fundamentally similar, no matter how different their message. If one were to attempt excision of either his Stoicism or his Skepticism from Erasmus' works, for instance, or from Montaigne's, or from the utterances of Hamlet, there would be little left, for the ideas were interrelated and inseparable. Erasmus, Montaigne, and Hamlet, together with the host of Stoic writers concerned with knowing themselves, were engaged in something other than the moral self-examination required by religious tradition and exemplified in manuals of devotional meditation, but in something more cutting, the self-conscious effort to understand understanding, their own and that of mankind. In late renaissance England, this enterprise became the subject of poetry, in such works as Sir John Davies' *Nosce Teipsum*,[22] Fulke Greville's *Treatie of Humane Learning*,[23] John Davies of Hereford's *Mirum in Modum, Summa Totalis,* and *Witte's Pilgrimage*;[24] and John Donne's *Anniversary* Poems. These strongly Christian poems are all in the stoical tradition and owe a debt to their skeptical inheritance; their poets were engaged in fulfilling their Christian-humanist obligation to know themselves, and to know how they knew what they knew.[25]

Sir John Davies' poem, published in 1599, begins with the traditional antithesis between principle and practice, between form and appearance:

> Why did my parents send me to the schooles,
>   That I with Knowledge might enrich my mind?
> Since the *desire to know* first made men fooles
>   And did corrupt the root of all mankind?[26]

Flawed by that first tricky "desire to know," "What can we know? or what can we discern?" Can man hope to know more than "the wisest of all Morall men," who said of himself that *"he knew nought, but that he nought did know"*? (p. 4) One after another, Davies dismisses the vanities of learning, to return ultimately to the proper study of mankind:

> My self am *Center* of my circling thought,
> Onely *my selfe* I studie, learne, and know. (p. 8)

For Davies, as for Montaigne, Charron, Scaliger, and the other memorialists of human limitation, human existence was made up of contrarieties:

> I know my Bodi's of so fraile a kinde
>   As force without, feavers within can kill;
> I know the heavenly nature of my minde,
>   But tis corrupted both in *wit* and *will*:
>
> I know my *Soule* hath power to know all things,
>   Yet is she blind and ignorant in all;

> I know I am one of *Natures* litle kings,
> Yet to the least and vilest things am thrall.

> I know my life's a paine, and but a span,
> I know my *Sense* is mockt with every thing;
> And to conclude, I know my selfe a *Man,*
> Which is a *proud,* and yet a *wretched* thing. (p. 8)

External nature provided for Davies a less sure guide to truth than the natural law had provided the antique Stoics. Furthermore, the sixteenth-century world, undergoing its geographical and cosmographical reconstruction, inevitably delivered such contradictory data to the senses and the judgment that a man had slight chance at arriving at a just assessment of the physical and intellectual world. The soul, however, has deeper perceptions than the mind and is capable of reaching fundamental truths: the soul can know substances, not merely skins of things: can know the nature of, say, a tree, not just the look of a particular bark or leaf; can recognize true concords, not just the heterogeneous noises of natural things. The senses have their inadequate uses (Davies followed Du Plessis Mornay in regarding as "senseless" those Epicurean advocates of sense-experience alone), but only the soul can transcend human contradictions. The soul is both substantial and spiritual, active and passive, reflective and creative; only the soul possesses the nobly paradoxical qualities and functions that Davies defends with all his wit and will:

> When without hands she thus doth Castels build,
> Sees without eyes, and without feete doth runne,
> When she digests the World, yet is not fild,
> By her owne power these miracles are done. (p. 14)

Under the exercise of the soul's power, material limitations disappear, and with them, definitions also disappear. As the image of God in man, the soul contains everything in its proper place. It travels with all imaginable speed, like the deity is at once here and there, combines the separate empires of wit and will into the single search for the true wisdom of God:

> Now God the *Truth* and *first of causes* is,
> God is the last *goodend,* which lasteth still,
> Being *Alpha* and *omega* nam'd for this,
> *Alpha* to wit, *omega* to the will. (p. 59)

The puns indicate Davies' need for a rhetoric to transcend ordinary descriptive, even metaphorical, statements, and to express the transcendence which is his subject. "The last good end" and "alpha to wit" begin and end, without setting limits to, the idea of God's perfect knowledge of Himself and all His works.

In spite of occasional syntactical tricks, though, Davies' basic lesson is as direct and unparadoxical as he could make it. Since his subject, the soul, is by traditional definition ultimately unknowable, the poet must

rely upon both the general epistemological tradition of paradox and its
special development in the paradoxes of theological definition, called the
negative theology.[27] Because of its platonic likeness to the deity, the One
in Whom the many are subsumed, the soul and all its operations could
also be expressed in the paradoxes of the negative theology.

Like his courtly namesake, John Davies of Hereford was a deeply religious
man deeply concerned in the organization of knowledge under God.
Though he too believed that "The 'externall *Sences* serve the common
Sence," and that Reason "useth every *Sences* facultie,"[28] the deficiencies
of sense were perfectly evident to him:

> But yet in cases of our constant faith
> Wee *Faith* beleeve, and give our Sence the lie,
> Nay, whatsoe're our humane reason saith,
> If it our faith gainesay, we it deny:
> On highest heights Faith hir foundation laith,
> Which never can be seene of mortall eye.
> For if *Faith,* say, a *Maid* may be a *Mother,*
> Though *Sence* gainesay it, wee beleeve the other.
> If *Faith* affirme, that God a man may bee,
> (A mortall man and live, and die with paine)
> We it believe, though how, we cannot see,
> For heere strong *Faith* doth headstrong *Reas'n* restraine:
> And with the truth compells hir to agree,
> Lest she should over-runne hir selfe in vaine:
> So, if *Faith* say one's three, and three is one,
> Though *Sence* say no, we *Faith* believe alone.[29]

Only God, the *summa totalis* of a later poem by the same man, could
finally compose the contradictions all men invariably experience in their
sublunary lives. Didactic poetry, this is: even less than Sir John Davies
does Davies of Hereford show the transcendence of truth.

In 1633 Greville's *Treatie of Humane Learning,* which deals with the
same problems as those raised by the other poets, was finally published.
Stoic, platonist, and Christian determinist, Greville knew and set down
at once the difficulties of his task:

> The Mind of Man, is this worlds true dimension;
> And *Knowledge* is the measure of the minde:
> And as the minde, in her vast comprehension,
> Containes more worlds than all the world can finde:
> So *Knowledge* doth it selfe farre more extend
> Than all the minds of Men can comprehend.[30]

Unknowable knowledge demands the paradoxical expression to which Sir
John Davies had had to turn earlier:

> A climbing height it is without a head,
> Depth without bottome, Way without an end,
> A Circle with no line environed;
> Not comprehended, all it comprehends;
>> Worth infinitude, yet satisfies no minde,
>> Till it that infinite of the God-head finde. (I, 154)

After such a beginning, an encomium of knowledge and of the human mind, Greville then proceeds—by rhetorical rather than syntactical paradox—to argue against the perfections of the human mind and to present, not its marvellous transcendent wholeness, but its defects in all its parts. He too exposes the vanity of all the arts and sciences, as well as the vanity of the creature who, in his temerity, thinks that he comprehends them. In failing to clarify precisely, the human understanding may positively mislead:

> Againe, we see the best Complexions vaine,
> And in the worst more nimble subtilty;
> From whence *Wit, a distemper of the braine;*
> The Schooles conclude, and our capacity;
>> How much more sharper, the more it apprehends,
>> Still to distract, and lesse truth comprehends. (I, 159)

No man has ever been able to prove a single thing past doubt—

> Of perfect *demonstration,* who yet gave
> One clear example? Or since time began
> What one true *forme* found out by wit of Man; (I, 160)

Astronomy, philosophy, rhetoric, music, geometry—all is vanity. Practitioners of these arts are mere quarrelers for personal preeminence. If the arts and sciences, those tools of truth, are based on error, how can a man choose among truths to reach any final, ultimate truth? He is required, after all, by the reality he cannot fail to recognize, to put the dangerous, destructive, skeptical question:

> A *Science* never scientificall,
> A *Rhapsody* of questions controverted;
> In which because men know no truth at all,
> To every purpose it can be converted:
>> Judge then what grounds this can to others give,
>> That waved ever in it selfe must live? (I, 166)

Greville was too religious—and too stoical—a man to rest upon the skeptical question; nor, like Montaigne, did he make the leap directly from Skepticism into fideism without concern for the truth of physical "reality." In Greville's view, however insecure a man might be among the paradoxical pieces of information afforded him by his limited sources of knowledge, he must never allow himself to contemplate only the inevitable flux of things; for contemplation (says this platonist!) destroys, "Transformes all beings into Atomi: / Dissolves, builds not." Social reality demands that the sciences be reformed along empirical lines, according to Bacon's doctrine of utility (I, 171). The universities, the law courts, medicine, logic, rhetoric—all must be stripped of their wayward terminology to conform to man's immediate and simple needs. Only by the way of humility can man hope to reverse, or even to modify, the general doom incurred for his original intellectual pride. His soul must "raise herselfe again, / Ere she can judge all other knowledge vaine" (I, 191). By knowing all things, without being puffed up, a man may legitimately come to reject his knowledge in order to come into perfect knowledge.

Greville's paradoxes, like those of the two Davies', are the traditional ones of Stoical, Skeptical, and Christian self-examination. What is interesting about these poems is the richness of the traditional paradoxes of content, as well as the poetic tentative toward their proper expression. The poems deal, after all, with the major unanswerable questions of human speculation, the nature of the transcendent God and the nature of human thought; and they deal with them, albeit often awkwardly, in poetry. The subject demanded and the poets attempted to supply a rhetoric appropriate to the complications of such speculation. Without some realization of the nature and variety of the traditional paradoxes of epistemology which exercised such fascination for these poets, we run the risk of overstating the poets' philosophical and rhetorical originality and thereby of failing to recognize their peculiar and original solutions to the poetic problems raised by the subject of transcendence. These poets were engaged in a heroic enterprise—to make as plain as possible the mysteries of human understanding. It remained for another poet to do more, to dramatize rather than to describe human understanding, to bring his readers into that understanding by performing the poetic act of understanding rather than by outlining the process in verse: John Donne in his *Anniversaries*.

II

JOHN DONNE'S ANNIVERSARY POEMS AND THE
PARODOXES OF EPISTEMOLOGY

Donne's *Anniversary Poems*[31] have been greatly illuminated by having been read against the various traditions which they exploit and of which they are a part. They are poems of meditation,[32] with medieval, reformation, and counter-reformation analogues; they are poems of the old[33] and the new science;[34] they are cosmic eulogies of a dead maiden and (perhaps; though perhaps not) of a dead Maiden Queen;[35] they are a document in Skepticism[36] and in natural law;[37] they are companion-pieces drawn to a pattern, the *quaestio* and *responsio* of medieval argument. They are, too, a body-soul debate, the first poem a *contemptus mundi* and the second a *consolatio philosophiae,* or *consolatio spiritualis.* They are poems about sacred love, the power of which in part derives from the poems' delicious reference to profane love—they are, then, sell-disguised poems in the traditional line of the *dolce stil nuovo*.[38] Anti-petrarchan, the poems out-do the Petrarchan rhetoric.

What is remarkable about these poems is that, though all these readings concern such very different sets of ideas, they do not contradict, but rather enhance each other. The poems' extraordinary quality resides in their resis-tance to final definition: when all the separate explications and interpreta-tions are added up, the Anniversary *Poems* prove to be more than the sum of their parts. They hold in balance many oppositions and contradictions: they are, in short, paradoxical poems, poems about paradoxes and poems within the paradoxical rhetoric.

It is in two traditions of paradox, the self-conscious reflections of classical and renaissance epistemology and the meditative Christian paradoxes of mystery, that I propose to read the *Anniversay Poems*. Like Sir John Davies' *Nosce Teipsum* and Fulke Greville's *Treatie of Humane Learning*, Donne's poems are about the difficulties inherent in understanding one's self, the world, and God. As Mr. Bredvold has demonstrated, all these poems derive a great deal from Montaigne's *Apologie* and from the skeptical tradition in general; Mr. Ornstein's argument grounds them thoroughly in their Stoic background of natural law.[39] Like the epistemological poems of his contem-poraries, Donne's *Anniversary Poems* work within the contradictory tradi-tions of Stoicism and Skepticism; like the poems of Davies and Greville, they deal with the paradoxes necessarily attendant upon epistemological speculation. Like them, too, Donne exploits the traditions of Christian self-knowledge, with its paradoxes of the transcendent spirit. But where Davies and Greville reflect chiefly upon the intellectual difficulties involved in un-derstanding the human understanding. Donne operates within an additional paradoxical area as well, that of individual psychology. Assuming the exis-tence of a tradition of epistemological poetry, this paper attempts to point to Donne's many-sided use of a many-sided tradition and to his peculiar mastery of an expression appropriate to it, especially in comparison to the rather tentative poetic experiments of his contemporaries engaged upon the same problem.

The *Anniversary Poems* consistently work within the most obvious kind of rhetorical paradox, since they regularly cheat the reader's expectation. For example, in the first poem, after a beginning conventional in its elegiac despair, Donne springs it on his readers that it is not the death of a lady only that he laments, but the death of the whole conceivable world. The poem, with its companion-piece, propounds a lament for a world mortally wounded because of the death of one particularly gracious spirit. The sub-ject of the poem had, in her life, been in her bodily form the soul of the world, its "Cyment," its "intrinsique balme," the "preservative" that kept it sweet, the "Magnetick force" that gave coherence to its parts. The soul gone, the world's body has no choice but to die. The decay of the world, presented with such ominous enjoyment in Greville's *Treatie*, actually takes place in Donne's poem: Donne's "anatomy" is performed upon a crooked

and putrid corpse. In every way, the world has lost its nature—it is un-
balanced, disproportionate, colorless, askew. Man has a shorter life, a smaller
stature, a narrower mind than ever before. He is still the measure of all
things, but by that fact all things have lost their glory: crooked and shrunken
himself, he measures a world correspondingly skewed. That "stedie and
settled order" of creation, celebrated by Du Plessis Mornay,[40] the cheerful
study of which he enjoined his readers to undertake, served to demonstrate
to variable and doubting man that God's purpose was fixed in the beautiful
patterns of natural law operating upon the creation. Donne's animate, an-
thropomorphized universe has partaken to the last degree of man's sin, has
become as variable as wicked man himself.

A crooked mind cannot measure a crooked world; man's ways of knowing
are as skewed as the world they seek to know. The nets man throws over the
firmaments, those astronomical charts designed to fix the heavenly patterns,
prove worthless, both because they are the inadequate inventions of weak
minds and because the firmament itself has lost its originally regular pattern.
None of the sciences has an ordering value any more—astronomy, medicine,
natural philosophy progressively reveal how awkward the creation is, just as
the arts and sciences reveal the mistakes of human life. Amidst all this, as
Davies and Greville complained, knowledge is impossible—for Donne, it
seems, impossible for the soul as well as the mind.

"Poore soule, in this thy flesh, what dost thou know?" Where Davies had
asserted that it was possible for the soul to know, and organized his theory
of knowledge around the soul, Donne denied the soul knowledge even of
itself:

> Thou know'st thy selfe so little, as thou know'st not,
> How thou didst die, nor how thou wast begot.
> Thou neither know'st, how thou at first cam'st in,
> Nor how thou took'st the poyson of mans sinne.
> Nor dost thou, (though thou know'st, that thou art so)
> By what way thou art made immortall, know.
> Thou art too narrow, wretch, to comprehend
> Even thy selfe. (*Second Anniversary,* 255-62)

The most the world can do is to set riddles. All kinds of apparently ordinary
questions appear to have no answer—who knows how the stone came into
the bladder, or how the blood circulates? In the world of learning, nothing
can be known either:

> What *Caesar* did, yea, and what *Cicero* said.
> Why grasse is greene, or why our blood is red,
> Are mysteries which none have reach'd unto.
>   (*S.A.,* 287-89)

The world "dissolves into its Atomies," particles of disorganized matter;
and its forms dissolve into an eternal mutability, until men are not, genuinely,
what they are. The fact that lovers' vows are impermanent—as Donne else-

where emphasized, that impermanence is the only permanent thing about lovers—is appropriate enough, since lovers' vows are the utterances of bodies terrifyingly fluid:

> Poore cousened cousenor, *that* she, and *that* thou,
> Which did begin to love, are neither now;
> You are both fluid, chang'd since yesterday;
> Next day repaires, (but ill) last dayes decay.
> Nor are, (although the river keepe the name)
> Yesterdaies waters, and to daies the same.
> So flowes her face, and thine eyes, neither now
> That Saint, nor Pilgrime, which your loving vow
> Concern'd, remaines. . . . (*S.A.,* 391-99)

Even lovers cannot know one another, though the idiom may dupe them into thinking that they can: and lovers are not the only variable people on the planet. No man has constant qualities—that man who "thinkes that he hath got / To be a Phoenix" has not even a personal identity. Like everything else, man is an illusion:

> whilst you thinke you bee
> Constant, you'are hourely in inconstancie.
> (*S.A.,* 399-400)

In this attack upon individual and personal integrity, Donne owes a considerable debt to Montaigne's *Apologie,* and some to Heraclitus. Donne administers, though, a thoroughly Christian warning to men: his is an Augustinian and "counter-renaissance"[41] antidote to man's pride in himself.

For willy-nilly man unmakes himself.[42] The blind passage of time is not the only thing that produces irrevocable decay; man connives at his own decadence. Man is "borne ruinous," comes "headlong" upon an "ominous precipitation," all brought upon himself by his inherited behavior. Woman, "sent for mans reliefe," is the instrument of his destruction, the "cause of his languishment." With its legacy of mortality, "that first marriage was our funerall"—the day of joy is the day of death. Love, elsewhere a redeemer, in these poems merely hastens the lover's inevitable death—

> One woman at one blow, then kill'd us all,
> And singly, one by one, they kill us now.

In this particular suicide, man can be counted on to cooperate enthusiastically:

> We doe delightfully our selves allow
> To that consumption; and profusely blinde,
> We kill our selves to propagate our kinde.
> (*First Anniversary,* 106-10)

The paradoxes of love are turned upside down, in an ominous precipitation of their own—in "The Canonization," the act of love, called "death" in the voluptuary's slang, brought ecstasy and resurrection; in the *Anniversary Poems*, a man seeking to secure his future in an heir simply shortens his life.

In every other way, man seeks his own annihilation. He takes pride in his ingenuity and works perversely to his own end:

> Wee seeme ambitious, Gods whole worke t'undoe;
> Of nothing hee made us, and we strive too,
> To bring our selves to nothing backe. . .
> (F.A., 155-57)

All this, from the creature who even in his fallen state is the object of God's extraordinary love:

> This man, whom God did wooe, and loth t'attend
> Till man came up, did downe to man descend,
> This man, so great, that all that is, is his,
> Oh what a trifle, and poore thing he is!
> (F.A., 167-70)

Death is hidden everywhere in life; spring-times are tombs, and in a fine pun, "false-conceptions fill the generall wombes." Man is doomed by his situation and further doomed by his behavior.

There appears to be no room for anything but despair in the picture Donne draws. However prepared readers are to expect death in an elegy, few could have been ready for so complete an elaboration of that morbid theme as these poems afford, evidently offering no way out from general and total condemnation. At the end of the *First Anniversary*, the world has had its qualities and attributes stripped off, like the gradually reduced man of Vesalius' drawings, until it is a dry cinder, lifeless, without substance, and without future.

But just at this point the paradoxist takes hold. We reasonably expect the poem to end, for the worse, on the grim note so long sustained, of death and annihilation. Our expectation is cheated, though, not merely by the reversal of tone and message, but by the simplicity of the reversal. By a rhetorical topos and a doctrinal paradox so familiar as to be commonplace, Donne turns the poem around, upon a future whose existence he has apparently hitherto denied. His own works, he says,

> Will yearely celebrate thy second birth,
> That is, thy death. . . ,

until, in truth, kingdom come. All Donne's readers, trained to the paradoxes of orthodoxy,[43] knew that death was not death, knew that

> though the soule of man
> Be got when man is made, 'tis borne but then
> When man doth die; our body's as the wombe,
> And, as a Midwife, death directs it home.
> (F.A., 450-54)

This particular paradox was no longer a "wonder," in Puttenham's word,[44] by the early seventeenth century. What is remarkable is Donne's manipulation of so "simple" a paradox—for, in fact, we discover rather to our chagrin, we have been prepared for just this turning from the very beginning of the poem, listening to a ground bass of argument accompanying the whole catalogue of disease, decadence, death, and despair. Donne tells us at the start that the lady's death raised "a perplexed doubt, / Whether the world did lose or gaine in this"; but the poem moved so fast through such sensational images and speculations that the reader was not permitted to linger over the perplexities of that doubt. Though Donne appears to have been in no doubt that the world lost and lost mortally by the lady's death, his question could be answered another way. The title of the first poem, *An Anatomy of the World,* implies a limited optimism, since anatomies are undertaken in the hope of an ultimate understanding of the body, even of a cure for bodies not yet dead. At the heart of one simile, fairly early in the poem, lies the promise of resurrection:

> For as a child kept from the Font, untill
> A prince, expected long, come to fulfill
> The ceremonies. . . ;
>
> (*F.A.,* 33-35)

baptism promises the chance of a future state of bliss. Even the lines suggesting total annihilation carry deep within them their hope of a better life—

> We'are scarce our Fathers shadowes cast at noone:
> Onely death addes t'our length: nor are wee growne
> In stature to be men, till we are none.
>
> (*F.A.,* 144-47)

The *Second Anniversary* begins with the death so fully described in the first poem; this death is particularly suitable to the moral condition of the world, since it is the violent retributive death of a criminal:

> Or as sometimes in a beheaded man,
> Though at those two Red seas, which feely ranne,
> One from the Trunke, another from the Head,
> His soule be sail'd, to her eternall bed,
> His eyes will twinckle, and his tongue will roll,
> As though he beckned, and cal'd backe his soule,
> He graspes his hands, and he pulls up his feet,
> And seemes to reach, and to step forth to meet
> His soule. . . .
>
> (*S.A.,* 9-17)

The long meditation, so brilliantly established in its traditional form by Professor Martz' analysis of the poem, follows properly upon the simile of the executed criminal. Each man dies for his mortal sin, but even so he may "step forth to meet His soule," trusting that "th'immaculate blood" of a

far greater victim of execution will "wash his score." Indeed, the terrible
death of Donne's lady, which has reduced the world and all its wonders to
a dry cinder, is seen to be the exemplum of a proper death. Man is exhorted
to "thinke" himself into a good death, like the lady's, with all the strength
he has. No matter how closely a man may be in possession of righteousness
while he lives (and some men are, as even Donne admits), "Death must
usher, and unlocke the door" for the imprisoned soul. Death is the birth
into eternal life, into beatitude, into real knowledge. The soul's curious
perplexed doubt in the *First Anniversary*—

> For who is sure he hath a Soule, unless
> It see, and judge, and follow worthinesse,
> And by Deedes praise it?
>
> (*F.A.*, 3-5)

—comes to resolution in the *Second Anniversary*, where in the very symptom of its illness lies the hope of a cure. "O my insatiate soule," the poet
cries out,

> Be thirstie still, and drinke still till thou goe
> To th'only Health, to be Hydroptique so.
>
> (*S.A.*, 47-48)

Man's ignorance turns in his hand to become a weapon of his salvation
("To be thus stupid is Alacritie" in the search for God); his very lethargie
is actually memory disguised. The lady has proved stronger in her going
than in her staying, for though in her life she had preserved the world, in
her death she was still medicinal, "More Antidote, than all the world was
ill" (*S.A.*, 378). She was impossibly miraculous, that lady

> To whose proportions if we would compare
> Cubes, th'are unstable; Circles, Angular. . . .
>
> (*S.A.*, 141-42)

Because of her transcendent qualities, literally, her perfection, she had left
behind "a kinde of world remaining still," a new world of the imagination
with new creatures settled in a "weedlesse Paradise": or, the image of a
future heaven.

That image was literally regenerative. Under the prevailing narrative of
death and anatomy run the images of creation and recreation. As Davies
had said,

> Then doth th'aspiring *Soule* the bodie leave,
>   Which we call *death*; but were it knowne to all,
>   What life our *Soules* do by this death receave;
>   Men would it *birth*, or *Gaol-delivery* call.[45]

Death is the midwife to the soul's birth, sending it into its newly-perceived
world. In the *Second Anniversary*, the lady is invoked as the poet's co-
operative muse:

> Immortall Maid, who thou thou would'st refuse
> The name of Mother, be unto my Muse
> A Father, since her chast Ambition is,
> Yearely to bring forth such a child as this.
>
> (*S.A.,* 33-36)

In such a context, poetry, the living victor over time, is of consummate importance, in particular for a poet determined to paint the hyperbolical ills of the world. Rhetoric as an instrument of paradox becomes the instrument of transcendent meaning. In Davies' and Greville's epistemological poems, Donne might have found, had he needed it, some rudimentary suggestion of his own technique. In a rather elementary use of simile and metaphor, for example, Davies reinforced his concept of the truth of poetry: God is at once "the rising Sunne" (which in one of His hypostases He actually is) and is like the sun; the soul-as-substance is "a *Vine*" and "a Starre," in illustration of its form and function.[46] For the soul-as-spirit, a concept familiar to his readers, Davies needed no particular metaphorical support, and could simply explicate his view, as a prose-writer might do. Greville, like his friend Lord Bacon, distrusted the arts, including rhetoric, in which he considered that words were too often merely drugs, and language an imprecise and misleading means of communication. But the friend of Sir Philip Sidney could not denounce words altogether, and in the end he permitted to poetry (as well as to music) a particular place in the worship and service of God. Poetry is "like a Maker"; like the Maker, poetry creates worlds and states of mind.[47]

In spite of his friendship for Sidney, who endowed poetry with the highest powers, one feels a certain niggardliness in Greville's praise of the art of verse. Donne invests poetry with unqualified power. For him, the "name" of a thing, the *logos* glorified in both stoic and Christian traditions, was all-important.[48] From the *logos,* the originating word of God, all things took their form; the lady whose death had robbed the world of its soul, and thus of its life, had a name whose divine properties exceeded the "naming-magic" of Agrippa. Her name, Donne tells us, defined the world, gave it form and grace; when the world forgot her name, it forgot its own and thus ceased to know itself. Lost to the world though the sovereign power of her name is—and in a splendid practical illustration of his notion, Donne never assigns the lady a name, nor ever calls by their proper names her subsidiary representatives, Astraea, Queen Elizabeth, and the Virgin Mary[49]—that secret name has the power, in poetry, to "refine coarse lines, and make prose song." Across the wastes of despair in both poems echoes the image of song. The *First Anniversary* begins with the image of the lady in the angelic choir. Throughout the dirge for the world's ugliness, colorlessness, lack of taste, and bad smell, there is no hint that sound and speech have lost their power. So at the end of the *First Anniversary* the prose of complaint turns into song, the particular proud song of the Renaissance that sounded louder than mortality, and the religious song from which all spiritual life derives:

> Vouchsafe to call to minde that God did make
> A last, and lasting'st peece, a song. He spake
> To *Moses,* to deliver unto all,
> That song, because hee knew they would let fall
> The Law, the Prophets, and the History. . . .
>
> (*F.A.,* 461-65)

In emulation of that original song of revelation, the poet dared "this great Office to invade" in order to imprison in verse the lady's liberation. As the final couplet of the first poem says,

> Verse hath a middle nature: heaven keepes Soules,
> The Grave keepes bodies, Verse the Fame enroules.
>
> (*F.A.,* 473-74)

The poem does not ask blindly for eternal fame, as in the Horatian topos: his poems are not destined to live "forever." From the conjunction of the lady's spirit and his Muse, he wishes to produce a child a year, a poem in anniversary which shall create as the generations of man recreate, out of its own power, to

> worke on future wits, and so
> May great Grand children of thy prayses grow. . . .
> For thus, Man may extend thy progeny,
> Untill man doe but vanish, and not die.
> These Hymnes thy issue, may encrease so long,
> As till Gods great *Venite* change the song.
>
> (*S.A.,* 37-38, 41-44)

Song is constant, but songs are made on earth, and even divine subjects share their end with death.

All the same, words have a power transcendent over things. They are, certainly, all too subject to human abuse, as Donne well knew. The "spungie, slack divines" vent falsehoods and vanity as if they were the word of God. Libellers mis-speak and thus fatally distort the truth, undo the good done in the world. But words also make possible the lesson the lady teaches: her form and name make up the world's "worthiest booke," of which all human virtuous actions are "but a new, and worse, edition." That book was a bargain, too—

> rather was two soules,
> Or like to full on both sides written Rols,
> Where eyes might reade upon the outward skin,
> As strong Records for God, as mindes within; . . .
>
> (*S.A.,* 503-06)

The lady's ineffable name was properly holy, not falsely so, like the false saints of the Roman Church, but a true pattern for posterity, since

> what lawes of Poetry admit
> Lawes of Religion have at least the same
> (*S.A.*, 514-15)

Finally, in the conceit, the lady herself, not just the poet's description of her, becomes the lesson read to the people, with the poet as her reader: since her image "makes prose song," the poet's images become music. The final lines of the poem proclaim the lady's identity with the poem itself:

> Thou art the Proclamation; and I am
> The Trumpet, at whose voyce the people came.
> (*S.A.*, 527-28)

The miraculous lady, alive and revivifying even in her death, is the pattern for and the image of the life to come. She is its whole idea; preparation for that life is best achieved in "reading" her, or in listening to her proclamation —in reading, then, the poet's poems. He is her trumpet, an instrument announcing her reign and the end of the old world. His poems are to go on, as the herald's trumpets resound, proclaiming the sovereign from generation to generation, "untill Gods great *Venite* change the song," and another Trumpet shall sound, to announce the great change of Doomsday.

At that final resurrection to grace, body and soul shall fuse again, this time into a permanent perfection where decay is impossible. In that state, indescribable, like all ideas of heavenly bliss, the frontiers of the senses shall be breached for the achievement of total experience. Man shall no longer be partial, but whole and indivisible. Donne's rhetoric reaches out to express such supernatural unity in, for instance, the lines so often quoted as his "metaphysical" denial of the limitations of sense:

> her pure, and eloquent blood
> Spoke in her cheekes, and so distinctly wrought,
> That one might almost say, her body thought; . . .
> (*S.A.*, 244-46)

But this is not simply a stylistic trick performed for its own sake, as the Sophists might have done: Donne is making a metaphysical, a theological, and a poetical statement. The lady's significant perfection permits her to think by a grosser part than is usually granted mortals to think by. The interpenetration of body and mind in this lady is not just the poet's *epideixis:* Donne means exactly what he says. The daring of his image proceeds from the concept it seeks to express. When we look at the poems closely, we see that throughout their long length, Donne makes a fusion, even a confusion, of part and whole, to indicate the total fusion of experience to which his poems are to lead. He does not rely, as most poets must, on the rhetorical devices of metonymy and synecdoche merely; from first to last, he commits significant solecisms to point to his paradoxes. In heaven, he tells us at the very beginning, "that rich Soule" is "now a part of both the Quire, and song": she is, then, both container and thing contained. Of the joys in heaven, she is both "partaker, and a part"; she has gone to heaven "as well t'enjoy, as get perfection." Nor is she a passive recipient of grace—in heaven, "shee receives, and gives addition."

Such devices are rhetorical modes of expressing supernal unity, and that perfect knowledge promised in heaven, where the sight of God unites object and subject, "is both the object and the wit," and where beatitude is at once "a full, and filling good." In spite of terrestrial evidence to the contrary, the container and the thing contained, by logical predestinarianism forever separate, must in ultimate salvation be one. Single is double, multiple is single. So the world, which took its form from the lady and which once contained her body and soul as the human body contains its immortal soul, may expect to live in her dying and to die into her new life. At her death, the world sings its swan's song, which is the poem; but the poet, good Christian that he is, does not sing all alone, like the swan. He sings specifically to other men, utters his "full, and filling good" for their salvation as well as his own. The poem, moving from a single death to the general judgment, moves toward the fulfillment of human understanding. It moves from a moment in time, one year after a certain lady's mortal death, to that last moment in time when time, the sum of parts, becomes eternity, the indivisible whole. In the *Anniversary Poems* the laws emulate the laws of religion, attempting to transcend the merely physical and intellectual incompatibilities that lead men into despair. The world's variety and change frighten the poet, alarm him into a skeptical questioning of his and all men's stoical security, and stir him to understand variety, change, and contradiction. These poems do not try to set things straight, to make contradictions orderly: they accept contradiction and paradox as the basis of human existence and of human understanding, and simply build upon that acceptance. The contradictions and paradoxes are the point in these poems, are the poems themselves, make up a whole at once active and passive, giving and receiving, full and filling. These peoms are a dirge that lies about itself, although like a good paradox it leaves the reader in no doubt about fundamental truth: these poems are a song of triumph, both of God's glory and the art of verse.

PARADOX IN DONNE

Michael McCanles

A letter which Donne wrote to Sir Henry Wotton in 1600 accompanying
a copy of his early *Paradoxes* reads in part:

> S^r. Only in obedience I send y^o some of my paradoxes; I loue y^o & my-
> self & them to well to send them willingly for they carry wth them a
> confession of there lightnes. & y^r trouble & my shame. but indeed they
> were made rather to deceaue tyme then her daughth^r truth: although
> they haue beene written in an age when any thing is strong enough to
> overthrow her: if they make y^o to find better reasons against them they
> do there office: for they are but swaggerers: quiet enough if y^o resist
> them. if pchaunce they be pretyly guilt, y^t is there best for they are not
> hatcht: they are rather alar$\bar{u}$s to truth to arme her then enemies: &
> they haue only this advantadg to scape fr$\bar{o}$ being caled ill things y^t they
> are nothings: therfore take heed of allowing any of them least y^o make
> another.[1]

A. E. Malloch in an article which called my attention to this letter comments:

> Donne's statement that his paradoxes are nothings has this much truth,
> that they only seem to represent a conceptual argument, but, in fact,
> do not. They achieve and sustain this appearance by means of a fabri-
> cated argument which consists of discrete statements equivocally united.
> But Donne also says that the paradoxes have a nature which is revealed
> in the act of meeting (or, more accurately, resisting) them. And their
> nature is revealed then because their being remains unfulfilled until they
> become part of a dialectic action. They do not become themselves until
> they are overthrown. They are written to be refuted, and unless they
> are refuted their true nature is hidden. Thus the paradox may be said
> to present one part in a verbal drama (truly a word play); the other part
> is not written out, but is supplied by the reader as he tries 'to find better
> reasons.'[2]

The point to be made about Donne's paradoxes is that we are simultaneously aware both of their internal (though sophistical) consistency and of their
inconsistency with reality: in short, they demonstrate the discrepancy be-

Reprinted from *Studies in the Renaissance,* 13 (1966), 266–87, by permission of the
author and The Renaissance Society of America.

tween concept and object in the very attempt to reduce object to concept. This discrepancy, implying as it does 'the wars of truth',[3] is at first unsettling, because we discover that the mind is capable of making arguments which have a certain self-consistency but which yet reach conclusions manifestly violating common-sense reality. If Donne's paradoxes as Malloch says 'are written to be refuted' by the reader's taking another look over the head of the paradox, as it were, at the reality which it purports to describe, this second look only confirms the initial impression: that the mind may contradict itself when faced with the existential. Or, to put it another way, the order of the conceptual is capable of going its own way with internal consistency quite independently of things.

This is not a new observation about human knowledge, whether from a philosophical viewpoint or from that of common experience. What is noteworthy nevertheless is the perennial interest we take, from Zeno to Chesterton and Shaw, in discovering anew the curious ways in which words and concepts can diverge from the world of the existential. This conflict seems interesting to us primarily because we all assume, with varying degrees of conscious precision, that minds do come in contact with matter and in fact reflect it to some extent at least. It would be fairly easy to show, furthermore, that even attempts to prove the separation between thought and reality, such as Ockham's and Hume's, operate within the context of a (thwarted) demand that mental concepts reflect material reality with univocal completeness. The dialectic which Malloch interprets Donne as setting up between reader and paradox is in reality a dialectic between concepts and things, and the result is not a synthesis of the two but rather an affirmation of their separation.

The structure and intention which Donne ascribes to his early *Paradoxes* are likewise fulfilled in many of his poems, chiefly some of the *Songs and Sonets* and *Divine Poems*. In fact, certain poems of the *Songs and Sonets* seem to be not essentially different in these respects from the *Paradoxes,* and it will be chiefly from these that I will draw examples. Lying behind Donne's paradoxes, however, is a long and involved philosophical tradition, which for convenience's sake one might call 'conceptualist', and which assumes as the criterion for true knowledge a correspondence between the modes and structures of both mental concepts and material objects. It is not my contention that Donne's 'paradoxical' poems are in the direct line of this conceptualist tradition. What is interesting to note, however, is the light which the ideas that occur at various points within this tradition, particularly the 'place logic' of Agricola and Ramus, throw on the peculiar exigencies and structure which give these poems their effect. As will become apparent, it is only within a context of a conceptualist demand for concept-object correspondence that the Donnean paradox delivers its unsettling suggestion of concept-object discrepancy. What follows is less a systematic tracing of the changing forms of conceptualism than a sketch of certain examples which illustrate most clearly the conceptualist demand for concept-object correspondence as it is relevant for understanding Donne's paradoxes.

II

The basis of St. Thomas Aquinas' criticism of Plato was that, 'wishing to save the certitude of our knowledge', he demanded that the object known exist according to the same mode as the mental concept of the object:

> Now it seems that Plato strayed from the truth because, having observed that all knowledge takes place through some kind of similitude, he thought that the form of the thing known must of necessity be in the knower in the same manner as in the thing known itself. But it was his opinion that the form of the thing understood is in the intellect under conditions of universality, immateriality, and immobility; which is apparent from the very operation of the intellect, whose act of understanding is universal, and characterized by a certain necessity; for the mode of action corresponds to the mode of the agent's form. Therefore he concluded that the things which we understand must subsist in themselves under the same conditions of immateriality and immobility.[4]

As a result of this demand for corresponding modes of existence in thing and in the mind, the modes of mental conception were ontologized and the structure of the universe was seen as formed according to the exigencies of the genus-species mechanism.[5] That is, since the relation of concepts in the mind is one of subsumption of the less general under the more general, the universe was likewise seen as consisting of material entities 'composed' by 'participation' in (i.e., subsumption under) various Forms. From Aquinas' viewpoint the genus-species structure properly exists only in the mind and refers only to an order among concepts abstracted from individual things,[6] and corresponds to no actual order outside the mind.

The important point regarding the Platonic ontologization of the genus-species mechanism is that it is the result of a demand, as Aquinas says, that mind and matter bear a univocal relation to each other. Plato, though differing with Parmenides on some of the inferences to be drawn from the latter's doctrine of the One, nevertheless agreed with him on the basic thesis that 'it is the same thing that can be thought and that can be'.[7] As a result, just as concepts are abstract predicates referring to classes which can be stated univocally of many singulars, so the Platonic 'Forms' are participated in univocally by the changing sensible things of the material world. Despite F. M. Cornford's disclaimer that the science of dialectic which Plato defines in the *Sophist* is not logic, we can only note that the structure of that dialectic corresponds to the central mechanism of a class logic, the hierarchy of genera and species.[8] In this fashion does Plato come fully under Aquinas' criticism that he had guaranteed certain knowledge only by turning the extra-mental universe into a direct reflection of the structure of concepts in the mind.

The implications of this demand for concept-object correspondence become quite explicit in certain of the Neoplatonists. Plotinus' disciple Porphyry platonized Aristotle's logic when he propounded in the *Isagoge* what he considered the fundamental question concerning the status of the genus-species mechanism:

> First of all, as to what concerns genus and species, the question is to know if they are realities subsisting in themselves, or are merely simple conceptions of the mind, and supposing them to be substantial realities, whether they are corporeal or incorporeal, and finally whether they exist separately or only in sensible things and with regard to them?[9]

Such a question, unintelligible from an Aristotelian viewpoint, is easily understood once we understand Porphyry's conceptualist inheritance from Plato. That Porphyry found the question too involved to go into is beside the point: that he could ask it at all is enough.

One of the most full-blown extrapolations of Platonic conceptualism is Proclus' *Elements of Theology,* where we find a cosmology arranged hierarchically according to the genus-species mechanism.[10] For example: 'Prop. 19: Everything which primitively inheres in any natural class of beings is present in all the members of that class alike, and in virtue of their common definition.'[11] Here Proclus is commenting on the main property by which singulars are related to a universal concept abstracted from them all: that the concept is predicated univocally (extension) of all these singulars and according to some common notes (intension). This quality of the relation between mental concepts and material things, however, is later transposed into a relation between higher and lower planes of being; for example, 'Prop. 29. All procession is accomplished through a likeness of the secondary to the primary.'[12] 'Prop. 28. All that is produced by a greater number of causes is more composite than the product of fewer causes', concerns the notion of the 'plurality of forms' referred to in footnote 9. That is, one might take the distinction between an individual man and the concept 'man', and find that the first is lower in the hierarchy of being because the number of concepts which can be abstracted from it (of which it is 'composed' by participation) is greater than those which go to make the composed concept 'man', namely 'rational, sensitive, living, material being'. 'Prop. 62. Every manifold which is nearer to the One has fewer members than those more remote, but is greater in power',[13] comments on the fact that more general concepts (those nearest to the most general concept, the One) have comparatively broad extension but correspondingly narrow intension ('members'). The result of ontologizing the genus-species mechanism is the famous Neoplatonic doctrine of emanations, the pyramidally structured universe in which, as Henle says of the Platonic world, there are 'objects of knowledge which, in content, in modality, in mode of existence and in point of any qualification whatever will exactly, point-by-point, correlate to and parallel the concept and intentional existence'.[14]

The next area of western thought where we can find further changes worked on the conceptualist demand for concept-object correspondence is late-medieval scholastic formal logic. The most influential treatise on logic, as Father Ong has shown,[15] was the *Summulae logicales* of Peter of Spain,

written some time during the middle of the thirteenth century.[16] Joseph P.
Mullally's introduction to a translation of the seventh treatise of the
Summulae logicales advances the thesis that Peter of Spain was heavily influenced by formulations of medieval grammarians before him, and that his
logic is worked out according to the formal structure holding between
words in grammatically correct syntactical compositions.[17] Something of
a naive realist, Peter of Spain went so far as to ontologize the relation between noun and adjective. In speaking about what nouns and adjectives (or
verbs) signify when they stand in a sentence, he says:

> This is not, in the strict sense, substantival or adjectival signification, but
> is rather the signification of something substantively or adjectivally, be-
> cause to signify something substantivally or adjectivally are [sic] modes
> of words, while adjectivity and substantivity are modes and differences
> of the things which are signified and which do not signify.[18]

In the basically nominalist approach to the relation of terms as signs to
extra-mental things signified of which Peter of Spain was a major forerunner, the realist ontologization of the genus-species mechanism was
simply reversed. Instead of grounding the structure of things on the structure of mental concepts and thus enforcing complete concept-object correspondence, nominalists such as Ockham found a simple but sharp distinction between the two realms of being. What is to be noticed, however,
despite the noisy controversy which they carried on, is that the positions
of both realists and nominalists in the middle ages were founded on the
same demand for concept-object correspondence.[19] Mental concepts become 'universals' when they are looked upon as connoting a content which
is derived from and can be predicated of many individual substances ('man'),
or of an accident ('rational', 'white') separated from the substance in which
it inheres. For the nominalists none of these contents could refer to an
actual object of immediate experience: there are only men, not 'man', and
'rational' and 'white' exist only in individual rational animals or white substances.[20] Therefore, taking the individual, discrete, and irreducible material
things of the sensible world as their ground, while assuming still that conceptual knowledge, to be true, must be univocally coextensive with things,
the nominalists came to the conclusion that mental concepts bear an equivocal relation to things.

Two Renaissance academicians whose roots are firmly in nominalist
logic and who bring us well up within shooting distance of Donne are
Rudolph Agricola and Peter Ramus. Agricola's *Dialectical Invention in
Three Books* (1479) is notable for a wrenching of medieval scholastic
machinery in the interests of a simplified rhetoric, and the keynote is
sounded when he crashes together the three areas of scientific demonstration, dialectic (argument concerning probabilities), and rhetoric, and insists
that all discourse deals only with scientific demonstration.[21]

Traditionally each mode of discourse had its own 'topics'. For instance, scientific demonstration was formed in terms of the Aristotelian categories. Dialectic, on the other hand, dealt not with demonstration but with argument *sic-et-non* about opinions and probabilities. The dialectical topics were simply 'headings one is to run through when one has to say something on any subject'.[22] Agricola, by asserting that all discourse dealt with scientific demonstration and establishing the topics of dialectic as the foundation of discourse, merely stated that whatever could be connected with something else by being found joined in a topic common to both was in fact connected with that thing in reality. Agricolan rhetoric falls into two parts. The first, invention, is the searching out of 'the middle term or argument' which will allow two ideas or things to be connected; the second step, judgment, is that by which we confirm the liaison so made. All this means in essence is that the mind working along lines prescribed by Agricola searches for some topic, or place (*locus*), in terms of which two things or ideas are similar and joins them accordingly. Actually this process is merely a variation on the genus-species mechanism. One has simply to find a generic idea under which the two things are subsumable univocally and the similitude so arrived at is taken as objectively true.[23] What we have is a theory of discourse which in effect makes the linking of ideas and things through a higher genus or place directly correspondent to the structure of things. To have 'invented' a common place and then 'judged' that two things were really united in terms of this common place was to have made a statement scientifically demonstrable, i.e., existentially valid. That such a mode of conceiving has little or nothing to do with the truth of things is obvious. It is entirely dependent on the manipulation of concepts in the mind within the exigencies of a univocalist and conceptualist genus-species mechanism. On that basis literally anything could be 'connected' with anything and the result 'judged' as true.

Rudolph Agricola's so-called 'place logic' was absorbed by Peter Ramus when he was a student at Paris under Johann Sturm, who brought Agricola's theories from Germany to Paris in 1529.[24] Ramus took the doctrine of places and blew it up to a revolutionary theory embracing not only all kinds of verbal discourse but all sciences as well; indeed, he took his so-called 'natural dialectic' to be the structure of all reality.[25]

The essential note is sounded immediately by Ramism: when dealing with the status of the universal (that hoary problem) it manages to have it both ways:

> The whole matter can be settled briefly this way. If you regard the words themselves, genus and species are notions within our souls, and thus are not substances, neither participating in nor lacking body or sensation. On the other hand, if you understand things themselves as genera and species of men, birds, fishes, cattle, colors, magnitude, virtues, vices, then, just as these things themselves are substances and accidents, so genera and species will be substances and accidents.[26]

This wholesale identification of concepts and things, by which concepts become things and things concepts, represents historically perhaps the nadir of the conceptualist demand for concept-object correspondence.

As it was for Rudolph Agricola, the system of places and the linking of arguments by univocal similarity founded on various places was the keystone of Ramus' logical theory. Invention became the search for generic categories within which two ideas could be connected by similarity; judgment was the comparing of ideas within various places and really constituted nothing more than the construction of a syllogism with the generic place as the middle term.[27] The last step by which single concepts (or things: they were interchangeable), having been built into propositions and linked by syllogisms, were made into a connected discourse was the so-called Ramistic 'method'. This meant beginning a discourse with a definition, and then subdividing or dichotomizing in descending order of generality, drawing out link after link in a manner similar to Neoplatonic emanation.[28]

The key to this business is Ramus' allowing idea and thing to be interchangeable. In this way he assumes that any collection of ideas into one group is likewise a grouping of things. Thus mental judgments about similarities are really judgments about reality. On the other hand, all statements about reality are in fact grounded on the modes of mental conception, i.e., the genus-species mechanism, where the relation is of common to proper. Therefore any univocal grouping of concepts under a higher genus becomes likewise the grouping of many real singulars into a real group.

The main significance for Donne's paradoxical poems of this conceptualism shared by such diverse philosophers as Plato, Ockham, and Agricola lies mainly in the changes which each rings on the central demand for concept-object correspondence. In this respect the Platonic, realist tradition which ontologizes the structure of mental concepts and the nominalist, empirical tradition which divorces the mental from the material can be seen to be operating as dialectical opposites on the ground of the same demand. However, the point to be made here is not primarily philosophical, but rather illustrative of something else which seems prior to both philosophy and poetry, namely, 'the fear of this evil that is ignorance', as L. M. Regis calls it.[29] This fear is wholly human and does not simply arise as the result of philosophical speculation, but rather is at the root of it. It is possible then to look at certain occurrences of the conceptualist demand for concept-object correspondence in European philosophy as perhaps only the clearest and most available examples of attempts to assuage the fear of the evil of ignorance. We may with the Platonic tradition surreptitiously insert the structure of the mental universe into the world outside of our minds, thereby guaranteeing that we will be able to find it again; or we may with Ockham despair of any complete correspondence of mind with matter, and turn the mind into a manufacturer of signs capable of signifying the outside world as best it can. Or, with Agricola and Ramus, we may simply crash the two realms together and consider both concepts and objects as 'things' capable of manipulation. In all three cases it is under the pressure of the demand for concept-object correspondence that the conclusions have been arrived at.[30]

III

Most relevant for Donne's paradox is Ramism, but the strange implications of this method, by which propositional unions and disjunctions of ideas are made directly reflective of the outside world and the vehicles of scientific demonstration, become intelligible only when seen against the centuries-long tradition of conceptualism that I have sketched briefly. From this viewpoint, one ought to see Ramism not so much as the overt cause of radical changes in Renaissance conceptions of thought and discourse as Father Ong tends to do, but rather as a symbolic form, to borrow Ernst Cassirer's phrase, manifesting these changes. In this respect, Renaissance Neoplatonism and Ramism become twin streams by which the conceptualism of late scholastic philosophy traveled into the seventeenth century to influence continental idealism and British empricism respectively. If, in relation to Donne's paradoxes, prose and verse, this container seems far too large for what it contains, that is inevitable. For such basic motifs and patterns of thought manifest themselves only in the aggregate, so to speak, and what I am defining here is less direct influences in the usual sense of the word than a *gestalt*, a pattern, and a milieu which manifest, with differences, basic guidelines and grooves within which European thought was moving at this time. For purposes of labeling, then, one might well be a 'Ramist' without having heard of Ramus or a 'conceptualist' without knowing anything about epistemology, just as today one may be an Einstinian 'relativist' without ever having read Einstein. What is significant here is the usefulness of philosophical formulations as heuristic devices for bringing to focus latent and amorphous contemporary thought patterns and tendencies, not an original idea to be sure.

The place to Donnean paradox in the context of conceptualism is a bit oblique but clear. On the one hand, the speakers or *personae* strive valiantly to think as if the conceptualistic demand for concept-object correspondence were indeed a fact. On the other, the very strictness with which the chain of conceptual argument is worked out demonstrates through contradiction, paradox, reversal, and dialectic the ultimate inability of the mind to reduce the real wholly to itself. One of the main notes which all have recognized in Donne's poetry in general is its tendency to carry a given idea, metaphor, or assertion out to its logical extreme. As far as the poems which I am going to survey are concerned, this extension of the logical argument has as its primary purpose the pushing of a given argument to the point where its inadequacy for reflecting reality becomes fully recognizable. As such it then becomes an 'alarum to truth', as Donne says, and requires the mind of the reader to take a new look not only at the reality but also at its own capabilities for grasping that reality.

Here are two excerpts from the first of the prose *Paradoxes*, 'A Defence of Womens Inconstancy':

That Women are *Inconstant*, I with any man confess, but that *Inconstancy*
is a bad quality, I against any man will maintain: For every thing as it is one
better than another, so is it fuller of *change*; The *Heavens* themselves continually turn, the *Stars* move, the *Moon* changeth; *Fire* whirleth, *Aire* flyeth,
Water ebbs and flowes, the face of the *Earth* altereth her looks, *time*
staies not; the Colour that is most light, will take most dyes . . .
For as *Philosophy* teacheth us, that *Light things do always tend upwards*,
and *heavy things decline downward*; Experience teacheth us otherwise,
that the disposition of a *Light* Woman, is to fall down, the nature of women
being contrary to all Art and Nature.[31]

The first passage is similar to part of the argument in 'Confined Love':

> Are Sunne, Moone, or Starres by law forbidden,
> To smile where they list, or lend away their light?
> Are birds divorc'd, or are they chidden
> If they leave their mate, or lie abroad a night?
>   Beasts doe no joyntures lose
>   Though they new lovers choose,
> But we are made worse then those.[32]

The method of argument in both cases is quite simple and moves according to
the place-logic developed by Agricola and Ramus out of logicist conceptualism. What women and heavenly bodies have in common would be some
higher genus called perhaps 'substances which change'. The various comparisons in the discourse not only establish this place implicitly but also invest it
with the added notes derived from heavenly bodies. In a word, women are
grounded on and defined by the sun and the moon and of course only those
notes which they share univocally with these objects are illuminated for the
purposes of the argument. Having insisted explicitly on the univocal similarity
between women and the stars, however, the speaker pushes his conclusion
that since women change, and since it is the nature of stars to do so, it is
the nature of women also. Having followed out to its logical conclusion
this conceptual manipulation and found it correct in the terms given, the
reader must immediately jump to the conclusion that though the reasoning
is correct there is something wrong about the application of this reasoning.
One line of argument has generated its dialectical opposite, the realization
of some of the ways in fact in which women are not like the sun and stars.
In the second passage Donne simply reverses the previous argument by a pun
on 'light' by which he proves that women do not conform to natural law.
Yet in a sense this is an argument founded, if only by reverse, on natural
law by the very fact that 'light' women become an exception to it. Our attention is focused on the pun, and we are reminded that there is a difference
between physical and moral 'lightness', just as there is a real difference
between the realm of physical and moral law. Again, the connection between
woman and physical bodies, explicitly affirmed by the pun on 'light', only
serves to indicate the ways in which the connection is invalid. The passage

from 'Confined Love' works essentially the same way: a 'place' which we might call 'things which change' is established as a supreme genus by the speaker's citing such 'species' as 'Sunne, Moone, or Starres' and birds and beasts; implicitly the speaker asserts that human love falls within these places and thereby shares commonly with stars and birds the notes character-istic of these logical places. The last three lines of the poem (19-21) shift the grounds of the argument, although the basic method is the same:

> Good is not good, unlesse
> A thousand it possesse,
> But doth wast with greedinesse.

As a general statement we might well agree with it, until we ask just what particular things the concept of 'good' is going to subsume. The poem has already told us: ships, trade, houses, and women. 'Good' here really means 'commodity', and by univocally subsuming women under this concept of good defined by the other examples as a commodity, we have the desired conclusion: women, by definition, should bestow their favors on as many as possible. Asked to act as if the conclusions of this poem were 'true', to take action in the world of existences on the basis of a purely conceptual manipulation, the reader revolts. But what he is revolting against is not simply promiscuity; he is also forced to revolt against the arguments for such promiscuity and ultimately to call into question the sources of these arguments, namely, the mind's capability of manufacturing structures of concepts in complete disregard of the full nature of the existential. Finally, it should be clear that the arguments, in both 'A Defence of Womens In-constancy' and 'Confined Love', operate on the Ramistic assumption that in fact mental concepts and the extra-mental world mirror each other exactly, and that the finding of common qualities between two things in the conceptual order is to assert a real connection in the existential.

'The Flea' was among Donne's contemporaries one of his most famous poems, and still is the prime example of one kind of his ingenuity. It is justly famous for the intricacies of its arguments, intricacies which, from our point of view, by sheer ingenuity only point up their removal from facts.

> Marke but this flea, and marke in this,
> How little that which thou deny'st me is;
> It suck'd me first, and now sucks thee,
> And in this flea, our two bloods mingled bee;
> Thou know'st that this cannot be said
> A sinne, nor shame, nor losse of maidenhead,
>   Yet this enjoyes before it wooe,
>   And pamper'd swells with one blood made of two,
>   And this, alas, is more then wee would doe.
>
> Oh stay, three lives in one flea spare,
> Where wee almost, yea more then maryed are.
> This flea is you and I, and this

Our mariage bed, and mariage temple is;
Though parents grudge, and you, w'are met,
And cloysterd in these living walls of Jet.
　　Though use make you apt to kill mee,
　　Let not to that, selfe murder added bee,
　　And sacrilege, three sinnes in killing three.

Cruell and sodaine, has thou since
Purpled thy naile, in blood of innocence?
Wherein could this flea guilty bee,
Except in that drop which it suckt from thee?
Yet thou triumph'st, and saist that thou
Find'st not thy selfe, nor mee the weaker now;
'Tis true, then learne how false, feares bee;
Just so much honor, when thou yeeld'st to mee,
Will wast, as this flea's death tooke life from thee.[33]

　　We have in the flea itself a kind of ribald Ramistic 'place', a common point where the two lovers have already mingled their two bloods. The rhetorical end of the poem is of course seduction, and to that end the facts noted in the first stanza can hardly be denied; in microscopic fashion the bloods of both lovers are already mingled inside the flea. The logical twist comes in the second stanza when we ask what interpretation is to be given to this marriage of bloods. If marriage means a physical joining of separate bodies, then the flea has joined them in something that is more than marriage, because now there is 'one blood made of two'. Only by reducing the concept of marriage to the mingling of bloods can the speaker assert that 'this flea is you and I'. Needless to say, more is involved than blood in an actual marriage, though the speaker has conveniently left this out. The 'we' in the lines

　　　　　　　　　　　　　　w'are met,
　　　　And cloysterd in these living walls of Jet

represents a reduction of the persons to their blood, and a further reduction to that blood which is inside the flea. The lady, like the reader, reacts to the logical conclusion of this argument that killing the flea will involve murder, suicide, and sacrilege by simply testing it against the facts. She finds that the argument is meaningless and that she is no 'weaker' after having 'killed herself' than she was before. Then the speaker pulls off an ingenious equivocation. From the point of view of his own argument throughout the poem the lady should be dead. That the consequence is palpably untrue in fact should mean that the chain of reasoning is untrue also. Yet the argument that the flea's death should have resulted in her death (but did not) depends precisely upon this chain of reasoning's being true. Either both she and the flea are dead, or she is still living, and if she is, then the statement that 'this flea is you' is pure fantasy. And if it is, then he has no business attempting to argue logically in the last line that the flea's death has anything to do with her at all. In a word, he tries to have it both ways, and in doing so catches himself in his own logic.

But the destruction of logic by logic in this poem is only part of its wider purpose, which is to display comically the complete independence of the rational argument from the nature of real things. 'Men and women are blood', which means that they are nothing else, is a univocal placement which ignores all differences and facts which the ground does not comprehend. If all blood is homogeneous then we can say that men and women 'are' not only all their blood but every part of it as well. Thus

> This flea is you and I, and this
> Our mariage bed, and mariage temple is.

Palpable nonsense in reference to the facts, but not so in Ramistic logic. Granting the continual denial of whatever facts do not enter into the links of the argument at every step, we can have no recourse but to agree with the conclusion. But when the exercise in definition moves out of the logical realm and into the existential one of rhetoric we, like the lady, triumphantly crush the flea with no consequences. In a real sense 'The Flea' asks to be crushed. The very ingenuity of its argument, ruthlessly cutting across all facts of the matter by strict deduction of concept from concept, cries out that the mental mechanism which composed it is easily and readily capable of manipulating mental entities in total separation from the objects from which they were abstracted. Like the *Paradoxes* 'The Flea' is also an 'alarum to truth', asking only to be knocked down in order to reveal not only its true nature but, more importantly, the nature of the human intellect capable of creating it.

Another poem similar in both theme and technique to 'Confined Love' and 'The Flea' is 'Communitie'. The poem begins with a series of statements which are really definitions of the relations between good, evil, and 'things indifferent'.[34] The conclusion, that the last 'wee may neither hate, nor love', is then applied to women, and the speaker reasons (ll. 10-12) that since Nature

> did them so create,
> That we may neither love, nor hate,
> Onely this rests, All, all may use.

The argument proceeds to point out the reasons why women are neither good ('Good is as visible as greene') nor evil ('If they were bad, they could not last, | Bad doth it selfe, and others wast'), and the final stanza concludes that women are like another indifferent object, fruit, and closes (ll. 22-24):

> Chang'd loves are but chang'd sorts of meat,
> And when hee hath the kernell eate,
> Who doth not fling away the shell?

In other words, the speaker proceeds to test the particular case, women, according to the ways it fits within the structure of concepts already established.

Since he finds that women are neither good nor evil he can ground them
securely on the only other place left, the indifferent. In simplified logical
statement, the speaker's argument moves this way: X is subsumable under
any one of concepts A, B, or C. It is not subsumable under A or B, therefore it must be subsumable under C. Formally the argument is flawless, and
even valid materially once one grants a correspondence between the speaker's
invention and disposition and the existential facts of women themselves. The
discrepancy between logic and fact, however, while calling attention to itself,
points in another direction as well. That is, the speaker's cynicism regarding
women ends in a withdrawal into himself and an attempt to rationalize
the situation in a way wholly controlled by his own mind. Logic becomes an
instrument of personal triumph; nevertheless it undercuts itself by driving
concepts too hard and attempting to force itself on the reality. So likewise
the speaker's cynicism dramatizes itself implicitly as a partial view. Here the
logical process of the poem and the ambiguous emotion which lies beneath
it meet in one poetic whole.

A final poem of this type, 'The Paradox', is interesting here mainly because it is a version of one of the traditional *insolubilia* of medieval logic,
namely, the liar paradox.[35] This paradox exists in many forms, one of the
simpler being 'Socrates says "Socrates says what is false".' The problem is
obvious. We have two propositions to judge the truth of, the first being the
whole proposition 'Socrates says "Socrates says what is false"' and the
second being 'Socrates says what is false'. If the first proposition is true
then the second is false; and if the second proposition is false, then presumably the statement which says that it is true is also false, in which case the
second proposition becomes true again. This problem exercised the talents
of many late medieval logicians. It is quite obviously a problem which exists
only within the realm of strict logical formulation, for it is wholly conceivable
that a man whose every statement has been a lie should for once tell the
truth in affirming that fact. The question is whether or not the second proposition can be taken as referring also to the first proposition which affirms
the second to be true. Paul of Venice (d. 1429) deals with the problem at
length, presenting a number of possible solutions. The one Bochenski favors
makes a distinction between the suppositions of the two propositions:[36]

> Second thesis: no mental proposition properly so-called can signify
> that itself is true or that itself is false. Proof: because otherwise it would
> follow that some proper and distinct cognition would be a formal cogni-
> tion of itself, which is against the first thesis [where Paul had proved that
> a concept is always of something other than itself].
>
> From this thesis it follows that the understanding cannot form a uni-
> versal mental proposition properly so-called which signifies that every
> mental proposition is false, such as this mental (proposition): 'every
> mental proposition is false', understanding the subject to suppose for
> itself; nor can it form any mental proposition properly so-called which
> signifies that any other is false which in turn signifies that the one
> indicated by the first is false; nor any mental proposition properly so-

called which signifies that every mental proposition is false, such as this mental (proposition): 'every mental proposition is false', understanding the subject to suppose for itself; nor can it form any mental proposition properly so-called which signifies that any other is false which in turn signifies that the one indicated by the first is false; nor any mental proposition properly so-called which signifies that its contradictory is true, as this one: 'this is true' indicating its contradictory. . . .

The third thesis is this: a part of a mental proposition properly so-called cannot suppose for that same proposition of which it is a part, nor for the contradictory of that proposition; nor can a part of a proposition that signifies in an arbitrary way suppose for the corresponding mental proposition properly so-called.[37]

The distinction which Paul draws is based on Ockham's distinction among the various kinds of suppositions. In essence he is saying that a proposition within a proposition may suppose for every other proposition except that one in which it is contained. Therefore the proposition 'Socrates says "Socrates says what is false"' contains no contradiction, because the truth of the affirmation 'Socrates says' is not referred to by the truth of proposition which it affirms. The total proposition supposes for the one act of saying, while the proposition within it supposes (possibly) for every other act of saying but this one. This *insolubilium* becomes a problem only when all concepts are taken as referring directly to things, as they are in the conceptualism of Plato and Ramus. In that case the propostion 'Socrates says what is false' may just as well refer to the statement Socrates makes in affirming that proposition as any other. Ockham's differentiation of various levels of supposition, which is in turn based on the separation of concepts both as mental entities and as signs of real things from these real things, makes it quite easy to solve this problem without any logical contradiction. At best this *insolubilium* is founded on a confusion between concepts (and propositions) which stand for real things (personal supposition) and those which stand for other concepts (simple supposition).

The Paradox

No Lover saith, I love nor any other
    Can judge a perfect Lover;
Hee thinkes that else none can, nor will agree
    That any loves but hee;
I cannot say I lov'd, for who can say
    Hee was kill'd yesterday?
Love with excesse of heat, more yong then old,
    Death kills with too much cold;
Wee dye but once, and who lov'd last did die,
    Hee that saith twice, doth lye:
For though hee seeme to move, and stirre a while,
    It doth the sense beguile.
Such life is like the light which bideth yet

> When the lights life is set,
> Or like the heat, which fire in solid matter
> Leaves behinde, two houres after.
> Once I lov'd and dy'd; and am now become
> Mine Epitaph and Tombe.
> Here dead men speake their last, and so do I;
> Love-slaine, loe, here I lye.[38]

This poem is based on the Petrarchan convention that the lover is 'killed' by love. If the speaker is really dead, of course, then he cannot speak. The whole poem is thus reduced to an *insolubilium*, 'I say "I cannot speak".' The point of the poem is the obvious one that lovers have died from time to time but not for love, and that there is an equivocation here. However, as I have pointed out elsewhere, Donne points up the equivocation between what the speaker says and the reality by driving home to its farthest reach one side of the equivocation, thereby producing the realization in the reader of its opposite. The implied statement in the poem 'I cannot speak' is founded on the literal meaning of 'death', whereas the fact of the 'I say' (which is the poem itself) drives home the transferred meaning of the term in Petrarchan convention. According to the solution of the liar paradox given above, the most he can say is that he is speechless in every instance except this one, but this one case in effect denies the validity of every other. If he is really in love there should be no exceptions. Thus the whole poem, which can be reduced to the proposition 'I say "I cannot speak",' is an attempt to force the reference of this proposition to every instance of fact. The foundation of the 'paradox' in the poem is the assumption that every statement and every concept in that statement must correspond to a reality in the actual world (cf. Parmenides' 'It is the same thing that can be thought and that can be'). The supposition of the whole proposition is the poem itself where the speaker 'speaks'. But that the proposition within the proposition negates that speaking is a conceptualist illusion. On the contrary, as was pointed out, the contradiction is a pure product of conceptualist manipulation and assumes a false existential validity only when the demand for concept-object correspondence is made. Donne in effect is requiring the reader to solve the *insolubilium* in a manner similar to that outlined by Paul of Venice. He forces the reader to make a distinction between the exigencies leading to contradiction in the logical order and those which are independent of that realm, one of which is the palpable existence of the poem itself, the record of the (living) speaker's speech.

All of these poems are 'rather alarums to truth to arme her then enemies' and 'if they make you to find better reasons against them they do there office'. The discovery that better reasons are needed and that reasons which the mind invents can diverge from reality in proportion to their self-consistency are simultaneous discoveries. The shock of the poems comes to the extent that the reader had assumed that 'logical' and 'real' are coextensive, and that deductions from the invention and disposition of a logical argument are by their very necessity valid for the existential. On the contrary, we find instead that internal consistency may be the sign of just the reverse. Nor, however, does this discovery lead necessarily to skepticism, at least for Donne. The alternative to the Platonic assumption of univocal concept-object correspondence was the nominalist insistence on the equivocation between the two, and skepticism may well be no more than the result of the thwarted demand that mind and matter correspond completely—an all-or-nothing situation. For Donne the issue is not so simple. In the poems examined here the mind reacts simply to them, destroying their arguments in the spirit of cerebral joking. Nevertheless, the dialectic between poem and reality, and poem and reader, which shows itself in these comparatively uncomplicated poems, can be found also in more serious poems of the *Songs and Sonets,* such as 'The Extasie', 'A Valediction: forbidding mourning', and 'Lovers infinitenesse'. In these poems the dialectic between reader and writer and mind and matter ends not simply in a destruction of the poem's argument, but rather results in a balanced, unresolved dialectic by which both sides coöperate in holding in solution existential situations which defy clear conceptualization and which can be defined only in paradox. Such situations include the body-soul and the lover-lover relations, relations which are analogical rather than univocally simple; in these poems there is neither conceptualism nor skepticism but a careful balance of the two. However, these poems will be the subject of another study. As for the purely 'paradoxical' poems discussed here, the pattern is clear and simple: paradox is seen to be the function of a previous demand and assumption about the relation of mind to matter by which they correspond completely. Nevertheless, 'there is an ancient axiom, which runs: the more bitterly and acutely we formulate a thesis, the more irresistibly it clamours for the antithesis'.[39]

V. LOVE POETRY

THE ARGUMENT ABOUT 'THE ECSTASY'

Helen Gardner

Whenever opinion is sharply divided on a question it is worth asking what the opponents are agreed upon. This will usually show what are the genuine grounds of disagreement and narrow the dispute to particular points. But sometimes such an inquiry has a more interesting result. It may show that the opponents are arguing from a common position which is itself false; and correction of this common basic misconception may make it possible to put forward a new view which can take into account elements in the opposing views which had appeared irreconcilable. The dispute over the significance of 'The Ecstasy' is, I think, a case in point. There is no short poem of comparable merit over which such completely divergent views have been expressed, and no lover of Donne's poetry can be happy to leave the question in its present state of deadlock. For it is obvious that those who assert that the poem is the supreme expression of Donne's 'philosophy of love' and those who declare that it is a quasi-dramatic piece of special pleading have now no hope of converting each other. The one side merely adduces fresh parallels from various Italian Neo-Platonists and from Donne's own works; the other continues to insist on the sexual overtones of the imagery and to point out sophistries in the argument. Neither side will recognize that there are elements in the poem which contradict its interpretation.

To Coleridge 'The Ecstasy' was the quintessential 'metaphysical poem': 'I should never find fault with metaphysical poems', he wrote, 'were they all like this, or but half as excellent'.[1] And to a poet-critic of our own day, Ezra Pound, it is equally, beyond question, a great 'metaphysical poem' in the truest sense. After printing the poem in his *ABC of Reading*, he commented: 'Platonism believed. The decadence of trying to make pretty speeches and of hunting for something to say temporarily checked. Absolute belief in the existence of an extra-corporal soul, and of its incarnation, Donne stating a thesis in precise and even technical terms.'[2] But among scholars there has been flat disagreement over the genuineness of the poem's 'Platonism'; and, even among those who regard it as seriously intended, there has been a recurrent note of reserve in their praise of the poem. Thus Sir Herbert Grierson, in his chapter on Donne in the *Cambridge History of English Literature,* declared that 'The Ecstasy' 'blends and strives to reconcile the material

Reprinted from *Elizabethan and Jacobean Studies presented to F.P. Wilson,* eds. Herbert Davis and Helen Gardner (Oxford: The Clarendon Press, 1959), pp. 279-306, by permission of the author and The Clarendon Press.

and the spiritual elements of his realistic and Platonic strains'; but added the comment, 'Subtle and highly wrought as that poem is, its reconciliation is more metaphysical than satisfying'. Three years later, in his introduction to his edition of Donne's poems, he expanded this view in a passage which may be taken as the classic statement of the orthodox view of the poem:

> The justification of natural love as fullness of joy and life is the deepest thought in Donne's love-poems, far deeper and sincerer than the Platonic conceptions of the affinity and identity of souls with which he plays in some of the verses addressed to Mrs. Herbert. The nearest approach that he makes to anything like a reasoned statement of the thought latent rather than expressed in *The Anniversarie* is in *The Extasie,* a poem which, like the *Nocturnall,* only Donne could have written. Here, with the same intensity of feeling, and in the same abstract, dialectical, erudite strain he emphasizes the interdependence of soul and body.

But, after quoting some lines, he added:

> It may be that Donne has not entirely succeeded in what he here attempts. There hangs about the poem just a suspicion of the conventional and unreal Platonism of the seventeenth century. In attempting to state and vindicate the relation of soul and body he falls perhaps inevitably into the appearance, at any rate, of the dualism which he is trying to transcend. He places them over against each other as separate entities and the lower bulks unduly.[3]

Against Ezra Pound's 'Platonism believed' we have to set Grierson's 'Platonism modified and transcended, and yet perhaps not fully believed'.

A wholly different view was put forward by Professor Pierre Legouis in *Donne the Craftsman* in 1928. He denied that the poem had any philosophic intention and declared that it was, within a narrative framework, quasi-dramatic, the representation of a very skilful piece of seduction. He regarded the Platonism as a transparently cynical device by which a clever young man, pretending that their minds are wholly at one, is persuading a bemused young woman that there can be nothing wrong in her yielding to him. After a detailed examination of the poem, Professor Legouis summarized his view of it by saying:

> Donne does not set out to solve once for all the difficult problem of the relations of the soul and body in love. He considers the particular case of a couple who have been playing at Platonic love, sincerely enough on the woman's part, and imagines how they would pass from it to carnal enjoyment; whether he thinks this *in abstracto* a natural consummation or a sad falling-off matters little; the chief interest of the piece is psychological, and character being represented here in action, dramatic. The heroine remains indeed for the reader to shape, but the hero stands before us, self-revealed in his hypocritical game.[4]

M. Legouis's interpretation was strongly contested by many scholars, notably by Professor Merritt Hughes and by the late Professor G. R. Potter.[5] Professor Hughes contested it by referring to Italian and French Neo-Platonists. He showed that the argument for the body's rights in love was a common topic in writers such as Benedetto Varchi, and declared that Donne's poem clearly descended from the casuistry of the Italian Neo-Platonists. Professor Potter supported Grierson's interpretation by a mass of quotations from Donne's poetry and prose to prove that Donne did indeed hold the views which Grierson said that the poem put forward. Neither of these writers, nor, as far as I am aware, any other opponent of M. Legouis, attempted to refute in detail his close analysis of the poem and his criticism of the sophistries of its supposed argument.

The controversy flared up in a slightly different form when Professor C. S. Lewis and Mrs. Joan Bennett skirmished over 'The Ecstasy' in the course of a general battle over Donne's merits as a love-poet.[6] Professor Lewis, classing the poem with 'poems of ostentatiously virtuous love', declared that it was 'nasty'. If the idea of 'pure' passion has any meaning, he said, 'it is not like that'; and he concluded by exclaiming, 'What any sensible woman would make of such a wooing it is difficult to imagine'. Mrs. Bennett took up the challenge and reaffirmed Grierson's view of the poem's philosophy. The debate had rather shifted its ground here to the value of the philosophic views put forward, or assumed to be put forward, by the poem; but Professor Lewis appeared to take for granted that we may disregard, as M. Legouis does, the poem's statement that the man and the woman thought as one and take it that the poem, in fact, presents a 'wooing'. Later, Professor Lewis, while 'still unable to agree with those who find a valuable "philosophy" of love in "The Ecstasy"', confessed that he had 'erred equally in the past by criticizing the supposed "philosophy"'. Asserting that ideas in Donne's poetry 'have no value or even existence except as they articulate and render more fully self-conscious the passion' of a particular moment, he declared that the real question was 'how that particular progression of thoughts works to make apprehensible the mood of that particular poem'.[7]

In spite of all the parallels from Italian Neo-Platonists and all the references to Donne's views on the relation of soul and body which have been brought against him, M. Legouis has not retracted. On the contrary he has more than once reaffirmed his view. He must have been encouraged in this obstinacy by the accession of a notable recruit in Professor Frank Kermode who, in his British Council pamphlet on Donne, informs the general public, as if the case did not need arguing, that 'The Ecstasy' may be classed with 'The Flea' as an example of Donne's 'original way of wooing by false syllogisms'. He says of 'The Ecstasy': 'The argument, a tissue of fallacies, sounds solemnly convincing and consecutive, so that it is surprising to find it ending with an immodest proposal. The highest powers of the mind are put to base uses, but enchantingly demonstrated in the process.'[8]

Professor Kermode's quip that the whole argument leads to 'an immodest proposal' finds certain echoes among those who claim that the poem's

Platonism is seriously intended. Thus, Professor Mario Praz, who spoke of
'The Ecstasy' as 'un compendio della metafisica d'amore quale la concepiva
il Donne', and repeated Grierson's view that 'Questa poesia tratta della mutua
dipendenza del corpo e dell' anima', confessed to finding disconcerting notes
in the Platonic poetry of Donne and cited, as an example, 'il contrasto tra la
macchinosa argomentazione metafisica e il pratico realismo della perorazione'
in 'The Ecstasy'. He thought that one would be inclined to think this the invention of a mocking spirit if one did not recall parallel statements from
Donne's letters.[9] Even Professor Merrit Hughes, by using such a phrase as
'the casuistic idealism of the Italians', and by calling Donne's poem 'frankly
carnal', shows that he believes the poem finds its culmination in a plea, or a
'proposal', that the lovers should turn from the enjoyment of spiritual communion to the pleasures of physical. This is the common ground on which
the dispute about the poem's meaning has arisen. Both sides take it for
granted that the main point of the poem is a justification of physical love
as not incompatible with the highest form of ideal love. The point of disagreement is whether the justification is seriously meant (and, if so, is it to
be taken seriously or is it worthless), or whether the whole argument is intentionally sophisticated and the poem shows somebody 'being led up the
garden path'.

The whole dispute has arisen, in my opinion, from a misreading of the
last section of the poem (ll. 49-76). The only 'proposal' which is made in
these lines is the perfectly modest one that the lovers' souls, having enjoyed
the rare privilege of union outside the body, should now resume possession
of their separate bodies and reanimate these virtual corpses. The phrases

> But O alas, so long, so farre
>   Our bodies why doe wee forbeare?
> To'our bodies turne wee then,

and

> . . . when we'are to bodies gone,

have as their obvious and main meaning, and this we must establish before
we start listening for overtones, or hunting for ambiguities, the sense 'But,
O alas, why do we for so long and to such a degree shun the company of
our bodies?', 'Let us then return to our bodies', and 'When we are gone back
to (our) bodies'. The final and, one must suppose from its position, the conclusive reason for such a return of the separated souls is not that it will in
any way benefit the lovers; but that only in the body can they manifest love
to 'weake men'.[10] The fact that an ideal lover is invited to 'marke' them
when they are 'to bodies gone' surely makes the notion that the poem culminates in an 'immodest proposal' absolutely impossible.[11] M. Legouis
himself thought it particularly shocking that 'the hypothetical listener of
the prelude re-appears and turns spectator at a time when the lovers as well
as we could wish him away. But the lovers, far from wishing him away,
actually invite his presence. They wish to display the mystery of their love

to one of 'love's clergie' as well as to the 'laity', to one who is 'so by love refin'd' that he can understand 'soules language', as well as to 'weake men', who can only glimpse these mysteries through the reports of their senses, and who need, therefore, the body for their book.

My own position combines elements from both views. I regard the poem as wholly serious in intention. (Whether it is wholly successful I must leave undiscussed for the moment.) But if the conclusion really meant what it has been supposed to mean, I should be on M. Legouis's side, since the arguments put forward, regarded as arguments leading to the supposed conclusion, are beneath contempt. None of the analogies work if taken as elements in an argument designed to justify the body's claims in love. I am not, on the other hand, wishing to deny that, as a corollary to its main line of thought, the poem implies the lawfulness and value of physical love. I should also not deny that separate lines and stanzas of the poem, if taken in isolation, are susceptible of a fuller and richer meaning than they have within the limits of the poem, and that we can legitimately quote them as expressing more than the lovers in the poem intend. I am only denying that the poem is in the least concerned to argue to this particular point. In other poems, as in the passages which have been quoted from his letters and sermons, Donne does declare that

> as all else, being elemented too,
> Love sometimes would contemplate, sometimes do;

but in this poem he is concerned with something else. As Professor Lewis justly says, one of Donne's greatest gifts as a lyric poet is the intensity with which he abandons himself to the exploration of a particular mood, or experience, or theme. In this poem, as the title[12] tells us, his subject is ecstasy. He is attempting to imagine and make intellectually conceivable the Neo-Platonic conception of ecstasy as the union of the soul with the object of its desire, attained by the abandonment of the body. Unlike the great majority of Donne's lyrics 'The Ecstasy' is a narrative, relating an experience which took place in the past. But by means of the hypothetical listener it turns into a poem in the dramatic present, Donne's habitual tense, in the long 'speech' of the lovers, which occupies two-thirds of the poem. Both the unusual narrative form, with its exceptionally detailed setting and its description of the lovers' poses, first seated, then prone in ecstasy, and the introduction of the hypothetical listener are made necessary by the nature of the experience while Donne is trying to render. It is the essence of ecstasy that while it lasts the normal powers of soul and body are suspended, including the power of speech, and the soul learns and communicates itself by other means than the natural. Ecstasy can then only be spoken about in the past tense. Donne has shown both a characteristic daring and a characteristic ingenuity in attempting, by means of his ideal listener, to render the illumination of the soul in ecstasy as a present experience. The conception of such a listener being refined, beyond even his own high stage of refinement, by his contact with the lovers in their ecstatic union is in keeping with

a recurrent note in those lyrics of Donne which deal with the mysteries of
mutual love: the claim that he and his mistress can give 'rule and example'
to other lovers, that they have a kind of mission. If we take the poem as
concerned with ecstasy and read its arguments as designed to illuminate
the conception of love as a union by which two become one, we can explain
the meaning of passages which have baffled commentators and have been
passed over silently by most disputants over the poem's meaning. I hope to
demonstrate that my hypothesis as to the poem's central intention[13] can,
as the older one could not, thus 'save the phenomena.'

I

Before considering the poem in detail I wish to establish that Donne
derived his conception of 'amorous ecstasy' from a definite source. Donne
actually wrote two poems on the ecstasy of lovers. Ironically, Gosse, who
has been the butt of scholars for his fantastic attempt to treat Donne's love
poetry as autobiographical, saw the connexion between them. There is often
much sense in Gosse's nonsense and in a single sentence on 'The Ecstasy' he
hit the mark twice. He connected it with the poem which has, since the
edition of 1635, been printed as the tenth elegy, under the title 'The
Dreame', and he owned to being puzzled by 'the obsession with the word
"violet"', which he thought 'had, unquestionably, at the time of its (the
poem's) composition an illuminating meaning which time has completely
obscured'.[14] The tenth elegy is not, in fact, an elegy at all, but a lyric. It
should be printed in stanza form, and its title, given to it by whoever edited
the edition of 1635 and placed it with the Elegies, should be altered. I wish
it could be called simply 'The Image'; but a wholly new title would be in-
convenient. I propose, therefore, to call it 'Image and Dream', which both
preserves a link with the older title and serves to connect the poem with,
and differentiate it from, the poem called 'The Dream' which appears among
the Songs and Sonnets. The poem puzzled Grierson, who was misled by the
title 'The Picture' which is given to it by one unreliable manuscript. His
error in taking the opening words, 'Image of her', to mean 'picture of her',
instead of 'intellectual idea of her',[15] led him to dismiss the poem in his
commentary as 'somewhat obscure', and it has never received much attention. Since it is not generally familiar, I print it in full.

Image and Dream

Image of her whom I love, more than she,
    Whose faire impression in my faithfull heart,
Makes mee her *Medall,* and makes her love mee,
    As Kings do coynes, to which their stamps impart
The value: goe, and take my heart from hence,
    Which now is growne too great and good for me:
Honours oppresse weake spirits, and our sense
    Strong objects dull; the more, the lesse wee see.

When you are gone, and *Reason* gone with you,
    Then *Fantasie* is Queene and Soule, and all;
She can present joyes meaner then you do;
    Convenient, and more proportionall.
So, if I dreame I have you, I have you,
    For, all our joyes are but fantasticall.
And so I scape the paine, for paine is true;
    And sleepe which locks up sense, doth lock out all.

After a such fruition I shall wake,
    And, but the waking, nothing shall repent;
And shall to love more thankfull Sonnets make,
    Then if more *honour, teares,* and *paines* were spent.
But dearest heart, and dearer image stay;
    Alas, true joyes at best are *dreame* enough;
Though you stay here you passe too fast away:
    For even at first lifes *Taper* is a snuffe.

Fill'd with her love, may I be rather grown
Mad with much *heart,* then *ideott* with none.

The importance of this poem to my argument is that it can be shown to depend directly upon a source, and the same source lies, I believe, behind 'The Ecstasy'.

I cannot believe that Donne could have written 'Image and Dream' if he had not very recently been reading one of the most famous and beautiful works of the Italian Renaissance, Leone Ebreo's *Dialoghi d'Amore.*[16] Written about 1502 and published in 1535, the *Dialoghi d'Amore,* if we judge by the number of editions, rivalled Ficino's commentary on the *Symposium (De Amore)* and Pico's commentary on some sonnets by Beneviente as a main source of sixteenth-century Neo-Platonism. It was twice translated into Spanish, and twice into French, as well as into Latin and Hebrew. The distinction which 'Image and Dream' turns on, between the 'dulling' of the senses by 'strong objects' and the 'locking up' of the senses in sleep, is handled at length in the third and last of the dialogues in which Philo instructs his mistress Sophia in the mysteries of love.

The dialogue opens with the lover, Philo, being reproached by Sophia for being oblivious of her presence. He excuses himself by saying that his mind was rapt in contemplation of her beauty, whose image 'impressed' upon it has made him dispense with his external senses.[17] Sophia asks how something so effectively impressed on the mind cannot, when present, enter the eyes. Philo acknowledges that it was through the eyes that her radiant beauty pierced into the very midst of her heart and the depth of his mind ('nel centro del cuore e nel cuore de la mente'). Sophia recurs to her point later, when in reply to Philo's saying that if she must complain she should complain against herself, since she has 'locked the door' against herself, she answers, 'Nay I lament rather that the image of my person has more sway over you than my person itself': the paradox with which Donne begins his poem. Philo agrees that the image has more power, since an image within the mind is stronger than one from without.[18] This is stock Neo-Platonic doctrine and parallels could be adduced from Ficino, Pico, Bembo, and many others. What makes it certain that Donne read it in Leone Ebreo is that Philo's first defence against Sophia is that she would not have blamed him for being unaware of her presence if he had been asleep. She owns that sleep would have excused him, since its custom is to remove all sense-perception (*che suole i sentimenti levare*). He declares that he has a better excuse than sleep and she asks what can blot out perception more than sleep which is a semi-death (*che è mezza morte*). He retorts that ecstasy brought about by a lover's meditation is more than semi-death. When she protests that thought cannot divorce a man from his senses more than sleep does, which lays him on the ground like a body without life, he answers that sleep restores life rather than destroys it, which is not true of ecstasy.[19] This leads to a long comparison between the physiology of ecstasy and the physiology of sleep. In the one, the mind withdraws, taking with it the greater part of its powers and spirits ('la maggior parte de le sue virtú e spriti'), leaving only the vital spirit to keep the body just alive. In the other, the spirits are drawn to the lower regions of the body to perform the work of nutrition, the mind is deprived of its reasoning power, and the imagination (*la fantasia*) is disturbed by dreams engendered by vapours arising from the concoction of food.[20] Both sleep and ecstasy, that is to say, discard and inhibit sense and motion; but in the one case the spirits are withdrawn and collected, either in the midst of the head, the seat of all knowledge, or in the centre of the heart, the abode of desire ('in mezzo de la testa, ove è la cogitazione, o al centro del cuore, ove è il desiderio'); in the other they are drawn down to the lower regions of the body. The heart is the link between the head and the belly, and is the seat of the soul, the intermediary between the intellectual and the corporal in man. The vital power of the heart preserves the mind and body from dissolution. But in ardent ecstasy it may happen that the soul will wholly enfranchise itself from the body, and the spirits, the soul's instruments, will be dissolved, or loosened or untied (*resolvendosi i spiriti*), by reason of the force and closeness with which they have been gathered together.[21] This is the blessed death of ecstasy. Philo, whose mistress will not confess that she loves him, declares that her image is acting upon him like poison, which goes straight to the heart and will not leave until it has consumed all the spirits. Her image, which he contemplates in ecstasy, arouses in him insatiable desire, and this desire would destroy the spirits which it has gathered in his heart, if her presence did not save him from death by restoring his spirits and senses to their natural functions. But the return to waking life does not take away the pain of desire which her beauty, contemplated or perceived, arouses.[22]

In his poem Donne has combined the conception of the image in the lover's heart, greater than the beloved in her person, whose contemplation 'shuts out' sense, and which 'oppresses the spirits', with an old familiar poetic theme, deriving from Petrarch: the theme of the sensual love-dream, in which the lover finds in sleep the satisfaction which his mistress denies him waking. The image is 'too great and good', and the lover turns from contemplation which may destroy life to sleep which restores it, bidding farewell to his heart as seat of reason and rational desire and allowing 'fantasy' and sensual appetite to reign. But at the close he decides that of the two ways of being 'out of one's senses', he prefers the madness of ecstasy, born of rational contemplation of her image, to the irrationality of sleep, in which he may enjoy the pleasures of fantasy and escape the pain of truth.

In discussing this poem we can point to a definite passage which provided Donne with his basic idea, the likeness and difference between ecstasy and sleep, as well as with certain phrases. The relation of the 'The Ecstasy' to the Italian treatise is less immediately obvious but more interesting. The long discussion of the physiology of ecstasy and sleep, as well as with certain phrases. The relation of 'The Ecstasy' to the Italian treatise is less immediately obvious but more interesting. The long discussion of the physiology of ecstasy, culminating in the description of the 'blessed death of ecstasy' and including an analysis of the nature of the soul and of its relation to the spirits, is patently the source of Donne's conception of ecstasy, as will be apparent shortly when I use it to explicate the poem. But Donne found much more than this in the *Dialoghi d'Amore*. The discussion of ecstasy does not arise out of the experience of an ecstatic union of the lovers, but from the lover's experience of an ecstatic union with the idea of the beauty of his beloved. The charm and strangeness of Leone Ebreo's book lies in its combination of metaphysical, theological, and cosmological speculation of the most daring kind with a delightful battle of wits between two persons; for Philo, while instructing Sophia in the mysteries of love,[23] is also wooing her, and Sophia is both the very clever pupil, asking leading and often awkward questions, and also the mistress who denies. The work, as it was printed, is unfinished. The close of the third and last dialogue looks forward to a fourth, in which Philo will teach his mistress about the effects of love.[24] It is clear from the close of the third dialogue that Sophia is weakening fast and that the whole work was intended to move towards the blissful moment when Philo and Sophia will be no longer the one the Lover and the other the Beloved, but both will be equally Lover and Beloved. This happy consummation is continually looked forward to and anticipated throughout the work as we have it; but it has not been achieved by the time the book ends. There is then no single passage describing an ecstatic union of lovers to which we can point as the source of 'The Ecstasy'. Instead, we find scattered through the whole work ideas and phrases which have been woven into the substance of the poem.[25]

The first dialogue, which is much the shortest, handles the fundamental problem of the relation of love to desire. Although short, it ranges over the whole subject of love, raising the questions which are to be treated extensively in the subsequent dialogues. The second dialogue deals with the universality of love and is concerned with love throughout the cosmos; the third

is one the origin of love, and treats of the love of God. Love between
human beings is left to be treated in the missing fourth dialogue, on the
effects of love. We can form a good idea of what it was to contain, for the
first dialogue contains a brief treatment of love between human beings,
and there are references in the others which relate human love to Leone
Ebreo's definition of love as the desire for union: 'an affect of the will to
enjoy through union the thing judged good'.[26] Thus in the first dialogue
he proceeds from this general definition to define 'the perfect love of a
man for a woman' as 'the conversion of the lover into the beloved together
with a desire for the conversion of the beloved into the lover'. And he adds
'when such love is equal on both sides, it is defined as the conversion of
each lover into the other'.[27] This mutual and equal love is the love which
Donne is writing about in 'The Ecstasy'.

What has convinced me that the poem was directly inspired by the reading of the *Dialoghi d'Amore* is that phrases which have puzzled me and
other commentators and readers cease to be obscure or doubtful in meaning when we read similar phrases in Leone Ebreo, and that, while it is possible to find illustrative and explanatory parallels for separate ideas referred
to in the poem in a wide variety of authors, once an editor can turn to
Leone Ebreo the task of annotating 'The Ecstasy' is child's play. Almost
all the *idées recues* to which Donne refers to in the poem are referred to or
handled at length by Leone Ebreo. Finally, one of the most striking statements of Donne's lovers echoes a fundamental and distinctive idea of Leone
Ebreo. This idea, which is directly opposed to the orthodox view as it appears in the writings of such Platonic doctors as Ficino and Pico and such
popularizers of Platonism as Bembo, is exactly what is usually referred to
as 'Donne's philosophy of love'.

The best example of a difficulty which can be solved by reference to the
Dialoghi d'Amore is the doubt which most readers in my experience feel as
to what Donne's lovers mean by saying that love mixes souls

> And makes both one, each this and that.

In the first dialogue Philo, at Sophia's request, speaks briefly of human friendship, differentiating those lesser friendships which are for the sake of utility
or pleasure from true friendship which generates the good and conjoins the
virtuous. This is the 'friendship of perfect union':

> Such union and conjunction must be based on the mutual virtue or
> wisdom of both friends; which wisdom, being spiritual, and so alien to
> matter and free from corporeal limitations, overrides the distinction of
> persons and bodily individuality, engendering in such friends a peculiar
> mental essence, preserved by their joint wisdoms, loves and wills, un-
> marred by divisions and distinctions, exactly as if this love governed but
> a single soul and being, embracing,—not divided into,—two persons. In
> conclusion I would say that noble friendships make of one person—two;
> of two persons—one.[28]

This notion that in the union of love one becomes two and two become one is recurred to in the third dialogue when Philo repeats that 'two persons who love each other mutually are not really two persons'. Sophia, in her role of Dr. Watson, asks how many they are, and receives the answer that they are 'only one or else four', since

> Each one being transformed into the other becomes two, at once lover and beloved; and two multiplied by two makes four, so that each of them is twain, and both together are one and four.

'I like this conception of the union and multiplication of the two lovers', comments Sophia.[29] These mystical mathematics also pleased the author of 'The Primrose', who not only rendered them succintly in the line

> And makes both one, each this and that,

but also remembered that the union of love was a multiplication when he supplied an analogy from nature in the violet which, when transplanted, 'redoubles still and multiplies'.

As for passages illustrating the poem, the following topics, given in the order in which they occur in the poem, are handled by Leone Ebreo; that sight is by means of rays emitted from the eye;[30] that although the soul is one and indivisible, it is also 'compounded', that is, it contains 'mixture of things'; that intelligences love the spheres which they animate, a conception which is discussed at great length to explain why the spiritual intelligence of man is united to his body. Reference to the *Dialoghi d'Amore* supports Grierson's adoption of the reading of the manuscripts against that of the editions in line 55, where the plural 'forces' renders 'le virtú' in the recurring phrase 'le virtú e i spiriti', and supports an emendation which I had intended to propose independently in line 67. In discussing the soul's relation to the body, Leone Ebreo uses the metaphor of gold and alloy.

More exciting is the fact that the first thing which is revealed to Donne's lovers in their ecstasy is something which Philo was at great pains to teach Sophia:

> This Extasie doth unperplex
> (We said) and tell us what we love,
> We see by this, it was not sexe,
> We see, we saw not what did move.

Philo first 'unperplexes' Sophia by teaching her that love and desire are not opposites. In arguing this Leone Ebreo sets himself against orthodox Platonism, as expressed in Ficino's commentary on the *Symposium* or in Bembo's *Asolani*, where the young man who puts forward this view is corrected later by the wise hermit. Sophia, who ably argues for the view that love and desire, or appetite, are clean contrary, is converted by Philo who explains that there are two kinds of love. Imperfect love is engendered by sensual appetite, and since desire, as soon as it is satisfied, dies, this love, which is the effect of desire, dies with its cause. But perfect love 'itself generates

desire of the beloved, instead of being generated by that desire or appetite:
in fact we first love perfectly, and then the strength of that love makes us
desire spiritual and bodily union with the beloved'.[31] Sophia then asks 'If
the love you bear me does not spring from appetite, what is its cause?' and
Philo replies:

> Perfect and true love, such as I feel for you, begets desire, and is born
> of reason; and true cognitive reason has engendered it in me. For knowing
> you to possess virtue, intelligence and beauty, no less admirable than
> wondrously attractive, my will desired your person, which reason rightly
> judged in every way noble, excellent and worthy of love. And this, my
> affection and love, has transformed me into you, begetting in me a desire
> that you may be fused with me, in order that I, your lover, may form but
> a single person with you, my beloved, and equal love may make of our
> two souls one, which may likewise vivify and inform our two bodies.
> The sensual element in this desire excites a longing for physical union,
> that the union of bodies may correspond to the unity of spirits wholly
> compenetrating each other.[32]

When the desire which is born of this perfect love is satisfied and ceases, the
love which inspired it does not cease, nor is the desire to enjoy the fullest
union with the beloved lessened by the temporary satisfaction of physical
desire. The first thing which Donne's lovers learn in their ecstasy is that
theirs is this 'perfect love', not born of desire or appetite, but of reason.

It may now very well be pointed out that having as I hope proved the
close dependence of 'The Ecstasy' on *Dialoghi d'Amore*, I have ended by
producing a passage which makes the same point as it has been assumed
that Donne was making in his poem: that lovers who are united in soul
must, in order that their union should be complete, unite also in body.
Here in Leone Ebreo is what has been called 'Donne's metaphysic of love'.
I would agree; but I would not agree that in this particular poem this conclusion is being argued for, although it is implied. I would say that 'The
Ecstasy' originated in Donne's interest in Leone Ebreo's long description
of the semi-death of ecstasy and in the idea that the force of ecstasy might
be so strong that it would break the bond between soul and body and lead
to the death of rapture. This death in ecstasy his lovers withdraw from, to
return to life in the body. What they are concerned to argue, in the concluding section of the poem, is that the bond of the 'new soul' will still subsist
when their souls once more inhabit their separate bodies, and that they
have a function to fulfil in the world of men which justifies their retreat
from the blessed death of ecstasy.

II

'The Ecstasy' falls into three parts. The first twenty-eight lines are a prelude. They set the scene, the 'pregnant banke' which rests 'the violets reclining head'; they describe the pose of the lovers; they tell how their souls
went out from their bodies; and they introduce the hypothetical ideal lover

who is capable of 'hearing' the wordless communication of the separated
souls. The scene is unusually detailed for Donne, and M. Legouis has commented on it sarcastically as showing Donne's incapacity as a poet of nature:
'Even when for once he lays the scene of his action outdoors, his metaphors
take us back to the boudoir or the rake's den. The epithet "pregnant",
though not voluptuous, is also sexual, and the drooping violets suggest
languor.' The violet, which puzzled Gosse, is not here because of any symbolic associations; but it may be as well to add that, although in classical
poetry it has erotic associations, in Elizabethan literature it is invariably
'modest', 'pure', and the 'virgin of the year'. It is here because it is a flower
which is found in two forms, the single and the double violet, and Donne
is going to refer later to this phenomenon of nature in an analogy which
he did not find in Leone Ebreo. The setting is a natural one. It is spring,
the traditional season for a dialogue of lovers. The bank is pregnant with
new life and the wild, or uncultivated, single violet grows upon it. The
word 'entergraft' which is used to describe the clasp of the lovers' hands,
is taken from horticulture; and 'propagation' has horticultural connotations
also. It is to horticulture and not to boudoirs that we must look for the
explanation of the presence of 'the violets reclining head'. The language of
the first twelve lines is 'pregnant' with sexual meanings. The 'balme' which
'ciments' the lovers' hands, as M. Legouis rightly pointed out, implies that
they are young and fit for all the offices of love. I have no objection at all
to his suggestion that the stanza

> So to'entergraft our hands, as yet
>   Was all the meanes to make us one,
> And pictures in our eyes to get
>   Was all our propagation[33]

implies that, although these are so far the only physical means which the
lovers have employed, they will soon enjoy that union in the body which
perfect love desires. But the main meaning is that so far their only union
is through the corporal sense of touch and the spiritual sense of sight. It is by
these means, particularly through their gazing into each others' eyes, that soul
is being 'conveyed' to soul and such an ardent desire for union is being engendered
as will cause the souls of each to abandon their bodies.

  This ecstasy, or 'going out' of the souls, is described in the first of the
analogies which Donne found for himself and not in his source. They have
all puzzled commentators. Their difficulty lies in the precise sense of the
connectives 'as' and 'so'. A paraphrase, 'As Fate suspends uncertain victory
between two equal armies, our souls hung between her and me', shows we
need to expand 'as'. The parallel is not between Fate's action and the souls
hanging in the air. The connexion there is purely verbal—between the old
Homeric metaphor of the scales of battle 'hung out' in the heavens and
the souls being 'suspended' above their bodies. This is an extra adornment
of wit over and above the point of the simile whose sense is 'Just as when
two equal armies are locked in battle so that neither side is advancing or

retreating, so our souls hung motionless, face to face, in the air.' The point
which is being established is the absolute equality of the souls and their
immobility. While the souls thus 'negotiate' or confer, the bodies lie inanimate on the ground, like statues on a tomb. They are 'her' and 'me'.
This is the only use in the poem of the singular pronouns. Elsewhere there
is an almost monotonous insistence on the plural pronouns 'we', 'us', and
'our', repeated, at times within a single line, and continually given metrical
stress.

So far there has been no suggestion of a union of souls. Indeed, the implications of the souls being like 'two equall Armies', and of the word
'negotiate', hint at the opposite. The notion that equality implies identity
does not occur until line 25, when it is stated that this was no parley between opposing sides, but a 'dialogue of one', as it is called at the close:
'both meant, both spake the same'. In order that we may know what the
souls said, the hypothetical bystander, another perfect lover, is introduced.
He is sufficiently 'refin'd' to understand; but, even so, he will receive a new
'concoction' from his experience, and 'part farre purer then he came'. This
is the language of alchemy. The only other use of the word 'concoction'
in Donne's poetry is in *The First Anniversary* (l. 456), where the 'example'
and 'virtue' of Elizabeth Drury works upon her 'creatures' to give them
'their last, and best concoction'. But the idea that gold, the perfect metal,
can be refined into a tincture which will transmute baser, that is less pure
or more mixed, metals to its own perfection is common in his verse. The
soul, as Leone Ebreo, citing Plato, teaches in his discussion of ecstasy, is
of a mixed nature, 'compounded of spiritual intelligence and corporeal
mutability'. But it can at times withdraw from the exercise of its bodily
functions and unite itself wholly to its intellectual nature.[34] It is then, as
he says elsewhere, like gold without alloy.[35] The souls of Donne's lovers,
which have thus withdrawn from their bodies, in order to enjoy 'true intellectual light', can, like tincture of gold, give a new concoction to the soul
of anyone capable of receiving it, making it 'farre purer'. The conception
of the soul as containing 'mixture of things', which underlies the use of
the alchemical terms 'refin'd' and 'concoction', is referred to explicitly
in the next section of the poem (ll. 29-48), which contains the illumination
which the lovers received in their ecstasy.

The first thing which the lovers learn is 'what they love'. By a supernatural
experience they learn what is hidden from the lovers of 'The Relic' who
'loved well and faithfully',

> Yet knew not what they lov'd, nor why; and from the lovers
> of the 'Valediction: forbidding Mourning', who loved with a love
> so much refin'd
> That our selves know not what it is.

(It is a Neo-Platonic commonplace that perfect lovers do not know what it
is they love.) Donne's lovers here see that it was 'not sexe', the 'difference

of sex', what distinguishes man from woman, that each loved in the other. It was something invisible, what they did not see, which drew them to each other, or 'moved' them both. By the mingling of their two souls, the invisible essences which drew them together, there has arisen by the power of love a 'new soule', and this new and 'abler soule' is, unlike all separate and individual souls, gifted with complete self-knowledge. It understands its own essence, or nature. The final ecstatic revelation which the lovers receive is the answer to the question which Lord Herbert of Cherbury's lovers debated in a poem which, as Grierson noted, is plainly inspired by 'The Ecstasy'. They learn that their love 'will continue forever'.

The 'new soul' has come into being through the action of love upon individual souls, which alone or 'separate' contain 'a mixture of things'. 'When the spiritual mind (which is heart of our heart and soul of our soul), through the force of desire, retires within itself to contemplate a beloved and desired object, it draws every part of the soul to itself, gathering it into one indivisible unity.'[36] It is two such 'recollected' or 'reconcocted' souls, 'mixed again' by love or desire for union, which love unites to make of two one and of each one two. This union is indissoluble because it is the union of perfect with perfect, or like with like. It is only those things which are unequally mixed which are subject to decay or mutability. The force of love has united all the diverse parts of each soul wholly to its own intellectual nature, which is its true essence, and the 'new soul' of their union, being wholly intellect, knows itself. The union of the lovers is the union of their intellectual souls, or spiritual minds. In their triumphant certainty the lovers borrow a word from the contrary philosophy of materialism, the Epicurean doctrine that the world came into being and exists through the chance congruence of atoms. It is by 'congruence' that they exist, but the atoms from which they grow are souls, and they have not come together by chance but by the force of love, which is the desire for union. Such a congruence is, according to Leone Ebreo, the secret of the whole universe.

In a parenthesis Donne provides an analogy from the natural world. I take the stanza on the transplanting of violets as parenthetical, pointing to the existence of something in nature which is both one and multiple, and regard the 'so' of the line 'When love, with one another so' as referring back, beyond the parenthesis, to love's making 'both one, each this and that'. Like a modern scientist, trying to explain some scientific mystery to laymen, Donne refers to something rather similar in nature to the union which love effects in souls. The idea, often referred to in this period, that certain flowers, including the violet, will grow double by frequent transplantation is perfectly true: 'It is a curiosity', writes Bacon, 'also to make flowers double, which is effected by often removing them into new earth; as on the contrary part, the double flowers, by neglecting and not removing, prove single.'[37] Marvell gives the right reason, in speaking of the 'double pink': 'the nutriment did change the kind'.[38] The richness of the new soil stimulates the growth of a superabundance of petals. But in Elizabethan

writers I have found certain hints that the 'doubling' of single flowers, and
the production of parti-coloured flowers, such as Perdita calls 'nature's
bastards', was the result of the mingling of seeds in the earth, and that the
'double' flower, or the 'streaked' flower, was actually two flowers in one.
Since it was not recognized until late in the seventeenth century that stamens
and pistils were sex organs, the phenomenon of hybridization was not understood. The passage in *The Winter's Tale* describes grafting as a means of producing pied flowers and Bacon wonders whether 'inoculating', that is grafting, might not make flowers double.[39] But he also refers to another method
of making shoots 'incorporate': the putting of divers seeds into a clout and
laying it in well-dunged earth.[40] This method of planting seeds together in a
bag is referred to by the sixteenth-century botanist, Giambattista Porta, in
his *Magia Naturalis*.[41] He appeared to think that by this method parti-coloured
flowers could be produced by 'commixtion of seeds'. And Puttenham, who
distinguishes between 'aiding nature', by enriching the soil in which plants
grow, and 'altering nature and surmounting her skill', gives as an example
of the latter the production of double flowers from single, as if more were
involved in this than mere mulching.[42] I believe that some such notion of
'commixtion' of seeds in the earth lies behind Donne's reference to the
'single violet' which, when transplanted, 'redoubles still and multiplies'. If
so, the analogy is a very good one, because the so-called 'double violet' has
far more petals than twice a single violet would produce. Union has produced
not 'two violets in one', but something much nearer the 'one and four' of
the lovers' union.

With the revelation that their love is immortal, the ecstasy of the lovers
reaches its climax. Unless they are to enjoy the 'blessed death' of ecstasy,
they must now return to their bodies. The conclusion of the poem (ll. 49-76)
justifies this return by reference to the doctrine of the circle of love. The
heart of Leone Ebreo's doctrine is that the world as it exists and was
created is such a circle. The inferior desires to unite itself in love with what
is superior; but equally the superior desires to unite itself in love with what
is inferior. The inferior desires the perfection which it lacks; the superior
desires to bestow its own perfection on what lacks it. The final cause of love
in each is the desire for perfection, for the union of all the parts of the
Universe so that it may perfectly realize the divine Idea of its being, and
be itself united to its perfect Source and End. The illustration which Philo
gives at some length to show the love which superior bears for inferior is
the love of intelligences for the spheres which they move and govern, and
Sophia comments: 'I suppose it is for the same reason that the spiritual intelligence of man unites with a body as frail as the human: to execute the
divine plan for the coherence and unity of the whole Universe.'[43] The same
force, love or the desire for union, which has united the lovers' intellectual
souls brings those souls back to their bodies. 'Love is the condition of
existence of the world and all in it'; and intelligent souls would not 'unite
with human bodies to make them rational, if love did not constrain them
thereto'.[44]

The souls of the lovers yearn towards their bodies, which are 'theirs', though not 'they'. They own their debt to them. By the joining of hands and the gazing of the eyes the desire for union became so strong that soul was conveyed to soul. (The word 'thus' in line 53 is meaningless unless we take it that the 'thankes' for the bodies' aid refers to the experience of the poem and not to some remote first meeting.) It was because the bodies yielded up their own faculties, the powers of the senses, and allowed the 'sensible soul' to be wholly united to the intellectual soul, leaving themselves deprived of motion and sense, that the ecstasy came to pass. The lovers turn to their own purpose the metaphor of gold and alloy, to declare that the body is alloy and not dross, and find an analogy to support them in their belief that they need not fear that the descent of their souls from ecstatic union to inhabit their separate bodies will make it impossible for soul to flow into soul. Donne is here referring, I think, to the fundamental Paracelsian doctrine that the influence of the heavenly bodies, whether good or evil, is the 'smell, smoke or sweat' of the stars mixed with the air.[45] It is, like the analogy with violet, an illustrative parallel: 'heavenly bodies cannot act upon man without the material intermediary of air, so we may believe that souls which are in the body can communicate through the body's aid'. The famous lines which follow display the working of the cosmic principle of the circle of love in the microcosm, or little world of man:

> As our blood labours to beget
> Spirits, as like soules as it can,
> Because such fingers need to knit
> That subtile knot, which makes us man:

> So must pure lovers soules descend
> T'affections, and to faculties,
> That[46] sense may reach and apprehend,
> Else a great Prince in prison lies.

The blood strives to become spiritual, to produce the spirits, or powers of the soul, which are necessary to unite the intellectual and corporal in man. Conversely souls must condescend to the affections and faculties of the body in order than man's sense organs may become rational. The mind, as Philo teaches Sophia, 'controls the senses and directs the voluntary movements of men'. 'For this purpose it must issue from within the body to its external parts and to the organs of sense and movement, in order that man may approach the objects of sense in the world around him, and it is then that we are able to think at the same time as we see, hear and speak.'[47] If the soul does not thus inform all the activities of the body, it is abandoning its task which is 'rightly to govern the body'.[48] Its duty is to take 'intellectual life and knowledge and the light of God down from the upper world of eternity to the lower world of decay' and thus realize the unity of the Universe. A soul that does not perform this divinely appointed function is like a prince in a prison. The concordance to Donne's poems shows how fond he is of the metaphor of the soul as prince and the body, with its limbs, as his province. If the soul does not thus animate the body in all its parts, it is imprisoned in a carcass instead of reigning in its kingdom. Donne is contrasting the Platonic view of the soul imprisoned in the flesh with the Aristotelian conception of the union of the soul and body in man. A prince is no prince if he does not rule his kingdom and a kingdom without a prince is a chaos. Prince and kingdom need each other and are indeed inconceivable without each other. In the final lines of the poem the lovers find a further justification for life in this world, in the duty to reveal love to men, and declare that, if one of 'love's Divines' has heard their 'dialogue of one', he will not be aware of much difference between their union when 'out of the body' and their union when they have resumed possession of their kingdoms.

III

It remains to ask how successful 'The Ecstasy' is in what it attempts, and this question is connected with the problem of why it has given rise to such contradictory interpretations. 'The Ecstasy' is remarkable among Donne's lyrics for its length and for its lack of metrical interest and variety. Although it has fine lines and fine passages, it lacks, as a whole, Donne's characteristic *élan,* and at times it descends to what can only be described as a dogged plod. It is also remarkable for an excessive use of connectives, such as 'as' and 'so'. It was this which first suggested to me that it depended on a written source. (Anyone who has ever corrected large numbers of *précis* knows how hard these little words can be worked in summarizing discursive arguments.) The word 'argument', I think, holds the clue both to the slight sense of dissatisfaction which Grierson expressed and also to the variety of misinterpretations which the poem has suffered. There is a tone of argument throughout the lovers' speech which is out of keeping with the poem's subject. The essence of any illumination received in ecstasy, if we accept the conception of such illumination being possible, is that it is immediate and not arrived at by the normal processes of ratiocination. In ecstasy the rational faculty is laid aside and in a holy stillness the intellect rests in the contemplation of what is, and in the peace of union. Donne's lovers seem very far from this blissful quiet. Their minds are as active as fleas, hopping from one idea to the next. Although we are told that the two souls speak as one and that we are listening to a 'dialogue of one', the tone is that of an ordinary dialogue in which points are being made and objections met. When Donne was inspired by the *Dialoghi d'Amore* to write a poem showing the achievement of union in love, he caught from his source that tone of persuasion which has misled readers. The poem *sounds* as if someone is persuading someone. The defect of 'The Ecstasy' is that it is not sufficiently ecstatic. It is rather too much of an 'argument about an ecstasy'. It suffers from a surfeit of ideas.

For all that it is a wonderful poem and a poem that only Donne could have written; and it holds the key to Donne's greatest love-poetry. No poet has made greater poetry than Donne has on the theme of mutual love. He has no predecessors here and virtually no successors of any stature. The poems which Donne wrote on the subject of love as the union of equals, such poems as 'Good-morrow,' 'The Anniversary,' or 'A Valediction: Forbidding Mourning' are his most beautiful and original contribution to the poetry of human love; for poets have written very little of love as fullness of joy. I am in no way depriving Donne of his glory when I suggest that it was in Leone Ebreo's book that he found this conception, which he made so wholly his own, of love as not being love 'till I love her that loves me'. I do not believe that Donne was very deeply moved by the conception of ecstasy. He too often in his sermons disparages the idea of ecstatic revelation for me to feel that it had ever had a strong hold on his imagination. He was, on the other hand, profoundly moved by the conception of love as union. 'Image and Dream' and 'The Ecstasy' would seem, from their closeness to their source, to be the first poems which Donne wrote on this theme. In other poems on the same subject we can explain ideas and phrases by referring to Leone Ebreo,[49] but we cannot in the same way speak of the *Dialoghi d'Amore* as a source. I cannot at present suggest when Donne first read Leone Ebreo, though I think it may be possible to discover this. But it seems likely that Donne's love poems, like his divine poems, came in bursts, a new theme leading to a group of poems, and that we can legitimately think of his poems on love as 'peace', like his youthful poems, the Elegies, on love as 'rage', as having been written fairly close to each other in time. More than one of the poems of mutual love assumes the presence of a king on the throne, and so must have been written after 1603. I do not wish to follow Gosse in trying to make Donne's love-poetry autobiographical and deprecate attempts to connect particular lyrics with Mrs. Herbert or with Lucy, Countess of Bedford. At the same time I cannot believe that we can divorce a man's intellectual life and the sources of his creative inspiration from his experience. Certain books, and certain ideas which we meet with in our reading, move us deeply and become part of our way of thinking because they make us conscious of the meaning of our own experience and reveal us to ourselves. I find it impossible not to connect Donne's marriage with his discovery of a great new subject for poetry in Leone Ebreo's discourses on love as union.

It is the fashion today in scholarly circles, in reaction against earlier idolizing of Donne, to exalt his wit at the expense of his artistic and intellectual integrity, and to deny that ideas had any value to him as a poet except as counters to be used in an argument. Donne's greatness needs restating. One element in that greatness is that certain ideas mattered to him intensely and that he made them wholly his own. It is characteristic of his intellectual stature that his Platonism was derived, not at second-hand from fashionable poets, but directly, from one of the great books of the early Renaissance. The *Dialoghi d'Amore* is an ambitious attempt to bring into a synthesis all the intellectual traditions of Europe. It attempts to include in its doctrine of a living universe, moved and united by love, the cosmology and physiology of Aristotle, the Platonic doctrine of Ideas, the Neo-Platonic doctrine of the Transcendence of the One and of procession from and conversion to the One by means of the Emanations, and the Jewish doctrine of Creation. Anyone who is familiar with Donne's religious writings knows how deeply he meditated the doctrine of Creation. It is the stress on this distinctively Judeo-Christian doctrine—that the High and Holy One Himself loves the world which He made—which distinguishes Leone Ebreo from the other masters of Neo-Platonism, Ficino and Pico, making him give the material universe and the body a greater dignity. We are not depriving Donne of his greatness and originality as a poet of love if we think of him as inspired in part by a book which, in its Hebrew translation, was in the library of Spinoza, and from which, it has been suggested, he took the idea which we most associate with him of 'the intellectual love of God'. In 'The Ecstasy' Donne is too tied to his source. It smells a little of the lamp. In other, more wonderful, poems he was able to tell in his own language and in his own way what he had learned in his experience, as illuminated by the Jewish Platonist, of love's power to 'interinanimate two souls'.[50]

SOME OF DONNE'S 'ECSTASIES'

Merritt Y. Hughes

I

It is still undecided in what sense, if any, the ecstasy in Donne's most famous poem should be regarded as mystical. Even if we evade the problem of defining mysticism, there is still the question of what ecstasy meant to the poet. In 'The Extasie' the word keeps its literal meaning of *ekstasis* or exodus of the souls of the two lovers from their bodies, for Donne tells us that they "Were gone out"[1] so as to unite into the "abler soul" which "Defects of lonelinesse controules" (ll. 43–44), and makes the discovery that sex was not the source of their love. Recent interpreters have stressed the change which comes over the poem at line forty-nine, where the lover, or as Pierre Legouis insists,[2] the seducer, ends the literal *ekstasis* of the two souls with a plea for their return to the physical senses of their bodies "Else a great Prince in prison lies" (l. 68).

A choice is also given us between the view of Leo Spitzer[3] that the literal *ekstasis* of the lovers' souls is "a mystic union of a Neo-Platonic order," and that of A. J. Smith[4] that the *ekstasis* is "the wittiest possible play" upon "the popular figure of ecstasy, the current physiology, and the Thomist doctrine of hypostasis as it was then generally accepted." On the choice depend both our conception of the ecstasy and the Prince and also our esthetic judgment of the poem.

If Smith is right in regarding the first part as reaching its climax in "the play of conceit . . . which has moved from the stock notion of refined love, and its figurative expression in fused minds, or souls . . . to the analogically supported position that the new, fused soul has insight denied to ordinary souls,"[5] it is easy to concur in his higher rating of the latter part of the poem simply as poetry. A reader who shares his view of the first part simply as a brilliant exhibition of wit, though he may admire the love-trance, must also agree with E. M. W. Tillyard[6] that it is "pretty coolly described" and seems to be "rather an academic affair." If our preference is reversed in favor of what Spitzer calls[7] the "allegorical figure of Ecstasis," with "the flexible figures of speech" circling around it, we are likely to agree with him that the last part of the poem, "in which the justification of the body is offered, . . . is poetically less successful than the first."

Before the ecstasy of Donne's lovers is accepted as a mystic union of a

Reprinted by permission of Grace D. Hughes and the Modern Language Association of American from *PMLA*, 75 (1960), 509-18.

definitely Neo-Platonic order, some of his less famous ecstasies ask for review. The least mystical of them occurs in *Ignatius his Conclave*[8] where his "little wandring sportful Soule" has "liberty to wander through all places and . . . all the volumes of the heavens." In *Ignatius* Donne, the space-man who William Empson thinks[9] should be more with us, momentarily contemplates the newly mapped skies of the astronomers as Cowley was to do in his "Extasie" as his spirit left "*Mortality,* and things below" to follow the track of Elijah the prophet past "th' *Moon* and *Planets.*" But unlike Cowley and unlike John Hughes, whose later "Ecstasy" almost forgot the earth[10] in its interest in the starry heavens, Donne's *animula blandula vagula* is not interested in the spectacle of the modern skies. Still less is it intent upon emancipation from mundane interests to pursue a mystic vision. It appears simply to play a minor part in the satiric strategy of *Ignatius,* and its appearance anticipates the part which ecstasy was to play in the metaphysical strategy of several of Donne's poems.

II

The strategy of several of Donne's best and worst poems depends upon the mystery of the soul's literal *ekstasis* from the body either at death or in moments of what may be called television in life. The single case of the use of the word *ecstasy* in a different sense is the insignificant one in the "Elegie upon the untimely death of the Incomparable Prince Henry" (ll. 26-28), where Henry's foreign reputation is said to have been so great that it

> was an extasie
> On neighbour States, which knew not why to wake,
> Till he discover'd what wayes he would take.

Here the word means a kind of amazement or paralysis of thought, as it does in *Eikonoklastes* when Milton says[11] that Parliament's "horrid proposition" to end episcopacy in the English Church struck King Charles "into an ecstasie." In the same Elegy the departure of the soul of the Prince is treated as if it were in fact the *ekstasis* of the soul of Britain or of the entire world: "Nor hath our world now, other Soule than that" (l. 58). In closing, Donne extended the compliment to include the girl who might have been Henry's queen and fancies the pair as potentially "two mutual heavens" upon whom he might look down like an angel to sing their loves.

In "A Funerall Elegie" and in both "Anniversaries" Donne again used the conceit of a departed soul as having left the world unanimated. Elizabeth Drury's soul was once "the forme, that made it [the world] live."[12] The conceit was familiar,[13] and in identifying Donne's subject with the bright occidental star which set in 1603 Marjorie Nicolson[14] regards it as none too hyperbolic praise for the queen "which did inanimate and fill the world."[15] For Donne her death was an ecstasy in the literal sense that every death was an *ekstasis* of a soul from a body. Fancifully mourning over the departed soul in "A Funerall Elegie,"[16] he reproached it for running away from the "busie noyse" of the world, taking "so much death, as serv'd for opium,"

and yielding to "too long an extasie." In "The Second Anniversary," since
he regarded his meditations on the departed soul as an annual *ekstasis* of his
own soul to contemplate a nobler one, he warned himself (ll. 321-323) to

> Return not . . . from this extasie,
> And meditation of what thou shalt bee,
> Of earthly thoughts.

In the "Anniversaries" Donne explored all the possibilities of the assumption that in temporary *ekstasis* from the body a poet's soul may contemplate
the permanently disembodied soul of his subject. The result is poetry that
stirs both the mind and the emotions. But in the inflated encomium of the
"Obsequies to the Lord Harrington, brother to the Lady Lucy, Countesse
of Bedford" the result falls short of poetry when Donne professes to hear
Harrington's voice as a "part of God's great Organ," and then—speaking to
him directly (ll. 9-15)—asks him to

> See, and with joy, mee to that good degree
> Of goodnesse growne, that I can studie thee,
> And, by these meditations refin'd,
> Can unapparell and enlarge my minde,
> And so can make by this soft extasie,
> This place a map of heav'n, my selfe of thee.

Grierson bracketed[17] the "Obsequies to the Lord Harrington" with Donne's
laments for Elizabeth Drury as a kind of passionless writing which too easily
accumulated "monstrous and disgusting hyperboles," though he also declared
that no English poem combined them with "more splendid audacities" than
does the "Second Anniversary." In several of his verse letters Donne used the
convention or perhaps what he sincerely regarded as the experience of
ekstasis with varyingly convincing effects. When in "A letter to Lady Carey,
and Mrs. Essex Rich, from Amyens" he imagines himself transported to their
presence and actually seeing them visibly

> in this my Extasie
> And revelation of you both,[18]

the conceit seems a transparent pretense in the service of compliment. The
falsity of the pretended revelation contrasts oddly with Izaac Walton's
solemn story[19] of Donne's vision of his suffering wife when he was on a
continental trip.

If Donne can be believed, absent friends seemed to him to be present in
absence, as he protested to Sir Henry Goodyere was his experience after
their parting in London:

> Riding I had you, though you still staid there,
> And in these thoughts, although you never stirre,
> You came with mee to Micham, and are here.[20]

The doubtful seriousness behind Donne's play with literal *ekstasis* in his correspondence emerges in a letter to Sir Henry Goodyere which Grierson quoted[21] in his notes to "The Extasie" for what light it may throw upon that poem. It is a long letter[22] touching the disagreements of great authorities on several doctrines, and finally regretting that, though faith has established the soul's immortality, "there is . . . no opinion in Philosophy, nor Divinity, so well established as constrains us to believe, both that the soul is immortal, and that every particular man hath such a soul." The letter opens with the words which Grierson quotes: "I make account that this writing of letters, when it is with any seriousness, is a kind of extasie, and a departure and secession and suspension of the soul, which doth then communicate itself to two bodies . . ." Although the interminable sentence later refers to Donne's obviously frequent impulses to write to his friends as rather casual "extasies," Grierson compared its opening reference to them with "ecstasy in Neo-Platonic philosophy . . . in which the soul escaping from the body, attained the vision of God, the One, the Absolute." Then returning to the poem, he compared the *ekstasis* of the lovers' souls with Plotinus' famous account of ecstasy as a rare experience—attained only four times in his life —of "a simplification, an abandonment of self, a perfect quietude, a desire of contact, a wish to merge oneself in that which one contemplates in the sanctuary" (*Ennead VI,* ix, 11).

III

It is, to say the least, strange to find the epistolary "ecstasy" which Donne once invoked to compliment two ladies whom he had never seen, abruptly identified with the Plotinian ecstasy which is the rare reward of the soul which turns away from visible things to make itself resemble the Absolute, the One, and may sometimes even unite with the One in a perfect union of which that of earthly lovers is a mere simulacrum.[23] Yet in a devious way Donne's conceited play with the ecstasies of letter-writing may be more definitely related to Plotinus that is "The Extasie." In two passages (*Ennead IV,* iv, 5 and 8) remote from the famous account of ecstasy at the close of the *Enneads* which Grierson quoted, the intercommunion of souls is discussed as an aspect of Plotinus' doctrine of the linkage of all human souls to the absolute One through their common life in the All-Soul and its contact with the Divine Mind, the first emanation from the primal One above all being. P. O. Kristeller has pointed out[24] that Ficino was very fond of these passages in the *Fourth Ennead* and of the debate in Plato's *Lysis* about the possible source of friendship in friends' common love of the *summum bonum*. Plato, said Ficino in his commentary on this passage,[25] ". . . Amicitiam esse vult honestam perpetuae voluntatis communionem. Huius finem esse vitam unam. Principium eius cognationem. Medium autem amorem . . . Cognitio convenientiam in idaea, sidere, genio & quandam animae corporisque affectionem significat."

A corollary which Kristeller notes[26] to Ficino's doctrine of friendship as communion of will and thought was the union or interchangeable identity of the souls of friends. It implied that, however far apart friends might be, their souls were constantly, reciprocally present with each of them. So Donne wrote from Mitcham to Sir Henry Goodyere in London to say that they were not separated by distance. And so he playfully began a poem which had no real concern with friendship by writing to Sir Henry Wotton:

> Sir, more than kisses, letters mingle Soules:
> For, thus friends absent speake.[27]

Ficino himself had set the example of play with the communion of the souls of his friends with his own by using the idea to explain his lapses of memory when he confused their names or was slow in answering their letters. If his friends' souls were constantly with him, what need was there to write to them? Or again, he turned it into a double-faced compliment in a letter to Pico della Mirandola by protesting that by long dwelling in his body his young friend's soul had actually rejuvenated him physically so that they resembled each other. When in an "extasie" Donne turns a more extravagant though similar compliment to Lord Harrington, we call it metaphysical wit.

IV

It would be unfair to Ficino and to the many Neo-Platonists of the Renaissance who believed deeply in the possible union of the souls of friends if Donne's casual epistolary ecstasies were traced to it while its possible connection with "The Extasie" was neglected. No satisfactory survey of the Neo-Platonic features of the poem has been made,[28] and the task is complicated by the fact that for centuries the basic idea had been a literary commonplace with often questionable Platonic overtones. They are faint indeed in Horace's salute to Virgil as *animae dimidium meae* (*Odes,* I, iii, 8), and they are hardly distinct in Augustine's borrowing of the phrase[29] in a passage which Aquinas quoted.[30] They are no necessary part of Montaigne's echo of it in speaking of his beloved Etienne de la Boetie.[31] In Tudor literature and Stuart drama Laurens Mills has spotted many echoes of it, but only a very few which trace the communion of souls back to Socrates or Plato, and none which clearly derive it from any Neo-Platonic writer. Plotinus, Ficino, Pico, and Leone Ebreo are not mentioned in *One Soul in Bodies Twain.* Behind the idea of the unifying communion of the souls of lovers Mills sees (p. 110) traditions of chivalry and courtly love as well as non-Platonic classical ideas. And it is worth noting that the non-Platonic authority of Aristotle and Cicero is cited by Leone Ebreo[32] in justification of his central doctrine "che l'amicizia onesta fa d'una persona due, e di due una." Honorable love and friendship seemed to him both to unite spiritual love with physical and to unite lovers and friends in a dual love because:

> ... (come dice Aristotile) ogni sapiente è buono e ogni buono è sapiente: di maniera che è gemino insieme nel corporale e nel spirituale. Ancora, la geminazione conviene a l'amore amicabile e a l'amicizia onesta, perché

sempre è reciproco: che (come dice Tullio) l'amicizia è fra li virtuosi e
per le cose virtuose, onde mutualmente gli amici s'amano per le virtú
d'oguno di loro: è gemino oncor in ciascuno degli amici e amanti, però
che ognuno è se stesso e quello che ama, che l'anima de l'anima de
l'amante è il suo proprio amato.

From the Neo-Platonic doctrine of the union of the souls of friends in
their common love of the good it seems an easy leap to the conclusion that
Donne was a pupil of Plotinus or Ficino. When Donne professed[33] his belief
in "a Religion of friendship" to "the Lady G" and in a letter (No. XXX,
p. 74) to Sir Henry Goodyere called it his "second religion," he was speaking the language of the Neo-Platonists. When he wrote reminding Lady Bedford that those "Which build them friendships, become one of two;"[34]
and when he addressed[35] Christopher Brooke as "Thou which art I," he
was using the traditional idea of the identity of the souls of friends for
which Kristeller notes[36] that Ficino drew support from Plotinus' *Fourth
Ennead*. If there is anything definitely Plotinian in Donne's professions of
faith in the literal union of the souls of friends in *ekstasis* from their bodies,
it should be traced to *Ennead IV* rather than to the passage which Grierson
quoted[37] from *Ennead VI* on the union of the purified and enlightened soul
with the One. Yet it was probably the famous passage at the close of the
last of the *Enneads* that Austin Warren had in mind when he described[38]
Donne's experience in "The Extasie" as "a mystical state."

To Warren's theory a sceptic might reply that "The Extasie" reveals
nothing more mystical than the carnal mystery of the boldest of all Donne's
religious metaphors in his early love poetry, the "mystick books" of *Elegy
XIX* (l. 41. *Poems*, I, 121). "The Extasie" begins with "The mystique
language of the eye" and "hands" of which Donne boasted (l. 4. *Poems*,
I, 89) his mastery in *Elegy VII*, and the role of that language in both poems
seems to many Christian readers to confirm Michael Moloney's conviction[39]
that "Donne is not a mystic by any standard which his own age would have
applied to him." For such readers the lovers in "The Extasie" are certainly
not "mystically joyn'd" in bonds at all comparable with those uniting the
bride and groom in the "Epithalamion made at Lincolnes Inne."[40] Yet their
union may be called mystical—as Moloney suggests—by analogy with "the
mystic conception of the ecstatic contact of the soul with Christ," or—as
Warren suggests—it may be a truly mystical development of the mysticism
which Donne probably first learned from teachers like St. Bernard rather
than Plotinus, though he associated it "not with the religion in which he
was reared, but with something literary and philosophical,—i. e., with
Neoplatonism."

If Warren is right, the question arises whether the union of the lovers in
"The Extasie" reaches as far as the genuinely mystic experience[41] which
Plotinus described in the closing chapters of *Ennead VI*. Or is the lovers'
union simply a metaphysical experiment with the idea of one soul in bodies
twain which contributed to Ficino's doctrine of mutual exchange or common
possession of souls by "Platonic" friends on the basis of *Ennead IV*? For

Ficino, says Kristeller,[42] such love was "a simple preparation . . . for the love of God, which is the true and real content of human desire, and is only deflected to persons and things by the reflected splendor of divine beauty and goodness in them." It is impossible not to see such a deflection in Donne's protests of the union of his soul with the souls of the ladies addressed in "A Valediction: forbidding mourning" and "The Canonization," which Margaret Willy ranks[43] with "The Good-morrow" and "The Extasie" as proof of his faith that "oneness of spirit is to be achieved only through the medium of the body." As the *ekstasis* of the lovers' souls in the first part of "The Extasie" assumes the momentary aspect of religious vision and reveals the sex-transcending origin of their love, it is easily mistaken for something more than human love. Up to line thirty-two Donne seems to be turning a potentially carnal love trance into a vision of the enjoyment of the beauty which Bembo taught in *The Book of the Courtier*[44] could be "sundred from matter" and become the inmate of the soul of the lover who learns that "the bodie is a most diverse thing from beautie, and not onely encreaseth, but diminisheth the perfection of it." But in the following seven lines the union of the lovers themselves becomes the end of their ecstasy. "The point of this seemingly tame issue," says Smith,[45] is in line forty-eight: "Are soules, whom no change can invade." So Donne's intention all along has been "to have the lovers announce their eternal fidelity, and prove it necessary by a conceited argument . . . linking a common figure for spiritual love with the metaphysical commonplace of the immutability of the soul."

V

Without trying to probe further into Donne's intention in "The Extasie," we may ask whether he was aware that the experience of his lovers was short of or counter to the fulfilment of the quest of the mystics, Neo-Platonic and Christian, whose works he knew. Did he consciously suffer from what has been called[46] complete failure to understand the solitude in which "les grands mystiques ont cherché Dieu—cette harmonie interieure que ce grand maître des mystiques, Plotin, a tenu pour condition essentielle de la vision mystique"? It is relevant to remember Donne's confessions of constant failure to concentrate in prayer, of which even more examples can be found in his *Sermons* than Herbert Umbach collects in his Introduction to the *Prayers*.[47] In his *Sermons* references to the doctrines of mystical theology are so rare, in contrast with their frequency in his love poems, that Helen Gardner makes no claim for him as a mystic of any kind—certainly not as a Christian mystic, for she regards him as sharing the weakness of many contemporary Anglican divines whose emphasis on liturgy "made them undervalue the place of private prayer in the life of the soul."[48] And she quotes Itrat Husain's remark that Donne's passages on Purgation, Illumination, and Union, "though paralleled by passages from the great mystical doctors, only serve to show how little Donne as a preacher has to say about the interior life." And in a chapter on "Donne as a Theologian,"[49] Evelyn Simpson also contrasts the mystical imagery of "The Extasie" with the "little that can be called mystical in the technical sense of the term in the *Sermons* and *Devotions*."

In recent discussion of Donne's mysticism there is some naive anachronism, for it would be absurd to expect to find something in any of his poetry or prose exactly tallying in terminology or feeling with modern treatments of the subject like Dean Inge's *Philosophy of Plotinus*. But it is a striking fact that Itrat Husain is doubtful "whether Donne himself reached the unitive stage of the mystical life,"[50] and that after quoting several passages from the *Sermons* he concludes that Donne regarded "the highest degree of knowledge and blessedness" as "reserved for the soul in heaven." But Husain does not mention a passage which gives Donne's reasons for that opinion and gives them in a way which may help us to understand both his reticence about religious ecstasy in his *Sermons* and perhaps also his fondness for irreverent play with its concepts in his love poems and letters. The sermon was preached at Easter, 1628, at St. Paul's, and was on I Corinthians, xiv.12: "For now we see through a glass darkly, but then face to face." Its message was that in this world we must be satisfied with the dark glass. Reviewing the record of men's visions of God in the Bible and in Church history, Donne said[51] that it might be

> fairly argued . . . That neither *Adam* in his extasie[52] in Paradise, nor *Moses* in his conversation in the Mount, nor the other Apostles in the Transfiguration of Christ, nor S. *Paul* in his rapture to the third heavens, saw the Essence of God, because he that is admitted to that sight of God, can never look off, nor lose that sight againe. Only in heaven shall God proceed to this patefaction, this manifestation, this revelation of himself.

In the confident denial that Paul in his ecstasy could have seen the essence of God, it is strange that Donne should contradict Aquinas' equally positive and carefully reasoned statement to the contrary. In an article[53] replying to objections to Paul's vision of the divine essence Aquinas reaffirms Augustine's assertion in *De videndo Deum* that Paul in his rapture did see God's essence and not the mere effulgence of divine glory. The same assertion is made about Moses: "and these things agree, for as Moses was the first teacher of the Jews, so Paul was the first teacher of the gentiles." Aquinas distinguishes the vision of God's essence from contemplation of divine truth *per similitudines quasdam imaginarias* and *per intelligibiles effectus*—lesser kinds of vision vouchsafed to David, Peter, and other biblical worthies whose visions never transported them out of their bodies into the third heaven, the *locus contemplationis beatorum*. And in another context,[54] Aquinas distinguished Paul's *ecstasis* from his body and all physical sensation, *per vim apprehensivam,* from the two ecstasies of love, one of which is the outgoing love of friends, while the other is the concupiscence which ends in madness (*furiam vel amentiam*). Bernard of Clairvaux, from whom Husain thinks[55] that Donne learned much about the mystic way of Purgation, Illumination, and Union, agrees with Aquinas about the possibility of union with God by *ekstasis* from the body in this life. Donne cannot have differed from Augustine and his Scholastic masters on this point without knowing why.

His reason for differing, as he immediately stated it himself, was his sweeping objection to medieval thought about the ways of "The School" to "union with God." All were over-valued by the Scholastic doctors, he said, except the way of open vision (*per apertam visionem*), "by his clear manifestation of himself in heaven." In speaking so Donne was perhaps more influenced than he was aware by a many-sided reaction against popular degradation of the mystic's ideal. Evelyn Underhill has noted[56] that "the greatest mystics, Ruysbroek, St. John of the Cross, and St. Theresa herself in her later stages" protested against the identification of mysticism "with visions, voices, and supernatural favours." Popular interest in ecstasy had become mainly confined to the perversions which Aquinas had attributed to concupiscence, but which many readers in the sixteenth century regarded as Jean Bodin did in his chapter "Du Ravissement ou Ecstase, des Sorciers, & des frequentations ordinaires, qu'ilz ont avec les Daemons."[57] Donne wrote for an audience which had rejected its faith in ecstasy as Aquinas understood it and was ready to accept Montaigne's view in his essay on "The Force of the Imagination"[58] that its "visions" and "enchantments" alike proceeded "from the power of imaginations, working especially in the mindes of the vulgar sort." People who liked to think neatly and scientifically were grateful for Charron's analysis[59] of ecstasy into three kinds, "Divine, Diabolicall, or Humane," and for his quick disposition of the divine kind, of which Paul's was the accepted example, by quoting the Apostle's words, *"Whether in the body, or without, I know not, God knoweth,"* as "An instruction that may serve for all others, and for other separations of lesse quality." By the end of the sixteenth century, if ecstasy in any of its meanings was to be taken seriously, it had to be turned into flights of imagination like Donne's "Anniversaries" or into ingenious compliments or courtships like his letter to Sir Henry Goodyere or "The Extasie." In them he worked in the tradition of the Platonic union of souls which Ficino and Bembo had taught was a step toward the final mystical experience itself, but he was always too averse to the doctrine of mystical union of the soul with God to take the final step with Bembo's lovers of universal beauty into "the most holy fire of true heavenly love," which is "the fiery bush of Moses . . . which doubleth grace and happinesse in their soules that be worthie to see it, when they forsake this earthly basenesse, and flee up into heaven."[60] Perhaps Donne knew that some Neo-Platonists had reservations, and that Leone Ebreo had said[61] in his discussion of the "copulation" (*coppulazione*) with God to which intellectual love leads that alone among the prophets Moses had reached that final peak of divine vision.

VI

It should be clear by this time that, however solemn a revelation of the nature of their love Donne's lovers may have had in "The Extasie," he could not have regarded it as something literally equivalent to the final mystical experience of Plotinus. We may see in their trance something as lovely as Amoret's embrace of Scudamour,[62] "overcommen quight Of hugh affection," melting in pleasure and pouring out her spirit "in sweet ravishment":

> No word they spake, no earthly thing they felt,
> But like two senceles stocks in long embracement
> dwelt.

Or we may see in the love trance a situation as equivocal as Tasso's picture of Rinaldo in Armida's arms, feeding his eyes upon her face and sighing

> . . . as if his Soul had fled
> With her beloved Sprite.[63]

If in Donne's question recalling the lovers from their trance—

> But O alas, so long, so farre
> Our bodies why doe wee forbeare—

we agree with Spitzer[64] that *forbeare* means "endure, tolerate," we may have to agree with him also that, "Donne knows, in fact, no true answer to that tormenting question." If we agree with Pierre Legouis that *forbeare* means "restrain, control," it is easy to interpret the following dialectic leading to that image of the "great Prince" to be released from his prison by the return of the souls to "sense" as the rhetoric of seduction. The poem is then degraded to a level close to that on which Cowley, frankly in the role of seducer in "The Gazers,"[65] asks his mistress to sit no longer "gazing only . . . As *Man* and *Wife* in *Picture* do." She should rather

> Mark how the lusty *Sun* salutes the *Spring*
> And gently kisses everything
> . . . .
> Then on the Earth with *Bridegroom* Heat
> He does still new *Flowers* beget.
> The *Sun* himself although all *Eye* he be,
> Can find in *Love* more pleasure than to *See*.

A sure answer to Donne's tormenting question may be no more possible than is a neat interpretation of his "great Prince" who must lie in prison until the right answer is found. But by ignoring the context of the *ekstasis* and union of the souls of Donne's lovers it is possible to reach confident and absurdly similar but incompatible answers. C. S. Lewis' verdict[66] that "The Extasie" is a poem of "ostentatiously virtuous love," "much nastier than the nineteenth *Elegy*" may be read either as confirmation or contradiction of Clay Hunt's admiring interpretation[67] of it as a "wholehearted acceptance of sensual satisfaction as an act which entails taking up a philosophic option, which forces one to embrace a philosophic materialism and to reject completely the doctrines of philosophic idealism." The only escape from the dilemma of treating Donne as a crude sensualist or as a materialist philosopher less at home in his own century than in ours is to look at him in his own intellectual tradition.[68] His contemporaries assumed man's central position in the cosmic hierarchy between the perishing beasts and the angels. Few, if any, of them would have denied Aquinas' doctrine[69] that the soul is united with the sensitive body for the sake of its own perfection, and that all souls are indebted to their bodies for having—in Donne's words—"Yeelded their forces, sense" to them. Probably none of Donne's readers would have challenged Aquinas' hierarchy of the senses[70] with touch at the bottom and the spiritual sense of sight at the top.

Contemporaries sharing Donne's interest in Neo-Platonic thought would know Bembo's doctrine[71] that by "correction of the senses" men might climb "the stayre of love" to "beholde the beautie that is seene with the eyes of the minde," but they would also have been aware that several famous Italian dialogues of love[72] had no less firmly asserted love's debt to the flesh as well as to the spirit. If it occurred to them to compare the ecstasy of Donne's lovers with that of Scudamour and Amoret, they would remember Spenser's comparison of his entranced pair with a certain "faire hermaphrodite," and they might recall the use of the hermaphrodite together with the centaur by Speroni to symbolize the fact that love is a compound[73] not only of animal with spiritual elements, but also of countless contraries. And the best read of Donne's audience might have known that this dualism went back behind the Italian Neo-Platonists as far as Guido Cavalcanti's recognition in his *Canzone d' Amore* that Love is[74] "both intellectual and sensual," and that beyond its first perfection in a cherished memory of ideal feminine beauty, "its second perfection is when it moves with the appetites of sense to the conquest of a living woman who has been recognized as similar to the ideal image in the memory." The doctrine resembles Joan Bennett's defense[75] of Donne's statement that

> Love's not so pure, and abstract, as they use
> To say, which have no Mistresse but their Muse.

For Donne love, "like everything else on earth, is composed of diverse elements."

Whatever violence—if any—may have been intended in "The Extasie" to the Neo-Platonic doctrine of a "stayre of love" leading to a perhaps ecstatic vision, Donne's proposal to liberate his "great Prince" can hardly be regarded as a revolt against the hierarchy of the senses. His prince is better seen as a relative of a less famous royal personage. In Chapman's allegory in *Ovid's Banquet of Sense* release is proposed for an imprisoned king who represents the sense of touch in a conversation about the virtues of the five senses between Ovid and the lady Corynna, whom he finds bathing in a garden. In the dialogue, says Chapman, the poet's object is to make his "intellectual life, or soule, passe into hys Mistres conceit," as "The Philosopher saith, *Intellectus in ipsa intelligibilia transit.*"[76] The last of the senses about which he shares his meditations with the lady is touch—"Sweete touch the engine that loves bow doth bend" (Stanza 113, l. 1. *Poems*, p. 81). It is an imprisoned monarch for whom the poet makes a specious plea:

> For if wee be allowd to serue the Eare
> With pleasing tunes, and to delight the Eye
> With gracious showes, the Taste with daintie cheere,
> The Smell with Odors, ist immodestie
>   To serue the sences Emperour, sweet Feeling,
> With those delights that fit his Emperie?[77]

Corynna's ladies interrupt the dialogue and "the sences Emperour" is not released in action.

Donne's imprisoned prince is a kindred but a different image. He is the soul that can perfect itself only through the life of the senses. In the image as it comes in the "Elegie on M^ris Boulstred" their hierarchy can be assumed: "Her Soule and Body was a King and Court" (l. 39. *Poems,* I, p. 283). In "The Anniversarie" the super-soul uniting the souls of the lovers is a prince who accepts the senses as a condition of love which will die only when the body dies:

> Alas, as well as other Princes, wee,
> (Who Prince enough in one another bee,)
> Must leave at last in death, these eyes, and eares.
>   (ll. 13-15. *Poems,* I, p. 241)

In "The Extasie" the super-soul is in a position somewhat like that of the "two souls . . . which are one" in "A Valediction: forbidding mourning" (l. 36. *Poems,* I, p. 50). The trance must end in resumption of ordinary consciousness by the lovers. But the banquet of sense to which they return need be no debauch. At worst it will be such a debauch as Jan Breughel the younger painted in his allegories called *Los Sentidos Corporales* in the Prado at Madrid.[78] All five of his scenes are voluptuous, but touch is not preeminent. Sight is the most interestingly treated of the five, and the traditional hierarchy is not challenged. At the banquet of sense—of "affections" and "faculties"—to which Donne's lover invites his lady in "The Extasie" the presiding "great Prince" need not be a voluptuary. He may turn out to be a patron of the arts, or even a devotee of the learning which John Donne himself loved; though, like Donne, he may not aspire to the ecstasy which Plotinus called "a flight of the alone to the alone."

*   *   *

This paper was read at the meeting of the Modern Language Association in Chicago in December 1959 and was in the hands of the Editor of *PMLA* before the publication of Helen Gardner's "The Argument of 'The Ecstasy'" in *Elizabethan and Jacobean Studies Presented to Frank Percy Wilson in honour of his seventieth birthday* (Oxford: Clarendon Press, 1959), pp. 279-306. Speaking from a more careful reading of Leone Ebreo's *Dialoghi d'Amore* than mine, and giving him unique importance among the Neoplatonists whom Donne may have read, she throws a steadier and more flattering light upon the poem than does my survey of Donne's other experiments with the ecstasies and unions of the souls of friends and lovers.

"THE CANONIZATION"—THE LANGUAGE OF PARADOX RECONSIDERED

William J. Rooney

At the end of *The Well Wrought Urn*[1] Cleanth Brooks tells us that the generalizations which he makes depend for their validity upon the adequacy of his reading of particular poems.

> The reader will by this time have made up his mind as to whether the readings are adequate. (I use the word, advisedly, for the readings do not pretend to be exhaustive, and certainly it is highly unlikely that they are not in error in one detail or another). If the reader feels that they are seriously inadequate, then the case has been judged; for the generalizations that follow will be thoroughly vitiated by the inept handling of the particular cases. (p. 177)

I propose, therefore, to examine the adequacy of Brooks' reading of "The Canonization," which he has offered as a kind of archetypal[2] illustration of his now famous thesis (almost a commonplace of American criticism) that "there is a sense in which paradox is the language appropriate and inevitable to poetry" (p. 3). I choose "The Canonization" because if Brooks' thesis is not verifiable there, it is probably verifiable nowhere. "Donne's 'Canonization,' he tells us, ought to provide a sufficiently extreme instance."

> The basic metaphor which underlies the poem (and which is reflected in the title) involves a sort of paradox. For the poet daringly treats profane love as if it were divine love. The canonization is not that of a pair of holy anchorites who have renounced the world and the flesh. The hermitage of each is the other's body; but they do renounce the world, and so their title to sainthood is cunningly argued. The poem then is a parody of Christian sainthood; but it is an intensely serious parody of a sort that modern man, habituated as he is to an easy yes or no, can hardly understand. He refuses to accept the paradox as a serious rhetorical device; and since he is able to accept it only as a cheap trick, he is forced into this dilemma. Either: Donne does not take love seriously; here he is merely sharpening his wit as a sort of mechanical exercise. Or: Donne does not take sainthood seriously; here he is merely indulging in a cynical and bawdy parody.

Reprinted from *English Literary History*, 23 (1956), 36–47, by permission of the author and The Johns Hopkins Press.

Brooks says:

Neither account is true; a reading of the poem will show that Donne
takes both love and religion seriously; it will show, further, that the
paradox is here his inevitable instrument. But to see this plainly will re-
quite a closer reading than most of us give to poetry. (p. 10-12)

"To see this plainly," Brooks gives "The Canonization" "a closer reading"
which consists principally in an anlysis of some of the *semantical* implications (1) of address ("The person" addressed "represents the practical
world which regards love as a silly affection"); (2) of the "metaphor" of
canonization "on which the poem is built" (Donne begins to suggest this
metaphor in the first stanza by the contemptuous alternatives which he
suggests to the friend"); (3) of the "conflict between the 'real' world and the
lover absorbed in the world of love" (It "runs through the poem; it dominates
the second stanza . . . is touched on in the fourth . . . appears again in the last
only to be resolved when the unworldly lovers, love's saints who have given
up the world, paradoxically achieve a more intense world"); (4) of the love
metaphors which begin in a "vein of irony" and shift "from ironic banter
into a defiant but controlled tenderness" ("The effect of the poet's implied
awareness of the lover's apparent madness is to cleanse and revivify metaphor; to indicate the sense in which the poet accepts it, and thus to prepare
us for accepting seriously the fine and seriously intended metaphors which
dominate the last two stanzas of the poem"); (5) of tone ("The poem opens
dramatically on a note of exasperation. . . . The tone with which the poem
closes is one of triumphant achievement, but the tone is a development
contributed to by various earlier elements"). Throughout the analysis is
of meaning and resonance of meaning, of what "we can imagine," of what
"runs through the poem," of the "suggestions" developed by words in
"contrast" with other words, of the support of "paradox" by the "dominant metaphor," of the "development of theme," its "complication," the
"powerful dramatization" of its paradox, etc. (pp. 10-14).

The most immediately striking thing about this analysis is that it begins
from, and never questions, the assumption that the poem is natural speech.
Petrarchan conventions are admitted, but no other conventions are recognized as operating conventionally in the speech (From the analysis it might
appear that Brooks considers conventions to be conventional only when
they are threadbare). And nowhere is there even a hint of the real possibility
of a distinction between a serious statement by a writer and manipulation
of verbal conventions, whether serious or otherwise, that is in itself pure
artifice.

Actually, the more closely one reads the poem, the more astonishingly
conventionalized as speech it appears to be. Conventional symbols referring
to human love (the Petrarchan conceits, the phoenix figure etc.), overlaid
by reference to consciousness that these are conventional, and themselves
in contrast to conventional symbols referring to worldly success, are merged
with conventional symbols referring to divine love and heavenly success,
the point of identity being the conscious fallacy of a univocal interpretation
of renunciation of the world. The lovers are used as the focal point for both

sets of symbols, especially the lover who is speaking, and the whole is set finally in the framework of a Renaissance interpretation of the Horatian convention of roughness of address characteristic of the *sermo* of satire. The fusion is, to use a phrase of Horace's in a sense broader than he intended, a *callida junctura.* It is unexpected. It is splendid metaphor, and largely because it is good riddle.[3]

This quality of conventionalization penetrates even the details of the experience as they are presented in the poem. The reference is to affective states of the speaker, but the presentation is in no sense psychologistic. The figures and images are drawn from (a) common artifacts, unspecified by particularizing detail (*wealth, ships, hermitage, tombs, hearse, urn, glasses, mirrors, spies, town, courts, Tapers*); (b) the world of literary art and learning (*Arts, wit, riddle, legend, verse, Chronicle, sonnets, hymnes, world's soul, neutral thing,* and *fly, eagle, dove, phoenix,* as standardized literary symbols); (c) professions cited generically (*soldiers, lawyers, merchants*); (d) generically presented diseases (*palsie, gout, colds, heats*). The number of these categories (most of them function as categories), together with the way the speaker jumps from one to another, like the recitation of a catalogue, and the generalized level at which the process of love itself is referred to— all push the poem more and more in the direction of intricately conventionalized verbal art rather than any real communication, so that when the reader comes to the truncated "collect" with which the poem closes he knows that this prayer is no prayer precisely because it is so perfectly manipulated as prayer.

Brooks' interpretation of "The Canonization," on the contrary supposes that the statements in the poem are universally evaluatory—that the poem speaks seriously about the superiority of choosing human love rather than secular success. He thinks the poem functions to present a conflict between the "practical world" of the addressee, "which regards love as a silly affectation," and "the lover absorbed in the world of love." That opposition of this sort is presented is beyond doubt ("For God's sake hold your tongue and let me love"). But is this opposition a matter of verbal art or is it real? What is affirmed *in the poem?* After a series of commands and rhetorical questions to his addressee, the speaker says: Call us what you will, we are made such by love; and if our story is unfit for chronicles, it is fit for verse; and by these hymns all shall approve us canonized for love. "We are made such by love" is a conjunction of terms. But how is the conjunction affirmed? What we have here is a statement of a matter of fact without any real assertion of value. It is significant that nowhere in the poem is there any request for the addressee's approval of this conjunction on, let us say, ethical or broadly political grounds. There is no positive statement about the absurdity or wisdom of either of the contrasting elements or their juncture. For example, the speaker in the poem nowhere rejects the addressee or the addressee's world. He affects impatience with him, it is true; the reason, if any, that is offered, however, is that his interference is impeding the rush of passion, and not that there is a radical breach of values. It is significant, in terms of

and the title — a show-off way that his poem will be canonized

the "argument" within the poem, that there is a good deal of "ethical"
reference, references to the speaker's own "state of soul," but none of
what the rhetoricians speak of as "pathetic argument"—there is no play
upon the addressee's feelings, no effort to win him over to the speaker's
state of mind. Even the last stanza, which might be construed in this way,
is not a "peroration," but the verbal fanfare of one striking a posture with
dissuading friends.

   This lack of real contrast between the speaker's world of love and the
addressee's world of success is confirmed by the sameness in the quality
of reference throughout the poem. For denotatively the words have the same
clarity from first to last. The double meaning which Brooks finds in the
word "die," if it is there, does not really constitute an ambiguity that affects
any qualitative changes in the meanings. A like qualitative consistency is to
be found in the connotations of the words of the poem. The world of
"countries, towns, courts" is the world of "gout" and "grey hairs," of
the "king's real and his stamped face"; the sonnets of the fourth stanza
are the familiar territory of the conceits of the second stanza. The "well
wrought urn" versus the "half acre tomb" of the fourth stanza, even in its
more generalized framework of semi-soliloquy, is a clear reflection of the
meaning of the first stanza; while the exaggerated conceits of the second
stanza come from the same tradition of rhetorical ornament as the stylized
metaphors of the third stanza. The fresh "turn" given the images in the
fourth stanza is possible only because they are of the same general lineage
as those in the preceding stanzas. A rhetorician like Geoffrey de Vinsauf
would be at home with the technique of this poem. He would recognize
in Donne a craftsman in the tradition of those for whom the practice of
their art was the varying of given material, who believed that novelty, to be
new, must be a change in what is old, and that freshness is always as here,
merely readjustment in the weight of convention.

   Brooks notes a shift in tone from the second stanza into the third and
through the rest of the poem, a shift "from ironic banter into a defiant but
controlled tenderness." Postulating such a shift is consistent on Brooks'
part. For the poem to say what he construes it to say, there must be such
a shift. But this avoids one problem only to raise another and more serious
problem. For is not the effect of such a change the destruction of the poem's
integrity as a poem? Would not a shift in tone so radical be an aesthetic flaw
rather than an excellence? It is a shift after all not just in degree but in kind
of meaning and direction of address. It supposes not only a shift from irony
to tenderness but the much more violent change of the addressee from
"the friend, who is objecting to the speaker's love affair" in the first stanza
to "us" in the last stanza. At the beginning of the analysis Brooks points out
that "the 'You' whom the speaker addresses is not identified. We can imagine
that it is a person, perhaps a friend, who is objecting to the speaker's love
affair. At any rate, the person represents the practical world which regards
love as a silly affectation." Towards the end of his analysis Brooks says
"The effect of the poet's implied awareness of the lovers' apparent madness

is to cleanse and revivify the metaphor; to indicate the sense in which the poet accepts it, and thus *to prepare us* for accepting seriously the fine and seriously intended metaphors which dominate the last two stanzas of the poem." (Italics mine.)

Actually there is no shift either in address or in tone. There is, it is true, a kind of modulation from the first stanza (developed through figures of balance) and the second (amplified through standard conceits) into the third, fourth and fifth stanza (prevailingly metaphorical)—the third stanza sharing with the second a hyperbolic quality in the figures. But the change is not "from ironic banter into a defiant and controlled tenderness." It is not a modulation from a "note of irritation" to a "tone . . . of triumphant achievement." The modulation which occurs is not in terms of the reality to which the signs refer, but in terms of the signs which are used; a modulation from signs (for erotic love expressed in the Petrarchan conceits) whose merely nominal function is perceived, to signs (for sanctity—the love of *agape*) which might be equally nominalistic in another context but which as signs are freshened by use in what has become a conventional love poem. The proof, if nowhere else, is in the theme, which, it should be noted, is the same, and conventionally so, as any hack sonnet of the period. Throughout the love is the romantic love or *eros*. The reference to the saints, the use of these signs, does not change the love to that of *agape*. Rather the reverse is true. The symbols for *agape* are controlled by the symbols for *eros*. To attain an effect of verbal art there is introduced the conscious fallacy of a univocal interpretation of renunciation of the world. That is why the speaker, as he introduces the symbols for sanctity, shifts neither address nor tone but the *immediacy* of address. For if the tone and the poem are to be saved the speaker's posture must be kept clear. And so he moves from the direct "I-You" relationship of stanzas one and two, into the "We-You" relationship of stanza three, and finally into the semi-soliloquy of stanzas four and five. The addressee is left standing there, with the speaker becoming absorbed in fantasy. In short, the speaker in the poem maintains a general consistency of address, shifting only its immediacy and introducing modulation not in that which is talked about but in the signs used in discussing this thematic material.[4]

All of this seems borne out, too, by grammatical and rhetorical details of the poem. For if the values which Brooks finds set forth with such "dignity," "precision," and "supernaturalism," were really there, the meanings would have to be combined with much more complication than the paractactically presented meanings of "The Canonization." Its most conspicuous relational words are "and" and "or"—especially in the first three stanzas. In these stanzas the structure of elements is coordinate. In stanza four there is more subordination of elements and there are more relational words, at least within the sentences, but from sentence to sentence the relationship is still that of coordination. Stanza five is one non-predicative exhortation with a piling up of parallel elements. This paratactical quality is helped along by the predominance of phrases of instrumentality over those of

5th stanza — not conclusive in terms of logical argument (sealing the argument)

Form-dreamt and in making solid argument other

qualification or modification. And the relative paucity of adjectives confirms the non-analytic, non-hypostatic nature of the speech. The sentence structure is non-intricate, built up principally by compounding and repetition of elements like imperative clauses.

The structure of the rhetoric corresponds to this grammatical structure. There is very little conceptual complication and little logical order. The opening and closing stanzas are volitional—commands in stanza one, and invocation in stanza five. Stanzas two, three and four, dealing with the past, present and future respectively, are affective in reference and develop inductively through exemplifying details. From stanza to stanza the relation is not syntactical. Rather each stanza is a separate unit connected aggregatively with the others. From a rhetorical point of view, the total effect is loosely syndetic.

Such agglomerative development is quite properly consistent; Donne makes out of this material the structure of a fine poem. The point to be made here, however, is that such a structure, successful for Donne's artistic purposes, is inconsistent with the meanings which Brooks purports to find in the poem.[5] What Brooks does in his reading is supply syntactic articulation for meanings which in the poem are actually juxtaposed in a relationship fundamentally paratactic. He thus does not really face the text but uses it to suggest what for him is an important set of meanings.[6]

Brooks concludes his "close reading" with an important summation of his thesis:

> I submit that the only way by which the poet could say what 'The Canonization' says is by paradox. More direct methods may be tempting, but all of them enfeeble and distort what is to be said. This statement may seem the less surprising when we reflect on how many of the important things which the poet has to say have to be said by means of paradox: most of the language of lovers is such—'The Canonization' is a good example; so is most of the language of religion—'He who would save his life, must lose it'; 'The last shall be first.' Indeed, almost any insight important enough to warrant a great poem apparently has to be stated in such terms. Deprived of the character of paradox with its twin concomitants of irony and wonder, the matter of Donne's poem unravels into 'facts,' biological, sociological, and economic. What happens to Donne's lovers if we consider them 'scientifically,' without benefit of the supernaturalism which the poet confers upon them? Well, what happens to Shakespeare's lovers, for Shakespeare uses the basic metaphor of 'The Canonization' in his *Romeo and Juliet*? In their first conversation, the lovers play with the analogy between the lover and the pilgrim to the Holy Land. Juliet says:
>
> > For saints have hands that pilgrims' hands do touch
> > And palm to palm is holy palmers' kiss.
>
> Considered scientifically, the lovers become Mr. Aldous Huxley's animals, 'quietly sweating, palm to palm.' (pp. 16-17)

Brooks thinks that "The Canonization" does not unravel into scientific "facts" because the poet has conferred a "supernaturalism" on the lovers by means of an insight that must be stated in paradox with its accompaniment of irony and wonder. To bolster his argument he introduces the parallel of the language of religion and the language of lovers as examples of the same kind of need and use for paradox. But the languages of lovers and of the New Testament do not really support Brooks' assertion about the language of poetry. Rather they betray his argument and reveal a fundamental contradiction at the basis of his analysis. To support Brooks' argument, the passage which he quotes from the Bible would have to resist unraveling into facts. But it is of the essence of the Biblical language to unravel into facts, not biological or sociological or economic facts, it is true, but theological facts. The New Testament language is primarily a statement about something. "The first shall be last" points to a reality for which it asks approval and acceptance. It is aimed at turning its hearer's mind to an order of thought and his will to a program of action. By its nature it does not maintain wholeness *as speech*, but surrenders itself in a context of instruction and persuasion. As speech it is not autotelic but *per se* useful, with its end outside itself. In short, as speech it secures its end by unraveling.

Brooks has insisted that "deprived of the character of paradox with its twin concomitants of irony and wonder, the matter of Donne's poem unravels into 'facts,' biological, sociological and economic." But has he precluded the possibility that in his interpretation the poem unravels into facts of another kind—humanistic facts, statements about an ultimate unity which can only be expressed with "dignity" and "precision" through paradox? I think he has not. As "The Canonization" has been read by Brooks what emerges as important is the poet's meaning and not what the poet has *made* out of this meaning. The integrity at stake for Brooks in his actual reading of the poem, is not the integrity of a linguistic construction but the integrity of a vision that "apparently violates science and commonsense" and "welds together the discordant and contradictory."[7] But in communicating this vision is not the poem serving an end outside itself? Is it not, in short, "unravelling"?

To read "The Canonization" as such a vehicle of paradoxical insight is, however, not the only way to read the poem, as I have tried to show above. In fact, "The Canonization" can be read as such a vehicle only by ignoring the actual philological details of the poem, details which point not to the identity of the speech of "The Canonization" with that of lovers or of Biblical parables, but to its essential diversity from such speech. Attention to such details reveals that "The Canonization" stands detached as an integral aesthetic whole in a way that Biblical speech, functioning as an instrument, never could be detached. The function of "The Canonization" is primarily non-instrumental. No matter what its meaning is, its end is obviously that it be read with delight and for delight. There is paradox in the poem. The meaning of the poem could not be what it is without the paradox. The paradox functions, however, primarily for the sake of the total verbal structure of which it is a part and which has its own end in being a poem—a beautiful speech.

It is one thing to say that a poem is *made of paradoxical meanings* and quite another thing to conclude that the poem *functions to convey* a paradox, serious or otherwise. Effective reading of "The Canonization" cannot start from the assumption that paradox has a single effect. Effective reading must recognize that paradox can be fitted indifferently to different effects. The use of paradox varies as the context varies from the scientific to the logical to the rhetorical to the poetical. The use in the instance of "The Canonization" is a distinctly poetical one, and from such use nothing can be concluded about whether "Donne takes both love and religion seriously." In apprehending this poem, the reader, modern or otherwise, is not faced with the philosophical dilemma, "Either: Donne does not take love seriously . . . Or: Donne does not take sainthood seriously," as Brooks asserts. But he is quite clearly faced with the philological problem of being sensitive to the functional variation of traditional components of speech.

DONNE'S "VALEDICTION: FORBIDDING MOURNING"[1]

John Freccero

In the twelfth chapter of Dante's *Vita nuova,* Love appears to the poet in the form of an angel and gives himself a mystic definition: "I am as the center of a circle, to which all parts of the circumference stand in equal relation; *you, however, are not so.*"[2] For Dante, as for most thinkers of his time, the spatial and temporal perfection represented by the circle precluded its use as a symbol for anything human. The perfect circularity of the *Paradiso* was a gift awaiting the man who had been through Hell; it could never be considered a birthright, for perfect circles transcend the human just as the heavens transcend the earth. So great was the gap between perfection and humanity that it could be spanned only by the Incarnation.

Dante and the early Florentine humanists were the last Italians for several centuries to take Love's admonition very seriously. Later thinkers of the *Quattrocento* would not accept any such limitation and with their rhetoric attempted to set man free from the great chain which bound him to the angels above and to the beasts below. By attributing to the human soul an angelic perfection, they attempted to divorce it from its body, which they were prepared to leave to the protective custody of Lorenzo de' Medici. While they claimed for the soul eternity's symbol, the infinite circle, they surrendered to *Il Magnifico* the more limited space around the Square of the *Signoria,* thus making of God's circular hieroglyph not only an emblem of man's dignity, but also of his solipsism. This metamorphosis of the circle from the transcendent to the mundane, recently and brilliantly traced by Georges Poulet,[3] was historically coincident, at least in Italy, with the metamorphosis of the human soul from incarnate reality, to angelic abstraction, to poetic fiction. The beast which was left behind, however, remained substantially unchanged.

Among English poets who underwent the influence of Italian love poetry of the Renaissance, John Donne stands out as one who sought to reconcile the errant soul to its body once more. This meant rescuing human love from both the angelic mysticism and the erotic formalism of the Italian tradition and restoring it to its proper domain: humanity. Donne was primarily concerned neither with the angel nor with the beast, but rather with the battlefield separating them, long since vacated by the Italians; insofar as he defended that middle ground in the question of human love, his poetry

Reprinted from *English Literary History,* 30 (1963), 335-76, by permission of the author and The Johns Hopkins Press.

marked a return to a more "medieval" sensibility. It is the thesis of this
paper that his most famous image, that of the compass in "A Valediction:
Forbidding Mourning," protests, precisely in the name of incarnation,
against the neo-Petrarchan and neoplatonic dehumanization of love. It
makes substantially the same point made by Love to the young Dante
three hundred years before: angelic love is a perfect circle, while beasts
move directly and insatiably to the center; *tu autem non sic.*

Human love is neither because it is both; it pulsates between the
eternal perfection of circularity and the linear extension of space and time.
The compass which Donne uses to symbolize it, therefore, traces not merely a circle but a dynamic process, the "swerving serpentine"[4] of Donne's
poetry and of his thought. This is the essence of the love celebrated in
the "Valediction: Forbidding Mourning," a vortical reconciliation of body
and soul. At the end of its gyre, on the summit where time and eternity
meet, stands the lovers' Truth: "hee that will / Reach her, about must, and
about must goe . . ." (Satyre III, 80-1). Because Love's truth is incarnate,
however, its celestial apex is at the same time the profound center of an
interior cosmos which is governed by its own laws and bounded by the
lovers' embrace. For such lovers there can be no breach between the macrocosm of space and time and the microcosm of Love because all of reality
is circumscribed by the point upon which their love is centered. With its
whirling motion, Love's compass describes the expansion of the lovers'
spirit from eternity to time and back again.

This motion is the archetypal pattern of Love's universe, the principle
of coherence joining matter and spirit throughout all levels of reality. The
first part of this study will show that this is the motion traced by the
compass. We shall see that the principle of motion in Love's universe is
patterned upon what was considered the principle of motion in all of
reality. By itself, however, this principle is purely formal. The image of
the compass cannot convey the vital reality which underlies it and gives to
the poem its symbolic substance. The second part of this study is therefore
concerned with describing the "vehicle" itself, the "spirit" of Love to which
motion is imparted. Finally, the last part of this study will examine the literal
significance of the symbolic statement in terms of the relationship of the
lover to his beloved.

*   *   *

In his sermons, Donne expresses the incarnate dynamism of humanity
with the figure of married love: "As farre as man is immortall, he is a married
man still, still in posession of a soule, and a body too."[5] "Death," he tells
us, "is the Divorce of body and soule; Resurrection is the Re-union. . . ."[6]
It is from this exegetical commonplace that the argument of the "Valediction: Forbidding Mourning" derives its force. If incarnation is not simply an
abstraction, but rather the informing principle of reality, then the terms of
the analogy are reversible and the union of body and soul may serve as a

figure for the love of husband and wife. Donne the preacher wrote of death
and resurrection in figurative terms of the separation and reunion of husband
and wife; as a lover, in the poem we are about to discuss, he had written to
his beloved of their separation and eventual reunion in figurative terms of
death and resurrection: "As virtuous men passe mildly away . . . So let us
melt. . . ." The poem reversed a traditional figure and gave to the neo-
Petrarchan dialectic of presence and absence a new metaphysical meaning.
As the soul is indissolubly linked to the body, so the husband is linked to
his faithful wife. The "Valediction" is a *congé d'amour* which precludes
grief in the same way that the death of a virtuous man *forbids mourning;*
that is, the simile with which the poem begins glosses the poem's title by
hinting that, just as the righteous soul will at the Last Judgement return to
its glorified body, so the voyager will return to his beloved.

The ironic reversal of a traditional theme is not mere flippancy. Donne
characteristically pushes the analogy to a fine philosophical point. If the
union of husband and wife, their love, is like the union of body and soul,
then it too is a "hylomorphic" entity which cannot be simply reduced to
the carnality or to the spirituality of which it is nevertheless composed. It
is Love incarnate, possessed of a single soul ("Our two soules . . . which are
one") and, in its perfection, of a single body: Adam and Eve cleave unto
each other and are one flesh (Gen. 2, 24). The doctrine of the Resurrection
can be of little comfort to lovers whom death parts, since there is no marriage in heaven.[7] In the case of these lovers, however, who part only temporarily, the Resurrection lends considerable force to the poetic statement
of their inseparability because, by inverting the whole theological structure
and balancing it on a personification—the body and soul of Love-Donne
gives the entire weight of Revelation to his promise to return. Love dies a
physical death when the lovers part, for their bodies "elemented" its body.
Its soul lives on, however, in the comfort of the Resurrection, when husband
and wife, the components of Love's body, will cleave together once more.
It is because their Love is like a just man that it can "passe mildly away,"
"care lesse" (but like the lovers still *care*) to miss its body, knowing that it
will end where it began, reconciled to the flesh once more.

The beginning of the poem states the relationship of the lover to his beloved in terms of the union of body and soul. The ending of the poem traces
the emblem of that union, the geometric image of a soul that cannot be perfect while it remains disembodied and therefore cannot be represented in
the same way that Dante represented angelic love. In other words, the
"circle" which ends the poem is no circle in the ordinary sense, but is rather
a circle joined to the rectilinear "otherness" distinguishing man from the
angels. This explains the apparent inconsistency in Donne's image, a poetic
inconsistency, it would seem, compounding the obscurity of the final verses.
Two different movements are executed by the compass:

> An though it in the center sit,
>   Yet when the other far doth rome,

> It leanes and hearkens after it,
> And growes erect, as that comes home.

These verses clearly describe motion along a radius, from a center to a circumference and back to the center again. On the other hand, the last stanza of the poem clearly describes circular motion:

> Such wilt thou be to mee, who must
> Like th'other foot, obliquely runne;
> Thy firmnes drawes my circle just,
> And makes me end, where I begunne.

Together, these two movements comprise the dynamism of humanity. With its whirling motion, the compass synthesizes the linear extension of time and space with the circularity of eternity.

The metaphysical importance of the geometrical problem presented by these verses becomes apparent when we examine a passage from the sermons in which Donne distinguishes between the circle of eternity and the human circle which is in the making: "This life is a Circle, made with a Compasse, that passes from point to point; That life is a Circle stamped with a print, endlesse, and perfect Circle, as soone as it begins."[8] We are not told what the radius of eternity's circle is, for the stamp is merely intended to convey its simultaneity, not its dimensions. No finite circle can express the all-encompassing dimensions of eternity, nor can any localized center give a hint of its omnipresence. Like the God of the mystics, eternity is an infinite circle whose center is everywhere, circumference nowhere. In terms of earthly co-ordinates, it can be represented only by the dimensionless point which is both a center and a circumference. The human circle, on the other hand, has its limits. Both its radius and its sweep are measured by time and space. Nevertheless, it tends toward eternity as its goal. Geometrically speaking, then, it moves toward the circular perfection of the center; when the circle is finally closed, its radius will no longer have finite extension but will coincide with the limitless point of eternity. The compass of the human soul opens with time and closes toward eternity all the while that it whirls around the central point which is both its beginning and its end.

The epigrammatic quality of the last verse suggests that the harmonization of the circle and the line is indeed complete and that both motions end at their point of departure. Like Plato's star-soul,[9] the soul of Love ends with the perfect circularity with which it began. Its movement is therefore a pulsation, a contraction following an expansion ("Our two soules . . . endure not yet / A breach, but an expansion . . ."), a synthesis of two distinct motions: circular, but with an ever-increasing radius until a maximum circumference is described, whereupon the radius decreases and the circle contracts, approaching the point as its limit ("Thy firmness drawes my circle just"). The word "just" certainly refers to circular perfection; at the same time, however, it recalls the virtuous men of the first stanza and therefore underscores the analogy between the soul of Love and the soul of a "just" man.

The dimensionless *point* of dying coincides with the central point of return, the transition between a "just" life and the infinite circle of glory. Thus, like the Aristotelian circle,[10] Donne's has no beginning or end along its circumference, but is rather contracted and expanded along its radius, so that the beginning and end of its pulsation coincide at the center. Were it otherwise, we would have difficulty applying the resultant image to the two lovers who part and are reunited. If we were to take "end" to mean some point on the circumference, then the feet of the compass would remain equidistant throughout such an image, whereas the meaning is that the lover begins from the center, beside his beloved, is separated from her and finally will return. No matter how far he "romes," however, his thoughts revolve about her. Such a movement is at once linear and circular.

In antiquity, the spiral was considered to be the harmonization of rectilinear motion with circularity. Chalcidius, in his commentary on the *Timaeus*, describes spiral motion precisely in terms of the two-fold movement of a compass: radial, from center to circumference, and circular, around the circumference. This passage is probably the ultimate source of Donne's compass image:

> We usually call "spiral" that genus of circle which is described when one foot of a compass is fixed and the compass is either stretched out or closed up, either by chance or intentionally, so that circles are described such that not only does the extremity of the circular line not return to its place of origin but is even deflected a given amount either above or below the previous circular line so as to make either wider or narrower circles.[11]

The spiral is therefore a kind of circle whose outline is unfixed until outward motion ceases and inward motion begins, retracing the same gyre in the opposite direction toward the central point of origin. When we consider the figure, our attention is directed toward the center as beginning and end of all movement, while the periphery remains undefined and vague. So in the poem, our attention is directed not toward Donne's destination abroad but rather toward his wife, to whom he will return, no matter how far he roams.

A similar focus is characteristic of most of the *lemmata* that were illustrated in Donne's day with the emblem of the compass. *Donec ad idem,* for instance, stands for a meditation on death and its accompanying compass image serves to illustrate God's condemnation of Adam, that he will end where he began: *donec revertaris in terram* (Gen. 3, 19). The poet or preacher's promise to return to his central theme is pictorially represented with the compass and the *lemma: non vagus vagor.* Even the Jesuit missionary's obedience to his superior can be similarly illustrated: *si jusseris, ibit in orbem.*[12] Most of the similies in love poetry of the sixteenth century which are based on the compass also stress central constancy in spite of circumstantial vicissitudes. So the explicit compass image from Guarini's madrigal: "un piede in voi quasi mio centro mi fermo, / l'altro patisce di fortuna i giri,"[13] or the sub-

merged compass image of Maurice Scève, of which we shall have more to
say later: ". . . ma pensée à peu pres s'y transmue, Bien que ma foy, sans
suyvre mon project, Ça et là tourne, et point ne se remue."[14] Insofar as
these compasses have their origin in the tradition of Chalcidius' image,
they trace spirals, whether their authors knew it or not.

We can however be sure that John Donne knew it. The word "rome" in
the verse, "Yet when the other far doth rome," cannot refer to circular motion, anymore than can the finite verb *vagor* in the emblem books, for a
circle does not wander. Donne used the compass image in precisely the same
way that Chalcidius used it in the passage we have quoted; that is, to describe
a wandering path which is nevertheless rooted in circular regularity. The
exemplar of all such orbits is the path described by the planets, or "wandering" stars.

Plato used the movements of the heavenly bodies in order to "spatialize"
his conception of intellectual process; it was in this way that he managed to
give to his idea of *paideia* a symbolically dynamic dimension. In his microcosmic analogy, the perfect circling of the fixed stars represented the perfect
movement of the speculative reason, whereas the rectilinear motion characteristic of the elements represented the lowest human faculties. Between these
upper and lower limits of human potentiality there lay the human composite
itself, a synthesis of both circle and line. Like the planets, the human soul
partakes of the movements of both the outermost sphere, rationality, and
of the sublunary world of matter.[15]

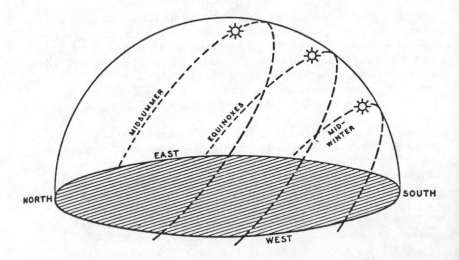

Fig. 1. The Path of the Sun (after a sketch by M. A. Orr, *Dante and the Early
Astronomers* [London, 1913], p. 23)

Planetary movement was considered to be spiral because it seemed to be composed of at least two opposing movements. Like the sun and moon, the planets rise and set each day, moving from east to west. At the same time, they move along the Zodiac from west to east. The resolution of these two motions, from the perspective of the earth, described a slow-moving spiral from one tropic to the other. In other words, from what we know to be the earth's rotation and revolution, the sun, moon and planets seem to follow a spiral course (fig. 1). Chalcidius continues the passage containing the compass image as follows:

> . . . [Plato] has correctly called them [the planets] errant stars, rotating in a spiral, because of the inconstant and unequal circular movement. If, for example, the star of Venus is in the sign of Aries and then is rapt by the course of the universe so that it is carried further and further away from its previous progression, there will certainly be some declination away from Aries; and as many more turnings as it makes, so much the more will it descend from Aries to Pisces, the next sign, and from there it will be impelled to Aquarius. On the other hand, if it were rapt the other way it would proceed from Aries to Taurus and thence to Gemini and Cancer, its gyre becoming ever smaller in due measure; which gyre the Greeks call *helix* . . .[16]

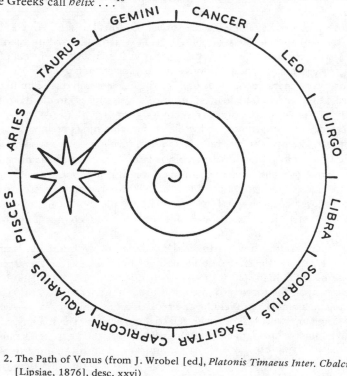

Fig. 2. The Path of Venus (from J. Wrobel [ed.], *Platonis Timaeus Inter. Chalcidio* [Lipsiae, 1876], desc. xxvi)

In most of the redactions of Chalcidius' commentary, this passage is accompanied by a diagram of Venus' orbit, viewed from the pole and projected onto the plane of the ecliptic (fig. 2).[17]

The word "rome" suggests the planetary, or at least "wandering," character of the lover's journey away from his beloved. We shall see that several other words in Donne's last verses prove that the imagery is basically astronomical. For the moment, our suggestion seems confirmed by a phrase in the second verse of the last stanza, "obliquely runne." This phrase not only describes planetary motion quite accurately, but also points toward the platonic analogy which we have been discussing and hence to the significance of the spiral form. In the first place, the word "oblique" is still used as a substantive in English to denote the ecliptic, the imaginary line which runs along the center of the Zodiac and traces the path of the planets, sun and moon. In the Middle Ages, Dante used a form of the word as an adjective to describe the ecliptic: "l'oblico cerchio che i pianeti porta," while in the Renaissance Théophile de Viau speaks of the sun's path as an "oblique tour,"[18] thereby giving to the word the meaning of "spiral," at least implicitly. Of particular interest to us, however, is that Donne here uses an adverbial form, "obliquely," which indicates not a path or a line but a *kind* of motion, the motion which in the Latin neoplatonic tradition was referred to as the *motus obliquus.*

Plato's geometric analogy for the three "motions" of soul, circular (divine), spiral (human) and rectilinear (animal), from which is derived his theory of microcosm and macrocosm, enjoyed a great vogue in subsequent neoplatonic writings. According to the pseudo-Dionysius, for instance, the three "conversions" were characteristic not only of the heavens and of the human soul, but also of the angels. The highest order of angels moves circularly around God and the lowest order moves directly toward man. Between these, the middle order rotates around God while at the same time pursuing its terrestrial missions. In like manner, the human soul can turn directly to God by divine intuition (*supra nos,* St. Bonaventure was later to say), or to the outside world (*extra nos*); but since the "unitive" way is given to few men, most must proceed to God with a combination of those two movements (*intra nos*). This last movement, the spiral, is emblematic of the soul incarnate, of the soul whose inner life is a continual contemplation of God in spite of worldly vicissitudes.[19]

In the Latin translations of the Dionysian corpus, from the ninth to the fifteenth centuries, the translation usually offered to describe the "spiral motion" of the human soul is the Latin adverb "oblique."[20] Marsilio Ficino comments upon the three movements of the soul under the rubric, "De motu angeli et animae triplici id est, circulari, recto, obliquo."[21] Elsewhere, he uses the same words to describe celestial movement. The planets, he tells us, move "sinuosa quadam obliquitate, velut in spiram."[22] It seems most likely that this tradition, at once astronomical and mystical, underlies Donne's use of the words "obliquely runne." If this is the case, then Donne himself alludes to the geometrical solution of the problem presented by his own lines. A compass can lean or grow erect *at the same time* that it describes a circle only if that "circle" is in fact a spiral. The next to the last line of the poem does indeed indicate diurnal, circular motion, the fixity of love, while the last refers to a dyastolic and systolic pulsation, the "zodiacal" exigencies of life, for these two patterns are combined in the figure that "obliquely" runs.

To return to our summary of the strategy of the poem, with which we began this paper, we said that the "body" of Love dies when the lovers part and is "resurrected" when they are reunited. The compass image manages to span these two moments and thus provides us with an emblem of duration, a fixity of being (insofar as it is a single image) in the process of becoming (insofar as it moves). That duration is literally the time of the lovers' separation from each other and figuratively the history of the disembodied soul of Love, awaiting its glorification at the end of time. In the universe of Love, the time measured by the compass' whirling is the *marking* of time between one moment of eternity and the next, between the creation of time and its dissolution. It cannot be a circle for it is as yet incomplete, as the soul is incomplete without its body, as the lover is incomplete without his beloved. When the restoral is finally achieved, however, the lovers will be reunited, the soul of Love will be reconciled to the body of Love and the planets will end their wandering at their points of origin.

To a modern reader, planetary imagery may seem gratuitous in a poem which is primarily concerned with the relationship of body and soul as a figure for the relationship of two lovers. To thinkers of the Renaissance, however, there seemed to be an intimate connection between the life of the cosmos and the life of man. The exile of the soul from its body was thought to last precisely as long as the exile of the planet from its home. According to the doctrine of "universal restoral," which is platonic in origin,[23] the life of the entire universe is measured by the Cosmic Year. All of the heavenly bodies will return to precisely the same positions from which they began at the end of 36,000 solar years. Ausonius is one among many in antiquity who describe this *apocatastasis*; his verses call to mind the *lemma* of Death's compass, *donec ad idem:*

> Donec consumpto, magnus qui dicitur, anno,
> Rursus in antiquum veniant vaga sidera cursum
> Qualia dispositi steterant ab origine mundi.[24]

By an association which seemed to Christian astrologers inevitable, in spite of the protestations of critics such as Pico della Mirandola, the *apocatastasis* of the ancients was taken to be coincident with the Christian Apocalypse and hence with the resurrection of the body.[25] Thus, when the human soul ends where it began, the planets, *vaga sidera*, will return to the positions they occupied at the Creation. Marsilio Ficino, characteristically, defends the religious doctrine with the astrological "fact" in order to bolster his own somewhat shaky belief in the Resurrection:

Nor should it appear absurd that souls, after they have left their natural state, should return again to the same place, for indeed the planets leave their natural homes [*domicilia*] and seek them again. Further, particles of elements which are expelled from their natural place return again to it. Nor is it difficult for the infinite virtue of God, which is everywhere present, which created everything *ex nihilo,* to bring together those elements of a body which had once been dissolved.[26]

The homes of the planets, their *domicilia* or *klairoi* in the celestial sphere, mark the beginning and end of planetary motion. Donne the lover, metamorphosed into a planet wandering from his beloved, also begins and ends at "home" (line four, stanza eight). The poet has once more reversed a traditional argument, reversing signifier and thing signified and interposing a concrete image increasing the distance between them. As the soul will return to the body, so the soul of Love (the lovers' two souls) will return to its body (the lovers' two bodies), as the planets come "home."[27]

If our contention that the compass image has primarily astronomical reference is correct, then there are a series of words in the next to last stanza that still require interpretation. The stanza says of "Thy soule the fixt foot":

> And though it in the center sit,
> Yet when the other far doth rome,
> It leanes, and hearkens after it,
> And growes erect, as that comes home.

We have suggested that "rome" characterizes the motion of the wandering stars and that "home" designates their *klairoi* or *domicilia.* Another position which astrologers felt obliged to determine was the planetary *exaltatio,* or as the word is still translated, the "erect" position.[28] Vittoria Colonna, for example, describing the auspicious moment of her lover's birth, says that the planets were in that position:

> Gli almi pianeti in propria sede *eretti*
> Mostravan lieti quei benigni aspetti,
> Che instillan le virtù nei cor più rari . . .[29]

In the history of astrology there was considerable disagreement about how the "homes" and the "exaltations" of the planets were measured. According to Pliny in the passage which is the *locus classicus* for the discussion of the *exaltatio* of the planets, the critical point on the Zodiac was reached by the planet when its orbital arc was at its highest elevation from the center of the earth. Using this criterion, he provided a catalogue of planetary domiciles: "Igitur a terrae centro apsides [i. e., planetary arcs] altissimae sunt Saturno in scorpione, Iovi in vergine, Marti in leone . . .[etc.]."[30] Later thinkers, and especially the Arabs, disagreed, and insisted that the measurement of the *altitudo* was to be taken not from the earth but from the center of the Zodiac to the zodiacal sign. From this new form of calculation they put together a totally different catalogue of "exaltations."[31] For our purposes, however, it should be noted that the measurements themselves, according to a probably spurious passage in the text of Pliny, were taken precisely by means of the compass: "Omnia autem haec constant *ratione circini* semper indubitata."[32] The point on the Zodiac diametrically opposed to a planet's *exaltatio* is the point of *deiectio*; if the former be described in terms of a compass which is tracing a spiral and is at its maximum erection, then the *deiectio*[33] will be the point of the compass' maximum depression. It is at this point that the compass "leanes," when the moving foot is at its greatest distance from the foot fixed in the orbit's center. In the context of the "Valediction," the suspicious lines "It leanes, and hearken after it, / And growes erect as that comes home" are primarily a geometric indication that, at the end of the exile of Love's soul, the planets will be exalted in their homes, awaiting the final consummation and the lovers' eternity.

A word must be said here about the literal meaning of the phrase, "It leanes . . . and growes erect" as it applies to the woman, in order to lay to rest the erotic interpretation sometimes given it. Whatever else the poem may be, it obviously constitutes a song of praise to the woman. In the Middle Ages, the most famous of such *encomia* was the praise of the virtuous wife taken from Proverbs 31, 10-31: "Who can find a virtuous woman . . . for her price is far above rubies." The verses in the original form an acrostic, each verse beginning with a letter of the alphabet in order from Aleph to Sin. Verse 20 reads: "She stretcheth out her hand to the poor." Albertus Magnus in his *De Muliere forti* notes that the verse begins with the letter Caph (כ) which he interprets *inclinatio,* referring to the compassion which inclines the hardness of the heart.[34] Verse 24, "She maketh fine linen," is introduced by the letter Samech (ס), which he interprets *erectio,*[35] the hope which raises us up. Donne may have been using the words "lean" and "erect" as similar compliments to his faithful beloved; this would explain why he uses the words with respect to her in spite of the fact that the purely literal meaning of the words is necessarily applicable to both legs of the compass. More interesting, however, is the fact that the Hebrew letters standing for the words *inclinatio* and *erectio* constitute ingenious hieroglyphs for separation and reunion. Caph, the broken circle (כ), marks the separation of the feet of the compass, whereas Samech brings them together and closes the circle (ס) as the compass becomes erect. This interpretation of the words has the advantage of doing violence neither to the poem nor to its context and, if it strains our credulity about how much Donne could put into a single line, it at least avoids the physiological naiveté required for an erotic interpretation of the words.

We have seen that the souls of the lover and the beloved together constitute the soul of Love, tracing humanity's emblem in a spiral course around the center which is their common possession, much like a planetary orbit around the axis of the universe. It happens that the gyre of the planetary soul is the archetype of motion in the human soul as well. The compass stands for a principal of motion that is common to humanity and to the heavens.[36] It is this analogy which relates the beginning of the poem to its ending, for if the soul of Love moves like a planet, it also moves like a *human* soul. Further, once we understand this movement, we shall also understand how a soul can be one and yet logically two-fold ("Our two soules ... which are one") in literal, as well as figurative terms. We shall have to discover why the compass is a perfect image of the soul.

In order to clarify the interrelationship of the cognitive and appetitive powers of the soul, Aristotle in the *De Anima*[37] described its workings mechanistically in terms which recall "stiffe twin compasses." All movement consists of three factors: 1) that which originates movement; 2) the means whereby it originates it; 3) that which is moved. In locomotion, the origin of movement is the soul, working through the heart (1). The means (2) are the vital spirits, pushing and pulling against a stationary point which provides thrust: the "fixt foot" (stanza 8 of the "Valediction"). The thing which is moved is the other foot. If we analyze the origin of motion, the heart, we find that it is where the beginning and end of motion coincide, the center of articulation, a joint between two extremities. Aristotle compares it to a ball-and-socket joint (*gigglimus*),[38] or to the elbow.[39] This is because it is the mid-point between the alternate movements of pushing and pulling in the motions of an animal. When a human being walks, one side remains fixed while the other moves, the latter in turn becoming fixed while the former moves. An interesting poetic description of the first steps of Adam is given to us in the *Microcosme* of Maurice Scève, where the word for "measure," *compas,* is perhaps used as a pun:

> Dresseé sur piés branchus, une jambe en avant,
> L'autre restant, se vit à cheminer savant,
> Et se conduire droit en tous lieux pas à pas
> Mesurant son alleure avec grave compas.[40]

According to Averroes, the pushing and pulling movements are not precisely straight because the vital spirits themselves, which are responsible for transmitting the heart's impulses to the limbs, move in a gyre: a *motus gyrativus* around the heart.[41]

The movement of the soul is precisely analogous to the local motion of the body. It is the appetitive faculty, the will, which, like the left foot, provides thrust, while the reason steps out first, like the right foot. They are joined to each other by the faculty of choice itself, whose "highest" point came to be called the *apex mentis.*[42] The link between all of these and the body is *pneuma* or *spiritus,* the mysterious substance which is the locus of contact between body and soul. If the *apex mentis* is like the heart, the joint of a compass, then the will is its fixed foot while the reason is the other. The *pneuma* which joins them traces its gyre on the plain of human action.

In the compass of the human soul, it is the will which remains fixed in its constancy while the reason moves out. So in Scève's submerged compass image, the lover's "pensée" may be diverted, but "ma foy, sans suyvre mon project, / Ça et là tourne, et point ne se remue."[43] So too, the Plantin device serves as an image of constancy in action: *Labore et constantia.*[44] To this is doubtless related Cesare Ripa's use of the compass as an emblem for "pratica," by which he probably means the practical reason.[45] Donne chose to compliment his beloved on her constancy, her faith, with this emblem. At the same time he consoled her by suggesting that they were as the will and reason respectively of a single soul, "inter-assured" of the apex of the mind. For all of its dazzling virtuousity, the conceit is analogous to an ancient exegetical commonplace. As Adam represents *ratio,* or the highest faculty of the soul, so Eve represents *appetitus,* which is in direct contact with the body. Together, they are one.[46]

We have so far been concerned with establishing the principle which governs the movement of the poem, symbolized by the compass image. It is this universal principle which gives the "Valediction" its coherence upon so many analogical levels of reality. In the second part of this paper, we shall turn to a close reading of the poem in order to examine its multilevelled coherence. Before we proceed, however, something must be said of the poem's relationship to the literary tradition from which it takes its point of departure. It will be seen that Donne's originality here, as so often, consists in the startlingly new form that he bestows upon time-worn banalities. Thematically, the "Valediction: Forbidding Mourning" resembles the medieval *congé d'amour,* wherein a lover takes leave of his lady and consoles her by claiming that they are not really two individuals, but rather affirms that they are one, or that he has left with her his heart.[47] In Renaissance treatments of the presence-absence antithesis, elements of the *congé* are combined with Petrarchan and stilnovistic themes and often expressed in terms of Plotinian theories of ecstasy, as has been pointed out recently by Merritt Hughes.[48] Among the *trattati d'amore* of the *cinquecento,* Sperone Speroni's is almost exclusively concerned with the antithesis of presence and absence, although he does not mention the Resurrection,[49] as does Marsilio Ficino in a similar context.[50] Nor is the consolation of a reunion at the end of a cosmic year entirely original; Giordano Bruno, in a rare fabulist mood, pokes fun at the idea of "universal restoral" and Plotinian ecstasy with a bizarre *congé d'amour* of his own, written thirty years before Donne's poem:

The flea, which had been educated according to the dogma of the divine Plato, was consoling the bedbug with loving words from the height of the roof, while a cruel fate was dividing the two companions: the chamber-boy, shaking the mattress, was already at the point of casting them down and throwing them off to diverse fates, for he was rolling up the sleeve of his shirt from his naked arm. The bedbug's face was lined with tears as it said: "Not my fate, not my cruel fate bothers me, that this my spirit should abandon these ugly and miserable members, but rather does that violent separation disturb me because you, dear Flea, are forced by iniquitous fates to leave me, fates which tear me away and cannot give you back to me." The flea answered, "Do not torment yourself, for this your torment transfixes me, consumes me and makes me unhappy. My spirit and yours are not twin, o bedbug of one soul with me, for you are more intimate to me that I am to myself; where-

fore my worry for you bothers me while I have no worry for myself.
Therefore, even if thundering Jove himself separate these our two bodies
iniquitously, nevertheless, only when he makes me leave my very self
can he cause my spirit to leave you, my fate, my death, once my life
and my hope. But even making me forgetful of myself, I find it difficult
to believe that he can make me forgetful of you. Weep not, my life's
blood, I know certainly that our two bodies will one day be together
again. I should like to say more, but already we are torn apart. Ahi!
ahi! Now farewell, sweet love! After two times, three times, one hundred
thousand years, added to which two other times three and two times
three hundred thousand (which I hope will come to pass auspiciously
and happily), you will look for me a second time and I myself will see
you a second time.[51]

It is however the Resurrection, not the cosmic year, that Donne offers to
his wife as a consolation forbidding mourning. This is not simply an attempt
to adapt a platonic banality to the Christian revelation, but rather has the
effect of transposing the theme of "restoration" from the universe of space
and time to an interior dimension. The criticism of Bruno, which is to say
the criticism of the "layetie" who do not understand that the entire universe
and its mystery are recapitulated in the microcosm of Love, is groundless
here; the "Valediction" establishes a *symbolic* cosmology, Love's universe,
where time begins at the lovers' parting and ends at their reunion. The poem
and the duration it spans seem at first to be a breach of eternity's circle; as
we read, however, we come to realize that time is eternity's moving image
—its end is its beginning—and the 36,000 years of its reign (measured in
Donne's 36 verses) constitutes merely a pause for lovers who are eternally
one. Similarly, space is transcended in Love's symbolic cosmos by the assurance that, thanks to the constancy of Love's faith, the centrifugality of
any separation will be overcome by the centripetal force that binds all of
reality to the same Center.

The neo-Petrarchan antithesis of presence and absence underlies the
simile of the dying man with which the poem begins,[52] but its banality is
here transcended by what Albert Béguin has called love's "chemin vers
l'intérieur."[53] As each of the lovers is the life of the other, separation is
tantamount to the death of their superficial identity. The absence of his
beloved forces the lover into himself to begin the spiral descent toward
the void where his life once was. At the center of his being, he discovers,
not his heart, nor even the heart of his beloved, but rather the "heart" of
the entire universe, the Center about which all of reality revolves. It is here,
in the depths of his subjectivity, that death is transcended and the whole
universe interiorized around the pole-star of Love.[54] Upon this transcendence, the death "intra nos" that ultimately leads "supra nos," a new, more
authentic identity is established. The miracle of Love's askesis is that in
thought, by participation in the "mind" which transcends them, man and
woman are joined together and transmuted above the sphere of the moon,
"refin'd" to await their glorious reunion. All of the heavens are embraced

by the soul of their love, for at Love's center is the point which is in fact a cosmic circumference.

*   *   *

Insofar as the compass stands for the archetypal movement of the soul (whether celestial or human), it is a symbol, a formal image standing for the instrumentality whereby spiritual movement is accomplished. It is the rational principle underlying that movement, or its formal cause. The movement itself, however, must be a movement of *something*; it is to this something that we must now turn our attention. Just as scientists, before the theory of relativity, believed that motion in the cosmos had to be through some sort of vehicle which they called *aether,* so metaphysicians believed that the interraction of soul and body had to be through a medium which combined the properties of both. This medium they called *pneuma.* Similarly, in Donne's poem, a symbolic *pneuma* joins the body and the soul of Love, and therefore is the symbolic medium through which the poem moves.

The vital reality underlying the compass image is *pneuma,* or *spiritus,* the mysterious substance which was considered to be the medium of the soul's action on the body, as well as the medium of the planetary soul's action on the heavenly body. In effect, this "breath of the universe" represented antiquity's attempt to find a single explanation for all movement in the cosmos, a primordial "field theory" which the Stoics used to interpret the pulsations of both air and aether and which the Christians did not hesitate to associate with the God-head.[55] It was because *pneuma* represented the locus of contact between body and soul that its movement was composed "ex recto et circulari," a movement which Averroes chose to call the "motus gyrativus."[56] The vital "spirits" move in their gyre around the heart as the planetary aether moves around its soul. Albertus Magnus equates the two movements: "Motus autem horum spirituum in corpore sunt sicut motus luminarium in mundo."[57] "Breath" was for the ancients the *hegemonikon* of the universe; in Donne's poem, it is the pulsating reality. The compass is an image which stands for an archetypal movement as universal as the heavens and as commonplace as respiration. We may turn now to see *what* it is that actually moves.

The poem opens with an important statement that identifies the "spirit" of Love by comparing it to life's "pneumatic" principle:

> As virtuous men passe mildly away,
>   And whisper to their soules, to goe,
> Whilst some of their sad friends doe say
>   The breath goes now, and some say, no:

Virtuous men pass away mildly because they are convinced that their death is no definitive separation; it is simply a pause in the life of body and soul. The resurrected body is precisely the same body, but glorified and made immortal; the soul which leaves it, therefore, endures "not yet / A breach, but an expansion," since an ideal link (however tenuous) still joins the two.

We shall see that this subtle link, of "ayery thinnesse," is the *pneuma* of Love's cosmos, the "spiritus" of Love, refined from the sublunary world to the heavens.

The sad friends of virtuous men lack an intimate assurance of the Resurrection and therefore cannot be sure that they will ever see the dying man again. This may well be the moment of definitive separation and it therefore seems a matter of some importance to watch the purely material breath (which is all they can perceive) as it leaves its body once and for all. Their debates are however irrelevant to the dying man who, like the historian of ideas, knows that the "breath" which is expired in time is intimately connected with the soul which is "inspired" in eternity.[58] With a confidence he cannot communicate to the "layetie," he whispers his *congé* to his soul. The effect of that whisper is that it gives substance to his soul and spirituality to his breath. His last breath is impressed with the seal of rationality, the *words* which are the physical manifestation of thought, a link between body and soul. Material breath is transformed by speech into *spiritus,* the God-given efflatus (Gen. 2, 7), which is the symbol of humanity.[59] Were it not for this link, the body could say nothing—a man whose soul departs is no longer a man but a corpse. The point is that here there is no separation. Body and soul are eternally related to each other by the "pneumatic" whisper which is "exhaled" to a cosmic dimension before coming home. We shall have more to say of this sublime mystery.

The expansion and contraction of this breath are the diastole and systole of both human and cosmic life, the *motus gyrativus* of man and the planets. This is the analogical link between the opening and the closing of the poem. Marsilio Ficino describes the mechanics of "breath":

> [The body's extension in space and time] might cause it to be drawn apart in rectilinear fashion [i. e., centrifugally], so that it would perhaps dissipate itself were it not drawn back by the intellectual soul. Hence, nature gives it a propensity to circularity. Think of the heavenly body in the same way, as if it were the breath [*spiritus*] expelled by the soul's exhalation, most certainly subject in the same way to rectilinear dispersion, but alternately contained again immediately afterward by the soul's inhalation. Therefore, since the soul cannot ever cease its breathing, it is necessary that [the heavenly body] be turned back within the heavens around the soul and, indeed, within it.[60]

The analogical structure of *pneuma* accounts for the poetic connection between the expiration of virtuous men and planetary movement. The rectilinear impulsion of the heavenly *spiritus* is overcome by the circular force of the Soul in the same way that a human soul holds sway over the vital spirits. These cycles are mechanically recapitulated in every human breath. In Donne's poem, however, the analogous structure is not simply a static juxtaposition of the two opposite states of *pneuma,* a simile comparing the breath of man to the "breath" of the universe; it is rather a dynamic continuum joining the two poles. As the soul leaves the body, the *spiritus* is gradually released from the flesh which contains it, rises by a continual refinement to the celestial dwelling-place of the soul and joins the heavenly *spiritus* in the cosmic "respiration."[61] When the planets return to their starting place at the end of the cosmic year, the soul then descends to the glorified body, gradually contracting its *pneuma* so that both may again be contained within the resurrected flesh. Because of the doctrine of the Resurrection, then, the final breath of an expiring soul is separated by a cosmic diffusion from the first breath of the glorified body. Nevertheless, they are simply the two phases of a single cycle. In the odor of sanctity, the last breath of time virtually coincides with the first breath of eternity.[62]

The third stanza of the poem is the macrocosmic counterpart of the first, for it contrasts definitive separation with the diastole and systole of death and Resurrection:

> Moving of th'earth brings harmes and feares,
>   Men reckon what it did and meant,
> But trepidation of the spheares,
>   Though greater farre, is innocent.

C. M. Coffin was incorrect when he supposed that this stanza was a juxtaposition of the old cosmology with the new, a Copernican moving of the center of the earth with the Ptolemeic trepidation of the spheres.[63] "Moving of th'earth" is simply Donne's translation of *terrae motus*, the earthquake, believed to be caused by a violent expulsion of winds (*pneuma*) trapped within the earth. According to Aristotle, it is the macrocosmic parallel of death: in both cases, the *pneuma* is expelled by the separation of the body's elements.[64] The parallel is implicit in a passage from *Henry IV* Pt. I:

> Diseased nature oftentimes breaks forth
> In strange eruptions; oft the teeming earth
> Is with a kind of colic pinch'd and vex'd
> By the imprisoning of unruly wind
> Within her womb; which for enlargement striving
> Shakes the old beldam earth, and topples down
> Steeples and moss-grown towers.[65]

It is therefore a definitive rupture of "body" and spirit, a *breach* full of evil portents (which is the point of the passage in the context of Shakespeare's play) and calamitous consequences. Since it is a departure of "breath," the men who reckon its consequences are much like the sad friends of the first stanza, who see death from a purely earth-bound perspective and similarly discuss what seems to them an imminent breach ("Some . . . doe say, / The breath goes now, and some say, no"). Moreover, earthquakes are caused by the same pneumatic turbulence which is responsible for floods and tempests, a point worth remembering for our discussion of the lovers' silent parting in the last section of this paper ("No teare-floods, nor sigh-tempests move"). In all of these ways, but above all *spatially,* moving of the earth is the antithesis of trepidation of the spheres.

The essential difference between the trembling of the earth and the "trembling" of the eigth sphere is that the latter movement is no break but simply a going and coming, an "access and recess."[66] The two movements differ in exactly the same way that a purely physical death in the sublunary world differs from the death of a virtuous man seen from the perspective of eternity; the first is an occasion for sadness and "feares," the second, which measures the universe's life in a single pulsation of immense extension in space and time, can do no hàrm ("is innocent") to the man who virtuously submits to it, who has no reason to fear the end of time and the Last Judgement. When, after thousands of years, the pole of the heavens returns to the true pole in its sinuous curve,[67] all of creation will arise from death. The *pneuma* which leaves the body (of men or of the world)[68] joins the cosmic respiration until the Resurrection.

Because its pulsation rules both the microcosm and the macrocosm, the "spirit" of Love is the vital bond which gives to the lover's universe its coherence and its continuity. That universe is purely poetic and Donne therefore has license to disregard contemporary cosmology and to take liberties with contemporary theology when he describes Love's *hegemonikon*. Nevertheless, the assertion of a universal continuity, in an epoch which had long since been shaken from such dreams, seems painfully naive even when its validity is restricted to the closed world of human love. Furthermore, the poem seems poetically unsatisfying while its fundamental principle lacks the symbolic concreteness which we have come to expect from Donne. Finally, unless the "spirit" of Love is somehow rooted to the real world, the hope and consolation which it offers seem equally insubstantial and purely poetic.

There was at least one science in Donne's time, however, which still held to a theoretical continuity between matter and spirit: the science of alchemy. Donne borrowed some of its principles in order to give a symbolic consistency to his "Valediction: Forbidding Mourning." An allegory based upon the Hermetic science resolves the complexity of the poem into a unified and poetically meaningful statement because it gives to the "spirit" of Love a symbolic grounding by equating it with something real and—very nearly—tangible. The allegory is a subtle answer in kind to the cynicism of "Loves Alchymie."

We have seen that the first and third stanzas of Donne's poem trace the expansion of "breath" from the world of time to the heavens and back again in a diastolic-systolic movement of death and resurrection. The poet refers to this process indirectly as a refinement, for he compares it with the refinement of the two lovers ("But we by a love, so much refin'd"): As virtuous men pass away, so let us melt and be refined to a celestial expansion, "Like gold to ayery thinnesse beate." This refinement is exactly analogous to the refinement or sublimation practiced by the alchemists in their search for the philosophers' stone. The volatile "spirit" of a metal is extracted by liquefaction, transmuted by sublimation and subsequently "fixed" by settling. The all-important sublimation was considered to be a transmutation of the "spirit" of a metal from one level of reality to another; what made it possible was the alchemist's unshakeable faith in the doctrine of *pneuma*. Because alchemy was a "child of Greek philosophy," it regarded all of reality as a continuum between the poles of mind and matter, or of body and soul. *Pneuma* was considered to be the universal link, at once the substance of the heavens and the "breath" of the human soul, marking the transition between the two by its varying degrees of subtlety.[69] According to a commonplace as old as Diodorus Siculus, it was the Quintessence, ontologically located between the four elements and pure immateriality.[70] Ever since Aristotle, men had believed that metals were produced by the action of *pneuma* trapped within the bowels of the earth; it followed that *pneuma* could bring any metal to the perfection of pure gold.[71] All that was necessary was to solidify *pneuma* into usable form: the Philosophers' Stone.

Because the doctrine of *pneuma* was historically not only a physical and metaphysical principle, but also a religious tenet, a description of it was perforce three-fold in its reference. To discuss the nature of *pneuma* was to discuss not only the relationship of body to soul, but also the relationship of the earth to the heavens and even the relationship of the universe to God, the Holy Spirit. This accounts for the almost limitless possibilities at the disposal of the practical alchemist to hide his true meaning under the guise of cosmic or religious allegories. Thus, the removal of the volatile "spirit" from a metal was the severing of body and soul, the chemical "death" necessary in order to bring about the "resurrection" of the philosopher's gold. The vehicle of this process was the "breath" of the universe; its principles were repulson, attraction and circularity. The end product was a gold of such subtlety, incorruptibility and purity that it could be compared only to the glorified body.[72]

J. A. Mazzeo has discussed Donne's reversal of signifier and signified in these alchemical allegories and has quoted several examples of Donne's "spiritual alchemy" in the sermons.[73] It should be stressed that the reversibility of spiritual and chemical orders was built into the language of all of the alchemists. We cite Nicholas Flammel as one example among many:

> You should also know that in our Art we distinguish two things—the body and the spirit; the former being constant, or fixed, while the other is volatile. These two must be changed, the one into the other. . . . Then the body loses all its grossness, and becomes new and pure; nor can this body and soul ever die, seeing that they have entered into a eternal union, such as the union of our bodies and souls shall be at the last day.[74]

By a further association which we first noted at the beginning of this paper, the relationship of the body to the soul was itself allegorized in terms of the relationship of man and woman, or husband and wife. So too in alchemy, where a kind of generation or birth was the object of the art, an additional allegorical dimension was provided by sexuality, the physical analogue of all generation in the cosmos. Albertus Magnus, for instance, discussing the components of all metals, reduces them to two, mercury and sulphur, and says of them: "quasi universalia metallorum sunt sicut pater et mater." In later alchemical works, we find that the union, dissolution and subsequent restoration of chemical elements is allegorized by death and resurrection in both the spiritual and the sexual senses of the words.[75]

Donne used the arcane process of the alchemists as an allegory of what was for him a much more profound mystery—the quintessence of human love. He did this by making a prime reality of what the alchemists considered a mere figure of their art. This is apparent as soon as we consider the second stanza of the poem. The opening simile of the poem ends with the exhortation: "So let us melt. . . ." The first stanza provides us with the metaphysical analogue of separation and reunion while the second introduces a literal situation: the relationship of a man to a woman. The word "melt," however, points to the symbolic reality underlying both of them, the physical analogue of separation: liquefaction.

The ambiguity of the much discussed word "melt" in this context is a function of its ambiguity in the purely physical sense: it can mean both dissolution or blending, at once a separation and a union. Thus, in the allegory of the alchemists it is variously represented as death and sexual union, while the still or "limbick" is alternately designated as a sepulchre or a marriage-bed.[76] The most famous of all "metaphysical" *double-entendres,* "to die," might therefore be equally well rendered "to melt," or, as Donne himself sometimes renders it, "to dissolve."[76a] This ambiguity is no bawdy joke to the alchemists; the "death" of volatilization is like the marriage of man and wife, for from the "putrefaction" of the "Hermaphrodite" is generated the seed of a new creature. Like the death of a Christian, this decomposition is also a birth:

> Amen, Amen, I say to you, unless the grain of wheat falling into the ground die, itself remaineth alone. But if it die it bringeth forth much fruit. (John 12, 24-5.)

In the context of the "Valediction," however, the death of virtuous men and the severing of a metallic spirit from its "body" stand for a physical *separation* and a *spiritual* union; the usual erotic values seem to be reversed by the context's literal meaning. We shall explain this at length in the last part of this paper. For the moment, it is necessary to point out only that the word "melt" stands for the departure of "breath" in all of the dimensions we have so far discussed: physically, as the *pneuma* leaves the metal; metaphysically, as the bodily *pneuma* leaves the flesh; literally, as the lovers part in the flesh and join in "breath." Nor do all of these meanings strain the word beyond its traditional capacity. Brother Joseph has observed that Shakespeare used the word "melt" in precisely the same way that it is used by Donne: in order to describe a peaceful and quiet departure which seems a "pneumatic" dispersion. In *Macbeth,* the witches are said to vanish

Into the air; and what seemed corporal *melted* as breath into the wind.[77]

The dispersion of the "spirit" of Love will ultimately be followed by a final condensation.

The diastole-systole of *pneuma* is a refinement because its absence serves the purpose of glorifying the body it leaves behind. Its point of arrival is the same as its point of departure, except infinitely more pure and incorruptible. This is obviously the case in the theological meaning of the process, for the glorified body will be more agile, more subtle, more perfect than the mortal body it once was. Like a seed, the human soul is "sown in corruption, [but] it shall rise in incorruption" (I Cor. 15, 42). This is also true in the alchemist's art. In order to obtain the "philosopher's gold," one must begin with earthly gold and extract its spirit. The essential ingredient of any transmutation is the "seed of gold," "for barley engenders barley and the lion, a lion, and gold, gold." In the words of Basil Valentine, one must begin with "gold . . . beaten into the greatest possible thinness."[78] When once the melting of the gold begins, its "spirit" is driven away uniformly and quietly precisely because it is so perfectly wedded to the body. It is in this way the antithesis of base metals such as lead, which melt noisily and with much smoke because they are imperfect mixtures. This lack of uniformity led Aristotle to characterize them as "stuttering mixtures." Albertus Magnus explains: "for in some parts of the mixture they attain uniformity and in some parts not, but are rather scarcely mixed at all, like a stuttering man who arrives at some words and at some words not."[79] It might therefore be said that perfect mixtures, such as gold, lose their "spiritus" in an even stream of words analogous to the whisper of virtuous men.

The process of refinement must be attended by both water and air, in very careful measure. Giano Lacinio says, "the experience of sigh is essential." Too much air and floods of water, however, will produce a tempestuous condition and ruin the experiment:

> For though the soul of the metal has to be extracted, it must not be killed in the operation; and the extraction of the living soul, which has to be reunited to the glorified body, must be carried on in a way very different from the violent method commonly prevailing among alchemists.[80]

The "death" of the metal must therefore be like the death of a Christian, accompanied, not by "teare-floods" or "sigh-tempests," but by a faith in the Resurrection:

> This separation of body and soul is brought about by a spiritual dying. For as the dissolution of body and soul is performed in the regenerated gold, where body and soul are separated from one another, and yet remain close together in the same phial, the soul daily refreshing the body from above, and preserving it from final destruction, until a set time: so the decaying and half-dead bodily part of man is not entirely deserted by the soul in the furnace of the Cross, but is refreshed by the spirit from above . . . (for our temporal death, with is the wages of sin, is not a real

death, but only a *natural and gentle serving of body and soul*). The indissoluble union and conjunction of the Spirit of God, and the soul of the Christian, are a real and abiding fact.[81]

This is the profound mystery that sad friends, "layetie" and "dull sublunary lovers" will never understand. So a great a secret was the recipe considered by some alchemists that it could be whispered by the philosopher only on his death-bed.[82]

It remains for us now, before we discuss the literal meaning of the poem, to show how Donne's alchemical allegory is related to the geometric statement with which the poem ends. W. A. Murray has shown that the current symbol for gold in Donne's time suggests the compass image: . .[83] The lovers are therefore compared to a circle "to ayery thinnesse beate," or, as we have stated the matter, to a circle which is expanded and ultimately contracted with two-fold movement: radially, from center to circumference and circularly, with an ever increasing circumference. Because the lovers begin as gold and "endure not yet a breach, but an expansion" until they come together as glorified gold, their movement is a regular expansion of a small circle and a regular contraction back to it. Because the terminal point coincides with the lovers' eternity, however, the final circle approaches the minimum point, the center which the mystics identified with the infinite circle of eternity.[84] In the world of space and time, the only way that such a movement can be formally represented with a mathematical figure that captures both its essence and its duration is by means of a compass whose circlings never cease (the fixity of Love) while its radius expands and contracts (the exigencies of life).

We have however shown that the compass traces a planetary orbit, and not just any regular spiral. It is obvious to even the most casual student of alchemy that the continuity of *pneuma* throughout the cosmos had the effect of linking experiments on earth with the movement of the heavenly bodies. The philosophers' Quintessence (which we have called the "spirit" of Love) was itself considered to be the incorruptible material of which the heavenly bodies are composed.[85] In a general way then, one would have expected Donne to give a cosmic circumference to the poetic refinement represented in his poem. It is Donne's genius, however, never to leave the matter at a merely general stage of coherence. His poetic precision narrowed the focus to a particular planet and thereby linked the symbolic statements to the real world. In order to demonstrate this, we must return for a moment to our analysis of planetary movement in the first part of this paper.

We have tried to show that Donne used the words "erect" and "home" in a technical sense to indicate the *exaltatio* and *domicilium* respectively of his planetary orbit. These are two different points of the planetary course through the Zodiac. The "home" of a planet is always the mid-point of an arbitrary constellation in which the planet was believed to have been at the moment of creation. Since the arc of a constellation is $30°$, the "home" of a planet is always $15°$ of the given constellation. On the other hand, the *exaltatio* is mathematically determined. The point of the Sun's erection, for instance is 19° Aries, of the Moon 3° Taurus, of Saturn 11° Libra, etc. Of only one planet is it true that the point of *exaltatio* coincides exactly with the planetary *domicilium,* and that is the planet Mercury. Its *exaltatio* is 15° Virgo; its "home" is in the same constellation—at 15° Virgo. Only of a mercurial orbit may it be said that its altitude

> . . . growes erect *as* that [i. e., the planet itself] comes home.

The movement of the "spirit" of Love therefore moves as does the "subtle" Mercury, the "Hermaphrodite" planet.[86]

Since the lovers begin and end as gold, it is clear that their "spirit" must be the "spirit" of gold, the tincture. In the blundering confusion of formulae and recipes in the history of alchemy, the importance of mercury as a constituent of all metals remains constant. In medieval metallurgy all metals were considered to be composed of sulphur and mercury, the latter being the volatile principle. Gold's purity and uniformity was due to the purity and the perfect homogeneity of its elements; its "spirit" was identified with *spiritus* itself, the fifth essence. Thus, in the fifteenth and sixteenth centuries, mercury was considered the essential element in the production of the "spirit" of gold and of the "philosophers' stone."[87] Paracelsus' famous innovation, the theory of the *tria prima* which made such an impact on Donne, did not shake mercury's pre-eminent position; on the contrary, his assertion that all of matter was composed of sulphur, salt and mercury made of the last substance the perfect analogue of bodily and heavenly *pneuma.* Mazzeo states the analogy succinctly: "To the mystical interpreters of the 'tria prima' mercury became the human spiritual principle [i. e., *pneuma*] and sulphur and salt corresponded to the human body and its soul."[88] By having his compass trace a mercurial orbit, Donne identified the *pneuma* of Love's universe with the *Mercurius Philosophorum.* Its quintessential *motus gyrativus* contains within it all of reality, for "est in Mercurio quicquid quaerunt Sapientes."[89] Thanks to celestial Mercury, the "spirit" of Love (". . . we by a love so much refin'd . . ."), the earthly gold of the two lovers is refined into the immortal and incorruptible gold of the glorified body and soul.

It may be useful to recapitulate the alchemical process which Donne uses as an allegory of his love. The homogeneous mixture of mercury and sulphur which is gold is prepared by being beaten into gold-leaf. It is melted gently and carefully in the presence of some air and some moisture. Its mercurial "spirit" and its soul are thereby extracted gently from the body, but remain in contact with it from afar, refreshing it from time to time. In some experiments, the "spirit" of mercury was sometimes "refined" by being whirled in a spherical container;[90] in Donne's macrocosm, the container is of course the vault of heaven, while "Trepidation of the spheares" is the gentle whirling of refinement. When the "spirit" reaches its point of celestial purity, both it and the soul return to the body which is thereby coagulated, "fixed" in the form of celestial, glorified gold, now capable of turning into gold all that it touches. It is gold's *pneuma,* the "breath" of the two lovers, which has undergone a cosmic expansion and contraction.

*   *   *

To conclude this reading of the poem, it will now be necessary to determine the literal terms of the contrast between the initiate-lovers and the dull sublunary "layetie." This contrast is at the heart of the poem's literal meaning.

The first two stanzas are a simile comparing the death of virtuous men to the parting of the two lovers. The exhortation "So let us melt . . ." relates both of the stanzas to a physical reality which provides them with a metaphoric analogue of separation: the melting of a metal. Moreover, the simile places the words "melt" and "whisper" in parallel, an association which seems confirmed by the Aristotelian comparison of the uniformity of metallic mixture to the uniformity of speech. The meaning of the word "melt" as it applies to the literal situation must therefore also be a "pneumatic" dispersion which is physical (insofar as it is a "melting") and spiritual as well (insofar as it is analogous to the whisper). Another simile, antithetical to the first, is also presented in the first two stanzas: sad friends who cannot determine when the separation is definitive because they cannot discern the breathing are like the "layetie" who cannot understand the mystery of love. The use of the word "layetie," however, suggests that the process is hermetic and therefore associates both the soul's whisper and love's whisper with the secret of "refinement" in the alchemist's art.

The third stanza shifts the focus of attention to the macrocosm rather abruptly by adding still another set of dichotomies to the poem's dialectic. The spatial tension which it introduces (earth-spheres) matches the logical tensions we have just examined. Moving of the earth, the earthquake, is a fortuitous breach in the sublunary world which brings with it tempests and floods. It is a macrocosmic analogue of death in the purely physical sense and an analogue of the separation of elements in ruined or "flooded" experiments. Trepidation of the spheres, however, is an access and recess, a departure followed by a return. The analogue is metaphysically apt, for the movement measures the life of the cosmos and of the soul from the moment of death to the Resurrection: it is a harmless ("innocent") respiration. Its alchemical equivalent is also a necessary trembling, for the gentle whirling of the "spirit" of gold in a spherical container is the refinement prior to a fixation in the glorified composite. The problem seems to be with the relevance of this stanza to the literal situation.

The cosmic restatement of the third stanza is a development which is familiar to us within the context of both physical and metaphysical statements. Because of the doctrine of *pneuma* and the universal continuity which it implies, any alchemical occurrence has a dimension of meaning in the universe. Similarly, because of the theory of macrocosm and microcosm, the soul's processes have their universal counterparts. These multiple associations, however, are scarcely enough to account for the abruptness of the transition between the first two stanzas and the third. Logic seems to require an amplification of the first simile as it applies to the two lovers

rather than a shift to a universal dimension. This is in fact what Donne provides. His macrocosmic language simply underscores the importance he gives
to the laws of Love and serves to make a universe of the two lovers. In order
to make his literal meaning apparent, we must reverse his procedure and reduce the statement to microcosmic proportions, interpolating what he says
of the world's body to apply to the body of Love.

This is clear in retrospect when we come to the fourth stanza. The phrase
"Dull sublunary lovers love" telescopes microcosm and macrocosm and
brings to the surface the submerged literal meaning of the preceding stanza.
The earthquake is the love of sublunary lovers "because it doth remove
those things which elemented it." It is a "fatal" release of *pneuma* which
culminates in absence. Lovers who are merely carnal couple only to separate; their violent coming together can have disastrous consequences. Coitus
is a collision of "elements" accompanied by floods and outbursts of noise,
the *strepitus* which is the sign of the animal.[91] It is ended in an orgasmic
death which, like the earthquake, is a burst of *pneuma* from the organic
depths of the body, a definitive "going."[92] This is how sad friends conceive
of death and how dull sublunary lovers love—only with their earthy selves.

If the "earth" of a lover is his body, then his "sphere" is his head. The
analogy between the spherical shape of the head and the spherical shape of
the celestial vault is probably the origin of Plato's theory of macrocosm
and microcosm.[93] It is at any rate the most familiar of the *Timaeus'* analogies.
So in Donne's poem, the spheres stand for the highest part of incarnate, rational lovers. In spite of their physical separation, they are still joined by
the mind, the pivot of Love's compass. Because of its rational quality, their
love is a "virtuous" melting: an "innocent" trepidation of "breath." It is a
blending of souls in an ecstatic whisper: the farewell kiss of rational lovers.
In a famous passage of the fourth book of the *Courtier*, Castiglione analyzes
the kiss in rational love:

> For since a kiss is the union of body and soul, there is danger that the
> sensual lover may incline more in the direction of body than in that of
> soul; whereas the rational lover sees that, although the mouth is part
> of the body, nevertheless it emits words, which are the interpreters of
> the soul, and that inward breath which is itself called soul. Hence, a man
> delights in joining his mouth to that of his beloved in a kiss, not in order
> to bring himself to any unseemly desire, but because he feels that that
> bond is the opening of mutual access to their souls, which, being each
> drawn by desire for the other, pour themselves each into the other's
> body by turn, and mingle so together that each of them has two souls;
> and a single soul, composed thus of these two, rules as it were over two
> bodies. Hence, a kiss may be said to be a joining of souls rather than of
> bodies, because it has such power over the soul that it withdraws it to
> itself and separates it from the body. For this reason all chaste lovers
> desire the kiss as a union of souls; and thus the divinely enamoured Plato
> says that, in kissing the soul came to his lips in order to escape from his
> body. And since the separation of the soul from sensible things and its

complete union with intelligible things can be signified by the kiss,
Solomon, in his divine book of the Song, says: "Let him kiss me with
the kiss of his mouth," to signify the wish that his soul be transported
through divine love to the contemplation of heavenly beauty in such
manner that, in uniting itself closely therewith, it might forsake the body.[94]

This is the ecstasy that Donne and his beloved enjoy, precisely like the ecstasy
of a virtuous man dying. According to a tradition of the *Midrash* which
entered Renaissance treatises of love through Pico della Mirandola, virtuous
men die like Moses: "Thereupon God kissed Moses and took away his soul
with the kiss of his mouth."[95] They "melt" ecstatically in the same way
("So let us melt . . ."), with a tenderness that releases their *spiritus* from
their mouths in the form of a kiss.[96] They whisper into each other the quintessence of their love and begin their physical separation. That quintessence
recapitulates the gyre of their lives in the "spiraculum vitae" which joins
them for all time of exile in the universe of Love. At the end of that exile,
the lover's journey, their refined soul will reanimate a glorified body in the
perfect golden circularity of an eternal embrace.

*   *   *

The vortex of John Donne's poem has no carefully defined and static
structure, but is simply a repetition of its basic theme through all the analogous planes of reality. It obliterates space by pulsating from a center of
consciousness toward an infinity in which it might perhaps be dissipated,
were it not for its point of fixity. Similarly, it has no time, for its 36 verses
divide a circumference which constitutes both an instant and a sidereal
period of 36,000 years. It whirls around in its path the wreckage of the
poetry and philosophy of three centuries and, like the kaleidoscope, gives
a simple form to the complex of its pieces only by shaking them together.
Part of its complexity is the work of history; our reading has been at times
involved because it was necessary to reconstruct a pattern of thought before
identifying its fragments. In part, however, its complexity is a deliberate
reflection of the love of the poet, in all of its vital historicity. Underlying
the fragile complexity, however, the bewildering flux rests on an ontological
certainty. At the center of the human vortex, in profundity, is the Center
of all reality. Because the poem rests on that Center, it is safe, as long as
Love is safe, from the angels which would flatten it to circular perfection
and from the beast which tightens the coils. Like the kiss which is its emblem,
it is an incarnate (although ephemeral) reality, neither pure body nor pure
soul. In this way, it resembles both the man who wrote it and, as far as we
can tell, the men who read it.

DONNE'S "A NOCTURNALL UPON S. LUCIES DAY" AND THE NOCTURNS OF MATINS

Clarence H. Miller

Donne's "A Nocturnall upon S. Lucies day, Being the shortest day" stands apart from the rest of the *Songs and Sonets* not only because it is a quintessence, as it were, of his subtle lyrical manner, but also because it strikes a different balance between the two kinds of love, sacred and profane. Unlike "The Canonization," in which profane love is transformed into sacred, or "The Anniversarie," in which the poet imagines that he and his lady "shall prove / This, or a love increased there above,"[1] the "Nocturnall" presents the poet crushed by the death of his lady and seeking to find comfort in the thought of reunion with her in heaven. Not content to remain in bitter disillusion and despair, as in "Farewell to love" or "Loves Alchymie," he abandons the love of earth for the love of heaven. The skewed violence of the poem is an index of the huge labor of recreating (or at least beginning to recreate) a mind utterly destroyed by absolute desolation. Hence, like the potent but elusive elixir of the alchemists, the poem is powerful but problematic,[2] so problematic that some critics have been willing to accept it as merely an expression of unqualified despair.[3]

But lately it has been recognized that the "Nocturnall" moves from despair toward resolution. For example, Richard Sleight, in a detailed analysis, points out how

> the poet travels through a series of destruction-creation units, whereby he approaches a negative existence, ending where destruction and creation are not two opposed and complementary events succeeding one another in time, but where destruction becomes a mode of creation.[4]

Arnold Stein contrasts the "surface rhythms of the ordinary world of love, which go about their cyclical business," with "the slow, deep, resolute movement" of the poet's own rhythm, so that he finds the poem to be "a kind of ritual (and that in itself is most rare in Donne) through which he empties himself, and his love, of concern with self and love."[5] Louis Martz and Theodore Redpath have both noted that the movement toward regeneration is implied in the liturgical overtones of "her Vigill, and her Eve" (44), suggesting "an intending Easter communicant"[6] or "the ancient

Reprinted from *Studies in English Literature*, 6 (1966), 77-86, by permission of the author and the publisher.

ecclesiastical usage of the term 'nocturnal,' or 'nocturn,' . . . a midnight
service, a 'Vigill.'"[7]

The significance of this ritual movement can be seen more clearly if we
notice that "nocturnall" in the title and the phrase "this houre her Vigill"
suggest a specific ritual well known (and much discussed) in Donne's time:
the divine office, and in particular the canonical "hour" of matins, consisting of three nocturns, originally recited at (or near) midnight and often
called *vigiliae nocturnae*.[8] To compare the poem with the nocturns of
matins can provide us with a more definite view of the poem's content and
structure. It is not unreasonable to apply the traditional implications of
"nocturn" to this poem, since some of Donne's poems clearly depend on
liturgical forms. He chose a liturgical pattern for "A Litanie" (and defended
his choice by citing two obscure examples he found "Amongst ancient
annals").[9] In fact, as Helen Gardner has shown, the first sonnet of "La
Corona" takes its "leading ideas and much of its phrasing from the Advent
Office in the Roman Breviary,"[10] and in the second and third sonnets of
"La Corona" Donne recalls the *Horae B.V.M.*"[11] These parallels are especially significant because the feast of St. Lucy (December 13) occurs in Advent
within the octave of a major feast of the Blessed Virgin (Immaculate Conception, December 8) which is commemorated in St. Lucy's office.[12]

If we consider the form or pattern of matins, we find some authority
for a five-fold plan comparable to the five stanzas of the "Nocturnall."
Baronius, an author cited by Donne, matches five features of matins with
five functions listed by St. Paul:

> *Cum convenitis, unusquisque vestrum Psalmum habet, doctrinam,*
> *Apocalypsim, linguam, interpretationem* [I Cor. 14:26]. Et vere in
> Matutino habemus Psalmos, Lectiones prò doctrina; Responsoria pro
> Apocalypsi, idest, revelatione; Evangelium pro lingua; Homiliam pro
> interpretatione. . . .[13]

In the tradition of meditation, the number "five," especially because of its
association with the Virgin, was connected with praising the "heroicall"
virtue of an Ideal Woman, as in Donne's "The First Anniuersary," which
has a five-part structure.[14] In "The First Anniuersary" this theme is joined
with *contemptus mundi,* as it is in the "Nocturnall," which not only
honors a sainted lady but also dismisses with contempt the dead world
and the lustful lovers.[15] Moreover, in the "Nocturnall" (14-18) Love's "art
did expresse / A quintessence [or 'fifth essence'] even from nothingnesse,"
which is itself subdivided into five terms: "privations . . . emptinesse . . .
absence, darknesse, death." The opposite of this nothingness is also expressed in five terms: "Life, soule, forme, spirit, whence they beeing have" (20).

But neither matins nor the "Nocturnall" is basically quintal in structure,
but rather trinal. The *Pilgrimage of Perfection* (1531) gives a simplified but
accurate description of matins: "In matyns communly be iii orbes, otherwise called iii nocturnes, of yᵉ whiche euery orbe conteyneth iij psalmes,
iii lessons, and iii responsories."[16] The nine psalms of matins were regularly

paralleled to the "trinall triplicities" (as Spenser calls them) of the nine angelic choirs. On the feasts of saints, the nine psalms were thought to be appropriate "eo quod digni facti sunt illi [sancti] ascendere usque ad altitudinem Caeli, in quo habitant iidem Chori Angelici."[17] The nine lessons of matins,[18] each followed by its responsory, are said to be significant because "conjungunt nos dostinae et conversationi novem ordinum Angelicorum: sicut et gaudiis ipsorum conjungunt nos novem, quae sequuntur, responsoria."[19] These overtones from the nocturns of matins are appropriate to the "Nocturnall" (which is written in a nine-line stanza) because Donne there prepares for his "conversation" (to use a term from "The Second Anniuersary," 325) with the sainted (and possibly virgin) soul which now enjoys her heavenly reward: "Since shee enjoyes her long nights festivall, / Let mee prepare towards her . . ." (42-43).

According to the traditional interpretation, the triplicities of the nocturns of matins also signify the movement from a dead world to renewal through grace, a movement reflected in the three periods of history (before the law, under the law, after the Incarnation) and paralleled in the three nocturns. This is why the lessons of the third nocturn consist of commentaries on the gospel, "tempori gratiae congruum." It is also the reason why the hymn "Te Deum" is usually sung after the third nocturn: "Et quia tempore gratiae, laetitiae locus est magis, quam in aliis stantibus ante legem, & sub lege: ideo in fine tertii Nocturni, si dicendus est, cantatur Hym[n]us *Te Deum.*"[20] Moreover, the conclusion of matins leads naturally into the joyful dawning "hour" of lauds.[21] There is, of course no joyful exaltation at the end of the "Nocturnall," nor has the time changed from midnight. But it is clear that in the last four lines the poet is looking "towards her," the Lucy whose name means "light"; and the midnight is now "deep," not because it expressed despair greater than that in the first stanza, but because it betokens a profounder understanding of darkness. Similarly, Crashaw[22] in his "In the Glorious Epiphanie of our Lord God" follows, like Donne, the way of withdrawal and praises Dionysius for teaching

> obscure Mankind a more close way
> By the frugall negatiue light
> Of a most wise & well-abused Night
> To read more legible thine originall Ray,
> [*Cho.*] And make our Darknes serue Thy day; . . .
>
> (209-213)

And in "Obsequies to the Lord Harrington," which gives a full and explicit version of the kind of preparation merely mentioned in the conclusion of the "Nocturnall," Donne himself finds revelation and self-knowledge in the enlightened darkness of midnight.

> Thous seest mee here at midnight, now all rest;
> Times dead-low water; when all mindes devest
> To morrows businesse . . .

Thou at this midnight seest mee, and as soone
As that Sunne rises to mee, midnight's noone,
All the world growes transparent, and I see
Through all, both Church and State, in seeing thee;
And I discerne by favour of this light,
My selfe, the hardest object of the sight.

(15-30)

In the "Nocturnall" the withdrawal is accomplished in the three central
stanzas, framed by the first and the last, which provide the transition from
the dead darkness of despair to the deep darkness of resigned expectation.
They are marked off from the rest of the poem by the two addresses to the
worldly lovers: "Study me then, you who shall lovers bee" (line 1 of stanza
2) and "You lovers" (line 2 or stanza 5). The poet admonishes the lovers to
"study" him and proceeds to read a lesson, a meditative analysis, on his own
nothingness. As Herbert directs his body "To spell his elements" on tombs
in "Church-monuments" and proceeds to tell the body what it will learn,
here Donne commands the lovers to study the "Epitaph"[23] of dead nature,
himself, and goes on to pursue the real meaning of the words of the epitaph
(they are, one would imagine, "I am nothing") with a persistent subtlety
reminiscent of much patristic exegesis of biblical texts in the homilies which
make up the lessons of the third nocturn of matins. Thus in the lessons for
the third nocturn of St. Lucy, St. Gregory the Great "expresses" the meaning of the text "Simile est regnum coelorum thesauro abscondito in agro"
and concludes:

> Thesaurus autem coeleste est desiderium: ager vero, in quo thesaurus
> absconditur, disciplina studii coelestis. Quem profecto agrum venditis
> omnibus comparat, qui voluptatibus carnis renuntians, cuncta sua
> terrena desideria per disciplinae coelestis custodiam calcat.[24]

Donne's middle stanzas are a sort of "disciplina studii coelestis," and the
last stanza certainly treads down all earthly desires.

But these three middle stanzas are framed not only by the first and last
stanzas, but also by the repetition (with variation) of the first line as the
last. Refrains are not uncommon in Donne's poetry, and "La Corona" is
woven together by a carefully wrought scheme of repeated lines; but only
in the "Nocturnall" does Donne frame a poem by repeating a line. The
nocturns of matins offer a precedent for this, since one of their most
characteristic features is the repetition of a different antiphon, usually a
single verse, before and after each of the nine psalms. (The same is true of
lauds and vespers.) In fact, the rank "duplex" to which St. Lucy's feast
belongs takes it name from this fact: "Haec vox: *Duplex apud Durand*[um]
. . . habetur. Apud antiquiores non habetur. Et ex eodem Durand[o] significat, Antiphonas in Officio duplicari, hoc est integras recitari ante & post
Psalmos."[25] To read the office for a week means reading about 150 psalms,
each framed by an antiphon. The practice was thought, and probably also

felt, to be symbolic: the antiphon "sua combinatione seu repetitione, ante,
& post Psalmum, significat diversorum unionem, & charitatem."[26] But the
more frequent practice is to say only the first half of the antiphon before
the psalm and the whole antiphon after it—in other words, repetition with
a sense of resolution and completion. Hugh of St. Victor says that this fuller
repetition "significat inchoatam in hac vita charitatem, consummandam esse
in fine vitae; sicut integra dicitur antiphona in fine Psalmi."[27] In his stylistic
analysis of the opening and closing lines of the "Nocturnall," Richard
Sleight reaches a parallel conclusion on purely aesthetic ground. Pointing
out the rhythmic dissonance of the first line, he adds:

> Not until the end do the year and the day achieve harmony and cease
> to pull in opposite directions. The intervening lines reduce the diver-
> gences by regarding the past love, the intervening misery, and the
> present state, as parts of one experience. Once the unity has replaced
> the sharpness of each part of the experience, as the dominant feature,
> then that unity leads directly to its full completion, to the restoration
> of a perfectly balanced union. The threads that seemed to lead in so
> many different directions in the body of the poem have linked up:
> >   since this
> > Both the yeares and the dayes deep midnight is.[28]

The material of Donne's poem, apart from its structure, seems to owe
nothing to the legend of St. Lucy in the lessons for the second nocturn of
her feast, though her story does present the contrast between the lustful
lovers and the sainted lady, as Donne does in the last stanza.[29] But the
regular course of scripture readings in the lessons of the first nocturn of
matins may have provided Donne with some hints for his "Nocturnall."
These lessons were originally designed to cover most of the Old and New
Testaments in one year, but the gradual accretion of saints' offices, which
displaced the regular office for the day, cut out much of the reading from
the Bible. This conflict was probably the most important reason for the
heated discussion and frequent revision of the breviary during the sixteenth
century.[30]

As he tells us in the preface to the *Book of Common Prayer,* one of
Cranmer's purposes in simplifying and recasting the canonical hours into
matins and evensong was to restore the sequence of Bible readings. The
Church fathers, he says,

> so ordered the matter, that all the whole Bible (or the greatest part there-
> of) should be read over once in the year. . . . But these many years passed,
> this godly and decent order of the ancient fathers hath be so altered,
> broken, and neglected, by planting in uncertain stories, Legends, Responds,
> Verses, vain repetitions, Commemorations, and Synodals, that common-
> ly when any book of the Bible was begun, before three or four chapters
> were read out, all the rest were unread. And in this sort, the book of
> Esaie was begun in Advent, and the book of Genesis in Septuagesima: but

they were only begun and never read through.[31]

Cranmer left the readings from Isaias in Advent, but he moved the readings from Genesis back to January.[32] In "La Corona" Donne drew upon passages from Isaias in the Advent Office;[33] and chapter 32 of Isaias, assigned in the Book of Common Prayer to matins of St. Lucy's day, contains one of those powerful images of desolation, frequent in Isaias, which is close to the mood of the "Nocturnall":

> Super humum populi mei spinae et vepres ascendent: quanto magis super omnes domos gaudii civitatis exultantis? Domus enim dimissa est, multitudo urbis relicta est, tenebrae et palpatio factae sunt super speluncas usque in aeternum. (vv. 13-14)

More striking, however, is Donne's stupendous reversal of Genesis in lines 22-29 of the "Nocturnall," where he sweeps back from the flood, to the creation of the world, to the chaos out of which it was formed, to the nothing before chaos, to the "Elixir" or quintessence of that nothing.

> ... Oft a flood
> Have wee two wept, and so
> Drownd the whole world, us two; oft did we grow
> To be two Chaosses, when we did show
> Care to ought else; and often absences
> Withdrew our soules, and made us carcasses.

> But I am by her death, (which word wrongs her)
> Of the first nothing, the Elixer grown; ...

Thus in content, but especially in structure, Donne's "Nocturnall" draws upon the nocturns of matins in the divine office. The quintal, trinal, and antiphonal form of these nocturns provided an allegorical pattern—what might be called nowadays a mythic scheme—of recreation and regeneration which Donne adapted in a "ritual" lyric which traces with great subtlety and power the recreation of a mind destroyed by grief, the arduous course from utter desolation to expectant resignation. The "Nocturnall" provides evidence that Donne might well have shared the opinion of a modern writer who is speaking from personal experience when he says of the Night-Office that "its chief grace is that it stimulates the mind to serious reflection."[34]

VI. RELIGIOUS POETRY

JOHN DONNE'S *HOLY SONNETS* AND THE ANGLICAN DOCTRINE OF CONTRITION

Douglas L. Peterson

The recent work of Louis Martz and Helen Gardner with the tradition of religious meditation is an important contribution to literary history and thus to criticism.[1] It has provided us with valuable insights into the ways that Donne and certain of his contemporaries adapted traditional meditative disciplines to the writing of devotional verse. Of no less importance to those who are interested particularly in Donne is Miss Gardner's additional contribution—a rearrangement of the *Holy Sonnets* suggested by the most authoritative manuscripts and early editions and confirmed by the sequential order that is thus revealed in the twelve sonnets of the edition of 1633.[2] She has enabled us to see things in the group which have been obscured since Grierson's standard edition.

In certain respects, however, the arguments on which Miss Gardner bases her four groupings—the "two contrasting groups of six" which make up the edition of 1633, the four "penitential" sonnets of 1635, and the three "occasional" sonnets that appear only in the Westmoreland manuscript—require further qualification. Her arguments on the basis of manuscripts and dates seem indisputable; equally convincing is the evidence she has drawn up to show that the twelve poems of 1633 form a sequence following certain progressive steps of meditation proposed in Loyola's *Spiritual Exercises.* On the other hand, her classification of the four groupings according to theme is arbitrary.[3] It violates the essential unity of the *Holy Sonnets* as a group, misconstruing Donne's intentions and distorting, in several instances, the meaning of individual poems.

J. B. Leishman perceives something of these difficulties in his review of Miss Gardner's edition:[4]

> According to Miss Gardner's classification, the fifth sonnet (first group), 'If poysonous mineralls, and if that tree,' is a sonnet on death, while the ninth sonnet (second group), 'What if this present were the worlds last night?' is a sonnet on God's love; nevertheless, are not both themes equally present in each sonnet—or rather, is not each sonnet concerned with the twofold theme of the love which alone can save us from eternal death? (p. 75)

Reprinted from *Studies in Philology,* 56 (1959), 504-18, by permission of the author and the publisher, the University of North Carolina Press.

He notes a similar overlapping in the classification of the four "penitential" sonnets: "Miss Gardner declares that they are related by their common emphasis on sin and tears for sin, although it is perhaps difficult to perceive any very clear and obvious difference between them and the last six of the original twelve" (p. 75). Leishman suggests, therefore, that in spite of Donne's indebtedness to the Ignatian art of meditation, "his sonnets still remain so personal that it is perhaps easier to classify them according to phrases and images than according to clearly distinguishable themes" (pp. 75-6).

The source of difficulty here is that neither Miss Gardner nor Mr. Leishman recognizes a controlling principle for all nineteen of the sonnets. Leishman assumes that because the same subjects reappear in different groups, classification according to theme is impossible. Miss Gardner assumes that because one group is concerned primarily with fear, another with love, and another with repentance, each group is distinct. Donne, himself, discloses in one of his sermons the principle that unifies the sequence as a whole. He is discussing fear and love as essential preliminaries to repentance:[5]

> Place the affection . . . upon the right object, God, and I have, in some measure, done that which this Text directed, (*Taught you the fear of the Lord*) if I send you away in either disposition, *Timorous*, or *amorous*; possessed with either, the fear, or the love of God; for, this fear is inchoative love, and this love is consummative fear; The love of God begins in fear, and the fear of God ends in love; and that love can never end, for God is love.

Thus it is that the stimulation of fear in the first half of the sequence of 1633 is in the interest of the stimulation of love in the second half, which is essential in turn to the "contrite" sorrow that is the theme of the four sonnets of 1635 and the three Westmoreland sonnets. In short, the controlling principle in all nineteen of the *Holy Sonnets* is the Anglican doctrine of contrition.

Both Catholic and Anglican doctrines agree that contrition is essentially a state of feeling, a "sorrow of heart and detestation for sin committed, with the resolve to sin no more."[6] But the demands upon the Anglican penitent are more stringent than those made on the Catholic. The Council of Trent established a formal distinction between perfect and imperfect contrition (attrition) in terms of what has motivated "sorrow of heart." Sorrow motivated by a fear of divine punishment was defined as attrition; sorrow motivated by a hatred of sin itself and a love for God was defined as contrition. Although the latter is the more desirable, either, according to the Catholic church, is sufficient for salvation. Anglican doctrine, however, insists absolutely that sorrow must be motivated by a hatred for sin in itself and that it must be precipitated by love for God. Donne is simply quoting orthodox doctrine when he insists that sorrow must issue from love and that fear is only a preliminary to love. Fear is merely attrition and, in itself, not sufficient for salvation:[7]

> Our new *Romane Chymists* . . .can change any foulness into cleanness
> easily. They require no more after sin, but . . . A little slight inward sor-
> row, and that's enough. For, they have provided an easier way then *Con-
> trition*; for that which they have induc'd, and call Attrition, is not an
> affection . . . That hath proposed God, for the mark, that it is directed
> to . . . but it is such an affection as may be had without any concurrence
> or assistance of grace, and is onely . . . a natural sorrow, proceeding onely
> out of a servile fear of torment. And yet, a Confession made with this
> Attrition and no more, is enough for salvation, say they; and he that
> hath made a confession with such a disposition as this . . . shall never
> need to repent any farther for his sins. . . . This is Attrition, to be dis-
> pleased with our sins, but not more with our sins, then with any thing
> else . . . To have a purpose to leave a sin, but not the sin rather then any
> thing else, this is their *Attrition,* and this is their enough for salvation.
> A sigh of the penitent, a word of the *Priest,* makes all clean, and induces
> an absolute pureness.

As Donne implies in this passage, the Anglican's penitence must be made
directly to God; he cannot rely on any church intermediary; he receives no
assurance from his priest that he has satisfied the requirements of contrition.
Assurance is entirely a matter of conscience.

The consequences of such doctrine for a man whose belief is as rigorous
as Donne's are an intensive and sometimes tortuous examination of conscience and equally intensive meditation upon the consequences of sin and
those Christian commonplaces that ought, God willing, to stimulate proper
love and sorrow. But the effort toward saving sorrow is fraught with difficulties. Such sorrow can be only an effect of grace; and since it is a state
of emotional conviction, not merely a rational acknowledgment of sin and
of the debt of love that man owes God, the question of assurance is exceedingly difficult. To be too easily convinced of saving sorrow is to risk the
sin of complacence; to be overly scrupulous is to risk despair. The avoidance
of either extreme is doubly difficult, since contrition is a supra-rational
experience—a state of feeling that can not be confirmed by rational means.
The penitent's only recourse, therefore, is to follow disciplines advocated
by the church and designed to help him co-operate with God in the hope
that with their aid his efforts will be rewarded with saving grace.[8]

Those disciplines coincide exactly with the disciplines employed in the
Ignatian art of meditation for the stimulation of religious fervor, and it is
in the interest of experiencing contrition that Donne employs the Exercises
in the sonnets of 1633. He has not composed "two contrasting sets of six
[sonnets]" to "create an image of himself at prayer;" nor is he committed
"to showing himself as he would be rather than as he is,"[9] except in the
obvious sense that any man of Donne's religious convictions prefers salvation to damnation. The *Holy Sonnets* represent a series of efforts to experience those states of feeling that either precede or are concomitant with
contrition. Once this is recognized, the stages of progression in the sequence
of 1633 are clearly evident for the first time.

The introductory poem, "As due by many titles I resigne," poses the problem that the sequence attempts to resolve. The penitent, having satisfied the preliminary requirements of repentance by a declaration of faith and an acknowledgement of sin (ll. 1-10), must now seek the grace that is essential to contrite sorrow:

> Except thou rise and for thine owne worke fight,
> Oh I shall soone despaire, when I doe see
> That thou lov'st mankind well, yet wilt'not chuse me,
> And Satan hates mee, yet is loth to lose mee.

But grace is not immediately forthcoming. The penitent must first dissuade his will from sin; and it is to this end that fear of punishment is stimulated in the next three sonnets. Donne's procedure here is confirmed by Richard Hooker, who stresses the function of fear as prerequisite to repentance: Although "fear is impotent and unable to advise itself; yet this good it hath, that men are thereby made desirous to prevent, if possibly they may, whatsoever evil they dread. . . . Fear of divine revenge and punishment, where it taketh place, doth make men desirous to be rid . . . from that inward guiltiness of sin, wherein they would else securely continue."[10] For the stimulation of fear Hooker advises meditating on the Ignatian topics, "The Last Things": "The resurrection of the dead, the judgment of the world to come, and the endless misery of sinners being apprehended, this worketh fear." (p. 241). Such meditation, however, must also include a consideration of both the means and possibility of avoiding "revenge and punishment":

> Howbeit, when faith hath wrought a fear of the event of sin, yet repentance hereupon ensueth not, unless our belief conceive both the possibility and means to avert evil: the possibility, inasmuch as God is merciful, and most willing to have sin cured; the means, because he hath plainly taught what is requisite and shall suffice unto that purpose (p. 241).

Donne's employment of the Ignatian topics is thoroughly in accord with Hooker's instructions. "Oh my blacke Soule! now thou art summoned" meditates in the octet upon "the endless misery" that confronts the sinner at the point of death and in the sestet contemplates the possibility and means of averting punishment. The possibility is made manifest, of course, through Christ; the means is repentance or, more exactly, that proper sorrow, as well as the acceptance of the Atonement, which allows grace to be operative:

> Yet grace, if thou repent, thou canst not lacke;
> But who shall give thee that grace to beginne?
> Oh make thy selfe with holy mourning blacke,
> And red with blushing, as thou art with sinne;
> Or wash thee in Christs blood, which hath this might
> That being red, it dyes red soules to white.

It should be noticed here that "holy mourning blacke" and "red with blushing" imply sorrow for sin itself rather than sorrow occasioned by fear of punishment. The procedure in the next poem, "This is my playes last scene, here heavens appoint," is the same except for one interesting variation. This time the means and possibility of avoiding the punishment demanded by absolute justice are founded on a deliberately fallacious argument which dates back at least to the medieval "Debate of the Body and Soul": Since it has been my body that has sinned, and since at the moment of death my body will be separated from my soul, I shall be thus purged of evil and may therefore legitimately hope that God will "impute me righteous." What is particularly interesting is that Donne rejects this argument as fallacious in the following poem on "the resurrection of the dead" by pointing out that it is the whole man—not the soul alone—that will be judged on Doomsday:

> At the round earths imagin'd corners, blow
> Your trumpets, Angells, and arise, arise
> From death, you numberlesse infinities
> Of soules, and to your scattred bodies goe. . . .

Furthermore, it is futile to hope for pardon on the Day of Judgment. There is only one way of receiving pardon: full repentance "here on this lowly ground":

> 'Tis late to aske abundance of thy grace,
> When wee are there; here on this lowly ground,
> Teach mee how to repent; for that's as good
> As if thou 'hadst seal'd my pardon, with thy blood.

At this point in the sequence the first phase of the discipline is concluded. The following two poems, "If poysonous mineralls, and if that tree" and "Death be not proud, though some have called thee," are transitional sonnets in the sequence which look forward to the next phase of contrition, the transcendence of fear through love. "If poysonous mineralls, and if that tree" questions the justice and mercy of God in order to dramatize the futility of attempting to resolve by reason the mystery of God's justice:

> If lecherous goats, if serpents envious
> Cannot be damn'd; Alas; why should I bee?
> Why should intent or reason, borne in mee,
> Make sinnes, else equall, in mee, more heinous?
> And mercy being easie, and glorious
> To God, in his sterne wrath, why threatens hee?

To argue such questions—to dispute the paradoxical concept of a deity who is at once absolutely just and infinitely merciful—is pointless. The penitent is obliged to accept God and His decrees on faith and to throw himself upon His mercy. Thus the stimulation of fear by meditating upon God as absolute justice brings home to the penitent the need to make full repentance. The poem ends with a plea for the grace that will, in effect, transform sorrow incited by fear to sorrow incited by love:

But who am I, that dare dispute with thee?
O God, Oh! of thine onely worthy blood,
And my teares, make a heavenly Lethean flood,
And drowne in it my sinnes blacke memorie.
That thou remember them, some claime as debt,
I thinke it mercy, if thou wilt forget.

"Death be not proud, though some have called thee" dismisses death as a
valid motive of fear. Fear of death is a "natural fear" and, according to
Donne, natural fears are invalidated by "Feare of the Lord": ". . . though
fear look upon evill, (for affliction is *malum poenae*, evill as it hath the
nature of *punishment*) yet when the feare of the Lord is entred into my
naturall feare, my feare is more conversant, more exercised upon the contemplation of *Good*, then *Evill*, more upon the glory of God, . . . then upon
the afflictions of this life, how malignant, how manifold soever."[11]

The sequence now proceeds to the final prerequisite to contrition, the
love for God.[12] The first three poems are devoted to the goodness and
mercy of God, subjects which, according to Hooker, are the best means
of stimulating the love that "moveth unto repentance":

Our love and desire of union with God ariseth from the strong conceit
which we have of his admirable goodness. The goodness of God which
particularly moveth unto repentance, is his mercy towards mankind,
notwithstanding sin: for let it once sink deeply into the mind of man,
that howsoever we have injured God, his very nature is averse from
revenge, except unto sin we add obstinacy; otherwise always ready to
accept our submission as a full discharge or recompense for all wrongs;
and can we choose but begin to love him whom we have offended? or
can we but begin to grieve that we have offended him whom we now
love? (p. 242)

The first of these three poems, "Spit in my face yee Jewes, and pierce my
side," expresses for the first time in the sequence a sorrow that is not
motivated by fear. By considering sin as cruelty to Christ, Donne approaches
the sorrow for which he had prayed in "If poysonous mineralls, and if that
tree." The sestet then moves to what is also the subject of meditation in
the next two poems, a consideration of divine mercy:

Of let mee then, his strange love still admire:
Kings pardon, but he bore our punishment.
And *Jacob* came cloth'd in vile harsh attire
But to supplant, and with gainfull intent:
God cloth'd himselfe in vile mans flesh, that so
Hee might be weake enough to suffer woe.

The next poem, "Why are wee by all creatures waited on?", reconsiders
the hierarchical creation, which had been the subject of "If poysonous
mineralls, and if that tree." Whereas the earlier poem had considered reason
only as the faculty whereby man was made responsible for his transgressions,

it is now treated as the gift that enables man to rule the natural world and second only to the Atonement as an indication of God's love. The progression from reason as a source of culpability to reason as a source of nobility is directly the result of the different phase of repentance involved. The same thing occurs in the next poem, "What if this present were the worlds last night?", which, like "This is my playes last scene, here heavens appoint," imagines the imminence of Doomsday. In the earlier poem fear was stimulated by contemplating God as judge. Now, to dispel fear, the subject of meditation is the mercy and love of God that is evident in the Crucifixion. The face of God "whose feare already shakes my every joynt" is supplanted by the face of Christ, mercy suffusing wrath:

> Marke in my heart, O Soule, where thou dost dwell,
> The picture of Christ crucified, and tell
> Whether that countenance can thee affright,
> Teares in his eyes quench the amasing light,
> Blood fills his frownes, which from his pierc'd head fell,
> And can that tongue adjudge thee unto hell,
> Which pray'd forgivenesse for his foes fierce spight?

With a final declaration of assurance, "This beauteous forme assures a pitious minde" (l. 14), another step toward contrition has been taken. The next step is to return God's love. This once accomplished, proper sorrow ought to follow. Thus it is the debt of love to God that provides the subject for the final three poems of the sequence.

"Batter my heart, three person'd God; for, you" is a prayer for the grace that is necessary for the consummation of contrition. The penitent has co-operated in so far as he is able:

> I, like an usurpt towne, to 'another due,
> Labour to 'admit you, but Oh, to no end,
> Reason your viceroy in mee, mee should defend,
> But is captiv'd, and proves weake or untrue. . . .

Sufficient love for God requires divine aid:

> Divorce mee, 'untie, or breake that knot againe,
> Take mee to you, imprison mee, for I
> Except you 'enthrall mee, never shall be free,
> Nor ever chast, except you ravish mee.

The plea here is nearly identical to the plea made in the introductory poem, "As due by many titles I resigne." It differs only in the intensity of feeling. The penitent has experienced the full implications of what in the earlier poem was stated simply as a truism:

> Oh I shall soone despaire, when I doe see
> That thou lov'st mankind well, yet wilt'not chuse me,
> And Satan hates mee, yet is loth to lose mee.

The spiritual effort undertaken in the intervening eight sonnets has cul-
minated in this more intense desire and more urgent need to satisfy the
requirements of contrition. After the next sonnet, "Wilt thou love God, as
he thee! then digest," which only reaffirms the tenet that grace will not be
forthcoming until the penitent's love for God is sufficient, the sequence is
concluded by "Father, part of his double interest"—a summarizing affirmation of the tenet that mercy transcends justice and that the command to
love, by which God's law is abridged, offers the only means and possibility
for hope to the penitent.

The sequence ends, therefore, with no indication that the efforts it represents have been successful: each of the preliminary stages which ought
to lead to contrition is represented, but so far there has occurred no expression of contrite sorrow. There are indications of such success, however,
in the "penitential" sonnets of 1635. These four poems, while not sequen-
tially related to the sequence of 1633, consummate, nevertheless, the
disciplines represented by it. Richard Hooker concludes his discussion of
the methods of bringing about contrition by describing what are in effect
the subjects and feelings of the sonnets of 1635:

> From these considerations, setting before our eyes our inexcusable
> both unthankfulness in disobeying so merciful, and foolishness in provok-
> ing so powerful a God, there ariseth necessarily a pensive and corrosive
> desire that we had done otherwise; a desire which suffereth us to fore-
> slow no time, to feel no quietness within ourselves, to take neither sleep
> nor food with contentment, never to give over supplications, confessions,
> and other penitent duties, till the light of God's reconciled favour shine
> in our darkened soul (p. 243).

The first three sonnets of the 1635 group are clearly expressions of that
"pensive and corrosive desire" described by Hooker. 'Thou hast made me,
And shall thy worke decay?" is both a "supplication" and "confession." "I
am a little world made cunningly" and "O might those sighes and teares
returne again" are lamentations for sin, expressing "a desire that we had
done otherwise" and prayers for "God's reconciled favour." The fourth and
concluding poem, "If faithfull soules be alike glorifi'd," on the other hand,
is not an expression of contrition, but a summarizing commentary on the
success of the disciplines undertaken in the preceding fifteen sonnets. The
admission here is one of assurance: "captive reason" (Sonnet 10) is now
capable of "white truth"; sorrow is now "true griefe." The penitent is in a
state of grace: "valiantly I hels wide mouth o'rstride."[13]

There is, then, a clearly realized principle of unity and of progression
in the sixteen sonnets that have so far been discussed. The sequence of
1633 is devoted to those preliminary stages of feeling, of fear and of love,
that ought to lead to contrite sorrow; the first three of the sonnets of
1635 are expressions of contrite sorrow, and the fourth is a statement of
success. Furthermore, it is also evident that the next group, the Westmoreland sonnets, are about contrition and hence are neither "entirely uncon-

nected with each other" nor "distinct in their inspiration from the sixteen
which precede them in the manuscript."[14]

"Show me deare Christ, thy spouse, so bright and cleare" fulfills one of
the obligations of the Anglican who would properly love God: to love God
is also to love Christ's "bride," the spiritual church.[15] Donne mourns the
state of the temporal church abroad and in England and then prays that the
true church, the "mild Dove," be revealed and accepted by "most men."

> Betray kind husband thy spouse to our sights,
> And let myne amorous soule court thy mild Dove,
> Who is most trew, and pleasing to thee, then
> When she'is embrac'd and open to most men.

Love and sorrow; again Donne's concern is with feelings proper to contrition. The penitent is obliged to feel the weight of the sins of all humanity,
of which the abuses in the temporal church are a part. The obligation is accepted by David in Psalms 79 and 80, it is accepted by Fulke Greville in
"*Syon* lyes waste, and thy *Ierusalem*," and it is here accepted by Donne.[16]

The other two Westmoreland sonnets, "Since she whome I lov'd hath
payd her last debt" and "Oh, to vex me, contraryes meete in one," round
out the *Holy Sonnets* as a group of poems dedicated to the experience of
contrition by considering difficulties that are apt to arise if the penitent
is inclined to excessive scrupulosity.[17] "Since she whome I lov'd, hath payed
her last debt" has customarily been read as a lament for the poet's deceased
wife; but her death is only incidental to the real subject of the poem, a condition Donne introduces to explain his present feelings toward God:

> Since she whome I lov'd, hath payd her last debt,
> To Nature, and to hers, and my good is dead,
> And her soule early into heaven ravished,
> Wholy in heavenly things my mind is sett.

Through her the poet's longing for God has been sharpened, but the real subject of the poem is a kind of spiritual sickness:

> Here the admyring her my mind did whett
> To seeke thee God; so streames do shew the head,
> But though I have found thee, and thou my thirst hast fed,
> A holy thirsty dropsy melts mee yett.

The sickness is an inordinate desire that God provide him with further indications of His love, some assurance that he is in a state of grace. The sickness
is correctly diagnosed in the sestet:

> But why should I begg more love, when as thou
> Dost wooe my soule, for hers offring all thine:
> And dost not only feare least I allow
> My love to saints and Angels, things divine,
> But in thy tender jealosy dost doubt
> Least the World, fleshe, yea Devill putt thee out.

It is sufficient assurance, Donne concludes, that the penitent feel in his
heart that God desires his love and would see him remain free from sin.

It may be that the spiritual difficulty treated by Donne in this poem
arose as a consequence of his wife's death. One would suppose that for
the Christian a loss such as Donne's would be more easily interpreted as
an indication of God's displeasure than as an indication of His love. Nevertheless, Donne's main concern is clearly not with his wife's death but with
his inordinate desire for assurance.

The difficulty confessed in "Oh, to vex me, contraryes meete in one"
is even more serious. Inconstancy in devotion has become habitual; hence,
contrition is imperfect:

> As humorous is my contritione
> As my prophane love, and as sonne forgott:
> As ridlingly distemperd, cold and hott,
> As praying, as mute; infinite, as none.

The initial "contraryes" are defined clearly enough: "inconstancy" has become "a constant habit." But it is only after we are aware of the theological
doctrines behind the poem—those formulations from which the precise
definitions of the key terms, "love" and "fear," depend—that we recognize
the source of inconstancy and thus are able to appreciate the full range of
the sonnet's implications. The inconstancy of Donne's devotions are the
result of his failure to resolve another set of contraries, contraries which he
had defined in "If poysonous mineralls, and if that tree." He is confounded
by a deity who is at once absolutely just and infinitely merciful; his feelings
waver between "true fear" and an insincere love that can express itself only
in "flattering speaches":

> I durst not view heaven yesterday; and to day
> In prayers, and flattering speaches I court God:
> To morrow I quake with true feare of his rod.
> So my devout fitts come and go away
> Like a fantastique Ague: save that here
> Those are my best dayes, when I shake with feare.

Unless we realize that for the Anglican fear alone is not sufficient for salvation, that in fact, unless fear is transcended by love, it is damning, we are
unable to appreciate the terrible irony of the concluding line or to recognize
that the sonnet is an admission of near-despair, reflecting a moment of
spiritual dryness, brought on, perhaps, by the scrupulosity that appears to
have been a characteristic of Donne's asceticism.[18]

Thus, in spite of their diversity of subject, the Westmoreland sonnets
are not "entirely unconnected with each other" or "distinct in their inspiration from the sixteen which precede them in the manuscript." They are
not related schematically to the sonnets of 1633 and 1635; nevertheless, as
comments upon the experience of contrition, they depend for a full realization of their implications upon the spiritual efforts represented in the earlier

sonnets and have their place in a complete representation of the Anglican experience of contrition. Finally, the problem of dating the *Holy Sonnets* has no bearing upon the argument that all nineteen of the sonnets are to be considered as a unified group. Whether one accepts Grierson's conjecture that all of the sonnets were written after the death of Anne Donne in 1617, or Gardner's theory that the first sixteen were written between 1609 and 1610 and the last three between 1617 and 1620, the unity of theme and purpose apparent throughout the entire group is sufficient evidence for considering them together. The unity of the group does not presuppose that the poems were written necessarily within a period of three years or that they could not have been written over a period of eleven years; nor, for that matter, need it be supposed that the sonnets of 1633 and 1635 were written in the order dictated by the progressive steps of the discipline they represent.

To show that the *Holy Sonnets* have a unity of purpose and theme is not to argue that their value as poetry is thereby enhanced, but, ultimately, responsible criticism will have to take into account the ramifications in individual poems of the theological doctrine which informs the sonnets as a group. The reasons for this should be obvious. For one thing, the meaning of individual sonnets is qualified by their relationships with other sonnets in the group. For another, the terminology of individual sonnets is given finer definition by their theological context than is otherwise possible. Finally, we are brought closer to understanding the sonnets on Donne's terms. Such a reading ought, at least, to lead to certain revisions of contemporary commonplaces about Donne's neurotic and melancholy faith. Certainly it is rash to assume from the subject matter and emotional quality of these poems that their author was the victim of an overwrought religiosity. For those who, in keeping with the current fashions, insist upon Donne's uniquely "modern" sensibility, it may seem less ingenius to read the *Holy Sonnets* according to prescribed habits of thought and feeling; but since such a reading comes closer to respecting Donne's intentions, it has its compensations in the more accurate and profound reading it has provided.

HOLY SONNETS VIII AND XVII: JOHN DONNE

M. E. Grenander

Writing in 1930, George Williamson pointed out that "the two subjects in which [John Donne] went deepest are those which try the understanding most—love and religion. From these twin sources . . . flow significant currents in English poetry. Love poetry could never be quite the same after him, and religious verse that is also poetry descends from him."[1] Most modern critics for many years focussed on one of these currents—the *Songs and Sonets.* More recently, however, they have turned their attention to the other— Donne's sacred verse. This shift in critical emphasis undoubtedly owes much to the appearance of two exhaustive and extremely informative works of contemporary scholarship: Helen Gardner's edition of the *Divine Poems*[2] and Louis L. Martz' *The Poetry of Meditation.*[3] Miss Gardner pointed out (p. xvii) that the divine poems are "great poems of their kind," and she remarks in her Preface (p. vi):

> No poet more needs or more repays commentary than Donne. . . . With a poet so difficult as Donne the plain meaning is sometimes overlooked, and a wrong explanation may at least provoke someone else to provide the right one. The attempt to understand the exact meaning of the words, and to recognize the sources or the field of reference of a poem brings great rewards. Indeed it places some poems in quite a fresh light.

Among the *Divine Poems,* the nineteen "Holy Sonnets" are of particular interest. Mr. Martz has demonstrated their intimate relation to the Jesuit tradition of meditation, concurring (p. 216) with Miss Gardner's division of them, on the basis of an exhaustive textual study, into three groups. With the first of these, which she treats as a sonnet cycle, I am not here concerned. The remaining poems she has put into two categories: a set of penitential meditations on sin (I, V, III, and VIII); and a group of three unrelated sonnets from the Westmoreland MS (XVII, XVIII, and XIX). I have chosen to consider for analysis one poem from each of these two latter groups, as contrasting examples of two instances of Donne's "wit" pointed out by Louis I. Bredvold: "a plain and straightforward reasoning about his subject," and symbolism, the "most characteristic form" in which Donne's poetic genius expressed itself.[4] I do not intend to suggest that an interpretation of these poems is, in any sense, a substitute for the poems themselves, or an

Reprinted from *Boston University Studies in English,* 4 (1960), 95-105, by permission of the author and the editor of *Studies in Romanticism* (holder of rights).

intellectual puzzle to be played with for its own sake. But the relationship between understanding and appreciation is an intimate one, and a precise explication may even contribute toward clearing up textual problems.

The text of both poems is taken from *The Poems of John Donne,* ed. Sir Herbert J. C. Grierson (Oxford: Clarendon Press, 1912), Vol. I. Holy Sonnet VIII is from page 325. Miss Gardner's text differs from Grierson's only in the substitution of "to" for "by," line 8. Holy Sonnet XVII, however, poses a textual problem. Since the interpretation I will offer differs notably from Miss Gardner's in at least two respects, and since the interpretation is radically affected by certain emendations, I have followed the reading of the Westmoreland MS on some disputed points. The text to be given is essentially Grierson's (p. 330), with the following exceptions: I have omitted the comma, which is not in *W,* at the end of line 2, though Hayward, Gardner, and Martz have all followed Grierson in adding it; and in lines 4 and 6, I have followed Miss Gardner in changing "on" to "in" and "their" to "the," both of which were misread from *W* by Gosse and Grierson.

I

Sonnet VIII, which Miss Gardner characterizes (p. liv) as "an individual moralization," is a good illustration of "plain and straightforward reasoning":

> If faithfull soules be alike glorifi'd
> As Angels, then my fathers soule doth see,
> And adds this even to full felicitie,
> That valiantly I hels wide mouth o'rstride:
> But if our mindes to these soules be descry'd
> By circumstances, and by signes that be
> Apparent in us, not immediately,
> How shall my mindes white truth by them be try'd?
> They see idolatrous lovers weepe and mourne,
> And vile blasphemous Conjurers to call
> On Jesus name and Pharisaicall
> Dissemblers feigne devotion. Then turne
> O pensive soule, to God, for he knowes best
> Thy true griefe, for he put it in my breast.

This is a non-symbolical poem portraying the protagonist in a mood of troubled searching, pondering a question of vital import to himself. His thought progresses from one doubtful solution of his problem to a second and certain, hence preferable, solution. This change in thought from doubt to certainty involves an accompanying series of changes in emotion from mild confidence to anxiety through angered frustration to serenity. As Williamson remarks (p. 23), "thoughts were not thoughts for Donne till they were proved upon his pulses."

If we judged the poem according to conventional sonnet structure, we would say that in the octave the speaker asks, "Can my father's soul know the inner workings of my mind?" and that in the sestet he answers his own question: "No, he cannot, with certainty, know the essential me. Therefore I will turn to God." But the mode of analysis which I shall consider here, although it also regards the poem as having two major divisions, interprets the break between them as coming, not at the end of the octave, but at the end of the first eleven and a half lines. The whole sonnet then represents a search for someone with insight enough to penetrate to the speaker's true religious attitude, his "mindes white truth." At first the speaker considers the possibility that the insight required may be found in his father's soul. Then, realizing that at best his father's insight is of doubtful validity, he turns to God as being most certain to know his "true griefe." This interpretation gains some weight from the fact that the sonnet, although for the most part conventionally Petrarchan in form, closes with what comes very close to being a Shakespearean couplet.

In the first four lines the speaker states the most hopeful side of the hypothesis that his father's soul may understand his spiritual struggle and victory, the belief that, if his father's soul be glorified as an angel's, then his father will add to his heavenly felicity the knowledge that the speaker valiantly bestrides hell's wide mouth.[5] But this is purely hypothetical comfort: the father's soul will be able to penetrate to the son's mind only if the father has the insight of an angel. The speaker must therefore also consider the other alternative. If souls do not know immediately the minds of those of us who are still on earth, but must deduce them from outward circumstances, the speaker realizes that there is no sure way they can comprehend his mind and its "white truth," for the outward show does not always reveal the inner conviction.

To support this thesis, the next four lines of the sestet give examples of various kinds of misleading signs, in order of their seriousness. The weeping and mourning of "idolatrous lovers" in the Petrarchan convention of profane love may give an illusory semblance of piety. Blasphemous conjurers, who call on Jesus' name in their rites of black magic while abjuring Christ, may give a false impression that they are true believers. And finally, "pharisaicall dissemblers," whose sin is hypocrisy *per se*; "feigne devotion."

At this point, the speaker has exhausted the possibilities of his earthly father's realizing his religious grief and devotion; he has taken up and developed the only two possible alternatives. Either his father's soul can know his mind directly, in which case the speaker would need to search no further; or the "faithfull soules" cannot know minds immediately, but must judge by external circumstances, which can be painfully misleading. Hence the protagonist seeks a positive comfort, not dependent on a hypothetical premise: he turns to his heavenly Father, God, who is sure to know his soul's "true griefe."

Here one may ask, What potentialities does the beginning of the poem offer for this development? These are to be found in the first object intro-

duced, the father's soul, two aspects of which deserve notice: first, the relationship with the speaker (father-son); and second, its spirituality. The
final object on which the speaker's attention is centered has both these aspects, though in a glorified form. First, God is the protagonist's heavenly
Father (as the speaker's father gave him his body, so God gave him the
"true griefe" in his breast); and second, God is the very essence of spirituality.

The relative lengths of the two divisions of the poem are appropriate to
the exigencies of each. The number of lines devoted to the possibility that
the father's soul may know the speaker's mind (eleven plus) far exceeds
the number (two plus) devoted to the fact that God knows the speaker's
mind. This is not, however, a disproportion. The first phase of the poem
expresses doubt; the second, certainty. In any case involving doubt, both
sides of the question must be weighed with great care. On the other hand,
a case of certainty can be expressed concisely, the number of words required
being determined only by the complexity of the idea about which the opinion is held, not by any considerations as to the validity of the opinion itself
or as to the grounds of its truth or probability. Therefore, it is appropriate
that the ending of the poem is relatively short, since the speaker, a devoutly
religious man trained in scholastic philosophy and the Jesuitical tradition
of meditation, believes there can be no doubt about the omniscience of God.

But not only is the number of lines devoted to each of the major divisions
demonstrably appropriate; the proportionate lengths of each of the subsections of the first division are equally appropriate. The first phase of the poem,
the hypothesis that the father's soul may have the insight of an angel, takes
only four lines, relatively few. The second phase, the hypothesis that souls
may not be able to penetrate minds immediately, takes the next four lines;
then, as a corollary to that, the following three and a half lines consider
examples of men whose actions may lead the souls, if they have to judge
by external signs, to judge wrongly. The second hypothesis, altogether,
takes up almost twice as much space as the first. This is fitting for two reasons.
First, the second hypothesis involves two parts, a question and an answer;
the first four lines pose the question; the next three and a half answer it.
Second, the protagonist has to give examples to prove that, under this hypothesis, souls would misjudge the minds of at least some men on earth,
and almost half the space devoted to the second hypothesis is given over to
these examples.

This sonnet, then, involves a change in both thought and emotion. The
speaker first thinks his earthly father can know his mind, then realizes that,
possibly, such insight is not within the power of his father's soul; and so
he turns to his heavenly Father, who he is certain can know the true grief
in his breast. Accompanying this change in the thought is a series of emotional changes from troubled searching to mild confidence to anxiety, which
develops into angered frustration, but is resolved by catharsis to serenity.
And the relative number of lines devoted to each aspect of these changes
is demonstrably appropriate.

II

The second sonnet to be considered, characterized by Williamson (p. 16, n. 2) as "an intimate revelation of mind," is the XVIIth, a brilliant instance of the peculiarly daring and subtle symbolism which characterizes much of Donne's poetry.

> Since she whom I lov'd hath payd her last debt
> To Nature, and to hers, and my good is dead
> And her Soule early into heaven ravished,
> Wholly in heavenly things my mind is sett.
> Here the admyring her my mind did whett
> To seeke thee God; so streames do shew the head;
> But though I have found thee, and thou my thirst hast fed,
> A holy thirsty dropsy melts mee yett.
> But why should I begg more Love, when as thou
> Dost wooe my soule for hers; offring all thine:
> And dost not only feare least I allow
> My Love to Saints and Angels things divine,
> But in thy tender jealosy dost doubt
> Least the Worlde, Fleshe, yea Devill putt thee out.

The second line posed a problem in explication to Miss Gardner, who wrote (p. 79):

> The words "to hers, and my good is dead" may amplify the preceding clause: Death ends the possibility of doing good to oneself or to another. Or they may point forward: her death is for her good and his, since by it she has entered heaven early, and his affections are now all in heaven. The first interpretation seems strained; the second almost intolerably harsh.

But I would argue for a third reading, which is supported by the MS omission of the comma at the end of the line. "And to hers" is parallel with "To Nature." "My good" then becomes the subject of "is dead." In other words, the woman, by dying, has paid her debt to Nature, since all natural things must die; and she has also paid her debt to her (human) nature, which is mortal. (Milton has a similar construction in *Eikonoklastes:* "To descant on the misfortunes of a person fallen from so high a dignity, who hath paid his debts both to nature and his faults, is neither of itself a thing commendable, nor the intention of this discourse.") The speaker's "good" (*i.e.,* the woman; there may even be a pun on "god" here) is now dead, and her soul is ravished into heaven. To read the line as if "hers" modified "good" ("to hers . . . good is dead") simply does not make sense to me, grammatically or otherwise.

Holy Sonnet XVII is a symbolic poem involving a change in thought and an accompanying change in emotion. The first attitude on the part of the protagonist is revealed in the octave: he has found God, knows that God loves him, and yet he wants more love. In the sestet, however, his thought changes to a realization of the all-sufficiency of God's love. Accompanying this change is the change from an emotion of desire to one of serenity.

The progression of the poem depends upon the manner in which the change is brought about. Besides the two chief divisions of the poem, there are three further subdivisions in the octave. In the first of these, lines 1-4, the speaker presents his attitude since the death of the woman he loved: his mind is devoted completely to heavenly things. In the second part, lines 5-6, the chronological sequence is broken to show his thoughts and emotions before the death of his loved one: his admiration of her while she was here on earth led him to a search for that which was the source of all that he admired in her; that is, God. Then, in part three, lines 7 and 8, he comes again to a consideration of his present attitude, but treats a new aspect of it. Though he has found God, and God has satisfied his longing, yet paradoxically he feels a holy "thirst" for yet more love. These three parts conclude the first major division of the poem, the octave. Then in the sestet the speaker realizes that his desire for more of God's love is ill-founded, that God's love is already sufficient.

In order to understand how this change is brought about, one must inquire into the relationships involved in the poem. There are three characters: the woman, the protagonist, and God; and there are various and changing relationships among them. In the first four lines, the speaker reveals the love relationship which had existed between him and the woman before her death. He also reveals that this relationship no longer exists between them: her soul has been "ravished" into heaven. This suggests that he has a rival for the possession of the woman, the divine ravisher, God. But the implication is that the speaker no longer wants the woman; his mind is now "wholly in heavenly things." In order for a reunion to take place, his attitude must change so that he desires it; and the divine ravisher must either be overcome (obviously impossible), or cease to be a rival.

The implications of line 4, which purports to indicate the speaker's turning away from the woman, are significant. His mind is set "wholly in heavenly things," but the line just preceding this reveals that the woman has been taken into heaven, so that she is now (presumably) one of the heavenly things in which his mind is set. In other words, line 4 is equivocal in meaning, a fact which suggests a possible solution: that the lovers will be reunited in heaven. The two problems remain, however, of the speaker's becoming *consciously* desirous of a reunion with the woman, and of a change in God's attitude toward the lovers.

In the next two lines, an analogy is set up between the profane love the protagonist felt for the woman and the divine love he feels for God. "Here [on earth] the admyring her my mind did whett | To seeke thee God; so streames do shew the head." In other words, God was the source of all that he found admirable in the woman, and the profane love he felt for her was merely a reflection of the divine love he now feels for God. Donne sets up the following proportion: the woman he loved is to God as a stream is to its head. Now a stream is essentially the same as the head which is its source. Analogically, therefore, at this stage of the poem, the woman is essentially the same as God, who is the source of that which the speaker admired in her. His admiration for the woman has led the protagonist to seek God as the ultimate object of his admiration. This conception of God represents a distinct change from the "ravisher," or rival of the speaker's, who was introduced in the first four lines. The second barrier to the speaker's reunion with the woman—God's acting as a rival for her possession—begins to crumble here.

In these first six lines, the divine love the speaker has felt for God has been one of the mind, revealed by the lines "Wholly in heavenly things my *mind* is sett. | Here the admyring her my *mind* did whett . . . " The emotion felt is a Platonic one: "admiring." But in the next two lines the element of physical passion is introduced. The speaker's love is described in terms of a physical appetite, "thirst," "a holy thirsty dropsy."[6] This image of thirst is united to the preceding sections of the poem on the level of diction by the last half of line 6: "so streames do shew the head," the image of water suggesting the thirst which enters in the following two lines.

At this point, God has ceased to be the object of a Platonic admiration of the mind and has become the object of a physical passion which the speaker feels for him. And the speaker's attitude toward the woman has also changed. At first he thought God alone was the "heavenly thing" toward which his mind was directed. But by the time the octave is over he realizes that something besides God is necessary to fulfill his longing. His thirst cannot be satisfied simply by God's love, if that love is no more than a sublimated analogue to earthly love. He has that, and yet he is still melted by a "holy thirsty dropsy." Significantly this desire is, at the completion of the octave, unspecified as to its object. The ambiguity is useful. In one sense, the desire may be for more love from God, or love of a different kind. On the other hand, the desire may be for love from an object other than God; that is, from the woman. In order to satisfy his emotional longing, therefore, the speaker must enter into a new relationship with the other two characters in the poem.

At the conclusion of the octave, then, both barriers to the reunion of the speaker and the woman have been broken down. The speaker is in a frame of mind to desire the reunion, and God is no longer a rival. But the reunion cannot yet be accomplished, for the woman is in heaven, and the speaker is still on earth. As stated above, however, there is in lines 3-4 the suggestion that the meeting of the two lovers will be a "heavenly" one, that there will be something divine about it.

In the sestet, indeed, a divine intercession occurs, and the imagery shifts again. God becomes a mediator, whose function is to bring about the reunion of the man and woman in heaven. At this point, where the analogy between God and the woman has been broken down, the woman re-enters the poem, and a new relationship is set up among the three.

God woos the speaker's soul in order to unite it with the woman's, even going to the extent of offering all his own soul in exchange. As a consequence of God's jealous mediation, the speaker can be sure that he will be reunited with the woman; not only does the deity take care lest the protagonist give his love to things divine (the remnants of the "heavenly things" of line 4); he disputes with the world, the flesh, and the devil for the speaker's love. To explain the tremendous emphasis given by the last four lines to the "jealous" quality of God's mediation, one must explore the character of God as presented in the poem. Throughout, the woman has been the medium through which the protagonist was led to God. But a love of God which was merely a sublimation of the speaker's earthly love for the woman was not enough to satisfy the protagonist. In death as in life, her hold on the speaker's emotions is so strong that no pietistic fervor which does not in some sense include her, too, will suffice for him. God, therefore, in order to woo the speaker's soul, must do it through the strongest emotional appeal that can be made to the protagonist: his love of the woman. And since this love was in part a spiritual one, the promise of an ecstatic reunion of the lovers' souls in heaven is God's strongest and surest claim on the speaker's religious devotion. Miss Gardner (p. 79) emended line 10 from "soule for hers;" (*W* and *Gr*) to "soule, for hers"—a change which destroys the symbolic development of the poem. In her note on the emendation, she says:

> The line apparently presented no difficulty to Grierson and Hayward, but Bennett punctuated as I do. As the line stands in *W*, I can give no sense to "for." Repunctuation gives not the meaningless antithesis between "my soule" and "hers," but a proper antithesis between "hers" and "thine": "How can I ask for more love, when Thou art my wooer, who in place of *her* love offers me all *thine*."

Clearly, in order to "give sense" to the line as it stands in the MS, one must read the sonnet as a symbolic poem, and as a poem of change.

Having analyzed in detail the connections among the three characters of the poem, one can see that accompanying each section or subsection of the sonnet is a change in relationship. In the first four lines, though he is not mentioned by name, God is revealed as a "ravisher" who has taken the woman into heaven, thus destroying the earthly love relationship which had existed between the two humans. In the next two lines of the octave, God is a deity whom the speaker "admires" with his "mind." In the third subsection of the octave, the relationship between God and the speaker is described as one of fulfillment of a physical appetite: God has "fed" the speaker's "thirst." Finally, in the sestet, God becomes an intercessor who strives to reunite the speaker and the woman, not in an earthly love, but in a holy Love between their souls, meeting in the common ground of God's soul. The relationship at the end of the poem, as in the beginning, is love, but heavenly instead of earthly.

This sonnet, then, is one involving a change in thought and emotion which is expressed imagistically, with the image changing at intervals corresponding to the changes in thought and emotion. The speaker's attitude toward both the woman and God is altered. His emotion for the woman

changes from earthly love to a sublimation of his love for her in a passion
for God to a heavenly Love for her. His conception of God passes through
successive changes, noted above, expressed imagistically throughout.

The chief symbol employed in the poem is that of profane love, and
the imagery is built around this symbol.[7] In the first four lines of the poem,
the woman is expressed as having "payd a debt" by being "ravished."
Specific instances of the imagery of profane love are revealed in the following passages: line I: "lov'd"; line 3: "ravished"; line 5: "admyring"; line 9:
"Love"; line 10: "Wooe"; line 12: "Love"; line 13: "jealosy." "Begg more
Love" (line 9) is appropriate to the image of a lover not satisfied with the
love his mistress has given him.

To sum up, the progress of the poem is as follows: first a problem is
stated, the separation of the speaker from the woman he loves; then the
solution is suggested, but not amplified, by the statements that she is in
heaven and that his mind dwells wholly in heavenly things. The implication
here, obviously, is that, in some manner, the two will be reunited in heaven,
but the manner in which this reunion will come about is not indicated in
the octave. The speaker has three conceptions of God in the octave, none
of which is correct; in the sestet comes the correct conception of God, that
of a divine mediator, and the revelation of how the reunion of the two lovers
will be accomplished through the medium of God's intercession. The problem stated in the opening lines of the poem is solved, with the solution stated
imagistically, and the sonnet is logically over.

GOODFRIDAY, 1613. RIDING WESTWARD THE POEM AND THE TRADITION *

A. B. Chambers

When John Donne rode westward on Good Friday, 1613, he travelled in large company; most of the universe—as he knew it, at least—was moving westward too. The heliotrope, a favorite example, arched its stem in order to follow the course of the sun.[1] Gasparo Contarini had noted that the ocean flowed to the west; Peacham said that only the Mediterranean refused to obey this general law; and Donne himself discovered that the currents of the south-west straits never flow eastward.[2] Westward, too, the course of empire took its way, in Donne's time as well as in Bishop Berkeley's.[3] Indeed, Donne's early readers may well have remembered that the journey of Aeneas to Rome was a significant example of this *translatio imperii.* If they did, they may also have recalled Dante's use of the theme in the *Paradiso*. In the sixth canto we learn that Constantine, moving the empire from Rome to Byzantium, reversed Aeneas' path and

> turned the Eagle's head
> Against heaven's course which it of old pursued
> With him who took Lavinia to his bed.[4]

For the medieval and Renaissance reader, to go contrary to *pius* Aeneas was of course unwise, and as Dante's early commentators pointed out, movement against the course of heaven was folly. Benvenuto of Imola, Landino, Vellutello—all explain that we are to understand "heaven's course" both literally and metaphorically: Aeneas went west, Constantine went east; one followed the divine will and one did not.[5] It is Francesco da Buti who provides the cosmological details. The primum mobile, he says, whirls all things westward, and since the primum mobile is moved by God, such movement is "natural, uniform and direct"; the eighth sphere and the planets struggle to move from west to east, contrary to heaven's will, and this motion is "accidental, divided and oblique." Aeneas followed "natural" motion, Constantine did not.[6]

Buti's commentary is the most helpful of these four because it tells us why seas, plants, and empires move the way they do: the spheres below are ultimately controlled by the primum mobile—and by God—above. Yet Constantine did move the declining empire eastward for a time, and the sea—swayed by an inconstant moon—has its eastward moving tides. "Natural"

Reprinted from *English Literary History*, 28 (1961), 31-53, by permission of the author and The Johns Hopkins Press.

motion prevails no more completely on earth than it does in the skies above, for microcosm and macrocosm are ever alike. Thus Sir Thomas Browne found a plant—"the great Convolvulus or white flower'd Bindweed"—in which the correspondence was complete: "while the flower twists Æqui-noctionally from the left hand to the right, according to the daily revolution, The stalk twineth ecliptically from the right to the left, according to the annual conversion."[7] Moreover, as the separate parts of his world are micro-cosms of the heavens, so is man himself, and this is the way Donne begins his poem: "let man's soul be a sphere."

The origin of this particular kind of microcosmic correspondence is supplied by Browne himself, a few pages beyond those on the bindweed:

> Of this figure [the quincunx] *Plato* made choice to illustrate the motion of the soul, both of the world and man; while he delivereth that God divided the whole conjunction length-wise, according to the figure of the Greek X, and then turning it about reflected it into a circle; By the circle implying the uniform motion of the first Orb, and by the right lines, the planetical and various motions within it. And this also with application unto the soul of man, which hath a double aspect, one right, whereby it beholdeth the body, and objects without; another circular and reciprocal, whereby it beholdeth it self. The circle declaring the motion of the indivisible soul, simple, according to the divinity of its nature, and returning into it self; the right lines respecting the motion pertaining unto sense, and vegetation, and the central decussation, the wondrous connexion of the several faculties conjointly in one substance.[8]

Browne's paraphrase, controlled by his own quincunctial purposes, shifts Plato's emphasis slightly, but it does lead us to Timaeus' account of the creation of the world. The demiurge formed the universe by joining to-gether the circle of the Same (the fixed stars) and the circle of the Other (the planets), and he set one whirling to the right, one to the left. When the lesser gods created man, they imitated the work of the master builder, and thus

> The divine revolutions, which are two, they bound within a sphere-shaped body, in imitation of the spherical form of the All, which body we now call the "head," it being the most divine part and reigning over all the parts within us.[9]

This is the first example of what might be called spherical analogy.[10] In a sense, therefore, it is the point of origin for Donne's poem. But only "in a sense," for linking Plato and Donne is an unbroken bridge over the centuries, and upon that bridge stand many illustrious names.

One of these is Plutarch, who paraphrases the *Timaeus* in order to dis-cuss moral virtue; he understood that the circle of the Same represents reason, while that of the Other indicates passion. So too with Philo, and in greater detail:

Our mind is indivisible in its nature. For the irrational part of the soul received a sixfold division from its Maker who thus formed seven parts . . . But the rational part, which was named mind, He left undivided. In this he followed the analogy of the heaven as a whole. For we are told that there the outermost sphere of the fixed stars is kept unsevered, while the inner circle by a sixfold division produces the seven circles of what we call the wandering stars. In fact I regard the soul as being in man what the heaven is in the universe.

Many Neoplatonists were probably thinking in these terms. Hermes Trismegistus tells us that "The Kosmos is a sphere, that is to say, a head," while Plotinus adapts the analogy in this way: "Since God is omnipresent the Soul desiring perfect union must take the circular course: God is not stationed. Similarly Plato attributed to the stars not only the spherical movement belonging to the universe as a whole but also to each a revolution around their common center." Shortly after Plotinus, commentaries on the *Timaeus* appear; in them these analogous spheres are inescapable. Proclus' work breaks off about half-way through, but not before he has said that the Other pertains to sense, the Same to intellect. Chalcidius gives us a choice: in the cosmos the two circles represent reason and sense, while in man "alter intelligentia est, alter opinio." In twelfth-century Chartres we encounter William of Conches. The movement, he says, of the firmament and the parallel movement of the intellect are controlled by divine providence. And an anonymous commentary of a century later pronounces that rational motion follows the circle of the Same. By Renaissance times, Ficino apparently thought these ideas too common to warrant extended treatment; he paraphrases briefly and passes on to less obvious material.[11]

Commentaries on the *Timaeus* are the obvious, but not the only, source for Platonic spheres. Macrobius took up the subject to discuss the seven possible movements of heavenly and earthly spheres, and Boethius included the analogy in his *Consolation:*

> Tu [God] triplicis mediam naturae cuncta mouentem
> Conectens animam per consona membra resoluis
> Quae cum secta duos motum glomerauit in orbes,
> In semet reditura meat mentemque profundam
> Circuit et simili conuertit imagine caelum.

Medieval commentaries explain Lady Philosophy's enigmatic hymn in varying ways, but all agree upon the meaning of the *duos orbes.* Pseudo-Aquinas introduces a comparison between rational souls and stars, while Dionysius the Carthusian later refers the two orbs to the fixed stars and the planets. For my purposes the best of the commentators is pseudo-Johannes Scotus, since his comments could be used to explain the lines from Dante with which this discussion began:

Dvos Orbes uocat rationabilem et irrationabilem motum. Rationabilis dicitur motus qui fit ab oriente per occidentem et iterum in orientem. Irrationabilis uero motus est qui nititur contra firmamentum sicut motus planetarum, que fit ab occidente per orientem iterum in occidentum.[12]

Plato's students and their commentators thus represent an important locus for the appearance of analogous spheres. There is also an important line of discussion stemming from Aristotle. In the *De anima,* III.xi, Aristotle includes a discussion of appetite and will, arguing that while all creatures capable of deliberation necessarily have appetites, the possession of appetite itself does not at all imply capacity for deliberative choice. Moreover,

νκᾷ δ' ἐνίοτε καὶ κινεῖ ὁτὲ μὲν αὕτη ἐκείνην, ὁτὲ δ' ἐκείνη ταύτην, ὥσπερ σφαῖρα ⟨σφαῖραν⟩, ἡ ὄρεξις τὴν ὄρεξιν, ὅταν ἀκρασία γένηται.

Translation of this passage is difficult, for its obscurity casts doubt on all interpretations. Aristotle may mean that desire overcomes deliberation, or that rational choice overcomes irrational appetite, or that one irrational desire overcomes another. Some one of these three states, it seems, is comparable to a σφαῖρα, a simile which confuses matters the more. Does the word refer to a "ball" (that is, a child's toy) or to a celestial "sphere"? The Greek commentators could not agree. Sophonia assumed that Aristotle was comparing a man torn by conflicting desires to a ball bouncing up and down. Simplicius believed this interpretation to be correct but was aware that "others" thought the word meant "sphere." One of these others was Themistius; his Greek is cryptic, but the spherical analogy is clearly present:

> The irrational [desire] sometimes conquers the rational, but sometimes the reverse [occurs], and [in either case] the conquering [desire] moves the overcome [desire], not stopping from its own impetus but carrying [the overcome desire] around with itself, just as in the heavenly spheres that of the fixed stars does not stop that of the planets, but nevertheless moving in its own way it draws [that of the planets] about with itself.[13]

Plato and Aristotle thus joined hands in a union which later times were loath to part. Averroes, for example, entertained no doubts as to the meaning of σφαῖρα; for him the spherical analogy was undoubtedly meant. A century later, Themistius became semi-official through the translation of William of Moerbeke, and in Moerbeke's translation of Aristotle, the sphere is retained:

> Vincit autem et movet aliquando appetitus deliberationem. Aliquando autem movet et hunc illa, sicut sphaera, appetitus appetitum, cum in continentia fuerit.

This is, moreover, the form in which Aristotle reached the thirteenth-century commentators. Aquinas therefore explains that "the lower appetite which is without deliberation, conquers deliberation and removes man from that which he deliberates upon. Sometimes, conversely, appetite moves appetite, that is the superior appetite, which partakes of deliberative reason, moves that which partakes of *phantasiae sensibilis*; as in celestial bodies, the higher sphere moves the lower." Albertus Magnus, commenting on the *Physics,* says that these internal spheres exist only "rhetorice . . . & per similitudines," but in his *De anima* the reservation does not appear. Three centuries later, the analogy is still present in Suarez but is so suppressed that only those aware of the tradition will see it. When, however, the university of Coimbra published its commentary in 1600, the attraction of the microcosm proved strong. Fist we are given a translation which preserves the reading "sphere"; next a paraphrase which echoes Aquinas and Albertus; then a discussion in terms of the body politic; and finally a parallel between Angelic intelligences in the spheres above and intellectual faculties in the microcosm below.[14]

There is still another convenient locus for these analogous spheres in medieval times, and that is Sacrobosco's popular textbook:

> Be it understood that the "first movement" means the movement of the *primum mobile,* that is, of the ninth sphere or last heaven, which movement is from east through west back to east again, which also is called "rational motion" from resemblance to the rational motion in the microcosm, that is, in man, when thought goes from the Creator through creatures to the Creator and there rests. The second movement is of the firmament and planets contrary to this, from west to east back to west again, which movement is called "irrational" or "sensual" from resemblance to the movement of the microcosm from things corruptible to the Creator and back again to things corruptible.

This passage, lengthy enough in itself, becomes the basis for prolix discussion in Sacrobosco's commentators. Michael Scot is the most elaborate, introducing scripture, quoting Boethius, and working out the correspondences with considerable care. Robertus Anglicus and Cecco D'Ascoli are almost as detailed. All agree that both heaven and man have a twofold movement; that the rational motion is from east to west, the sensual from west to east; that divine movement follows the primum mobile and ignores the wandering stars.[15]

These sources, separately distinct so long as one looks steadily at a particular tradition, begin to merge in the scattered references to analogous spheres and westward movement, until it is impossible to decide what line of development lies behind any given writer. The "natural, uniform and direct" motion which Buti found in Aeneas' journey could thus depend on Plato's circle of the same, or on scholastic interpretation of Aristotle, on Sacrobosco, or—in fact—on none of these. The spirit of analogy which worked so powerfully with other images caused also an endless whirling of these spheres. There is Moses Maimonides; aware of man the microcosm, he adapts the analogy to say that God, the primum mobile, corresponds to man's vital force, the heart. Or Alain de Lille, who gives one of the clearest expositions both in the *De planctu naturae* and in the *Distinctiones:*

Mundus. Dicitur homo qui in multis similis est mundo: sicut in mundo
majori firmamentum movetur ab oriente in occidentem et revertitur in
orientem, sic ratio in homine movetur a contemplatione orientalium,
id est coelestium, primo, considerando Deum et divina, consequenter
descendit ad occidentalia, id est ad considerationem terrenorum, ut per
visibilia contempletur invisibilia, deinde revertitur ad orientem iterum
considerando coelestia. . . .

In the *Speculum naturale,* Vincent of Beauvais necessarily takes up the
movements of the stars, and this leads him to the parallel movements of
the soul. Duns Scotus knows of these analogous spheres, John of St.
Geminiano remarks in passing that divine motion—like that of the primum
mobile—is from east to west, and Bonaventura adapts the figure in this
mystic way:

> As the sun moving through the twelve signs [of the zodiac] gives life, so
> the sun of wisdom, shining and moving in the hemisphere of our mind,
> orders our life through these twelve parts of virtues; and what other
> knowledge so ever a man may have, unless he has virtues he has not life;
> so whatever stars he has, unless he has the sun in their midst, he shall
> have no day.[16]

These spheres continued to revolve throughout the Renaissance. Ficino
remembers Aristotle in the *Theologia platonica*: "Quemadmodum sphaera
mouet sphaeram: sic concupiscentia voluntatem." His younger friend Pico
found room for the image both in arguing against the astrologers and in
describing the manifold creations of Genesis:

> Man is composed of body and a rational soul. The rational soul is called
> heaven; for Aristotle calls heaven an animal moving by its own motion,
> and our soul (as the Platonists prove) is a substance moving itself.
> Heaven is circular and the soul likewise is circular; or rather, as Plotinus
> writes, heaven is circular because its soul is circular. Heaven is moved in
> a circuit; the rational soul, moving from cause to effect and back again
> from effects to cause, is revolved around in the circuits of reasoning.

In the *Occult Philosophy* of Cornelius Agrippa, this spherical theology is
retained. "Grace," he says, "which the theologians call charity or infused
love, is in the will like the primum mobile above, for if it is absent the
harmonious universe lapses into dissonance." The spheres are given their
strangest guise by Paracelsus:

> It should be known that all monstrous signs are not produced only by
> the progenitor, but frequently from the stars of the human mind, which
> perpetually at all moments, with the Phantasy, Estimation, or Imagination,
> rise and set just as in the firmament above. Hence through fear or fright
> on the part of those who are pregnant, many monsters are born, or chil-
> dren signed with marks of monstrosity in the womb of their mother. The
> primary cause of these things is alarm, terror, or appetite, by which the

imagination is aroused. If the pregnant woman begins to imagine, then her bosom is borne round in its motion just as the superior firmament, each movement rising or setting. For, as in the case of the greater firmament, the stars of the microcosm also move by imagination.

Giordano Bruno apostrophizes the wandering stars, saying that he too begins the circular course. And Kepler, despite his Copernicanism, apparently thinks that astronomical knowledge is possible only because of the correspondences:

> That relation which the six orbs have to their common center and thus to the center of the world, is the same as the relation of discursive intellect to mind . . . and, again, the local revolutions of the individual planets about the sun are to the unchanging rotation of the sun in the middle part of the whole system . . . as the multiple discursive processes of reasoning are to the most simple intuition of mind. . . . Moreover, so connected and bound together among themselves are the motions of the planets about their central sun and the discursive processes of reason, that if the earth, our dwelling-place, did not measure out its annual course amidst the other orbs, changing from place to place and station to station, then human reasoning would never have risen to an understanding of the truest intervals between the planets nor to the other things dependent on these; never would it have created astronomy.[17]

By this time, however, the image had lost most—if not all—of the theological implications which it once possessed. The adaptations of the analogy are more frequent, the "pure" form rarely found. More significantly, "natural" motion no longer need be in imitation of the primum mobile above, a fact which Joseph Hall makes abundantly clear. He knows that in the tradition the movement from east to west is rational and divine; he writes:

> In the motion of thine [God's] Heaven, though some Starres have their own peculiar, & contrary courses, yet all yeeld themselves to the sway of the main circumvolution of that first mover; so, though I have a will of mine owne, yet let me give my selfe over to be ruled, and ordered by thy Spirit in all my ways. Man is a little world; my Soule is heaven, my body is earth; if this earth be dull and fixed, yet O God, let my heaven (like unto thine) move perpetually, regularly, & in a constant subjection to thine holy Ghost.

Yet the traditional force of the image is not enough to keep Hall from turning its meaning inside out should his purposes so demand. His version at another time is therefore this:

> Good men are placed by God as so many stars in the lower firmament of the world. As they must imitate those heavenly bodies in their light and influence, so also in their motion; and therefore, as the planets have a course proper to themselves, against the sway of the heaven that carries them about, so must each good man have a motion out of his own judge-

ment contrary to the customs and opinions of the vulgar, finishing his course with the least show of resistance.

When Plato's circles could become a figure of speech to be manipulated at will, their usefulness to discussions of the human condition was over. Those forces which broke the circle caused also the spherical movements in man to stop. In the latter case, however, the revolutions were started up again by two notable poets. The first was Pope:

> On their own Axis as the Planets run,
> Yet make at once their circle round the Sun:
> So two consistent motions act the Soul;
> And one regards Itself, and one the Whole.

The second was Wordsworth; within his mind

> each airy thought revolved
> Round a substantial centre, which at once
> Incited it to motion, and controlled.[18]

The rest is silence.

*   *   *   *

Within this tradition of spherical analogy "Goodfriday, 1613" quite clearly has a place, and yet the poem itself is evidence that in 1613 the tradition was a dying thing. Donne cannot unquestioningly assume that man's soul is a sphere which imitates the motion of the heavens above. Rather, he must put a case in suppositional form: "*Let* man's soul be a sphere." Let us assume, he says, that the old notion is in fact correct in order to explore its possibilities.

> Let mans Soule be a Spheare, and then, in this,
> The intelligence that moves, devotion is,
> And as the other Spheares, by being growne
> Subject to forraigne motions, lose their owne,
> And being by others hurried every day,
> Scarce in a yeare their naturall forme obey:
> Pleasure or businesse, so, our Soules admit
> For their first mover, and are whirld by it.
> Hence is't, that I am carried towards the West
> This day, when my Soules forme bends toward the East.[19]

Some of these possibilities look strange to one with the tradition firmly in mind, but not all. Reason—which traditionally looks to God—here becomes Good Friday's devotion looking to Christ; passion—traditionally concerned with earthly affairs—becomes the business or pleasure which takes Donne westward. But even as what should have been Donne's lower sphere has become his primum mobile, so the direction of the two movements has been reversed. Devotion leans eastward, while that motion which should have been "natural, uniform and direct" is apparently wrong. The lines are, however, considerably different from those passages in Bishop Hall which they may seem to resemble. Hall alternatively advocates the motion of the primum mobile or that of the planets in order to point up a different moral. Donne, remaining closer to traditional forms, says not that he should follow the motion of the planets but that his primum mobile is wrong. His reasoning is this: since the upper sphere must always move the lower, and since passion seems to rule, the "irrational" must have become the upper sphere. This reversal of symbolic directions is therefore not an arbitrary manipulation of the figure but a reinterpretation from the point of view of a man who thinks he is going the wrong way. The curious thing about the lines is therefore not the change in direction, but the poetic premises which dictate it. Why should Donne assume that westward movement is the result of pleasure or business? Why should devotion try to lean to the east? These assumptions result, I think, from the force brought to bear upon the poem of another traditional symbolism, geographical rather than astronomical in origin. This symbolism, as it affects "Goodfriday, 1613," is specifically Christian in its development, but in order to perceive that fact some knowledge of pagan geography is necessary too.

In non-Christian tradition, symbolic geography is found in fragmentary form or as a detail incidental to more important matters. The Greeks knew of the Hyperboreans, living in their blessed land to the far north, and they spoke also of the western isles, the fortunate Hesperides.[20] One might therefore suppose the west and north to be the favorable quarters of the globe, but this was not always the case. Plutarch reports that the Egyptians conceived of the Nile as flowing from left to right, south to north, birth to dissolution; and Proclus tells us that these same peoples believed the west to be a place of evil demons.[21] Nor did the Greeks or Romans themselves consistently favor the west and north, as we can tell from even a rudimentary examination of the many conflicting statements on directions in augury.

The question of first importance in augury is whether signs on the left or signs on the right are favorable. As Cicero noted, the Greeks and Romans had different notions on the matter.[22] As early as Homer the Greeks had normally favored the right; as early as Ennius the Romans had chosen the left.[23] Even if the meaning of right and left should be decided, there was the further problem of which direction was "right." Homer—Hector, at least—considered the east to be the right, a judgment with which Plato and Aristotle were later to concur.[24] The attraction of east and right as the favorable parts was so strong to Aristotle, in fact, that he attributed them to heaven and was thereby led inescapably to the conclusion that the south pole is the top of the world.[25] The Hermetic Asclepius thus pictures the world as a man stretched out with his head to the south and his feet to the north—the right hand, of course, falling to the east; Chalcidius, swayed by similar beliefs, quotes the Iliad to show that the right-hand east is best.[26] Juba, however, had reported that Romans believed the left-hand side was to the north, "which some think the superior [καθυπέρτερον] part," and

Dionysius of Halicarnassus devoted considerable space to proving the correctness of such a view.[27] Livy's description of the taking of omens supports the Greek historians of Rome, and Servius later uses this symbolism to gloss the *Aeneid*.[28] Yet Pliny the Elder, contradicting Greeks and Greek historians of Rome and Romans alike, wrote that "Flashes [of lightning] on the left are considered lucky, because the sun rises on the left-hand side of the firmament."[29]

These examples of pagan geography do no more than exhibit the principal possibilities, but they may serve to indicate the internal contradictions to be found outside Christianity. Indeed, within Christianity remnants of this kind of thinking can sometimes appear. Rabanus Maurus, for example, writes that

> Aquilo is the harsh wind, which by its other name is called "right," from the fact that Satan takes to himself the name of "right"—of "good" so to speak; or because to those looking westward, that is to sin, he is on the right.[30]

Or in another branch of Christian thought, all directions are good because they symbolize the four cardinal virtues.[31] Thanks, however, to a few scriptural texts, there came into being what might be called a standard Christian geography rather different from any symbolism so far mentioned. The first of these texts is the well-known passage in Isaiah on Lucifer, the fallen star of the morning:

> For thou hast said in thine heart, I will ascend into heaven, I will exalt my throne above the stars of God: I will sit also upon the mount of the congregation, in the sides of the north (xiv. 13).

As early as Origen this speech becomes the proud utterance of Satan, but the tradition depends most strongly on Augustine. In the *Enarrationes in Psalmos,* Lucifer's speech is quoted as "Ponam sedem meam ad Aquionem, et ero similis Altissimo." Forever thereafter the biblical commentaries, putting these words in Satan's mouth, gloss north as symbolic of the devil and of the spiritual ice of sin.[32] Thus Dante reserves hell's coldness for the chief of all sinners; accounts of the rebellion in heaven, both Old English and Miltonic, represent Lucifer as withdrawing to the north; when Spenser's Archimago performs his vanishing act for Braggadocchio, he calls upon the north winds to spirit him away; and Joseph Beaumont writes that "S. Philip"

> hies him to ye North, ye place
> Stamp'd with *Proverbiall* disgrace.[33]

The second text of importance is Canticles iv.16:

> Surge, aquilo; et veni, auster;
> perfla hortum meum, et fluunt aromata illius.

North as a symbol for Satan carries over into this text too. "Surge," which the King James translates "awake," is thus interpreted in medieval commentaries as "arise and depart." The south wind is correspondingly glossed as the Holy Ghost. The *sponsa,* who speaks these lines, prays that the winter of sin depart and the reviving breath of God be felt. Symbolically speaking, north and south are therefore poles apart.[34]

West occasionally appears as a separate geographical symbol. Mâle tells us that the west window of churches was given over to scenes of the last judgment.[35] More usually, west is the implicit contrast to the Christian east, and the east is the most important of the four directions, for Christ himself is *Oriens.* Again, the Bible provides a basic text:

> Ecce vir Oriens, nomen ejus, et subter eum orietur,
> et aedificabit templum Domino (Zach. vi. 12).

Origen refers to this passage in connection with baptism, but it was Jerome who supplied the most frequently repeated gloss. Christ is *Oriens* because "in diebus ejus orta est justitia."[36] He is therefore the Sun of Justice referred to also in Luke i. 78. The association of Christ with the east entered the liturgy with the fifth of the Seven Great Antiphons for Advent, attracted Donne so strongly that it appeared in his self-chosen epitaph, and achieved a kind of apotheosis in the poems of Joseph Beaumont:

> Epiphanie Oblation
> (To a Base & 2 Trebles)
> 1. Our Gold, rich King of Poverties,
> Xss 2. Our Incense Infant Dietie,
> 3. Our Myrrh for thy Humanitie,
> *Chorus.*—And Our poore Selves we bring to Thee.
>
> Xs
> In Us our East is hither come.
> *Chorus.*—To meet thine Eyes, its fairer Home.
> 1. O let this Gold wait on thy Crowne:
> Xss 2. This Incense let thine Altar owne;
> 3. And this Myrrh on thy Tomb be throwne:
> And our East be thine Eyes Sweet Dawne.
> *Chorus.*—So shall our East & We
> Adore no Sun, but onely Thee.[37]

The interesting results of this symbolic geography occur when the round earth's imagined corners meet together in one text. Lactantius's *Institutes* successively compares and contrasts not only the various geographical directions, but also their associations with day and night, heat and cold, fire and water, and the seasons of the year. For Eucherius and Rabanus Maurus the world and most of its peoples and things can be understood by means of these symbols. Hugh of St. Victor's geographical exposition embraces the fall and degeneration of man as well as the four possible ascents to the mystical Ark of Wisdom: the whole of human history—from our departure

out of paradise to our entrance into paradise regained—is thus summed up
in east, west, north and south. So also of our religion, for Durandus explains
the liturgy in geographical terms.[38]

In the Renaissance, discussion of the globe's four quarters does not necessarily follow these traditional lines. Pico, possibly infuenced by that lesser
strain in medievalism which saw the cardinal virtues dispersed in every direction, attributes this parable to Zoroaster:

> God's paradise is laved and watered by four rivers, from whose same
> source ye may draw the waters of your salvation. The name of that in
> the north is Pischon, which meaneth the right. The name of that in the
> west is Dichon, which signifieth expiation. The name of that in the east
> is Chiddikel, which expresseth light, and of that in the south Pareth, which
> we may interpret as piety.

Paracelsus departs still further from Christian geography, yet his conclusion
will not seem totally strange: "As Boreas coagulates, so the south wind dissolves, the east preserves the west putrifies." Donne is more recognizably
Christian than this when he writes that

> Christ calls upon the North, as well as the South, to blow upon his Garden,
> and to diffuse the perfumes thereof. Adversity, as well as prosperity, opens
> the bounty of God unto us; and oftentimes better. . . . The Eastern dignity,
> which we received in our first Creation, as we were the work of the whole
> Trinity, falls under a Western cloud.[39]

This geographical tradition, peculiarly Christian in origin and development,
is the modifying force brought to bear on the non-Christian tradition of
spherical movement. The modification is apparently necessary in order that
Donne's devotion may look eastward to *Oriens.* And if Donne himself could
move in that direction, there in the east, he says,

> There I should see a Sunne, by rising set,
> And by that setting endlesse day beget;
> But that Christ on this Crosse, did rise and fall,
> Sinne had eternally benighted all.

The westward journey thus becomes not a rational movement but a departure
from the Christian path, a turning from light to enter the ways of darkness.
Yet at the end of the poem, Donne will argue that he moves westward not
in the wilfullness of sin but because of penitential desire to be scourged. The
preparation for this reinterpretation requries most of the poem's remaining
lines, and it consists of this:

> Yet dare I'almost be glad, I do not see
> That spectacle of too much weight for mee.
> Who sees Gods face, that is selfe life, must dye;
> What a death were it then to see God dye?
> It made his owne Lieutenant Nature shrinke,

It made his footstoole crack, and the Sunne winke.
Could I behold those hands which span the Poles,
And tune all spheares at once, peirc'd with those holes?
Could I behold that endlesse height which is
Zenith to us, and to'our Antipodes,
Humbled below us? or that blood which is
The seat of all our Soules, if not of his,
Make durt of dust, or that flesh which was worne
By God, for his apparell, rag'd, and torne?
If on these things I durst not looke, durst I
Upon his miserable mother cast mine eye,
Who was Gods partner here, and furnish'd thus
Halfe of that Sacrifice, which ransom'd us?

There is much in these lines for the conscientious editor to annotate: the theological doctrine behind "who sees God's face must die"; the conception of Nature as God's lieutenant; belief and disbelief in the existence of the Antipodes; ideas concerning the locus of souls, whether ours or Christ's; the difference between dirt and dust.[40] But to discuss these matters would require the expansion of these pages to twice their present number, and the returns upon this invested space would not be great. I shall discuss one couplet only, therefore, in order to illustrate the means by which these lines progresss.

The couplet I choose is

Could I behold those hands which span the Poles,
And tune all spheares at once, peirc'd with those holes?

The apparent sense of these lines requires that "pierced" modify "hands": Christ's creating hands, pierced by the nails of the crucifixion, nevertheless span the very poles of the earth. They also tune the spheres, because Christ is the new string required, as Donne says elsewhere, to remedy Adam's dissonance in the world harmony.[41] The crucifixion would thus be too terrible for Christian eyes to view. The answer to Donne's question is—implicitly—no. Yet the position in these lines of "pierced" syntactically demands that it modify not "hands" but either "spheres" or "I." The syntax, that is, suggests that the crucifixion must affect not Christ alone, that the spheres which revolve within Donne's soul and the spheres which constitute the framework of the world are materially altered by the Passion. The suggestion can be made because it is true in many ways: the death of the Logos within the world did cause the earth to crack and caused the eclipsed sun to wink; each man, like Christ, must bear his individual cross; and the Passion is the means by which man is the recipient of mercy and grace. Indeed, the crucifixion is everywhere; like the Cross, in Donne's poem of that name, it is visible in its effects in all places and times, including the human and celestial spheres. Donne asks "Could I behold?" The answer—implicitly—is that, pierced with those holes, he can scarcely do otherwise. Donne answers his question with both yes and no.

This, I think, is the key to the whole series of questions which Donne asks. In each case, the apparent answer is no, but in actual fact the answer must be yes. He inevitably beholds the endless height and casts his spiritual eye upon the *Mater dolorosa.* Donne thus begins with the assumption that westward movement makes impossible the looking toward Christ. He progresses to an internal argument of the soul in terms of which he is physically unable but spiritually compelled to look. The self-questioning must take the form it does because only thus can Donne simultaneously affirm the impossibility and the inevitability of seeing what he cannot and yet must see. By the end of this section, however, the spiritual answers have become so obvious that the poetic fiction breaks down; the equality of negative and positive responses to these questions can no longer be maintained. Hence the rhetorical questions are at length concluded in order for this increasingly apparent fact to emerge:

> Thou these things, as I ride, be from mine eye,
> They'are present yet unto my memory,
> For that looks towards them; and thou look'st towards mee,
> O Saviour, as thou hang'st upon the tree.

The conflicting answers to Donne's questions prove to be a preparation for, a transition to, the realization that the crucifixion is visible to the memory, that faculty—as we know from Spenser's House of Alma—which is in the back of the mind, the side of Donne toward the east. And, of course, it is only the mental eye that could possibly see these things, for on Good Friday, 1613, Christ was crucified not in Palestine but in the sinful heart of everyman. Donne simply cannot ride away from Christ; he carries within him a daily re-enactment of the Passion. Once this fact is realized, therefore, a new argument for tergiversation must be found. The one which is discovered concludes the poem:

> I turne my backe to thee, but to receive
> Corrections, till thy mercies bid thee leave.
> O thinke mee worth thine anger, punish mee,
> Burne off my rusts, and my deformity,
> Restore thine Image, so much, by thy grace,
> That thou may'st know mee, and I'll turne my face.

Donne rides westward, then, that he may be scourged, but the scourge is to be a burning by the refiner against whom none may stand; the restoration of God's image is to be accomplished through the final destruction from fire. Two things necessarily follow: first, Donne will continue riding westward—riding "waste-ward" perhaps—until death; second; only by riding westward can he arrive at the east. One must reduce the "flat Map to roundnesse," for then "East and West touch one another and are all one";[42] one must ride to Last Judgement in the West to receive an oriental resurrection. Once this conclusion is achieved, the specific images of the poem fall more significantly into place. Donne at first refuses to look to Christ with his

outer eye, but in fact he has no choice in the matter. Since the vision of
Christ in this life is necessarily metaphorical, only devotional memory can
look to the east. Thus Donne fulfills one kind of "natural form" at once:
he does turn devotion in the proper direction. The turning, of course, pre-
sumes the presence in the east of *Oriens,* for without the day which the
Son begets, devotion and memory could not see—all would be "benighted."
This Son is therefore a "spectacle": a sight which memory beholds but
also the means by which the seeing is done. And the act of viewing must
be performed. The sun can only wink—an image which can now be seen
as an echo of that twinkling of an eye in which we are all changed—and
man's willful blindness to truth cannot last. Devotion, then, must "behold"
the hands of Christ, his blood, his flesh. It does look toward Christ upon
the tree, and Christ looks back. For Donne to turn his face, however—for
him to see God directly—the spectacle and the viewer must become one:
"Who sees God's face must die." Donne must be pierced, must assume the
"rag'd and torn" apparel of God, and must then be scourged of the de-
formity thus put on. The corruptible must be refined by fire that it may
put on incorruption. The journey westward to death is both right and inevitable.

Donne has therefore followed natural, uniform and direct motion
throughout his poem. That movement, we recall, begins with the Creator
in the east, progresses westward in order to view the Creator in visible and
created things, and returns to rest with the Creator in the east. This well
describes Donne's hoped-for progress. His origin is as an image of God,
planted—like Adam—in oriental climes; he rides westward through the world
but carries within him an image of the crucifixion and sees the effects of
the Passion all about him; and on the other side of death he returns to
Oriens and the life everlasting. In the final analysis, rational, uniform, direct
and natural motion moves westward through Donne's universe too. If this
is true, then that reinterpretation of spherical analogy which began the
poem must have been mistaken. Donne says, we remember, that pleasure
or business whirls him westward; yet in fact he is vividly aware of Christ,
and his primum mobile ultimately agrees with God's. He follows heaven's
course. Devotion, leaning to the east, thus becomes the irrational motion
within Donne's sphere, becomes a "passionate" and "sensual" movement
toward Christ. The divine contemplation of Good's Friday's Passion creates
in Donne the irrational desire to move eastward at once, the desire to avoid
that longer and harder westward path. This devotion can scarcely be called
bad; indeed, it is that which makes the westward movement good, for
only Donne's awareness of Christ at his back makes possible the final
touching of east and west. Yet that vivid consciousness does for the moment obscure Donne's judgment, causes an initial mistake which the rest
of the poem sets right. It would be too much to say that Donne finally
rejects the geographical symbolism of Christian tradition in favor of non-
Christian spheres; for him, the east of heaven is good for reasons other
than Plato's. Yet the Christian geography, no less than the paradoxically

"irrational" devotion to Christ, is responsible for that first erroneous re-interpretation of the movements of internal spheres, a reinterpretation which the poem must ultimately reject in order to affirm a tradition which could at first be stated only argumentatively: Let man's soul be a sphere.

THE MEANING OF THE "TEMPLE" IN DONNE'S *LA CORONA*

A. B. Chambers

Donne's *La Corona* is a poem of "prayer and praise" upon the life of Christ. It is composed of seven sonnets, six of which can be readily accounted for. The first, clearly, is introductory, and five of the remaining encompass Christ's temporal beginning with the "Annunciation," his temporal end with the "Ascension," and three principal events in between: the "Nativitie," the "Passion," and the "Resurrection." All of these are of critical importance to a summary of the life of Christ, and each fittingly receives a sonnet of its own. There is, however, no apparent reason for the intrusion of the sonnet which deals with the story of Jesus and the Doctors. Finding the incident recorded in only one of the Gospels (Luke 2: 42-52), we are likely to assume its relative insignificance, and while a glance at the Missal and Prayer Book finds the story in its proper place (First Sunday after Epiphany), no relevant interpretation meets the eye. John Boys, as early as 1611, in fact, explained that the Prayer Book lesson "is a direction how parents ought to carrie themselues toward their children, and how children also should demeane themselues toward their parents."[1] More recent explanation, no more enlightening, has seen the service as a celebration of the Holy Family.[2] Now if this is the interpretation to be made, then the "Temple" is sadly out of place in *La Corona;* the poem collapses into disjunctive incidents artificially joined by metrical means. One saving explanation, dependent on the Rosary, has thus far been offered. The fifth of the Joyful Mysteries of Mary is the Finding in the Temple; the first of the Sorrowful Mysteries is the Agony. Hence, argue Miss Gardner and Mr. Martz,[3] the appearance of Jesus in the Temple is not surprising, nor is the rapid transition to the Crucifixion. The vitiating factor in this suggestion is that *La Corona* quite clearly devotes itself to Christ and not to such specifically Marian material as the Mysteries of the Virgin. Hence, while Rosary meditations are surely a strong force behind the popularity of the incident and perhaps an explanation for Donne's remembering it, the poem's thematic development should demand a fourth sonnet important not to the life of Mary but to the life of Christ. The proper question therefore asks what the presumed significance of the story was, and the answer necessarily requires an examination of the Biblical commentary.

Reprinted from *Journal of English and Germanic Philology*, 59 (1960), 212-17, by permission of the author and the publisher, The University of Illinois Press.

The tradition is full and comparatively persistent. Within it are the inevitable interpretive variations, including the practical homiletics of Dr. Boys. "Learn where those who seek Jesus find him," writes Origen; "not everywhere, but in the Temple. And do you too seek Jesus in the Temple of God. Seek him in the Church."[4] And Jeremy Taylor, later than Boys, learns from the story that "whoever seeks Jesus must seek him in the offices of religion, not amongst engagements and pursuit of worldly interests."[5] Writing with different intent, Abbot Wernerus discovered that Jesus' twelve years were a type for the twelve degrees of humility to be practiced by the abbot's monks—and, strangely, a type for the twelve degrees of pride they were to avoid.[6] Yet the main outlines of belief transcend such individual usages as this last one, and we may approach Donne's point more nearly by summarizing the principal topics into which the outline divides.

The commentaries are agreed that the incident in its totality affirms the first of those "three most mystical unions" of which Sir Thomas Browne speaks:[7] the man-God which is Christ. The point is made in Augustine and Ambrose but is most fully developed by Bede.[8] Christ's going up to Jerusalem at the feast of Passover represents the man's observance of the law which the God had ordained; to show his humanity, Jesus listened humbly to the Doctors and returned home with his parents; to demonstrate his divinity, he taught wisely and spoke of his Father's business, says Bede. This doctrine behind the story goes far toward explaining the presence of Donne's ninth line: "His Godhead was not soule to his manhood." More important, because the belief in Christ as both man and God is central to the Christian faith and because Jesus in the Temple confirms that faith, a logical progression can now be seen. "Annunciation" promises that the Word shall be made flesh, "Nativitie" fulfills that promise with fact, and "Temple" confirms the fact with the actions of Christ himself. Hence Donne can say "The Word but lately could not speake" (l. 5) to refer back to the human frailty of the Nativity and can continue with "It sodenly speakes wonders" (l. 6) to recollect the divine power now seen.[9] Already, then, one basis for the inclusion of the "Temple" is clear: "thus," as the *Glossa* summarizes, "was the double nature of Christ shown."[10]

This much, however, is only one of the commentary topics; other glosses are equally helpful. As Miss Gardner points out, if we look for a reference to the Ministry of Christ in *La Corona,* we shall be disappointed. Yet the interpreted story of Jesus in the Temple supplies the omission by implication and thereby provides another basis for its inclusion. Because I find no explicit reference in the poem, I pass over the number symbolism which sees Jesus' age as a type for the twelve apostles "necessary to preach the faith."[11] Instead I consider two other closely related matters: the belief that this incident marks the first entry of Christ into that for which he came and that this beginning is distinguished by a miracle. Jesus came to the Temple, says Nicholas of Lyra, "that he might show forth his zeal concerning spiritual things"; Dionysius remarks that thus "he began to demonstrate his wisdom to the glory of his Father"; this was the first manifestation of his power for the anonymous Greek; he began his teaching at twelve, says Epiphanius; and Hugh Latimer saw the event as witnessing "wherefore he was sent into the world, namely to teach the way to heaven."[12] Origen and Chrysostom called such demonstration of wisdom a "wondrous" thing; Jeremy Taylor saw it as being "beyond the common spirits of the best men, discoursing up to the height of a prophet, with the clearness of an angel, and the infallibility of inspiration";[13] and Donne himself was later to write:

> Let us aske his Miracles, and they will make us understand Christ . . . In his Miraculous birth of a Virgin, In his Miraculous disputation with Doctors at twelve years of age . . . Christ spoke in himselfe, in the language of miracles.[14]

And here in *La Corona,* he concludes this sonnet with "He in his ages morning thus began"—and what Christ began can only be his and his Father's business—"by miracles exceeding power of man."

There are other incidental details in the sonnet which could be discussed; for example, the paradox in lines 3-4—that Christ eclipses the knowledge which he himself bestowed—can be paralleled by a sermon from Augustine or a contemplation from Bishop Hall.[15] But only one important matter remains, and it concerns the belief that the Finding in the Temple implies the whole of Christ's work. The commentaries make the point by means of another number symbolism: Jesus is found by Joseph and Mary on the third day either because after an equal interval he would arise from the dead or because the third day represents the time of grace as opposed to the times before the law and beneath the law.[16] Only in the twelfth-century Bruno Astensis do I find a more general basis for the belief: the rites Jesus came to Jerusalem to observe signified "his Passion, his Resurrection, and all other things written of him."[17] Now whether Donne depended on Bruno, upon a suppressed number symbolism, or upon a personally derived belief, it would be impossible to say, but in some way the connection was made between Jesus in the Temple and the whole of Christ's work. It emerges in the imagery of lines 11-12: "But as for one which hath a long taske, 'tis good, / With the Sunne to beginne his businesse." Now in one respect, this is a paraphrase of Christ's own words: "wist ye not that I must be about my Father's business?" In another respect, the image is of the rising sun as metaphor for the early start. But more precisely, the reference is to Psalm 19:4-5: "In them hath he set a tabernacle for the sun, Which is as a bridegroom coming out of his chamber, and rejoiceth as a strong man to run a race." The allusion is appropriate first because the strong man (or *Gigas,* as the Vulgate puts it), like the Temple scene, is universally taken to be emblematic of the double nature of Christ;[18] secondly, because the sun coming from his chamber, again like the Temple scene, is a clear parallel to the entry of Christ into his ministry; and finally, because the image of beginning the race is conventionally interpreted as a forecast of all the events in Christ's life.[19] Clearly, then, Donne has not employed the number symbolism of the commentaries on the Temple, but the implication is retained by means of another allusion which is appropriate in two other ways as well. Writing later in the Sermons, Donne was to connect the Temple scene and the Psalm in precisely the same terms with exactly the same import; he begins by quoting the closing words of Luke's account and continues with the image from the Psalm:

> Christ himself, *increased* in wisdome, and in stature, and in favour with God, and Man; . . . and it was prophesied of him, *Exultavit ut Gigas ad currendam vim* [*sic*], He went forth as a Gyant, to run a race . . . and the end of his course was, to be obedient unto death.[20]

These various glosses, taken together, make it possible to see that the subject matter of the fourth sonnet looks back to the human frailty of the birth of Jesus, signifies the first manifestation of his divinity, marks his entrance into the ministry, and forecasts the end for which he came. Because this is the case, one final—and by this time obvious—statement can be made: the "Temple" appears in a poem of prayer and praise upon the life of Christ not as an extraneous element but as a thematic part which is in effect a précis of the whole.

VII. THE ANNIVERSARIES

THE ARGUMENT OF DONNE'S *FIRST ANNIVERSARY*

Harold Love

Donne's *Anniversaries,* after having been dismissed by most twentieth-century critics as fitfully brilliant failures, have recently begun to look like something considerably more valuable. The process was inaugurated by Marjorie Nicolson's advocacy in *The Breaking of the Circle* (New York: Columbia University Press, 1950) and Louis L. Martz's demonstration in *The Poetry of Meditation* (1954)[1] that these supposedly formless poems actually made use of a precise, even rigorous form derived from that of the Ignatian meditation. It has been continued most notably by Frank Manley who, in the Preface to his excellently annotated edition of *The Anniversaries* (1963),[2] has been able to relate Donne's hyperbolic inflation of Elizabeth Drury into a kind of neo-Platonic demiurge to a long series of allegorical representations of the figure of Wisdom. While Manley's claim that the poems are perhaps Donne's greatest has yet to be seconded authoritatively, there seems to be growing agreement that *The Second Anniversary,* at least, is far more successful than earlier writers were prepared to recognize.

In the case of the first, *An Anatomy of the World,* opinions have been much more divided, and some impenitently hostile. The best-argued criticism (which is not to say the most convincing) is that of Martz, who has accused Donne of failing to relate his panegyric of Elizabeth Drury properly to the more substantial theme announced on the poem's title page—the representation of "the frailty and decay of this whole world." Attempts to answer this criticism have been made by both Manley and George Williamson,[3] the first asking us to extend Martz's theories of meditative structure, the second to abandon them entirely, and neither, it seems to me, managing to more than half persuade. The result is that, while readers of the sixties are in a position to gain a far better understanding of what Donne was trying to do in the poem than those of previous decades, I doubt whether they would receive a strong enough sense of a coherent purpose fulfilled to justify the high claims made for it by Manley. Part of the fault for this may easily be Donne's, but I suspect that much of it is ours and that it can be traced back to a series of crucial misreadings which between them have given rise to a mistaken idea of the poem's rhetorical

Reprinted from *Modern Philology,* 64 (1966), 125-31, by permission of the author and the publisher, The University of Chicago Press.

organization. I would like to develop this theme through a more detailed
examination of Martz's criticisms.

Martz's analysis of the *Anatomy* begins with a plausible enough division
of the poem into an introduction, a conclusion, and "five distinct sections
which form the body of the work."[4] Each of these sections is in turn divided
into three subsections, the first a "Meditation" on some aspect of the decay
of the world, the second, which Martz calls the "Eulogy," a panegyric of
Elizabeth Drury, and the third, the "Refrain and Moral," a direct address
to the reader exhorting him to abandon the world whose decay has been
so thoroughly demonstrated in the Meditation. Martz's own summary of
one of these sections will show his intentions more exactly:

> Section II, 247-338: "how ugly a monster this world is."
> 1. Meditation, 247-304. Proportion, the prime ingredient of beauty, no
>   longer exists in the universe.
> 2. Eulogy, 305-24. The girl was the "measure of all Symmetrie" and
>   harmony.
> 3. Refrain and Moral, 325-38. Human acts must be "done fitly and in pro-
>   portion."[5]

The chief weight of Martz's criticism falls on the second and third subsections, particularly the Eulogies, which he feels to be insufficiently connected with the rest of the poem to justify the prominence they have been
given. Donne's starting point is, of course, the hyperbolic claim that the
death of Elizabeth Drury has caused the death of the world, the principal
function of the Eulogies being, in Martz's analysis, to provide periodic recapitulations of this idea. Where Empson[6] had seen the critical challenge
posed by the *Anatomy* as the need to rationalize this central hyperbole
(e.g., by equating Elizabeth Drury with the Logos, or, as Manley has done,
with *Sapientia*), Martz denies that it performs any essential function in the
poem at all. Despite the elaborateness with which the image of the death
of the world is presented, both it and the Eulogies which are its vehicle
turn out on inspection to be merely decorative. Martz's conclusion is that
"Elizabeth Drury has, basically, nothing to do with the sense of decay in
the poem."[7] It is in the so-called Meditations that he locates the real poetic
substance of the *Anatomy,* and these are not only structurally but also
thematically self-contained, drawing on seriously held religious and philosophical ideas which refuse to harmonize with the frivolous "Petrarchan
hyperbole of the world's death."[8] When, at the end of each Meditation,
Donne insists on returning to the initial hyperbole, the effect is unavoidably
one of clumsiness and evasion. Martz does not object to the hyperbole in
itself. He feels that if Donne had been prepared to use it more consistently
it might easily have been able to give unity to the poem by functioning as
a "dominant symbol of virtue's power."[9] Donne, however, has not chosen
to do this, and Martz, as a consequence, has had no option but to accuse
him outright of bad poetic carpentry: "The very fact that the poem is
rigidly divided into sections and sub-sections gives us another aspect of its

failure. Nearly all the joints between sections and sub-sections are marked by strong pauses or by clumsy transitions; while the Morals are strained in an attempt to bring Meditation and Eulogy into some sort of unity. The parts will not fuse into an imaginative organism."[10] *The First Anniversary,* Martz concludes, would be a better poem all round if the Eulogies, Morals, introduction, and conclusion were simply omitted. The suggestion is rather alarmingly Bentleyesque, but one can hardly deny that Martz's argument has been conducted with remarkable efficiency. Neither Manley's defence nor Williamson's—the latter sparked off by justified doubts as to whether Martz's "Meditations" satisfy his own criteria for the form—really gets to grips with his central charge of lack of integration.

That Martz is basically wrong about the poem I take to be self-evident. *An Anatomy of the World* has an authority of statement and a singleness of effect that simply cannot be explained away. Even while allowing it faults, it is impossible to deny it greatness, and nothing in Martz's analysis explains or even allows for that greatness. The problems still remain, however, of where Martz has made his mistake and why his critics have not been able to correct it. To the second question, at least, the answer seems fairly obvious—Manley and Williamson share too many of Martz's assumptions about the poem to be effective critics of his conclusions. Despite the valuable insights mediated by all three, none seems to me to have been able to recognize the full complexity of the role played in the poem by the figure of Elizabeth Drury, and I would suggest that it is this, above all, that has prevented them from reaching a final settlement of their differences. Martz was quite right about the central concern of the poem being the representation of "the frailty and decay of this whole world." He was at least half right in his claim that the initial hyperbole that the death of the world was caused by the death of Elizabeth Drury never really becomes organically involved in this central concern. His mistake—which has been that of most writers on the poem—lay in his assumption that the Eulogies were mere recapitulations of this hyperbole and that Elizabeth Drury was nothing more in Donne's system of images than a kind of cosmic embalming fluid. The essential point that he has overlooked is that Donne's initial conceit is really a double one—or rather a conjunct one, like the combined theme-counter-subject of a double fugue. Besides telling us that the death of the world has been caused by the death of Elizabeth Drury, Donne has also gone to some pains to state the apparently contradictory proposition that the death of Elizabeth Drury has been caused by the death of the world. Elizabeth Drury exists in the poem not only as the soul of the world whose withdrawal from it has caused its corruption but as the heart of the world, a heart that despite its perfections has been finally unable to avoid becoming involved in the universal process of corruption that began with the fall. It is from the periodic collision of these images that a good part of the fascination of the poem derives. Discussion of the role of the Eulogies has been conditioned by the assumption that they were recapitulations of the first image. I would claim that they are also intended as recapitulations of the second and that once they are recognized as such they will be seen to play a far more significant role in the poem as a whole. To show how this applies, however, it will be necessary to approach the structure of the poem in rather different terms from those used by Martz, terms that, needless to say, are meant to supplement rather than to supplant those of his analysis.

Quite apart from its relationship to the Ignatian meditation, *The First Anniversary* also exhibits features of another traditional form, the *oratio iudicialis* in six (or four, or five, or seven) parts of the classical rhetoricians. It opens with an easily recognizable *narratio* (of the type that the rhetoricians would have called *fabula*[11]), follows this with a copybook *refutatio* (ll. 63-90) and a *probatio* which, while it contains no formal *partitio,* is divided into the recommended three divisions (i.e., ll. 91-248 demonstrating the decay of nature, ll. 249-376 arguing the want of beauty, and ll. 377-434 demonstrating the "Weaknesse in the want of correspondence of heauen and earth"—the first two having two subsections each, the third remaining undivided). The only serious absence is that of a formal *exordium,* but this, like the suppression of the *partitio,* was an acknowledged licence,[12] and in any case its function, described by Cicero as *animum auditoris idonee compar[are] ad reliquam dictionem*[13] was quite adequately performed by the prefatory "To the Praise of the Dead, and the Anatomy" attributed by Jonson to Joseph Hall. The presence in the poem of such clear traces of a form whose whole raison d'être was the establishment of proof suggests that Donne may easily have been as much concerned with arguing an issue as with representing a state, and looking where we would expect, according to Thomas Wilson,[14] to find the *propositio* (i.e., at the very end of the *narratio*), we discover the following couplet, the thirtieth of the poem:

> Her death hath taught vs dearely, that thou art Corrupt and mortall in
> thy purest part.

It would be perverse to try to present the poem as a full-scale proof of this proposition, but it is highly instructive to observe the consistency with which the various sections of the *probatio* refer back to it. The key word here, though it does not occur in the couplet itself, is *heart,* and the key concept is that of Elizabeth Drury as the heart of the world. The first suggestion of this comes in the passage beginning with line 171:

> If man were any thing, he's nothing now:
> Helpe, or at least some time to wast, allow
> T'his other wants, yet when he did depart
> With her, whom we lament, he lost his hart.

Here Elizabeth Drury is the heart of *mankind*; a few lines further on the "purest part" of line 60 is identified as a heart, and the dead girl becomes the heart of the corpse that is the world:

> Shee, shee is dead; shee's dead: when thou knowest this,
> Thou knowest how poore a trifling thing man is.

And learn'st thus much by our Anatomee,
The heart being perish'd, no part can be free.
[ll. 183-86.]

The idea is echoed in lines 240-42, once more close to the refrain:

. . . this worlds generall sickenesse doth not lie
In any humour, or one certaine part;
But, as thou sawest it rotten at the hart . . .

The word "heart" also appears in association with the third refrain ("Corruptions in our braines, or in our harts . . .")[15] and again following the fifth (". . . those rich ioyes, which did possesse her hart . . ."[16]—this also recalling the "rich soule" of l. 1). The last two examples are repetitions of the word rather than restatements of the proposition, but they serve to draw attention to the fact that the contexts in which they occur are such restatements. The long catalogues of the perfections of Elizabeth Drury which Martz was prepared to dismiss as "Eulogies" are simultaneously preparations for the staggering realization foreshadowed in the thirtieth couplet that even this woman, the "purest part" of the physical creation, has proved "corrupt and mortall."

Donne's rhetorical strategy in the *Anatomy* is a little slapdash but basically quite straightforward. His purpose, as an anatomist, is argument, and the topic that he sets out to argue is the corruptness of the world. In doing this he makes use of three distinct proofs. The first and most direct involves the division of the principal generalization into three subsidiary ones, each of which is then supported by the adduction of evidence drawn from philosophy, theology, and science. It is this that provides the rhetorical shape of the sections that Martz has described as "Meditations" and Williamson, much more helpfully for the present analysis, as "statement and proof of a thesis."[17] The second proof is that based on the analogy between the world after the death of Elizabeth Drury and the body after the departure of the soul. This can be taken either at its face value as a typical—and perhaps in its context rather vapid—piece of seventeenth-century wit (Martz) or as an allegory of considerable profundity (Empson, Nicolson, Manley). The third and least often recognized proof is that built up round the crucial instance of the general thesis—the fact that even the most perfect thing in the world, Elizabeth Drury, has been unable to escape its corruption and has had to suffer death. If the purest part is rotten, there can be no hope of soundness anywhere. The force of the argument will depend, of course, on the intensity with which the vision of purity is presented, and it would seem to be this, rather than mere amplification of the image of Elizabeth Drury as the soul of the world, that is the real point of Donne's emphasis on what we might describe as her "demiurgic" powers. Each of the sections of the *probatio* begins with a general statement of the aspect of the "frailty and decay of the world" that is to be its special topic and moves steadily toward the statement of the culminating particular fact that even the heart of the world

is rotten. The heart of the world, as I have shown, is Elizabeth Drury, or
rather the body of Elizabeth Drury. This represents the most perfect state
to which matter can aspire. Its perfection is so complete that it has succeeded
in disrupting the established boundaries between the spiritual and the physical,
boundaries that were, in any case, far more fluid for Donne than they could
ever be for inhabitants of a post-Cartesian universe:

> Shee that was best, and first originall
> Of all faire copies; and the generall
> Steward to Fate; shee whose rich eyes, and brest,
> Guilt the West Indies, and perfum'd the East;
> Whose hauing breath'd in this world, did bestow
> Spice on those Isles, and bad them still smell so,
> And that rich Indie which doth gold interre,
> Is but as single money, coyn'd from her:
> She to whom this world must it selfe refer,
> As Suburbs, or the Microcosme of her,
> Shee, shee is dead; shee's dead . . .
>   [ll. 227-37].

So superior was the matter of which Elizabeth Drury was composed to other
matter that it seemed for a while that it might have been capable even of re-
generating it. In the event, however, it could not overcome the innate corruptness of all matter. The fact that a creature so perfect had to die is the
strongest impeachment of the physical world it was possible for Donne to frame:
it is also the most cogent single argument advanced in support of his thesis.

With this in mind, we are now able to identify Martz's principal mistake
as his failure to recognize the existence of this third process of proof.
Excusably dubious of the tonal (and logical) congruence of the second
proof, the bizarre image of the world as a body deprived of its soul, with
the more conventional processes of the first, he chose to dismiss as superfluous the Eulogies that were its vehicle. What he overlooked was that these
Eulogies were also the vehicle of another vision, half contradictory, half complementary: a vision of the girl's death not as the cause but as the consequence
of the innate corruption of the natural world and hence the culminating argument for it. In denying the Eulogies a meaningful function in the poem, he
not only missed a significant aspect of its thesis but robbed it of what should
be its strongest assault on the imagination—Donne's stammered horror ("Shee,
shee is dead; shee's dead . . .") at the sheer fact of this death—at the realization that, despite the miracles of beauty and order of which it was capable,
the natural world was ultimately irredeemable. The horror is perhaps more
philosophical than personal (in the sense of involving any genuine emotion
toward Elizabeth Drury as an individual), and the religious vision underlying
it is one that is extraordinarily hard for a twentieth-century reader to share.
It is impossible, however, not to feel the force with which this horror is felt
and expressed.

Martz's failure to recognize the full importance of the Eulogies is shared by Manley and Williamson, and it is because of this that they have not been able to contradict him as effectively as they meant to. To Williamson the function of the Eulogies is reduced to that of an "Elegiac antithesis" or relevant contrast" that "crowns" the proof but does not play any essential part in it.[18] To Manley the relationship of the death of Elizabeth Drury to the decay of the world is an extra-logical one: it "makes sense of sorts,"[19] but it is not a sense that can be fitted into rhetorical moulds. In his concentration on the connotative aspect of the juxtaposition, he has completely overlooked the denotative. Each of these critics, despite the value of his individual contribution to our understanding of the poem, has fallen into a simple semantic trap arising from the ambiguity of the logical relationship of the refrains to the long catalogues of the "demiurgic" powers of Elizabeth Drury that are used to lead up to them and to the moral conclusions that follow them. Within the refrain itself the danger point is "when thou knowest this."

> Shee, shee is dead; shee's dead: when thou knowest this,
> Thou knowest how poore a trifling thing man is   [ll. 183-84] .

Donne indicates a relationship between two pieces of knowledge but does not specify in any way what it is. He tells us what we should know but refrains from telling us why we should know it. The reader has to choose between (or harmonize) two possible interpretations—to decide whether man is a trifling thing because he is now deprived of the enlivening force of the perfections of the Elizabeth Drury or because he is in bondage to an inherently corrupt natural order which has been responsible for the destruction of these perfections. The point can be made more clearly by comparing the two most obvious ways of paraphrasing the refrain. Approached in terms of the first interpretation, the force of the refrain would be something like, "Because she is dead whose perfections made her the source of the world's life, the world has now become . . ." A reader alerted to the second, on the other hand, would also be able to interpret the refrain, "Because even she is dead who represented the highest perfection to which the world could aspire, the world cannot be denied to be . . ." He might not want to do so in every case—indeed it is only in a minority of instances that such a reading would be actually forced on him by the text—but he would find himself doing it enough to become aware of structural patterns of a kind not allowed for by Martz. Martz, having restricted himself to the first interpretation, found he was unable to give the Eulogies any really meaningful place in the poem as a whole. The second interpretation is not so immediately obvious but once recognized allows us to integrate the Eulogies and refrains much more effectively into a continuing process of argument.

Not all the loose ends, of course, will let themselves be tied up. The gap between the two visions of Elizabeth Drury advanced in the poem—animating spirit and vulnerable body—is too wide not to set up serious strains and, indeed, it could be argued that Donne has been far less careful than he should have been about keeping them distinct from one another. In *The*

Second Anniversary he tries to make amends for this. Elizabeth Drury is considered specifically as spirit in the first and fourth "Meditations" and body in the second and third. To achieve this added clarity, however, Donne has been forced to abandon the provocative indeterminacy of the spirit-matter relationship that is central to *The First Anniversary* for a neater but far less stimulating vessel analogy.[20] There must be many for whom the earlier poem with all its rough edges is still the most satisfying.

THE *ANNIVERSARIES*: DONNE'S RHETORICAL APPROACH TO EVIL

Patrick Mahony

The full nature of Donne's *Anniversaries* can be better understood by a clear analysis of their rhetorical situation. Specifically, the sequel poems are formal examples of deliberative-epideictic rhetoric,[1] and as such, they are primarily poems of process rather than fixity, of argumentation rather than exposition.[2] Summarily, the rhetorical problem of the *Anniversaries* is a dynamic one: what type of rational approach must one take to address and persuade a mankind whose very mental powers have been diminished by sin?[3] In other words, the rhetorical treatment of evil is a key to the understanding of the sequel poems. The two poems as a whole constitute a profound examination of evil in three aspects, namely, its causes, its effects or manifestations, and the remedies for evil. Comparatively, the remedies are of both foremost and inclusive importance, for the diverse references to the causes and effects of evil are occasioned by the specific remedy applied. Because of a desire for clarity, however, I shall treat the three aspects of evil individually.

Donne lists three general causes of physical and moral evil in the companion poems. First, there is the death of the heroine, who thereby deprived man of virtuous force and energy (*FA*, 409–12) and who as the almighty World Soul took from the world its last remaining coherence. The couplet,

> If this commerce twixt heauen and earth were not
> Embarr'd, and all this trafique quite forgot,   (*FA*, 399–400)

indicates the other two causes of evil. The "embarr'd commerce" is primal "Corruption"; this nearly Manichean concept of creation is spelled out in some earlier lines:

> Then, as mankinde, so is the worlds whole frame
> Quite out of ioynt, almost created lame:
> For, before God had made vp all the rest,
> Corruption entred, and deprau'd the best:
> It seis'd the Angels, and then first of all
> The world did in her Cradle take a fall,
> And turn'd her braines, and tooke a generall maime

Reprinted from *Journal of English and Germanic Philology*, 68 (1969), 407–13, by permission of the author and the publisher, the University of Illinois Press.

Wronging each ioynt of th'vniuersall frame.
The noblest part, man, felt it first; and than
Both beasts and plants, curst in the curse of man.
So did the world from the first houre decay. . . .
                                                        (FA, 191-201)

Corruption is, then, a primal force that first "seis'd the Angels" with the result
that some of them revolted and sinned against God. A chain reaction ensued.
The world's whole frame suffered a "generall maime." Then each "ioynt"
of the world's frame was affected. The noblest "ioynt," man, was the first
affected, as he committed original sin; this "curse of man" in turn blighted
beasts and plants. The "trafique quite forgot" (FA, 400) points to the third
cause of evil, that is, actual sin or sin subsequent to original sin. If original
sin diminished man's mental faculties, actual sin has deadened these
faculties—it has caused man to lose his "sense and memory" (FA, 28).

For purposes of convenience rather than of strictly logical separation,
three effects or manifestations of evil may be named. First, there is the
death of the heroine, which is not only a cause of evil but also a manifestation.[4] Her death is at the very core of Donne's De contemptu mundi attitude:

Her death hath taught vs dearely, that thou art
Corrupt and mortall in thy purest part.   (FA, 61-62)

In other words, since the purest part of the world is mortal and corrupt, a
fortiori the world is corrupt. The second effect of evil is the corruption in
man and in the cosmos, described at length in FA's first meditation and
second to the fifth meditations respectively.[5]

The third effect of evil in the Anniversaries is the loss of operativity of
man's three mental faculties, as seen in FA, lines 3-6. What is most neglected
in the criticism of the Anniversaries is this: the primary grief of the sequel
poems, their central lament as elegies, is not the death of any incarnation
of the Idea of Woman,[6] nor of the death of her as the World Soul; it is
rather that the soul's three faculties (the heroine's second symbolization
as moral force for man) have been deadened:

Her death did wound, and tame thee than, and than
Thou mightst haue better spar'd the Sunne, or Man;
That wound was deepe, but 'tis more misery,
Than thou hast lost thy sense and memory.   (FA, 25-28)

Sin deadens the efficacy of the sense and memory. The best definition for
"sense" here is: "Mental apprehension, appreciation, or realization of (some
truth, fact, state of things). Also, comprehension, perception of the meaning
of" (OED, sb. 15). Accordingly, "sense" alludes in Donne's poem to both
the understanding and the will, whose perfection was the basis of Socratic
virtuous perception.

Donne's limitation of his rhetorical audience characterizes his remedy
for evil in the Anniversaries. The audience is not all mankind, but rather
the chosen. Here Donne is similar to Moses, who delivered a song of remem-

brance not to the pagans (the *ever* spiritually dead world) but to the
Israelites:

> . . . God did make
> A last, and lastingst peece, a song. He spake
> To *Moses,* to deliuer vnto all,
> That song: because he knew they would let fall,
> The Law, the Prophets, and the History,
> But keepe the song still in their memory.
> Such an opinion (in due measure) made
> Me this great Office boldly to inuade.   (FA, 461-68)[7]

Hence Donne primarily addresses the "new world" (*FA*, 76), that is, only
those who understood the worth of the Idea of Woman (*FA*, 72).[8]

In rectifying evil, Donne made about one-half of *FA* appeal to the
memory, whereas *SA* is overwhelmingly concentrated on the understanding
and the will. As Manley points out, the memory, understanding, and the
will relate to *FA*'s meditations, eulogies, and morals respectively.[9] As veritable lectures on the effects or evidences of evil, *FA*'s five meditations,
totaling over two hundred lines and thereby constituting the poem's major
section, produce a principal focus on the faculty of memory; these meditations are an effort to remedy evil by laying bare some of its nefarious effects.
Most significantly therefore, *FA* is not merely a companion poem but a
necessary preparatory poem to *SA*. In light of this, one may readily see
that Donne's rhetorical strategy to combat evil in a spiritually amnesic
society is to ground the complementary nature of his poems on meditative
practice: first, stimulate largely the memory, and then the understanding
and the will. Consequently, *FA*'s meditations, written in the third person
of the indicative mood, are anatomies revealing material to be immediately
accepted by the memory. On the other hand, *SA*'s meditations may even
appeal to the will—they are direct addresses to the soul and are characterized
by many exhortations, imperatives, and submerged imperatives found in
challenging questions.

As antidotes to evil, *SA*'s first three meditations consider the body and
soul in terms of earthly and celestial existence; meditations 4 and 5 contrast
earthly and celestial knowledge; earthly and celestial joy are compared in
the last two meditations. Thus, for example, Donne, in a series of ten commands, in the first meditation orders his soul to forget "this rotten world";
unlike the submissive forgetfulness or lethargy of *FA* (l. 24), the forgetfulness here is willed and is constructive as well. In the fourth meditation,
Donne bids his soul to ameliorate its epistemological perspective:

> Thou look'st through spectacles; small things seeme great,
> Below; But vp vnto the watch-towre get,
> And see all things despoyld of fallacies. . . .
>   (FA, 293-95)[10]

Finally, the most subtle distinctions for the understanding—those between

earthly and celestial or essential joy—are shrewdly reserved for *SA*'s last
two meditations.

In conclusion, an adequate understanding of the *Anniversaries* must take
into account their full rhetorical nature, including their chief cause of lament,
their restricted audience, and their nuanced harmonization and mutuality as
rhetorical argument based on the meditative tradition. As epideictic rhetoric,
the *Anniversaries* praise the heroine and what she represents, and dispraise
worldliness; as deliberative rhetoric, the poetic diptychs persuade the new
world to become virtuous like and through the heroine. The magic of these
poems is that they possess an ultimately indissoluble union of epideictic
and deliberative rhetoric, a union most strikingly announced in the opening
eighteen lines of the first poem.

Some passages in Donne's sermons present an interesting gloss on the
rhetorical problem in the *Anniversaries* as a whole. Donne once more is profoundly aware of the argumentative difficulty of exhorting sinful man to
do good, for his mental powers are deadened:

> But if it [sin] be above our head, then the brain is drownd'd, that is, our
> reason, and *understanding,* which should dispute against it, and make us
> asham'd of it, or afraid of it; And our *memory* is drown'd, we have for-
> got that there belongs a repentance to our sins, perchance forgot that
> there is such a sin in us; forgot that those actions are sins, forgot that
> we have done those actions; and forgot that there is a law, even in our
> own hearts, by which we might try, whether our actions were sins, or
> no. If they be above our heads, they are so, in many dangerous accepta-
> tions. (II, 110)[11]

A question immediately presents itself: if man is immersed in sin and is
therefore gravely afflicted in his mental faculties, how may he be brought
to goodness? Donne finds the initial solution in the memory. It has a central
importance in the learning process, and of all the faculties it is the most
accessible:

> For the rectifying of the *will,* the *understanding* must be rectified; and
> that implies great difficulty: But the *memory* is so familiar, and so
> present, and so ready a faculty, as will always answer, if we will but
> speak to it, and aske it, *what God hath done for us, or for others.* The
> art of *salvation,* is but the art of *memory.* (II, 73)

> *Plato* plac'd *all learning in the memory*; wee may place *all Religion* in
> the memory too. (II, 74)

> The memory, sayes St. *Bernard,* is the stomach of the soul, it receives and
> digests, and turns into good blood, all the benefits formerly exhibited to
> us in particular, and exhibited to the whole Church of God: present that
> which belongs to the understanding, to that faculty, and the understand-
> ing is not presently setled in it. (II, 236)

> And truly the memory is oftner the Holy Ghosts Pulpit that he preaches

in, then the Understanding. How many here would not understand me . . .
if I should spend the rest of this houre in repeating, and reconciling that
which divers authors have spoken diversly of the manner of Christs
presence in the Sacrament. (VIII, 261)

In trying to safeguard a people weakened by sin, Donne recalls God's solution
with respect to the Israelites. God gave Moses a song of remembrance to be
delivered unto the Jewish tribes:

> God himselfe made *Moses* a Song, and expressed his reason why; The
> children of *Israel,* sayes God, will forget my Law; but this song they will
> not forget; and whensoever they sing this song, this song shall testifie
> against them, what I have done for them, how they have forsaken me.
> (IV, 179-80)[12]

As God instituted this song of remembrance, so Donne composes his
Anniversaries or remedies for evil:

> The *Iewes* did, we may institute new *Holy dayes.* And not onely transitory
> daies, for a present thanks giving for a present benefit, but *Anniversaries,*
> perpetuall memorials of *Gods* deliverances. And thats our next step. . . .
> God by *Moses* made the children of *Israel* a *Song,* because, as hee sayes,
> howsoever they did by the Law, they would never forget that *Song,* and
> that *Song* should be his witnesse against them. (IV, 368)

DONNE'S *ANNIVERSARIES* AS CELEBRATION

Dennis Quinn

Donne's *Anniversaries* are celebratory in so far as they are commemorative, public, and joyful songs of praise. For Donne commemoration meant bringing the past to bear on the present and establishing a pattern for the future; hence the *Anniversaries* urge the reader to remember Elizabeth Drury as a pattern of virtue. Since all celebration is a public and communal act, Donne's poems place particular emphasis on death as the process in which all Christians participate. Although festivity occurs, then, at the junctures between life and death, the dominant note of celebration is joy. The *Anniversaries*, therefore, confront the full horror of death only to emerge into the light of Elizabeth's joy. The element of praise which dominates the poems is that part of celebration which affirms the goodness of the order of things. Hence, while Donne dispraises sin and "the world," he does not reject God's order but rather emphasizes its restoration in the virtue of Elizabeth. Donne is conscious, moreover, of declaring his praise in the lofty genre of celebratory song, the high standards of which poems sustain.

Dylan Thomas gave a rough but illuminating definition when he said that, "The joy and function of poetry is, and was, the celebration of man, which is also the celebration of God."[1] Some poems and some poets, however, are more immediately and directly celebratory than others—as, say, Spenser's *Epithalamion* and Milton's *Hymne on the Morning of Christ's Nativity* are more properly celebrations than are *The Canterbury Tales* and *King Lear* and *The Wasteland.* Similarly, the celebratory or festive character is more striking in certain of Donne's poems than in others. The *Anniversaries* are celebratory in the fullest sense of the term, and the epithalamia are more festive than has been commonly appreciated. For the present, however, I shall confine my remarks to the poems celebrating Elizabeth Drury.

At the end of the *First Anniversary,* Donne asserts that he "As oft as thy feast sees this widowed earth, / Will yearely celebrate thy second birth[2] (ll. 449-450)." And in the second line of the poem he has said that all men who know they have a soul, "celebrate" "that rich soule which to her Heaven is gone." In this latter case Donne is using the term in the sense of praise, which was unusual at the time in English, although, of course, the Latin verb had always had that sense. Celebration is, however, a much broader activity than praise. In the first place, celebration involves commemoration, as the use of the term in the lines first quoted above suggests, and the *Anniversaries* are Donne's only truly and fully commemorative poems.[8]

Reprinted from *Studies in English Literature*, 9 (1969), 97-105, by permission of the author and the publisher.

The meaning of commemoration and its association with celebration appears frequently in Donne's sermons preached on church feasts. On Whitsunday of 1627, for example, Donne begins by saying, "And this very particular day, in which we now commemorate, and celebrate that performance of Christs promise, in that Mission of the Holy Ghost upon the Apostles, are all these Scriptures performed again, in our eares, and eyes, and in our hearts."[4] Even more pertinently, in his "Commemorative Sermon" for Lady Danvers in 1627, Donne invokes her spirit, saying,

> But wee doe not invoke thee, as thou art a *Saint in Heaven;* Appeare to us, as thou didst appeare to us a moneth agoe; At least, appeare in thy *history;* Appeare in our memory; that when every one of us have lookt upon thee, by his owne *glasse,* and seene thee in his owne *Interest,* such, as thou wast to him, That when *one* shall have seene thee, the *best wife,* And a larger number, the *best mother,* And more then they a whole *Towne,* the best *Neighbour,* . . . And more then *all they, all the world,* the *best example* . . . bee still content, to bee one of this Congregation. . . .
> (VIII, 85-86)

Commemoration, then, is the act of bringing a past event into the lives of men in the present. It is obvious that the *Anniversaries* seek to make the death of Elizabeth relevant to those who survive her, to make her the best example to all the world. At the end of the *First Anniversary,* Donne explicitly declares that poetry is superior to "Law, Prophets, and History" in that song stays in the memory. I have pointed out elsewhere the connection traditionally made between memory and self-knowledge;[5] similarly, in the *Anniversaries* it is important to note that Donne's main purpose in recalling Elizabeth is to cause the reader to remember himself—what he is now and what he can be. It is important, too, that the reader not mistake this traditional view of memory, formulated mainly by St. Augustine, for the conventional post-Hobbesian conception, which presents the memory as a receptacle for fading sense impressions, rather than as a faculty which not only makes present the past, but also brings into view a pattern of the future.[6] Hence Donne's poems re-present Elizabeth as she was, is, and will be, tracing through her the history of man as he was, is, and will be.

Besides being commemorative, celebration is also a public act—as the etymology of the word (L. *celebritas,* crowd) suggests. Donne may have regretted having "descended to print anything in verse," but in publishing the *Anniversaries* his instinct was entirely sound. They are pre-eminently public poems, addressed to the world at large. One cannot, after all, properly celebrate or commemorate privately. All Saints Day, says Donne, "is truly a festivall, grounded upon that Article of the Creed, *The Communion of Saints,* and unites in our devout contemplation, The Head of the Church, God himselfe, and those two noble constitutive parts thereof, The Triumphant and the Militant" (X, 42). Birthdays and death days, Christmas or Good Friday, all beginnings and endings, whether of marriages or wars, the Christian Sunday or the Jewish Sabbath—all are occasions

which are eminently public and communal in character. It is so because
such events remind men of what they share at the deepest level of their
humanity.

In the face of the conventional view of Donne the egotist, the individual-
ist, it may be useful to emphasize especially the communal character of the
Anniversaries. The most profound expression of Donne's sense of community appears later, in the *Devotions,* in a passage too famous to quote,
when Donne hears the passing bell from his sickbed. The roots of the
famous words, it is too often forgotten, are in the beginning of the seventeenth "Meditation": "The Church is Catholic, universal, so are all her
actions; all that she does belongs to all. When she baptizes a child, that
action concerns me; for that child is thereby connected to that body which
is my head too, and ingrafted into that body whereof I am a member."[7]
To the faithful Christian it is no matter of hyperbole to say that all fellow-
Christians suffer and die when a member of the Body of Christ dies. All
Christians participate in that death just as they share in the redemptive
death of Christ, thus dying to sin. In the *Anniversaries,* Donne represents
the process of death as it infects all created being, from the angels to the
cosmos, from Adam to Elizabeth Drury. It is precisely the universal character of death and its mother, sin, which Donne chooses to emphasize.
And when Donne turns to the positive meaning of the death of Elizabeth,
it is to her becoming "a part both of the Quire, and Song" in the communion
of saints. Indeed, very near the end of the *Second Anniversary,* Donne devotes a substantial section to contrasting "our company in this life, and in
the next," where the saints enjoy the society of Mary, the Patriarchs, the
Prophets, Martyrs, Apostles, and Virgins. Elizabeth Drury's death, in the
end, serves not to divorce her from "the world" in the sense of her fellow
Christians or the created universe, but only from that "world" whose un-
holy companions are the flesh and the devil—i.e., sin.[8]

Celebration and festivity occur, as I have observed, in conjunction with
beginnings or endings. Or, to be precise, they mark endings which are also
beginnings—the old year dies, the new is born; a child baptized dies to sin
and enters into the new life of grace; Christ emerges from the tomb at
Easter. Festivity always occurs at junctures between life and death, although
we incline at present to neglect the element of death. Whereas Donne can
speak freely of "celebrating Christs Funerals" (VII, 277), present usage
reserves the word for "purely" joyous occasions; but a moment's reflection
reminds us that an integral element of our rejoicing at the new lies in our
simultaneous recognition that the old must die before there can be a new.
"I joy," says Donne, "that in these straits, I see my West." Hence the paradox that a poem commonly considered notorious for its gloom and for its
morbid immersion in death can be called festive and celebratory.[9]

But after all is said, is not joy an essential feature of all festivals? Certainly
it is, but as I have insisted, it is a joy born of a certain sadness, a joy which
bursts out of the heart of darkness. Good Friday must be experienced before
Easter, and the long harsh expectation of the Messiah must be endured be-

fore Christmas. So also for the Christian the terrors of death must be experienced before the joys of the new life. Donne's *Anniversaries* represent the whole process, confronting death in its total physical, psychological, metaphysical, and theological horror, only to emerge into the light of joy. Donne certainly does not portray the Christian's earthly life as joyless, "for," as he affirms in the sermons, "he that feeles no joy here, shall finde none hereafter" (X, 214); and "here in this world, so far as I can enter into my Masters sight, I can enter into my Masters joy" (V, 287). Similarly, Elizabeth

> had Here so much essential joy,
> As no chance could distract, much lesse destroy;
> Who with Gods presence was acquainted so,
> (Hearing, and speaking to him) as to know
> His face in any natural Stone, or Tree.   (ll. 449-453)

But since "*Solum Deum vere festum agere,* That only God can be truly said to keep holy day, and to rejoyce" (V, 287), so only in heaven can man enter into the eternal festival. Hence it is the "essential joys" of Elizabeth Drury after death which dominate the end of the *Second Anniversary.* After a general definition (ll. 443-446) and a contrast of transient earthly joys (ll. 471-486), Donne ascends to the last great summit of the poem:

> Ioy of a soules arrivall neere decaies;
> For that soule ever ioyes, and ever staies.
> Ioy that their last great Consummation
> Approaches in the resurrection;
> When earthly bodies more celestiall
> Shalbe, then Angels were, for they could fall;
> This kind of ioy doth every day admit
> Degrees of grouth, but none of loosing it.
> In this fresh ioy, tis no small part, that shee,
> Shee, in whose goodnesse, he that names degree,
> Doth iniure her; (Tis losse to be cald best,
> There where the stuffe is not such as the rest)
> Shee, who left such a body, as even shee
> Onely in Heaven could learne, how it can bee
> Made better; for shee rather was two soules,
> Or like to full, on both sides written Rols,
> Where eies might read upon the outward skin,
> As strong Records for God, as mindes within.
> Shee, who by making full perfection grow,
> Peeces a Circle, and still keepes it so,
> Long'd for, and longing for'it, to heaven is gone,
> Where shee receives, and gives addition.   (ll. 489-510)

Commemorative, public, and joyful—to these festive notes, I should add another, and that the most significant of all. It is praise. But after Professor Hardison's exposition,[10] one need not prove that Donne's poems are centrally poems of praise. Some further questions might be asked, however, concerning the nature of praise and how it is related to festivity and celebration.

In a sermon Donne cites the brief definition of glory (i.e., praise of God) given by St. Ambrose—*clara cum laude notitia,* "an evident knowledge, and acknowledgement of God, by which others come to know him too" (IV, 306). By praising Elizabeth Drury, making "evident" her character as a champion of virtue and grace, Donne intends simply to make her (and through her, God) known to others. Praise is a deeply affirmative act involving positive assent to the object of praise. It is here, as Josef Pieper observes, that praise intersects festivity.[11] In religious festivals there is always a fundamental motif of praise of things as they are ordered by God. The ultimate goodness of God is acknowledged by assent to the order which prevails in nature. Commenting in another sermon on the definition of St. Ambrose, Donne says, "the glory of God, is the taking knowledge, that all that comes, comes from God, and then the glorifying of God for whatsoever comes" (IV, 123). And, defending Protestantism against the Roman charge of negativism, Donne praises the "Affirmative man, that does acknowledge all blessings, spirituall and temporall, to come from God . . ." (IX, 405).

But how can a poem be called affirmative which is so much a "just disestimation of the world" and which relentlessly and corrosively indicts a world steeped in sin and death? The correlative of praise is dispraise, and the two acts are seldom separated; for to dispraise what is bad is a way of praising what is good. What Donne dispraises is not God's created order but rather man's attempt to uncreate that order through sin and its consequence, death. The emphasis of Donne's poems does not fall upon dispraise of sin and "the world," however, but upon praise of Elizabeth Drury and her virtue, which is truly the ordering principle, the soul, of the universe. This emphasis is especially clear in the *Second Anniversary*, where it is shown how exactly the virtue of Elizabeth nourished a harmony, beauty, balance, and proportion in *this* world. By her virtue, in fact, she "Who made this world in some proportion / A heaven" (ll. 468–469), was able to restore, at least temporarily, the order of nature. Nor, it should be emphasized, was this restoration effected by a renunciation of the body. Donne's famous lines on the body of Elizabeth are more than a passing flash of metaphysical wit; if anything, the *Second Anniversary* broods more upon her body than upon her soul. "Shee, whose faire body no such prison was" (l. 221), brought back into nature that harmony of body and soul, the disruption of which was one of the chief consequences of the Fall. It is too seldom noted that, for all its castigation of the sinful flesh, the *Second Anniversary* concludes with the resurrection of the body rather than with the immortality of the soul. In explaining his famous comparison of the body to a prison, St. Augustine says, "Our body too might be said to be a prison, not because it is a prison which God hath made, but because it is under punishment and liable to death . . . If then the flesh is a prison to thee, it is not the body that is thy prison, but the corruption of thy body. For God made the body good.

. . ."[12] Surely the same explanation fits Donne's *Anniversaries.* While rejecting the corruption of the world, he affirms its ultimate goodness.

This affirmation of the natural order, however, extends ultimately to an acceptance of, a submission to death itself. It is a Christian attitude, having nothing to do with Stoic resignation nor with the death wish, and it is an attitude which is present in all Christian celebration. The death of Christ is greeted with a mourning but not with a rejection; at last it must be embraced and assented to, not simply as an act on the part of Christ, but as an act in which Christians participate. The same is true in all Christian funerals, which reflect the view that death is not a meaningless surrender but a free act of the will. This positive assent to an order of which death is a strangely essential part is one of the strongest emphases of the *Second Anniversary.*

The principal means by which celebration and festivity manifest and express themselves is song or poetry. While there may be poetry which is not celebratory, there is no celebration without poetry, public poetry of commemoration, joy, and praise. We recall at once the last seven poems of the Book of Psalms, the Olympian Odes of Pindar, the chants, litanies, and hymns which contribute to the Sunday celebration of the resurrected Christ. Or we might recall, as did Donne several times in his sermons, the songs of Deborah and Moses upon occasions of God's deliverance of his people.[13] Donne's own consciousness of his role as celebrant singer is most strikingly manifested at the end of the *First Anniversary,* in a passage which, at the same time, shows an awareness of all the aspects of celebration which I have treated here—if one accepts joy as being implicit in praise:

> And you her creatures, whom she workes upon
> And have your last, and best concoction
> From her example, and her vertue, if you
> In reverence to her, doe thinke it due,
> That no one should her prayses thus reherse,
> As matter fit for Chronicle, not verse,
> Vouchsafe to call to minde, that God did make
> A last, and lastingst peece, a song. He spake
> To Moses, to deliver unto all,
> That song: because he knew they would let fall,
> The Law, the Prophets, and the History,
> But keepe the song still in their memory.   (ll. 455-466)

Donne does not exactly presume to compare his poetry with that of Moses, and he modestly qualifies the comparison in the next two lines: "Such an opinion (in due measure) made / Me this great Office boldly to invade." Nevertheless, if Donne's great poems are to be classified by genre and tradition, they may best be regarded as celebratory and festive. It is a high and ambitious genre, always written in high, even extravagant, style and on the grand scale. Donne's poems in their own unique fashion meet these lofty demands.

DONNE'S TIMELESS ANNIVERSARIES

Carol M. Sicherman

Yeats told Anne Gregory that only God could love her for herself alone, and not her yellow hair. Literary scholars tell us that we can never know, or begin to know, rich poems of a past era unless we first learn as much as possible about their historical milieu, and even then we can't know the poems "for themselves." But need we in fact take the hair and leave the girl, take the history and leave the whole poem? If we learn the golden sayings of literary historians, is it then so hubristic to read the poems—Donne's *Anniversaries,* in this case—for themselves alone? Perhaps it is not impossible to have our cake and eat it too, to love both the essential Anne and her yellow hair, to read the *Anniversaries* with that "historical sense . . . of the timeless and of the temporal together" of which Eliot speaks in "Tradition and the Individual Talent."[1]

What would happen if we read Donne's *Anniversaries* in learned ignorance? What would happen if we took as a *donnée* the knowledge of the "temporal" aspects of the poems provided by scholars in recent years, and if we concentrated our attention on the "timeless" *Anniversaries,* pushing hard at the imperfectly resolved questions of the poems' coherence and meaning, knowing about, yet unsatisfied by, previous interpretations? The present essay is an attempt to show at least some of the things that could happen. These happenings may contain answers complementary to those offered by other writers, may cause modification of conclusions reached through more directly historical readings.

The scholars whose works are in one way or another implicit in this essay all imitate Donne's "Anatomy of the World" in their method and assumptions.[2] When Donne complains that this present world is pocky and bumpy, he compares it with an unblemished sphere of perfection, a perfect body. When these scholars analyze the historical context of the *Anniversaries* —whether in terms of the genre(s) to which the poems belong, or in terms of various currents of intellectual history—they imply an ideal model to which they compare Donne's poems. As "this whole world" in the poems is an imperfect and distorted copy of the ideal world, so the poems themselves are seen as imperfect realizations of scepticism, or of religious meditations, or of the elegiac mode; or else the poems are distorted by the critic to make them into perfect realizations. No one, even the most admiring

Reprinted from *University of Toronto Quarterly,* 39 (1970), 127-43, by permission of the author and the publisher, University of Toronto Press.

lover, has succeeded in loving the *Anniversaries* for themselves alone. As such love is my present aim, I must avoid paying two distracting tributes, one to Donne and the other to his past admirers: unwitting emulation of Donne's own model, and syncretic analysis which gets no farther than the commendable contributions made by past explorers of the poems. The tribute I mean to pay is simpler: response to the strange stimulation Donne offers, and analysis, clarification, and explanation of that response.

Donne's two long poems occasioned by the death of Elizabeth Drury form a single argument, a single poem. The two parts of the poem relate to each other as draft to revision, as problem to tentative solution. Like many of Donne's divine poems, the *Anniversaries* show us a speaker debating with himself, a speaker who craves a calm and full resolution of his spiritual vacillations—and who achieves at best a willed and implicitly temporary cessation of his inner strife.

The antagonists in the battle, separate yet fatally linked, are secular Donne and holy Donne, body and soul, reason and faith, or (to quote the subtitle to *The Second Anniversarie*) "this life and . . . the next";[3] all these pairs, and more like them, clash in the *Anniversaries*. The critic-referee has a difficult job in adjudicating the winner in poems like these; only the Last Judgment can settle the score indisputably. In some of Donne's most successful divine poems—successful both as art and as attainments of decision —paradox alone can provide a conclusion:

> for I
> Except you'enthrall mee, never shall be free,
> Nor ever chast, except you ravish mee.[4]

Transcending reason, Donne attains the certainty of faith, but the denial of reason fails ultimately to satisfy so rational a man; victory is temporary.

In its 1002 lines the poem of the *Anniversaries* is the most extended version of Donne's battle with himself;[5] to call the speaker "Donne" is not merely a convenience but a reasonable conjecture. Again and again in other of Donne's poems we have heard this voice, arguing, confessing, proclaiming, searching: above all, searching. In *The First Anniversarie* Donne is searching not so much for an answer as for a question; confusion and inconsistency increase until at last he emerges into the realization upon which the second poem is founded, that this world "is not worth a thought" (*PS*, 1. 83). Considered as an effort to reach intellectual clarity concerning his world and his place in that world, the poem fails—that, *ex post facto,* is Donne's point, and Louis Martz's,[6] yet whatever the poet-speaker's original idea of success may have been, the poem succeeds artistically, in two ways. First, as a separate poem it succeeds simply as an eloquent expression of the anguished discovery of failure. Second, as half of a diptych, its culminating discovery enables its sequel to attain a better balance of intellect and emotion, to attain the ultimate insights which unify the entire bipartite poem.

"The Progres of the Soule"—to give *The Second Anniversarie* its significant title—shows Donne by an act of will refusing to think about the world he still occupies and, at least for the moment, finally succeeding in achieving that certainty expressed in the paradox of Holy Sonnet XIV. In the *Anniversaries*, as in all of Donne's religious poetry, the claims of this and the other world cannot be reconciled, unlike the harmony of body and soul sometimes attained in his secular poems. Donne wrote no divine "Exstasie," no religious reconciliation of body and soul; in "The Progres" he tells his soul that the best thing she can do is to remain outside the body in her "extasee, / And meditation of what thou shalt bee" (ll. 321-2). But before she can do that, she must understand by "earthly thoughts" (l. 323) what she now is on earth; the *Anniversaries* are those "earthly thoughts."

In the first poem, Donne attempts to find a meaning, a justification for life on earth, by performing "An Anatomy of the World." By the end of the poem he has discovered that he must break off the anatomy; if he continues, "the worlds carcasse would not last," would instead rot (l. 439). His analysis has reduced the world from a "lame . . . cripple" to an "ugly . . . monster" to a "wan . . . Ghost" to, finally, a "drie . . . Cinder" (ll. 238, 326, 370, 428). Lifeless, the world holds no meaning for our life, a negative conclusion which reveals itself gradually. At the opening of the poem Donne grants no more than that the world is "sicke . . . in a Letargee" (ll. 23-4), and only after much strained argument does he admit the reduction from cripple to cinder, from sickness to death. This reduction—one cannot speak of a development, for Donne's stubborn confusions persist until nearly the end—can be traced; but first a word about Elizabeth Drury, sponsor of the *Anniversaries*.

The titles of the two poems clearly inform us that Elizabeth Drury's "untimely death," her "religious death," provided the "occasion" for Donne to represent "the frailty and the decay of this whole world" and to contemplate "the incommodities of the soule in this life and her exaltation in the next." Most readers today agree that Elizabeth Drury is merely the "occasion," not truly the subject, of the poem. Many elegiac elements are of course present in the poem, but other possible, indeed expectable, elegiac topics are either slighted or entirely omitted: her virginity, her youth, the grief of her parents and close friends[7]—in short, incentives for and expressions of personal sorrow. Similarly, if one compares the praise accorded the "she" of the *Anniversaries* with Donne's compliments in verse letters to ladies, one finds many parallels in metaphor and conceit,[8] yet parallels which militate against a particularly personal reading of the memorial. Donne himself knew the problems of conventions: "But these" metaphors (he remarks in concluding a letter to Lady Bedford) "Tast of Poëtique rage, or flattery, / And need not, where all hearts one truth professe"—and so he stops, for he knows that "Oft from new proofes, and new phrase, new doubts grow . . ."[9] Precisely; and where Donne stops in writing to Lady Bedford he starts in writing of his "impossible shee,"[10] filling the *Anniversaries* with new proofs and phrases. New doubts, necessarily, grow.

If "she" is not, centrally, Elizabeth Drury, who then is she? At the start

Donne himself—it might be clearer here to say the speaker himself—does not know who "she" is. All he knows is that something—"she"—is gone, something which when present gave life meaning, which "defin'd" the world and gave it "forme and frame" (AW, l. 37). The hypnotic repetition of "she," especially in the "refrains,"[11] anaesthetizes both speaker and reader into temporary suspension of the demand to know who "she" is, but the demand remains, for both reader and speaker. Under the cover of pronominal hypnosis or anaesthesia, Donne makes in the "Anatomy" a series of attempts to discover her identity, attempts rendered all the more difficult by his initial hypothesis that her very name is lost, and with her name, her meaning. For he tells the world, "Thou hast forgot thy name" (AW, l. 31).

The world to whom Donne speaks is his world, is himself, notwithstanding his use of "thou." In both the "Anatomy" and "The Progres" Donne imagines a listener—the world in the first poem, his soul in the second, "she" at times in both poems—but throughout he himself is the person addressed. The poems are interior debates, debates with shifting personae, as Donne tries on mask after mask in order to find one that fits. If the world's name and meaning are lost, so are Donne's; he searches for a central stability, for an immutable relationship. The repeated metaphors of glue, cement, and magnet attest to his effort to recover his lost sense of relation.

For his definition of the world's definer and for his description of what is left after her departure, Donne needs words; he needs metaphors. Much of the "Anatomy" consists of attempts to find metaphors adequate to Donne's meaning. The metaphors of carcasses and embalming that the poem shares with Donne's complimentary addresses to ladies, most prominent in "the entrie into the worke," fade out as the poem goes on: they are discarded, unable to carry Donne's meaning. The trouble—and it is a trouble both to Donne and to us his readers—is that much of the time he is uncertain of his meaning. The major opening metaphor of sickness shows him reluctant to accept the fact that "she" is gone absolutely from the world, that she is dead. The world bleeds away its "strongest vitall spirits"; its consumption turns to a fever; it feels a wound; it is "sicke . . . , yea dead, yea putrified" (AW, ll. 12-56). "Yet"—and the "yet" reflects not rational demonstration but simple assertion—"there's a kind of world remaining still," a "new world" with "new creatures" brought into being by "the twi-light of her memory" (ll. 69, 67, 74-6).

Here, towards the end of the introductory section, Donne announces both the governing metaphor of the anatomy and the source of the knowledge which enables him to perform the anatomy. He knows what he knows because he remembers what he has lost. Recalling that lost "she," he can enlighten the world as to its past and present conditions. Memory is the metaphor which provides the ostensible mode of the "Anatomy of the World," the means by which Donne expects at the start to arrive at his definition.[12] In losing "that rich soule" the world has lost its "sense and memory," forgotten its name (ll. 1, 28, 31). Donne will repair the omission; he will tell the new world that its name is still "she," for "her virtue" affords

"the matter and the stuffe of this" new world (ll. 77–8). He will, furthermore, prudently inform the new world about the old; knowledge of the evil
past will forestall its reenactment.

But this desperate fiction of a new world peopled by "so many weedlesse
Paradises" (l. 82) breaks down no sooner than it is erected. By an exercise
of memory, so the hypothesis goes, Donne will dissect the old world's
"infirmities" (l. 65). Grammatical logic requires the past tense, yet Donne
begins the anatomy proper in the present: "There is no health . . ." (l. 91).
Clearly the present world is continuous with the past: Donne is not remembering; he is looking at his present surroundings, his present condition. His
first trial metaphor has burst, allowing the hot air of optimism to escape
while the sick putrefaction remains. He forgets the "new world" but remembers in his later metaphors "this worlds generall sickenesse" (l. 240).[13] Man
and his world are helplessly deformed. The idea of physical, intellectual, and
spiritual disintegration, felt not as argument but as fact, dominates the rest
of the poem.

We see soon enough that the present is but an intensification of the past.
"Almost created lame," the world did "from the first houre decay," and
today "freely men confesse, that this world's spent" (ll. 192, 201, 209).
"This is the worlds condition now," Donne says (l. 219), and all he can
think to do is to rehearse more sensuously than before the lost perfections
of that "she" whom he celebrates, that Platonic "originall / Of all faire
copies," that macrocosm of our self-distorted "Microcosme" (ll. 227–8,
236). Instead of recreating in her image a rich and spicy paradise, we seek
new worlds in an effort that Donne mocks as a foolish misdirection of
"mans wit" (l. 207).

Donne's own wit turns to sour mockery frequently in the "Anatomy":

> We seeme ambitious, Gods whole worke t'undoe;
> Of nothing he made us, and we strive too,
> To bring our selves to nothing backe . . . (ll. 155–7)

He makes hectic jokes on stale subjects—"that first marriage" of Adam and
Eve

> was our funerall:
> One woman at one blow, then kill'd us all,
> And singly, one by one, they kill us now.
> We doe delightfully our selves allow
> To that consumption; and profusely blinde,
> We kill our selves, to propagate our kinde. (ll. 105–10)

—and breaks off in contempt: "And yet we doe not that; we are not men:
/ There is not now that mankinde, which was then" in the heroic days
when there were giants in the earth.[14] Sardonic, contemptuous, Donne
measures man's presumptuous intellect and finds it worth but a hollow
laugh:

> For of Meridians, and Parallels,
> Man hath weav'd out a net . . .
> We spur, we raine the stars, and in their race
> They're diversly content t'obey our pace. (ll. 278-9, 283-4)

The sound, bitter and dismissive, is the laugh of a man beyond hope.
Donne has, after all, found no replacement for the abandoned metaphor
of a new world; looking backward has only forced his eyes to look more
closely—and, inevitably, more despairingly—at the present. By the end of
the "Anatomy," even the once beautiful if obscure metaphor of the dead
"she" has become tainted.[15] She who earlier was the mint from which
"that rich Indie" derived its gold (l. 233) is at the end no more than the
gilding which prettifies sinful men. In the final "eulogy," Donne's accumulated bitter futility breaks out in a tirade of intensifying disgust; thanks
to her, he says with shocking contempt,

> some Princes have some temperance;
> Some Counsaylors some purpose to advance
> The common profite; and some people have
> Some stay, no more then Kings should give, to crave;
> Some women have some taciturnity;
> Some Nunneries, some graines of chastity. (ll. 419-24)

The purest are almost entirely corrupt.

Donne has written himself into a corner. Attempting to teach and con-
sole himself and all who remain in that "kind of world" which is our world,
he has learned only "how drie a Cinder this world is" and

> That 'tis in vaine to dew, or mollifie
> It with thy Teares, or Sweat, or Bloud: no thing
> Is worth our travaile, griefe, or perishing,
> But those rich ioyes, which did possesse her hart,
> Of which shee's now partaker, and a part. (ll. 428, 430-4)

What then can Donne do? He can write himself out of his corner. He can
reaffirm that she is still herself, still that image of perfection, still that

> blessed maid,
> Of whom is meant what ever hath beene said,
> Or shall be spoken well by any tongue,
> Whose name refines course lines, and makes prose song . . .
>   (ll. 443-6)

He can perceive that, like the world he was questioning, his queries were
impotent, misdirected. He can proclaim that "our body's as the wombe"
of the soul and that death is really the soul's "second birth" (ll. 450-3). He
can now recognize that the only consolation for past loss is future gain:
the proper mode for celebration is prophecy, not memory. And so, having
come to these realizations, Donne ends by seeing himself as a Moses about

to sing the Lord's word to his people—about to sing "The Progres of the Soule." Donne has at last found his subject; the light wit of the concluding lines (the parenthetical "in due measure"; the joke about "trying to emprison her") shows a poise achieved by, and achievable only by, the preceding 442 wavering, painful, and purgative lines. Now he can begin.

Early in "the entrance" to "The Progres," Donne makes his changed tone apparent. No longer does he picture the world as a man afflicted by sickness; instead the world is like "a beheaded man," "Red seas" of blood running from his trunk and head, his eyes twinkling, his tongue rolling, his hands and feet jerking convulsively (*PS*, ll. 9-15). Donne focuses in the second poem not on the world *per se* but on its end, on that Pauline moment when "in the twinkling of an eye . . . we shall be changed" (1 Cor. 15:52). The violent assurance of the opening is characteristic of "The Progres," in which the grotesque and the surrealistic suit the supranatural journey of the soul. Having found his metaphors and his meaning, Donne can easily describe Beauty as a flowing face or "her . . . growen all Ey" (ll. 397, 200). This is not that playing with images which we saw in the "Anatomy"; there are no more uneasy jokes in "The Progres."

From the start of the second poem, Donne knows what he has to say, and his tone becomes increasingly confident. The timid, vague advice of the "Anatomy"—"Be more then man" (l. 190)—modulates, as "The Progres" proceeds, to urgent encouragement: "Up, up, my drowsie soule" (*PS*, l. 339). After a casual allusion to the old metaphor of memory ("All have forgot all good, / Forgetting her," ll. 28-9), Donne turns the anxious complaint of the "Anatomy" that the world has forgotten its soul into a command to his own soul to "forget this rotten world" (l. 49). Abandoning his earlier metaphor of her memory acting as the world's preservative,[16] Donne counsels his soul to lump past and present together: "Let thine owne times as an old story be," adding ironically: "Men thus lethargique have best Memory" (ll. 50, 64). Lethargy, in the "Anatomy" a sick condition impeding recognition of the world's very name, is seen now as a convenient assistant in forgetting the world.

Because he has lost all desire for an accommodation with the world, Donne rejects his former attempts to define it. His assumption now is that "this world . . . is not worth a thought" (ll. 82-3). With a strong anti-intellectual thrust, "The Progres" urges upon the soul the irrelevance of all earthly knowledge: "study not why, nor whan; / Do not so much, as not beleeve a man" (ll. 51-2). There is no need to recall the history of man, to trace (as the "Anatomy" traces) his physical and spiritual diminution since the world's "first houre" (*AW*, l. 201); man's present state is deterrent enough.

"The entrance" (ll. 1-44) and the first section (ll. 45-84) of "The Progres" constitute a direct reply to the "Anatomy" and a forecast of what is to come. Even in the necessary and somewhat inconsistent formalities of "the entrance" Donne's mastery of a new tonal complexity can be heard. His

tone now has that blend of wit and solemnity that characterizes the best
of his shorter poems. He can not only make the "immortal Mayd" act as
father to his muse, bringing forth each year a hymn (him); but he can maintain the metaphor in decency and unite it with the most solemn evocation
of the Last Judgment, praying that "These Hymns thy issue, may encrease
so long, / As till Gods great Venite change the song" (ll. 43-4).

Control such as this enables Donne to make the transition from the
"Anatomy" to "The Progres." The turn from the first to the second poem
occurs sixty-five lines into "The Progres," as Donne makes explicit and
emphatic the advice which had been so cautiously offered in the "Anatomy":
"Looke upward; that's towards her, whose happy state / We now lament
not, but congratulate" (ll. 65-6). Now that we understand the subject,
thanks to the explorations of the "Anatomy," we can properly "celebrate"
her "rich soule," as the first poem asked us to do (AW, ll. 1-2). Section I
of the second poem brings the first to an end by using the familiar formula
of the "morals" or "refraine" of the "Anatomy." The only section of "The
Progres" to preserve the full structural formula of the "Anatomy,"[17] it provides the world's quietus: the "Cinder" of the "Anatomy" has disintegrated
to "fragmentary rubbidge," and the world can be put aside as irrelevant
(PS, ll. 81-4).

At the same time that he is concluding the movement of the "Anatomy,"
Donne is establishing the direction of "The Progres." Whereas to perform
the anatomy he had to look around him, in order to perceive the ascent
of the soul he has to "looke upward" (l. 65). The discouraged, confused,
sometimes hectic meditations of the "Anatomy" have been silenced; now
we hear a man who knows what he is about and who conveys his hortatory
assurance through insistent imperatives and loaded rhetorical questions.
Donne now knows his soul has great powers; he teaches us what the soul
can do, not (as in the "Anatomy") what feeble man cannot do. The "glimmering light" of "her Ghost," which lit the "Anatomy" (l. 70), Donne now
perceives as emanating directly from heaven. We see it only at the end of
our earthly existence, when Death comes like a groom bearing "a Taper . . .
a little glimmering light" (PS, ll. 86-7). In the first poem we groped about
in "the twi-light of her memory" (AW, l. 74); now we follow the light of
Death's taper, eager for him to "usher, and unlocke the doore" to the full
light of heaven (PS, l. 156).

Taking for granted the knowledge analytically achieved in the "Anatomy"
(the world is "fragmentary rubbidge . . . not worth a thought"), Donne
bases "The Progres" on knowledge intuitively attained. "In this low forme"
—the form of its body and its form in the school of life—Donne's "poore
soule" can do nothing, so long as it adheres to "this Pedantery, / Of being
taught by sense, and Fantasy" (ll. 290-2). In heaven, he assures his soul,
knowledge is immediate, intuitive:

> Thou shalt not peepe through lattices of eies,
> Nor heare through Laberinths of eares, nor learne

> By circuit, or colections to discerne.
> In Heaven thou straight know'st all, concerning it,
> And what concerns it not, shall straight forget. (ll. 296-300)

True, only "shee, / Shee who all Libraries had throughly red / At home, in her owne thoughts," could, while still on earth, grow "in th'Art of knowing Heaven . . . to such perfection" that actually coming to heaven was but to "read the same" (ll. 302-14). Yet we can imitate her, exchanging "earthly thoughts" (l. 323) for an imaginative anticipation of our life in heaven. We can extend our soul in an "extasee, / And meditation" (ll. 321-2) of its future state until we picture it traveling to heaven, quite without earthly "desire to know" about earthly matters such as the scientific questions bothering Donne's contemporaries, and arriving with incomprehensible speed at the bright room of heaven (ll. 185-218). "Thinke . . . thinke . . . thinke," Donne insists, reiterating the command thirty-three times in a hundred lines,[18] and the culmination of thought will be the annihilation of thought, when the soul will at last take its "long-short Progresse" "twixt Heaven, and Earth" (ll. 219, 189).

But we have not yet "chang'd our roome"; we remain in "our living Tombe / Oppress'd with ignorance" (ll. 251-3). Having described the perfection of our future knowledge, Donne pauses to consider our present ignorance. In the "Anatomy" he had dwelt with contempt upon man's pretended knowledge and actual ignorance of the world. That topic is at best peripheral, he now realizes; the central, the pitiful ignorance, is man's ignorance of himself. Not only is man ignorant of his spiritual nature (ll. 257-60), but he is "to[o] narrow . . . to comprehend" his body, the mere physical details of his being (ll. 261-3). And if "wee / Know not the least things, which for our use bee," how can we hope "to know our selves" (ll. 279-80)? If the knower knows not himself, how can he know other men, know "what Caesar did, yea, and what Cicero said" (l. 287)?

What is true of intellectual activity is true as well of social activity. "The cheefest parts" of society are corrupt—the court, of course, but also God's ministers who, Donne scornfully says, "Drinke and sucke in th'Instructions of Great men, / And for the word of God, vent them again" (ll. 336, 329-30). "The poyson of sinne" infects society as much as it does "this poore unlittered whelpe / My body" (ll. 338, 165): formidable evidence leads Donne once again to urge his soul to join the fulfilled hosts in heaven. More exultant and assured still, he has performed the earlier demand to "thinke," and now can command: "Up, up . . . up . . . up" (ll. 339-56).

The upward movement cannot by definition be completed in the poem, for Donne is still on earth. He returns necessarily, after explaining how her just acts "made her a soveraigne state, religion / Made her a Church," once more to compare this life and our expectations in the next: "But pause, My soule, and study" essential joy (ll. 374-5, 383). Again Donne raises a question concerning knowledge; again he treats the problem through rhetorical questions; again he pities the soul, "poor couse'ned cose'nor" (l. 391). This

time Donne considers the two most laudable focuses of earthly love: "Beauty
worthyest is to move . . . Honour may have pretense unto our love" (ll. 390,
401). If essential joy is attainable on earth, it will be attained through love
of beauty and honour. But beauty, Donne shows, in a remote and errie image,
is transitory:

> that she, and that thou,
> Which did begin to love, are neither now.
> You are both fluid, chang'd since yesterday;
> Next day repaires, (but ill) last daies decay.
> Nor are, (Although the river keep the name)
> Yesterdaies waters, and to daies the same.
> So flowes her face, and thine eies . . . (ll. 391-7)

As an observer of the earthly scene, Donne is already far up the "watch-
towre" (l. 294); this vision, though not divinely intuitive, does not come
through "lattices of eies." At the start of "The Progres," while still trying
to break away from the barren mood of the "Anatomy," Donne saw decay
as violent; he saw a dead and maggoty world struggling "in corruption"
(ll. 21-2).[19] Having proceeded imaginatively up, up to heaven, Donne from
his new distance can calmly watch the beauty of fluid dissolution. Yet
dissolution it remains, and both lover and beloved beauty "are howrely in
inconstancee" (l. 400). Honour, too, proves illusory, subject to that "rise,
and fall, to more and lesse" that characterizes all earthly things (l. 411).
All happiness on earth is "casuall" or "accidentall"; none is "essentiall"
(ll. 412, 384).

But Donne has still not given earth its due; he must explore one last possibility of earthly happiness. Having considered essential joy he must fulfill
his promise to "study . . . accidentall ioyes" (ll. 383-4). He first admits that
we partake on earth of accidental or casual joys. Immediately rhetorical questions prick the bubble:

> What should the Nature change? Or make the same
> Certaine, which was but casuall, when it came?
> All casuall ioye doth loud and plainly say,
> Onely by comming, that it can away. (ll. 483-6)

Again, the only assurance lies in heaven, where, paradoxically, "accidentall
things are permanent" (l. 488).

And so, having exhausted his angry dismay at earthly failure and having
surveyed the possibilities of mortal happiness, Donne concludes his *Anniversaries* with an address to the "Immortall Maid" (l. 516), an address which,
like the opening appeal, combines wit and solemnity. He plays with the idea
of invoking her name—for he writes from France, where "mis-devotion"
allows such invocation—but decides against it: she herself would reject his
poem, his "second yeeres true Rent," were it dedicated to any name other
"then his, / That gave thee power to doe, me, to say this" (ll. 511, 520-2).
Her name is never once uttered; as all vestiges of the occasion of the poem

disappear, it is her Idea which becomes "for life, and death, a patterne" (l. 524), a pattern which God has commanded Donne to make known: "Thou art the Proclamation; and I ame / The Trumpet, at whose voice the people came" (ll. 527-8).

The quiet triumph of this conclusion proceeds from Donne's discovery of his own meaning, which is the discovery of hers. He now knows who she is and thereby knows who he is, for she is that cohesive force which makes him spiritually whole. Donne has solved the problem which partly caused, partly resulted from his confusions in the "Anatomy." In the first poem Donne tries to relate "that rich soule which to her Heaven is gone" to the world (l. 1); she is to be the "glue" for the broken world, the preserving balm, the "Magnetique force" (ll. 50, 57, 221). But absolute perfection cannot be linked unaffected with rotting sin. "That rich soule" was bound to seem tained, and in Donne's last attempt to speak her eulogy the taint became manifest: she, "though she could not transubstantiate / All states to gold, yet guilded every state" (AW, ll. 417-18). She had been asked to serve as a last desperate resort, but this world is seen to be beyond last resorts. This glue would not, could not stick; her influence fails because the world is incapable of receiving it. The metaphor itself has come apart, imitating the world it describes.

In "The Progres" the metaphor has been made whole by being made separate from the corrupt world. Possibly Donne had not distinguished, at the start of his enterprise, between hyperbolic praise (like the grand assertion of "The Sunne Rising": "She is all States") and metaphoric representation of an ideal. Such confusion had been banished when he came to pay his "second yeeres true Rent."[20] In The Second Anniversarie Donne allies her with "some Figure of the Golden times," Astraea, the personification of justice (l. 70). He declares that "shee was the forme" of the world (l. 72); that to her "person Paradise adhear'd" (l. 77); that she was perfectly proportioned in every respect (ll. 123-42); that her body was so fit a vehicle for her perfect soul "that one might almost say, her bodie thought" (l. 246); that she encompassed all the virtues of both an ideal "soveraigne state" and "a Church; and these two made her All" (ll. 374-5); that she enjoyed so much of heavenly essential joy on earth that she "made this world in some proportion / A heaven" (ll. 468-9); finally that, on arriving in heaven, she performed the miracle of "making full perfection grow" (l. 507).

To effect this revelation of the "blessed maid" as a thoroughgoing symbol of spiritual perfection, Donne had to sever her connection with an actual dead girl, to make it plain that the death of Elizabeth Drury was but the occasion for the poem. This he does, as we have seen, partly by simple denial: name-dropping, he does not dwell on the topics necessary to an orthodox memorial poem devoted to Elizabeth Drury. His chief positive method of making the "maid" represent all-encompassing spiritual perfection is through using increasingly abstract and conceptual vocabulary in the "eulogies." In the passage describing her as a state, for example, we hear that "reson . . . rectifie[d] her will," that "shee made peace" where "beauty and chastity to-

gether kisse," that "shee did high iustice" and "gave pardons" and "protec-
tions" (ll. 361-71). In these lines Donne makes her serve perfectly as a metaphor for ideal self-control.[21]

The revelation of the significance of "she" is gradual; the abstraction of
the diction proceeds as Donne discovers or unfolds her meaning through
the *Anniversaries*. The measure of his ultimate achievement of consistency
appears if we compare passages in the two poems which apparently deal
with the same subject and which use similar vocabulary. In the "Anatomy,"
Donne eulogizes the "best, and first originall / Of all faire copies; and the
generall / Steward to Fate" (ll. 227-9)—certainly an abstract statement, and
very much like the abstractions in the second poem. He then continues:

> shee whose rich eyes, and brest,
> Guilt the West Indies, and perfum'd the East;
> Whose having breath'd in this world, did bestow
> Spice on those Isles, and bad them still smell so,
> And that rich Indie which doth gold interre,
> Is but as single money, coyn'd from her:
> She to whom this world must it selfe refer,
> As Suburbs, or the Microcosme of her,
> Shee, shee is dead . . . (ll. 229-37)

Sensuously breathing perfume over the world, she is still physical, the metro-
polis or macrocosm to our still earthly suburbs or microcosm. In "The
Progres" she has become far more abstract:

> Shee, in whose body (if wee dare prefer
> This low world, to so high a mark, as shee,)
> The Westerne treasure, Esterne spiceree,
> Europe, and Afrique, and the unknowen rest
> Were easily found, or what in them was best . . .
> Shee, of whose soule, if we may say, t'was Gold,
> Her body was th'Electrum, and did hold
> Many degrees of that; we understood
> Her by her sight, her pure and eloquent blood
> Spoke in her cheekes, and so distinckly wrought,
> That one might almost say, her bodie thought,
> Shee, shee, thus richly, and largely hous'd, is gone . . .
> (ll. 226-30, 241-7)

She is such that, while still on earth, she could be intuitively apprehended,
understood without words, her body a perfect symbol of her soul. Donne
has conquered the problem of describing her physically by making her
physical appearance entirely symbolic, for she "is not such as the rest" of
us on earth (l. 500). Inconsistencies such as the over sensuous spicy scent
of the "Anatomy," which like the imagery of carcasses and balm may betray
the poem's occasion, vanish in "The Progres," which has moved as far from
the historical Elizabeth Drury as the soul does from the carcass.

Finding his metaphor, Donne finds his subject, his meaning. His harmony with his subject in "The Progres" is the perfect relation of singer to song; the poem he makes conveys her meaning. No longer does he speak of her verse as enrolling her fame, as he does at the end of the first poem; rather he sees himself as the mere but essential means to relate her vital message, the instrument making audible the music of her "Proclamation."

Earthbound, we need Donne's explication. His thoroughly achieved metaphor is when most inclusive also most abstract. "Shee's now a part both of the Quire, and Song," "partaker, and a part" of heavenly joy (*AW*, ll. 10, 434). The paradoxes increase with the growing abstraction of the second poem: she has gone to heaven, "where shee receives, and gives addition," where she will "as well . . . enioy, as get perfectione," where she meets "such a full, and such a filling good" as "essentiall ioye," joy which is "both the obiect, and the wit" (*PS*, ll. 510, 318, 442-5). Donne has perceived her supernatural perfection, her Yeatsian unity of the abstract and the concrete. He has answered Yeats's question, "How can we know the dancer from the dance?" In heaven we cannot know, for there is no difference: she is both at once, "a part both of the Quire, and the Song." Here on earth we can at least attempt to understand the separate parts, although their whole remains an inexplicable mystery. Donne interprets for us that embodied and comprehensive perfection he discerned while meditating upon the "untimely" and "religious death of Mistris Elizabeth Drury." We do our part by listening, for he is "the Trumpet, at whose voice the people came."

"ESSENTIALL JOYE" IN DONNE'S ANNIVERSARIES

P. G. Stanwood

The Anniversary poems of John Donne are at once the longest and the most complex and elusive of his poetic works. A judge usually so perceptive as Ben Jonson thought that they might properly be about the Blessed Virgin Mary but instead unfortunately described Elizabeth Drury, who could hardly be worthy of such effusive compliment. Jonson is reported to have said "that Dones Anniversarie was profane and full of Blasphemies."[1] The *Anniversaries*, indeed, still trouble readers who search too far for historical, allegorical, structural, or secular meaning without understanding enough of their devotional significance. Of course, these are poems with various concerns and numerous confusions, but above all else they give triumphant expression to God's glory and to the art of verse.[2] Here is a single ambition with a "divine" end—to celebrate God's grace and His glory by means of the verse which itself is the offspring of the very grace being celebrated.

My wish is to explore the essentially religious and Christian quality of the *Anniversaries,* and especially their teaching about grace, a term which I use in its theological sense, particularly to indicate "sanctifying," rather than "actual" grace. The latter is a passing help for the production of some good act, but sanctifying grace is a permanent quality inhering in the soul. It is "the reality produced in man by God's creative love . . . [and] the result of the gracious love of God . . . received by man as a favor or free gift."[3] Man's redemption and salvation depend upon the sacramental life made possible by the Incarnation; for God through Christ restores man to his original state by His Passion and Resurrection, and God thus makes the free offering of grace. The *Anniversaries* likewise reveal the same bounteous gift of grace by their redeeming of time. By this I mean that they mediate for God on behalf of Christ, with the poet himself acting a priestly office by turning his poetry and himself into a holy sacrifice, into which and out of which grace may flow. Donne's language is often oblique, for it tries to express the ineffable; but we must, at the last, know the faith which the poet has declared is possible for us to have by means of grace. Like Elizabeth Drury, we, too, must let our bodies think.

Although Donne's *Anniversaries* are poems of meditation in the way that Louis L. Martz has shown, they are also poems of vision, giving them a special

Reprinted from *Texas Studies in Literature and Language*, 13 (1971), 227-38, by permission of the author and the publisher, University of Texas Press.

kinship with the work of such later poets as Yeats and Eliot. The traditional patterns of prayer, however, of the sort that evidently inspired the structure of the *Anniversaries*, appear only tentatively in such modern poets. Poetry of meditation becomes something freer in them, though no less rigorous an exercise in introspection. Yet even poetry like the *Anniversaries*, while remaining "Ignatian," certainly cannot be defined by its formal structure, for its external plan both encloses and releases its inner movement, that "interior drama of the mind" that produces an action leading to the consciousness of a moment of illumination.[4] Such inner and progressive movement leads to and overtakes the climax and so lets our appreciation of extrinsic form disappear into a higher wisdom. And it is this illumination itself, rather than the formal means for disclosing it, that underlies my theme.

I

The narrative voice of the *Anniversaries* searches for colorful, strident and dramatic tones. Above all, the *Anniversaries* are allegedly about someone, the person of Elizabeth Drury being always plainly before us (although she is never actually named). Yet few readers have been content to take Donne at his literal word. Surely Elizabeth Drury, a young girl whom Donne never knew, cannot be herself but rather an emblem for Queen Elizabeth, or for the Blessed Virgin, or for Justice and Truth and Divine Wisdom. O. B. Hardison, Jr., is close to the best sense when he says that "she is a virtuous young woman concerning whom Donne had received 'good report' and whom he undertook to celebrate in two elegies based on traditional topics and images."[5] While Hardison is right in appreciating the relationship of Elizabeth Drury to Renaissance epideictic theory, and consequently in recognizing that Donne meant us to take her historically and not as a *figura* of the *logos* or of anything else, he inadequately characterizes Elizabeth's full role in the poems.

Elizabeth Drury remains herself—she is not allegorical. But Donne does use her in order to describe the life of grace in its fullness and in its withdrawal. The world is a carcass for the anatomist to dissect and Donne's autopsy has shown foul disease in the old world that Elizabeth had inhabited; that world which only Elizabeth could keep alive is dead with her own death. She had provided sweetness and joy when in the world, though she herself was not altogether free of its corruption (for it was, after all, fatal): "Shee, shee embrac'd a sicknesse, gave it meat, / The purest Blood, and Breath, that ere it eat" gives testimony of the disease (*The Second Anniversary. Of The Progres of the Soule*, ll. 147-148).[6] Donne thus gives report of the world uninformed by grace. Having once been so lavishly embodied in Elizabeth Drury, grace retired with her, and now that it is deprived of its richest expression, the world can exist only as a dead thing, "a dry cinder." This is what Donne meant by the Idea of a Woman: Elizabeth Drury stands for herself, who is the idealized, the saintly embodiment of God's free gift of sanctifying grace. Once this is gone, or seems to have disappeared, life cannot wholly function again.

Donne's *First Anniversary,* or *An Anatomy of the World,* therefore, re-calls the Old Dispensation, the Law uninformed by grace. Although Eliza-beth Drury belonged to the old world, she provided it with a glimpse of the new one to come by leaving the old with her instructive model. Donne expresses such a view in these lines from *The First Anniversary:*

> And though she have shut in all day,
> The twi-light of her memory doth stay;
> Which, from the carcasse of the old world, free,
> Creates a new world; and new creatures be
> Produc'd: The matter and the stuffe of this,
> Her vertue, and the forme our practise is.
> And though to be thus Elemented, arme
> These Creatures, from hom-borne intrinsique harme,
> (For all assum'd unto this Dignitee,
> So many weedlesse Paradises bee,
> Which of themselves produce no venemous sinne,
> Except some forraine Serpent bring it in)
> Yet, because outward stormes the strongest breake,
> And strength it selfe by confidence growes weake,
> This new world may be safer, being told
> The dangers and diseases of the old.

(ll 73-88)

The old world is dead; the new one is not in fact the world of Donne's poem, but one, discovered through grace, within ourselves. Donne again has in mind the old world in the concluding lines of *An Anatomy of the World* where he sees himself, with Moses, as the instrument of God's song. He thus recalls the Old Covenant, which the *Anatomy* has analyzed, and Moses' commandments and "last, and lastingst peece, a song":

> [God] spake
> To *Moses,* to deliver unto all,
> That song: because he knew they would let fall,
> The Law, the Prophets, and the History,
> But keepe the song still in their memory.
> Such an opinion (in due measure) made
> Me this great Office boldly to invade.
> Nor could incomprehensibleness deterre
> Me, from thus trying to emprison her.

(ll. 462-470)

In the *Essayes in Divinity,* Donne refers again to Deut. 32.4, the Scriptural passage alluded to in these lines, and comments on its further implications: "One benefit of the Law was, that it did in some measure restore them [Abraham and his children] towards the first light of Nature: For, if man

had kept that, he had needed no outward law; for then he was to himself
a law, having all law in his heart."[7] *The First Anniversary* concludes with
the poet looking back to a dark and graceless world. But with the pun on
"fall," he can also look forward to being celebrant once more, both as poet
and priest, of a joyful world where grace has returned to revitalize all and
make of man's heart a paradise within, happier far. Such an office can
hardly comprehend or encircle all God's fullness. But "of his fulness have
all we received, and grace for grace. For the law was given by Moses, but
grace and truth came by Jesus Christ" (John 1.16, 17).

II

I have mainly referred to *The First Anniversary*, an almost unrelieved
rehearsal of the calamitous state of the world. Donne has performed an
anatomy by stripping away, layer by layer, the skin and tissue of its body,
and shown at last, as Vesalius did his man, only the skeleton to be left.
That is, Donne would perform so complete an anatomy if the world's carcass would outlast its own putrefaction (ll. 435-440). What remains afterwards is our sense of corporal and spiritual darkness. Our physical senses
remind us of the present rottenness of the inmost parts, a world of stinking
flesh, a world deprived of grace: the smell is unpleasant to hear, Donne
wittily observes; the outward expression of the interior ruin tells us of
the abundance of corruption. This is the fallen world in need of the grace
which Elizabeth embodied. *The Second Anniversary* builds upon this frail
base; the progress is upward, starting from the "fall"—the fall of the world
from grace (partly because Elizabeth Drury left the world, but mostly because of man's intrinsic sinfulness) and the death-fall of the poet as well
as of Elizabeth. We must "trust th'immaculate blood to wash [the] score"
(l. 106), a wretched one, indeed. *The Progres of the Soule* is not only about
such a movement; it is the movement itself. Donne does not commonly
refer in his poetry to the poet in the process of writing: he does not look
over his shoulder to see what it is that the creative process is in the very act
of creating.[8] In being forced to go beyond Elizabeth Drury herself—or
better to say, to accompany her on her progress—one recognizes that the
poetic act embodies her, as she embodied all virtue. *The Second Anniversary*
is a poem about Elizabeth Drury, but it is also, and more important, about
the creative power of the soul itself, above all about the power of the poet
who interprets and prophesies and gives form to the highest truth. This
truth is the life of grace made possible by God, through the Incarnate
Christ, in the Holy Spirit—and it infuses everything.

Donne ended *The First Anniversary* by referring to the Old Law, to life
in the Old Dispensation. "Fall" appears at several points in *The Second
Anniversary*, and first of all at its beginning where the term acts as a bridge
for bringing us from the previous poem into this next one:

> Nothing could make mee sooner to confesse
> That this world had an everlastingnesse,

> Then to consider, that a yeare is runne,
> Since both this lower worlds, and the Sunnes Sunne,
> The Lustre, and the vigor of this All,
> Did set; t'were Blasphemy, to say, did fall.
>
> (ll. 1-6)

The pun on "fall" is multiple—the fall of man, the fall of Elizabeth, the fall of the Sun-Son, the fall of the world.[9] These fallings prepare us for the bold simile that follows, of the beheaded man whose head drops from his body and leaves a double jet of blood, "One from the Trunke, another from the Head" (l. 11). Still his eyes "twinckle" and his tongue "will roll, / As though he beckned, and cal'd backe his Soul" (ll. 13-14). The truncated body still seems to grasp and try to reach its departing soul. This, with the other similes that immediately follow, is proof that there is "motion in corruption," that the "fall" is not final.

Later, when Donne is enjoining his soul to go up, and from its position in the watch-tower to "see all things despoyld of fallacies" (ll. 294-295), he aims to go

> Up to those Patriarckes, which did longer sit
> Expecting Christ, then they'have enjoy'd him yet.
> Up to those Prophets, which now gladly see
> Their Prophecies growen to be Historee.
>
> (ll. 345-348)

The direction is the forward one for which the lines about Moses and the prophets in *The First Anniversary* have prepared us. *The First Anniversary* had looked to the past and present world, but *The Second Anniversary* to the present and to the future one. Donne is embracing all time in these poems. His subject is grace, made possible by Incarnation, or, in T. S. Eliot's expression, by the "intersection of the timeless moment" (*Little Gidding*, I). Donne is revealing the new life of love in the progress of a soul that makes an ending which is also a beginning, and he is fascinated by just proportion and the fitting together of the embracing circle. He complains in the *Anatomy* (especially ll. 249-324) that the world's beauty is gone and disproportion has become true form:

> nor can the Sunne
> Perfit a Circle, or maintaine his way
> One inche direct . . .
>
> (ll. 268-270)

But *The Second Anniversary* answers by revealing the vision of the saint:

> Shee, who by making full perfection grow,
> Peeces a Circle, and still keepes it so.
>
> (ll. 507-509)

Elizabeth Drury, whose soul has immigrated to Heaven, possesses endur-

ing joy. Donne, who speaks for his own and the world's soul, sees the lesson
to be learned: she who has shown us the way must inspire us to work even
harder, for the knowledge that grace increases in Heaven should move us
toward realizing the grace here within us all the more. The spiritual and
intellectual effort required recalls Satyre III, where Truth, the object of all
our search stands

> on a huge hill,
> Cragged, and steep, . . . and hee that will
> Reach her, about must, and about must goe.
>
> (ll. 79-81)[10]

From *The Progres of the Soule*:

> whither who doth not strive
> The more, because shee'is there, he doth not know
> That accidentall joyes in Heaven doe grow.
> But pause, My soule, and study ere thou fall
> On accidentall joyes, th'essentiall.
>
> (ll. 380-384)

Manley's interpretation of these lines is incomplete: "The essential joy of
heaven is the everlasting possession of the Beatific Vision; all others are its
accidents."[11] The Beatific Vision, which forms the end of all our striving
and the end of these poems, is *essential* because it is complete and continuing,
and we can never be deprived of it. Donne had said at the beginning of *The
Progres,* "Thou seest mee strive for life" (l. 31). Surely this is the life of grace,
"the seed of glory," the "positive share or participation in the life of God
Himself."[12] Grace, too, is traditionally understood, as Donne would have
known, to be *accidental.* It is, in orthodox theology, a given reality or entity,
an "accident," something added to a man who is already a completely constituted being and inhering in him. Grace adds a divine quality, a supernatural
and additional abundance. In our earthly life, we may live in the life of grace
intermittently; but in our heavenly existence, we live fully within it. Accidental joys grow, or increase, in Heaven because they flourish uninterruptedly,
and there our sight of God's love and grace cannot be darkened by mortal
sin and the corruption of a primitive and fallen world. One may "fall" on
accidental joys—Donne is characteristically punning—in the sense that having
made a beginning in the life of grace, having started his study, one may not
see how to complete it. The answer comes in the sight of the essential joy
of heavenly grace. Donne is thus saying that we should study the vision,
the essence, the object of grace, even before we start, and perhaps fail or fall
along the way. There is essential joy on earth, of course, as well as in Heaven,
but here it is transitory, and Donne is eager in the next fifty lines to demonstrate this fact:

> whil'st you thinke you bee
> Constant, you'are howrely in inconstancee. (ll. 399-400)

Thus "accidentall" means "but a casuall happiness" (l. 412) while it also defines in a technical way the meaning of grace as taught by the Fathers and the Schoolmen.

The climactic lines of *The Second Anniversary,* indeed of both poems, for they are one long poem united by a single purpose and direction, begin at l. 435:

> Then, soule, to thy first pitch worke up again;
> Know that all lines which circles doe containe,
> For once that they the center touch, do touch
> Twice the circumference; and be thou such.
> Double on Heaven, thy thoughts on Earth emploid;
> All will not serve; Onely who have enjoyd
> The sight of God, in fulnesse, can thinke it;
> For it is both the object, and the wit.
> This is essentiall joye, where neither hee
> Can suffer Diminution, nor wee;
> Tis such a full, and such a filling good;
> Had th'Angels once look'd on him, they had stood.
> To fill the place of one of them, or more,
> Shee whom we celebrate, is gone before.
> Shee, who had Here so much essentiall joye,
> As no chance could distract, much less destroy;
> . . . .
> Whose twilights were more cleare, then our mid day,
> Who dreamt devoutlier, then most use to pray;
> Who being heare fild with grace, yet strove to bee,
> Both where more grace, and more capacitee
> At once is given: . . .

(ll. 435-450, 463-467)

The passage is a brilliant one: the first pitch to which the soul is enjoined to work up again recalls its Edenic state, its highest elevation before the Fall. Pitch is a musical image, too, and appropriate here for the fact that it recalls other musical references, central to the purpose of both poems. In *An Anatomy,* Elizabeth Drury was seen as "a part both of the Quire, and Song," one who sings and is sung about; in *The Progres,* Donne indicates that he will propagate a child each year by writing a hymn in Elizabeth's honor. Punning on hymns, Donne says that he shall continue to let his verses be Elizabeth's children: she, as much as the poet, makes this issue possible, and so her posterity will be enriched until "Gods great Venite change the song" (l. 44), until the Resurrection of the body and the end of time. Elizabeth Drury thus teaches us the first pitch, the best harmony. Pitch also leads into the next metaphor by carrying a geometrical meaning, for one pitches a circle—pitch in this sense (see *OED,* sb., III.10) is the point from which one describes the circle—here the point or center is Donne's soul itself. Again, we may recall the numerous images in these poems that have

relied upon and called for the harmony of the circle. Elizabeth has pieced
the circle together, or shown how it is complete (l. 508), for the circle,
indeed, represents the Beatific Vision for which we all long. Donne, who
speaks for us, lives on earth, not always with the sight of God, and his life
is the line which transects the center, the soul on earth, longing to touch
Heaven (the circumference) twice. "Double" is an imperative, associated
with thoughts; in touching the circumference with them, our time crosses
earth, where the soul presently stays, and links it with Heaven. "All" is
opposed to "Onely," in line 440. But "all" suggests that to have one's
thoughts on Heaven in double the number of one's thoughts on earth is
insufficient; only the whole circle the whole vision of God is enough, and
only those who have had it can "thinke it." Here *think* is related to Elizabeth Drury, whose body thought (l. 246)—she did have "the sight of God,
in fulnesse." This sight is both *object,* the known thing, seen in itself, and
the *wit,* the very mode of perceiving. Object is realization complemented
by wit, or the means of realizing. And such is essential joy, or grace unending,
where one has a reciprocative share in the supernatural life. Indeed, had
all the angels looked on God, none of them would have fallen. "No chance"
could distract Elizabeth, who lived in grace, no accident. Her twilights were
clearer than our brightest hours (the same image occurs in the passage of
The First Anniversary, ll. 73-74, quoted earlier), but still she laboured for
more grace.

The *Progres of the Soule* ends by recalling its beginning: *An Anatomy
of The World* showed the disease of earthly life under the Old Dispensation;
The Progres, of life in grace, which the poet will continue to celebrate until
God's last Venite. The image of "great Grand-children of [her] praises,"
the role of the verse itself described at the beginning of *The Progres,* Donne
recalls at the ending of the poem. By being Elizabeth's child, this poem is
also Donne's, for he asks her to be the father of his chaste muse (ll. 33-36).
Elizabeth, having pieced the circle of harmony in which we may see and
discover the embodiment of grace, would be worthy of an invocation. But
Donne does not invoke her name; he remembers his purpose has been to
commemorate Elizabeth by declaring that God has given her power to be
well remembered and him the poetic ability to write well of her:

> Since his will is, that to posteritee,
> Thou shouldest for life, and death, a patterne bee,
> And that the world should notice have of this,
> The purpose, and th'Autority is his;
> Thou art the Proclamation; and I ame
> The Trumpet, at whose voice the people came.
>
> (ll. 523-528)

The poet merges with the poem and its subject; the voice of Moses with which
Donne identified at the end of *An Anatomy* is now God's song of the New
Dispensation of grace whose pattern Elizabeth was able to proclaim. Both
of the *Anniversaries* have been tied together by the motif of song, at first

struggling to be heard (Moses knew the people would not hear), and at the last triumphantly sounding—the people come to hear the sound of the last trumpet which announces the general resurrection (I Cor. 15.52, 55). The poems are a performance in which the poet has been both conductor and subject. Yet he still waits for God's last calling of the faithful together, His last *Venite* when all voices shall join in a hymn of praise: "O come, let us sing unto the Lord: let us heartily rejoice in the strength of our salvation."[13]

The trumpet commonly signifies the inspired prophet. Donne again calls all men to a general resurrection at the conclusion of one sermon where he compares his own "lower and infirmer voice" to the last trumpet: "as at the last resurrection, all that heare the sound of the Trumpet, shall rise in one instant, though they have passed thousands of years between their burialls, so doe all ye, who are now called, by a lower and infirmer voice, rise together in this resurrection of grace." Moreover, in the Second Prebend Sermon, Donne points to Christ's joyous *Venite*: "The everlastingnesse of the joy is the blessednesse of the next life, but the entring, the inchoation is afforded here. For that which Christ shall say then to us, *Venite benedicti, Come ye blessed*, are words intended to persons that are coming, that are upon the way, though not at home; Here in this world he bids us *Come*, there in the next, he shall bid us *Welcome*." Beginning, entering, coming, welcoming—*Venite* has many voices.[14]

But there is a further point, and that is to see the poet as priest, who, through God's grace, has offered up his performance to God. As priest, Donne has taken the ordinary world and consecrated it so that *The Progres* can end with joy, harmony, and heavenly wisdom. When opposing accidental to essential joy, and yet mingling them, Donne intends a Eucharistic meaning. Joy is grace, and grace, as we have seen, is an accident, an objective *quality*; the dull and common world is also an accident, but of *quantity*, in need of priestly blessing. Donne, who himself accompanies Elizabeth on a progess, and identifies himself with her, transforms, by means of the grace available through Christ and embodied in Elizabeth Drury, the vulgar world; for he has made possible its transubstantiation. While appearances remain the same, the substance of life is totally altered. *The Second Anniversary* declares the new life of power in grace, the essential and substantial life of the spirit, the real presence of Christ; and earlier, in *The First Anniversary*, Donne had dwelt primarily upon insubstantial, accidental forms. If the Beatific Vision, and the harmony that accrues and belongs to it, is the end of this poem, then we may say that the poet has consciously played his part both as poet in describing this new life and as priest, by God's power, in consecrating it and making it holy. Although Donne does not use the term, he is fully conscious of it: Incarnation makes possible, through Christ, a sacramental way for the stream of grace to flow to us all.[15]

In embracing all experience, from decay and disorder through joy and grace, from old convenant to new order, these extraordinary poems speak on different levels, but in one harmony. While Elizabeth Drury always remains herself and the world goes on being corrupt, both can be informing and informed through the creative acts of poetry and of grace. Donne has shown the turning of sorrow into joy and offered up himself and his poetry to the God of grace as a fit sacrifice of praise and thanksgiving; having cried out from the depths of his experience, he heard at first his own voice in this calling, but at last only Love's, drawing him with promises of plenteous redemption, and revealing what he had always known, in speech which never began and has no ending. Donne takes us where we may know "the souls bloud, / The land of spices; something understood."

VIII. MISCELLANEOUS POEMS

'BLANDA ELEGEIA': THE BACKGROUND TO DONNE'S 'ELEGIES'

A. LaBranche

The sudden impetus which Catullus gave to elegiac love poetry was lost a few decades after his death. Among Roman authors the genre ran its course swiftly.[1] Certain themes and motifs were perpetuated, of course, through the songs, epistles and complaints of the middle ages, but they rarely appeared in that perfect balance which we attribute to the Roman genre: the elegiac metre, the importance attached to the subjective predicament of the speaker, the realistic, at times frantic recriminations between lover and lady, and the sustaining contrasts drawn from the worlds of mythology or of everyday occurrence. Not until the neo-Latin poets of the sixteenth century and Ronsard can we find a programme, however haphazard, of recapturing the action and tone of the love-elegy as it was developed by Propertius, Tibullus, and Ovid.[2]

This discovery of the dramatic element in the elegy is one principal triumph of Renaissance imitation—the kind of imitation which adapted classical rhetorical conventions to English soil and quickly made them into a native ornament. It is in this context that I wish to consider Donne's *Elegies* and to describe their intensely dramatic monologue. We cannot unravel here all of the perplexed influences which Professor Ellrodt has recently gathered in his immense study.[3] But by reviewing some of the more striking conventions of Latin love-elegy, we will prepare ourselves to recognize in the *Elegies* all those traits which have long been isolated and institutionalized as hallmarks of Donne's manner: the careful dramatic contexts of the poems, the speaker's 'scapes and shifts', the reversals and tentative resolutions, the surprising self-discoveries. All of these attributes accompany the study of essential human relationships which is a principal theme of the love elegy, and which bears a strong hand in the fashioning of its dramatic techniques.

I

The mixed environment out of which the *Elegies* grew indicates the combination of attitudes, amatory and satiric, which is their mark. Professor Grierson asserts that Donne was writing love elegies as early as 1593 and that the

Reprinted from *Modern Language Review*, 61 (1966), 357-68, by permission of the editors and the Modern Humanities Research Association.

bulk of his elegiac production lies between 1593 and 1598.[4] The remaining
seven of his twenty elegies were composed probably at various moments
prior to 1610. Such pieces as XIX ('Going to Bed'), XVI ('On his Mistris'),
XI ('The Bracelet'), III ('Change') were being devised at the same time as
some of the *Songs and Sonets,* with which the elegies were traditionally
grouped by virtue of style and content. According to three MSS, *Elegie X*
('The Dreame') is placed among the *Songs and Sonets* (where there is a poem
of the same title),[5] and Mrs. Simpson has uncovered a MS which presents
fourteen of the *Elegies* interspersed with such lyrics as 'The Flea', 'The
Legacy', 'The Extasie', and 'Goe and catch'.[6] Clearly the *Elegies* are an important step in Donne's dramatic-amatory work.

The same period saw the beginning of the *Satyres,* Davies's *Epigrams*
(published together with Marlowe's translation of Ovid's *Amores*),[7] and in
1597 the vogue of the 'heroicall epistle' (*Sapho to Philaenis*). It is difficult
to separate any of these from the elegy, so flexible is the Elizabethan concept of that genre[8] and so intricately bound are all to the literary penchant
of the late 1590's for pronounced dramatic stances, for obscurity, cynicism,
and the laboured effect of 'strong lines'.[9] All of these attributes, Professor
Ellrodt remarks,[10] are manifestations of a growing self-consciousness—that
is, manifestations of a speaker who fills the intellectual framework of his
poem more dramatically, more individually than was previously the rule.
Such attributes are bound to cut across genres, and to avoid a narrow and
misleading view of one genre we should, ideally, study all. A case in point is
the relation of the epigram to love elegy, which has been a puzzle ever since
the Greek Anthology and Catullus.[11] Both genres show a taste for observing
the subjective predicament, for sententiousness, and for witty paradox.
Two, at least, of Donne's elegies occupy a middle soil between elegy and
epigram, *Elegie V* ('His Picture'), and in Martial's vein *Elegie XIII* ('Julia').
Like the elegy, the epigram generally proposes either a topic or a visual object upon which to focus its sense of incongruity. It is this procedure of
vivid, external focus (the 'bracelet of bright haire') which becomes a serious
dramatic technique during these years and which is as noticeable throughout
Donne's poetry as is the traditionally ingenious 'epigrammatic turn.'

The genre of the love-epistle also requires some passing mention since it
shares a background of dramatic techniques with the love elegy. The relationship between love-epistle and elegy reaches back to Propertius 4.3, whence
it is thought Ovid derived his notion of the *Heroides.* The style here is
not that of the moral epistle, the Horatian *sermo* or plain style which
Mr. Wesley Trimpi has meticulously traced in Jonson's poems,[12] but belongs to a more dramatic and oratorical tradition. This tradition—the *sua-
soria,* or advice offered to an arbitrary, fictitious situation—was practised in
the declamatory schools which Ovid attended[13] and goes some distance in
describing the rhetorical techniques of the Latin elegists, and of Donne as well.
Not only did the *suasoriae* teach the speaker to dramatize his appeal rapidly and
vividly, but the whole artifice was an exercise in sympathetic communication

and persuasion, or as one scholar memorably puts it, an exercise in 'sympa-thetic schizophrenia'.[14] Under Ovid's touch in the *Heroides,* and in the *Amores* where the love epistle is turned in upon itself, the poetry often takes the form of a personal appeal, or of an 'interview' as so variously true of Donne. There are other attributes which may accompany this convention: the style will tend to be hyperbolic with much 'ocular demonstration' or vivid amassing of detail,[15] there will be a rapid shifting of ground, and on occasion bitter reproach joined to exhortation.[16] Such rhetorical gestures as these, touched at moments by wit and a sense of perspective, furnish the central action of the love-epistle as well as of elegy.[17] In each case the world of lovers is intent upon fashioning an urgent mode of self-expression—otherwise the truths of their narrow intense experience will remain unspoken.[18]

II

From the background of occasional practitioners of the elegy in English, like Surrey, of the adapters or translators, like Marlowe, and of the profes-sional forgers of style, like Jonson, Donne's *Elegies* stand out as the most original and carefully fashioned imitation of the classical genre. This superi-ority becomes apparent when we examine the group of elegies included by Jonson in *Under-woods* (XXXVIII-XLII), into which crept one of Donne's, XV, 'The Expostulation'. Donne's poem (*Under-woods,* XXXIX) distinguishes itself by a stronger emotional and dramatic fluidity; all of Jonson's elegies lack, by comparison, dramatic cogency and a discursive probing of the love situation.[19] These strictures are not advanced as a criticism of Jonson's powers of imitation,[20] but in order to indicate that Donne's accomplishment, from the outset, lies in a full understanding and use of the dramatic speaker. Without this, the elegy falls at the mercy of whatever idiom—be it Petrarchan or satiric—in which it is conceived. Donne's discovery is an extreme innovation, even when we propose its possible inspiration by Mar-lowe's translations of the *Amores.*

Marlowe's *Elegies* are uniformly pedestrian exercises, always rendering flatly the more delicate dramatic turns in Ovid's psychological portraits. The first two Books of *Amores* are largely wasted on the English poet, for Marlowe has a knack of transmuting dramatic self-expostulation (as in 2.4, 'The Indifferent') into a set piece—a tendency noticeable in many Renais-sance imitators, including Donne. But if he misses the spirit of semi-serious invocation and conjuration which fills Ovid's complaints, Marlowe does respond occasionally to tenser emotional situations by coarsening his language and adopting a satiric manner (2.19, 'Foole if to keepe thy wife thou hast no need'). Especially in Ovid's last Book, in which a keen edge of bitterness shows through the convention, Marlowe adopts at times a vigorous and exclamatory idiom, though the over-all effect of his pieces is to drone on forever in couplets.[21]

It is not surprising, then, that in addition to drawing from the conven-tions of epigram and love epistle, Donne's *Elegies* should strike us as essays in sarcasm and invective, as rather self-conscious attempts to overthrow orthodox taste, fashion, and the appearance of morality—in fact, as thoroughly traditional adherents to the role of elegy. But the elegiac point of view differs from the satiric in that the elegiac poet does not sing 'high and aloof' nor set himself in a position of retirement or of moral advantage; rather, he is intimately involved in the society of lovers which is being criticized. Ovid's perverse reprimand of the husband who refuses to turn jealous, and so threatens to spoil the delight of the intrigue (2.19) rises immediately to mind, or the delightful self-appraisal of his own inconstancy (2.4) which reappears as Donne's 'The Indifferent'. One must discriminate between the satire of Hall, Marston, or of Donne himself, and the satiric content and manner of the *Elegies* where the speaker is engaged in a drama of shifting involvement with the situation at hand.[22] The difference seems to receive emphasis when we compare the *Elegies* to the *Satyres*: the 'fondling motley humorist' of *Satyre I* and the numberless mock-courtly, mock-religious, mock-learned figures which flit through the succeeding poems, all try to involve the speaker in a torrential stream of argument and activity. The world of chaos has burst in upon the speaker's study, and to keep aloof he must defend himself with sarcasm and invective. But in the *Elegies* the speaker has from the beginning committed himself to and associated himself with the erotic world, and all satire strikes closer to home, forcing him to revise continually his relationship to that world.

For the present I would like to probe a little further into the conventions which govern the drama and rhetoric of elegy and show what resources they might supply a young man intent on fashioning a new poetic manner.

I. *Self-Awareness*

Catullus is considered the first Roman poet to make the revolutionary discovery that love matters—that is, love matters as a literary topic and provides a valid body of manners and material for a poet to take some pains in articulating.[23] All of the elegiac poets took pride in asserting this proposition and in practising the genre against prevailing critical opinion. What concerns us here, however, is the rapid growth in the elegiac convention between Catullus and Ovid; the theme of the latter is not so much the flesh-and-blood mistress as the Muse *Elegeia* herself. Ovid, the final exponent of the genre and the most certain source of elegy for Donne and his contemporaries, is intent on presenting the elegiac convention as an area of valid psychological insight.[24] Herman Fränkel writes:

> His subject was *The Story of Love,* and that, after all, is what the title *Amores* means. . . . By a number of concrete examples the poet tried to present a comprehensive image of what a young man's existence is like when it is dominated by a passionate attachment. Of the lover's existence he would draw an ideal picture which boldly challenged comparison with the lives of nonlovers.[25]

'The lives of nonlovers'—the phrase calls to mind the basis in sarcasm of 'The

Good-morrow', 'The Sunne Rising', 'The Canonization', and 'The Relique'. But before we leave Ovid's interpretation of the genre, let us note one more of its implications. In transmuting the personal nature of elegy into a dramatic representation, Ovid has rendered uncertain or ambivalent the speaker's position on stage. There alternates an assurance with an uncertainty of self, in Fränkel's words 'the notion of dubious or fluid identity',[26] in Donne's case the painful self-awareness which accompanies a drama of shifting involvement.

Elegie I ('Jealousie') proves to be such a case. In spite of the reduction of the poem to a set piece by the title—this was the practice in sixteenth century editions of Ovid—the speaker shows several attitudes to the wronged husband and to the mistress. The first fourteen lines present a cool appraisal of the emotional situation: the mistress is foolish and inconsistent in her grief over her husband's jealousy, for if he actually lay dying,

> Thou would'st not weepe, but jolly, 'and frolicke bee
> As a slave, which to morrow should be free;
> Yet weep'st thou, when thou seest him hungerly
> Swallow his owne death, hearts-bane jealousie.
>
> (ll. 11-14)

But the focus shifts immediately to include the speaker's own involvement in the adulterous deception.

> O give him many thanks, he'is courteous,
> That in suspecting kindly warneth us.
> Wee must not, as wee us'd, flout openly,
> In scoffing ridles, his deformitie. . . .
>
> (ll. 15-18)

The attitude to the husband has, until now, been one of transparent disgust, following the portrait of him given by Ovid (1.4) and following the convention of the resentful illicit lover. At this moment, and beginning with this ironic compliment (l. 15), the speaker breaks away from the intimate, sensual predicament of the two lovers and begins to evaluate, albeit tentatively, the legal and moral rights of the offended party.

> Now I see many dangers; for that is
> His realme, his castle, and his diocesse.
>
> (ll. 25-6)

The lovers still can play, but henceforth they must do so as exiles, counterfeiters, London low-life, or minority religious groups (ll. 26-34). As in Ovid, the husband, *vir,* or man in possession, has a certain legal or moral status which affects the pleasure of the lovers; it is impossible to deny his existence, and his 'rights' to the lady render the affair sordid. This situation lies behind the puzzled and pathetic state of self-deception which we find at the end of Ovid's poem (1.4.59 ff.).[27] There is also the possibility, of course, that Donne's speaker is scoffing at all authority, that the lovers through wary

practice will remain as safe as 'Germans from the Pope's pride'. A threat
has been uncovered, nevertheless, and the speaker balances precisely between a scoffing and a sober view of the predicament; he seems to sense
the strengths and fallacies of his pose. From close scrutiny of Ovid's
speaker he has learned the habit of self-awareness.

Another diatribe or set piece is *Elegie IV*, 'The Perfume'. Far from being
what Ellrodt might propose, a poem which exalts masculine values and
derides the 'effeminate perfume',[28] this is the story of a lover who has been
insufficiently self-aware. His too complacent acceptance of the erotic world
has betrayed him to the world outside; he has understood too late the pre-
cariousness of the elegiac situation. Like the 'selfe-traytor' in 'Twicknam
garden', each lover carries within him the seeds of his own undoing.

> But Oh, too common ill, I brought with mee
> That, which betray'd mee to my enemie:
> A loud perfume, which at my entrance cryed
> Even at thy fathers nose, so were wee spied.
>
> (ll. 39-42)

And like so many of Donne's lovers, this speaker has attained to his moment
of self-awareness or of self-evaluation through a summary of the love story
(ll. 1-38). The downfall here, typically, is precipitated by some minute
detail, some 'too common ill', and the resultant self-awareness mixes resignation with a sense of particular loss. The whole treacherous situation of man
in the world finds expression on a small scale in the story of love, and these
two poems show a speaker awakening, ever so slightly, to this reality.

Two further rhetorical traits emerge from the dramatic, elegiac position,
and both play frequent roles in Donne's poetry. Since the main drama is
one of self-evaluation, it is not surprising to find that Donne's descriptions
are heavily laden with adjectives expressing some value judgment, satiric,
pejorative, or approving.

> I taught my silkes, their whistling to forbeare,
> Even my opprest shoes, dumbe and speechlesse were,
> Onely, thou bitter sweet, whom I had laid
> Next mee, mee traiterously hast betraid,
> And unsuspected hast invisibly
> At once fled unto him, and staid with mee.
>
> (ll. 51-6)

Indeed the principal action of the *Elegies* lies in depicting a sensitive and
evaluative state of mind, one which would recognize, for example, the
speaker's 'opprest shoes'. A second peculiarity of rhetoric is associated with
this: the plurality of audiences within a single poem. 'The Perfume' begins
with an address to the mistress, recalling the story of their love, but some
fifty lines later switches to address the perfume, with a fine associative irony.

> Onely, thou bitter sweet, whom I had laid
> Next mee, mee traiterously hast betraid.

Then after twenty lines of invective against the perfume, the speaker returns to the original 'thou' of the love-situation and ends abruptly.

> All my perfume's, I give most willingly
> To 'embalme thy fathers corse; What? will hee die?

The ability, perhaps even necessity, to shift attitude and perspective is a trait of style which Lowry Nelson has described recently[29] and which is central to the concept and movement of elegy.

This section has served only to sketch some possible ways in which the elegiac speaker may be animated dramatically so as to serve the purpose of a young poet intent on overriding current love conventions. More material can be gleaned from *XI* ('The Bracelet') and *XV* ('The Expostulation'). We have noted that several traits of style arise from self-awareness: one is a tendency to evaluate, by adjective or metaphor, the descriptive material through which elegy presents its drama. Another may be called the appearance of sincerity—that is, the apparent sincerity of those moments in which the speaker, through circumstantial review of his history, has arrived at self-evaluation. Finally, we can observe that self-awareness recurs frequently in those two most famous of Donne's lyric genres, the valediction and the interview. The interview, as Shakespeare also uses it in his comedies, is a dramatic method of measuring self-awareness[30]—a superbly flexible technique which tests a speaker's ability to remain sensitive and clear-headed in a given love situation.[31]

2. Praeceptor Amoris

The role of *praeceptor amoris*, tutor in love, is part of the elegiac scheme to overthrow conventional worldly values and substitute for them a relationship stripped of all but the essential truths.[32] Donne's insistence on 'love interviews' reflects such a plan: how often his speaker appears intent on only the most essential kind of communication between man and woman and how often the most direct route, love, turns out to be mined with pitfalls and barriers, and the speaker is turned back to debate with himself. The dramatic virtue of the role of *praeceptor* is that it is half-mocking, half-serious, precisely what is contained in the whimsical notion that love need be 'taught' at all[33] and in the serious notion that to be 'schooled' in it is greatly urgent. In Catullus and Propertius, the two poles of a relationship establish themselves in the respective pleasures of illicit eroticism (*furtivus amor*) and holy friendship (*sancta amicitia*);[34] and these poles also begin to describe the area of vacillation in Donne's *Elegies* and in many of his lyrics. Three of the *Elegies* are outright presentations of the *praeceptor* theme, *XVIII*, *XIX*, and *XX*, but it is important to notice that Donne's speaker constantly refers to his position as tutor: 'Natures lay Ideot, I taught thee to love' (*I, II, IV, VII,*

XII, XVI). More than serving a satiric blow to the traditional love poetry
and moral epistle, the pose underscores the ironic predicament of the
speaker, for often, as in Ovid (2.5.47 ff.), his tutelage backfires and the
tables are reversed.

> Natures lay Ideot, I taught thee to love,
> And in that sophistrie, Oh, thou dost prove
> Too subtile.
>
> (*VII*, ll. 1-3)

This privileged knowledge is, in part at least, self-mocking, for it not only
asserts the superiority of the erotic world in the face of the dull and quotidian,
but it also represents through its 'sophistries' how painful is the search for
satisfactory human relationships.

In this light the poems of seduction seem to have occasioned some mis-
apprehensions, largely because readers have forgotten Ovid's particular kind
of serious make-believe. The facetious erotic instructions of *XIX*, or the
sophistries of 'The Flea', are elegiac conventions, and we must leave it to
Professor Legouis and to successive generations of students to wonder if the
lady is actually present and if the speaker's tutelage is taking effect.[35] The
literary reality is both less and more serious than this, for the speaker's facile
knowledge of female geography and of erotic psychology calls attention to
its own superficiality—no matter how seriously practised it remains a divertise-
ment—and this implies in turn the difficulty of coming to a true knowledge
of love. The whimsical grotesqueries ending *Elegie XVIII* and the famous
'What needst thou have more covering then a man' of *XIX* both suggest
their opposites: the whole position of *praeceptor* and of 'free love' has
turned out rather a sham, and the road to a true union is longer and more
difficult than expected.

Placed in such a context, the essential communication between man and
woman reduced to terms of nakedness and erotic adventure seems to the
modern taste, rather grotesquely witty. We are reminded of Donne's famous
comment in his letter to Sir Robert Ker: '. . . you knew my uttermost when
it was best, and even then I did best when I had least truth for my subjects.'[36]
If too many of the *Elegies* and of Donne's other poems appear to be calculated displays of wit, it is useful to remember that the elegiac speaker
takes refuge from involvement behind his wit, behind his facetious rationalizations, and that often the way of wit leads back into emotional involvement.
As we have observed of Elegies *I* and *IV*, Donne's speaker best performs his
humorous 'scapes and shifts' at the brink of seriousness. He demands liberty,
even libertinism, of belief and manners, and yet this seems to raise more
questions that it answers. Discoursing on change in *Elegie III*, the speaker
reproves his mistress:

> Thou lov'st, but Oh! canst thou love it and mee?
> Likenesse glues love: and if that thou so doe,
> To make us like and love, must I change too?

> More then thy hate, I hate'it, rather let mee
> Allow her change, then change as oft as shee. . . .
>
> (ll. 22-6)

Variations of this predicament appear in 'Womans Constancy' and in others of the *Songs and Sonets*. It is not surprising that Donne also should have discovered, as one more dramatic possibility, the serious-minded *praeceptor* of *Elegies VII, XII, XVI,* 'The good-morrow' and 'The Sunne Rising'.

3. *Intimate Recrimination*

> Yet let not thy deepe bitternesse beget
> Carelesse despaire in mee, for that will whet
> My minde to scorne; and Oh, love dull'd with paine
> Was ne'r so wise, nor well arm'd as disdaine.
>
> (*VI*, ll. 35-8)

What is often taken as a sense of melancholy or discouragement in Donne is, dramatically speaking, a scene of intimate recrimination. 'The spirit of love sets up its own code of propriety', remarks Fränkel,[37] and it is obvious that the failure of the mistress, or the intrusion of some unhappy chance, will occasion a particularly painful reproach from the speaker. The very narrowness and intensity of the elegiac world begets the intimate nature of this reproach, for such displays are directed against not only the mistress, but any close associate which has betrayed the speaker, the perfume of *Elegie IV,* the treacherous third party of *XV,* Love itself in *XII* and the speaker's own sophistries in the *Songs and Sonets.* Such scenes are frequent in Donne, and the impact of the speaker's disenchantment always seems the greater for its having been delivered to him at point-blank range, either by the failure of a trusted friend or by the discovery of an unpleasant flaw in the erotic world itself.[38]

Closely related to the moments of self-awareness, these scenes of recrimination are unusually plentiful and compelling in the *Elegies.*[39] The rhetorical technique they employ is found throughout Donne's poetry. The complaint or reproach must appear well founded and appropriate; in many instances, therefore, it is mingled with selected intimate details of a carefully recalled biography. We have noted already the situation of *praeceptor* in *VII* ('Natures lay Ideot. . .'); the poignancy of the adulterous drama is furthered, as in 'The Perfume', by tiny recollected details.

> Natures lay Ideot, I taught thee to love,
> And in that sophistrie, Oh, thou dost prove
> Too subtile: Foole, thou didst not understand
> Thy mystique language of the eye nor hand:
> Nor couldst thou judge the difference of the aire
> Of sighes, and say, this lies, this sounds despaire:
> Nor by the'eyes water call a maladie
> Desperately hot, or changing feaverously.

> I had not taught thee then, the Alphabet
> Of flowers, how they devisefully being set
> And bound up, might with speechlesse secrecie
> Deliver arrands mutely, and mutually.

(II.1-12)

Or again, in XII the speaker recreates the dramatic circumstances of the affair and draws himself, and us, into a deeper involvement with the story.

> Was't not enough, that thou didst hazard us
> To paths in love so dark, so dangerous:
> And those so ambush'd round with houshold spies,
> And over all, thy husbands towring eyes
> That flam'd with oylie sweat of jealousie:
> Yet went we not still on with Constancie?

(II.39-44)

The focus becomes more intense and intimate through the rapid transition from the first 'thou' (the speaker is addressing Love) to the second, the flesh-and-blood mistress ('*thy* husbands towring eyes').

Upon this narrowing of the situation, there follows in rapid succession sentimental recollection, disenchantment, and an awareness of self-deception. Propertius and Ovid are masters of this particular phase of the elegiac story, and it offers great scope to self-criticism tempered with the recollection and regret which characterize the 'elegiac tone'.[40] Still another dramatic possibility occurs within this convention, and it is fully exploited by Donne in some of his most effective pieces. Sometimes the speaker will pervert his recrimination of the mistress by a conscious act of sophism, a conscious act of self-deception, if only to suggest how far arguments fall short of expressing the realities of any love situation and how necessary is something more than logic. Fränkel shrewdly remarks this argumentative position in Ovid's speaker: 'While trying to convict his mistress of a breach of faith, he sadly overrates the stringency of his arguments; but his gratuitous reproaches show how highly he treasures the integrity of their association.'[41] The speakers of *Elegie VI* (in the passage given at the head of this section), 'Womans constancy', 'Loves exchange', 'A Valediction: of weeping', 'A Ieat Ring sent', arise from similar dramatic situations, although the contents of their arguments are more carefully turned than is usual in elegy. One recurrent tension in Donne's poems is that created between the sophistic abilities and the practical self-awareness of the speaker.

So well has Donne adapted these rhetorical gestures to his purpose that it is entertaining to observe them arise *ab ovo* in an unidentified elegy which Chambers has printed and attributed to Donne on the basis of verbal similarities with *Elegies VI* and *VII*.[42] This curious draft of a poem reminds us of Donne not only in its choice and handling of imagery, but also, and most strikingly, in the managing of elegiac conventions. First, here is a classical instance of reproach, Ovid's address to the guardian of the door (1.6.41-6).

You are unyielding; or does sleep—and may it be the ruin of you!—give
to the winds the lover's words your ears repulse? Yet at first, I remember,
when I wished to escape your eye, you were wakeful up to the midnight
stars. It may be that you, too, have a love, who is resting even now at
your side—alas, how much better your lot than mine!

Donne combines his recrimination with the pose of *praeceptor*.

> Yet I had thy first oaths and it was I,
> that taught thee first, loues language t'vnderstand
> and did reueale pure Loues high Misterie
> and had thy heart deliuered by thy hande. . . .
>
> (ll. 21-4)

> O I appeale
> vnto thy soule wheather I haue not cause
> to chainge my happiest wishes to this curse
> that thou from chainging still might neuer pause
> and euery chainge might be from worse to worse.
> Yett my heart cannot wish nor thoughts conceiue
> of ill to thine nor can thy falshood whett
> my dull minde to reuenge; that I will leaue
> to thee, for thine owne guilt will that begett.
>
> (ll. 36-44)

Here in unlicked form is a full recognition of the dramatic depth of the conventions and of a speaker who creates the illusion that 'the author composed
his own life and lived his own verse'[43]—in the projection of a scene from a
drama as old as humankind.

4. Resting-Point

Eventually, after many disputes, recollections, and self-discoveries, the
elegiac speaker must reach a state of concrete, if temporary, equilibrium,
something strong and inviolate in his intensely disrupted world. This position
is achieved after extensive biographical recollection, and it resembles a
precariously asserted belief or faith.

> . . . and by the memory
> Of hurts, which spies and rivals threatned me,
> I calmly beg: But by thy fathers wrath,
> By all paines, which want and divorcement hath,
> I conjure thee, and all the oathes which I
> And thou have sworne to seale joynt constancy,
> Here I unsweare, and overswear them thus,
> Thou shalt not love by wayes so dangerous.
> Temper, ô faire Love, loves impetuous rage,
> Be my true Mistris still, not my faign'd Page;
> I'll goe, and, by thy kinde leave, leave behinde
> Thee, onely worthy to nurse in my minde,

Thirst to come backe; ô if thou die before,
My soule from other lands to thee shall soare.

(XVI, ll. 5-18)[44]

This growth toward assurance is present also in *Elegie XII, XVII,* 'The
Relique', 'The Dreame', 'The good-morrow', 'The Sunne Rising' and in various of the valedictions. There is no need to labour the importance of this
device in its ability to suggest that a certain emotional distance has been
traversed and that the speaker, by suffering or experiencing intensely within
a fairly narrow convention, has achieved a perspective or resting-point. Ovid's
witty phrase here acquires a deeper significance: 'ingenii est experientis
amor' (1.9.31), in Marlowe's words 'love tries wit best of all'. The life of
wit and balance in Donne is inextricably bound to the story of love, and if
ever we doubt the reality of the situation we do not doubt the reality of
wit and feeling which emerges from it and which affirms the significance
of the poem. Like the pastoral, the elegiac world ends by viewing a horizon
much wider than we anticipated, and again like pastoral the convention
achieves this end by insisting on retelling its own narrow history and simultaneously implying a universal story of quarrels and of broken relationships.

It is this convincing dramatic cohesiveness that enables Donne's love
poems to appear homogeneous though they resist all efforts of classification.
They are episodes and variations of a single drama, which chronicles the
lover's mode of existence. Such a view renders unnecessary Arnold Stein's
recent distinction between personality and idea in the *Songs and Sonets*
and helps to explain the 'poetry of presence' which so occupies Professor Ellrodt.[45] The presence of a resting-point does suggest that elegiac poetry is
contemplative as well as dramatic, and in actuality we are often impressed
by a sense of deliberateness hidden beneath a surface of urgency and dis-
array. As in Propertius, we suspect that the widely diversified materials
and extended digressions are dramatic indications of mind; they represent
a kind of dramatic reaching-out of the speaker toward certainties and toward
things only hopefully certain. One sees such drama in Donne's use of the
word *great,* which sometimes means *dread* (as in XI, l. 35) and sometimes
indicates any violent emotional reaction to a situation—an assertion that the
elegiac world contains *multum in parvo.*

In view of the drama we have been witnessing, it seems strange that the
Muse *Elegeia* should have acquired the epithets 'smooth', 'light', and 'blandish-
ing'.[46] Her antique story of the arguing, suffering lover stands behind such
varied dramatic gestures as the *Songs and Sonets* record and is in itself a kind
of romance in rhetoric, dominated by the problem of human relationships.
Following in this tradition, the *Elegies* impress us with their struggle to reduce
life to its essential predicaments and with their struggle, at the same time, for
tolerance of human failure. Their whole effect is a miraculous transcending
of narrow social and literary conventions.

THEME AND STRUCTURE IN DONNE'S *SATYRES*

N. J. C. Andreasen

Because Donne's *Satyres* are among his earliest works, they have a special interest for anyone who wishes to study the poetic techniques which he tried during his literary apprenticeship. Yet, oddly enough, no detailed study has been made of them. Critics have commented on them in passing, it is true, but the enormously varied nature of the responses these *Satyres* have aroused suggests that a more careful examination of them is needed. Typical of one extreme is C. S. Lewis, who damns them as shaggy and savage, unmetrical in versification, disgusting in diction, and obscure in thought.[1] Alvin Kernan, on the other hand, maintains that they are among the least savage of the satires of the period and that they are also the most consistent and ordered.[2] Surely someone must be wrong. One should think twice before tilting lances with C. S. Lewis, but in this case it must be done, all the more because he is *not* a windmill. For Donne's *Satyres,* important because of their historical interest, are also of considerable intrinsic literary merit as well.

These five satires, far from being incoherent, are all built upon a single thematic principle of organization; they are all concerned with presenting an idealistic defense of spiritual values against the creeping encroachment of sixteenth-century materialism. Donne's dramatic situations, satiric pose, diction, and imagery are all employed, in each of the five satires, to point up this contrast between the sacred and the profane. Each individual satire is put together with great care, and each depicts a different kind of material-istic deviation from the spiritual ideal. Each individual satire illuminates the others, for the whole sequence rests upon a single unifying principle which is treated from five different aspects. Once we realize that the *Satyres* are a dramatization of the contrast between the sacred and the profane, their obscurity vanishes, their roughness is justified, their organic unity is clear, and their vivid humor is delightful.

Before looking at the individual satires more closely, however, we would do well to observe in general the satiric methods which are employed in all of them. Following the precedent set by the former masters of satire, whether Horace or Chaucer, Donne has made them all dramatic in tone and technique.[3] Each has a speaker who delivers a tirade to a listening adversary. The adver-sary often merely listens without responding, but he may occasionally break in and turn the dramatic monologue into a dialogue. Both speaker and

Reprinted from *Studies in English Literature,* 3 (1963), 59-75, by permission of the publisher.

antagonist are living characters, revealing their personalities by their comments on society and upon one another. The personality of the speaker is
characterized more fully, however, since he reappears in each satire, while
his antagonist changes from satire to satire. Their conversation is played
against some background such as a street full of passers-by or a royal court
full of courtiers, and this background provides a setting for the drama and
an inspiration for the angry remarks of the speaker. Sometimes a situation
is also briefly sketched in; in the first satire, for example, the studious protagonist is enticed away from his books by a foppish young friend. This
combination of setting, situation, living characters, and interaction among
them, makes each satire a drama-in-miniature.

Donne produces continuity from satire to satire through the pervasive
presence of the speaker himself, who consistently defends the spiritual
values of simplicity, peace, constancy, and truth. This idealistic protagonist,
who combats the materialistic and profane antagonists he encounters, is a
satiric mask which Donne adopts, just as Swift later puts on various masks in
his various satires. But Donne's use of the mask is somewhat different from
its use in, for example, *Gulliver's Travels.* Unlike Swift, Donne speaks directly
through his mask, permitting his protagonist to advocate the very position
Donne himself wishes to advocate. Nevertheless, the *Satyres* are literature
rather than life and the fully characterized protagonist is Donne's spokesman
rather than Donne himself, however much Donne's own views shimmer behind him. So I shall distinguish between the two by referring to the mask as
the protagonist, the speaker, or Donne's spokesman.

This protagonist has a personality in his own right. In accordance with the
over-all thematic purpose of defending spiritual values against creeping
materialism, he is presented as a retiring scholar who is occasionally persuaded to venture out of his study to observe the sights which arouse his
wrath. The first lines of the first satire set forth this aspect of his personality:

> Away thou fondling motley humorist,
> Leave mee, and in this standing woodden chest,
> Conforted with these few bookes, let me lye
> In prison, and here be coffin'd, when I dye;
> Here are Gods conduits, grave Divines; and here
> Natures Secretary, the Philosopher;
> And jolly Statesmen, which teach how to tie
> The sinewes of a cities mistique bodie;
> Here gathering Chroniclers, and by them stand
> Giddie fantastique Poets of each land.[4]
>
>   (I.1-10)

Although these lines might also suggest that he has a touch of the misan-
thrope, a suggestion further substantiated by the harsh terms that he sometimes uses to condemn vice, we gradually realize that, like all outspoken
idealists, he only hates men insofar as they fail to conform to the spiritual
realities which he envisions. He is betrothed to his "Mistresse Truth" (IIII.163),

his "Mistresse faire Religion" (III.5). He wishes to commend these mistresses
to other men and to chastise them for giving their devotion to mistresses
more earthly and more inconstant. Thus when he slips into angry vituperation, as he sometimes does, it is not because he hates mankind, but because
he hates mankind's failure to fulfill the spiritual potentialities which make
them fully human and mankind's tendency to dwell on more transient
values. But he never permits anger to interfere with his awareness that
mockery is the best weapon. The speaker, in spite of the fact that he is a
contemplative scholar, can also debate skillfully with the most quick-witted
worldling. In the first satire, for example, he begins by preaching gray-
beardedly to his degenerate young friend; but when the ambitious youth
continues to ogle noblemen, sophisticates, and prostitutes, the protagonist
drops gray-bearded piety and uses the crude humor that the fop is more
capable of comprehending. Their dialogue runs:

> But Oh, God strengthen thee, why stoop'st thou so?
> Why? he hath travayld; Long? No; but to me
> (Which understand none,) he doth seeme to be
> Perfect French, and Italian; I replyed,
> So is the Poxe . . . .

(I.100-104)

The fop's eyes and mind have wandered off while the protagonist is deliver-
ing his crushing retort, however, and so he neither answers it nor is deterred
from lechery and ambition. As we follow him through the five satires, the
speaker thus reveals himself as an idealistic but troubled scholar, eager to
give paternal advice to others; he is sometimes angered by their failure to heed
it or by the social abuses he observes, sometimes aroused to mockery, sometimes to astonished bitterness, never to inarticulate silence.

   In addition to the continuity provided by the personality and idealism
of the protagonist himself, a further link and a further sharpening of the
contrast between the spiritual and the material is provided by a system of
interlocking imagery which recurs within individual satires and from satire
to satire. This imagery forms two main strands, one abstract and the other
grossly material; the two strands become joined in the later satires as concrete imagery, especially water, is used both for its visual suggestiveness and
for its abstract spiritual significance. The abstract strand of imagery is essentially conceptual and is drawn from religion and religious philosophy,
employing the ideas of sin, law, conscience, virtue, and truth. In the first
satire, for example, the pious protagonist playfully extends the concept
of adultery when he warns his young friend not to desert him for someone
who is nobler or better dressed when they venture out on the street together:

> For better or worse take mee, or leave mee:
> To take, and leave mee is adultery.

(I.25-26)

He concludes his warning by metaphorically making himself an indulgent
priest and his young friend a repentant sinner:

> But since thou like a contrite penitent,
> Charitably warn'd of thy sinnes, dost repent
> These vanities, and giddinesses, loe
> I shut my chamber doore, and come, lets goe.
>
>   (I. 49-52)

And later when the young friend wanders off after a brightly-dressed fellow
fop, the protagonist calls him "my lost sheep."

But since Donne's object is to depict and chastise the bestial aspects of
man which may interfere with the fulfillment of the spiritual ideal, there is
a second strand of imagery, concrete and vivid, which is drawn from man's
physical life. Through these images Donne emphasizes the coarser aspects
of gratifying the senses by eating, drinking, love-making, being clothed, and
obtaining money. It is this strand which has tended to repel or offend critics,
for Donne is trying to make vice vividly repulsive and succeeds in doing just
that. In condemnation of the bad poets who borrow and steal from the
stored nourishment of others' brains, for example, his spokesman says:

> But hee is worst, who (beggarly) doth chaw
> Others wits fruits, and in his ravenous maw
> Rankly digested, doth those things out-spue,
> As his owne things; and they are his owne, 'tis true,
> For if one eate my meate, though it be knowne
> The meate was mine, th'excrement is his owne. . . .
>
>   (II.25-30)

This is one of the most brutal images in all the five *Satyres*. It would be
difficult to find a phrase more ugly to the ear than "Others wits fruits." But
it would also be difficult to make more vivid the ugliness of literary fraudu-
lence.

Such superb ability to make vice repulsive to both the ear and mind is its
own answer to those who object to the unpleasantness of the *Satyres*. It is
motivated not by hatred of mankind, nor by Manichaean contempt for the
physical, but by hatred of sins and evils to which man's incipient bestiality
may lead. It proceeds by making that incipient bestiality vividly apparent.
But the superficial negativeness of the *Satyres* is redeemed by their affirmation of the high human values of truth, constancy, and virtue. And their
superficial ugliness is redeemed by the lightning speed of their movement
and the intellectual humor of their wit. In spite of all the condemnation
and vituperation which they contain, they are driven on by a rollicking *jeu
d'esprit* which the reader can hardly fail to find delightful.

With these general principles of organization and technique in mind, we
can observe their operation in individual satires in more detail; for the five
satires, whether they are intended to be organically joined to one another

or not, share the same structure and the same fundamental attitude toward life. Each satirizes a different aspect of society: I, the opportunism and lechery of a young rake; II, corrupt lawyers; III, religion; IIII, courtiers and the court; and V, officers and suitors. I is closely related to IIII, and II is closely related to V; III, containing the great paean to Truth, is central in both position and theme.[5]

The first satire is concerned with contrasting the constancy which adherence to virtue produces and the inconstancy which results from commitment to profane and material values. This contrast is dramatized through the personalities of the admonitory protagonist and the madcap young rake who has appeared and is trying to drag him away from his studies. Their opposition is apparent from the outset; after surveying the books in his library, the contemplative scholar asks:

> Shall I leave all this constant company,
> And follow headlong, wild uncertaine thee?
>
> (I.11-12)

In terms of virtues and vices the protagonist stands for simplicity, peaceful contemplation, and the constancy which they possess and produce; the antagonist for fashion, lechery, and social-climbing, and the inconstancy which they possess and produce.

The imagery is directly related to the theme, drawn from religion, fashions in clothing, and prostitution. These are all compressed together in the following passage, where the simple and high-minded scholar criticizes the rake for pursuing whores and following changes in fashion:

> Why should'st thou (that dost not onely approve,
> But in ranke itchie lust, desire, and love
> The nakednesse and bareness to enjoy,
> Of thy plumpe muddy whore, or prostitute boy)
> Hate vertue, though shee be naked, and bare?
> At birth, and death, our bodies naked are;
> And till our Soules be unapparrelled
> Of bodies, they from blisse are banished.
> Mans first blest state was naked, when by sinne
> Hee lost that, yet hee was cloath'd but in beasts skin,
> And in this course attire, which I now weare,
> With God, and with the Muses I conferre.
>
> (I.37-48)

Virtue is simple, bare, and unchanging; it is achieved by conferring with God and with the Muses, reflected in a contemplative life and coarse clothing. But the young rake, however much he may enjoy nakedness at some moments, is as fickle and inconstant as the fashions which he follows. The protagonist attempts to convince him of his error by appealing to religious doctrine: prelapsarian Adam wore no clothes at all and desired to put them on only after

he had fallen from grace; and until souls shed in death the bodies with which
they are clothed in life, they cannot ascend to the bliss of heaven.

But the young fop is almost incorrigibly committed to the material value
of fashion, and the protagonist is also aroused to rebuke him for judging his
friends by their appearance:

> Oh monstrous, superstitious puritan,
> Of refin'd manners, yet ceremoniall man,
> That when thou meet'st one, with enquiring eyes
> Dost search, and like a needy broker prize
> The silke, and gold he weares, and to that rate
> So high or low, dost raise thy formall hat. . . .
>
> (I.27-32)

As Donne's spokesman implies, to judge people so cursorily on superficial
appearances is a form of superstition, a quality shared by the over-scrupulous,
over-precise, and hypocritical Puritans.[6] But the protagonist knows his young
friend well enough to realize that he is not likely to heed these warnings and
admonitions. Before venturing out, he predicts the fop's behavior on the
street in lines which compress and combine the now-familiar inconstancy
images of whores and fashions:

> But sooner may a cheape whore, who hath beene
> Worne by as many severall men in sinne,
> As are black feathers, or musk-colour hose,
> Name her childs right true father, 'mongst all those. . . .
> Then thou, when thou depart'st from mee, canst show
> Whither, why, when, or with whom thou would'st go.
>
> (I.53-64)

Part of the irony of the poem derives from the fact that the protagonist,
aware of the inconstancy of the young man's friendship, goes off with him
anyway after having charitably warned him of his sins. He admits that he
sins against his own conscience in going (65-66), but this admission only
increases his effectiveness as a protagonist. By admitting that he too sins,
he establishes himself as an honest and human man, a man who can be
believed and whose charitable warnings should be heeded, all the more because they grow out of his own experience of sin.

When they go out on the street, his prediction comes true. Although
they follow a wall on their walk and the protagonist takes the outside track
to prevent his friend from running off, the young man is still able to ogle
and grin. He looks around with amorous smiles for every painted fool,
servilely stoops before the great, and completely ignores the men who are
grave and virtuous. As they walk and the protagonist comments on what
he sees and his friend's behavior, we are given a fast-moving, vivid, panoramic,
and dramatic view of Elizabethan London, its inhabitants, and its vices. The
action is fully visualized, from the foppish "many-coloured Peacock" whom

the young man chases momentarily to the seductive beloved whom he spies in a window and chases at greater length. The drama is further increased by several dialogues which break into the protagonist's monologue of complaint. The young rake bows before some high personage:

> Now leaps he upright, Joggs me, & cryes, Do you see
> Yonder well favoured youth? Which? Oh, 'tis hee
> That dances so divinely; Oh, said I,
> Stand still, must you dance here for company?
> He droopt, wee went, till one (which did excell
> Th' Indians, in drinking his Tobacco well)
> Met us; they talk'd; I whispered, let'us goe,
> 'T may be you smell him not, truely I doe. . . .
>
> (I.83-90)

The satire comes to a natural end when the young man runs off to visit his inconstant beloved and finds her surrounded with other young men. Pressing his case, he is beaten up by them. At last he is forced to do something constantly, although not by choice; as the protagonist remarks ironically:

> He quarrell'd fought, bled; and turn'd out of dore
> Directly came to mee hanging the head,
> And constantly a while must keep his bed.
>
> (I.110-112)

In the second satire, dealing with corrupt lawyers, Donne treats vices far more serious than the inconstancy produced by social-climbing, fashion-fascination, and lechery. In this satire his object of attack is fraud, a spiritual sin rather than a sin of the flesh, although rooted in the material because it is rooted in a desire for secular wealth and power. For this reason, the imagery of prostitution continues, but is given a new twist. Donne uses it to build up gradually to the accusation that those who commit fraud are spiritual prostitutes who sell their souls for secular gain. The main object of attack is the lawyer who uses fraud on his clients, and this form of fraud is personified in Coscus, the young man who plays the antagonist in this satire. But Coscus is also a former poet, and the protagonist is thus led to attack those poets who are frauds and spiritual prostitutes, those who write for Lords for the sake of advancement or because it is the fashionable thing to do, those who plagiarize the fruits of others' wits and produce mere excrement. After his sideglance at the abuses of poetry, however, he goes on to say:

> . . . these do mee no harme, nor they which use
> To out-doe Dildoes, and out-usure Jewes;
> To out-drinke the sea, to out-sweare the Letanie. . . .
>
> (II.31-33)

Although at first glance this may seem "light-hearted tolerance of sin,"[7] he makes it clear a few lines later than he is simply after bigger game. These sins are their own punishment, he tells us (39); his vehemence against Coscus is aroused because this lawyer uses his position and profession to harm others as well. Following traditional moral theology, he regards compound sins and spiritual sins as the worst of all and attacks them with more virulence than the simple sins of lechery and gluttony.

Having thus set up his ethical and moral standard, the protagonist now summons up the figure of Coscus for indictment and judgment. Again, the scene is depicted dramatically, employing personal interaction and dialogue. The protagonist is apparently a guardian or advisor to Coscus, who when called to account for himself immediately launches into a description of his success in his current love affair. Interrupted by the protagonist's "spare mee," he goes on to describe his success in his law career. The older man rebukes him angrily:

> When sicke with Poetrie, and possest with muse
> Thou wast, and mad, I hop'd; but men which chuse
> Law practise for meere gaine, bold soule, repute
> Worse then imbrothel'd strumpets prostitute.
>
> (II.61-64)

And he fills the remainder of the satire with a monologue on the theme that the corrupt lawyer who practices law for gain, for the acquisition of secular power and wealth, is a spiritual prostitute. Such a lawyer is worse than "carted whores" who lie to judges to save themselves for the corrupt lawyer consistently and conscientiously lies in order to achieve personal success. Further, he thrives on the existence of sin with selfish delight, because it is grist to his gainful mill. The protagonist embeds such fraudulent lawyers in the ninth circle more deeply than Satan himself:

> And spying heires melting with luxurie,
> Satan will not joy at their sinnes, as hee.
>
> (II.79-80)

Encouraging his clients in their vices, the corrupt lawyer manages to defraud them and gain their property for himself. Or if this opportunity is not present, he may intentionally and secretly alter wills or deeds in order to reap some potential advantage for himself. This lawyer may also be compared with another set of frauds who commit a similar sin in the area of religion—the religious controversialists who "in vouch'd Texts, leave out / Shrewd words, which might against them cleare the doubt" (II.101-102).

After this flaying of the vice of fraud in many of its forms, the protagonist briefly asserts the necessity of virtue and the way it can be attained. In his eyes, it resides in the golden mean, in the avoidance of the corrupting forces of deficiency or excess. Lust for great secular wealth and power is the prime temptation for men such as Coscus, but the protagonist realizes that total deprivation of wealth is also a temptation to sin. Thus he hates equally "Carthusian fasts, and fulsome Bachanalls" (106) and advocates simple moderation, for "None starve, none surfet so . . ." (109). And in spite of the overwhelming presence of evil in his contemporary world, he refuses to despair; he stoically sees "Good workes as good, but out of fashion now, / Like old rich wardrops . . ." (110-111). So we return again to the virtues of simplicity, tradition, and constancy which were asserted as the ideal in the first satire.

The first two satires are long in their condemnation of vice, short in their praise of virtue, often coarse in diction and imagery, and highly visual, dramatic, and concrete. The third satire marks a partial departure from many of these characteristics. The first two, with their manifold skirmishes with every manifestation of vice within eye-range, have some of the superficial chaos of an impressionistic montage. Not so with *Satyre III*, every line of which has an obvious organic and thematic appropriateness. Unlike every other satire in the group, this one is a soliloquy conducted in meditative isolation.[8] In place of the usual interlocutor, the protagonist counsels with his own better self. He begins in a state near despair, reasons himself through a series of negative possibilities, and finally rises to an affirmation which enables his will to act, concluding with a great paean to Truth.

His theme in this satire is "our Mistresse faire Religion." Setting himself a series of questions and then answering them, he distinguishes between the secular courage of straw which enables men to explore the unknown seas of a brave new world or to fight battles from the wooden sepulchers of ships and the genuine spiritual courage which prompts them to explore the mysteries of religion and do battle with the Devil himself. Bidding himself to seek true religion, the protagonist looks around to find it, but discovers instead only a confused variety of warring creeds. Mirreus chooses Roman Catholicism; Crantz, Genevan Calvinism; Graius, English Anglicanism; Phrygius, no religion; Graccus, all. What is truth, he asks himself, and pauses for an answer. Believing that man must choose only one religion, and that the right one, he suggests a way to go about choosing, though he does not completely resolve the problem of which religion is the right one. His basic appeal is to tradition:

> . . . ask thy father which is shee,
> Let him aske his; though truth and falsehood bee
> Neare twins, yet truth a little elder is. . . .
>
> (III.71-73)

But most important is the sincerity and persistence of the search itself. Truth, like all ideals, resides at the top of a rugged pinnacle, and the ascent to it is a difficult one:

> On a huge hill,
> Cragged, and steep, Truth stands, and hee that will
> Reach her, about must, and about must goe;
> And what the hills suddennes resists, winne so;
> Yet strive so, that before age, deaths twilight,
> Thy Soule rest, for none can worke in that night. (III.79-84)

Thus the protagonist affirms the supreme importance of the individual search for spiritual truth; for him the claim upon every man to save his immortal soul is a far higher one than the secular claims to excel in fashion, to scramble for place, to gratify physical desires; this belief is, of course, the motivation behind the vehemence with which he attacks secular abuses in the other satires. Parallel to this view of the importance of the spiritual search is his assertion that God's law stands above mere human law; if there is a conflict between them, then the individual must choose to follow God's law. Material and secular power is viewed in all these satires as a great potential threat and temptation, for it causes men to use human law to gratify their own evil desires, to ignore the supremacy of divine law, and to blind themselves to more immutable and constant spiritual values. So, returning to the water imagery which he used at the beginning of this satire, he concludes with a superbly effective image which unites all the varying emphases of the five satires:

> As streames are, Power is; those blest flowers that dwell
> At the rough streames calme head, thrive and do well,
> But having left their roots, and themselves given
> To the streames tyrannous rage, alas, are driven
> Through mills, and rockes, and woods, and at last almost
> Consum'd in going, in the sea are lost:
> So perish Soules, which more chose mens unjust
> Power from God claym'd, then God himselfe to trust.
>
> (III.103-110)

At the top of the cragged and steep hill where truth stands, all is peaceful, calm, and good; religion, divine power, and virtue—all the immutable values—reside there. But if men abandon this height for the tyrannous rage of secular desires and injustices, they are buffeted and tossed and torn, perishing in the sea of iniquity. This underlying attitude toward secular and spiritual matters, common to all five satires, ultimately works to give them a unity greater even than their carefully conceived dramatic structure creates.

From this high point, the protagonist descends in the fourth satire to consider again the purgatory which is secular life and to chastise the folly of secular desires and accomplishments. More particularly, he satirizes the court and courtiers. Having been led away by a foppish bore to visit the court, he writes this satire as a recollection in tranquility after he has escaped from its temptations; thus he is able to unite the drama of his visit with reflections on its significance. The antagonist of this satire who incarnates most of the sins Donne wishes to condemn is a threadbare young courtier, a personification of most of the characteristics of the Gallicized or Italianate Englishman. He babbles on about his ability as a linguist, his knowledge of fashion, his love of a Lord. Their dialogue is extremely humorous, since the protagonist mocks his egoism at every turn, and the young fop is too obtuse and self-centered to understand him. When he boasts of his knowledge of languages, he is told that his skill is an anachronism, that he would have made a good interpreter to the bricklayers of the Tower of

Babel. When he exclaims, "'Tis sweet to talke of Kings" (74), the protagonist recommends him to the company of the keeper at Westminster Abbey. Still the bore sticks like a burr, and still he echoes the cry of the sixteenth-century pseudo-sophisticate:

> He's base, Mechanique, coarse,
> So are all your Englishmen in their discourse.
>
> (IIII.81-82)

Changing his subject matter, the young worldling begins to talk of court life, unwittingly giving a detailed and accurate account of its iniquities; he speaks of the sale of offices, entailed until the Day of Judgment; which ladies paint themselves; who loves whom, and who boys and goats; who is going bankrupt because of ostentation; why the wars thrive ill.

Finally ridding himself of the bore by lending him a crown, the protagonist still cannot rid himself of the awful vision of court life, and so he goes on to give his own description of it. The technique is a clever one, since we are given dual views of court life—that of the admiring inside-dopester and that of the revolted man of honor; yet both the admirer and the despiser present pictures which disgust. The protagonist (who is much brighter than the fop) gives an account full of epigrammatically devastating touches:

> As fresh, and sweet their Apparrells be, as bee
> The fields they sold to buy them. . . .
>
> (IIII.180-181)

He objects to the same qualities at court as were personified in the young fop himself—affectation, corruption, and false values—all the result of emphasizing secular aspirations instead of spiritual ones. Those who live at court are:

> . . . men that doe know
> No token of worth, but Queenes man, and fine
> Living, barrells of beefe, flaggons of wine. . . .
>
> (IIII.234-236)

Totally disheartened with it all, he returns to the sea imagery with which he concluded the last satire, calling upon preachers ("Seas of Wit and Arts" [238]) to drown the sins of the court. He, a dweller in the peace and isolation of the stream's head, is but a tiny brook, sufficient only to wash his own stains away.

The fifth satire returns again to the theme of the law, already considered in the second satire. This time, however, the object of attack is officers who take advantage of suitors, rather than lawyers who deceive their clients. The protagonist now speaks to a young man who has fruitlessly bribed corrupt officials and who quietly listens to the angry tirade. And, as in *Satyre II*, the speaker also regards this perversion of the law as the prostitution of a worthy ideal; he pleads:

> Oh, ne'r may
> Faire lawes white reverend name be strumpeted,
> To warrant thefts. . . .
>
> (V.68-70)

But he knows too well that it has been strumpeted already. The young man has bribed a judge without success, and the money he used for bribery was itself ill-gotten. The protagonist taunts him:

> Why barest thou to you Officer? Foole, Hath hee
> Got those goods, for which erst men bar'd to thee?
> Foole, twice, thrice, thou hast bought wrong, and now
>   hungerly
> Beg'st right. . . .
>
> (V.79-82)

Having stripped others of their wealth, the young man has now been stripped of his own by the judge. Ironically, this time the youth himself has been unjustly treated.

But the protagonist's anger is directed more toward the officers than toward the wretched suitor. His attack on them is linked to the previous satires through a pervasive use of stream and sea imagery. Now it is Law, God's Law, which dwells at the stream's head; officials who abuse the power delegated to them by God suck in and drown those who appeal to the law:

> . . . powre of the Courts below
> Flow from the first maine head, and these can throw
> Thee, if they sucke thee in, to misery. . . .
>
> (V.45-47)

He sees all mankind as a world:

> . . . in which; Officers
> Are the vast ravishing seas; and Suiters,
> Springs; now full, now shallow, now drye; which to
> That which drownes them, run. . . .
>
> (V.13-16)

When officers abuse their delegated power to increase their own wealth, there are only two possible ways to deal with them: to swim against the stream by protesting, the likely result of which is fruitless exhaustion; or to build golden bridges over it through fees and bribes, the likely result of which is the fruitless drowning of the money, a result only slightly better than the drowning of the suitor through exhausted opposition. These considerations bring the protagonist to proclaim an impassioned denunciation of the perversion of divine power for secular ends:

> Judges are Gods; he who made and said them so,
> Meant not that men should be forc'd to them to goe,
> By meanes of Angels; When supplications
> We send to God, to Dominations,
> Powers, Cherubins, and all heavens Courts, if wee
> Should pay fees as here, Daily bread would be

> Scarce to Kings. . . .
>
> (V.57-63)

God's justice is free, not bought with bribery; God may use angels as mediaries between Himself and mankind, but He never intended that His counterparts on earth be appealed to through metallic angels. The angels of God and the angels of man should not be used so differently, but they are. And so again we find in this satire the customary contrast between the righteous ideal, and the way in which it has been perverted by man's greed for material wealth and power.

Close analysis indeed reveals that these *Satyres* are finely unified works of art in their own right, not incoherent and unpolished as some critics have described them. Donne has wrought them with care, consciously using roughness when it is necessary for his purpose, but also infusing a lofty strain of idealism which compensates for the necessary roughness. Imagery, drama, and dialogue are all united to work toward a single end: a contrast between the spiritual values which men ought to seek and the material and secular temptations which cause men to ignore or pervert the spiritual idea. The *Satyres* show that Donne was an accomplished craftsman even in his apprentice work.

Although interesting in their own right, the *Satyres* have an important secondary interest for the Donne specialist because of what they reveal about the techniques and fundamental assumptions which inform his other better-known poetry. The *Satyres* are among Donne's earliest works,[9] and they anticipate many of the themes of his religious poetry, indicating that there was no great dichotomy between the rakish "Jack Donne" and the pious Dr. Donne. They reveal that the young Donne was deeply concerned with moral questions, that the *contemptus mundi* strain to which he gave expression in the *First* and *Second Anniversaries* was not a passing mood but a continuing preoccupation. The young man who wrote the *Satyres* saw very early that the Things of the Spirit offered more enduring satisfactions than the Things of the World. Still more important, however, is what the *Satyres* tell us about Donne's experimentation with technique. They provide concrete evidence for the view of some modern critics, predominantly Leonard Unger,[10] that many of the *Songs and Sonets* are to be read as dramatic monologues spoken by a *persona*, not as direct statements of Donne's own personal experience. Donne was in his very early twenties when he wrote these satires; their protagonist is an older man who gives grey-bearded advice to young men about town. Although this protagonist seems to state Donne's own views, none of Donne's contemporaries would have identified him as John Donne. The fact that Donne used the techniques of the mask and the dramatic monologue in the *Satyres* gives us some partial evidence for what has hitherto been presented as a useful hypothesis or an unproved impression, that the *Songs and Sonets* (many of which were written at about the same time) may also be read as dramatic monologues. Perhaps the phantom of Jack Donne, resurrected to account for their cynicism and lustiness, can at last be laid to rest and these poems can again be read as poetry rather than autobiography.

THE PERSONA AS RHETOR:
AN INTERPRETATION OF DONNE'S *SATYRE III*

Thomas O. Sloan

Nowadays if we find a poem that has been *recognizably* structured by considerations of a real audience, we hesitate to call it poetry at all. A real audience, we know, is always central in rhetorical discourse, and the only sort of rhetoric we wish to allow in the house of poetry is the imitative sort, the dialogue or monologue in which an imaginary speaker attempts to persuade an imaginary audience. Even higher than that in our estimation is poetry like certain of Donne's songs and sonnets, in which an imaginary speaker manages to be introspective while ostensibly attempting to persuade an imaginary mistress. What happens, then, when we read a poem by Donne that was *subtly* structured, not even in imitation of rhetoric but for actual rhetorical considerations, to persuade a real audience? Considering our critical predispositions, and our esteem for Donne, it is no wonder that we are tempted to read the poem as if it were at a far remove from actual rhetoric, and that we are tempted, further, to ignore the possibility that the poem might bear a greater resemblance to oratory than it does to dialogue, monologue, or soliloquy.

Let us look at a recent dramatic analysis of *Satyre III*, one of Donne's most famous and most rhetorical poems. My basic argument is that our use of the dramatic approach—of proven usefulness to oral interpreters[1] and to students of Donne[2]—needs the troubling which only the rhetorical dimension can provide in our analyses of Donne's poetry. We seem overly tempted to place all poetry in a kind of "another worldness," our critical refinement on Sidney's defense whereby we see the poem both as separable from the mind in which it was created and as only incidentally involved in its own milieu. This is a fault not of the dramatic approach but of its coupling with our critical predispositions, for all the dramatic approach does is raise questions (Who is speaking? To whom? What does he say? How? Why? Where? When?) and offer the important concept that poetic meaning inheres in the complex relationships of the answers. But it would apparently involve a real troubling of our critical predispositions to imagine that the audience (To whom?) could be real, the speaker's intent (Why?) to persuade that audience, and the identity of the speaker (Who?) less significant than we suppose. It is just such a troubling that I believe all users of the dramatic approach need

Reprinted from *The Quarterly Journal of Speech*, 51 (1965), 14-27, by permission of the author and the publisher.

in order to understand, classify, and evaluate certain poems—among them,
Donne's *Satyre III*.

Satyre III is one of Donne's five satires, all written during the close of
the sixteenth century, when Donne was in his early twenties. N. J. C.
Andreasen's analysis of these five poems performs the important service of
defending them against critical complaints that they are shaggy or obscure
and against the critical notion that they are interesting mainly as autobiographical curiosities.[3] As mentioned earlier, Andreasen's approach is dramatic;
by his view, these five satires are related; though they differ in dramatic
situation, all are spoken by the same *persona* and all employ the same themes.
The *persona* who speaks the poems is "a retiring scholar who is occasionally
persuaded to venture out of his study to observe the sights which arouse his
wrath" (p. 61). He is an idealist, angered when society does not conform
to his ideals and eager to give advice, in a paternal, often "grey-bearded"
way, to others. A basic theme of all five poems is "an idealistic defense of
spiritual values against the creeping encroachment of sixteenth-century
materialism" (p. 59). In his defense, the speaker upholds the values of simplicity, peace, constancy, tradition, and truth. In discussing these points,
Andreasen shows that the five satires also employ similar imagery.

Andreasen's paraphrase of the poems is incisive, and most of his general
conclusions about their qualities are persuasive. Each poem, he states,
"satirizes a different aspect of society: I, the opportunism and lechery of
a young rake; II, corrupt lawyers; III, religion; IIII, courtiers and the court;
and V, officers and suitors. I is closely related to IIII, and II is closely related to V; III, containing the great paean to Truth, is central in both position
and theme" (p. 64). Andreasen states that *Satyre III* differs from the others
in two ways: first, as compared with the first two satires, *Satyre III* is much
more tightly organized, every line has an "organic and thematic appropriateness," whereas the first two send arguments skirmishing off to do battle
"with every manifestation of vice within eye-range" (p. 69). Secondly,

> Unlike every other satire in the group, this one is a soliloquy conducted
> in meditative isolation. In place of the usual interlocutor, the protagonist
> counsels with his own better self. He begins in a state near despair, reasons
> himself through a series of negative possibilities, and finally rises to an
> affirmation which enables his will to act, concluding with a great paean
> to Truth (p. 69).

It is mainly with the second difference which Andreasen draws between
Satyre III and the others that I disagree. It is true that this satire does not
depict a definite adversary or interlocutor, whose presence would turn the
utterance into a monologue. Nonetheless, it is misleading to call this work
a "soliloquy." First, as a soliloquy, the poem lacks probability, for, as we
shall see, it does not employ methods the supposed protagonist would most
likely use to reason with himself. Second, the poem reveals no palpable
evidence of a soliloquizing intent. In referring to the mask the dramatic approach discovers, Andreasen claims, "Although this protagonist seems to

state Donne's own views, none of Donne's contemporaries would have identified him as John Donne" (p. 75). Perhaps true; yet even though we may accept the notion that Donne's contemporaries may have read this poem as being spoken by a retiring scholar, who is more explicitly identified in the other satires, must we also accept the notion that these contemporaries would have regarded this poem as a soliloquy? While it is true that one of the major poetic achievements of the sixteenth century was the soliloquy, or lyric spoken in ostensible isolation, it is also true that soliloquies were created, read, and heard by men to whom the principal forms of discourse were rhetorical, men who practised literary criticism by means of rhetorical analysis. It seems improbable that, given the expectations of his audience, the poet would provide clues so strongly oratorical in naturè if his intent was to soliloquize. For one thing, there is little "I"-saying or self-searching or debating of alternatives. For another, almost any rhetoric textbook of the period contains descriptions of deliberative oratory that are strikingly similar to effects in this poem.

Consequently, I propose that we view the spoken form of this poem as more like an oration than like a soliloquy, more like the *persona's* attempt to persuade a real audience than like his attempt to persuade himself. Having looked at the discourse in this way, we shall then examine the character of the speaker.

Classically, deliberative oratory was political oratory, aimed at influencing the judgment of policy-determining assemblies. It was concerned with honorable action, the most honorable courses for men to take when faced with decisions. The classical rhetoricians knew that audiences are usually misled by prospects offering material advantage; therefore, they advised the orator that it would usually be necessary for him to distinguish for his audience between what is honorable and what is merely expedient. In the Renaissance, classical principles of deliberative oratory were applied to almost all the processes of public advice-giving, exhortation, even sermonizing. According to Thomas Wilson, "the whole compasse of this cause is, either to aduise our neighbour to that thyng, whiche we thynke most nedeful for hym or els to cal him backe frō that folie, which hindereth muche his estimacion."[4] Of course, in constructing a deliberative oration one will use topics, or "places," that also pertain to demonstrative oratory, as in praising or dispraising, and that pertain to judicial oratory, as in the interpretation of law. Two principal, specific functions of deliberative oratory are persuasion and exhortation, the latter usually primary:

> The places of exhortyng and dehortyng, are the same whiche we vse in perswadyng and dissuadyng, sauyng that he which vseth perswasiou [sic], seeketh by argumetes to compasse his deuise: he that laboures to exhorte, doeth stirre affections.
>
> Erasmus sheweth these to be the most especiall places that do perteine vnto exhortation.
>
> Praise, or Commendacion.

> Expectation of al men.
> Hope of victorie.
> Hope of renowme [sic].
>
> Feare of shame.
> Greatnesse of rewarde.
> Rehersall of examples, in all ages and
> especially of thynges lately doen.[5]

But anyone may write a discourse exhorting or persuading, using as Donne does the places advised by Wilson, and still fail to write in the oratorical mode. It is in the art of *dispositio* that we find the most striking similarities between this poem and oratory. By applying the principles of *dispositio* to this poem we may see clearly (1) the rhetorical function of each section of the poem, (2) the actual thesis of the poem, and (3) indications of the audience for which the poem was written. Wilson lists seven parts of an oration: entrance, narration, proposition, division, confirmation, confutation, and conclusion (fol. 4). But the best rule to follow for arrangement, he states, is the orator's own wit in adapting his discourse to his hearers (foll. 84-85). The following is an attempt first to analyze *Satyre III* by means of traditional, primarily Wilson's, principles of *dispositio* and second to study Donne's possible adaptation of traditional arrangement.

1. Entrance

The purpose of the entrance is to gain the audience's understanding and attention, and to make them well-disposed; for victory rests "firste, in apt teachyng the hearers, what the matter is, next in gettyng them to geue good eare, and thirdly in winnyng their fauour."[6] To gain the audience's understanding and attention the orator may explain the nature of the case and its importance. One of the ways he may get their good will is to reveal his own good character.

> Kinde pitty chokes my spleene; brave scorn forbids
> Those teares to issue which swell my eye-lids;
> I must not laugh, nor weepe sinnes, and be wise,
> Can railing then cure these worne maladies?[7]

The speaker begins *Satyre III* by indicating that his feelings toward the matter he is about to discuss are a compound of "kinde pitty" and "brave scorn": pity prevents him from laughing; scorn prevents him from weeping; therefore, in order to show sound judgment, he must neither laugh nor weep for these sins. Wilson advises preachers "sometimes to begynne lamentablie with an vnfained bewailyng of sinne, and a terrible declaryng of Goddes threates" (fol. 58ᵛ). But the speaker of this satire, a studious man (according to Andreasen) but no preacher, to be true to his own feelings may not employ the lamenter's response to this subject nor even the rebuker's laugh. Since these are matters that call forth strong emotions, perhaps he can cure them by "railing." Yet, that course is of doubtful efficacy,

since vigorous handling could not repair anything worn—and Donne soon
shifts from railing to exhortation.

Thus, in one sentence, the speaker has opened his case by revealing at
least three aspects of it. He has shown his own good character, as a man
with a concern for the expression of sound judgment. He has shown that
the case by its nature belongs to the general class of "sinnes" and "worne
maladies" but that, considering his character and his own strong feelings,
he finds the matter, though in part ridiculous, too serious for ridicule. It is
this second aspect of the entrance that sets the tone for the entire poem,
making its satiric elements texturally different from those found in the
other four satires. Moreover, this aspect rationalizes the speaker's "railing"
by means of which he constructs the second part of his discourse (the narration). Finally, he shows the unfavorable light in which the case for the
opposition will be displayed, as provoking both "spleene" and "teares,"
"scorn" and "pitty."

2. Narration

The narration of the case is the full presentation of the subject of the
oration, plus all necessary explanatory or background material. In cases in
which the audience is familiar with the subject, the orator is faced with
the question of either omitting the narration or using it as introduction,
to bring his subject into sharp focus. Wilson notes the following has been
the use of the narration by demonstrative and deliberative orators: to "cal
the whole summe of their matter to one especial poincte, that the rather
the hearers may better perceiue whereat they leauel al their reasons" (fol.
59ᵛ).

Donne's subject is that we should engage the full measure of our soul's
devotion in the service of religion. His places are mostly comparisons
and contraries; his "figure" is amplification, "which cōsisteth mooste in
Augmentynge and diminishynge of anye matter"[8] and whose beauty
"standeth most in apte mouyng of affections."[9] His method of organization is primarily dichotomy or twofold division, a manner of disposition
for which the Ramists were creating renewed interest in Donne's day.

Is not our Mistresse faire Religion,   5
As worthy of all our Soules devotion,
As vertue was to the first blinded age?
Are not heavens joyes as valiant to asswage
Lusts, as earths honour was to them? Alas,
As wee do them in meanes, shall they surpasse   10
Us in the end, and shall thy fathers spirit
Meete blinde Philosophers in heaven, whose merit
Of strict life may be imputed faith, and heare
Thee, whom hee taught so easie wayes and neare
To follow, damn'd? O if thou dar'st, feare this;   15
This feare great courage, and high valour is.

Dar'st thou ayd mutinous Dutch, and dar'st thou lay
Thee in ships wodden Sepulchers, a prey
To leaders rage, to stormes, to shot, to dearth?
Dar'st thou dive seas, and dungeons of the earth?   20
Hast thou couragious fire to thaw the ice
Of frozen North discoueries? and thrise
Colder then Salamanders, like divine
Children in th'oven, fires of Spaine, and the line,
Whose countries limbecks to our bodies bee,   25
Canst thou for gaine beare? and must every hee
Which cryes not, Goddesse, to thy Mistresse, draw,
Or eate thy poysonous words? courage of straw!
O desperate coward, wilt thou seeme bold, and
To thy foes and his (who made thee to stand   30
Sentinell in his worlds garrison) thus yeeld,
And for forbidden warres, leave th'appointed field?
Know thy foes: The foule Devill (whom thou
Strivest to please,) for hate, not love, would allow
Thee faine, his whole Realme to be quit; and as   35
The Worlds all parts wither away and passe,
So the worlds selfe, thy other lov'd foe, is
In her decrepit wayne, and thou loving this,
Dost love a withered and worne strumpet; last,
Flesh (it selfes death) and joyes which flesh can taste,   40
Thou lovest; and thy faire goodly soule, which doth
Give this flesh power to taste joy, thou dost loath.

That "our Mistresse faire Religion" deserves "all our Soules devotion" is proved in two parts: by comparing our (that is, the audience's) religious devotion with philosophical devotion in the "first blinded age," and by comparing our devotion to religion with our devotion to the pursuit of worldly gain and honor. In the first part the speaker compares means, then ends. First comparing means: religion is as worthy of devotion as virtue in the ancient philosophy; "heavens joyes as valiant to asswage/Lusts, as earths honour." In drawing these four terms together, Donne means that the former should at least be able to perform the offices of the latter, because the former (religion, heaven's joys) are greater. The force of his argument is strengthened by the epithet "first blinded age": that age (B.C.) was the *first* "blinded age," Donne's age is the second, for the second age is as blind to the Truth as it would be without the Light, or Revelation of God's Truth. Then, comparing ends: shall the ancients' love of "earths honour" be accounted more virtuous, more like the practice of Christian faith, than our "wayes"—shall they be saved, while we are damned? We learned from our fathers to follow "neare" to ways that are "easie" and "neare"—in the light of the thesis of this satire, I think he means conformity ("neare/To follow") to religious ways that are politically ("neare" in time and place) expedient ("easie").

In the second part, the speaker compares our devotion to religion with our devotion to the pursuit of worldly gain and honor, by proving this argument: fear of being damned involves greater courage and valor than do worldly pursuits, for indulging "Lusts" is actually a cowardly relinquishing to foes. Fear of being damned involves greater courage and valor than (1) adventurous enterprise, undertaken for gain—on the sea, aiding "mutinous Dutch" or becoming prey to the mysterious and unpredictable actions of man and nature, and on land, braving the extreme cold or the extreme heat, and (2) the exaggerated honor in amorous pursuits. The lover insisting that his mistress be called "Goddesse" places his worldly mistress in ironic juxtaposition not only to "our Mistresse faire Religion" but also to the ancients, whose mythological imagery was the rage of Renaissance lovers. Finally, the speaker reasons that fear of being damned involves greater courage and valor than do these pursuits, for these pursuits are the workings of our foes—the devil, the world, and the flesh. Relinquishing ourselves to these foes is cowardice; it is a yielding to those forces God gave us life and strength to battle.

Thus the speaker provides the background for his case. In the entrance he stated that his subject is one of "worne maladies," thereby implying that his audience is already only too familiar with the background of the case he is about to present. However, he does not omit the narration. Rather, he asks questions—the sort that nowadays we call "rhetorical questions"—designed to bring the subject into focus and to narrow his case to the precise points at issue.

In this section we get the clearest indication of the audience for which this discourse was intended. It is an audience whose fathers had taught them to break with tradition. It is a lusty audience, eager for adventure and romance. It is a youthful audience, to whom courage and valor must be expressed in terms of action, battle, and dueling. The speaker, it would seem, has adapted his discourse to reach young courtiers and gentlemen, the young men about London who are so prominent in Donne's other satires. Considering the amplification, particularly the comparing terms, it seems far less likely that this is discourse used by a retiring scholar to reason with himself in isolation!

3. Proof

Under the head "proof" I shall combine the three classical parts, proposition, confirmation, and confutation. The speaker states his proposition clearly and plainly, logically following the establishment of his subject in the narration: "Seeke true religion." By "true religion" the speaker means both a church, a system of Christian faith and worship, and a deep conviction concerning the existence of God—the close relationship of the two would hardly be questioned by Donne's audience. In most orations, supporting the proposition takes two courses: confirmation, the demonstration of the validity and truthfulness of the orator's case; and confutation, the demonstration of the fallacies in the opponent's case. Normally, the two courses are taken in that order, but confutation may be taken first; if our adversary's "reasons be light, and more good maie bee doen in confutyng his, then in confirmyng our awne:

it were best of all to sette vpon hym, and putte awaie by arte, all that he hath fondely saied without witte."[10] Donne places confutation first.

> Seeke true religion. O where? Mirreus
> Thinking her unhous'd here, and fled from us,
> Seekes her at Rome; there, because hee doth know   45
> That shee was there a thousand yeares agoe,
> He loves her ragges so, as wee here obey
> The statecloth where the Prince sate yesterday.
> Crantz to such brave Loves will not be inthrall'd,
> But loves her onely, who at Geneva is call'd   50
> Religion, plaine, simple, sullen, yong,
> Contemptuous, yet unhansome; As among
> Lecherous humors, there is one that judges
> No wenches wholsome, but course country drudges.
> Graius stayes still at home here, and because   55
> Some Preachers, vile ambitious bauds, and lawes
> Still new like fashions, bid him thinke that shee
> Which dwels with us, is onely perfect, hee
> Imbraceth her, whom his Godfathers will
> Tender to him, being tender, as Wards still   60
> Take such wives as their Guardians offer, or
> Pay valewes. Carelesse Phrygius doth abhorre
> All, because all cannot be good, as one
> Knowing some women whores, dares marry none.
> Graccus loves all as one, and thinkes that so   65
> As women do in divers countries goe
> In divers habits, yet are still one kinde,
> So doth, so is Religion; and this blind-
> nesse too much light breeds; but unmoved thou
> Of force must one, and forc'd but one allow;   70
> And the right; aske thy father which is shee,
> Let him aske his; though truth and falshood bee
> Neare twins, yet truth a little elder is;
> Be busie to seeke her, beleeve me this,
> Hee's not of none, nor worst, that seekes the best.   75
> To adore, or scorne an image, or protest,
> May all be bad; doubt wisely; in strange way
> To stand inquiring right, is not to stray;
> To sleepe, or runne wrong, is. On a huge hill,
> Cragged, and steep, Truth stands, and hee that will   80
> Reach her, about must, and about must goe;
> And what the hills suddennes resists, winne so;
> Yet strive so, that before age, deaths twilight,
> Thy Soule rest, for none can worke in that night.
> To will, implyes delay, therefore now doe: 85
> Hard deeds, the bodies paines; hard knowledge too

The mindes indeavours reach, and mysteries
Are like the Sunne, dazling, yet plaine to all eyes.
Keepe the truth which thou hast found; men do not stand
In so ill case here, that God hath with his hand   90
Sign'd Kings blanck-charters to kill whom they hate
Nor are they Vicars, but hangmen to Fate.
Foole and wretch, wilt thou let thy Soule be tyed
To mans lawes, by which she shall not be tryed
At the last day? Oh, will it then boot thee   95
To say a Philip, or a Gregory,
A Harry, or a Martin taught thee this?
Is not this excuse for mere contraries,
Equally strong? cannot both sides say so?
That thou mayest rightly obey power, her bounds know;   100
Those past, her nature, and name is chang'd; to be
Then humble to her is idolatrie.
As streames are, Power is; those blest flowers that dwell
At the rough streames calme head, thrive and do well,
But having left their roots, and themselves given   105
To the streames tyrannous rage, alas, are driven
Through mills, and rockes, and woods, and at last, almost
Consum'd in going, in the sea are lost:
So perish Soules, which more chuse mens unjust
Power from God claym'd, then God himselfe to trust.   110

The speaker dichotomizes his confutation of the answers given to the question, Where? into (1) one church and (2) not one church. The first part has two subparts: Catholic and Protestant; and the Protestants are two: Calvinist and Anglican. The second part (not one church) has two subparts: no churches, all churches. Throughout the confutation the speaker continues his "Mistresse" metaphor for religion, a metaphor that he introduced in the narration. However, in the narration "Mistresse" was used in an idealized way, in the way one might speak of a lady as the embodiment of virtue. In the confutation, "Mistresse" becomes mere woman, real, earthy, unidealized.

When the speaker takes up the confirmation of his proof, religion is transformed from church into faith, and the "Mistresse" metaphor continues. Thus, the "Mistresse faire Religion," like the "profane" mistresses of Donne's songs and sonnets, is both real and ideal: in this case, she is a real church and an ideal faith. The audience has forsaken the quest for the ideal, which, however, is attainable only through the real. In the narration he has argued that religion is "worthy of all our Soules devotion" and that therefore we must "Seeke true religion"; his confutation has deplored the answers men have given to the question, Where should true religion be sought? In the final part of his proof he confirms two right ways by which true religion should be sought: (1) by actively seeking Truth, deep assurances of our own convictions, or religious faith, and (2) by keeping the Truth which we have found. The difference between his confutation and his confirmation is the difference between the questions, Where should religion be sought? and, How should religion be sought?

Whether we follow the lead of our own stable judgment or whether we are "forc'd," we must acknowledge one church, and the honorable thing to do, in either case, is to follow our conscience and acknowledge the "right" church. As for which is the right church, we should turn to our fathers, not only that generation which taught us to protest, but our fathers' fathers, for "truth a little elder is" than the forced fashions and false passions of the age. Here, as in the narration, the speaker reveals his love of tradition, which Andreasen in examining all the satires has found is an important part of his character. In order to choose the right church, we must seek truth. In any "strange way," like the mysterious course of life, an active search for truth, not the blind acceptance of it or the course away from it, is the honorable path for man to follow. This is argued first in the allegory of Truth; and it is argued secondly in the exhortation to "therefore now doe," for the "mindes indeavours" attain "hard knowledge" and the work of sorting out truth.is the difficult job of seeking that whose contradiction another man may claim as truth. The speaker was being ironic as well as paradoxical and bitter when he claimed (ll. 68-69), echoing the narration (l. 7), that "this blind- / nesse too much light breeds"—allowed to fashion our own reasons, we give up the search for truth and willingly turn our paths into "easie wayes"; when he compares "mysteries" to the "Sunne," he means again that all men may claim knowledge but all are actually dazzled by the source of knowledge.

Second, the speaker argues, "Keepe the truth which thou hast found." Doing so is more honorable, more righteous, than following the dictates of temporal authority. This is proved in three ways: first, blindly following civil authority in spiritual matters could lead to damnation. Kings are not absolved of murder in killing those whom they hate; they are not deputies of God's will—Christ's "Vicars," a title used by popes but here applied specifically to kings—but executioners obeying the accidental laws of human destiny. It is wrong, then, for man to tie his soul to man's laws, by which the soul shall not be tried at the last day. Secondly, justifying one's choice by temporal authority, religious or civil—following the Catholic course simply because "a Philip, or a Gregory," or following the Protestant course simply because "A Harry, or a Martin," has taught one to—offers only reasons which all sides may use equally. Thirdly, these arguments lead Donne into a definition of power, which when obeyed in matters that do not pertain to temporal authority produces "idolatrie," the subversion of true religion. Power is likened to a stream, souls to flowers growing at the stream's edge; souls thrive, like flowers, when the "bounds" of power are kept, but perish in the "tyrannous rage" of the stream when the bounds are not kept. However, the flower is not the victim of its own choice; its vegetative principle is able only to select what it can feed on and avoid what it cannot (to "detest,/And love," *A Nocturnall Upon S. Lucies Day*, ll. 34-35). Flowers do not by their own force leave their roots or give themselves to the stream. But man's soul has this property. The difference—vivid to an audience brought up on the medieval doctrines of the vegetative, animal, and rational souls—enhances Donne's argument. Unlike flowers, man's soul has the property of moral choice, and by choosing man's power over God's the soul forfeits its immortality, a destruction as complete as that of a flower lost in the sea. Thus, with strong "stirring of affections" the poem ends.

4. Conclusion

It would appear, then, that there is no conclusion. The speaker has apparently concluded by confirming the righteousness of keeping "the truth which thou hast found" against all the laws and force of temporal authority. If there is no conclusion, its omission may be excused by arguing that its function is less necessary in a poem than in an oration. But even without a complete oratorical *dispositio,* the poem is improbable as a soliloquy; more likely the poem was designed, as deliberative orations are, to persuade and exhort a specific audience toward honorable actions and away from merely expedient ones.

However, there is another way of looking at the disposition of this poem, in which the last part does serve to conclude the actual thesis, particularly as it pertains to how true religion should be sought. Throughout the sixteenth century, there were two types of rhetorical disposition: "natural" and "discretionary." To traditionalists, like Wilson, "natural" arrangement consisted of entrance, narration, proposition, division, confirmation, confutation, and conclusion. Ramists, who were greatly in vogue during Donne's formative years, favored their own "natural method" over traditional arrangement. But even the Ramists left room for "discretionary" disposition; though they strongly preferred the "orderly distributions" of the Ramist-trained logician, they acknowledged the necessity of poets, orators, and such other "people pleasing men" to use their own discretion in achieving their purposes. In advice that echoes that given by Wilson, the Ramist Abraham Fraunce—a contemporary of Donne—states that orators, unlike logicians, often place their best arguments first and last:

> . . . leauing the worst, in the middle of their speech altogether, the one to help the other; that with forcible thinges in the beginning, the auditors may bee woonne; and with as good in the ending, haue their minde and memory wholy occupyed.
>
> This is called the concealed or hidden methode: the methode of wit and discretion, for that it is rather seene in the prouident conceipt of him that writeth or speaketh, then perceaued by any generall rule of art, or precept whatsoeuer.[11]

In speaking on a cause that may not be acceptable to our hearers, "it is not amisse, to imitate the cunning Surgeon, who hideth his knife, because his patient should not be discouraged."[12] Seen through this view, *Satyre III* has the following arrangement: (1) an entrance, to gain the good will of the audience, (2) the argument that religion is "worthy of all our Soules devotion" (which earlier we had called the narration), one of the strongest, sure to win the audience's assent, the one in which the most direct appeals are made to the specific audience; (3) the argument concerning where religion should be sought (confutation, the first part of the proof), evidently the weakest of the three—I would guess that it is the weakest because the speaker found that he could not himself take a positive stand for any one church, could only deplore and satirize the reasons men give for attending one, none, or all churches, and (4) the argument concerning how religion should be sought (confirmation, the final part of the proof). It is in this last argument that the surgeon reveals his knife.

By constructing rhetorical premises—preliminary arguments adapted to his audience—the speaker has reached a conclusion that in effect is not only bold but rebellious. He concludes by exhorting his audience of young gentlemen not to follow the Queen blindly and absolutely in religious matters—the sort of fealty the Queen herself desired, and the sort of allegiance most blindly or most fearfully given by the audience addressed.

By an act of supremacy Elizabeth had been given the same authority over the church as was assumed by her father. Like her father, she recognized the political advantage of this authority and sought to strengthen it by enforcing allegiance to the English Church throughout her realm, regarding all recusants as potential traitors, refusing university degrees to young students (Donne among them) who would not swear the oath of allegiance to the Queen's supreme ecclesiastical authority, punishing Romanists (like Donne's younger brother, who died of "gaol fever") and Puritans who refused to submit. Thus, the power of the throne is behind the phrase "forc'd but one allow" (l. 70).

At first, anxious to preserve her subjects' fanatical love for her while at the same time promoting internal harmony in the land (though any conjecture about Elizabeth's mind is at best problematical), the Queen did not deal ruthlessly with Catholics, as later she was slow to act against the parliamentary tactics of the Puritans. But events of the eighties—the discovery of the plots that surrounded Mary of Scotland, the Armada, growing agitation by Jesuits, the boldness of the Puritan Wentworth, Archbishop Whitgift's insistence on disciplinary measures—led her into an apparently firm resolve. As the nineties began, her course seemed to be firmly fixed on strengthening conformity to Anglicanism.

"Laws" were the weapons the Anglicans used against Catholics and Puritans as the nineties began. In 1593 "The Act Against Popish Recusants" considerably increased the efficiency of the surveillance and punishment of those Catholics who steadfastly refused to attend Protestant services. In the same year, Anglican defense of the English Church began reaching a culmination with the publication of the first four books of Hooker's *Laws of Ecclesiastical Polity,* followed in 1597 by the publication of the fifth book. Catholics, of course, insisted on the supreme ecclesiastical authority of the Pope. Though Puritans, on the other hand, argued for a separation of church and state, their arguments actually envisioned a state led by their church. But Anglicans, through legal actions and theological arguments, with the sanctions of the Queen, asserted the royal supremacy over church as well as state. It is in this scene—soon after 1593[13]—a scene of religious and political turmoil controlled into tense order by the magnificent but tyrannical Queen through "lawes/Still new like fashions," that the speaker of *Satyre III* delivers his exhortations to young men close to the Queen.

His thesis is not pro-Catholic, nor pro-Puritan, nor pro-Anglican. "To adore, or scorne an image, or protest,/May all be bad." His thesis is, rather, that in matters of religion we must follow the dictates of our conscience and that our conscience must be shaped by a firm conviction arrived at through reason ("the mindes indeavours"), tempered by tradition—and that the perversion of this truth-seeking is idolatry, such as following the false gods of material gain or idolizing the decrees of temporal authority, civil or religious, in spiritual matters. In shaping his argument, the speaker finally strikes the greatest blow against all forces of temporal authority in spiritual matters and specifically against the most fearsome, most immediate of these forces. Kings are not "Vicars," but the speaker qualifies the boldness of his statement by placing Kings with all who have assumed high authority over spiritual matters; the laws of man—Philip of Spain, Pope Gregory, Martin Luther, Henry VIII—take no precedence over the law of God, discoverable by the free, inquiring mind. But the most fearsome, most immediate obstacle to the activities of the mind embarked on such a search is subtly present and discernible to the audience: the power of Elizabeth. When Donne points directly he uses masculine terms: "Harry" (l. 97), "Kings" (l. 91), "Prince" (l. 48). But all the feminine references, which dominate the poem, are not to be explained away as poetic convention or as signs of Donne's own amorousness. He names Elizabeth for what she is: "Power," whose bounds we must know for the health of our souls—she is thus directly opposed to "our Mistresse faire Religion"—and calling Power "her" throughout ll. 100-102 would surely be, for the satire's audience, a sharply clear, even literal personification. Souls perish when men, so courageous and valorous in less vital quests, humbly give themselves to the "tyrannous rage" of the Queen in matters that are not part of her natural prerogative—when natural order is usurped, when power is not "rightly" obeyed. Added to the idea noted earlier in the final image—that flowers, unlike men's souls, cannot be victims of their own moral choice—may be added the picture of a stream allowed to overflow its banks.[14] With the power of Elizabeth as an adversary, with a thesis of religious freedom—freedom of mind and of conscience—and before an audience of his young contemporaries, the speaker displays his true "wit" and "discretion" in rhetorical proving.[15]

By using rhetorical possibilities for our answers to the questions, To Whom? and Why? questions of the dramatic approach, we would note that two things have been overlooked in the past: the speaker's method of thought, his reasoning from premises and images possessed by his audience; and his strategies in leading his audience to his final conclusion. Andreasen's analysis, as we have seen, identifies the speaker of this poem as a tradition-valuing, retiring scholar—but one whose characteristics are more clearly discernible in the other satires. One might combine the present rhetorical view of structure with Andreasen's description of the *persona,* and argue that part of Donne's rhetorical strategy in this poem is the mask he wears throughout his satires, a kind of surrogate ethos that makes up for the anonymity of circulating unsigned manuscripts. However, the reasons why the characteristics of that mask are difficult to discern in this poem may be the very reasons why the structure of this poem differs so perceptibly from the structures of the other satires: the poetical and rhetorical requirements of this satire differ from those of the others. Donne's strategy in this poem, so far as ethos is concerned, is not to call attention to the speaker's specific personality traits but to give evidence of his character through the moral values in his argument—a strategy that seems unlike the frequently "I"-saying Donne; yet the more we study Donne's *personae,* even in his sermons,[16] the more we are beginning to understand his subtle artistry in creating speaking roles that served the needs of his discourse.

Thus, while we need not confuse the *persona* with Donne, we also need not identify it with the *persona* in any one of his other discourses. The soundest analytical course is not to give Who? priority in our dramatic analyses but to carry our search for an answer only so far as our answers to the other questions (To Whom? What? Where? When? How? Why?) require. If Donne's contemporaries read this poem in terms of the *persona* so clearly established in *Satyre I,* or if they read it with no prior knowledge of Donne's satirical *persona,* the effect would most likely have been the same: Donne's ethical appeals depend not on some dramatized personality but on the moral values built into an argument carefully constructed to cause those young men at the rough stream's calm head to look within their own characters.

As mentioned at the first of this discussion, we need to add the rhetorical dimension to our dramatic approach not only for purposes of understanding but also for purposes of classifying and evaluating certain poems. Before we can evaluate a poem or see where it excels, we need to know what kind of thing it is and the possibilities for excellence within its class. This poem may be judged among formal satires, just as Marvell's ode "Upon the Return of Cromwell from Ireland" may be judged among Horatian odes. A general class, to which both the Donne and the Marvell poem belong, is rhetorical poetry: works that were structured to address a real audience, not the private emotions of the speaker or an imaginary audience—or even that hypothetical "general" audience that causes poetry to have "universality" —but a specific audience that existed at a certain time and in a certain place; works that are also poetical, at least in our modern conception of poetry, because their structures are clear, economical, definite, and so tightly knit that words and images are invested with that associative power we identify as poetical.[17] With the dramatic approach, Andreasen has already examined some poetical qualities of Donne's satire: he has noted the speaker-situation relationships in what appeared to be a closed, soliloquy-like situation, and has looked at the associative power of the words as they allow us empathically to participate in that situation. Employing the rhetorical dimension, we have looked at the speaker-situation relationships within an oration-like situation, and at both the associative and the implicative power the words might have had for a real audience. Furthermore, we need to know those values, at once poetical and rhetorical, by which to judge this poem. I suspect we shall not find those values so long as our critical sensibilities are victimized by the niceties of our distinctions between rhetoric and poetry, though unquestionably the *confusion* between rhetoric and poetry is far more pernicious than our rigorous distinctions.

Perhaps the concept of structure as revealed by the present analysis may help the oral interpreter find at least one of those rhetorical-poetical values, by showing him a way in which the poem might be read aloud. Following the present analysis, the interpreter would give his audience the impression that they are overhearing Donne's *persona* addressing the actual audience of the poem. The poem would sound like a speech being directly delivered to a certain audience. Making this poem sound oratorical is, I believe, the surest way to find that structural quality which Coleridge best described as Donne's "manly harmony," Donne's sense of symmetry whereby he gave vigorous argument an ordered beauty through rhythm and sound.

"Read even Donne's Satires," Coleridge advised, "as he meant them to be read, and as the sense & passion demand, and you will find in the lines a manly harmony."[18] Coleridge was speaking of reading the satires aloud, and he said "even" Donne's satires for of all the older poems, including plays, the meter of those poems must have sounded particularly rough to a post-Dryden age of metrical regularity. The appropriateness of the oral reading of *Satyre III* should be measured by its appropriateness to a speaker in a clearly rhetorical situation, for the components of a speaking situation are always the measure of appropriateness, either in structure of discourse or in oral delivery. Donne's contemporaries had definite notions about appropriateness, notions that can help us resolve doubts about the artistic intentions of his work, as hopefully the present analysis has shown.[19] Of the oral interpreter, the sense and passion in *Satyre III* demand an oratorical delivery.

Rhetorical dimensions in the dramatic approach to Donne's poetry should help all interpreters, oral or otherwise, become surer about Donne's poetic structures. As a poet of his time, Donne spoke to be heard by men of his time, and frequently utilized the methods and manners of rhetoric, even to the extent of building a poem in the way an orator might build a speech. No doubt these were some of the true causes of his manly harmony.

DONNE'S 'EPITHALAMION MADE AT LINCOLN'S INN': CONTEXT AND DATE

David Novarr

I

> That is some satire keen and critical,
> Not sorting with a nuptial ceremony.
>> (*A Midsummer Night's Dream*, v. i. 54-55)

Donne's 'Epithalamion made at Lincoln's Inn' differs from his 'Epithalamion . . . on the Lady Elizabeth and Count Palatine' and his epithalamion for the Earl of Somerset in that its occasion is not known. It differs from them, too, in that its wit seems more crudely licentious, harsher, less neatly integrated. This peculiarity of tone has not been entirely unnoticed. Grierson implied that the Lincoln's Inn epithalamion was 'reprehensible' when he coupled it with 'the most reprehensible' of the earlier elegies,[1] and he thought that its third stanza abounded in satire,[2] though some of the satire disappeared when he retracted his original reading of line 26.[3] But Grierson's comments on the poem have been largely neglected despite the fact that it has a number of puzzling elements which disturb the conventional epithalamic attitude.

One of these elements is Donne's reference to death in a marriage poem. This is odd, but the oddness has not disturbed readers unduly, perhaps because Donne refers to death several times in his other epithalamia. In the 'Epithalamion . . . on the Lady Elizabeth', 'The Sparrow that neglects his life for love' is conventional and apt for the occasion—St. Valentine's Day— and we are attracted, not repulsed, by so pleasant a way to die. Donne's suggestion that the noble lovers are a pair of phoenixes, that their 'motion kindles such fires, as shall give / Yong Phœnixes, and yet the old shall live' is delightful for its ingenious invention. His likening of the bride's jewels to a blazing constellation which signifies 'That a Great Princess falls, but does not die' pleases us not so much for the intensity of its visual imagery as for the felicity of its suggestion of the marriage-bed. Again, when Donne announces that 'A Bride, before a good night could be said, / Should vanish from her cloathes, into her bed, / As Soules from bodies steale, and are not spy'd', we are delighted by the aptness—and the incongruity—of his analogy. Similarly, in the epithalamion for the Earl of Somerset, Donne's introductory statement that the marriage reprieves the old year, due to die in five days, his

Reprinted from *Review of English Studies*, n.s. 7 (1956), 250-63, by permission of the author and The Clarendon Press, Oxford.

reference to the 'death bed' of the year in a poem celebrating the marriage-
bed, seems only to enhance the glory of the occasion. In his stanza of benediction, Donne addresses the couple as 'Blest payre of Swans', and he wishes
that they never sing until 'new great heights to trie, / It must serve your ambition, to die'. Here the eager desire for heavenly joy is wittily ambiguous;
the reference to death is properly improper, and it is followed, properly—
and improperly—enough, by the exhortation, 'Raise heires'. In referring to
the death of the swan, Donne makes his swans generate life; they are hardly
of the breed of the chaste swans greeted by the Jovelings of Spenser. When
Donne in his 'good-night' mentions the lamp which burned for fifteen
hundred years in Tullia's tomb, it is not the tomb that we remember but
the picture of the lovers as everlasting 'love-lamps'. He suggests that fire ends
in ashes, but only to contrast the everlastingness of the love of the couple:
'joyes bonfire' burns eternally, for bride and groom are both fuel and fire.

Donne starts the Lincoln's Inn epithalamion by comparing a single bed
to a grave: 'It nourseth sadnesse', and the body in it remains in one place.
But in his very expression, 'your bodies print / . . . the yielding downe doth
dint', Donne looks forward to a 'yielding' of another sort, and, indeed, his
next line is 'You and your other you meet there anon'. Later in the poem he
exploits a like idea: the marriage-bed is 'onely to virginitie / A grave, but, to
a better state, a cradle'. These references to the grave are somewhat blunter
than those in the other epithalamia. They are not so audacious, so witty, so
lovingly developed. Donne's further references to death in the poem disturb
us. One of them is not analogical at all; the other is a revolting analogy.
Donne writes

> Thy two-leav'd gates faire Temple unfold,
> And these two in thy sacred bosome hold,
>   Till, mystically joyn'd, but one they bee;
> Then may thy leane and hunger-starved wombe
> Long time expect their bodies and their tombe,
>   Long after their owne parents fatten thee.

It is conceivable that the church in which a marriage takes place may bring to
mind those buried there. It is conceivable, too, that tombs may be mentioned
in a wedding poem, but even Tennyson does not escape unscathed from a
rather inopportune morbidity in the Epilogue of *In Memoriam.* But Donne
does more than suggest that the church will receive the bodies of the lovers.
He is hopeful that the lovers' parents will die before they do, and his use of
'fatten' expresses an untoward relish. This seems like bad taste, but the passage
is offensive beyond this. Donne calls the marriage a mystical union, but his
words do not communicate a spiritual idea; they undercut it. The 'sacred
bosome' of the church does not bother us, but when it is conjoined with
'leane and hunger-starved wombe', we are distressed by the fleshly aspect
of the metaphor—all the more so since, after all, we remember the bride
standing by while Donne addresses the church. 'Leane and hunger-starved
wombe' outrages us not only because of its implication that the church

hungers for the death of the bride and groom, but also because we cannot help applying the words to the bride as well as to the church, and cannot help thinking that Donne wants us to do so. And what shall we make of the 'two-leav'd gates'? Our minds withdraw, and not into happiness. We are happier when Donne later compares the bride in her nuptial bed to a pleasing sacrifice on love's altar. But Donne's exploitation of this image is not wittily lascivious; it is grossly cruel. The bride lies like a sacrificial lamb while the bridegroom, like a priest, comes tenderly 'on his knees t'embowell her'. Tenderly? Is this the tenderness of the boudoir or the abattoir?

In each of the epithalamia, too, Donne refers to riches or money, but once again the references seem crude and tasteless only in the Lincoln's Inn poem. In the 'Epithalamion . . . on the Lady Elizabeth', the bride is ablaze with rubies, pearls, and diamonds. Donne's description is hardly startling, and to make it so he must turn the jewels into stars. His description (in stanza vii) of the activities of the wedding-bed in terms of a business transaction is discreetly coy. The analogy is conventional enough; its wit lies in Donne's extensive exploitation of the convention. To be in debt, for love, is no more serious than to 'die' for love. Lovers' 'debts' and their 'deaths' are paid in the same stock exchange, but Donne does not pull the occasion down to the level of the market-place. In the Somerset epithalamion Donne also mentions the bride's jewels, but only to suggest once more that they are stars and that the stars are not so pure as their spheres. So, too, his description of the bride's silk and gold serves to praise and elevate her, for, he says, silk and gold, 'the fruits of wormes and dust', are just objects for the sight of the common onlookers at the wedding ('dust, and wormes').

But in the Lincoln's Inn epithalamion, the description of the bride's flowers and jewels does not lead to such elaborate compliment. They are to make her fit fuel for love, 'As gay as Flora, and as rich as Inde'. If the analogies are conventional, the stanza in which they appear is hardly so. In it, Donne addresses the bridesmaids as 'Our Golden Mines, and furnish'd Treasurie'. To be sure he calls them 'Angels', but his reason follows immediately: they bring with them 'Thousands of Angels' on their wedding days. All we are told of the bridesmaids, then, is that they are rich. And the bride? In one line she is 'As gay as Flora, and as rich as Inde', and in the next she is 'faire, rich, glad, and in nothing lame'. The bride, then, is fair. At least she is 'in nothing lame'. And she, too, is rich. Donne seems preoccupied with this particular virtue. Is there not something a little ungentlemanly, a little crass and vulgar, in his attitude?

In the next stanza of the poem, some of the groom's attendants are called 'Sonnes of these Senators, wealths deep oceans', and again the overt reference to wealth seems adventitious and crude. In his last stanza, Donne refers to the bride's desire to exchange virginity for womanhood by talking about her preference for 'a mothers rich stile'. The emphasis on money in the Lincoln's Inn epithalamion seems far removed from the conventionally witty business of indebtedness in the Valentine epithalamion.

Donne's description of the bride in the Lincoln's Inn epithalamion also

seems different from the descriptions in the others. The Princess Elizabeth
is a blazing constellation, a phoenix. She and Frederick are two glorious
flames which meet one another. The beauty of Lady Frances is so brilliant
that she must powder her hair lest its intense lustre affect the onlookers
as Phaëton, not Phoebus, and, for the same reason, she must have a tear
of joy in her inflaming eyes. The Lincoln's Inn bride is conceitedly dressed,
adorned with flowers and jewels, and Donne writes of her as she approaches
the chapel,

> Loe, in yon path which store of straw'd flowers graceth,
> > The sober virgin paceth;
> Except my sight faile, 'tis no other thing.

Like the bride in Spenser's *Epithalamion,* this modest bride comes 'with
portly pace', but Spenser devotes some fifty lines to a description of his
bashful bride's charms. Shall we suppose that Donne's bride has both ravished
his sight and impaired his speech? Hardly. He says, nor can his blunt meaning
be mistaken, 'Unless I'm blind, that thing is the bride'. This is a strange
epithalamion indeed.

It is strange in its refrain. In the 'Epithalamion . . . on the Lady Elizabeth',
the refrain is an address to Bishop Valentine, and it integrates the bird
imagery and stresses all the romantic and holy aspects of the wedding day.
In the Somerset epithalamion, the 'inflaming eyes' and 'loving heart' of the
refrain apply equally to the bride and groom. But in the Lincoln's Inn poem,
the refrain '*To day put on perfection, and a womans name*' oddly concentrates attention on the occasion as it is important for the bride. The groom
seems slighted. The epithalamion is strange, too, in that the wedding guests
in their dancing are compared to 'toyl'd beasts'. Worse than this, the groom's
attendants are called 'strange Hermaphrodits'. In the last stanza the bride is
strangely likened to a faithful man who is content to spend this life for a
better one.

In Theseus's words (and Dr. Johnson's), How shall we find the concord
of this discord?

II

We shall not find it, I think, merely in assuming that the poem celebrates
a less memorable wedding than that of the Princess Elizabeth or of the Earl
of Somerset. The mere doffing of the party manners which Donne might
have used on those occasions would not lead to a strange indulgence in tone
and in wit on a lesser occasion. The crude, scoffing element in the poem
makes it unlikely, too, that it was an offering in jest from one smart young
man to another smart young man about to marry, even if we take into
account the differences in taste between Donne's day and our own. The
wit is too close to insult: it has not the cavalier geniality of Donne's other
epithalamia, but rather the heavy-handed raillery of his satires. Donne is here
crudely utilitarian in a genre which is customarily complimentary. It seems
very doubtful, then, that the occasion of Donne's poem is the actual wedding

of a rich maid of London and a gentleman of the Inns of Court. There is good reason to believe that Donne is not celebrating a real wedding at all.

The manuscripts of Donne's poems provide us with indistinct clues about the occasion of the 'Epithalamion made at Lincoln's Inn', and with more definite ones about its approximate date. Sir Herbert Grierson and Miss Helen Gardner agree that the presence of the poem in the Westmoreland manuscript, where it follows the elegies and precedes the verse letters, points to its being the only one of the epithalamia written when the first part of that manuscript was made.[4] Miss Gardner also suggests that since it is there entitled just 'Epithalamion', we have further reason to suppose that the epithalamia of 1613 were not yet written. Moreover, in the first part of the Westmoreland manuscript, all the verse letters but one belong to the time before Donne's marriage and are addressed to the circle of his friends at the Inns of Court. This part of the manuscript appears to have been copied from a collection of Donne's poems made about 1600. On the basis of the Westmoreland manuscript alone, it seems safe to assume that the epithalamion was 'made' at Lincoln's Inn while Donne was a student there.

Mr. I. A. Shapiro has admirably summarized Donne's career at Lincoln's Inn from his admission on 6 May 1592.[5] He assumes that since Donne was fined for not acting as Steward of Christmas in 1594 (he had been appointed to the office on 26 November) and since he is not mentioned in the *Black Books* of Lincoln's Inn as a student after he had been fined, Donne must have left Lincoln's Inn in December 1594. Mr. John Sparrow makes the same assumption and starts Donne on his travels.[6] But Professor R. C. Bald has discovered that on 20 July 1595 Donne agreed to take 'into his service to instructe and bring upp one Thomas Danbye of the age of fifteen yeres or there aboutes'.[7] Here is presumptive evidence that Donne was in England in the middle of 1595. There is no real evidence that he left Lincoln's Inn or England until he joined the Cadiz expedition at the end of May 1596. We may, then, suppose that the Lincoln's Inn epithalamion was written at some time between May 1592 and the middle of 1596.

The manuscripts of Donne's poems seem to show that Donne himself did not consider this epithalamion equal in worth or similar in kind to his others. It is not included in those manuscripts which Grierson and Miss Gardner call Group I (*D*, *H 49*, *Lec*, *C 57*, and *SP*). Miss Gardner argues convincingly that the manuscripts in this group derive from one which Donne himself unwillingly made just before taking orders, in compliance with Somerset's request that he should publish his poems. She suggests that Donne omitted from his collection such poems as he thought not worthy of a volume designed to win the favour of the great.[8] A large number of these were familiar verse letters addressed to the less distinguished circle of his youth, though Donne seems to have included the verse letters which he was particularly proud of—'The Storm', 'The Calm', and 'To Mr. Rowland Woodward' ('Like one who' in her third widdowhood'). We are, I think, forced to conclude that Donne himself considered the Lincoln's Inn epithalamion unworthy of inclusion not only because it was an intimate reminder of his Inns of

Court days but also because he felt that it lacked merit. Some of the manuscripts in which the poem does appear, however, may point more precisely
to the reason for its exclusion from Group I. In about half of the manuscripts in which the poem appears it is entitled 'Epithalamion on a Citizen'.
This title seems to imply that the occasion Donne celebrates is not a very
notable one. But it is odd that not one of the manuscripts gives the name
of the citizen. It is likely that the use of 'Citizen' is generic, and that though
some of Donne's contemporaries were unaware of the specific details of the
occasion of the poem, their use of 'Citizen' in the title of a poem written
by a young gentleman indicates their feeling that Donne's intent was not
entirely serious. It is hard to believe that in his Lincoln's Inn days Donne
could not have written, had he wanted to, an epithalamion, no matter to
whom it was addressed, which would merit inclusion in such a collection
as he was making in 1614. The manuscripts lead us to conclude that the
Lincoln's Inn epithalamion is a *jeu d'esprit* which Donne later cast aside.

The poem, then, may not celebrate a real wedding. Does it celebrate a
mock wedding? I think that Donne wrote it for just such an occasion, and
I wish to show, though the available materials are scanty, that such an
occasion is in harmony with the long tradition of Inns of Court revelling.

Inns of Court revelling is most frequently associated with the production
of lavish masques for specific occasions: with the 'Masque of Proteus' devised by the gentlemen of Gray's Inn for their extraordinary Christmas
festivity in 1594; with the masque composed by George Chapman and
designed by Inigo Jones which was performed by the gentlemen of the
Middle Temple and of Lincoln's Inn to celebrate the marriage of the Princess Elizabeth in 1613; with the spectacular *Triumph of Peace* of 1634,
acted by the four Inns for the King and the Court, with a script by James
Shirley, architecture by Inigo Jones, and music by Simon Ives and William
Lawes. But the Inns did not need an occasion for a masque. William
Browne's dedication of his *Inner Temple Masque,* or *Ulysses and Circe*
(1615) is interesting because it reveals that the masque is entirely independent of occasion. Browne reminds the gentlemen of the Inner Temple that
'it was done to please ourselves in private', and his reference to 'those
other the society hath produced' probably indicates that such performances
were not uncommon.[9] Masques were, on the whole, exceptional excrescences
which evolved from the normal procedure of revelling in which highly ritualistic 'solemn revels', marked by obeisance and stately parade, were followed
by 'post revels' or informal dancing by the younger gentlemen. Into this
standardized form of entertainment the high-spirited young men at the Inns
gradually introduced pageantry or a play, buffoonery, and burlesque.[10]

The amount of such revelling must have been remarkable. An entry in
1431 in the *Black Books* of Lincoln's Inn shows the frequency of revelling
in an order which restricts such occasions:

> . . . it is accorded by all the felawschip that ther schall be iiij revels in the
> yeere and no mo, that is to sayyng, in the fest off All Halowen oon, to

the wych schall be contributorie as well the persons wych were woned to paye to Seint William ys revell as tho the wych were woned paie to Seynt Hugh is Revell; and in the fest off Seint Arkenewold another, to wych schall be contributorie Seint Edmond is men. Item, the iij[de] in the fest off Purificacion off owre Lady, to wych all the remenaunt schall be contributorie savyng Seint Peter and Seint Thomas men. The Ferthe on Midsomer Day, to wych sall be contributorie Seynt Peter and Seint Thomas men.[11]

It is doubtful whether this order was followed to the letter, for in 1448 there is a reference to 'the revels at Christmas last'.[12] Attendance at the revels seems to have been compulsory, for there is a record of four men being put out of commons 'for goyng out of the Hall on Hallowmas evyn at the tyme of the Revelles'.[13] There is some evidence that the ritual of the revels palled on the gentlemen of Lincoln's Inn: on one occasion, one of them was put out of commons because he sang mockingly and irreverently at the revels,[14] on another occasion, all the fellows of the Inn refused to dance before the distinguished guests invited by the Benchers.[15] There is evidence, too, that it was hard to enforce discipline.[16] An entry on 14 November 1608 is illuminating: a committee of three Benchers and three others is appointed 'to conferr wth the younge gentlemen towchinge the time, manner and charge of the Revells and sportes intended'.[17] It is apparent that the young gentlemen took an active part in the planning of the revelling, and also that the revels were invariably combined with sports. Nor is it strange that the young gentlemen often confused the two. At Midsummer, for instance, ritualistic candles and reeds were ordered for the Inn,[18] and a light erected in the Hall to honour St. John; it is no surprise to find in an entry that 'Eldrington, Harrington, and Berners, aboughte Trynyte Sondaye laste, in the nyghte tyme, did take downe the lyghte of Sainte John in the Hall, and did hang in the stede therof a horsehede, in dyspite of the Sainte'.[19]

Although Saturday nights at the Inn seem to have been given over to card-playing and dicing, there is at least one indication that informal entertainment of other sorts also took place then. At a Council held on 2 November 1559, it was ordered that 'the Butler shall note every Saterdaye at night whoe faylyth at Revells that were at supper that night in the Howse, and that he that faylyth shall forfett iiijd. for every tyme, to be collectid by the Buttler, and therefore the Post Revelles to be agayne used as they have byn before this time'.[20] This entry shows the frequency of the informal entertainment put on at the Inn. The spectacular masques that are remembered are a small and unusual part of the playing and the dancing, the music and the buffoonery, the improvization and the burlesquing in which the young gentlemen of the Inn engaged.

III

If we view Donne's epithalamion in the context of Inns of Court reveling,

the strangeness of its tone and the oddness of its details disappear. We
should expect Donne to use broadly discordant effects, not subtly witty
ones. The tasteless references to death expressed in the images of the em-
bowelling priest and of the female organs of the church would convulse the
young gentlemen of the Inn. They would thoroughly enjoy Donne's jibes
at their mundane preoccupation with angels. In a mock-marriage, the part
of the bride would be played by one of the 'painted courtiers', and the
words on the bride's approach—''tis no other thing'—would be not only
fitting but funny. Moreover, under such circumstances, the refrain becomes
a jocular device: it serves as a continual reminder that the man playing the
part of the bride is literally putting on the name of woman for 'today' and
'tonight'. No wonder, then, that Donne focused attention in it on the bride
alone.

In a conventional epithalamion, the reference to the hermaphroditism of
the groom's attendants is out of place. But in a mock-epithalamion the reference becomes innocently salacious: the Inns of Court men are 'Of study
and play made strange Hermaphrodits' because at such performances they
must take the female parts. Donne's conceit at the end of the poem, which
compares the bride to 'a faithfull man content, / That this life for a better
should be spent', becomes still another device to emphasize the confusion
of sex caused by a man's playing the part of the bride. The final reference
to the bride as 'This Sun' becomes more than a conventional epithet for the
bride's transcendent beauty; it, too, takes advantage of the gender of the
bride, and Donne uses the stale sun-son pun freshly to call attention once
more to his unusual bride. 'Wonders are wrought', indeed, 'for shee which
had no maime', except that 'shee' is a 'he', *To night puts on perfection,
and a womans name*'.

In the context of an epithalamion 'made' or performed at Lincoln's Inn,
Donne is free to endow his 'Temple' with biological functions, for he is
alluding to a temple of the law. Such gross stress on the procreative capacities
of a church admits of no allegorical interpretation; to take a serious view of
the poem is to say that Donne's canticle here sings a song of sacrilege. But
to a group of students at Lincoln's Inn, 'Temple' would inevitably call to
mind the two rival institutions, and the gentlemen at Lincoln's would be
delighted by Donne's irreverence. They would not feel insulted when Donne
compared them to 'toyl'd beasts'; since they had a superfluity of dancing in
their solemn revels, they would enjoy Donne's oblique reference to their
'pleasing labours'. His lines about the chains and robes 'put on / T' adorne
the day, not thee' would remind them not only of the vestments which
adorned the man-bride but probably also of the ritualistic trappings in which
the Inn officials were bedecked. They would appreciate Donne's little professional joke in his mention of 'elder claimes', and they would delight in
his comparing the naked bride to the naked truth.

Donne's poem is not a serious epithalamion, but neither is it a 'satire keen
and critical'. It is closer to the 'palpable-gross play [that] hath well beguil'd /
The heavy gait of night'. To see it as a broadly satiric entertainment is to

rid it of its difficulties and to place it rightly, not with Donne's other epithalamia, but with his satires and love elegies.

IV

I should like to propose, though more tentatively, that Donne wrote his
epithalamion for a performance at the Midsummer revels of Lincoln's Inn
in 1595. The date is based on three assumptions which I shall try to show
to be fairly sound: (1) Donne's poem could have been written only after
the publication of Spenser's *Epithalamion*; (2) The Midsummer season is
peculiarly fitting for such a performance; (3) Donne was still at Lincoln's
Inn in June 1595.

It is difficult to see why Donne should have turned to the epithalamic
genre for a revels entertainment. In England the epithalamion was neglected
until the 1590's, and it seems strange that Donne should have satirized broadly in a genre with which his audience would not be very well acquainted.
Puttenham's discussion of the epithalamion in *The Arte of English Poesie*
conveniently shows us what the genre meant to the cultivated Elizabethan
gentleman.[21] For him, epithalamia were essentially 'ballades at the bedding
of the bride', and his description was based on his familiarity with the lyric
epithalamia of Catullus and one made 'of late yeares' by Johannes Secundus.[22]
Puttenham did not consider the great number of Latin epithalamia of the
Renaissance, which were predominantly not lyric, but, following the pattern
of Claudian and Statius, essentially narrative and descriptive.[23] The only epithalamion in English printed before Spenser's was Sidney's song of the shepherd Dicus at the marriage of Thyrsis and Kala, written in the early 1580's
and first published in the 1593 *Arcadia*. It was neither a bedding ballad nor
an 'epical' poem modelled after the epithalamia of Claudian and Statius, but
a pastoral benediction. Against the background of the epical character of the
major epithalamic tradition of the Renaissance and the paucity of models in
English, the startling originality of Spenser's poem stands out—despite
scholars' pointing to sources and analogues for hundreds of particular details.[24]
Spenser fused the narration of the events of the bridal day and the description of its many participants and places, typical of the epic or heroic epithalamion, with the bedding ballad and the personal appeal for benediction
in a poem glowing with lyricism.

Donne's Lincoln's Inn epithalamion has the same blending of the epic
narration of the bridal day with an essentially lyric intent, and this fusion
of the traditions was available to him only after the publication of Spenser's
poem.[25] If Donne had written his poem before he saw Spenser's, he would
probably have satirized in the neo-Latin epical fashion familiar to some in
his audience or in the pastoral-benediction fashion of Sidney. Something
caused him to satirize in the peculiar form he chose, and that was probably
the form recently used by the most highly regarded poet of his day. Spenser's
Amoretti and *Epithalamion* were entered in the Stationers' Register on
19 November 1594, and the first edition is dated 1595. The volume probably
appeared early in that year, though perhaps after 25 March. If we assume,

as I think we must, that Donne modelled his epithalamion on Spenser's, then Donne's poem was not written earlier than the first part of 1595.

I have implied that Donne turned to the epithalamic genre and to Spenser's design because he could assume that Spenser's poem would be fresh in the minds of his audience. A recent work by a popular writer is always fair game for parody, but more than recency may have drawn Donne to Spenser's *Epithalamion*. In Donne's poem, the line 'Hee [the sun] flies in winter, but he now stands still' seems to indicate a summer date, though conventionally in an epithalamion the sun never sets quickly enough. The most important revels at this time of year were held at Midsummer, and Midsummer seems the most likely occasion for the performance of Donne's epithalamion. If Donne were casting about for a subject for a Midsummer entertainment, he would find special relevance in Spenser's poem. Spenser makes it clear that his marriage took place on the feast of St. Barnabas, and the proverb 'Barnaby bright, Barnaby bright, / The longest day and the shortest night' shows that (with the calendar ten days out) the feast of St. Barnabas and Midsummer were frequently associated. I do not wish to suggest that Donne wrote a mock-Anniversary for Spenser, but I think it likely that the date of Spenser's wedding, a lovely detail which Spenser treats most charmingly, must have impressed Donne and tempted him to toy with the idea of Midsummer marriage. In June the newness of Spenser's poem would make Donne's burlesque topical and obvious. Moreover, the customary festivities of the Midsummer season make the Midsummer revels the perfect occasion for a mock-epithalamion.

When Spenser referred to the heavens 'In which a thousand torches flaming bright / Doe burne . . .', he may have been using a common conceit for stars, but his plea for darkness and for quiet has particular significance in the light of Midsummer tradition. The ancient sun-rites were celebrated by the lighting of bonfires, and the lights and reeds mentioned in the *Black Books* reflect a citified version of this.[26] Dekker mentions bonfires and triumphing on Midsummer Night in his *Seven Deadly Sinnes of London* (1606).[27] Although the latest surviving record of a pageant at Midsummer in London is for 1545,[28] provincial towns continued to have Midsummer Shows well into the seventeenth century.[29] The marching watch of two thousand in London at Midsummer was discontinued by the middle of the sixteenth century, but ensign-bearers still roamed the city at the end of the century.[30] In his *Popular Antiquities,* Brand says that the ritualistic dance around the coal fire in the Inns of Court may be connected with Midsummer festivity,[31] and we have already had an example of the horseplay which some gentlemen of Lincoln's Inn indulged in at this time of year. Brand further shows that at this season other customs were followed: fernseed was esteemed, love divinations of all kinds were popular, and boys dressed in girls' clothes.[32] The Midsummer tradition helped to create the special aura of *A Midsummer Night's Dream,* and Shakespeare's very title was an invitation to a giddy, vertiginous, and sublunary world.[33] The same tradition would make Donne's audience peculiarly susceptible to midsummer madness.

I think we may assume that Midsummer revels took place at Lincoln's Inn in 1595 despite the lack of documentary corroboration. They seem to have been customary, and there is no evidence in the *Black Books* that they were not held. In 1595 Trinity Sunday fell on 15 June (O.S.). Trinity Term usually began on the Wednesday after Trinity Sunday;[34] in 1595, then, term began on 18 June. Since Midsummer was customarily celebrated in conjunction with St. John's Day, 24 June,[35] it fell in 1595 during Trinity Term, and it, rather than Trinity Sunday, would be celebrated as a 'grand' day.

Was Donne at Lincoln's Inn as late as June 1595? Mr. Shapiro has examined in the manuscript *Black Books* of Lincoln's Inn (vol. v) lists of those who should have kept vacations and either did or did not, from the Easter vacation of 1589 to the Easter vacation of 1596. In these lists Mr. Shapiro has found that Donne's absence at the Easter vacation in 1593 is duly noted; he has found no record that Donne either kept or failed to keep a vacation after the notice of his keeping the autumn vacation of 1594. But Donne's being appointed Steward of Christmas on 26 November 1594 shows that he was at Lincoln's Inn at that time. That he was fined for not performing his duties as Steward, and that his name does not appear in the vacation lists after October 1594, do not prove that he left Lincoln's Inn between 26 November and 25 December 1594. He may have skipped attendance at a vacation or two while still maintaining his Lincoln's Inn connexion (we know, for example, that his absence at the Easter vacation in 1593 was no indication of complete severance). Nor does his defection as Steward indicate that he had left the Inn. Stewardships in the Inns must have been expensive and dull, and fines from men refusing to serve as stewards of various occasions seem to have constituted a staple sum of Inn income. There is no more frequent entry in the *Black Books* than that of Mr. So-and-so fined so much for refusing to serve as steward of this or that[36] (the fines were standardized, and that for the Steward of Christmas was smaller than most, 26s. 8d.).[37] Donne's defection as Steward need not mean, then, that he was absent from London and from Lincoln's Inn during and after Christmas 1594.[38] Indeed, Mr. Shapiro prints the part of the treasurer's record for (Nov.) 1594 to (Nov.) 1595 which shows that the Inn received from Donne the sum of 26s. 8d. for not acting as Steward of Christmas. Since it is not likely that Donne paid his fine in advance, we have here evidence that he was at the Inn after Christmas 1594. It is even conceivable that the very payment of the fine indicates that Donne planned to remain at the Inn for a time. Had he severed his connexion with the Inn before Christmas (or even after), he might not have been fined or felt obliged to pay his fine. The vacation lists inform us, I think, that Donne determined not to study law seriously about or after Christmas 1594, but they do not tell us that he left Lincoln's Inn at that time; in fact, from Mr. Bald's evidence that Donne was in London even in July 1595, we may probably assume that he spent Midsummer at Lincoln's Inn.

It is likely, then, that in the 'Epithalamion made at Lincoln's Inn' we catch Jack Donne in a carefree midsummer mood after he had decided that the law was not for him. We see in the poem not the serious poet of compliment but the roistering Inns of Court man of three and twenty, 'not dissolute, but very neat; a great visiter of Ladies, a great frequenter of Playes, a great writer of conceited Verses'.[39]

THE THEME OF VIRTUE IN DONNE'S VERSE EPISTLES

Laurence Stapleton

Among other qualities that set Donne's verse epistles apart as a distinct body of poetry, one must remark his preoccupation with the theme of virtue. In this, as in other respects, the *Letters to Severall Personages* represent a preparation for the more ambitious as well as more profound *Anniversaries*—and provide a sequel to them as well.

"Virtue" is a word that Donne rarely used except in the epistles and the *Anniversaries*. (It appears in these poems four times more often than in all the rest of his poetry.) Is the reason simply that in poems of friendship and of complimentary courtesy, Donne resorted too quickly to a facile Neoplatonism? Partly that is the answer, but it is an insufficient one, and potentially a misleading one.

For, if the theme of virtue furnished a ready pattern for the poem of compliment responding to a patron's kindness, it also became the instrument for Donne's anatomy of his own loyalties, his degree of commitment in the decade 1600-1610, the period of his inability to find employment, the period preceding his choice of the ministry as a profession. The *Anniversaries* register and explore the climax of his disappointment, dejection, and intellectual skepticism, while at the same time they celebrate the act of will which Donne made serve for faith. But in the verse epistles, we see the ambience, the serious debate and the courtly debate, the climate not so much of opinion as of temperament and identity, out of which Donne's choice emerged, and which it circumscribed and shaped to fit a new undertaking.

The term, as Donne handles it in those epistles written before 1600,[1] amounts to little more than a point of reference—a conversational clue, as it were, to the assumption by men of his circle, of a stoical attitude of detachment. He writes to Mr. R[owland] W[oodward] in 1597 that he loves the sense of retirement bred by a wise melancholy; if hope of adventure or gain may be frustrated, such a loss is not intolerable to the man of virtue:

> Perchance, these Spanish business being done
>
> . . . .
>
> Our discontinued hopes we shall retrive

Reprinted from *Studies in Philology*, 55 (1958), 187-200, by permission of the author and publisher, the University of North Carolina Press.

But if (as all th'All must) hopes smoake away
Is not Almightie Vertue'an India? (I, 210)

Or, in a discourse to Sir Henry Wootton (dated by Grierson 1598) he
expatiates on the corruption of court and city life: "Here's no more news,
than vertue. 'I may as well / Tell you *Cales* or *St. Michaels* tale for newes,
as tell / that vice doth here habitually dwell'." In this atmosphere, men
armed only with 'seely honesty' and 'neat integritie' are as sure to lose as
Indians fighting Spanish conquerors. The only strategy possible for the virtuous man is an ironical detachment in which he can laugh at courtiers "whose
deepest projects . . . are but dull Moralls of a game at Chests" (I, 187-8).
Here we have a point of view not too different from that of Montaigne's
early essays—or from Donne's Second Satire. In another epistle to Sir Henry
Wootton (which Grierson has shown to be part of a literary débat of some
wits of Essex's circle on the theme of two epigrams in the Greek Anthology)[2]
Donne finds court, town, and country equally hopeless, each a rock or "re-
mora" in life's voyage. Cities are sepulchres, courts theatres, and the country
a desert; in each, "virtue is barbarous" (a stranger). Men to whom outward
environment means much are incapable of self-knowledge; if they "durst
look for themselves . . . / They would like strangers greet themselves, seeing
then / Utopian youth grown old Italian." Instead, man must dwell in himself, to house his spirit, as the snail his body. "Bee thine owne Palace, or
the world's thy gaile." And with a courteous disclaimer that removes the
poem from the didactic to the reflective mood, Donne praises his friends
as those from whom he has learned this good counsel.

The reader feels indeed that in such verse as this Donne is but conning
over, genuinely enough, the social lessons of self-mastery. It reminds us of
the frame of mind in which "Michel de Montaigne, long weary of the servitude of the court and of public employments, while still entire, retired to
the bosom of the learned virgins . . . if the fates permit he will complete
this . . . sweet ancestral retreat, and he has consecrated it to his freedom,
transquillity and leisure."[3] If we are correct in accepting the dating of these
epistles as written before 1600, Donne had not, of course, retired to any of
the uncongenial country residences that he later owed to the help of relatives
or friends and resorted to through necessity. He was fashioning an attitude
of detachment which might save him from corruption in the world of
affairs.

It is, I think, merely a coincidence that in the last of these early epistles
touching on the theme of virtue, Donne refers to the doctrines of Paracelsus.
Yet he in all likelihood derived some special connotation of the term *virtus*
from Paracelsus, and, in a striking manner, combined it with Plato's conception of virtue as indivisible. From the conjunction of these two notions, he
originated an almost symbolic term that gives a common focus to his later
verse epistles and eventually results in the more animated structure of the
Anniversaries.

In a letter to Sir Henry Goodyere which was probably written in 1608,

Donne discusses his conception of virtue in somewhat studied language. No man, he tells us, is virtuous by reason of a single good quality, or by the effort to obtain a number of good qualities.

> Not he that doth all actions to the pattern of the most valiant, or liberall, which Histories afford: nor he which chooses from every one their best actions, and thereupon doth something like those. . . . For vertue is even, and continuall, and the same, and can therefore break nowhere, nor admit ends nor beginnings; it is not only not broken, but not tied together. He is not vertuous, out of whose actions you can pick an excellent one.[4]

Now, in brief, Donne is recapitulating Plato's argument in that elusive dialogue, the *Protagoras.* Socrates in his discussion with the famous Sophist has perhaps several aims, not only to show that the teaching of virtue by didactic discourse is impossible, but also to demonstrate the superiority of the dialectic method as an instrument of self-knowledge, and perhaps even to prove that he can, if need be, beat Protagoras at his own game. The opening discussion of virtue as a unity, and the closing section, in which this theme is resumed, are the parts of the dialogue which have a bearing upon Donne's use of the term. We shall therefore forego the pleasure of observing Socrates at work as a practical critic or as a precursor of Mill, both episodes in his encounter with the Sophist.

Socrates begins by asking Protagoras "whether virtue is one whole, of which justice and temperance and holiness are parts; or whether all these are only the names of one and the same thing?" Protagoras sees no difficulty in the problem presented, and replies that the qualities Socrates has enumerated are parts of virtue, "which is one." Upon this statement Socrates proceeds to his clever cross-examination. Is justice, or temperance, a part of virtue "in the sense in which mouth, nose, and eyes, and ears, are parts of a face?" Or do they resemble the parts of gold, which differ from one another only in being larger or smaller? Protagoras chooses the first, which we may call the functional, alternative.

To the next question—whether men may possess one of the "parts" of virtue but not the others—Protagoras is logically consistent as well as humanly realistic in answering that "many a man is brave and not just, or just and not wise." This leads him to maintain, under subsequent questioning, that "no other part of virtue is like knowledge, or like justice, or like courage, or like temperance, or like holiness,"[5]—a statement which his position did not require.

As a result of it, Protagoras—like many other opponents of Socrates—allows himself unwittingly to be led into a logical dilemma. He admits that each supposed virtue, such as justice or holiness, is self-identical (holiness is of the nature of the holy, justice of the just) and that each has only one opposite. Socrates then demonstrates that if Protagoras insists on maintaining that one part of virtue is unlike another, he will be forced to say that "holiness is not of the nature of justice, nor justice of the nature of holiness, but of the nature of unholiness, and holiness is of the nature of the not just, and therefore of

the unjust." He, Socrates, on the other hand, is able to maintain that justice
is holy, and holiness just, because to him virtue is one, not several. Protagoras
replies that he cannot agree to the proposition that justice is holy and that
holiness is just, "for there appears to me," he says, "to be a difference between them." But, whether out of uneasy politeness an impatience to get to
the main point (whether virtue can be taught) he allows Socrates to make
this assumption: "If you please I please," he says, "and let us assume, if you
will, that justice is holy and that holiness is just" (331-330).

Socrates, however, after the intervening diversions and digressions, returns
to state the fundamental question more plainly.

> Are wisdom and temperance and courage and justice and holiness five
> names of the same thing? or has each of the names a separate underlying
> essence and corresponding thing having a peculiar function . . . ? (349)[6]

But Protagoras never wholly abandons his basic opinion. Socrates disposes
of his reservation about bravery, as being more unlike justice and temperance
and holiness than any of these is unlike all the others. Protagoras then admits that the virtues are similar, although he still does not accept their identity.
For us, the significant point of the dialogue is that Socrates devotes himself
to maintaining the unity of virtue, not only because this is a necessary consequence of his belief that virtue is knowledge, but because the perfection
of knowledge and of being resides in the One, not in compound things or
multiplicity.

Plato's thinking on this subject finds expression in other dialogues, of
course. In the *Meno,* his emphasis falls more strongly on the definition of
virtue; in the *Laws,* his final attack on the problem, he strives to show that
the virtues may be regarded both as four, and as one; the Guardians must
understand "what is the identity permeating all the four, the unity to be
found, as we hold, alike in courage, in rectitude, in wisdom, and entitling
them all to be called by the one name, virtue."[7] Donne, who admired "that
great successive Trinity of humane wisdom, *Socrates, Plato,* and *Aristotle,*"
as he described them in *Biathanatos,*[8] probably obtained his knowledge of
Plato from reading Ficino's translation, as well as from various intermediate
sources. He once quoted from the *Laws,* in Latin, following Ficino's language
almost verbatim.[9] But the argument from the negative side—that virtue is
not several—emerges most sharply in the *Protagoras.* Since Donne's reasoning
stresses this point first and there is no reason to think that he had not read
this dialogue, I have used it as the best illustration to suggest the configuration
of an idea.

This aspect of Plato's theory of virtue seems to underlie Donne's synthesis,
in the later verse epistles, of the ethical concept (ἀρετή, *virtus*) with other
connotations of *virtus* in the work of Paracelsus. That Donne knew Paracelsus is beyond doubt, and has been commented upon by several critics.[10]
If, in *Ignatius his Conclave,* he satirized the fantastic claims of Philippus
Aureolus Theophrastus Paracelsus Bombast of Hohenheim, in *Biathanatos*
he had praised him as an "excellent Chirurgian."[11] Grierson, in his notes to

two of the poems I am about to discuss, had cited references in Donne's sermons to the *ideas* of Paracelsus. But the more usual view has been that acquaintance with Paracelsus furnished Donne with an occasional image or analogy. Evidence is at hand, however, in the prose letter to Sir Henry Goodyere from which I have already quoted, that Donne virtually *equates* the Platonic idea of virtue as necessarily indivisible, with the Paracelsian notion of a "balsam," "mummy," or life-force. If this interpretation is correct, the special Platonic-Paracelsian connotation of "virtue" in the later verse epistles makes these poems more important in the study of Donne's thought. In addition, new insight may be gained into the meaning of the *Anniversaries*.

For what Donne intends by the term "virtue" now appears to be something quite different from the traditional invocations of the word in the literature of "Platonic love" as we recognize it in Castiglione or, later, in Sidney or Spenser. Donne combines emphasis on its unity, as Plato had critically analyzed it, with its operative energy (the Paracelsian twist). Aware of the "scientific" implications, aware of Plato's logic, aware also of traditions connecting the two, he invests the word with more than merely complimentary associations. The technical problem involved in making such words come alive in verse he does not wholly solve. But he maintains independence about the poetic convention that he may seem superficially to have succumbed to.

We must return to his prose letter to Sir Henry Goodyere to observe how Donne specifically links the Platonic idea of indivisible virtue with the medical theories of an inborn preservative or life force. After the statement that "He is not virtuous out of whose actions you can pick an excellent one," he continues directly:

> Vice and her fruits may be seen, because they are thick bodies, but not vertue, which is all light, and vices have swellings and fits, and noise, because being extreams, they dwell far asunder, and they maintain both a forein war against vertue, and a civill against one another. . . . The later Physitians say, that when our natural inborn preservative is corrupted or wasted, and must be restored by a like extracted from other bodies; the chief care is that the mummy have in it no excelling quality, but an equally digested temper: And such is true vertue.[12]

In the great verse epistle to Mr. Rowland Woodward, "Like one, who in her third widdowhood doth professe," Donne does not avail himself of the image of a mummy or life-force, but he does associate other Paracelsian doctrines with the Platonic teaching that virtue is indivisible. The poem is concerned in some way with Donne's sense of a calling, with his sense of himself as a writer, and with an impending dedication to religion which will involve the sacrifice of part of his aims, ambitions and interests. The opening lines candidly suggest that his new disposition represents a response to disappointments of various kinds.

> Like one who' in her third widdowhood doth professe
> Herself a Nunne, tyed to retirednesse,
> So' affects my muse now, a chast fallowness. (I, 185)

We do not know with any certainty the date of this epistle, but I hardly think
it would have been addressed to Sir Rowland Woodward when he was in the
foreign service. From its tone and content, it would seem to be of the period
preceding the writing of the *Anniversaries,* the period Miss Gardner considers
to be the time when many of the *Divine Sonnets* were probably composed.[13]
Perhaps the fact that Sir Rowland entered the service of the Bishop of London in 1608 might justify the choice of that year or the year before as a
possible date. This would bring it very close to the time of the prose letter
to Sir Henry Goodyere on the theme of virtue.

The verse epistle "To Sir Rowland Woodward" develops its effort of persuasion (self-persuasion, as well as advice to a friend) with a greater intensity
of feeling than is common in poems of this kind. After the first ruminative
exploration of a divided mind, of regret that his Muse has grown satiric
thorns "where seeds of better Arts, were early sown," the poem moves firmly to record the resolve that "There is no Vertue, but Religion." The separate
virtues (wise, valiant, sober, just) are names which discreet men may gain,
but do not constitute true virtue. The traditional "cardinal virtues," then,
are in effect looked upon as insufficient, as even deceptive. True virtue is
one and unmixed. But Donne searches for it in self-knowledge, attention directed inward:

> So wee, if wee into ourselves will turne,
> Blowing our sparkes of vertue may outburne
> The straw, which doth about our hearts sojourne.

There is still, as we notice in the next to the last line ("and with vaine outward things be no more mov'd"), a trace of Stoicism in the philosophy of
this poem. Sir Herbert Grierson points out that in this line Donne is echoing
the very words of Epictetus. But it is a Stoicism reinforced, and transformed,
by the Platonic conception of virtue, here identified with religion, though
not with any dogma.

In the second half of the poem another Paracelsian doctrine furnishes
Donne with part of his quietly surprising, and forceful, sequence of images.
"You know, Physitians," he says in a disarmingly casual way,

> . . . when they would infuse
> Into any oyle, the Soules of Simples, use
> Places, where they may lie still warme, to chuse.
> · · · · · · · · · · ·
> So workes retirednesse in us. (I, 186)

Perhaps an association he was not wholly aware of, between the theme of
virtue as a unity and the notion of "simples," results from his general interest in Paracelsus. The image of the extraction of "Soules of Simples" seems
to continue the pattern suggested by sparks of virtue outburning "the straw

which doth about our hearts sojourne" and concluded by the statements, "Wee are but farmers of ourselves . . . Manure thyself then, to thyself be'approv'd" (I, 186). "To Sir Rowland Woodward" thus anticipates the theme of the *Anniversaries* in its eloquent plea for self-knowledge, without projecting a sense of failure upon the whole enterprise of humane learning.

The Paracelsian reverberations carried by the word "virtue" in the *Anniversaries* do not occur in "To Sir Rowland Woodward," but are markedly present in the group of epistles addressed to the Countess of Bedford and other noble ladies. To elucidate this, it will be desirable to introduce a few examples from Paracelsus himself. I cannot pretend to sufficient knowledge to comment upon the vocabulary of the alchemists. Indeed, I suspect that even for specialists in the history of science, or those really well read in this pseudo-science, it would be difficult to clarify the use of such terms as "balsam," "mummy," "tincture," and "virtue." But I am attempting simply to show their copresence and occasional interchangeability. We know that according to the teaching of Paracelsus, the "mummy," "balm," or life-force of a man might be used as a preservative of life in others. More broadly, however, it was an animating force of all nature. The terms "virtue" and "spirit," though in some cases distinguished from "mummy," or "balsam," are elsewhere conjoined with them or taken as synonymous.

In *De Origine Morborum,* the term "mummy" is coupled with "virtue" in its sense of "life-force" in several passages:

> According to one explanation: Mumia is man himself. Mumia is balsam, which heals wounds. (Lib. II, c. 2)
> The virtues of all herbs are found in this Mumia. (Lib. IV)[14]

Elsewhere, we find that the "tincture," the "arcanum," the quintessence of a substance "is not the virtue (*virtus*) but the essence (*vis*) and the potency (*potentia*), and is stronger than the virtue; *nevertheless, an old error of the doctors conferred the name of virtues upon the potential essences*" (*Paramirum,* Lib. IV).[15]

There is in Paracelsus also an identification of the term "spirit," "which holds within itself the virtue and power of the thing,"[16] with "balsam," which I believe to have been strongly present in Donne's mind not only in some of his later verse epistles but in the whole plan of his *Anniversaries.* In Paracelsus, the confused pattern of thought and the superstitious juggling of ritual words obscure the broad tradition of Renaissance Neo-platonism to which he is so obviously indebted. Fundamentally, he seems to be elaborating in a mystifying manner on the idea of the world-soul, which had been a part of the Neo-platonic and Hermetic schools of thought and is present in Ficino as well. As Professor Kristeller points out, "the broad stream of astrological and alchemical literature . . . also presupposes such notions as a world soul or the inner powers and affinities of things celestial, elementary, and composite, notions that go back to Arabic sources . . . but which derived new impetus and dignity from the Greek and modern Platonist writers and from the Hermetic works associated with them."[17]

Donne, as we know, would have encountered similar ideas in his reading of Hermes Trismegistus or, more rationally expounded, in Ficino. He was likewise an admirer of Pico and Reuchlin. In his poetry, nevertheless, the underlying Platonic and Neo-platonic ideas concerned obtain concreteness from the images provided by Paracelsus.

The conjunction of Platonic idea and Paracelsian image results in sheer bravura, not without serious accents, in the epistles addressed to the Countess of Bedford, "who only," as Donne wrote of her, had "power to cast the fetters of verse on [his] free meditations."[18] The energy of interest continues in verses addressed to the Countess of Huntington and finally in the "Letter to the Lady Carey and Mrs. Essex Riche, from Amyens." In 1607-8, when the Countess of Bedford first came to Twickenham, Donne's meditations on reason and faith combined to celebrate her as a symbol of virtue's strength, both spiritual and medicinal:

> In every thing there naturally grows
> A *Balsamum* to keep it fresh, and new,
> If 'twere not injured by extrinsinque blowes;
> Your birth and beauty are this Balme in you.
>
> But you of learning and religion,
> And vertue, 'and such ingredients, have made
> A methridate, whose operation
> Keepes off, or cures what can be done or said.
>
> Yet, this is not your physicke, but your food,
> A dyet fit for you; for you are here
> The first good Angell, since the world's frame stood,
> That ever did in woman's shape appear. (I, 190)

The Paracelsian identification of *virtus* with a balsamum or vital spirit is apparent and is used in a manner that anticipates the bolder plan of the *Anniversaries.* In a subsequent epistle to her, the equation of the *Anniversaries* is again tested:

> Therefore at Court, which is not vertues clime,
> (Where a transcendent height, (as, lownesse mee)
> Makes her not bee, or not show) all my rime
> Your vertues challenge, . . .
> For, as darke texts need notes: there some must bee
> To usher vertue, and say, *This is shee.* (I. 191)

The same theme in one of the poems addressed to the Countess of Huntington derives special interest from the alchemist's symbol, gold. Virtue, Donne writes, may seem to have declined if she has fallen so low as to inhere in a woman. (In this section of the poem, the suggestion of both the early *Progress of the Soul* and the later one is striking.) But virtue is not stooped, but raised, he continues;

>   . . . exil'd by men
> She fled to heaven, that's heavenly things, that's you. (I, 202)

Here the naming of a lady as a symbol of virtue, and the following lines, in which virtue is compared with the alchemist's gold or the elixir, shows that Donne has something more in mind than a fancy compliment, and the intellectual process here is stronger than analogy. The whole context shows that he is drawing upon his free meditations on the unity of virtue, at once the principle of life and the world's soul.

In this article, it is not possible to analyze recent debates concerning the interpretation of Donne's *Anniversaries.* But Donne's treatment of the theme of virtue in the epistles must be taken into account in considering the purpose and intent of *The Anatomy of the World* and *The Progress of the Soul.* In an appendix to his excellent study, *The Poetry of Meditation,*[19] Mr. Louis Martz argues against the views expressed by Miss Nicolson in her *The Breaking of the Circle,* his contention being that the central imagery refers to the Virgin Mary. Miss Nicolson's more broadly based interpretation of the symbol allows us to read in it a reference to Queen Elizabeth, to the general concept of virtue, to Astrea, or Justice, and perhaps to some unidentified woman as well.[20] When Ben Jonson uttered his famous criticism of the *Anniversaries* ("he told Mr. Donne if it had been written of the Virgin Marie it had been something") Donne had no reason to dissemble in replying to his friend and fellow poet. He could have disposed of the criticism by replying, "It was," had a meditation on the Virgin Mary been, as Mr. Martz argues, his aim. Instead he replied, "that he described the Idea of a Woman, not as she was." The last clause—if we accept Drummond's report of the conversation at all, as most scholars do—presents difficulties for Mr. Martz's position.

The Idea of a Woman as one type of virtue, his pondering on Plato's arguments for the unity of virtue, and the way in which Paracelsian doctrines interact gave Donne a fine sequential harmony to develop in his "Letter to the Lady Carey and Mrs. Essex Riche, from Amyens." This letter was written not long after the *Anniversaries* and is in part an apology for his having chosen Elizabeth Drury, a young lady unknown to him, as a central figure in poems casting into shadow his verse epistles to ladies of his own circle. In the opening lines he makes amends to the absent patronesses by satirizing the invocation of saints—as Donne often guards his own sincerity by double-barrelled description of his very means of praise. Then, in a series of terse punning lines he makes use of the theory of humors to lead to his central idea of the unity of virtue.

> Others whom we call vertuous, are not so
> In their whole substance, but, their vertues grow
> But in their humours, and at seasons show.
>
> For when through tastlesse flat humilitie
> In dow bak'd men some harmelessnes we see,
> 'Tis but his *flegme* that's *Vertuous,* and not Hee:

> So is the Blood sometimes; who ever ran
> To danger unimportun'd he was then
> No better than a sanguine Vertuous man.

> So cloysterall men, who, in pretence of feare
> All contributions to this life forbeare,
> Have Vertue in *Melancholy,* and only there.

> Spirituall *Cholerique* Crytiques, which in all
> Religions find faults, and forgive no fall,
> Have, through this zeale, Vertue but in their Gall.

The Galenist theory of humours had, as is well known, been rejected by Paracelsus. Donne plays with it here and puns upon the medical connotations of virtue, to lead to his more serious theme, that as there is no health in the predominance of one humour, neither is virtue divisible. And for the indivisibility of good he uses gold, the alchemist's mystery and Plato's own image in the *Protagoras.* If one quality, humour, or virtue is set apart, we are but "parcel guilt;"

> . . . to Gold we 'are growne
> When Vertue is our Soules' complexion;
> Who knowes his Vertues name or place, hath none.

> Vertue 'is but aguish, when 'tis severall,
> By occasion wak'd, and circumstantiall.
> True vertue is *Soule,* Alwaies in all deeds All.

Well might the Lady Carey and Mrs. Essex Riche have puzzled their wits to read Donne's meaning as he appears to compliment them in a transcendent flourish:

> This Vertue thinking to give dignitie
> To your soule, found there no infirmitie,
> For, your soule was as good Vertue, as shee;
> Shee therefore wrought upon that part of you
> Which is scarce lesse than soule, as she could do,
> And so hath made your beauty, Vertue too. (I, 222-23)

By tautologies well placed, Socrates had perplexed Protagoras. And, though seeming to attack the Sophist doctrine that virtue can be taught, Plato does not disown his own paradox when he has demonstrated that virtue is one, and is knowledge. The conclusion of this dialogue might furnish a fitting commentary on Donne's dialogue with himself, and others, on the theme of virtue. "If the argument had a human voice," says Socrates,

> . . . that voice would be heard laughing at us and saying: "Protagoras and Socrates, you are strange beings; there are you, Socrates, who were saying that virtue cannot be taught, contradicting yourself now by your attempt to prove that all things are knowledge, including justice, and temperance,

and courage. . . . Protagoras, on the other hand, who started by saying that it might be taught, is now eager to prove it to be anything rather than knowledge; and if this is true, it must be quite incapable of being taught." Now I, Protagoras, perceiving this terrible confusion of our ideas, have a great desire that they should be cleared up. (360)

So Donne might have reflected on some of the puzzling constructions placed upon his *Anniversaries*, his chiefest paradoxes constructed to maintain that "Vertue and shee / Is her own dower."[21]

WHAT WAS THE SOUL OF THE APPLE?

W. A. Murray

For to chuse, is to do. . . .

Since Donne added his mocking preface and discarded his unfinished first poem on the *Progresse of the Soule* it has received scant attention and less approval. Amongst this chorus of distaste, the solitary voice of De Quincey[1] seems little more than an eccentricity. Yet, although the poem is neither very good nor of much literary importance, it is by no means negligible for other reasons. It is the product of an important chapter in Donne's intellectual life; it is also not without interest to the historian of ideas.

The date of *The Metempsychosis* is established by Donne himself as 16 August 1601.[2] It falls therefore within the crucial period of his private life, the months which preceded his marriage. This is a fact of the first importance for our understanding of the poem. During the preparation for the decision which he had to make, he must have thought intensely about a variety of problems connected with his own situation. What then more natural than to write of choice itself, of the earthly progress of the soul from one dilemma to another?

I interpret *The Metempsychosis* as the result of his reactions to his own dilemma. It is an embryo Fall-poem, different in style and method from later developments of a similar theme in the *Anniversaries.* It is Donne on the subject of *Paradise Lost,* characteristically finding his symbols in the attempt of Philo Judaeus to allegorize the story of Genesis.

The Philonic element in this poem has not been sufficiently emphasized by scholars. Philo[3] as originator of a philosophical trend which leads through the Fathers of the Church to Thomas Aquinas has an obvious relevance to our study of Donne. He was a Jew, a contemporary of Christ, whom Christianity eventually almost adopted as its own.[4] He was a preacher, an eclectic philosopher, and a polymath. Donne's generation had an urge to reinvestigate the origins of their thinking, particularly in the domain of theology. Both Reformation and Renaissance contribute to a Philonic influence in European thought evident in the edition of Philo's *Quaestiones in Genesim* published by Budaeus in 1527, in the French translation of Philo's works by P. Bellier (1575), and in the Latin translation by Sigismundus Gelenius (1613). In these, the original texts of Philo, with some now recognized as spurious,

Reprinted from *Review of English Studies*, n.s. 10 (1959), 141-55, by permission of the author and the publisher, The Clarendon Press, Oxford.

were made available to a wide public, which could make direct contact with his ideas, not merely with the Philonic elements in the traditional philosophers, and in theologians such as St. Jerome.

Donne apparently did not rate Philo very highly, if we are to take his epigram *On an Obscure Writer* at its face value:

> Philo, with twelve yeares study, hath beene griev'd
> To be understood; when will hee be beleev'd?

Certainly there are few traces of reminiscence of reference, although the fact of Donne's familiarity with the manner of allegorical interpretation is proved by a passage in the letters.[5] It may be, too, that Donne's style of preaching owes something to Philo. The evidence, such as it is, would be covered without difficulty by assuming that Philo was a part,[6] possibly for a time an important part, of the theological inquiries which had their practical issue in Donne's choice of the Reformed religion.

While Philo, the assured believer in God, who was at the same time convinced of the philosophical consistency of the Pentateuch, is of obvious interest for anyone with Donne's religious problems, Philo the ascetic and preacher of asceticism has a special relevance to Donne in his year of crisis. Difficulties of decision about marriage, about the relationship of the sexes, are in themselves sufficient to explain the ironic mood, the bitter comments on Woman, the wry-mouthed humour of the poem. They may also partly account for the presence of the Philonic element. Although we know what was the outcome of Donne's agony of choice, and may guess how much more attractive to him would be a view of sex like that of Paracelsus, which emphasizes again and again the essential complementariness of Man and Woman, it seems quite reasonable to suppose that the stress of this period could create moods of ironic questioning in which an ascetic tendency was latent, and the Philonic associations in consequence more natural.

The interpretation of *The Metempsychosis* has hitherto been dominated by two biographical suppositions, neither of which has much supporting evidence. The first is that it was the product of Donne's Roman Catholic period. Sir Herbert Grierson in his edition of the poems says: 'Donne, who was still a Catholic in the sympathies that come of education and association, seems to have contemplated a satirical history of the great heretic in lineal descent from the wife of Cain to Elizabeth—for private circulation.'[7] The second is that the poem deals with the Essex revolt. Here the syllogism is perhaps, 'This is an obscure poem dated 1601. Everyone had to write obscurely about Essex in 1601. Therefore Donne was writing about Essex.' Professor Mahood takes this line and includes the first assumption also.[8]

It is not difficult to understand how these views arose. They combine a traditional misreading of the poem with a casual remark of Ben Jonson's to Drummond: 'The conceit of Donne's *Metempsychosis* was that he sought the soul of that apple which Eve pulled, and thereafter made it the soul of a bitch, then a she-wolf, and so of a woman; his general purpose was to have brought in all the bodies of the heretics, from the soul of Cain, and at last left in the body of Calvin: of this he never wrotte but one sheet. . . .'[9]

The tradition thus derived led Gosse to conclude: 'We have not yet advanced out of sight of the Garden of Eden, and at this rate of progress it would have taken millions of verses to get down to Queen Elizabeth.'[10] Professor Grierson remarks: 'The wit of Donne did not apparently include invention, for many episodes are pointless as well as disgusting.'[11] Such are representative opinions of those critics who have thought the poem worth noticing.

As Jonson's recollection of what Donne had written was inaccurate, his notion of its central idea may be no more than a misleading conjecture. I propose therefore to try the effect of discarding the traditional view and of applying in detail a new theory of the symbolism of the soul of the apple.

The initial step in this process is based upon internal evidence. Towards the end of the fragment some names of the children of Adam are used which do not occur in the Old Testament. All of these, except that of Tethlemite, are to be found in a history of the Jews[12] which in Donne's time was attributed to Philo Judaeus, and was bound along with the *Quaestiones in Genesim* in the edition of Budaeus. In the *De Opificio Mundi* of that author, a treatise which would naturally attract a student of Genesis, occurs the following passage which seems to bear upon the symbolism of *The Metempsychosis*:

> But in the divine park or pleasaunce all plants are endowed with soul or reason, bearing the virtues for fruit, and besides these insight and discernment that never fail by which are recognised things fair and ugly, and life free from disease, incorruption and all of a like nature. This description is, I think, intended symbolically rather than literally, for never yet have trees of life and understanding appeared on earth, nor is it likely that they will appear hereafter. No, Moses evidently signifies by the pleasaunce the ruling power of the soul, which is full of countless opinions as it might be of plants; and by the tree of life he signifies reverence towards God, the greatest of virtues, while by the tree that is cognizant of good and evil he signifies the middle thought ($\mu\acute{\epsilon}\sigma\eta$ $\phi\rho\acute{o}\nu\eta\sigma\iota\varsigma$), by which things of a contrary nature are distinguished from each other.[13]

The same terminology reappears, showing further associative links with our poem, in Chapter xi of the *De Plantatione* (*Noah's Work as a Planter*):

> We need, then, be at no loss to know why there are brought into the ark, which was built at the time of the great Flood, all the kinds of wild beasts, but into the Garden no kind at all. For the ark was a figure of the body, which has been obliged to make room for the savage and untamed pests of passions and vices, whereas the garden was a figure of the virtues; and virtues entertain nothing wild, nothing (we may say outright) that is irrational.

It is with deliberate care that the law-giver says not of the man made after God's image, but of the man fashioned out of earth, that he was introduced into the garden. For the man stamped with the spirit which is after the image of God differs not a whit, as it appears to me, from the tree that bears the fruit of immortal life: for both are imperishable and have been accounted worthy of the most central and most princely portion: for we are told that the tree of Life is in the midst of the Garden (Gen. ii. 9). Nor is there any difference between the man fashioned out of the earth and the earthly composite body. He has no part in a nature simple and uncompounded, whose house and courts only the self-trainer knows how to occupy, even Jacob who is put before us as 'a plain man dwelling in a house' (Gen. xxv. 27). The earthly man has a disposition of versatile subtlety, fashioned and concocted of elements of all sorts. It was to be expected, then, that God should plant and set in the garden, or the whole universe, the middle or neutral mind, played upon by forces drawing it in opposite directions and given the high calling to decide between them, that it might be moved to choose and to shun, to win fame and immortality should it welcome the better, and incur a dishonourable death should it choose the worse.[14]

It is true that the relationship between these extracts and the poem is not one of close parallel. Yet the occurrence, in texts which we have every reason to suppose that Donne had read, of the idea of 'neutral mind' and some suggestion of the allegorical images in *The Metempsychosis* is of obvious significance. In Philo we have the Ark, the beasts, the struggle between flesh and spirit, the agony of choice; in Donne the same elements appear, varied in detail and arrangement but subtly consistent with their probable source. This is well shown by the stanza on the Ark:

> Nor, holy Janus, in whose soveraigne boate
> The Church, and all the Monarchies did floate;
> That swimming Colledge, and free Hospitall
> Of all mankinde, that cage and vivarie
> Of fowles, and beasts, in whose wombe, Destinie
> Us, and our latest nephewes did install
> (From thence are all deriv'd, that fill this All,)
> Did'st thou in that great stewardship embarke
> So diverse shapes into that floating parke,
> As have been moved, and inform'd by this heavenly sparke.

This stanza says in fact that the 'neutral mind' (which Philo saw as a basic feature of the universe) has inhabited more shapes than those that derive from the ark. (It could, for example, be said to have been present in the heavenly host when Satan rebelled, or in living things which have appeared since the Flood.) Donne concentrates upon the institutions and creatures which maintain the existence of the fallen world, and especially on the Ark as the means of physical continuity. The allegorical and historical aspects

of the Genesis-theme are closely intertwined in what follows, as they were
in the 'double vision' of Philo himself.

It may be asked at this point what of the transmigration notion itself
which might seem from the Introduction to be one of the poem's main
ideas? The Pythagorean philosophy was an important element in Philo's
synthesis, so much so that both Eusebius and Clement of Alexandria
characterized him as a Pythagorean rather than a Platonist.[15] There is thus
no real incompatibility in the coexistence of Pythagorean and Philonic
elements in the same poem. None the less, I am convinced that transmigration is little more than an ingenious literary device to give some connexion
between episodes in the allegory. The essential thing is not the process of
metempsychosis itself but the allegorical meaning of the apple's soul which
undergoes it.

This attempt to interpret the poem rests therefore on the hypothesis
that it was planned as an allegory of the development of the knowledge of
good and evil in mankind, the separate episodes being related both to religious
or historical questions and to the circumstances of Donne's own predicament.

The method of the poem is related to Philo's as converse to proposition.
Where Philo worked from the Genesis narrative, to a statement of abstract
meaning, Donne states his abstract meaning as a Genesis-like narrative. His
imagery has an emblematic or iconographic quality. Spiritual and mental
states and events are shown as vegetables, beasts, fishes, children of Adam,
and occurrences in a Genesis world. Many of these images are found in
slightly different form in Donne's later poetry, and many have a currency
far beyond his works, appearing for example in the iconography of Dürer,[16]
and of Hieronymus Bosch,[17] whose preoccupation with the Genesis myth
Fränger has recently shown.[18] His symbolism is therefore not idiosyncratic,
though unusual.

Stanza 8 is an apt illustration of these wider associations and intercon-
nexions of Donne's imagery. It is specifically Christian rather than Philonic,
yet regards Christ Himself with the double vision of history and allegory,
in the manner characteristic of Philo:

> Yet no low roome, nor than the greatest, lesse,
> If (as devout and sharpe men fitly guess)
> That Crosse, our joye, and griefe, where nailes did tye
> That All, which alwayes was all, everywhere;
> Which could not die, yet could not *chuse* but die,
> Stood in the selfe same roome in Calvarie,
> Where first grew the forbidden learned tree,
> For on that tree hung in security
> This soule, made by the Maker's will from pulling free.

The symbolism of this verse is not unlike that of the plate of Dürer's *Great
Passion, The Harrowing of Hell.* On the left of this stands Adam, holding in
one hand the apple, and in the other a wooden cross over which floats the
glorified cross on a banner. Here the iconography suggests that the crucifixion

was implied in the first sin, and that it restored by the fate of Christ the possibility of right choice and redemption. A similar meaning, even closer to Donne, is to be found in Bosch's *Saint Jerome at Prayers*. The praying figure of the Saint lies on a round knoll, and clasps a crucifix on which the body of Christ appears in flesh-coloured miniature. Here is a symbolic Calvary to the right of which is a hollow tree trunk, while on the left, in a marshy pool, is the hollow rind of a large fruit. As Donne put it in his *Hymne to God My God, in my Sicknesse,*

> We thinke that Paradise and Calvarie,
> Christs Crosse, and Adams tree, stood in one place;
> Looke Lord, and finde both Adams met in me;
> As the first Adam's sweat surrounds my face,
> May the last Adam's blood my soule embrace.

Another image cognate with these, and sharing their quasi-historical, quasi-allegorical quality, appears in *The Litanie*:

> For that faire blessed Mother-maid,
> Whose *flesh* redeem'd us; That she-Cherubin,
> Which unlocked Paradise, and made
> One claim for innocence. . . .

In the person of Mary *the flesh* is restored to its incorrupt state before the Fall.

In her book on the *Divine Poems* Miss Helen Gardner, pursuing the traditional line of approach to the annotation of Donne, devotes a whole appendix[19] to confessing that no origin has been found for the notion of Christ's Cross and Adam's Tree standing in the same place. The iconographic parallel which I have discovered occurs in a famous picture which was probably known to Donne's contemporary Fra José de Siguença of the Order of Saint Jerome, writing on Bosch in 1599,[20] and which Donne himself could perhaps have seen. Even if Donne never saw or heard of the picture, its existence shows that this particular notion was not uniquely his invention as Miss Gardner claims, and that it may have been widespread in his time.

The central position, in Donne's thought, of the historical beginning of sin and its consequence in the temporal world around us is further demonstrated in the two Anniversaries, to which *The Metempsychosis* is directly related. From *The Second Anniversary* comes the following:

> Thinke further on thy Selfe, my Soule, and thinke
> How thou at first wast made but in a sinke;
> Thinke that it argued some infirmitie,
> That those two soules, which then thou foundst in me,
> Thou fedst upon, and drewst into thee, both
> My second soul of sense, and first of growth.
> Thinke but how poore thou wast, how obnoxious;
> Whom a small lump of flesh could poison thus.

This curded milke, this poore unlittered whelpe
My body, could, beyond escape or helpe,
Infect thee with Originall sinne, and thou
Couldst neither then refuse, nor leave it now.
Thinke that no stubborne sullen Anchorit,
Which fixed to a pillar, or a grave, doth sit
Bedded and bathed in all his ordures, dwels
So foully as our Soules in their first-built Cels.
Thinke in how poore a prison thou didst lie
After, enabled but to suck and crie.
Thinke, when 'twas grown to most, 'twas a poore Inne,
A Province packed up in two yards of skinne, . . .

To these examples of recurrent images it is necessary to add one passage
from *The First Anniversary*:

(For who is sure he hath a soule, unlesse
It see, and judge, and follow worthinesse,
And by Deedes praise it? hee who doth not this,
May lodge an In-mate soule, but 'tis not his.)

This is almost a description of the typical process in an episode of *The
Metempsychosis*. The soul of the apple becomes incarnate, expresses itself
in choice, direction, activity, and has its earthly mansion ruined by the
corruption of fallen nature, a process which also follows naturally from
my second quotation from Philo (above).

If this 'soul of the apple' or power of moral choice is central to the argument, only a little less important are the two forces of Destiny and Law.
'Fate, which God made, but doth not controule' conditions the circumstances in which choice must be exercised: Law, of God, of Nature, of Moses,
entails upon each choice its consequences.

These two conceptions appear substantially in the same form in the
philosophy of Philo. For 'destiny' he uses ὀπαδός, servant or Minister of God,
he also refers to the 'fixed rule of Fate', which determines the length of life. He
regards the laws of God, of Nature, and of Moses as essentially expressions of the
same Logos, and 'choice' as a special form of activity within this complex. Wolfson gives a thoroughly apposite summary of his views, from which I quote:

The determination of the mind to do or not to do is thus not the result
of natural causes which are 'of God' or 'according to God' and by which
the unalterable laws of nature established by God in the world are operated.
Such a determination by the mind is a break in the nexus of these natural
laws and in the established laws of the universe even as miracles are. This
power with which the human mind was endowed to choose or not to choose
refers not only to the choice of good, but also to the choice of evil, even
though the mind is by its very nature rational, for, as says Philo, there
are in our mind 'voluntary inclinations to what is wrong'. The essential

rationality of the mind does not preclude the possibility of its acting, by the mere powers of its free will, against the dictates of reason.[21]

Donne's thought seems consistent with this. As we shall see, in each episode of the poem a crucial error is followed by death from natural causes. 'Right' choice is given the rarity of the supreme miracle.

At the beginning Donne has invoked 'Destiny, the Commissary of God' in terms which reveal the autobiographical importance of his theme. He raises, only to dismiss, the ancient difficulty of reconciling God's fore-knowledge with Man's free will, and the problem of the justice of the Fall and of its penalty. To question revelation in these matters is to be drowned in what he later called 'the second deluge, Heresy'. Donne's solution is consistent with Philo's and also orthodox for both the Churches. He curtails abruptly his rebellious impulse, attributing it to the corruption of original sin, in a line which recalls the text, 'If thy tongue offend thee, pluck it out.'

By stanza 12, Donne has stated the elements of his argument, Choice, Destiny, and Law, and has suggested how these three are interrelated in the history of mankind and of individuals. He then proceeds to the narrative demonstration of his thought.

The history of the soul of the apple, in the temporal fallen world, is the history of sin accumulated upon the memory of innocence. Once Destiny has brought about the Fall, everything is corrupt, and liable to the penalty of the law of nature, death, which is also that of the moral law. The power of choice, in each predicament of its incarnations, becomes a prey to the instincts of fallen nature; in Donne's own terms, it feeds upon the (corrupt) souls of growth and sense, and is led to seek, as genuine goods, self-preservation and increase in the world of time. (Voluntary inclination to evil. The irrationality of fallen mind.)

The soul of the apple first encounters its environment as a mandrake,[22] in which it activates the soul of growth, and experiences the development of those passive sexual potentialities which belong, in the thought of Donne's time, to the lore of the mandrake. The episode of 'this living buried man' may be intended to represent, in the personal allegory, the fate of the innocent soul endowed with sexual properties, at the hands of the experi-enced, sinful, human being, the encounter of youthful latent sexuality with adult habits and motives. When the properties of the mandrake are exploited by Eve, the soul departs from it, having discovered that in the fallen world 'hee's short-liv'd, that with his death can do most good'. The plant which grows in the fallen world must expect its fate.

The next episode advances to the soul of sense, and to a more active stage of sexual life. Under the emblem of the sparrow,[23] bird of Venus, Donne shows the power of judgement seduced by a freedom which is licence, and lost in a consuming promiscuity, which not only destroys the body but demonstrates how necessary was the law of Moses, that first redeeming inter-vention of God, which set bounds to the sexual excesses of fallen nature.

These stanzas have an ambiguous atmosphere of levity (or is it irony?) which I shall discuss later, when considering how seriously this poem is to be taken.

In stanza 23 the centre of interest shifts from the morals of sex to the morals of survival in a world in which life is based upon the destruction of life. The first example in this category is parallel to that of the mandrake. The Soul endowed only with the minimum property of movement in the stream, and incapable of self-protection, is devoured by the Swan,[24] that whited sepulchre of the small and weak, obedient only to the law of the jungle. Both this episode and that of the mandrake represent the circumstances where choice is minimal: '. . . and unblam'd devoured there | All, but who too swift, too great, or well armed were.'

The next incarnation, another fish, is both somewhat larger, and, at first, somewhat luckier. 'To any new desire, Made a new prey' it goes down stream to the ocean of worldly life, beset by perils from which Destiny engineers its escape with almost diabolic ingenuity, so that it may arrive unscathed to face a more complicated choice than the embryo of stanza 23. This odyssey gives Donne the opportunity to underline the savagery of fallen nature, and its progressive degradation (stanza 26). There is an advantage in insignificance, which may prolong life, only to fail one at the crucial moment. One cannot escape the onus of choice, but how to choose between the fresh- and the salt-water factions? While the fish hesitates, it is lost:

> Exalted she is, but to the exalter's good
> As are by great ones, men which lowly stood.
> It's raised, to be the Raiser's instrument and food.

Having encountered the problems of the weak who try to preserve life in the world of this death, the soul of the apple is next involved in the experience of greatness. The emblem is Leviathan; the imagery was perhaps suggested by Donne's memories of the Essex expedition. The whole of this episode seems subtly relevant to the events of 1601:[25] the description of the growth of Leviathan would be an excellent allegory of the rise of the favourite. The law of self-preservation of greatness is increase and yet more increase, or so it seems to the aggressive great. How obviously appropriate to the political scene are these lines,

> O might not states of more equality
> Consist? and is it of necessity
> That thousand guiltlesse smals, to make one great must die?

and

> 'Tis greatest now, and to destruction
> Nearest; There's no pause at perfection:
> Greatnesse a period hath, but no station.

To be great is to be in mortal peril, but it is no safer to take envy of greatness as one's principle. The mouse, which does so, has the ironic misfortune

to destroy the only harmless great thing, and in so doing to make his foe
both his prey and his tomb.

The next and final series of incidents unites the themes of sexual and
social morality, in the emblems of the wolf, the wolf-dog hybrid, and the
ape. The wolf wishes to rule, and prey upon, the flock which Abel ('Who
in that trade, of Church, and kingdomes, there, | Was the first type') pro-
tects with the aid of his bitch. The method which the wolf uses to achieve
his purpose, for him an apparent good according to the law of his nature,
involves a more subtle and complex evil than those to which the power of
judgement has previously succumbed. Its essence is expressed in the tone
of Donne's words, '. . . . yet he called those | Embracements of love', a
trenchant comment on the perversion of love to selfish hypocrisy, preying
upon concupiscence.

The wolf having, as it were, invented hypocrisy, the wolf-dog hybrid exploits it. The evil of hypocrisy is natural to the hybrid creature: man himself
is a hybrid, both animal and divine, and attempts to satisfy both natures.
The symbolic duplicity of this episode leads to a new elaboration of sinful
behaviour, a further extension of the possibilities of the Fall. Not just a
straightforward criminal nature informed the monster, but a double hypocrisy
towards wolves and sheep, and so, in this treacherous isolation, he was deceived by his own deceit, invited pursuit by guilty flight, 'And, like a spie to
both sides false, he perished'.

In both these episodes the allegory has perhaps some relevance to Donne's
own recent experience of life. They might be summed up as problems of an
'outsider' who seeks preferment, or of a convert within his new church. The
next emblem, that of the ape, while partly of the same group, introduces
further the experience of profane love, distinguished from a naïve and generalized lust by having a specific object. In pursuing the satisfaction of this
desire the ape stumbles upon yet another extension of the scope of sin,

> . . . sinnes against kinde
> They easily do, that can let feed their minde
> With outward beauty.

The ape's sin against kind was of a different degree from that of the wolf.
The ape crossed the gulf between animal and human, from that which is not
in God's image to that which is.

The ape had sought to seduce the higher for the satisfaction of the lower;
it is therefore natural that the next stage of corruption of the power of judgement should illustrate the application of this process on the highest plane.
The soul's last incarnation in the poem is as Themech, through whom the
incestuous race of Cain was to be perpetuated. Themech stands, as Donne
makes clear, for that perpetual seduction of the higher by the lower, of man
by woman, of spirit by animal, through which temporal life maintains itself,
a process only to be interrupted by the virgin birth of Christ, and His crucifixion. Is not the body on the Cross the apple restored to its tree? (Goodfriday: 'O Saviour, as thou hang'st upon the tree.')

It remains, finally, to consider some of the critical aspects of *The Metem-psychosis,* apart from the obscurity which I have attempted to examine. The tone of the poem seems to vary from the grandiloquence of stanza 1, which is difficult to take seriously, through the genuinely impassioned

> O let me not launch out, but let me save
> The expense of brain and spirit; that my grave
> His right and due, a whole unwasted man may have

to the ironical jesting of

> Man to beget, and woman to conceive
> Askt not of rootes, nor of cok-sparrowes, leave:

It is, in fact, a fragment not of whole cloth, an experiment which its author discarded, and about which, for whatever reasons, he wove an atmosphere of deliberate mystification. It is very tempting to allow the strong influence of the tone of this poem to persuade one to accept it as 'the nadir of Donne's belief in God and Man'. Miss Mahood in her chapter on 'Donne: The Progress of the Soule' apparently does so, in a passage which shows the present state of the traditional interpretation:

> In the same spirit, Donne planned, in *The Progresse of the Soule,* to follow the transmigrations of the Pythagorean soul through many unattractive forms of life to its final sanctuary in the breast of Queen Elizabeth; and this obscure poem probably contains many now unintelligible covert slurs upon the Queen and her ministers. Beside his resentment of the Queen's treatment of Essex, Donne had another quarrel with the Court. Though he had himself ceased to be a Roman Catholic, natural tolerance, coupled with loyalty to his family and earliest friends, made him protest against the persecution of those who had kept to the older way of worship. So the tone of both *The Progresse* and *The Courtier's Library* is strongly anti-Protestant, although Donne's disillusioned frame of mind prevented his submission to either Rome or Canterbury. . . .
>
> Donne in his turn broods over the theory that a soul can pass through every kind of body, with the sardonic wit of Hamlet speculating how a king might go a progress through the guts of a beggar. There is no faith in man left in *The Progresse of the Soule;* and the scepticism of many passages, and especially of the concluding lines—
>
> > Ther's nothing simply good, nor ill alone,
> > Of every quality comparison,
> > The onely measure is, and judge, opinion
>
> suggests little faith in anything else. Yet in one passage of this poem, which critics have called profoundly irreligious and which certainly repre-sents the very nadir of Donne's belief in God and man, there sounds the note of determination already heard in the third *Satire.* The lines in ques-tion refer to *The Progresse,* but they have a wider significance than their

actual context; in them, Donne dimly perceives that the thirty years of
life which remain to him will be one arduous struggle to recapture, in a
new form, that faith which gave such conviction to his finest love poems. . . .

I think this is wrong in a number of ways. Donne was certainly tolerant,
he was equally certainly, as Miss Mahood admits, not a Roman Catholic
when he wrote this poem. There is no evidence to show that he ever designed
'now unintellibible covert slurs' against the Queen or her ministers, although
the suggestion is from its nature beyond disproof. I doubt if the poem is so
directly related to the events of 1601, or to public religious affairs. In my
opinion the public and private events of 1601 set going a train of thoughts
and feelings in the poet which were centred in the problem of choice. The
disillusioned, mocking, even cynical, tone is proof not of lack of faith, but
of acute, though sometimes grimly humorous, realization of the supreme
contrast between the decisions made by fallen man and that made by Christ,
the infinity of right choice.

Whether *The Metempsychosis* was intended as a public poem and was
still-born, or as a private poem and failed because of the clumsiness of its
structure or for some other reason, is difficult to determine. There is certainly
evidence in stanza 7 of an intent to conclude the poem with Queen Elizabeth,
and this I propose to examine in detail, since it is the basis of the interpretations which I regard as inadequate. If we substitute for 'soule' the
$\mu\acute{\epsilon}\sigma\eta\,\phi\rho\acute{o}\nu\eta\sigma\iota\varsigma$, or power of moral choice, stanza 7 may be paraphrased as
follows:

For that great power of choice, which is now incarnate in our Queen,
expressing itself in her acts, edicts, and thoughts, which control us with
certainty as the moon (Diana, Cynthia, Virgin Goddess), the tide, whose
story, an example of the neutral mind in operation, you will hear at the
conclusion of my poem, that power of choice which Luther experienced
and Mahomet (whether these chose well or ill, they still enshrined the
neutral soul if only briefly) that power of choice, which by its right or wrong
issue tore and mended the Empire and late Rome in its various crises, which
lived when every great change came, first existed in the apple, low enough
to be plucked from the fatal tree, on that first occasion when Man used his
free will to choose evil.

This seems to me to make sense. One may deduce from it that the poem
was not originally designed as a private one, whatever it may have become
before he abandoned it. I think that stanza 7 shows that Queen Elizabeth
is to this poem what Elizabeth Drury became for the Anniversaries. She
is to be seen as part of the formal occasional framework within which
Donne expressed things essentially personal to himself. Stanza 7 is thus
mainly elaborate compliment.

Paradoxically it is the fact that *The Metempsychosis* is unfinished, a
failure, that I find to be its greatest interest. Donne was seeking a terminology,
a manageable body of ideas and images in which to fix his physical, emotional,
and intellectual experience. Philo turned out to have been a blind alley.

Allegorical Judaism quickly lost its hold upon his imagination. He did not develop from this source the language in which he was eventually to write of the new world of his love and marriage, in images which show his imagination stirred by very different ideas.

Nevertheless there are in *The Metempsychosis* hints and foreshadowings of his future evolution. The tendency of his mind is revealed even in those very details which Grierson found pointless and disgusting, in descriptions of growth, and of physical organism, in lines such as

> And whether she leape up sometimes to breath
> And suck in aire, or find it underneath
> Or working parts like mills or lymbecks hath
> To make the water thinne, and airelike, faith
> Cares not;

His new experiences were emphasizing, as nothing can do so well as marriage, the intimate tangle of body and soul, flesh and spirit, which becomes his dominant subject.

NOTES

PRAZ, "The Critical Importance of the Revived Interest in Seventeenth-Century Metaphysical Poetry"

1. In the first edition of his well-known guide to the appreciation of painting, *Saper vedere.*

2. *Modern Poetry and the Tradition,* Editions Poetry, London, 1948, p. 60.

3. *Elizabethan and Metaphysical Imagery, Renaissance Poetic and Twentieth-century Critics,* The University of Chicago Press, 1947, *passim,* chiefly pp. 5, 95, 128.

4. 'Donne and the Rhetorical Tradition', in the *Kenyon Review,* Autumn 1949, pp. 571-89: 'Much of the haunting quality of Donne comes from writing about a total situation, without realizing quite how much of it he was getting into his language or even what all his cross-currents of feeling about it were; he broods like a thunder-cloud, as well as flashing like one.' 'Poor Mr. Eliot, not to mention minor figures, comes in for a good deal of teasing [on Miss Tuve's part] for having said that Donne felt his thoughts, or did not suffer from the peculiar separation between intellect and emotion which arose later. It was a time when "the intellect was at the tip of the senses", and so on. Admittedly these are literary phrases, therefore a kind of pot shot at the real point, but they seem to me good ones. As Miss Tube spends a great many pages in claiming that the old rhetoricians firmly avoided ever making the separation in view, it seems clear that she agrees with the point Eliot was making.'

5. Cleanth Brooks, op. cit., p. 199.

6. Op. cit., p. 60.

7. H. Read, *Wordsworth,* new edition, 1950, pp. 119, 126, 165.

8. 'Kidnapping Donne', in *Essays in Criticism,* Second Series, by Members of the Department of English, University of California, 1934. Tracing the influence of Donne on modern poetry, Mr. Hughes says: 'Above all, in Mr. T. S. Eliot's *poetry* we feel the justification of his recent assertion that it is the special glory of our time to have understood Donne.' See Eliot's essay in *A Garland for John Donne,* ed. Spencer, Harvard Univ. Press, 1931, p. 5.

9. *A Hope for Poetry,* 1934.

KEAST, "Johnson's Criticism of the Metaphysical Poets"

1. This paper was read before English Group VIII at the 1948 meeting of the Modern Language Association, as part of a symposium on "Dr. Johnson and the Seventeenth-Century Poets."

2. See *Rambler* No. 125 (Works [Oxford, 1825], III, 93); No. 156 (*ibid.,* p. 239); No. 158 (*ibid.,* p. 249); No. 23 (*ibid.,* II, 116); No. 121 (*ibid.,* III, 76-77).

3. Cf., e.g., *Rambler* No. 92 (*ibid.,* II, 431-32).

4. *Rambler* No. 125 (*ibid.,* III, 93); cf. *Rambler* No. 23 (*ibid.,* II, 115); *Lives of the English poets,* ed. G. B. Hill (Oxford, 1905), I, 18.

5. *Lives,* I, 458-59.

6. *Ibid.,* p. 59.

7. *Rambler,* No. 78 (*Works,* II, 367).

8. *Lives,* III, 438; II, 16; cf. III, 227; III, 235; *Rambler* No. 60 (*Works,* II, 286-288).

9. *Adventurer* No. 95 (*Works*, IV, 81); cf. *Rambler* No. 68 (*ibid.*, II, 322-23).

10. *Adventurer* No. 95 (*ibid.*, IV, 83).

11. *Johnson on Shakespeare*, ed. Raleigh (1931), pp. 158-59; *Lives*, III, 393; cf. Boswell, *Life*, ed. Powell, II, 87; *Rambler* No. 137 (*Works*, III, 147-48).

12. *Lives*, II, 202; I, 213-14.

13. *Ibid.*, III, 247; II, 16.

14. *Ibid.*, II, 76.

15. *Ibid.*, III, 394.

16. *Ibid.*, I, 441-42.

17. *Ibid.*, I, 42.

18. *Ibid.*, I, 21.

19. *Ibid.*, p. 35.

20. *Ibid.*, pp. 36, 37, 48.

21. The quotations from Donne in the *Life of Cowley* are drawn from the following poems (I give page and paragraph numbers to Vol. I of Hill's edition of the *Lives* and page and line numbers to the one-volume Grierson edition of Donne, Oxford, 1933): pp. 23-24; par. 68: "To the Countesse of Bedford," pp. 167-68. 21-28; p. 24, par. 69: "To the Countesse of Bedford," p. 175. 1-10; p. 24, par. 70: "To Mr R. W.," p. 186. 29-32; p. 26, par. 77: "A Valediction: of Weeping," p. 35. 10-18; p. 26, par. 77: "An Epithalamion, or Marriage Song on the Lady Elizabeth, and Count Palatine," p. 116. 85-88; pp. 26-27, par. 78: "Obsequies to the Lord Harrington," p. 248. 35-40; p. 28, par. 82: "A Valediction: of my Name, in the Window," p. 23. 1-4; p. 30, par. 86: "Elegie on the L. C.," p. 261. 13-16; pp. 30-31, par. 87: "Ecclogue. 1613. December 26," pp. 117-18. 23-32; p. 31, par. 90: "To the Countesse of Bedford," p. 173. 43-47; p. 31, par. 91: "To Mr. B. B.," p. 188. 10-14; pp. 31-32, par. 92: "The Second Anniversarie," p. 232. 173-84; p. 32, par. 94: "Twicknam Garden," p. 27. 19-22; p. 32, par. 95: "Elegie VIII," p. 81. 1-7; p. 33, par. 98: "Obsequies to the Lord Harrington," p. 247. 15-25; p. 34, par. 100: "A Valediction: Forbidding Mourning," p. 45. 21-36.

22. *Lives*, I, 454.

TILLOTSON, "Donne's Poetry in the Nineteenth Century (1800-72)"

1. Since the publication of this essay in 1959 I have found a few other relevant references to Donne; Godwin's and Scott's have been added to the text, and Kipling's parallel between Browning and Donne has been added in a footnote.

2. *PMLA*, LXVIII (1953), p. 658.

3. Interest in Donne's text is evident in *Notes and Queries* from the 1860's. In 1868 W. C. Hazlitt wishes that 'some competent person could be found to undertake [an edition] *con amore*'; a correspondent calling himself 'CPL' (doubtless the Rev. T. R. O'Flaherty, vicar of *Capel*, Surrey, and owner of important Donne manuscripts) agrees, and says that he has made large collections but 'cannot find time or courage to carry out my intention' (pp. 483, 614).

4. A. H. Nethercot, 'The Reputation of the "Metaphysical Poets" during the age of Johnson and the Romantic Revival', *SP*, XXII (1925), p. 81, deals mainly with the eighteenth century; see also the same author's 'The Reputation of John Donne as Metrist', *Sewanee Review*, XXX, (1922), p. 463.

5. His earliest known reference is in the 'Memoranda for a History of English Poetry' which Dr Coburn (*Inquiring Spirit*, 1951, p. 120) thinks may be 1796-8. See also the notebook quotations of 1800 and 1803-4 (*Notebooks*, ed. K. Coburn, 1957, i, nos. 698, 1786-7, 1789).

6. 'Of Persons one would Wish to have Seen' and 'The Conversation of Authors'.

7. He included no Donne in his *Select Poets of Great Britain*, 1824.

8. It would not have done so, for Cary's journal shows him reading Donne's satires in 1800.

9. There is also a brief and conventional reference to Donne's 'hobbling' verse in 'A Satire on Satirists', 1836.

10. *Leigh Hunt's Literary Criticism*, ed. L. H. and C. W. Houtchens, 1956, p. 358; see also pp. 498, 526, 561, and for the reference in *The Book of the Sonnet*, p. 318 below. Hunt also annotated a copy of Donne's poems which was borrowed by G. H. Lewes; see below, p. 319.

11. *Essays and Marginalia*, 2 vols., 1851, ii, 7, 10.

12. According to Kegan Paul, *William Godwin, his Friends and Contemporaries*, 2 vols., 1876, they were essays 'written during many previous years', probably in 1817-18 (ii, 248, 290). Godwin's reading in Elizabethan literature began in 1799, perhaps under the influence of his friends Lamb and Coleridge.

13. *Letters of William and Dorothy Wordsworth, The Later Years*, ed. E. de Selincourt, 3 vols, 1939, i, 469, ii, 652; cf. *Divine Poems*, ed. Helen Gardner, 1952, p. 69.

14. Compare Nathan Drake, *Literary Hours*, 1798, p. 452, and *Shakespeare and his Times*, 2 vols., 1817, i, 615.

15. Field's comments are quoted from the manuscript in the Houghton Library at Harvard, by Roberta Florence Brinkley in *Coleridge and the Seventeenth Century*, 1955, p. 519 n. This book includes some previously unpublished notes on Donne (pp. 527-8).

16. Lowell's annotated copy of this was used in the Grolier Club edition of 1895.

17. *Letters*, ed. R. L. Rusk, 6 vols., 1939, i, 10. On Emerson's interest in the metaphysical poets generally see Norman Brittin, *American Literature*, 1936, pp. 1-21, J. Russell Roberts, id., 1949, pp. 298-310, and Emerson's anthology *Parnassus*, 1875.

18. Such as an otherwise negligible article on Cowley, Donne, and 'Clieveland' [*sic*] by 'M. M. D.' in the *European Magazine*, August 1822, pp. 108-12.

19. Johnson knew Donne's poetry very well, and quoted from it constantly throughout his Dictionary, 'for instance, ninety-seven times under Q, R, S' (W. B. C. Watkins, *Johnson and English Poetry before 1660*, 1936, p. 80) and as the Dictionary long remained a standard work, this may have had considerable influence in familiarizing readers with Donne's poetry.

20. All follow 1719 (which follows 1669), each adding its own misprints. (The 1719 life, in accidental anticipation of the late Professor F. P. Wilson has 1572 as the date of Donne's birth.) Elegy XX was first printed from manuscript in Francis G. Waldron's *Collection of Miscellaneous Poetry*, 1802.

21. 2nd edition, 3 vols.; these poems were also in the one-volume edition of 1790, and in all later ones (1803, 1811, 1845, 1851).

22. The Rev. John Mitford's *Sacred Specimens*, 1827, has only the wrongly attributed Psalm 137.

23. *Atlas*, 25 June and 9 July 1826, and *Whims and Oddities*, 'The Marriage Procession', November 1827 (I owe the Hood and Barker references to Mr P. F. Morgan) Another wit, Douglas Jerrold, was also, according to his son's 'Memoir', a reader of Donne.

24. Vol. viii, pt. i, pp. 31-55. The essay is cited by Allibone, and was known to Grosart (*Notes and Queries*, 1870, p. 505), but the only modern critic who speaks of having read it is Wightman F. Melton, *The Rhetoric of Donne's Verse*, 1906, and no

attempt has ever been made to identify the writer. The editor of the *Retrospective*, Henry Southern (who also edited the *London Magazine* in 1825-8), wrote some articles, and so did Charles Wentworth Dilke, P. G. Patmore, W. J. Fox, and Thomas Noon Talfourd. On present evidence Talfourd seems a possible conjecture. (Since this article was sent to press I have seen the third edition of Keynes's *Bibliography of John Donne*, 1958, where the review is attributed to 'J. Spence'.)

25. S. C. Hall borrowed from this passage; see p. 285 above. It is also recalled in some anonymous *Lectures on the English Poets*, 1847, pp. 27-8.

26. This poem later became a favourite; it is in the selections of Southey, Hall, Alford, and in *Chambers's Cyclopaedia*, and is the only poem chosen from Donne in Dyce's *Early English Poems, Chaucer to Pope*, 1863.

27. Almost the only previous discussion of the satires is in John Payne Collier's *The Poetical Decameron*, 2 vols., 1820, and he is mainly concerned with questions of date.

28. Such as G. G. Cunningham, *Lives of the Most Eminent and Illustrious Englishmen*, 4 vols., 1837, iii, 240-2; Robert Bell, *Lives of the Most Eminent Literary and Scientific Men of Great Britain*, 2 vols., 1839, i, 50-3.

29. The sense in which Johnson used the word (see A. H. Nethercot, 'The term "Metaphysical Poets" before Johnson', *MLN*, xxxvii (1922), p. 11) is not understood, which is itself an interesting comment on its altered associations.

30. 4 vols., 1837-9; iii, ch. v.

31. This is probably the reason for its becoming a common quotation; I find it, for instance, in a paper by G. A. Sala in Dickens's *Household Words*, 19 June 1852, and in the Causton edition of Walton's *Life*, 1855.

32. In 1892 the entry shows no change except a reference to Grosart's edition; it was entirely rewritten, with the help of Edmund Gosse, in 1901.

33. The edition was prepared in 1838 at the request of the publisher, J. W. Parker; but Alford had been interested in Donne since his undergraduate days at Cambridge (*Life, Letters, and Journals*, edited by his widow, 1873, pp. 75, 112).

34. *Works*, ed. Masson, 1897, xi, 110.

35. 'Retrospective Reviews—No. VII' in the *National Magazine and Monthly Critic*, April 1838, pp. 373-8. Lewes's name is given at the head of No. 1 of the series, which is unknown to his biographers. He had borrowed a copy of Donne from 'L. H.' and quotes some of the owner's marginalia: this must be Leigh Hunt, whom Lewes knew well by 1837.

36. See Frederick Page, *Courage in Politics*, 1921, appendix ii, and J. C. Reid, *The Mind and Art of Coventry Patmore*, 1957. Patmore was writing for periodicals in 1845-6, but the evidence here is of the dubious sort called "internal'. Dr Samuel Brown contributed an essay on Herbert to *McPhail's Journal* in 1848, which has a slight resemblance to the Herbert article in *Lowe's*; Grosart's recollection probably confused the two.

37. *The Hero in Eclipse in Victorian Fiction* (translated 1956, first published 1952), pp. 431-9.

38. *Fortnightly Review*, June 1890, p. 805.

39. The *Lives* were constantly reprinted, and the edition of 1855 is very fully annotated (by Thomas Edlyne Tomkins) with many additional quotations from Donne's poetry.

40. Published 1885, but begun in the 1860's; see i, 183, 273, 288.

41. *Letters* [ed. W. A. Wright], 2 vols., 1894, ii, 26 (letter of 1861).

42. *Life of Landor*, 1869, ii, 183 n. Forster owned a copy of the 1633 Poems which had been in the Drury family.

43. chs. xxxix, lxxxiii.

44. *Quarterly Review*, October 1861, pp. 449-50, 456. His authorship is known from his copy of the article in the British Museum (*Opuscula*, I, press-mark 012274 ee. I).

45. 'Personal Recollections', contributed to Hallam Tennyson's *Memoir*, ii, 503.

46. Note in Palgrave's copy of Bell's *Songs of the Dramatists*, in the present writer's possession.

47. Palgrave included two verses of 'Absence' (from Davison's *Poetical Rhapsody*) which was approved by all the selectors, but did not attribute it to Donne until the edition of 1891, on Grosart's authority. In the edition of 1912 the name was removed.

48. Over thirty poems in all were added; some are mentioned in Colin J. Horne, 'Palgrave's *Golden Treasury*', *English Studies*, N.S. II (1949), pp. 54-63, the best account of the work.

49. Press-mark 2326 d. 3. It is not catalogued as Palgrave's, and his signature has disappeared in recent rebinding, but the marks are unmistakably his.

50. See Joseph E. Duncan, 'The Intellectual Kinship of Browning and Donne', *SP*, 1, (1953), p. 81; and Edward Dowden, *Fortnightly Review*, 1890. A writer in *Putnam's Monthly Magazine*, April 1856 (quoted in L. N. Broughton, *Robert Browning. A Bibliography 1830-1950*, 1953, p. 99) may be the first to draw the parallel. Kipling, who was interested in Donne's poems 'many years before they became a literary fashion', said that 'Donne was Browning's great-grandfather . . . with Browning's temperament for turning his mind upside-down and letting the ideas get out as they could'. (Charles Carrington, *Rudyard Kipling*, 1955, p. 477).

51. *Letters of E. B. Browning to R. H. Horne*, 2 vols., 1877, i, 136. But the quotation is not in Browning's letter to Horne (*New Letters*, ed. De Vane and Knickerbocker, 1950) and may have come from Miss Barrett, whose quotations from the Holy Sonnets in *The Seraphim*, 1838, and reference to Donne in *The Book of the Poets* (*Athenæum*, 1842) show that she had some knowledge of Donne before she met Browning.

52. Printed in editions of Donne (1650-1719), and also in Alford, but not in Anderson or Chalmers; this fact, taken with the early date of Browning's reading of Donne, and the presentation to him of a copy of 1719 in 1842, suggests that he used an early edition. (The particular lines are not in Walton's *Life*.)

53. D. G. Rossetti was reading Donne, evidently for the first time, in 1880 (*Family Letters*, ii, 356); Swinburne discovered the *Anniversaries* in 1876 (letter to Theodore Watts-Dunton, printed in T. J. Wise, *Autobiographical Notes by A. C. Swinburne*, 1920) and has several interesting references to Donne in his *Study of Ben Jonson*, 1889, e.g. pp. 99, 129, 142.

HUGHES, "Kidnapping Donne"

1. *Axel's Castle*, pp. 116-117.

2. *New Republic*, LXX, 51. The reviewer is Mr. Robert Penn Warren.

3. *A Garland for John Donne*, ed. Spencer (Harvard Univ. Press, 1931), p. 5.

4. *Dunbar*, p. 84.

5. *A Garland for John Donne*, p. 158.

6. *Studies in Philology*, XIV, 137.

7. Quoted by R. P. Blackmur in "T. S. Eliot," *The Hound and Horn*, I, 295.

8. *A Garland for John Donne*, p. 4.

9. George Williamson, *The Donne Tradition*, p. 47.

10. *Op. cit.*, p. 57.

11. *Op. cit.*, p. 294.

12. *Op. cit.*, p. 25.

13. *Op. cit.*, p. 200.

14. *Op. cit.*, p. 243.

15. *Op. cit.*, p. 94.

16. Helen C. White, "English Devotional Literature (Prose)," Univ. Wisconsin *Studies in Language and Literature*, no. 29, p. 243.

17. Evelyn M. Simpson, *A Study of the Prose Works of John Donne* (Oxford Univ. Press, 1924), p. 42.

18. *A Garland for John Donne*, p. 165.

19. *Op cit.*, p. 194.

20. E. E. Stoll, *Shakespeare Studies* (1927), p. 129.

21. G. Wilson Knight, *The Imperial Theme* (1931), p. 25.

22. *Op. cit.*, p. 185.

23. "Studies in Shakespeare, Milton, and Donne," Univ. Michigan *Language and Literature Series*, I, 203.

24. *Complete Poetry and Selected Prose*, ed. Hayward, p. 672.

25. Cf. Lynn Thorndike, *Science and Thought in the Fifteenth Century*, pp. 134-136.

26. Facsimile Text reproduction of the first edition, p. 146.

27. Hayward, *op. cit.*, p. 609.

28. Elegy XII, *His Parting from Her*, lines 99-100.

29. Book V, Prologue, stanza vii.

30. Hayward, *op. cit.*, p. 674.

31. Lines 37-39. *Poetical Works*, ed. Grierson (1912), p. 196.

32. Cf. J.-R. Charbonnel, *La Pensée italienne au seizième siècle* (Paris, 1919), p. 36.

33. *Paradoxes and Problems*, ed. Keynes (1923), p. 43.

34. *Essays in Divinity*, ed. Jessopp (1855), pp. 206-207.

35. Hayward, *op. cit.*, p. 619.

36. Keynes, *op. cit.*, p. 16.

37. Jessopp, *op cit.*, pp. 37-38.

38. Hayward, *op. cit.*, p. 733.

39. Keynes, *op. cit.*, p. 37.

40. *Aspects of the Italian Renaissance*, p. 288.

41. Canto IV, p. 44.

42. *Jour. Eng. Germ. Philol.* XVII, 471-502.

43. Keynes, *op. cit.*, p. 2.

44. Jessopp, *op. cit.*, p. 95.

45. Lines 263-285.

46. Lines 55-63. Professor Grierson's note on these lines indicates the practical knowledge of navigation and astronomy with which Donne varied the image of the ever fixed mark whose worth's unknown although its height be taken.

47. Blackmur, *op. cit.*, pp. 206-207.

48. Keynes, *op. cit.*, p. 64.

49. Book VI, stanzas 35-36.

50. Lines 79-81.

51. Lines 72-73.

52. Arthur O. Lovejoy, "The Parallel of Deism to Classicism," *Mod. Philol.*, XXIX, 281-299.

53. *Outflying Philosophy*, pp. 59-60.

54. *Donne the Craftsman*, pp. 59–69.

55. Henry Lanz in *The Fortnightly*, Vol. I, no. 6, p. 8.

56. George Wither, *Fair Virtue of the Mistress of Philarete*, London, 1818, p. 95.

57. *Ibid.*, p. 96.

58. "The Lineage of 'The Extasie'," *Mod. Lang. Rev.*, XXVII, 1–5.

59. Keynes, *op. cit.*, p. 6.

60. The confrontation is made by Elizabeth Holmes in *Aspects of Elizabethan Imagery*, p. 99.

61. *Jean Bodin*, by Roger Chauviré, Paris, 1914, p. 124. Vide Bodin's *Theatrum Naturae*, IV, 15, and *Demonomanie*, II, 5.

62. *The Criterion*, VIII, p. 464.

63. *A Garland for John Donne*, p. 4.

64. *The Religious Thought of John Donne*, p. 207.

65. Cf. *A Garland for John Donne*, pp. 53–55.

66. Hayward, *op. cit.*, pp. 113–114.

67. Cf. A. O. Lovejoy, "The Dialectic of Bruno and Spinoza," *Univ. Calif. Publ. Philos.*, I, 163–164.

68. Thorndike, *op. cit.*, p. 136.

69. Hayward, *op. cit.*, pp. 734–735. Cf. the use of the same thought in *Devotions upon Emergent Occasions* (ed. Sparrow), p. 4.

70. Hayward, *op. cit.*, pp. 628–629.

BATESON, "Contributions to a Dictionary of Critical Terms. *II. Dissociation of Sensibility*"

1. The quotation—from *The Prompter*, no. 63, June 17th, 1735—is the earliest use of the word in this specifically 'sentimental' sense that has so far come to light. See R. S. Crane, 'Suggestions towards a Genealogy of the "Man of Feeling",' *ELH*, December 1934, p. 220. *The Prompter* was edited and most of it written by Aaron Hill, the friend of Richardson, and the credit for the introduction of the term should probably go to him. For the later history of the word in this sense, see Edith Birkhead, 'Sentiment and Sensibility in the Eighteenth-Century Novel', *Essays and Studies*, XI, 1925.

2. 'Milton', p. 7 (*Proceedings of the British Academy*, vol. XXXIII, 1947).

3. Stopford A. Brooke, *English Literature*, 3rd edition, 1896, p. 115. What is essentially the same formula—'the emotional apprehension of thought' of Donne breaking down into a 'dualism' in Milton—is to be found in Herbert Read's 'The Nature of Metaphysical Poetry', *The Criterion*, April 1923 (reprinted in *Reason and Romanticism*, 1926, pp. 31–58).

4. Cf. 'Tradition and the Individual Talent' (*The Sacred Wood*, p. 49): 'The experience, you will notice, the elements which enter the presence of the transforming catalyst, are of two kinds: emotions and feelings.'

5. See Richard Fleckno, *Miscellania*, 1653, p. 102.

JOHNSON, "Classical Allusions in the Poetry of Donne"

1. E. M. Simpson, *A Study of the Prose Works of John Donne*, p. 46, and cf. Ramsay, *Les Doctrines Mediaevales chez Donne*, part II, Chs. 1 and 2, and Appendix I. Also *Donne's Poetical Works* ed. by Grierson, I, 35; Gosse, *Life and Letters of John Donne*, p. 14; and Jessopp, *John Donne*, p. 17.

2. The sonnet cycles referred to are: B. Griffin's *Fidessa*; H. Constable's *Diana*; B. Barnes' *Parthenophil and Parthenope*; W. Percy's *Coelia*; R. L.'s *Diella*; W. Smith's *Chloris*; Lord Brooke's (F. Greville) *Caelica*; R. Tofte's *Laura*; G. Fletcher's *Licia*; R.

Barnfield's *Cynthia*; N. Breton's *The Passionate Shepherd*; T. Watson's *The Passionate Centurie*; T. Lodge's *Phillis*; Daniel's *To Delia*; Drayton's *Idea's Mirror and Idea*; Sidney's *Astrophel and Stella*; and Spenser's *Amoretti*. The sonnets of Wyatt, Surrey and Shakespeare are also used.

3. Drayton, 31; Barnes, 37; Smith, 41. In actual references to the gods, Watson leads with 35; Drayton follows with 26; Barnes, 25; Donne, 23; the lowest are Percy, 3; Constable, 4; Daniel, 4; with a median of 14.

4. Mentioned also by Percy and Drayton.

5. By R. L.

6. By Spenser and Drayton.

7. By R. L., Smith, and Watson.

8. Phoebus is used by twelve; not by Constable, Percy, Barnfield, Lodge, Wyatt, Surrey, Daniel, and Drayton; Phaeton, by Griffin, Tofte, and Barnes. Donne uses more names than any of the sonnetteers except Watson, Barnes, and Drayton.

9, 10, 11. *Astrophel and Stella.*

12. Shakespeare, Sonnet 148.

13. Sonnet 137.

14. Sonnet 153.

15. Sonnet 154.

16. Donne, *Eclogue.*

17. *The Constant Lover.*

18. *Elegy XVIII.*

19, 20, 21. *Love's Deity.*

22. *Love's Exchange.*

23. *Elegy XIX.*

24. *Love's Exchange.*

25. *Second Anniversary.*

26. *Obsequies to Lord Harrington.*

27. *On Sidney's Translating the Psalms.*

28. "Fool, look in thy heart and write."

29. Muse is "dumb-born."

30. Sonnet 103: "What poverty my muse brings forth."

31. Letter to Rowland Woodward.

32. See above, footnote 2.

33. Sonnets 38 and 78. Donne subtly criticizes these writers in *Love's Growth:*

> Love's not so pure and abstract as they use
> To say, which have no mistress but their Muse.

34. *Eclogue.*

35. La Corona.

36. Letter to Mr. B. B. "If thou unto thy Muse be married." Cf. Spenser and Shakespeare in this. Spenser's muse was at times "absent in foreign lands." Shakespeare addresses her in Sonnet 101: "Oh truant Muse!" and like Donne speaks of the marital relation in connection with his muse; in Sonnet 82:

> I grant thou wert not married to my Muse.

37. *Satire V.*

38. "Muses scorn to dwell in vulgar brains."

39. Not of "pack-horse" breed; must have spirit and fire.

40. *Inferno*, Canto IV.

41. Love's Growth.
42. In the Eclogue of 1613:

> "And were the doctrine new
> That the earth mov'd, this day would make it true."

In a verse letter to Countess of Bedford:

> "As new philosophy arrests the Sunne
> And bids the passive earth about it runne . . ."
> "First seeds of every creature are in us"

In *The First Anniversary,* 1612:

> "The new Philosophy calls all in doubt,
> The Element of fire is quite put out;
> The Sun is lost, and th' earth, and no man's wit
> Can well direct him where to look for it. . . ."
> "They have impaled within a Zodiake
> The free-borne Sun . . .
> For his course is not round."
> "Man hath weav'd out a net, and this net throwne
> Upon the Heavens, and now they are his owne . . .
> And Oh, it can no more be questioned
> That beauties best, proportion, is dead."

Also, in Sermon "At Funeral of Sir William Cokayne, Knt." I need not call in new
Philosophy that denies a settlednesse, an acquiescence in the very body of the earth,
but makes the Earth move in that place, where we thought the Sunne had moved. . . ."
     3. From Sermon "At Funeral of Sir William Cokayne, Knt." *Love's Growth*:
"So many spheares, but one heaven make."
43. Love's Alchemy.
44. Good Friday.
45. Litany.
46. On the translating of the Psalms by Sidney.
47. "At St. Pauls upon Christmas Day." "To the King at White-hall," illustrate the
point.
48. Hymn to God the Father.
49. Elegy XII.
50. Holy Sonnets X.
51. Letter to R. Woodward.
52. Satire V.
53. Letter to Countess of Bedford.
54. *2 Henry, IV,* 3:1.
55. *Comedy of Errors.*
56. *Midsummer's Night's Dream.*
57. *Comedy of Errors.*
58. *2 Henry VI,* 4:1.
59. *Coriolanus,* 3:1.
60. *Anthony and Cleopatra,* 4:6.
61. Jove is mentioned by sixteen of the Elizabethans, omitting Griffin, Brooke,
Tofte, and Wyatt.
62. *Love's Deity.*

63. *Verse Letter to Countess of Bedford.*

64. *Anthony and Cleopatra.*

65. *As You Like It.*

66. *The Indifferent.*

67. Mentioned also by Shakespeare.

68. Brooke merely refers to Argus; Breton, "And Love in Argus eyes, Finds Jealousy a fiend"; Tofte wishes for Argus' eyes.

69. Drayton: "The furies cruel be."

70. Fletcher and Lodge refer to Python.

71. *Elegy XIX.*

72. "Go and Catch a Falling Star."

73. *Elegy XIV.*

74. Ode.

75. *Elegy XVIII.*

76. Hymn to Christ.

77. *The Storm.*

78. *The Comparison.*

79. *Elegy XIII.*

80. *Elegy XII.*

81. *Eclogue.* The myth of Prometheus is retold by Constable, Tofte, Barnes, and Sidney; Drayton merely refers to his aspiration. Smith and Watson repeat the myth of Acteon.

82. Satire IV. Other references to the myth of Circe are those of Griffin, Circe's rod; R. L., Circe's floods; Tofte, Circe changed to a fountain of tears.

83. Some of the sonneteers, for example, Watson, seem to pile reference upon reference merely to display a broad knowledge of classical learning.

84. Valediction to His Book.

85. *Elegy IV.*

86. *Elegy XIX.*

87. *Elegy XIV.*

88. *Elegy XII.* Daniel and Watson use term.

89. Letter to I. L. See Shakespeare's *Hamlet* for the most effective of his five references.

90. Sonnet IX.

91. *Second Anniversary.*

92. Valediction to his Book.

93. Commendatory Verses upon Mr. T.C.

94. Griffin and Daniel use the reference. Smith is the only one to refer to Lethe.

95. Obsequies on Lord Harrington.

96. Satire IV.

ALLEN, "John Donne's Knowedge of Renaissance Medicine"

1. *Op cit.* (Keynes, London, 1923), p. 64.

2. *Op cit.* (Merrill, New York, 1910), pp. 12-13.

3. A perfect example of this sort of historical essay is found in Columbus, *De Re Anatomica* (Venice, 1559), p. 256. The reader may apply what Columbus has to say about the importance of anatomies and dissections as a gloss on Donne's frequent allusions to this matter. Hundreds of medical works were published during the sixteenth and early seventeenth centuries, and though I shall mention other writers, I have tried to limit my investigations to the complete works of the following great physicians:

Jacques Dubois (Sylvius), 1478-1555; Gerard Columba (Columbus), 1494(?)-1559; Jean Fernel (Fernelius), 1497-1558; Andrea Vesalio (Vesalius), 1514-1564; Johannes Riolan (Riolanus), 1539-1605; Ambroise Paré (Pareus), 1500(?)-1590.

4. Greene, *Works* (Grosart, London, 1881-1883), III, 143; Harvey, *Works* (Grosart, London, 1884), II, 46; Nashe, *Works* (McKerrow, London, 1910), III, 13; Beaumont and Fletcher, *Works* (Waller, Cambridge, 1909), IV, 129; Dekker, *Works* (Grosart, London, 1884), I, 116, III, 348; Jonson, *Works* (Cunningham-Whalley, London, n. d.), II, 28-29, III, 96-98.

5. A typical aside of this sort is found in Riolanus, *Opera Omnia* (Paris, 1610), p. 10. Hanc Anatomen Hippocratis & Galeni doctrina stabilitam profitemur, eam tamen improbat Paracelsus, horrendam Lanienam, & Theatricam Carnificinam appellat: in cuius locum ridiculam & ad hunc diem inauditam Anatomen excogitavit, quam Formalem & Spiritualem vocat, non Materialem: Vivam, non Mortuam: Essentialem, non Localem. Haec Anatome hominis essentiam non ostendit in homine, sed extra hominem in universis partibus praesertim mineralibus: In cupro ostendit Anatomiam iecoris, quia igne separatur essentia, quae est iecur non corporeum & materiale, sed essentificatum; Pari ratione in argento ostendit cerebrum, in auro cor essentificatum, ita ut possis dicere argentum cerebrum minerale, vicissimque cerebrum argentum animale.

6. *Poetical Works* (Grierson, Oxford, 1912), I, 182.

7. *Biathanatos* (New York, 1930), p. 171; I called attention to this peculiarity of Donne in "Donne's Suicides," *MLN*, LXI, 129-34.

8. *Ibid.*, p. 216.

9. *Ibid.*, p. 215.

10. Sic luem veneream, diram Scortatoribus poenam a Deo Opt. Max. constitutam esse putandum est, adeo ut persuasam habeam, Sophistas ac Pseudomedicos istos quoque ceu carnifices divinae poenae adiunctos esse, ut scortatores falsis suis curationibus magis adhuc excrucient ac torqueant. *Opera* (Geneva, 1662), III, 1, 44-45.

11. *Biathanatos*, p. 172.

12. *Op cit.*, I, 658-63. In the *Paradoxes* (p. 38), Donne says that it is a belief of the Paracelsians that man could become immortal provided that he swallowed enough creatures alive. This is an ancient notion, but I have not been able to find any indication that Paracelsus subscribed to it. The discussion of immortality in Paracelsus' *De Vita Longa* (II, 46) suggests that this notion would be obnoxious to him.

13. *Op cit.*, I, 161, 275; II, 406; III, 1, 23, 52.

14. *L Sermons* (London, 1649), p. 165.

15. *Op cit.*, I, 422, 461.

16. *Ibid.*, I, 601.

17. *Ibid.*, I, 664.

18. *Ibid.*, III. 1, 206.

19. *Devotions* (Sparrow, Cambridge, 1923), p. 2.

20. His praeconceptis, scitote quod, eum homo caro ac sanguis existat, opus etiam Balsamo quodam habeat peculiare, a quo conservetur & sustineatur. Is in corpus salis positus est. Sic ergo a sale homo conservatur, veluti a Balsamo. . . . Simili ratione ipsa quoque terra Balsamum suum a sale habet, unde conservatur. *Op cit.*, I, 330. See also I, 51, 171, 328, 449, 467, 488, 529, 585, 633; II, 33, 62, 95, 127, 178, 193, 211; III. 1, 18, 64, 79, 90, 137, 148-49 *et passim*. See Roche Le Baillif, *Dictionariolum Vocum Quibus in Suis Scriptis Usus est Paracelsus*, appended to *Opera*, III.

21. *LXXX Sermons* (London, 1640), p. 313 and *L Sermons*, p. 214. Donne may

have read *A briefe and short discourse of the vertue of balsame*, London, 1585.

22. *Op. cit.*, III. 1, 19.

23. *LXXX Sermons*, p. 730: Pareus, *Les Oeuvres* (Lyon, 1652), p. 15.

24. *L Sermons*, p. 236; *Letters*, p. 246: Pareus, *op. cit.*, pp. 20, 529-31, 550; Sylvius, *Opera Medica* (Geneva, 1635), pp. 15-18; Riolanus, *Opera Omnia* (Paris, 1610), III. 1, 297, 318.

25. *Op. cit.*, p. 480.

26. *L Sermons*, p. 167.

27. *Op. cit.*, pp. 179-80.

28. *L Sermons*, p. 158.

29. *Op. cit.*, pp. 27, 424, 428, 588.

30. *Op. cit.*, p. 310.

31. *Ibid.*, p. 186.

32. *Op. cit.*, p. 563.

33. *Poetical Works*, I, 173.

34. *Op. cit.*, p. 256.

35. *Op. cit.*, p. 44.

36. *Op. cit.*, p. 127.

37. *Poetical Works*, I, 35: Riolanus, *op. cit.*, pp. 16-18.

38. *The Most Excellent Workes of Chirurgerye* (London, 1543), sig. Al.

39. Fernelius, *op. cit.*, p. 4; Riolanus, *op. cit.*, pp. 38-41; Pareus, *op. cit.*, p. 106; Columbus, *op. cit.*, p. 19; De Vigo, *op. cit.*, sig. A3v-A4.

40. *Opera Omnia* (Foesius, Frankfort, 1621), p. 410.

41. *Poetical Works*, I, 58.

42. *Ibid.*, I, 315.

43. Lanfrancus, *Science of Cirurgie* (Von Fleischhacker, *EETS*, 1894), pp. 24-25; Vesalius, *Anatomia* (Venice, 1604), pp. 323-24; Columbus, *op. cit.*, p. 194; De Vigo, *op. cit.*, sig. B6; Sylvius, *op. cit.*, p. 108; Fernelius, *op. cit.*, p. 100; Riolanus, *op. cit.*, I, 109-10, III. 1, 265; Pareus, *op. cit.*, p. 112.

44. *Poetical Works*, I, 257.

45. *Op. cit.*, p. 4; Pareus, *op. cit.*, p. 115; Vicary, *A Profitable Treatise of the Anatomie of Man's Body* (*EETS*, e. s., 1888), p. 74.

46. *Op. cit.*, pp. 2-3.

47. *Op. cit.*, p. 460.

48. *LXXX Sermons*, pp. 516-17.

49. *Poetical Works*, I, 259.

50. *Op. cit.*, p. 463.

51. *Op. cit.*, p. 177.

52. *Op. cit.*, p. 98.

53. For an elaboration of this notion see Fernelius, *op. cit.*, p. 72.

54. See also *Poetical Works*, I, 19, 67.

55. Pareus, *op. cit.*, pp. 18-19; Columbus, *op. cit.*, p. 191; Fernelius, *op. cit.*, pp. 72-74, 84-85.

56. *LXXX Sermons*, p. 714.

57. Pareus, *op. cit.*, p. 71; Columbus, *op. cit.*, p. 226; Vesalius, *op. cit.*, p. 431.

58. *Letters*, p. 116.

59. *LXXX Sermons*, p. 797.

60. Vassaeus, *In Anatomen Corporis Humani* (Venice, 1549), p. 30; Pareus, *op. cit.*, pp. 24, 76; Lanfrancus, *op. cit.*, p. 171; Vesalius, *op. cit.*, p. 395; Sylvius, *op. cit.*, p. 121; Fernelius, *op. cit.*, p. 19; Columbus, *op. cit.*, p. 231; Riolanus, *op. cit.*, I, 130; De Vigo,

op. cit., sig. B3v.

61. *Op. cit.*, p. 297.

62. *Poetical Works*, I, 259.

63. Fernelius, *op. cit.*, pp. 43, 51; Pareus, *op. cit.*, pp. 105, 142; Lanfrancus, *op. cit.*, p. 178; Vicary, *op. cit.*, pp. 23-24; Columbus, *op. cit.*, p. 255; Vesalius, *op. cit.*, pp. 109-10; Vassaeus, *op. cit.*, p. 147.

64. *Op. cit.*, p. 37.

65. *Op. cit.*, III. 1, 257.

66. *Op. cit.*, pp. 79. But probably derived from *Job* X:10.

67. Vicary, *loc. cit.* See also Pareus, *op. cit.*, pp. 591-92; Vassaeus, *op. cit.*, p. 35; Fernelius, *op. cit.*, pp. 164-66; Vesalius, *op. cit.*, pp. 403-404; Lanfrancus, *op. cit.*, p. 174.

68. *Poetical Works*, I, 256.

69. *Op. cit.*, pp. 591-92; Riolanus, *op. cit.*, I, 176.

70. *Op. cit.*, p. 168.

71. *Op. cit.*, p. 592.

72. *Op. cit.*, p. 79.

73. *Op. cit.*, p. 169.

74. *Poetical Works*, I, 234; *L Sermons*, p. 60.

75. Columbus, *op. cit.*, pp. 251-52; Pareus, *op. cit.*, p. 596; Fernelius, *op. cit.*, p. 170. On several occasions, Donne indicates that coitus shortens life (*Poetical Works*, I, 70-71, 234), and this view also had medical sanction. I cite the following from Riolanus, *op. cit.*, III. 1, 310. Immoderata autem illius profusio plus nocet vitae, quam si eo plus sanguinis centies effluxisset, hinc omnia animalia salacia sunt vitae brevioris. Ea causa passeres vix unquam duos annos excedunt, & mares quia femellis sunt salaciores, citius moriuntur. . . . Immodicae autem veneris haec incommodata memorantur, virium & spiritium exolutio, oblivio, visus hebes, foetor oris, nervorum & articulorum morbi, ut tremor, paralysis, arthritidis omne genus, Podagra, Chiragra, Gonagra, Ischias: praeterea Gonorrhoea, mictus sanguinis & urinae stillicidium, ut mittam luem veneream, & illius praecursores, cariem pudendi, virulentam gonorrhoeam, & bubonem venereum. See also Sylvius, *op. cit.*, p. 308; Fernelius, *op. cit.*, p. 196, 326; Cardanus, *De Subtilitate* (Basel, 1554), p. 363.

76. *Op. cit.*, pp. 48-49.

77. *Op. cit.*, p. 262.

78. *Poetical Works*, I, 178, 195.

79. *Op. cit.*, p. 5.

80. *Devotions*, p. 28.

81. *Op. cit.*, p. 439.

82. *L Sermons*, p. 328; De Vigo, *op. cit.*, sig. Qq4v.

83. *Ibid.*, p. 168.

84. *Op. cit.*, pp. 331, 302; Tagaultius, *op. cit.*, p. 49; Fernelius, *op. cit.*, p. 337; Riolanus, *op. cit.*, III. 1, 564-65, 623-24.

85. *Poetical Works*, I, 197.

86. *Op. cit.*, II, 516-17.

87. *Op. cit.*, pp. 471-73. In the "limits of knowledge" section of the *Second Anniversary*, Donne suggests that the means by which the stone enters the bladder is unknown. The medical authorities whom I have consulted do not consider it a problem, though Fernelius does disagree with the conventional explanations and offers one of his own (*op. cit.*, p. 311). In the same passage, Donne also says that the way in which the lungs attract mucous is unknown. Sylvius says that it is drawn from the air or produced by a disposition of the heart or lungs (*op. cit.*, p. 307); with this view Fernelius agrees (*op. cit.*, p. 128).

88. Fuchsius, *Ad Quinque Priores Suos Libros De Curandi Ratione* (Lyon, 1553), p. 155.

89. *LXXX Sermons*, p. 398: Sylvius, *op. cit.*, p. 268.

90. *Ibid.*, p. 715: "quelquefois rompt quelque vaisseau aux poulmons, dont ensuit flux de sang, qui abbrege la vie du malade." Pareus, *op. cit.*, p. 562.

91. *L Sermons*, p. 462; *Devotions*, p. 58; Sylvius, *op. cit.*, p. 513, 668; Fernelius, *op. cit.*, pp. 390-91.

92. *Biathanatos*, p. 171: Lanfrancus, *op. cit.*, p. 104.

93. *Op. cit.*, III. 1, 369.

94. *Op. cit.*, p. 719.

95. *Devotions*, p. 43; Sylvius, *op. cit.*, p. 730; Pareus, *op. cit.*, p. 708; Fernelius, *op. cit.*, pp. 452-53; Mathiolus, *Opera* (Basel, 1674), pp. 478-79.

96. *Ibid.*; Pareus, *op. cit.*, p. 708; De Vigo, *op. cit.*, sig. Hh4; Sylvius, *op. cit.*, p. 454; Fernelius, *op. cit.*, p. 454; Mathiolus, *op. cit.*, pp. 474-75.

97. *LXXX Sermons*, p. 645: De Vigo, *op. cit.*, sig. Nn3v; Sylvius, *op cit.*, p. 736; Fernelius, *op. cit.*, pp. 449-50; Mathiolus, *op. cit.*, p. 516.

98. *Poetical Works*, I, 248: Pareus, *op. cit.*, p. 504; Fernelius, *op. cit.*, p. 490; Sylvius, *op. cit.*, p. 480.

99. *LXXX Sermons*, p. 16: De Vigo, *op. cit.*, sig. Hh4; Mathiolus, *op. cit.*, p. 507; Fernelius, *op. cit.*, pp. 452-53.

100. *Poetical Works*, I, 186: Pareus, *op. cit.*, 722; Sylvius, *op. cit.*, p. 647.

101. *Ibid.*, I, 218: Pareus, *op. cit.*, p. 745; Gesner, *The Newe Jewel of Health* (London, 1576), p. 28.

102. *Ibid.*, I, 243.

103. *Op. cit.*, p. 495.

104. Since I have written on this in "Donne and the Bezoar," *MLN*, LVI, 609-10, I shall not discuss it here.

105. *Op. cit.*, pp. 240-55.

106. *Op. cit.*, p. 521.

107. *Op. cit.*, II, 44.

108. *Op. cit.*, I, 30.

109. *Op. cit.*, p. 135. Donne was also aware of the theory of the homunculus. "Man, whom Paracelsus would have undertaken to have made, in a Limbeck, in a Furnace," *LXXX Sermons*, p. 64.

110. *Letters*, pp. 84-85.

111. *Op. cit.*, pp. 486, 503.

112. *Op. cit.*, pp. 491, 626.

113. *Op. cit.*, pp. 294-99.

LEDERER, "John Donne and the Emblematic Practice"

1. *Studies in Seventeenth-Century Imagery*, vol. I, London, 1939 (translated from his *Studi sul concettismo*, Milan, 1934), p. 12.

2. The Italian academies, robbed of their scholastic arguments by the Renaissance, were discussing the difference between the emblem and the impresa at great length and the academicians did not hesitate to abuse each other on account of the finest points. Finally, one of them, the Abbot Ferro (*Teatro d'Imprese*, Venice, 1623), gave the judgment that the distinction was really quite negligible and therefore not justifiable, but only after having himself written several hundred pages on the subject. See E. N. S. Thompson, *Literary Bypaths of the Renaissance*, New Haven, 1924.

3. *The Worthy tract of Paulus Iovius, contayning a Discourse of rare inventions, both Militarie and Amorous, called Imprese*, London, 1585, 'To the Friendly Reader'.

4. I. Walton, *The Lives*, 1670, *The Life of Mr. George Herbert*, p. 68.

5. *Cf.* T. Tramer, *Studien zu den Anfängen der puritanischen Emblemliteratur in England* (Dissertation, Basle), Berlin, 1934, and A. Spamer, *Das kleine Andachtsbild vom XIV. bis zum XX. Jahrhundert*, Munich, 1930, pp. 157 ff.

6. The first and largest English emblem book, Geffrey Whitney's *Choice of Emblemes and other Devises*, was published abroad, in 1586 in Leyden. (Reprinted by H. Green, London, 1866.) It is an unoriginal book, a florilegium from the most popular Continental collections, but it represents the best emblematic work of its time. A year earlier appeared the already mentioned tract of Samuel Daniel, a translation of Paolo Giovio's *Dia logo delle Imprese militari e amorose* (Rome, 1555). The translator's preface shows that he was well acquainted with all the subtleties of the art. Then followed Abraham Fraunce with *Insignium, Armorum, Emblematum, Hieroglyphicorum et Symbolorum, quae ab Italis Imprese nominantur, Explicatio* (London, 1588). *The Heroicall Devises* of the French emblematist Claude Paradin appeared in P.S.'s translation in 1591 in London. Andrew Willet's *Sacrorum Emblematum Centuria Una* was a so-called 'naked' emblem book. It was published in Cambridge in the last decade of the sixteenth century, at a time when it was both difficult and expensive to procure in England good engravings. Henry Peacham published his *Minerva Britanna or a Garden of Heroical Devises* in 1612 in London. *The Mirrour of Maiestie* (London, 1618; reprinted by H. Green for the Holbein Society of Manchester with a part of *Minerva Britanna*, 1870) is ascribed to Sir Henry Goodyer, an intimate friend of Donne. The lines of emblem 28:

> Th' ascending Path that up to wisedome leades
> Is rough, uneven, steepe: and he that treades
> Therein, must many a tedious *Danger* meet,
> . . . . till he come at last
> Up to *Her* gate, . . .

are obviously a paraphrase of Donne's:

> . . . On a huge hill,
> Cragged, and steep, Truth stands, and hee that will
> Reach her, about must, and about must goe;

(Satyre III, ll. 79-81, Grierson, vol. I, p. 157. 'Grierson' refers throughout to H. C. J. Grierson's edition of *The Poems of John Donne*, 2 vols., Oxford, 1912.)

Further, there were printed Thomas Peyton's *The Glasse of Time in the First Age* (1620) and *In the Second Age* (1623), both in London. (Both reprinted in New York, 1886.) William Wyrley's *The True Use of Armorie* (London, 1592) is a semi-heraldic work and Francis Thynne's *Emblemes and Epigrames*, another 'naked' book, probably written in 1600, was not then printed. (Published by E.E.T.S., 1876.) Francis Quarles's *Emblemes*, the emblem book best known to-day, did not appear till four years after Donne's death.

7. See Thompson, *op. cit.*, p. 32.

8. *The Principles of Poetry*, London, 1943, p. 21.

9. The modern editor of Alciati, Henry Green, an enthusiastic Victorian bibliographer, used this deceptive method in his book *Shakespeare and the Emblem Writers* (London, 1870). He registered every instance where Shakespeare and some emblematist used a somewhat similar image or even the same word. Green's book, apart from having long been the only, though none too accurate, reference book for the student of emblematic literature, is therefore practically worthless as a critical study.

10. See Praz, *op. cit.*, pp. 193-207.

11. *Cf.* A. Warren, *Richard Crashaw. A Study in Baroque Sensibility*, Louisiana State University, 1939, pp. 71 ff.

12. T. O. Beachcroft in 'Quarles—and the Emblem Habit' (*Dublin Review*, January 1931, pp. 91-3) ascribes an emblematic meaning to various poems of Donne. His knowledge of emblematic literature is, however, negligible.

13. 'A Valediction: of weeping', l. 7, Grierson, vol. I, p. 38; 'Elegie XVIII.', l. 79, Grierson, vol. I, p. 119; 'To the Countesse of Bedford. On New-yeares day', l. 2, Grierson, vol. I, p. 198; 'Elegie upon . . . Prince Henry', l. 38, Grierson, vol. I, p. 268; 'The Annuntiation and Passion', l. 4, Grierson, vol. I, p. 334: 'A Hymne to Christ', l. 2, Grierson, vol. I, p. 352; *ibid.*, l. 4, Grierson, vol. I, p. 352.

14. *Il Canzoniere* I, cclvi, ll. 7-8, ed. M. Scherillo, Milan, 1908, p. 310.

15. 'The Legacie', ll. 17-18, Grierson, vol. I, p. 20.

16. 'The broken heart', ll. 29-31, Grierson, vol. I, p. 49.

17. See Praz, *op. cit.*, pp. 138-42.

18. B. van Haeften, *Schola Cordis*, Antwerp, 1635.

19. A. Wiericx, *Cor Iesu amanti sacrum*, plates reproduced in E. Luzvic and E. Binet, *Le Cœur devot*, &c., edition Douai, 1627. *Cf.* R. Sharrock, 'Bunyan and the English Emblem Writers', *R.E.S.*, XXI, April 1945, pp. 109-10.

20. D. Cramer, *Emblematia sacra*, Frankfort, 1624. *Cf.* also J. Mannich, *Sacra Emblemata LXXVI*, Nuremberg, 1625; F. Pona, *Cardiomorphoseos*, Verona, 1645, &c.

21. 'The Blossome', ll. 9-12, Grierson, vol. I, p. 59.

22. O. Vænius (van Veen), *Amorum Emblemata*, Antwerp, 1608. An English version (published also in 1608) was dedicated to William, Earl of Pembroke (Lord Herbert) and Philip, Earl of Montgomery.

23. For instance, F. Picinelli in the introduction ('Dell' Etimologia, ed Antichità dell' Imprese') to his enormous emblematic dictionary (*Mondo Simbolico formato d'Imprese*, Milan, 1669; first edition, Milan, 1653), a compendium of quotations from poetry and sermons of several generations of the 16th and 17th centuries, offering 'an infinite number of conceits for the use of orators, preachers, academicians, poets', cites the opinion of some writers that the Pentateuch should be read as 'abbozzatura d'Imprese'. 'Il rovo di Moise', he says, 'co'l soprascritto; ARDET, NEC COMBVRITVR, parole dell'Essodo, cap. 3.2. non è egli un impresa rappresentativa del popolo Israelitico . . .?'

24. 'Death', ll. 45-7, Grierson, vol. I, p. 286.

25. L. 14, Grierson, vol. I, p. 322.

26. 'Holy Sonnets', XIV, ll. 1-2, Grierson, vol. I, p. 328.

27. 'The Crosse', ll. 51-2, Grierson, vol. I, p. 333.

28. 'The Litanie', I, ll. 5-6, Grierson, vol. I, p. 338.

29. *Ed. cit.*, XXI, X, p. 763.

30. S. Bargagli, *Delle Imprese*, Siena, 1578. (Reprinted with parts II, III, Venice, 1594.)

31. 'The first Anniversary', ll. 129-30, Grierson, vol. I, p. 235.

32. 'A Funerall Elegie', ll. 38-40, Grierson, vol. I, p. 246.

33. *Devotions upon Emergent Occasions*, London 1624, Expostulation I, p. 14.

34. 'Obsequies to the Lord Harrington &c.', ll. 149-54, Grierson, vol. I, p. 276.

35. *Ed. cit.*, XXI, ix, p. 763.

36. *Essayes in Divinity*, London, 1651, p. 38.

37. *LXXX Sermons*, London, 1640, lxvii, p. 677.

38. *Op. cit.*, embl. 20, p. 39.

39. *Dialogo dell' Imprese*, edition Lyons, 1574, p. 90. *Cf.* Whitney, *op. cit.*, p. 43. William Drummond of Hawthornden describes in a letter to Ben Jonson (1 July, 1619) 'the *Impressaes* and Emblemes on a Bed of State' of 'the late Queen *Mary*' which were

embroidered by her own hand; 'the first is the Loadstone turning towards the pole, the word her Majesties name turned on an Anagram, *Maria Stuart, sa virtu, m'attire,* which is not much inferior to Veritas armate [*sic*]'. (*The History of Scotland,* 1681, pp. 395-6.)

40. H. Hawkins[?], or H. Aston [?], *Partheneia Sacra,* Rouen, 1633, pp. 114-25.

41. Ll. 8-10, Grierson, vol. I, p. 334.

42. See Grierson, vol. II, p. 238.

43. *Cf.* Chapman's *Tragedy of Byron,* v, iii, 13-14, *The Plays and Poems of George Chapman,* ed. T. M. Parrott, London, 1910, vol. I, p. 259.

44. *Ed. cit.,* IX, viii, p. 417.

45. See Praz, *op. cit.,* p. 63.

46. 'La Corona, Ascention', ll. 1-2, Grierson, vol. I, p. 321.

47. 'The Litanie', XIII, l. 117, Grierson, vol. I, p. 343.

48. 'A Hymne to God the Father', ll. 15-16, Grierson, vol. I, p. 369.

49. Ll. 15-16, Grierson, vol. I, p. 370.

50. 'Goodfriday, 1613', ll. 11-14, Grierson, vol. I, p. 336.

51. *Biathanatos,* London, n.d., p. 154.

52. *Ed. cit.,* I, V, p. 12.

53. *Ibid.,* p. 13.

54. See Grierson, vol. II, pp. 248-9.

55. *Cf.* L. Volkmann, *Bilderschriften der Renaissance,* Leipzig, 1923, pp. 26-8, 82-95 respectively.

56. Quoted from Grierson, vol. II, p. 92.

57. *Symbola Heroica M. Claudii Paradini et D. Gabrielis Simeonis,* edition Antwerp, 1583, p. 92. Paradin's *Devises heroiques* (Lyons, 1551) and Simeoni's *Imprese eroiche e morali* (Lyons, 1559) were first published together in 1562 in Antwerp.

58. 'An Epithalamion . . . on the Lady Elizabeth', ll. 23-6, Grierson, vol. I, p. 128.

59. *Ibid.,* ll. 101-2, p. 130.

60. The verse declares:

> '*The* Sonne's *and* Mothers *paines in one are mixt,*
> *His side, a Launce, her soule a Sword transfixt.*
> *Two harts in one, one Phenix love contrives:*
> *One wound in two, and two in one revives'.* (*Op cit.,* p. 266.)

61. M. Scève, *Delie obiect de plus haulte vertu,* Lyons, 1544, device 16. *Cf.* also Daniel, *op. cit.,* 'To the Friendly Reader'.

62. *Fifty Sermons,* London, 1649, xxxi, p. 275.

63. Ll. 19-20, Grierson, vol. I, p. 251.

64. *Op. cit.,* XXIII, iii, p. 805.

65. *Ibid.,* XXIII, vii, pp. 810, 811.

66. 'A Funerall Elegie', ll. 27-9, Grierson, vol. I, p. 246.

67. 'Obsequies', ll. 1-4, Grierson, vol. I, p. 271.

68. 'The Litanie', VIII, ll. 65-7, Grierson, vol. I, p. 340.

69. 'Upon the translation of the Psalmes', ll. 14-16, Grierson, vol. I, p. 348. *Cf. XXVI Sermons,* London, 1661, xxiv, p. 343.

70. 'To Sr Henry Wooton', ll. 22-4, Grierson, vol. I, p. 188.

71. *Hecatomgraphie,* Paris, 1540, quoted from Green, *op. cit.,* p. 321. *Cf.* also G. de la Perrière, *Le Theatre des bons engins,* Paris, 1539, embl. 27.

72. 'Elegie VIII', l. I, Grierson, vol. I, p. 90.

73. Ll. 19-27, Grierson, vol. I, p. 15.

74. H. Iunius, *Emblemata*, Antwerp, 1565, embl. 49. *Cf.* also Theocritus à Ganda (D. Heinsius), *Quæris quid sit Amor, Amsterdam*, n.d., embl. 8.

75. For instance, Paradin-Simeoni, *ed. cit.*, p. 283.

76. For instance, Vænius, *op. cit.*, embl. 52.

77. *Op. cit.*, embl. 39. This very common emblem is also mentioned by Drummond: 'A Bird in a *Cage,* and a *Hawk* flying above, with the word, *il mal me preme & me spaventa Peggio*'. (*Ed. cit.*, p. 396.)

78. Ll. 61-2, Grierson, vol. I, p. 297.

79. See Grierson, vol. II, p. 219.

80. *Op. cit.*, ll. 381-5, Grierson, vol. I, p. 310.

81. P. Valeriano, *Hieroglyphica*, Basle, 1556, Bk. 2.

82. *Op. cit.*, p. 150. *Cf.* J. Sambucus, *Emblemata*, Antwerp, 1564, p. 184.

83. *Op. cit.*, p. 195.

84. *Op. cit.*, ll. 394-6, 399, Grierson, vol. I, p. 311.

85. 'Meditation 12', p. 285. *Cf.* also *Paradoxes, &c.*, London, 1652, p. 56; *Fifty Sermons*, xl, p. 372.

86. Ll. 25-36, Grierson, vol. I, pp. 50-1.

87. Grierson, vol. II, p. 41.

88. Louise of Savoy, mother of Francis I, is portrayed in a miniature (Bibliothèque Nationale, Paris, MS. franç., 12247) with a large compass in her left hand. See Volkmann, *op. cit.*, pp. 61-2, fig. 56.

89. *Op. cit.*, LXXI, vii, p. 754.

90. *Rime*, Venice, 1598, Madrigali, xcvi, p. 106.

91. The date of Donne's travels remains a matter of conjecture. Walton, usually not too reliable, says Donne had travelled for 'some years', first in Italy and later in Spain, after the Island Expedition, that is to say, after October 1597. (See *ed. cit.*, 'The Life of Dr. John Donne', p. 16.) If this is true he would have arrived in Italy just in time for the publication of Guarini's *Rime*. The modern view, however, places the date of Donne's Continental tour between the years 1592 and 1596 (see E. Gosse, *Life and Letters of John Donne*, 1899, vol. I, pp. 55-6) or, more accurately, from November or December 1594 to June 1596, before the expeditions to Cadiz and the Azores. (See J. Sparrow, 'The Date of Donne's Travels' in *A Garland for John Donne*, Harvard, 1931.)

It is quite possible that Guarini's madrigal was widely circulated in Italian literary circles and that Donne frequented such society. Guarini, born in 1538, was already reaching the summit of his fame in the last decade of the cinquecento. His lyrical play *Il Pastor Fido* was published in 1589, but it had been finished in 1583. It was translated into English in 1602. (Dymock [?], *Pastor Fido: or The faithfull Shepheard*, London.) Guarini, a courtier of the house of Este, defender of the tragicomedy against the Aristotelians, was the parent of Italian Baroque poetry and the teacher of G. B. Marini. He wrote in a sophisticated style courtly, witty and sweet verse, but without Marini's capriciousness and occasional mawkishness. (*Cf.* V. Rosso, *B. Guarini ed Il Pastor Fido*, Turin, 1886.)

Donne's 'Valediction', like its companion song 'Sweetest love I do not go', had probably been addressed to his wife; it was not written until Donne's journey to France in 1612, the year of Guarini's death. (See Grierson, vol. II, p. 40.) Therefore Donne might have made acquaintance with Guarini's verse through Sir Henry Wotton, who was ambassador to Venice from 1604, and probably kept him informed of foreign literary novelties. Whatever the truth may be, there is little reason to doubt that Donne was familiar with the work of one of the most fashionable writers of his day, 'that wise knight, . . . whom learned Italy accounts one of her ornaments'. (Walton, *ed. cit.*, 'Life of Sir Henry Wotton', p. 11.)

92. 'Obsequies to the Lord Harrington', ll. 105-10, Grierson, vol. I, p. 274.

93. *Devotions*, Expostulation, 20, pp. 525-6.

94. *Fifty Sermons*, i, p. 3.

95. *Emblemata Sacra de Fide, Spe, Charitate*, Antwerp, 1636, embl. 38, p. 128. *Cf.* also C-F. Menestrier, *La Science et l'Art des Devises*, Paris, 1686, Devises sacrées, device 62, p. 257; 'Un compas couché sur un cercle achevé. PES EIVS STETIT IN DIRECTO. *Ps.* 25'.

96. *LXXX Sermons*, ii, p. 13.

97. The emblem delineated Christ nailed to an anchor taking the place of the cross. It was described by Walton. (See Grierson, vol. II, p. 261.)

MURRAY, "Donne and Paracelsus: An Essay in Interpretation"

1. Philip Aureolus Theophrastus Bombast von Hohenheim, called Paracelsus (*c.* 1493-1541), was the 'Luther of Medicine'. He introduced some new metallic drugs and ceremonially burned the works of Galen at Basle. His chief claim to greatness lies in his attempt to combine alchemy and medicine. He prescribed for Erasmus. All references to the works are to the folio edition *Paracelsi Opera Omnia* (Geneva, 1658), a reprint of the first general edition in Latin, that of Palthenius (Frankfurt, 1603). For further details see Stoddart, *Life of Paracelsus* (London, 1911), and Sudhoff, *Bibliography of Paracelsus* (Berlin, 1894).

2. Simpson, *A Study of the Prose Works of John Donne* (Oxford, 1924), p. 187 *n.*

3. Paracelsus, *Opera Omnia*, i. 99.

4. Ibid. 367.

5. Paracelsus, *Opera Omnia*, i. 91.

6. For Paracelsus's mining experience, see Stoddart, *Life of Paracelsus* (London, 1911), p. 43.

7. Grierson, *The Poems of John Donne* (Oxford, 1912), i. 182.

8. John Hester, *A Brief Answer of J. Quercetanus* (London, 1570), consists of alchemical recipes and apologetics. J. Du Chesne, latinized as Quercetanus (Quersitanus), was a Paracelsian. See Ferguson, *Bibliotecha Chemica* (Glasgow, 1906), ii. 236.

9. *All's Well that Ends Well*, II. iii:

> *Lafeu.* To be relinquished of the artists,—
> *Parolles.* So I say; both of Galen and Paracelsus.

10. It is worthy of notice in this connexion that the mediator between Donne and Ann More's father, after the secret marriage, was Henry Percy, ninth Earl of Northumberland, one of whose chief interests was alchemy and another medicine. [Gosse, *The Life and Letters of John Donne* (London, 1899), i. 99 f.]

11. See Tymme (Timme), *The Practise of Chymicall and Hermeticall Physike* (London, 1605), sect. iii, p. 168, and *O.E.D.*, *sub* 'mummy'.

12. Paracelsus, *Opera Omnia*, i. 52, 130 f.

13. Paracelsus, *Opera Omnia*, iii, sect. ii, p. 7.

14. Ibid. i. 368.

15. 'Angelica Ratio' is an expression occurring frequently in Paracelsus, e.g. 'The angelic and animal mind of man grow with him each according to its own nature and properties' (ibid. ii. 521).

16. There are two references in *Biathanatos* which show actual acquaintance with Paracelsus's works. See Donne, *Facsimile Text of Biathanatos* (New York, 1930),

pp. 172, 215.

17. Grierson, *Poems*, ii., p. xxii.

18. Paracelsus, *Opera Omnia*, ii. 91.

19. Ibid. 91-2.

20. For a summary of Paracelsus's ideas and their historical place, see Conger, *Macrocosms and Microcosms* (New York, 1922), pp. 55-60. The principal references in the works are at i. 99; ii. 532, which give the main ideas; i. 287, 405, and *passim*.

21. Paracelsus, *Opera Omnia*, ii. 562; cf. 'Nocturnall', ll. 35, 36.

22. Ibid. i. 127. For other ideas on this subject see above, in discussion of 'Love's Alchymie'.

23. Ibid. 654.

24. Ibid. 367 f. Paracelsus uses this symbolism very frequently for medical rather than alchemical purposes.

25. *O.E.D.*, *sub* 'Nocturnal', gives the following: 'All the Fryeres . . . say the Offices for the dead, and cause a Nocturnal to be rehearsed.' (Source dated 1670.)

26. Gruner, *Translation of the Canon of Avicenna* (London, 1930), p. 45.

27. *O.E.D.*, *sub* 'squib', 'small quantities of liquor'.

28. For light as a fluid compare *Paradise Lost*, vii. 362.

29. Compare Donne, *Fifty Sermons*, p. 214. I am indebted for this reference to Mrs. E. M. Simpson, who kindly read and criticized this article.

30. ἐπιτάφιος means literally 'on' or 'at a tomb'.

31. Both 'love's limbecke' (l. 21) and 'his flasks' (l. 3) conceal, possibly, sexual as well as alchemical images.

32. That Donne's love for Ann was not free from passionate disagreements is a possible inference from, for example, the poem 'Twicknam Garden', dated by Grierson 1608, which seems, although addressed to Lucy, Countess of Bedford, to have as its subject incidents of such a kind. To suppose so would at least offer a more straightforward interpretation than that of Grierson and explain the intensity of tone which he detects alike in the 'Nocturnall' and 'Twicknam Garden' (see Grierson, vol. i, p. xxii).

33. Paracelsus, *Opera Omnia*, ii. 276.

34. See Grierson, *Poems*, ii., p. xxii, where Gosse is quoted.

35. Note ecclesiastical use of 'prepare'. Donne, as is well known, had his likeness taken in his winding sheet. Perhaps a similar fancy underlies this phrase.

36. The phrase is from Walton's Life, but sounds like Donne himself. Perhaps he used such words to Walton, who thus describes him at Ann's death: 'for now his very soul was elemented of nothing but sadness'. Walton, *Lives* (London, 1674), p. 42.

37. 'For in the point the circle also exists not less than in the whole circle. For [no matter] how much greater the circle than the point, yet the two are integral. Thus, then, it comes about that *the fixed foot* of the compass gives the circle, the other the spatious periphery. So equally and in like manner is man in respect of the magnitude of the heavens' (Paracelsus, *Opera Omnia*, i. 201). Cf. 'A Valediction: Forbidding Mourning'.

ORNSTEIN, "Donne, Montaigne, and Natural Law"

1. *JEGP*, XXII (Oct. 1923), 471-502.

2. See, for example, R. C. Bald, "'Thou Nature art my goddess': Edmund and Renaissance Free-Thought," *Joseph Quincy Adams Memorial Studies*, ed. J. G. Mc-Manaway, et al. (Wash., D. C., 1948), pp. 337-50.

3. Bredvold, p. 498.

4. *Ibid.*, pp. 494-99.

5. It is generally assumed that *Biathanatos* was written several years after the ap-

pearance of Florio's translation of Montaigne (1603).

6. Bredvold, pp. 480 ff.

7. See Henry Cornelius Agrippa, *Of the Vanitie and Uncertaintie of Artes and Sciences*, trans. J. Sanford (London, 1575) pp. 160$^{r\&v}$. Agrippa's attack on natural law is, like the whole of his treatise, more obscurantist than skeptical in any philosophical sense. Because of the Fall, Agrippa asserts, the law of man's nature is corrupt and sanctions both Machiavellian expediency and "Epicurean" indulgence.

8. Diogenes Laertes, "Zeno," *Lives and Opinions of Eminent Philosophers*, trans. C. D. Yonge (London, 1853), pp. 290-92.

9. *The Republic*, trans. C. W. Keyes (London, 1928), p. 211.

10. I borrow the term from William L. Davidson, *The Stoic Creed* (Edinburgh, 1907), pp. 153 ff.

11. Individualistic rationalism is much more apparent in the thought of the Roman Stoics than in the thought of Zeno. But it is characteristic of classical Stoicism (see R. D. Hicks, *Stoic and Epicurean* [New York, 1910], p. 92).

12. See Seneca's description of the complete man in "On the Happy Life" (iii-viii), *Moral Essays*, trans. J. W. Basore (London, 1932), II, 107-21.

13. A. P. d'Entrèves, *Natural Law; An Introduction to Legal Philosophy* (London, 1951), p. 29.

14. *Ibid.*, pp. 24-26.

15. *Ibid.*, pp. 34-35.

16. See the discussion of justice in *De Legibus*, trans. C. W. Keyes (London, 1928), pp. 345-55.

17. Citations from the *Summa Theologica* are to the *Basic Writings of St. Thomas Aquinas*, ed. A. C. Pegis (New York, 1945), vol. II.

18. By making natural law contingent upon the Eternal Law of a supernatural God, the medieval theologian "perfected" the metaphysics of the Stoics. As Davidson points out (p. 103), "the physics and the ethics of the Stoics (more especially, the ethics of the Roman period) are not metaphysically of a piece: speculative materialism [a pantheistic worldview] rules the one, intense scorn of moral materialism dominates the other."

19. *Summa Contra Gentiles*, trans. Dominican Fathers (London, 1924), I, 4.

20. See Vernon J. Bourke's discussion of Thomistic ethics (*St. Thomas and the Greek Moralists* [Milwaukee, 1947], p. 40).

21. By "moral philosopher" I do not mean those Renaissance thinkers (like Pomponazzi or Bruno) who made important and relatively original contributions to the ethical thought of the age. I refer to those popular didacticists like Guillaume Du Vair and Pierre Charron, whose humanistic moral philosophy, drawn eclectically from classical sources, represents fairly well the commonplace moral attitudes of their period. It is difficult, of course, to generalize about the "commonplace" in so diverse an age as the Renaissance. And Charron, we must remember, expresses in somewhat attenuated form the skepticism of Montaigne. But his treatment of worldly virtue ("humane" probity) is, I think, characteristic of the Renaissance humanists' approach to practical moral problems (see Charron's Preface to *Of Wisdome*, trans. Samson Lennard [London, 1608]).

22. See Pietro Pomponatius, *Tractatus De Immortalitate Animae*, trans. W. H. Hay (Haverford, Pa., 1938), pp. 50 ff.

23. *The Boke Named the Governour* (Everyman edition), p. 47.

24. Léontine Zanta, *La Renaissance du Stoïcisme au XVIe Siècle* (Paris, 1914), p. 87.

25. Cf. Hardin Craig's discussion of Renaissance moral speculation in *The Enchanted Glass* (New York, 1950), p. 199.

26. *Biathanatos*, Facsimile Text Society edition (New York, 1930), p. 36. All citations from *Biathanatos* are to this edition.

27. Michel de Montaigne, *Essays*, trans. J. Florio (Everyman edition), II.xii.297. I use Florio's translation (unless otherwise noted) because it is the version of Montaigne which was best known to Donne's contemporaries. It is very probable, however, that Donne read Montaigne in the original.

28. Francisco Suárez, *De Legibus* in *Selections from Three Works*, II, "The Classics of International Law" (Oxford, 1944), p. 41, n. 20.

29. *Ibid.*, p. 42.

30. Richard Hooker, *Of the Laws of Ecclesiastical Polity, Works* (Oxford, 1875), I, 178.

31. *Ibid.*, I, 207.

32. Bredvold, p. 479.

33. Though Charron was bitterly attacked as a free thinker, Montaigne was almost universally acclaimed by contemporaries and succeeding generations as a moral instructor. In fact, there is practically no indication that any of Montaigne's early readers, who were, we assume, alert to any deviation from accepted moral principles, recognized his supposedly libertine philosophy. Those seventeenth-century readers who criticized Montaigne attacked his religious ideas and his skeptical attitudes, not his moral thought (see Alan M. Boase, *The Fortunes of Montaigne: A History of the Essays in France, 1580-1669* [London, 1935], pp. 1-47, 164-94). For an excellent corrective criticism of the libertine interpretation of Montaigne, see Arthur Tilley, *Studies in the French Renaissance* (Cambridge, 1922), pp. 246-58.

34. Because the passage in Florio is difficult to follow, I use the Charles Cotton translation in this instance (London, 1930), III.xii.313.

35. In *The Counter-Renaissance* (New York, 1950), Hiram Haydn reaches the astounding conclusion that Montaigne considered reason unnatural in man (p. 480). Yet one of the central ideas in the *Essays* is that the possession of reason makes man's nature essentially different from the rest of unrational nature. Indeed, how could a faculty which all men share to some extent be unnatural? In stressing Montaigne's freedom from contemporary dogmas, Mr. Haydn attributes to him one of the most absurdly dogmatic generalizations that could be made about man.

36. For a remarkable modern parallel to Montaigne's view of human reason, see Erich Fromm, *Man for Himself* (New York, 1947), p. 40.

37. In his excellent study, "The Libertine Donne" (*PQ*, XIII [July 1934], 276-91), George Williamson suggests that *Biathanatos* is a crucial intermediate point in Donne's movement away from youthful naturalism towards mature religious belief. I am not certain, however, that (as Prof. Williamson claims) the skepticism about natural law in *Biathanatos* stems from a naturalistic distrust of reason that eventually led to fideism. It is quite true that Donne's insistence on the need for "primary" ratiocination in moral judgments is based, paradoxically, on his recognition of the fallibility of human reason. But actually it is dogmatic unreason rather than reason which Donne argues against. It does not seem to me, moreover, that Donne's later fideism was necessarily a denial of, or development beyond, the *practical* ethical theory of *Biathanatos*.

MARTZ, "Donne and the Meditative Tradition"

1. T. S. Eliot, "The Metaphysical Poets," *Selected Essays* (New York: Harcourt,

Brace, 1932), p. 247; originally published as a leading article in the *Times Literary Supplement*. (The present paper represents a revision of a talk delivered at the meetings of the Modern Language Association, December, 1958.)

2. Joseph E. Duncan, "The Revival of Metaphysical Poetry, 1872-1912," *PMLA*, 68 (1953), pp. 658-71. Arthur Symons, "John Donne," *Fortnightly Review*, n.s. 66 (1899), p. 741.

3. T. S. Eliot, "Milton II," *On Poetry and Poets* (London: Faber, 1957), p. 152.

4. Frank Kermode, *Romantic Image* (London: Routledge, 1957), Chap. 8. Leonard Unger, "Fusion and Experience," *The Man in the Name* (Minneapolis: University of Minnesota Press, 1956), p. 123. Clay Hunt, *Donne's Poetry* (New Haven: Yale University Press, 1954), p. 148.

5. W. B. Yeats, *A Vision* (New York: Macmillan, 1938), p. 12.

6. I. A. Richards, *Principles of Literary Criticism* (New York: Harcourt, Brace, 1948), Chap. 32.

7. T. S. Eliot, "John Donne", *The Nation and the Athenaeum*, 33 (1923), pp. 331-2.

8. Eliot, *Selected Essays*, p. 247. George Williamson, *The Donne Tradition* (Cambridge: Harvard University Press, 1930), p. 48. John Crowe Ransom, *The World's Body* (New York: Scribner's, 1938), pp. 133-42.

9. Paul Claudel, *A Poet before the Cross*, trans. Wallace Fowlie (Chicago: Regnery, 1958), pp. 92-3, 150-1.

GUSS, "Donne's Petrarchism"

1. "Donne's Relation to the Poetry of His Time," *A Garland for John Donne*, ed. Theodore Spencer (Cambridge, Mass., 1931), pp. 51-56.

2. For several lyrics based on the comparison between poet and torch (and even between poet and votive candle), see Joseph Vianey, *Le Pétrarquisme en France au XVIᵉ siècle* (Montpellier, 1909), pp. 48, 55, n. 1. The lady-goddess conceit is, of course, common. Sometimes the theology according to which it is developed is classical or Neoplatonic rather than Christian: for example, in Son. XVIII, "O d'amor fredda, e di virtute ardente," Guarino compares his lady and himself to a goddess and the temple in which she is worshipped; and in Mad. 2, "Vien dal' onde, ò dal cielo," he wittily disputes whether his lady is the celestial or the terrestial Venus.

Unless otherwise noted, I use the following texts: for Jacopo da Lentini and Guido Guinizelli, *La poesia lirica del '200*, ed. Carlo Salinari (Turin, 1951); for Francesco Petrarca, *Le rime*, ed. G. Carducci and S. Ferrari (Florence, 1957); for the mid-fifteenth-century Neapolitans, *Rimatori napoletani del quattrocento*, ed. Mario Mandalari (Caserta, 1885); for Chariteo, *Lirici cortigiani del '400*, ed. Alessandro Tortoreto (Milan, 1942); for Serafino l'Aquilano's strambotti and epistles, *Opere* (Venice, 1502); for Serafino's sonnets, *Le rime*, ed. Mario Menghini (Bologna, 1894), I; for Guarino, *Rime* (Venice, 1598); for Thomas Watson, *Poems*, ed. Edward Arber (Westminster, 1895); for Philippe Desportes, *Oeuvres*, ed. Alfred Michiels (Paris, 1858); and for John Donne, *Poems*, ed. Sir Herbert J. C. Grierson (London, 1912). The translations are my own; though they are in prose, they are divided into lines to correspond roughly to their originals.

3. See Evelyn M. Simpson, "Donne's Spanish Authors," *MLR*, XLIII (1948), 185. On the compass image, see D. C. Allen, "Donne's Compass Figure," *MLN*, LXXI (1956), 256-57. On "The Extasie," see, for example, Merritt Y. Hughes, "The Lineage of the 'Extasie,'" *MLR*, XXVII (1932), 1-5, and Helen Gardner, "The Argument about 'The Extasy,'" *Elizabethan and Jacobean Studies Presented to F. P. Wilson* (Oxford,

1959), pp. 279-306. (I call the love tracts "Petrarchan" because when they treat love as a relation between two human beings they are primarily commentaries on the Petrarchan clichés.)

4. Jacopo, Son. VI, "Io m' aggio posto in core a Dio servire." Guido—in Can. III, "Al cor gentil repara sempre Amore," st. 6—says that, when God reproaches him for having adored his lady, he will cite in his defense her angelic appearance. (Since a personal God here condemns human love, despite traditional criticism this stanza cannot be a defense of Neoplatonic love.)

5. *Rimatori*, p. 48, "Se tu me aucidi et averamie morto," and pp. 12-15, "Per certo se troppo dura." On the punishment of reluctant ladies, see William Allan Neilson, "The Purgatory of Cruel Beauties; A Note on the Sources of the 8th Novel of the 5th Day of the *Decameron*," *Romania*, XXIX (1900), 85-93.

6. Luigi Tonelli, *L'amore nella poesia e nel pensiero o del rinascimento* (Florence, 1933), pp. 61-62. For imitations of the sonnet, see Tortoreto's comment, and also Vianey, p. 198.

7. Donne's suspicion that his lady may prove unchaste is far from unconventional. Sexual jealousy, a standard Provençal theme, is common in Neapolitan court poetry (see *Rimatori*, pp. 38-39, 147) and in late Renaissance Petrarchism—among Tasso's clichés about love are the statements that hate follows love, and that jealousy is a sign of ardent love (*Conclusioni amorose* 12 and 46).

8. See Josef Lederer, "John Donne and the Emblematic Practice," *RES*, XXII (1946), 194-95, and D. Philippi Picinelli, *Mundus Symbolicus* (Cologne, 1694).

9. See Mario Praz, "Petrarca e gli emblematisti," *Ricerche anglo-italiane* (Rome, 1944), pp. 303-19. Lederer (p. 185) attributes the similarities between Donne and the Petrarchans to the Alexandrian derivation of both emblem and Petrarchan conceit. But he does not show either that Donne draws upon the emblem rather than upon Petrarchan lyrics, or that the emblem uses Greek rather than Italian sources.

10. Rosemary Freeman, *English Emblem Books* (London, 1948), pp. 148-49, *et passim*.

11. Besides the interpretations provided by Picinelli, see Edgar H. Duncan, "Donne's Alchemical Figures," *ELH*, IX (1942), 270-71.

12. See, for example, Pet. 19, "Sono animali al mondo di sí altera," with the note, and Serafino, Son. I, "L'acquila che col sguardo affisa el sole" (cf. Watson, *Hec.* 78, "What scowling cloudes").

The emblem which Lederer notes is really a variation of a Provençal and Petrarchan conceit, the idea that the poet is the prey of the falcon love; see Francesco Flamini, *La lirica toscana del rinascimento* (Pisa, 1891), pp. 438-40, and Watson, *Hec.* 67, "When *Cupid* is content to keepe the skies." A much closer parallel is Serafino's *Epistola V*, ll. 38-39: "My constant love would certainly have paired / The eagle and the dove as friends." Donne may well have found a symbolic significance in this pun of l'Aquilano ("The Eagle-ite"). But the image is not unique—in "Ma petite columbelle," Ronsard says that he holds his lady as an eagle clasps a trembling dove.

13. Grierson, II, 15-16, and Williamson, "Textual Difficulties in the Interpretation of Donne's Poetry," *MP*, XXXVIII (1940-41), 45-46. Though Grierson's emendation—which his 1929 edition retains—is supported by good MSS, Williamson (pp. 37-72) and Grierson (II, cxiv-cxxi) agree that the 1633 text is to be followed wherever the sense permits it. Sir E. K. Chambers, reviewing Grierson's edition (*MLR*, IX [1914], 270), attacks Grierson's argument but agrees that 1633 is in fact the best text.

14. *Libro di natura d'amore* (Venice, 1536), fols. 131[v]-32[r]. Interestingly, on fol. 184[v] Equicola observes that Provençal poets often say that when their friends tell

them to renounce their fruitless love, they refuse—a situation like that of "The Canonization." And on fol. 44^v Equicola says that the eagle and the dove were an emblem at the marriage of Voluptuousness and Sorrow—a parallel of Donne's line 4 that has not to my knowledge been hitherto noted.

15. These sonnets appear in Fausto Montanari, *Studi sul Canzoniere del Petrarca* (Rome, 1958), pp. 79 and 83.

16. *Commentaire sur le "Banquet" de Platon*, ed. and trans. Raymond Marcel (Paris, 1956), Sp. II, ch. 8, pp. 155-58. Ficino's Platonic casuistry here is especially suggestive of Donne's logic; and his assertion that every lover dies, that he is resurrected only by returned love, and that to refuse his love is therefore to murder him, may explain "O murdresse" in "The Apparition," and perhaps Donne's use of amorous death in general.

17. See Jean Festugière, *La philosophie de l'amour de Marsile Ficin et son influence sur la littérature française au XVIe siècle* (Paris, 1941), pp. 96-98, 110, 116, *et passim*; and Watson, *Hec.* 44, 56, 57, 91, and *Tears* 40.

Though the phoenix image is sometimes used with a sexual meaning, it is primarily the symbol of holy mysteries, such as the union of the Virgin Mary with Jesus (see Henry Green, *Shakespeare and the Emblem Writers* [London, 1870], pp. 383-84). Donne's own use of the phoenix to represent the consummation of a marriage in the epithalamion "Haile Bishop Valentine," reveals his intention of exalting both the married couple and the miracle of marriage, and of considering sexual consummation as merely one element of spiritual union and spiritual rebirth. See also the exaltation implied by the phoenix symbol in a similar epithalamiom. "Ecco luce amorosa," *Biblioteca di letterature popolare italiana*, ed. Severino Ferrari (Florence, 1882), I, 184-85.

18. Ficino, Sp. V, ch. 9, p. 194, says that love results in the end of lawsuits, theft, homicide, and war. In st. 2, Donne ironically reassures his adviser, comforting him with the thought that the love of a mere two people will not so upset the profitable course of worldly affairs.

19. Quoted by Tonelli, p. 287. For the interpretation of Donne's stanza, it is interesting to note that Guarino (*Il Pastor Fido e Il compenio della poesia tragicomica*, ed. G. Bragnoligo [Bari, 1914], pp. 224-25) says that lovers' bodies cannot achieve the true, hermaphroditic union of which their souls are capable.

STEIN, "Meter and Meaning in Donne's Verse"

1. A stress-shift, reversing the normal flow of the rhythm, can be strong enough in its impulse to attract succeeding rhythmic waves into the new current.

2. All references are to Grierson's two-volume edition: to volume, page and line respectively.

3. "By," coming as it does just before "my," will be stressed a little more than might be expected in such a colloquial passage. In a passage where the basic pattern is strongly felt, a very light syllable may be reinforced by what is known as subjective stress; but not if two stress-compelling syllables follow immediately.

4. It is interesting to compare, for emphasis, a syllable that coincides with a stressed place in the pattern, and a syllable in which stress-shift occurs:

"Here Statesmen, (or of *them they* which can read,)"
A Valediction: of the booke, I, 31, 46.

The result helps explain why Donne never hesitates to use stress-shift when other metrical resources will not achieve the degree of emphasis he desires.

MOLONEY, "Donne's Metrical Practice"

1. *Discourse concerning the Original and Progress of Satire* (1693), in W. P. Ker, *Essays of John Dryden* (Oxford, 1926), II, 19; Gosse, *Life and Letters of John Donne* (New York, 1899), II, 334; Saintsbury, *A History of Prosody* (London, 1908), II, 159 and 161; Melton, *The Rhetoric of John Donne's Verse* (Baltimore, 1906), p. 148; Praz, *Secentismo e Marinismo in Inghilterra* (Firenze, 1925), pp. 97-98 (cited by Pierre Legouis, *Donne the Craftsman* [Paris, 1928], p. 45); Grierson, *Metaphysical Lyrics & Poems of the Seventeenth Century: Donne to Butler* (Oxford, 1921), p. xxv; Stein, "Donne's Prosody," *PMLA,* LIX (1944), 373-397; "Donne and the Couplet," *PMLA,* LVII (1942), 676-696.

2. "Donne's Prosody," pp. 389, 392-393.

3. G. Gregory Smith, *Elizabethan Critical Essays* (Oxford, 1904), II, 352; I, 119-120, 53-54.

4. Robert Bridges, *Milton's Prosody* (Oxford, 1921), pp. 15 ff.

5. The rules for elision which I believe Donne followed, with perhaps certain liberties, are essentially those set forth by Bridges, pp. 19-37. Donne's principal variation is a rather consistent tendency to elide unstressed internal *i,* e.g., the *i* in *medicine* (*Love's Growth,* l. 7); in *medicinall* (*Love's Alchymie,* l. 10); the initial *i* in *examining* (*Satyre IV,* l. 28).

6. "Donne's Prosody," p. 390.

7. Cf. Bridges, pp. 34-36.

8. *Ibid.,* p. 36.

9. Initial truncation and feminine endings as such are not here considered metrical irregularities in the *Songs and Sonets.* The effect of initial truncation in stanzaic patterns where it is recurrent is quite different from that of its occasional use in rimed couplets. In the latter it thwarts the expected rhythmic pattern, in the former it is a part of the pattern. Lines whose metrical difficulties I am unable to resolve occur in these poems: *The Indifferent; Song* ("Sweetest love, I do not goe"); *Aire and Angels; Loves exchange; Confined love; Witchcraft by a picture; The Primrose; Farewell to love; Sonnet. The Token; Self Love.*

10. In *Satyre IV* alone I find very nearly as many lines irreconcilable with the decasyllabic pattern as I find resisting the established metrical norms in all the *Songs and Sonets.*

11. Cf. John Crowe Ransom, *The New Criticism* (New Directions, 1941), pp. 268-325.

12. "The Metaphysical Poets," *Selected Essays: 1917-1932* (New York, 1932), p. 250.

13. The resemblance between lines 1-2 of Sonnet IX of the *Holy Sonnets* and the opening lines of *Paradise Lost* would seem scarcely accidental.

14. Cf. "At a Vacation Exercise," ll. 19-20, 5-6, 23-26; "On Shakespeare," ll. 14-15; "Another on the same," l. 5.

15. Cf. James Craig La Drière, "Prosody," *Dictionary of World Literature,* ed. Joseph T. Shipley (New York, 1943).

16. Smith, *Elizabethan Critical Essays,* I, 50.

SMITH, "An Examination of Some Claims for Ramism"

1. *The Enchanted Glass* (New York, 1936), p. 145.

2. *The New England Mind* (New York, 1939), p. 327.

3. *Elizabethan and Metaphysical Imagery* (Chicago, 1947). ch. xii.

4. There is a brief account in the introduction to Dr. Ethel Seaton's edition of

Fraunce's *The Arcadian Rhetorike* (Luttrell Society Reprints 9), pp. ix-xii.

5. *The Lawiers Logike* (London, 1588), Prefatory Letter. Mr. John Buxton suggests that Sidney's influence led Fraunce to study Ramus (*Sir Philip Sidney and the English Renaissance* (London, 1954), p. 147). But Fraunce unequivocally describes himself as Sidney's instructor, both in logic and in Ramism.

6. Buxton, op. cit., p. 46.

7. Orations *The Rhetor* and *Ciceronianus*, delivered in 1575 and 1576 respectively. See *Ciceronianus*, ed. H. S. Wilson and C. A. Forbes (Lincoln, Nebraska, 1945), pp. i-vii; and H. S. Wilson, 'Gabriel Harvey's Orations on Rhetoric', *ELH.*, xii (1945), 167-82.

8. 'R.F.', *Peter Ramus, his Logick* (London, 1632), A2^r-A3^v.

9. *The Logicians School-Master: or a Comment Upon Ramus Logicke* (London, 1629), p. 241.

10. A. Fraunce, *The Lawiers Logike* (London, 1588), f. 2^v.

11. *The Logike of P. Ramus* (London, 1574), p. 74.

12. A Fraunce, op. cit., f. 2^r.

13. Ibid., f. 3^r.

14. A. Richardson, op. cit., pp. 81-82.

15. A. Richardson, op. cit., p. 137.

16. 'R.F.', op. cit., p. 106.

17. Ibid., p. 107.

18. *The Lawiers Logike*, ed. cit., f. 40^r.

19. Ibid., f. 44^v.

20. 'M.R.M. Scotum', op. cit., p. 54.

21. A. Richardson, op. cit., p. 241.

22. Ibid., f. 120^r.

23. Fraunce, op. cit., f. 63^v.

24. Id., *The Arcadian Rhetorike* (London, 1588), B8^r.

25. Id., *The Lawiers Logike*, f. 72^r.

26. A. Richardson, op. cit., pp. 81-82.

27. Ff. 12^r, 15^v, 35^r, 42^v, 47^r, 93^v-93^r, 96^v, 108^r.

28. iii. 325, ed. Macray, p. 11. Fraunce was himself a St. John's man—a black sheep in that anti-Ramist fold.

29. Richardson, op. cit., p. 82.

30. Fraunce, *The Lawiers Logike*, f. 114^v.

31. Richardson, op. cit., p. 29.

32. Dudley Fenner, *The Artes of Logike and Rhetorike* (Middleburgh, 1588), C6^v.

33. *The Lawiers Logike*, ¶ 2.

34. R. Sherry, *The Figures of Grammar and Rhetorike* (London, 1555), f. lvii^r.

35. 'R.F.', op. cit., p. 55.

36. T. Wilson, *The Arte of Rhetorique* (London, 1553), f. 63^v.

SLOAN, "The Rhetoric in the Poetry of John Donne"

1. Or this concern may be regrouped according to a strategy employed by many New Critics: the analysis of a poem in terms of its "structure," which is its paraphrasable argument, and in terms of its "texture," which is the efficaciousness of its emotional appeal.

2. For a discussion of ancient and Renaissance definitions of "rhetoric," see Donald Lemen Clark, *Rhetoric and Poetry in the Renaissance* (New York, 1922), pp. 23-31, 43-55. One of the clearest discussions of the modern meaning of "rhetoric" is

Donald C. Bryant's "Rhetoric: Its Functions and Its Scope," *QJS*, XXXIX (1953), 401-424.

3. Wilbur Samuel Howell states that in the English Renaissance it was "the conviction of Renaissance learning that logic and rhetoric are the two great arts of communication, and that the complete theory of communication is largely identified, not with one, not with the other, but with both" (*Logic and Rhetoric in England, 1500-1700* [Princeton, 1956], p. 4).

4. Ramist disposition was meant to serve the purposes of both the *dispositio* of rhetoric and the *iudicium* of logic; as Abraham Fraunce states, "Disposition is the second part of Logike concerning the disposing of Arguments, thereby to iudge well of them: and therefore this second part is called both Judgement and Disposition" (The *Lawiers Logike* [London, 1588], fol. 86^r). These two procedures may be separated, without following Milton's teaching that judgment is a part of both invention and disposition, by noting that the step after invention involves two endeavors: framing thought (disposition) and testing validity (judgment). Donne uses "invention" and "judgment" to designate the first two parts of the creative process in *To E. of D. with six holy Sonnets.*

5. For a detailed explanation of this concept in the Ramist educational reform, see William Kempe, *The Education of Children* (London, 1588), Part 3; and *Gabriel Harvey's Ciceronianus,* introd. by H. W. Wilson and trans. by C. A. Forbes, "University of Nebraska Studies in the Humanities," No. 4, Lincoln, 1945.

6. See Pierre Albert Duhamel, "The Logic and Rhetoric of Peter Ramus," *MP*, XLVI (1949), 169; Perry Miller, *The New England Mind* (New York, 1939), p. 157; Norman E. Nelson, *Peter Ramus and the Confusion of Logic, Rhetoric, and Poetry* ("University of Michigan Contributions in Modern Philology," No. 2; Ann Arbor, 1947), p. 11; Rosemond Tuve, *Elizabethan and Metaphysical Imagery* (Chicago, 1947), ch. xii.

7. Rosemond Tuve, "Imagery and Logic: Ramus and Metaphysical Poetics," *JHI*, III (1942), 373-374, 376n.

8. Fraunce, fol. 4^v. Though I quote extensively from Fraunce, I have also examined such Ramist textbooks as Dudley Fenner, *The Artes of Logike and Rhethorike,* Middelburg, 1584; and Roland MacIlmaine, *The Logike of the Most Excellent Philosopher P. Ramus Martyr,* London, 1581.

9. *Elizabethan and Metaphysical Imagery,* p. 344.

10. "21. Meditation," *Devotions upon Emergent Occasions,* London, 1624; reprint ed. John Sparrow (Cambridge, Eng., 1923), p. 128.

11. See Fraunce, fol. 8^v.

12. Quoted by Charles Monroe Coffin, *John Donne and the New Philosophy* (New York, 1937), p. 119.

13. Walter J. Ong, S. J., *Ramus, Method, and the Decay of Dialogue* (Cambridge, Mass., 1958), p. 91.

14. Another approach to these same theories is merely to consider those aspects which serve memory. Hickey's discussion of Donne's belief in the power of constructing sermons which could be lodged in the memory stops short of discussing the means whereby memory was served; Robert L. Hickey, "Donne's Art of Memory," *Tennessee Studies in Literature,* III (1958), 29-36. To the Ramists, that discourse served memory best which was patterned after the operation of natural reason; of course, they also believed that the way to achieve this patterning was through the Ramist system.

15. "Method," Fraunce states, "descendeth alwayes from the generall to the specials,

euen to the most singular thing, which cannot bee diuided into any more parts" (fol. 113^v). And the best division is that whose parts "be most repugnant, which can bee but two, therefore *Dichotomia* is most excellent, a diuision consisting onely of two partes" (fol. 57^r). When these statements are juxtaposed, one has the doctrine of "method" in its simplest terms.

16. It was the question of the disposition of material in the two *Anniversaries* which caused Louis L. Martz to make his significant study of English religious literature of the seventeenth century (*The Poetry of Meditation*, New Haven, 1954). Martz shows that there existed at the time of Donne an abundant stream of meditative literature which Donne assimilated and which lent form to Donne's poetry. Martz's comparisons between meditative procedure and Donne's *Anniversaries* and *Holy Sonnets* are most convincing. However, the "methods of meditation," he states, "are in themselves adaptations of ancient principles of logic and rhetoric" (p. 38). A view through rhetoric is no less justifiable, rhetoric being another vital aspect of that ancient and continuing philosophic tradition which gave the Renaissance mind its habits of thought.

17. Fraunce, foll. 113^r and 116^v.

18. Fraunce gives an excellent example of the use of diagram in the analysis of Vergil's second eclogue on foll. 120^v-124^r. Though it is perhaps most Ramistic to cast all of the analysis of a poem in a diagram form, the purposes of this discussion are served by using the diagram to indicate only the basic structures. For a similar use of the diagram in analysis, see Thomas O. Sloan, "A Rhetorical Analysis of Donne's 'The Prohibition,'" in *QJS*, XLVIII (1962), 38-45.

19. Abraham Fraunce, *The Arcadian Rhetorike*, London, 1588; reprint ed. Ethel Seaton (Oxford, 1950), p. 15.

20. Of course, the compass image has vital connections with the rest of the poem: it is directly related to the dual being of virtuous men (body and soul), the simile which begins the argument; it has a visual relationship with "gold" (see W. A. Murray, "Donne's Gold-Leaf and his Compasses," *MLN*, LXXII [1958], 329-330), which is logically related to the "refin'd" elements of their love, which contrasts with the "Dull sublunary lovers love," and so on.

21. John Hoskins, *Directions for Speech and Style* [ca. 1599], ed. Hoyt H. Hudson (Princeton, 1935), p. 29: "Sometimes [hyperbole] expresseth a thing in the highest degree of possibility, beyond the truth, that it descending thence may find the truth; sometimes in flat impossibility, that rather you may conceive the unspeakableness than the untruth of the relation."

22. See *Elizabethan and Metaphysical Imagery*, esp. pp. 351-352. For arguments against her position, see Norman E. Nelson, *op. cit.*; A. J. Smith, "An Examination of Some Claims Made for Ramism," *RES*, new ser., VII (1956), 348-359; and George Watson, "Ramus, Miss Tuve, and the New Petromachia," *MP*, LV (1958), 259-262.

23. Certainly the only reference Donne makes to Ramus is hardly intended as praise; see *Catalogus Librorum Aulicorum*, ed. Evelyn Mary Simpson (London, 1930), pp. 27-28.

24. According to the Ramists, poetry differed from the rest of rhetoric merely on the basis of rhythm; see Ong. pp. 281-283.

25. "Donne and the Rhetorical Tradition," *KR*, XI (1949), 571-587.

COLIE, "The Rhetoric of Transcendence"

1. See particularly Frances A. Yates, *Sir John Florio* (Cambridge, 1933). I am indebted to conversations with John B. Jarzavek for a realization of the range and depth

of Montaigne's influence upon English literature in the seventeenth century.

2. The present paper is one of a series on paradoxes and paradoxology of the late Renaissance, of which several have already appeared: "Thomas Traherne and the Infinite," *Huntington Library Quarterly*, XXI (1957), 69-82; "Time and Eternity: Paradox and Structure in *Paradise Lost*," *Journal of the Warburg and Courtauld Institutes*, XXIII (1960), 127-38; "Some Paradoxes in the Language of Things," *Reason and Imagination: Studies in the History of Ideas 1600-1800*, ed. J. A. Mazzeo (Columbia University Press, 1962), pp. 93-128; and "Logos in the Temple: the Shape of Content in the Verse of George Herbert," *Journal of the Warburg and Courtauld Institutes*, XXVI (1963), 326-42.

All the papers owe a debt to several studies of paradox, in particular: Theodore C. Burgess, *Epideictic Literature* (University of Chicago Press, 1902); A. S. Pease, "'Things without Honour'," *Classical Philology*, XX (1926), 27-42; Warner G. Rice, "The *Paradossi* of Ortensio Lando," *Michigan University Publications in Language and Literature*, VII (1932), 59-74; Henry Knight Miller, "The Paradoxical Encomium, with Special Reference to its Vogue in England, 1600-1800," *Studies in Philology*, LIII (1956), 191-203; Howard Schultz, *Milton and Forbidden Knowledge* (New York, 1955), pp. 32-40; they owe a general debt to: Jurgis Baltrušaitis, *Anamorphoses, ou perspectives Courieuses* (Paris, 1955); Gustav René Hocke, *Die Welt als Labyrinth* (Hamburg, 1961); and above all, E. H. Gombrich, *Art and Illustion* (New York, 1960).

There is a serious methodological problem in dealing with paradoxes—types of paradox, though for a short time separable into specific categories, behave paradoxically and tend to overrun whatever barriers of definition are set up to contain them. In this paper, for example, I discuss three kinds of paradox: 1) paradoxes fundamental to metaphysical or epistemological speculation; 2) paradoxes (or contradictions) produced by the collision of different systems of thought; 3) the deeper paradox that, even in opposition, conflicting ideas or philosophies often coincide at the center (because of paradox 1). But since paradoxes have a magnetic attraction for one another, they do not remain independent or in categorical groups.

3. For renaissance readers the most readily available Stoical paradoxes, edited by Erasmus, were the *Paradoxa Stoicorum* of Cicero, a semi-satirical commentary on the moral standards of his day. Cicero had come a long way from the dialectical metaphysics of the Eleatics; like most subsequent Stoics, his emphasis was moral rather than metaphysical.

4. For a study of the conflicts of truth in the late Renaissance see Herschel Baker, *The Wars of Truth* (Harvard University Press, 1952).

5. For the literary background of renaissance Stoicism, see Robert Hoopes, *Right Reason in the English Renaissance* (Harvard University Press, 1962); for Skepticism, see Richard Popkin, *A History of Skepticism from Erasmus to Descartes* (Assen, Holland, 1960). Victor Harris' *All Coherence Gone* (University of Chicago Press, 1949), provides a fine account of naturalistic pessimism in the seventeenth century.

6. It includes the flower of Roman and Protestant orthodoxy: Erasmus, Calvin, Lipsius, the Scaligers, Agrippa, Du Plessis Mornay, La Primaudaye, Montaigne, Sidney, Greville, Spenser, Donne, and Milton, to name only some of the legitimate children of the titled line. Cadet branches are more difficult to number and bastards impossible.

7. Henry Cornelius Agrippa, *Three Books of Occult Philosophy*, trans. J. F. (London, 1651), "Life."

8. Agrippa's *Occult Philosophy* (*De occulta philosophia libri tres*, Cologne, 1533) contains his retractation of his earlier *Vanity of Arts and Sciences* (*De incertitudine*

et vanitate scientiarum et artium [Cologne, 1530]). See also his *Apologia adversus calumnias propter declamationem de vanitate scientiarum* ([Cologne,] 1533).

9. Philippe du Plessis Mornay, *De la verité de la Religion Chrestienne*, (Antwerp, 1581); I cite from the English translation by Sir Philip Sidney and Arthur Golding, *A Woorke concerning the Trewnesse of the Christian Religion* (London, 1587); and *The True Knowledge of a Mans Owne Selfe*, trans. A[nthony] M[unday] (London, 1602).

10. Pierre de la Primaudaye, *Academie Françoise* (Paris, 1577); trans. Thomas Bowes [?] (London, 1618).

11. Guillaume du Vair, *De la constance et consolation ès calamitez publiques* (Rouen, 1604), trans. as *A Buckler against Adversitie; or a Treatise of Constancie*, by Andrew Court (London, 1622); Du Vair, *The Moral Philosophie of the Stoicks*, trans. Thomas James (London, 1598).

12. Du Vair, *Moral Philosophie*, p. 188.

13. *Ibid.*, pp. 106-07.

14. Du Plessis Mornay, *Trewnesse*, "Epistle Dedicatorie."

15. See, *inter alia*, Du Plessis Mornay, *True Knowledge*, "The Epistle Dedicatorie," and *Trewnesse*, "Epistle Dedicatorie."

16. Du Plessis Mornay, *Trewnesse*, "Epistle to the Reader."

17. See Schultz, *Milton and Forbidden Knowledge*, for a discussion of the ethics of knowledge going far beyond the limits suggested in the book's title.

18. Michel de Montaigne, *An Apologie of Raymond Sebond*, *Essayes*, trans. John Florio (New York, n.d.), pp. 385-547.

19. Another paper in this series will deal with the "vanities of learning" of the Renaissance, chiefly Erasmus' *Encomium*, Montaigne's *Apologie*, and Agrippa's *Vanity of Learning*.

20. Pierre Charron, *De la sagesse* (Bordeaux, 1601); trans. as *Of Wisdom*, by Samson Lennard (London, [1608]), pp. 336, 467-68.

21. Such as Professor Bredvold hypothesizes for both Donne and Dryden: Louis I. Bredvold, "The Religious Thought of Donne in Relation to Medieval and Later Traditions," *University of Michigan Publications in Language and Literature*, I (1925), 193-232; *The Intellectual Milieu of John Dryden*, (University of Michigan Publications in Language and Literature, XII, 1934).

22. (London, 1599).

23. Fulke Greville, *A Treatie of Humane Learning*, in *Poems and Dramas*, ed. Geoffrey Bullough (London, 1945), I, 154-91.

24. John Davies of Hereford, *The Complete Works*, ed. Alexander B. Grosart, 2 vols. (London, 1878).

25. See Louis I. Bredvold, "The Sources Used by Davies in *Nosce Teipsum*," *PMLA*, XXXVIII (1923), 745-69.

26. *Nosce Teipsum* (London, 1599), p. 1. All further references to Sir John Davies are to this edition.

27. Another paper in this series will deal with seventeenth-century uses of the negative theology.

28. Davies of Hereford, *Mirum in Modum*, *Works*, I, 9.

29. *Ibid.*, I, 12.

30. Greville, *Poems and Dramas*, I, 154. All further references to Greville are to this edition.

31. *The Poems of John Donne*, ed. Herbert J. C. Grierson (Oxford; Clarendon Press, 1912), I, 229-66.

32. Louis L. Martz, *The Poetry of Meditation* (Yale University Press, 1954), pp. 211-48.

33. Joseph A. Mazzeo, "Notes on John Donne's Alchemical Imagery," *Isis*, XLVIII (1957), 103-23.

34. Marjorie Hope Nicolson, *The Breaking of the Circle* (Columbia University Press, 1960), pp. 81-122.

35. Nicolson, p. 96; Marius Bewley, "Religious Cynicism in Donne's Poetry," *Kenyon Review*, XIV (1952), 419-46.

36. Louis I. Bredvold, "The Naturalism of Donne in Relation to Some Renaissance Traditions," *JEGP*, XXII (1923), 471-502; see also his "The Religious Thought of Donne" previously cited.

37. Robert M. Ornstein, "Donne, Montaigne and Natural Law," *JEGP*, LV (1956), 213-29.

38. I owe the suggestion for this reading to Professor Maurice Valency of Columbia University. See *John Donne: The Anniversaries*, ed. Frank Manley (Johns Hopkins University Press, 1963), introduction, pp. 37-40.

39. Bredvold, "The Religious Thought of Donne," and Ornstein, "Donne, Montaigne, and the Natural Law."

40. *The Trewnesse of the Christian Religion*, "Epistle Dedicatorie."

41. The phrase is stolen from Hiram Haydn's *The Counter-Renaissance* (New York, 1950).

42. I am at work upon a study of the paradoxes of self-cancellation, of suicide, and of nothing.

43. The phrase is borrowed from Ralph Venning, *Orthodox Paradoxes* (London, 1650), a handbook of sacred paradoxology that went into several editions in the mid-seventeenth century.

44. George Puttenham, *The Arte of English Poesie* (London, 1589), p. 189.

45. *Nosce Teipsum*, p. 100.

46. *Ibid.*, p. 13.

47. Greville, I, 182.

48. See Colie, "Logos in the Temple," cited in note 2 above.

49. Nicolson, pp. 92-102.

McCANLES, "Paradox in Donne"

1. Quoted in Evelyn M. Simpson, *A Study of the Prose Works of John Donne* (2d ed., Oxford, 1948), p. 316.

2. 'The Technique and Function of the Renaissance Paradox', *SP* LIII (1956), 191-203. Donne's conception of the paradox was not unique; cf. the preface to a French translation of the *Paradossi* of Ortensio Lando made by Charles Estienne, *Paradoxes, ce sont propos contre le commun opinion: dabatus, en forme de declamations forēses* (Paris, 1553): 'A ceste cause ie t'ay offert en ce liuret le debat d'aucuns propos, que les anciens ont uoulu nommer paradoxes: c'est adire, contraires a l'opinion de la pluspart des hommes: affin que par le discours d'iceux, la uerité opposite t'en soit a l'aduenir plus clere & apparente: & aussi pour t'exerciter au debat des choses qui te contraignent a chercher diligemment & laborieusement raisons, preuues, authoritez, histoires & memoires fort diuerses & cachees' (quoted in Warner G. Rice, 'The *Paradossi* of Ortensio Lando', *Essays and Studies in English and Comparative Literature* (Ann Arbor, 1932), *Univ. of Michigan Publications, Language and Literature* VIII), pp. 59-74).

3. 'Paradox operates with especial vigour at the limits of discursive knowledge.

What ever else the riddling *Parmenides* is, it is a demonstration of the problems at the limit of knowledge and of the linguistic and rhetorical problems arising from the attempt to overcome those limitations. . . . Even the simplest form of paradox, the defence of a belief generally unpopular, is not really very simple, since it involves an unspoken assumption of the wars of truth, an acceptance of pluralism in the truth of sublunary situations and at the same time a conviction that truth is only one and all competing "truths" are at best but appearances.' (R. L. Colie, 'Some Paradoxes in the Language of Things', *Reason and the Imagination: Studies in the History of Ideas 1600-1800*, ed. J. A. Mazzeo, New York, 1962, pp. 109-110.)

4. *Summa Theologica*, I, 84, I (*Basic Writings of Saint Thomas Aquinas*, ed. Anton C. Pegis, New York, 1945).

5. '. . . the Platonic argument requires an exact correlation of knowledge and the objective world of Ideas. Consequently, there must be a single corresponding Idea wherever we understand a common nature, a *ratio communis*, an *unum-in-multis*, a universal, a distinct quiddity, or where we use a common predicate, predicating an *unum de multis*.' (R. J. Henle, *Saint Thomas and Platonism*, The Hague, 1956, p. 354.)

6. *S. T.*, I, 85, I, ad I; I, 85, 2, ad 2.

7. From Parmenides' *Way of Truth*, in F. M. Cornford, *Plato and Parmenides* (Indianapolis, n.d.), p. 31.

8. F. M. Conford, *Plato's Theory of Knowledge* (London, 1960), pp. 266-267. But Conford admits elsewhere (regarding *Sophist*, 249D-251A) that the Stranger 'has changed the subject from a metaphysical consideration of the nature of the real to a different field, which we should call Logic' (p. 252).

9. *The Age of Belief*, ed. Anne Fremantle (New York, 1955), p. 20. Cf. also Cornford, *Plato's Theory of Knowledge*, pp. 268-272, where it is shown how the Platonic dialectic leads to the doctrine of the plurality of forms, by which any material subsistent is 'composed' of the various Forms in which it participates.

10. In his introduction to his translation of Proclus' *Elements of Theology* (Oxford, 1933) E. R. Dodds comments (p. xxv): 'I will only say that its fundamental weakness seems to me to lie in the assumption that the structure of the cosmos exactly reproduces the structure of Greek logic [speaking of Proclus' system]. All rationalist systems are to some extent exposed to criticism on these lines; but in Proclus ontology becomes so manifestly the projected shadow of logic as to present what is almost a *reductio ad absurdum* of rationalism. In form a metaphysic of Being, the *Elements* embodies what is in substance a doctrine of categories: the cause is but a reflection of the "because", and the Aristotelian apparatus of genus, species and differentia is transformed into an objectively conceived hierarchy of entities or forces.'

11. *Ibid.*, p. 21.

12. *Ibid.*, p. 35.

13. *Ibid.*, p. 59.

14. Henle, p. 346.

15. Walter J. Ong, *Ramus, Method and the Decay of Dialogue* (Cambridge, Mass., 1958), pp. 55-65.

16. Joseph P. Mullally, *The* Summulae logicales *of Peter of Spain* (Notre Dame, Ind., 1945, *Pubs. in Medieval Stud.* VIII).

17. *Ibid.*, p. xl. One immediate source of Peter's terminist 'realism' is the *Metalogicon* of John of Salisbury, wherein he speaks of 'this reciprocity between things and words, and words and things, whereby they mutually communicate their qualities, as by an exchange of gifts' (*The Metalogicon of John of Salisbury*, tr. Daniel D. McGarry, Berkeley and Los Angeles, 1955, I, c. 16, p. 50).

18. Mullally, p. 3.

19. 'Ockham himself was the very reverse of a Platonist; in point of fact, he was the perfect Anti-Plato; yet, like all opposites, Plato and Ockham belonged to the same species' (Etienne Gilson, *The Unity of Philosophical Experience*, New York, 1937, p. 68).

20. William of Ockham, *Summa totius logicae*, I, c. XV (*Philosophical Writings*, ed. Philotheus Boehner, Edinburgh, 1957, pp. 35-37).

21. Ong, p. 102.

22. *Ibid.*, p. 104. Agricola lists twenty-four topics: definition, genus, species, property, whole, parts, conjugates, adjacents, act, subjects, efficient agent, end, consequences, intended effects, place, time, connections, contingents, name, pronunciation, compared things, like things, opposites, differences (*ibid.*, p. 122).

23. A typical argument can be found in Thomas Wilson's *Rule of Reason* (1551), a textbook heavily indebted to Agricola. The question is whether or not priests should marry. His technique is to draw the two words 'priest' and 'wife' through various topics in order to find a common term to unite them. As might be expected the argument devolves into a syllogistic chain. Having defined a preacher as one, among other things, who is 'desierouse to lyue vertuously', and a wife, also among other things, as one 'to auoide fornication', Wilson proceeds to set up his syllogism: 'Whosoeuer desireth to liue vertuously, desireth to auoide fornication. Whosoeuer desireth to auoyde fornication, desireth mariage. Ergo whosoeuer desireth to lyue vertuously desiereth mariage.' This argument is summarized with quotations in W. S. Howell, *Logic and Rhetoric in England, 1500-1700* (Princeton, 1956), pp. 25-27.

24. Ong, p. 21.

25. *Ibid.*, p. 197.

26. This passage is actually by Omer Talon, Ramus' *alter ego*, though Ong (p. 209) finds it 'the sum and substance of the Ramist position on universals'.

27. *Ibid.*, pp. 182-186.

28. '[Ramus] does not include in his logic any theory of the concept, without which it is impossible to have meaningful statements. By virtue of this omission Ramus's logic is indeed nominalistic, and lends itself to the rhetorical manipulation of words. However, as we read through the *Dialectica* we observe that it is soon tacitly proceeding on the basis of a corrupted Platonism. For in sweeping aside the categories as a means of analyzing experience and differentiating between types of predication, Ramus did not escape the necessity of ordering experience for the purpose of discourse. In place of the categories he offered his famous dichotomies, which are nothing but Porphyry's tree in rank and riotous growth.' (Norman E. Nelson, 'Peter Ramus and the Confusion of Logic, Rhetoric, and Poetry', Ann Arbor, 1957, *Univ. of Michigan Contributions in Modern Philology* no. 2, p. 7.) This study also throws light on Ramus' taking every statement arrived at by dichotomizing as reflecting the actual fact (p. 9): 'There seemed to Aristotle to be a significant difference between the statements: Man is a rational animal; Socrates is a philosopher; Socrates is at the seashore. Now Ramus by rejecting or ignoring these distinctions collapsed the terms—all words are logically equal in his vocabulary. There is no distinction in his logic between propositions which define essence and those which predicate property, or accidents of time, place, or condition.'

29. *Epistemology*, tr. Imelda Choquette Byrne (New York, 1959), p. 29.

30. One notable example of an answer to the problem of concept-object relation which avoids univocalist conceptualism is the epistemology of Aquinas. In brief his solution is this. The problem of the mental knowledge of material things, as Aquinas

saw it, was the problem of how an immaterial substance (the mind) can have knowledge of a material substance. He sets up the problem by opposing materialists such as Heraclitus to their polar opposite, Plato. For Heraclitus all reality is material and subject to eternal flux; as such the mind may know this shifting reality by being itself also material. Plato, on the other hand, hypostatizes the structure of mind and insists that the 'real' is disembodied 'Forms'. In both cases we find the demand for correspondence between mind and thing. Aquinas' position is midway between these two, and is founded upon the Aristotelian notion of man as a composite of body and soul, yielding this solution: 'So, too, the intellect, according to its own mode, receives under conditions of immateriality and immobility the species of material and movable bodies; for the received is in the receiver according to the mode of the receiver. We must conclude, therefore, that the soul knows bodies through the intellect by a knowledge which is immaterial, universal, and necessary' (S.T., I, 84, I). In other words, the concepts in the mind and the intelligible forms of material things bear, not a univocal, but an analogical relation to each other: the first reflects the second (thereby yielding truth), but according to its own modes.

31. John Donne and William Blake, *The Complete Poetry and Selected Prose of John Donne & The Complete Poetry of William Blake* (New York, 1941), pp. 277-278.

32. *The Poems of John Donne*, ed. Herbert J. C. Grierson (Oxford, 1912), I, 36, ll. 8-14.

33. *Ibid.*, I, 40-41.

34. *Ibid.*, I, 32-33, l. 3.

35. Extensive material on this problem is given in I. M. Bochenski, *A History of Formal Logic*, tr. Ivo Thomas (Notre Dame, Ind., 1961), pp. 238-247.

36. The theory of supposition was developed by late scholastic logicians to handle the various sign functions of concepts and words in propositions and in relation to extramental things. Some such theory was necessary once the equivocation between the structures of things and concepts was admitted. Thus it was necessary to distinguish among signs which stood for (*supponere*) real material entities (personal supposition), those which stood for mental concepts (simple supposition), and those which stood for terms (material supposition); this in order to avoid, for example, the realist interpretation of such propositions as 'Man is a species'. Cf. Ockham, *Summa totius logicae*, cc. lxii-lxiv, lxviii (Boehner, *Philosophical Writings*, pp. 64-74; Bochenski, pp. 163-176).

37. Bochenski, p. 245.

38. Grierson, I, 69-70. Cf. also 'A nocturnall upon S. Lucies day', to which the liar *insolubilium* is also relevant.

39. Hermann Hesse, *Magister Ludi*, tr. Mervyn Savill.

GARDNER, "The Argument about 'The Ecstasy'"

1. *Coleridge's Miscellaneous Criticism*, ed. T. M. Raysor, 1936, p. 138.

2. *ABC of Reading*, 1934, p. 126.

3. *Poems of John Donne*, 1912, vol. ii, pp. xlvi-xlvii.

4. *Donne the Craftsman*, Paris 1928, pp. 68-69.

5. Merrit Y. Hughes, 'The Lineage of "The Exstasie"', *M.L.R.* xxvii. Jan. 1932, and 'Kidnapping Donne', *Essays in Criticism*, Berkeley 1934, pp. 83-89; G. R. Potter, 'Donne's *Extasie*, Contra Legouis', *PQ*, XV, 1936.

6. In *Seventeenth-Century Studies presented to Sir Herbert Grierson*, 1938, pp. 64-104; see particularly pp. 76 and 96-97.

7. *English Literature in the Sixteenth Century*, 1954, p. 549.

8. *John Donne* (Writers and their Work, no. 86), 1957, p. 12.

9. *Secentismo e Marinismo in Inghilterra*, Florence 1925, pp. 28 and 27.

10. In his 'Platonic' poems Donne constantly, as here, makes distinctions between himself and his mistress, who are 'saints of love', worthy of canonization and capable of performing miracles; those who are capable of understanding these mysteries, Doctors, as it were, of Amorous Theology; and the 'laity', who either need simple instruction, or to whom it would be 'prophanation of our joyes' to speak.

11. It is one thing for a narrative poet to describe two lovers in passionate embrace oblivious of a bystander, as Spenser does at the original ending of Book III of the *Faerie Queene*; it is quite another for lovers themselves to call for an audience at their coupling.

12. 'The Ecstasy' always occurs with a title, and the same title in manuscript. We are, therefore, justified in assuming, as we cannot with most of Donne's poems, that the title is the author's.

13. In declaring that the poem does not conclude with a proposal to 'prove, while we may, the sweets of love', I have been anticipated by one critic, Donaphan Louthan, in *The Poetry of John Donne, an Explication*, New York 1951. I regret that I cannot agree with the details of his analysis.

14. *Life and Letters of John Donne*, 1899, i. 75-76.

15. The right interpretation was put forward by E. Glyn Lewis, the only critic who has discussed the poem at length; see *M.L.R.*, vol. xxix, Oct. 1934.

16. Translated, under the title *The Philosophy of Love*, by F. Friedeberg-Seeley and Jean H. Barnes, 1937. Page references are to this translation. Quotations in Italian are from the edition by S. Caramella, Bari 1929. The translators, in attempting to render the Italian into modern English, are often nearer to Donne's words than a literal translation would be. For a discussion of Leone Ebreo as a philosopher see Heinz Pflaum, *Die Idee von Liebe. Leone Ebreo,* Tübingen 1926.

17. P. 198: "La mente mia, ritirata a contemplar, come suole, quella formata in te bellezza, e in lei per immagine impressa e sempre desiderata, m'ha fatto lassare i sensi esteriori' (p. 172).

18. P. 229, *Filone.* 'Si che se lamentar ti vuoi, lamentati pur di te, che a te stessa hai serrate le porte.' *Sofia.* 'Pur mi lamento che possi e vagli in te, piú che mia persona, l'immagine di quella.' *Filone.* 'Può piú, perché giá la rappresentazione di dentro a l'animo precede a quella di fuore' (p. 197).

19. P. 199, *Sofia.* 'Come può la cogitazione astraere piú l'uomo de'sensi che 'l sonno, che getta per terra come corpo senza vita?' *Filone.* 'Il sonno piú presto causa vita, che la toglia: qual no fa l'estasi amorosa' (p. 173).

20. Pp. 200-3. See particularly p. 201: 'Ma quando la mente se raccoglie dentro se medesima per contemplare con somma efficacia e unione una cosa amata, fugge da le parti esteriori, e abbandonando i sensi e movimenti, si ritira con la maggior parte de le sue virtú e spiriti in quella meditazione, senza lassare nel corpo altra virtú che quella senza la quale non potrebbe sustentarsi la vita. . . ; questo solamente resta, con qualche poco de la virtú notritiva, perché la maggior parte di quella ne le profonda cogitazione è impedita, e perciò poco cibo longo tempo i contemplatori sostiene. E cosi come nel sonno, facendosi forte con virtú notritiva, arrobba, priva e occupa la retta cogitazione de la mente, perturbando la fantasia per l'ascensione de' vapori al cerebro del cibo che si cuoce, quali cansano le varie e inordinate sonniazioni, cosi l'intima ed efficace cogitazione arrobba e occupa il sonno, nutrimento e digestione del cibo' (p. 174).

21. P. 205: 'Cosi pungitivo potrebbe essere il desiderio e tanto intima la contemplazione, che del tutto discarcasse e retirasse l'anima dal corpo, resolvendosi i spiriti

per la forte e ristretta loro unione in modo che, afferandosi l'anima affettuosamente
col desiderato e contemplato oggetto, potria prestamente lassare il corpo esanimato
del tutto' (pp. 177-8).

22. Pp. 230-1; pp. 198-9 in Italian.

23. In spite of her name, she needs a great deal of instruction; but I suppose that we
can take it that she is instructing her lover in Socratic fashion.

24. It is uncertain whether the fourth dialogue, which contemporaries inquired for
in vain, was ever written. The last record of Leone Ebreo is in 1520, so that, since he
was born about 1460, he had probably been dead for some time when his book was
published in 1535.

25. Parallels for most of these can be found separately in other Neo-Platonic writers.
It is the collocation of these ideas in Leone Ebreo which is striking.

26. P. 12: 'affetto volontario di fruire con unione la cosa stimata buona' (p. 13).

27. P. 55: 'La propria diffinizione del perfetto amore de l'uomo e de la donna è la
conversione de l'amante ne l'amato, con desiderio che si converti l'amato ne l'amante.
E quando tal amore è eguale in ciascuna de le parti, si diffinisce conversione de l'uno
amante ne l'altro' (p. 50).

28. P. 31: 'E la causa di tale unione e colligazione è la reciproca virtù o sapienzia di
tutti due gli amici. La quale, per la sua spiritualità e alienazione da materia e astrazione
de le condizione corporee, remuove la diversità de le persone a l'individuazione corporale; e genera ne gli amici una propria essenzia mentale, conservata con sapere e con
amore e volontà comune a tutti due, cosi privata di diversità e discrepanzia come se
veramente il suggetto de l'amore fusse una sola anima ed essenzia, conservata in due
persone e non multiplicata in quelle. E in ultima dico questo, che l'amicizia onesta fa
d'una persona due, e di due una' (p. 30).

29. P. 260: *Filone*. 'Li due che mutuamente s'amano non son veri due.' *Sofia*. 'Ma
quanti?' *Filone*. 'O solamente uno, o ver quattro.' *Sofia*. 'Che li due siano uno intende,
perché l'amore unisce tutti due gli amanti e gli fa uno; ma quattro a che modo?' *Filone*.
'Trasformandosi ognuno di loro nell'altro, ciascuno di loro si fa due, cioè amato e amante
insieme: e due volte due fa quattro; si che ciascuno di loro è due, e tutti due sono uno
e quattro. *Sofia*. 'Mi piace l'unione e multiplicazione di li due amanti' (p. 222).

30. P. 215; pp. 175-6 in Italian. Philo explains that the eye sees by the transmission
of rays to the object, but that the representation of the object on the pupil is also
necessary, and that, further, the eye must direct its ray a second time on to the object
to make the form impressed on the pupil tally with the object. This is a highly characteristic attempt to combine two theories (sight by extramission and sight by intra-
mission), or to reconcile Plato and Aristotle on vision. It has suggested to Donne two
conceits: the twisting of the eye-beams and that the lovers were 'looking babies'.

31. P. 56: 'Ma l'altro amore è quello che di esso è generato il desiderio de la persona
amata, e non del desiderio o appetito; anzi, amando prima perfettamente, la forza
de l'amore fa desiderare l'unione spirituale e corporale con la persona amata' (p. 51).

32. P. 57: 'Il perfetto e vero amore, che è quello che io ti porto, è padre del desiderio
e figlio de la ragione; e in me la retta ragione conoscitiva l'ha prodotto. Che, conoscendo
essere in te virtù, ingegno e grazia non manco di mirabile attraizione che di ammirazione,
la volontà mia desiderando la tua persona, che rettamente è giudicata per la ragione in
ogni cosa essere ottima e eccellente e degna di essere amata; questa affezione e amore
ha fatto convertirmi in te, generandomi desiderio che tu in me ti converti, acciò che io
amante possa essere una medesima persona con te amata, e in equale amore facci di
due animi un solo, li quali simigliantemente de' corpi vivificare a ministrare possino.
La sensualità di questo desiderio fa nascere l'appetito d'ogni altra unione corporea, acciò
che li corpi possino conseguire in quella la possibile unione de li penetranti animi' (p. 52).

33. We may compare, if we choose, Ficino's description of how Lysias gazed on Phaedrus and Phaedrus on Lysias (*Commentary on the Symposium*, VII. 4); and indeed Ficino's description of the soul and spirits in ecstatic contemplation is much the same as Leone Ebreo's. But Ficino would hardly allow the lower, corporal sense of touch to play a part. Professor Mario Praz drew attention to a sonnet by Petrarch (Sonnet 63, *in vita*) which may have suggested to Donne the idea of two lovers united by the passionate intensity of their gazing on each other.

34. P. 206: L'anima . . . non è uniforme, anzi per esser mezzo fra il mondo intellettuale e il corporeo . . . bisogna che abbi una natura mista d'intelligenzia spirituale e mutazion corporea, altramente non potrebbe animar i corpi . . . Pur qualche volta si ritira in sé e torna ne la sua intelligenzia, e si collega e unisce con l'intelletto astratto suo antecessore. . .' (p. 178).

35. P. 396: 'E così come l'oro quando ha la lega e mescolanza de li rozzi metalli e parte terrestre, non può essere bello perfetto né puro, ché la bontá sua consiste in essere purificato d'ogni lega e netto d'ogni rozza mescolanza: così l'anima mista de l'amor de le bellezza sensuali non può esser bella né pura, né venire in sua beatitudine se non quando sará purificata e netta de l'incitazioni e bellezze sensuali, e allor viene a possedere la sua propria luce intellettiva senza impedimento alcuno, la quale è la felicitá' (p. 333).

36. P. 204: 'Quando . . . la mente spirituale (che è cuore di nostro cuore e anima di nostra anima) per forza di desiderio si ritira in se stessa a contemplare in uno intimo e desiderato oggetto, raccoglie a sé tutta l'anima, tutta restringendosi in una indivisibile unità' (p. 177).

37. *Natural History*, Century VI, section 513.

38. 'The Mower against Gardens.'

39. *Natural History*, ibid.

40. *Natural History*, Century V, section 478.

41. Translated as *Natural Magick*, printed for Thomas Young and Samuel Speed, 1658; see p. 70.

42. *The Arte of English Poesie*, edited by G. D. Willcock and A. Walker, 1936, pp. 303-4.

43. P. 189: 'Credo che per questa medesima causa l'anime spirituali intellettive degli uomini si collegano a corpo si fragile come l'umano, per conseguire l'ordine divino nella collegazione e unione di tutto l'universo' (p. 164).

44. P. 191: 'Siccome niuma cosa non fa unire l'universo con tutte le sue diverse cose se non l'amore, séguita che esso a more è cause de l'essere del mondo e di tutti le sue cose.' Also: 'Né mai l'intelligenzie . . . s'unirebbero con li corpi celesti . . . se non l'amassero; né l'anime intellettive s'uniriano con li corpi umani per farli razionali, se non ve le constringessi l'amore' (p. 165).

45. *Paramirum*, I. viii. *Der Bücher und Schrifften*, Basle 1589-90, i. 15.

46. Although I cannot claim support from the manuscripts, I am reading 'That' for 'Which'. 'Which' gives no sense, because 'sense' does not 'reach and apprehend' affections and faculties, but 'reaches and apprehends' objects of sense by means of them. I am assuming that 'which' has been substituted for 'that' under the mistaken notion that 'that' was a relative. Copyists tend to treat the two forms 'which' and 'that' as interchangeable. If we read 'That', as I do above, the action of the souls becomes purposeful, so that it parallels the purposeful action of the blood. I had decided that this emendation was necessary before I came upon the passage quoted below which supports it.

47. P. 201: 'La mente è quella che governa i sentimenti e ordina i movimenti voluntari degli uomini: onde per far questo offizio bisogna che esca de l'interior del

corpo a le parti esteriori, a trovare l'instrumenti per fare tali opere e per approssimarsi agli oggetti de' sensi che stanno di fuora, e allor pensando si può vedere, odire e parlare senza impedimento' (p. 174).

48. See pp. 189-90; p. 164 in Italian. The soul is able to mount to Paradise 'con rettitudine del suo governo nel corpo'. If it fails, 'resta ne l'infimo inferno, sbandita in eterno dalla unione divina e dalla sua propria beatitudine'. Donne's prison may be this 'lowest hell' to which the soul which has not fulfilled its function as a 'great Prince' is banished; but I prefer the interpretation suggested in the text, because of his use of the present and not the future tense.

49. In annotating some of the Songs and Sonnets I have found the *Dialoghi d'Amore* as useful as I found the Glossed Bible when I was editing the *Divine Poems*.

50. Since this Essay went to press I have read with great interest Mr. A. J. Smith's discussion of 'The Ecstasy' in 'The Metaphysic of Love', *R.E.S.*, Nov. 1958. Mr. Smith gives an admirable summary of amorous philosophizing in sixteenth-century Italy in order to demonstrate how little Donne's 'metaphysics of love' has the right to be called original. Although he makes more use of Leone Ebreo than of any other writer he does not suggest direct dependence, and his interpretation of the last section of Donne's poem differs greatly from mine. I must own that I think he has forced the sense of Donne's words.

HUGHES, "Some of Donne's 'Ecstasies'"

1. "The Extasie," l. 14.

2. In *Donne the Craftsman* (Paris, 1928), pp. 75-77, and in "L'Etat présent des controversies sur la poésie de Donne," in *Études Anglaises*, V (1952), 99.

3. Leo Spitzer, "Three Poems on Ecstasy" in *A Method of Interpreting Literature* (Smith Coll., 1949), p. 6.

4. A. J. Smith, "Donne in his Time: A Reading of 'The Extasie'," in *Rivista di Letterature Moderne e Comparate*, X (1957), 274. This important article is not included in the 1957 Bibliographies of either *SP* or *PMLA*.

5. "A Reading of 'The Extasie'," p. 265.

6. In "A Note on Donne's 'Extasie'," *RES*, XIX (1943), 67.

7. In "Three Poems on Ecstasy," pp. 12 and 15.

8. *Ignatius his Conclave*, ed. Charles M. Coffin. Pub. No. 53 of the Facsimile Text Society (New York, 1941), p. 2. Cf. Hadrian's *animula vagula blandula*, attributed to him in Aelianus Spartianus' *Augustan History*, p. 25.

9. William Empson, "Donne the Space Man," *Kenyon Review*, XIX (1957), 337-399.

10. As Marjorie Nicolson points out in *Mountain Gloom and Mountain Glory* (Ithaca: Cornell Univ. Press, 1959), p. 330.

11. *The Works of John Milton* (New York: Columbia Univ. Press, 1932), V, 184.

12. "The Second Anniversary," l. 72.

13. Maurice Valency, in his Introduction to the Love Poetry of the Renaissance, *In Praise of Love* (New York: Macmillan, 1958), p. 237, observes that the *stilnovisti* poets might treat a lady as "an organizing principle sent by God himself" into the world, and so might regard her as "the soul of the world," and thus prepare the way for Donne to treat Elizabeth Drury as he did in "An Anatomie of the World."

14. In *The Breaking of the Circle* (Evanston: Northwestern Univ. Press, 1950), p. 84.

15. "The First Anniversary," ll. 68-69.

16. "A Farewell Elegie," ll. 79-82.

17. In his Introduction to *The Poems of John Donne*, 2 vols. (Oxford: Clarendon Press, 1912), II, xxv and xxvii.

18. Ll. 20-21. In *Donne and the Drurys* (Cambridge Univ. Press, 1959), p. 94, Robert C. Bald notes that Donne "knew neither lady," and spoke of their charms as "Things which by faith alone I see."

19. See *The Lives of John Donne, Sir Henry Wotton, Richard Hooker, George Herbert and Robert Sandison*, by Izaac Walton, ed. S. B. Carter (London: Falcon Educational Books, 1951), pp. 22-24. In *Donne and the Drurys* (pp. ix and 97) Bald mentions this story without questioning Walton's account of the incident.

20. Letter to Sir Henry Goodyere, ll. 46-48.

21. In *The Poems of John Donne*, II, 42. The association of this letter with Sir Thomas Lucy is corrected by R. E. Bennett in "Donne's Letters from the Continent," *PQ*, XIX (1949), 75-76.

22. Letter vi in *Letters to Severall Persons of Honour*, by John Donne, ed. Charles E. Merrill, Jr. (New York: Sturgis & Walton, 1910), pp. 10-17.

23. *Ennead VI*, vii, 33 and 34.

24. Paul Oskar Kristeller, *The Philosophy of Marsilio Ficino* (New York, Columbia Univ. Press, 1943), p. 276.

25. In *Marsilii Ficini Opera* (Paris, 1641), II, 235. The quotation from the commentary is not given by Kristeller.

26. In *The Philosophy of Marsilio Ficino*, p. 282.

27. The lines compliment Wotton. Grierson regarded the poem as part of "a literary *débat* among the wits of Essex's circle" about the merits of life at court, in town, and country. In *The Poems of John Donne*, II, 411, he dated it not later than 1598.

28. A beginning was made in my "The Lineage of 'The Extasie'," in *MLR*, XXVII (1932), 1-7, and carried further by A. J. Smith in "The Metaphysic of Love," *RES*, IX, n.s. (1958), 362-375.

29. In a passage in the *Confessions*, IV, iii, which Laurens J. Mills quotes in *One Soul in Bodies Twain* (Bloomington, Ind.: Principia Press, 1937), p. 18.

30. S. Thomae Aquinatis *Summa Theologica* emendata de Rubeis, Billuart et aliorum notis selectis ornata, 6 vols. (Turin, 1937), II, I, xxviii, 1; Vol. II, p. 162.2.

31. In "Of Friendship," *The Essayes of Michael Lord of Montaigne*, trans. John Florio (Everyman ed.), I, 203.

32. *Dialoghi di Amore*, a cura di Santino Caramella (Bari: Laterza, 1929), pp. 30 and 289. Noting in *The Philosophy of Marsilio Ficino*, p. 278, that the "cult of friendship" was widely discussed in the Hellenistic schools of philosophy, Kristeller sees its starting point for Ficino in "this whole body of ideas" as it was expressed in Cicero's *De Amicitia*. On p. 281 Kristeller speaks of Ficino's conception as also being influenced by "the old Tuscan poets."

33. Letter lxxxviii in Merrill's edition of Donne's *Letters to Severall Persons of Honour*, p. 211. In "Donne's Letters from the Continent, 1611-12," p. 69, R. E. Bennett tentatively identifies the lady as Martha Garrard.

34. Letter to Lady Bedford, l. 6. *Poems of John Donne*, I, 227.

35. In "The Storme," l. 1. *Poems*, I, 175. A still more metaphysical example is Donne's verse letter to Mr. R. W. *Poems*, I, 207.

36. See p. 511 and n. 24 above.

37. See nn. 22 above and 40 below.

38. In "Donne's 'Extasie'," *SP*, LV (1958), 474.

39. In *John Donne: his Flight from Medievalism* (Urbana: Univ. of Illinois Press, 1944), p. 181.

40. L. 39. *Poems*, I, 142.

41. In *The Philosophy of Plotinus*, 2nd ed., 2 vols. (London: Longmans, Green,

1923), II, 142 and 144, William Ralph Inge declares that Plotinus' vision of the One, "as a description of a direct psychical experience . . . closely resembles the records of the Christian mystics, and indeed of all mystics, whatever their creed, date, or nationality," and that Plotinus rightly put it "at the apex of the pyramid which ascends . . . from the many and discordant to the One in whom is no variableness."

42. *The Philosophy of Marsilio Ficino*, p. 276.

43. In "The Poetry of Donne: Its Interest and Influence Today," *Essays and Studies of the English Association*, collected by Guy Boas (London: John Murray, 1957), n.s. VII, 97.

44. *The Book of the Courtier*, by Count Baldassare Castiglione. Done into English by Sir Thomas Hoby. Anno 1561. (Everyman ed.), p. 317.

45. In "Donne in his Time," p. 265.

46. By Mary Paton Ramsay in *Les Doctrines Médiévales chez Donne* (London, 1917), p. 242.

47. *The Prayers of John Donne*, Selected . . . by Herbert H. Umbach (New York: Bookman Associates, 1951). The same point is made, with several other illustrations, by Itrat Husain in *The Dogmatic and Mystical Theology of John Donne* (London: Society for the Promotion of Christian Knowledge, 1938), pp. 121-122.

48. Helen Gardner, "John Donne: A Note on Elegy V, 'His Picture'," in *MLR*, XXXIX (1949), 336.

49. In *A Study of the Prose Works of John Donne*, 2nd ed. (Oxford: Clarendon Press, 1948), pp. 91-92.

50. *Dogmatic and Mystical Theology of Donne*, pp. 141 and 143.

51. *The Sermons of John Donne*, ed. George R. Potter and Evelyn M. Simpson (Berkeley: Univ. of California Press. 10 Vols., 1953-1960), VIII, 232.

52. The word is used in the sense in which Jerome Zanchius explained in *De Operibus Dei* (Neustadt, 1591), III, i, 1, that the Greek word ἔκστασις was used in the Septuagint to render the Hebrew word which is translated as "a deep sleep" in the Authorized Version's translation of the account of the creation of Eve in Genesis ii. 21. Zanchius noted that the same word was used in the Septuagint of the visions of the Prophets and Apostles, especially of Paul: "& de se ait Paulus Act. 22 se fuisse in ἔκστασις, & vidisse Christum sibi dicentem: Festina, &c."

53. *Summa Theologica*, II, II, clxxv, 3; Vol. IV, 250-252.

54. *Summa Theologica*, II, I, xxviii, 3; Vol. II, 164-165.

55. *The Dogmatic and Mystical Theology of Donne*, p. 127.

56. In *Mysticism* (2nd ed., London: Methuen, 1911), p. 94. In *The Philosophy of Plotinus*, II, 149, Inge added Meister Eckhart, and quoted St. John of the Cross at length against perversions of belief in mystical experience through the bodily senses.

57. In *De la Demonomania des Sorciers* (Paris, 1580). Cf. Robert Burton's explanation of the "oracles" of the "Indian priests and the witches of Lapland" in the *Anatomy of Melancholy*, I, i, l. 4 (Everyman ed., I, 140), as "ecstasy."

58. *The Essayes of Michael Lord of Montaigne*, I, 94.

59. In *Of Wisdome*. Three Bookes Written In French by Peter Charron Doct[r] of Lawe in Paris. Translated by Samson Lennard (London, 1640), pp. 32-35. Charron professed scepticism about demoniacal ecstasy and described the human kind as "doubtelesse . . . no separation of the Soule but only a suspension of the parent and outward actions thereof."

60. *The Book of the Courtier*, pp. 319-320.

61. *Dialoghi d'Amore*, p. 275. In *Renaissance Theory of Love* (New York: Columbia Univ. Press, 1958), p. 94, John Charles Nelson says that Leone regarded direct knowl-

edge of divine beauty as "impossible in this life."

62. In the rejected conclusion to Book III of *The Faerie Queene. The Works of Edmund Spenser.* A Variorum Edition, ed. Edwin Greenlaw and others, 11 vols. (Baltimore: The Johns Hopkins Press, 1932-57), III, 181-182.

63. *Godfrey of Bulloigne: or the Recovery of Jerusalem.* Done into English by Edward Fairfax (Dublin, 1726). Canto XVI, stanza 19; p. 477.

64. In *A Method of Interpreting Literature,* pp. 19 and 17.

65. *The Works of Abraham Cowley* (11th ed., London, 1710, 2 vols.), I, 167.

66. In "Donne and Love Poetry of the Seventeenth Century." *Seventeenth Century Studies Presented to Sir Herbert Grierson* (Oxford: Clarendon Press, 1938), p. 76.

67. In *Donne's Poetry: Essays in Literary Analysis* (New Haven: Yale Univ. Press, 1954), p. 30.

68. As E. M. W. Tillyard does in "A Note on Donne's 'Extasie'."

69. *Summa Theologica,* I, cxix, 3; Vol. I, 744.2. Though this point is not made in Grierson's notes to the poem, he cites the *Summa,* I, lxx, 3, to illustrate lines 56-59 in the light of Aquinas' theory of the direct illumination of men's souls by the heavenly bodies.

70. *Summa Theologica,* I, lxxxviii, 3; Vol. I, 506.1.

71. *The Book of the Courtier,* pp. 321 and 318.

72. Examples are given in "The Lineage of 'The Extasie'." See n. 28 above.

73. *Dialoghi del Sig. Speron Speroni,* di nuovo ricoretti (Venice, 1606), p. 19 (misnumbered 21): Adunque non Amor solamente, ma noi ancora siamo Centauri, & Amore non pure è misto di huomo, & di brutto, ma d'infiniti contrarij, che sono uniti in lui solo, che troppo è lungo il contarli, & noi per proua li conoscete. Basti al presente, che sia Centauro, che fa gl'amanti Hermafroditi, dando alle parti di cotal misto la lor douuta felicità.

74. In J. E. Shaw's words in *Guido Cavalcanti's Theory of Love. The 'Canzone d'Amore' and Other Related Problems* (Toronto: Univ. of Toronto Press, 1949), pp. 11-12.

75. In "The Love Poetry of John Donne." *Seventeenth Century Studies Presented to Sir Herbert Grierson,* p. 100.

76. *The Poems of George Chapman,* ed. Phyllis B. Bartlett (New York: MLA, 1941), p. 59. Miss Bartlett notes (p. 431) Chapman's fondness for quoting this Aristotelian tag, but does not trace it to any source.

77. Stanza 103, ll. 1-6. *Poems,* p. 79. Following a suggestion of Leslie H. Rutledge, Miss Bartlett refers to Aristotle's treatment of touch as the first (*primum*) of the senses in *De Anima,* II, ii. But Aristotle thought of touch as first only in the sense that it was the basic faculty which man and all animals have in common. Aquinas, who more than once quoted the Aristotelian passage on touch as the prime sense, did not think of it as anything but the lowest in the hierarchy of the senses, though he recognized that the intellectual faculties of the soul depended upon its sensitive faculties. (*Summa Theologica,* I, lxxvi, 5; Vol. I, 486.)

78. The approximate date of the series is given as roughly between 1600 and 1615 by Fabrizio Clerici in *Allegorie dei Sensi di Jan Breughel* (Florence, Electa Editrice, n.d.).

ROONEY, " 'The Canonization'—The Language of Paradox Reconsidered"

1. New York, 1947.

2. He remarks that the poems examined in *The Well Wrought Urn,* other than those by Donne and the moderns, are, as a methodical principle, "to be read as one has

learned to read Donne and the moderns." (p. 117).

3. "And generally speaking, clever enigmas furnish good metaphors, for metaphor is a kind of enigma, so that it is clear that the transference is clever." Aristotle, *Rhetoric,* 1405b.

4. There is a corresponding phenomenon in the pattern of sound. The metrical cadence grows smoother in the fourth and fifth stanzas, but the groupings are still those of rough and colloquial speech. "We'll build in sonnets pretty rooms," is modulated from but not strange to the cadence of "Or chide my palsy or my gout."

5. It should also be noted that to present the meaning Brooks "discovers" the rhetoric of the poem would have to be symboleutic whereas it is pure epedeixis.

6. The kind of reading which Brooks has given to "The Canonization" he faithfully carries out with the other poems in *The Well Wrought Urn* so that there emerges a kind of method which might be described as the rumination of poems to discover whatever is paradoxical either in the material to which they refer or in the situation out of which they grow. The result is an emphasis not on the poet's craft but on his point of view. Examples can be multiplied from every page of *The Well Wrought Urn.* The analysis of Wordsworth's sonnet "Composed on Westminster Bridge," for instance, ignores that its structure is developed through something very much like what the logicians and rhetoricians of another age would call the argument of verbal fallacy (See Aristotle, *Rhetoric,* 1401a), where the form of wording causes the illusion of genuine reasoning—a series of statements, compactly put, each appearing to be the result of a previous line of reasoning, when they are merely collocated, create the impression of establishing a fresh conclusion. This spuriousness of enthymeme is a flaw not in the poetry (fallacies and good verse are not incompatible) but in the revelation which Brooks finds and offers as reason for the goodness of the poem.—"The city, in the poet's insight of the morning," Brooks says, "has earned its right to be considered organic, not merely mechanical. That is why the stale metaphor of the sleeping houses is strangely renewed. The most exciting thing the poet can say about the houses is that they are *asleep*. He has been in the habit of counting them dead—as just mechanical and inanimate; to say that they are "asleep" is to say that they are alive, that they participate in the life of nature. In the same way, the tired old metaphor which sees a great city as a pulsating heart of empire becomes revivified. It is only when the poet sees the city under the semblance of death that he can see it as actually alive—and quick with the only life which he can accept, the organic life of 'nature.'" (p. 6) Wordsworth's distinction between "poetry and matter of fact or science" seems wholly to have absorbed Brooks, making him oblivious to what structurally is the most interesting fact about the sonnet—the verbal craft which contrasts a strong background of academically conventional neo-classic rhetoric with a somewhat fainter foreground of realistically detailed sociology.

7. Brooks has a good many fine things to say about structure and about the fact that literary studies should take a direction that emphasizes structural analysis. He says, for example, that "the assumption" he has made in studying the poems discussed in *The Well Wrought Urn* is "that there is such a thing as poetry . . . and that there are general criteria against which the poems may be measured," and that he is against locating "the poetry" in a special doctrine or a special subject matter or a special kind of imagery . . ." The alternative, which he feels that he himself takes, is to emphasize "the way in which the poem is built, or—to change the metaphor— the form which it has taken as it *grew* in the poet's mind." If we do this, he thinks, "we shall necessarily raise questions of formal structure and rhetorical organization; we shall be forced to talk about levels of meaning, symbolizations, clashes of connota-

tions, paradoxes, ironies, etc." (p. 199) But in practice, as we have seen above, the analysis which Brooks presents is semantical rather than structural. And his theory, whatever thesis he proposes, in statements like those quoted above, seems reductively to support his practice. "The structure meant," he observes at one point, "is a structure of meanings, evaluations and interpretations; and the principle of unity which informs it seems to be one of balancing and harmonizing connotations, attitudes and meanings." (p. 178) At another point he says: ". . . The poet can make his poem *one* by reducing to order the confusions and disorder and irrelevancies of ordinary experience in terms of one unifying insight . . ." (p. 203) And at still another place: "It is not enough for the poet to analyze his experience as the scientist does, breaking it up into parts, distinguishing part from part, classifying the various parts. His task is finally to unify experience. He must return to us the unity of the experience itself as man knows it in his own experience. The poem, if it is to be a true poem, is a simulacrum of reality—in this sense, at least, it is as 'imitation'—by *being* an experience rather than any mere statement about experience or any mere abstraction from experience . . ." (p. 194) The emphasis made in these quotations certainly does not push toward analysis of objective structure made out of the material of speech; it moves rather toward a consideration of the structure of the poet's consciousness as that may be exposed by an enquiry into the words of a poem to find the extra sememes which the poet's usage has put into them and which are not there lexically. "I question," Brooks says, "whether the parts of any poem ever attain any tighter connections than the 'psychological' or that the coherence, even of the metaphysical poets, is not ultimately a coherence of attitude." (p. 221) It is true that the *mode* of connections in a poem may reflect the poet's psychological state; but is it not equally true, and infinitely more important to analysis of literary structure, that the actual connections in a poem are not psychological but philological—grammatical, rhetorical and poetical connections, the ligature of syntax, of narrative sequence, topical relations, etc.? And coherence of attitude, it must be objected, is not coherence of meaning; for attitudes are not meanings but one group of things about which meanings can be. To think of the search for structure of meaning as a search for balance of attitudes (heterogeneous or otherwise) fails to confront the fact that a poem, which refers to experience and attitudes, is not made out of experience and attitudes, but out of words.

FRECCERO "Donne's 'Valediction: Forbidding Mourning'"

1. In the preparation of this paper I have relied heavily upon the advice and collaboration of my friend A. B. Chambers of the University of California at Davis, not only for bibliographical help in an unfamiliar field, but also for background information on alchemy which proved to be crucial for an understanding of the poem. In a few instances Professor Chambers corrected my errors of interpretation; in several other instances, he provided me with notes which helped illuminate whole stanzas of the poem. I shall attempt to document my specific indebtedness to him at various points in the text. At this point, however, I should like to acknowledge my general dependence upon his specialist's knowledge throughout the writing of this paper and to express my gratitude for his help. The original version of this paper was read to the Johns Hopkins Philological Association in January, 1963.

2. *La Vita nuova* XII, 21-23, italics added. For an interpretation see C. S. Singleton, "*Vita Nuova XII, Love's Obscure Words*," *Romanic Review* XXXVI (April 1945), pp. 89-102. Translations throughout are the author's unless otherwise noted.

3. *Les Métamorphoses du cercle* (Paris, 1961), introduction.

4. The phrase "swerving serpentine" is from Mario Praz, *The Flaming Heart* (New

York, 1958), p. 190. Others have spoken of the "sensual character" of Donne's thought. The present study seeks to give a conceptual and historical basis to these critical expressions. Robert F. Fleissner does not consider the passage from the *Vita nuova* in his article "Donne and Dante: The Compass Figure Reinterpreted" (*MLN*, LXXVI, 4 [April, 1961], pp. 314-20).

5. *The Sermons of John Donne*, ed. Potter and Simpson (Berkeley and Los Angeles, 1953), VII, 257.

6. *Ibid.*, VI, 71; see also 1, 231: "this Divorce [death] is a new Marriage. . . ."

7. Matt. 22, 30; Mark 12, 25; Luke 20, 35.

8. II, 200. Cf. IV, 68: "In Him we move from the beginning to the end of our circle" and VIII, 97 for "Gods compasse."

9. *Timaeus* 44 c-d.

10. Aristotle, *De caelo* 269 b 1 ff; 286 b 15 ff. Cf. *Physics* III, 207a 8.

11. Plato, *Timaeus a Calcidio translatus commentarioque instructus*, ed. J. H. Waszink; Plato Latinus, ed. R. Klibansky, IV (Corpus Platonicum Medii Aevi), comm. CXVI (London [Warburg], 1962), p. 160.

12. For these and other compass emblems see Filippo Picinelli (Picinellus), *Mundus symbolicus*, trans. A. Erath (Cologne, 1687), II, 176-177 (s. v. *Circinus*).

13. The madrigal is given by Picinelli (*loc. cit.*). It has often been suggested as a "source" for Donne's image. See, among others, Josef Lederer, "John Donne and the Emblematic Practice," *RES*, XXII (1946), 198 ff. and *contra* Doris C. Powers, "Donne's Compass," *RES*, n.s. IX (1958), 173-5, as well as D. C. Allen, "Donne's Compass Figure," *MLN*, LXXI, 4 (April, 1956), p. 256 and M. Praz, *op. cit.*, p. 16, repeating an observation made in *Secentismo e Marinismo in Inghilterra* (Florence, 1925), p. 109 n.

14. *Délie*, CXXXII (*Poètes du XVIe siècle*, ed. A.-M. Schmidt [Paris (Pléiade), 1959], p. 119) The submerged compass is meant to show that Love "Par fermeté en inconstance esproeuve" its glory. Parturier (*Délie*, ed. E. Parturier [Paris, 1916]) reproduces it under the emblem of the weather vane, to which it of course bears a certain affinity. The words *pensée* and *foi*, however, seem to suggest that the "soul's compass" is here intended, as we shall later attempt to show. For a similar submerged image of Jean de Sponde, see note 54.

15. Plato called the two motions the "circle of the same" and the "circle of the other." See *Timaeus* 36d ff. and the remarks by A. Ölerud, *L'Idée de macrocosmos et de microcosmos dans le Timée de Platon* (Uppsala, 1951), pp. 32 ff., as well as J. Freccero, "Dante's Pilgrim in a Gyre," *PMLA*, LXXVI, 3 (June, 1961), pp. 172-3.

16. Chalcidius, *loc. cit.*

17. The diagram is not entirely accurate, for if it were a view from the pole, then the spiral would be off-center. The pole of the universe is approximately 23° from the pole of the *ecliptic* (the center of our diagram).

18. This use of the word probably arises from the fact that the ecliptic intersects the equator at an angle—"obliquely"—see *Timaeus, loc. cit.*, where the Demiurge places one piece of "soul-stuff" at an angle to the other. Dante's verse is from *Par.* X, 14; Théophile's from *Le matin* (*Oeuvres poétiques* ed. Streicher [Genève, 1951], p. 13).

19. Pseudo-Dionysius, *De div. nom. IV*, 8-9 (*PG*, III, 703-5). See remarks on this passage by W. Völker, *Kontemplation und Ekstase bei Pseudo-Dionysius Areopagita* (Wiesbaden, 1958), p. 191, who notes that Maximus the Confessor (*PG*, IV, 257B) develops the idea further. In the Middle Ages the *Liber de Causis* is often cited for a version of the three "conversions." For Bonaventure's doctrine see *Itiner. mentis in Deum* I, 2. The theme and its history are discussed by Freccero, p. 175. For the history

of the doctrine of the "circularity" of beatitude, see Bruno Nardi, "Sì come rota ch'igualmente è mossa," *Nel Mondo di Dante,* Storia e Letteratura V (Roma, 1944), 337-350.

20. The word ἐλικοειδῶς is rendered this way in four of the five translations known between 867 (Erigena) and 1492 (Ficino). Only the humanist Traversari offers a different reading. See Philippe Chevallier et al. (eds.) *Dionysiaca* (Bruges, 1937) I, 190.

21. Ficino, *Comment.* on *Div. Nom.* (*Opera omnia* [Basel, 1576] II, 1062-1063).

22. *Appendix Comment. in Timaeum,* cap. XIX (*Opera* II, 1467).

23. *Timaeus* 39d. See F. M. Cornford's notes *ad loc., Plato's Cosmology,* The Library of Liberal Arts (New York, 1957), pp. 116-7.

24. Quoted by E. Garin (ed.) in G. Pico della Mirandola *Disputationes adversus Astrol. Divin.* VI-XII, Ediz. naz. dei class. del. pen. ital. III (Florence, 1952), p. 537. Garin surveys the history of the doctrine from Cicero to Pico.

25. *Op. cit., Lib. VI,* cap. 1 (*ed. cit.,* p. 12). Pico describes the "astrologasters" as whispering to their followers the suggestion that *apocatastasis* and Resurrection are the same: "Quod quidam deinde astrologomistae profundius examinantes, consectaneis solent dicere in aurem: haec est illa Christianorum resurrectio, quam et Hebraei sperant et Mahumetenses." Pico refers his readers to Nicholas Oresme's refutation of the *apocatastasis,* cited by Garin as the *Tractatus de proport. proportionum,* Venice 1505. On the controversy in Dante's day concerning the relationship of *apocatastasis* and the Second Coming, see R. E. Kaske, "Dante's 'DXV' and 'Veltro,'" *Traditio* (1961), pp. 241 ff. One of the earliest and most famous attempts at a Christianization of *apocatastasis* was undertaken by Origen, who was condemned by the Council of Constantinople (V) for the doctrine of the pre-existence of souls and for "la monstrueuse apocatastase qui s'y rattache" (Vacant-Mangenot, *Dict. Théol. Cath.* (Paris, 1932), 11^2—col. 1581 (s.v. *Origénisme*).

26. *De immortal. animor.* XVIII (Opera I, 417).

27. For the doctrine of planetary homes (variously called *klairoi, loci, domicilia,* etc.), see Boll-Bezold, *Sternglaube und Sterndeutung,* 3 ed. W. Gundel (Berlin, 1926), p. 58 ff. and Garin, *op. cit.,* p. 538, who cites Manilius II, 788-970 and Firmicus Maternus II, 19-20.

28. The word is translated "erect" in modern English by Lynn Thorndike: "Every planet is erect in some one sign and falls in its opposite" (*A History of Magic and Experimental Science* [New York, 1923] I, 711.

29. Sonnet "Fiammeggiavano vivi i lumi chiari." *Lirici del Secolo XVI* (Milano, 1879), p. 118-9.

30. *Naturalis historiae II,* 16 (Rotterdam 1669), p. 26.

31. See notes and bibliography of Garin, p. 544 ff.

32. The passage is accepted by the variorum edition of 1669, *loc. cit.,* but modern editors reject it as probably spurious.

33. Boll-Bezold, *loc. cit.* They translate "Erniedrigungen." Marvell's *Definition of Love* exploits astrological doctrine in a similar way. See especially the lines ". . . conjunction of the mind, / And opposition of the stars."

34. Ed. Borgnet, xviii, 83 ff.

35. *Ibid.,* p. 109 ff.

36. Allen Tate has seen that Donne's compass traces the "Aristotelian circle of archetypal motion" ("The Point of Dying," SR LXI, 1 [Winter, 1953], p. 76).

37. The following passage is a resumé of a discussion in J. Freccero, "Dante's Firm Foot and the Journey without a Guide," *Harvard Theological Review* LII, 3 (October, 1959), p. 262, to which the reader is referred for fuller documentation.

38. *De anima III*, X, 433b, 19 ff. The word is retained by some commentators, *e. g.*, Averroes, *In Arist. de anima III* Corpus Comment. Averrois in Arist. VI, 1 (Cambridge, 1953), pp. 525 ff. Our expression "ball-and-socket" corresponds to the words "gibbositas et concavitas" in Latin translations.

39. Especially in the *De generatione animalium II*, 2 which G. Rodier considers the best commentary on the passage, whether it is spurious or not. See his translation and commentary for a lucid discussion of the Aristotelian principle: Aristote, *Traité de l'âme*, tr. G. Rodier (Paris, 1900), II, 547 ff.

40. Ed. Béguin, p. 57. Cf. François Sagon, "Le pied," *Blason du corps feminin:* "Pied qui suyt l'autre en ordre et *par compas* . . ." (Schmidt, p. 345). The analogy is implicit in the word "compass": **compassare* <L. *com*− + *passus*, a step.

41. "Et attractio et expulsio . . . non est in rectitudine sed secundum lineas non rectas, magis curvas quam rectas, et ideo assimilatur giro." *loc. cit.* Cf. Albertus Magnus: "his autem motus est gyrantis, quando motum membrum gyrum habet expulsionis et retractionis in eodem loco. In talibus enim motibus expulsio est sicut principium, et attraction est sicut finis ejus . . ." *Liber III de anima*, tr. iv, c. viii (*Opera omnia* ed. Borgnet [Paris, 1890] v, 405).

42. For the symbolic importance of the doctrine of the *apex mentis* or the *synderesis* see for instance Poulet, p. XIII f. For Thomas Aquinas' discussion, see *Summa Theologica* I, 79, 12. Harry V. Jaffa compares Thomas' use of the idea to Aristotelian principles in *Thomism and Aristotelianism* (Chicago, 1952), pp. 171-174.

43. See above, n. 14. Cf. Jean de Sponde's twin powers in the sonnet cited below, n. 54: "esprit" and "constance." Pietro Bembo's canzone "Quantunque in altro clima io giri il piede . . ." distinguishes "pensiero" and "core." Tasso's sonnet CIX similarly refers to "pensiero" and "costanza": "somiglia il mio pensiero / . . . / stella in cielo errante / per la costanza mia fatta incostante." (*Lirici del cinquecento* ed. C. Bo [Roma, 1945], p. 388). Finally see Jonson's "Epistle to Master John Selden": "And like a Compasse keeping one foot still / Upon your Center, doe your Circle fill / Of general *knowledge*." (*Works*, ed. Herford & Simpson [Oxford, 1947] VIII, 159).

44. Poulet remarks that Guy Le Febvre de la Boderie was in the "entourage" of Plantin. For the possible influence of the device on Donne's poem see the articles of Lederer and Powers (*cit.*) who, however, exaggerate its importance.

45. Cesare Ripa, *Iconologia* (Venice, 1669), p. 496.

46. Probably the most influential statement of the allegory is in St. Augustine's *De Trinitate* XII, 2 (*PL* 42, 1007-8).

47. For the *congé* and relevant bibliography, see Italo Siciliano, *François Villon et les thèmes poétiques du moyen âge* (Paris, 1934), p. 332.

48. "Some of Donne's 'Ecstasies,'" *PMLA*, LXXV, 5 (Dec. 1960), pp. 509-518. Professor Hughes' discussion of the use of Plotinian ecstasy as an epistolary conceit provides an excellent background for an understanding of Donne's verse "Inter-assured of the mind," which might be interpreted as "participating in the *Mens*" which transcends both the lovers. Such an affirmation would be the normal way for a neoplatonist to explain the fact that two souls are in fact one.

49. *Dialoghi* (Venice, 1544), p. 29:

> TUL. Il conforto della partita del Tasso sia la mia morte: che essendo tra lui, et me la medesima proportione, ch'è tra il corpo, e l'anima mia; partendo esso partirà l'anima, che mi tien viva . . . GRA . . . Percioche non sempremai, che l'anima nostra si discompagna dal corpo, noi cessiamo di vivere . . . adunque s'altrettanto in voi, e ne vostri amori vi mostrerò poter fare la partita del Tasso: onde viene che voi ve ne vogliate ramaricare? . . ."

This is one citation among many. In poetry, the theme of *congé* as "ectasy" is often repeated by Serafino dall'Aquila, with whom Parturier compares Scève's famous *dizain* CXLIV: "En toy je vis, où que tu sois absente: / En moy je meurs, où que soye presente . . ." (*Délie, ed. cit.,* p. 108). Cf. Petrarch, "Mira quell colle. . . ."

50. *Comm. in Convivium Platonis II,* 8 (ed. R. Marcel [Paris, 1956] p. 156): "In reciprocal love, there is only one death, but two resurrections. . . ." See the remarks on the passage by G. Saitta, *La Filosofia di M. F.* (Palermo, 1923), pp. 263-4. The passage is translated almost verbatim by Gilles Corrozet, *Le Sophologe d'Amour* (1542), fol. 15ʳ. Parturier, who does not seem to be aware of the source, calls this "un exemple, entre mille, du galimatias amoureux à la mode sous le règne de François I" (p. 101).

51. *De immenso et innumerabilibus* III, 7 (*Opere di G. B. e di Tommaso Campanella,* ed. A. Guzzo and R. Amerio, La Lett. Ital.: Storia e testi vol 33 [Milano, 1956], pp. 734-6). A serious use of the theme can be found in Scève's *Délie,* CCCLXVII, 1 ff: "Asses plus long, qu'un Siecle Platonique."

52. See, for instance, Serafino dall'Aquila's dialogue between the body and the soul (ed. M. Menghini [Bologna, 1894] I, 132): "Anima, su.—Che c'è?—Disgombra e vola [cf. Donne's ". . . and whisper to their soules, to goe"].—Dove?—A madonna.— A che? Ch'io son in via. —Tu mori?—Non.—Da te chi me desvia?—Quel crudo amor, che tutto el mondo invola—." The first lines of Louise Labé's *Elégie VI* are a classic example of the "body's lament for its "soul": "On voit mourir toute chose animee, / Lors que du corps l'ame sutile part: / Je suis le corps, toy la meilleure part: / Où es tu donq, o ame bien aymee? / Ne me laissez par si long tems pamee: / Pour me sauver apres viendrois trop tard. / Las! ne mets point ton corps en ce hazart: / Rens lui sa part et moitié estimee" (Schmidt, p. 283).

53. *Maurice Scève,* Choix des textes & préface par Albert Béguin (Paris, 1947), p. 16. Dante was of course the first to use this pattern of the mystics to celebrate his love for his Lady.

54. The simile of the lady as pole-star is a tired topos, often found in combination with the "ship of love" or the mariner's compass motifs. Two passages from 16th century French poems seem particularly suggestive for establishing an affinity between Donne's "Valediction" and Petrarchan currents (cf. Praz, *op. cit.,* pp. 186-203). In Jean de Sponde's *Amours* XVIII a submerged compass image is combined with the topos (Schmidt, pp. 905-6). Philippe Desportes specifically mentions zodiacal movement in a similar context: *Le cours de l'an* (Schmidt, p. 811).

55. For the history of the doctrine, see G. Verbeke, *L'Evolution de la doctrine du Pneuma* (Paris and Louvain, 1945).

56. *Loc. cit.*; cf. Albertus, *Liber VIII Physicorum,* tr. III (Borgnet, iv, 604). Cf. Aristotle's definition of "aither," *De caelo* I, iii (270b 15 ff).

57. *Summae de creaturis II,* II p., q. 78 (Borgnet, XXXV, 637).

58. The "layetie" who do not understand love's mystery are compared to those who do not know when the soul leaves the body in a number of Renaissance poems. We may cite: Philippe Desportes, *Les Amours d'Hippolyte* XII, line 7: "[Celuy] qui ne sçait quand l'ame est du corps divisee . . . Qu'il s'arreste pour voir . . . ma Deese" (Schmidt, p. 791); Scève, CCLXXVIII, line 4: "Comment du corps l'Ame on peult deslyer . . ." (Schmidt, p. 167), derived from Lodovico Martelli, *Rime* (Venice, 1533) f. A iiii v, cited by Parturier, p. 192 n. 2: "Come dal corpo l'anima si svia."

59. The association between breathing and speaking and the importance of both as symbols of the soul are as old as the Bible. A. Calmet notes that, although "mors corporis designatur emblemate spiraculi vitae," nevertheless the "breath" of Genesis II, 7 ("inspiravit in faciem ejus spiraculum vitae") indicates the "inspiration" of the

soul. He notes that "Chaldaeus vertit: *Factus est spiritum loquentem*" for the words, "factus est homo in animam viventem," since "Spirare et loqui vitae functiones sunt, quae non raro pro vita ipsa usurpantur." *Commentarius literalis,* trans. Mansi (Lucca, 1730), I[l], 20. See, on the matter of the Biblical variant, E. R. Wasserman, "Pope's *Ode for Musick,*" *ELH*, XXVIII, 2 (June, 1961), p. 170 f.

60. *In librum Enneadis* II, ii (Opera, II, 1605).

61. The "planetary home" of the soul is of course a Platonic theme. Plutarch speaks of the pure soul reaching the sphere of the Moon, which is possibly a Poseidonian innovation. See Cherniss' note to *Moralia* XII, Loeb (Cambridge, 1957), p. 209 f. The expansion and contraction of *spiritus* is the principle underlying the neo-platonic doctrine of the "pneumatic" body with which the soul "clothes" itself in its descent to earth. The doctrine is found as early as the *Pistis Sophia.* For its history in neo-platonism, see the appendix of E. R. Dodds, *Proclus: Elements of Theology* (Oxford, 1913); for a survey of the history of the idea in the Middle Ages and Renaissance, see R. Klein, "L'Enfer de Ficin" in *Umanesimo e Esoterismo,* Archivio di filosofia (Padova, 1960), pp. 64-67.

62. Luigi Tansilla compares love's despair to a man dying of a "grave mal" who "giace e piange lungamente . . ." *Sonn. XIX (Lirici del Cinquecento,* a cura di C. Bo [Roma, 1945], p. 248). The traditional identification of a peaceful death with virtue and a violent death with vice explains the association here of "virtuous men" and passing "mildly away."

63. C. M. Coffin, *John Donne and the New Philosophy* (New York, 1937), p. 98: "Of the new astronomy, the "moving of the'earth" is the most radical principle."

64. *Meteorologica* 366b 14 ff. (ed. H. D. P. Lee, Loeb [London, 1952], 204-5). See Festugière, *La Révélation d'Hermès Trismégiste* (Paris, 1950), I, 110 for the ps. Orphic *peri seismon,* a typical treatise on earthquakes and their interpretation.

65. Quoted by Lee, *ibid.*

66. "Access and Recess" is an alternate name for the movement of "trepidation." See, for example, Lynn Thorndike, *The Sphere of Sacrobosco* (Chicago, 1949), Index, s.v. "Access and Recess."

67. "The path of the pole among the stars is a slightly sinuous curve." *Ency. Brittanica* 11 ed. XVIII, 431 (s.v. *Precession*).

68. Leone Ebreo explains earthquakes by his theory of universal love; *pneuma* strives to return to its natural place (*Dialoghi d'amore,* ed. S. Caramella [Bari, 1929] p. 70).

69. For the importance of *pneuma* as a principle of alchemy, see F. Sherwood Taylor, *The Alchemists: Founders of Modern Chemistry* (New York, 1949), pp. 11-16.

70. Quoted by Taylor, p. 14. Albertus Magnus notes the traditional association but disagrees: "quidam dixerunt spiritus esse de natura quinti corporis: quod tamen non est verum." *Summae de creaturis* II, 78 (Borgnet XXXV, 637). Cf. *Summa* XI, 51, I (Borgnet XXXI, 538) where Costa ben Luca is cited and Verbeke, p. 148.

71. *Meteorologica III,* 6 (378c): "The vaporous exhalation is the cause of all metals, fusible or ductile things, such as iron, copper, gold," quoted by Taylor, p. 13 who explains the importance of the passage.

72. For alchemical allegory in general, see Taylor, Chapter XI: "Alchemical Symbolism" (p. 145 ff.). See especially Plate VI, no. 7 (p. 150 c), a reproduction from Mylius' *Philosophia Reformata,* labeled (p. 156): "Their souls depart: i.e., volatilization begins." For the principles of attraction, repulsion circularity see M. A. Atwood, *Hermetic Philosophy and Alchemy* rev ed. (New York, 1960), pp. 154 ff.: "Attraction

is the first principle of motion in nature . . . Repulsion is the second principle and a
necessary consequence of the first by reaction. Circulation is the third principle, proceeding from the conflict of the former two." The comparison of gold to the glorified
body is not restricted to the Alchemists; theologians use the comparison as well. See,
for example St. Thomas (*Summa Theologica* III [Supplement], Q. 83, Art. I, resp.) who
discusses the *subtilitas* of the glorified body: "thus we speak of subtlety in the sun and
moon and like bodies, just as gold and silver. . . ." He goes on to remark that some
"heretics" have suggested that the glorified body "will be like air on the wind," but of
course rejects the idea. He says that gold also resembles the glorified body by its
"claritas" and quotes Gregory the Great in support (*Ibid.,* ad 2. Cf. Gregory *Moralia
in Job* XVIII, xliv ff. and xlviii). I am indebted to Professor Chambers for the reference
from Thomas.

73. J. A. Mazzeo, "Notes on John Donne's Alchemical Imagery," *ISIS* XLVIII, pt.
2, 152 (June, 1957), pp. 113-114.

74. Nicholas Flammel, *The Glory of the World* in *The Hermetic Museum*, tr. A. E.
Waite (London, 1893), I, 47. For this and all future citations from Waite, I am indebted to Professor Chambers.

75. Albertus Magnus, *Mineralium* (Borgnet V, 83). Cf. Taylor, p. 148 ff.: "The
second great symbol of alchemy is that of a marriage." A few typical citations, provided me by Professor Chambers, will suffice: Nicholas Flammel, *His Exposition of
the Hieroglyphical Figures* . . . tr. Eirenaeus Orandus (London, 1624), p. 84: "In
this . . . operation [are] two *natures* conjoyned and married together, the *Masculine*
and the *Foeminine.*" Again, the anonymous *Golden Tract* . . . "they [husband and
wife] fell to embracing each other so passionately that the husband's heart was melted
with the excessive ardour of love, and he fell down broken in many pieces" (Waite
I, 47). Finally, Flammel, *His Exposition,* p. 78: "This dissolution is by the envious
Philosophers called *Death* . . . Others have called it . . *.Liquefaction.* . . ."

76. For the limbeck in Donne's poetry, see Mazzeo, pp. 110-111. In the plates
reproduced by Taylor (p. 150c), steps 5 shows the lovers (the "Hermaphrodite"
metal, composed of both a masculine and feminine principle) together in bed: "They
are married." The next step shows them in a grave: "The bodies putrefying in the
tomb of glass" (p. 155).

76[a]. The best demonstration of Donne's use of alchemy in an erotic context is Jay
A. Levine, "'The Dissolution': Donne's Twofold Elegy," *ELH,* XXVIII (1961). 301-315.

77. Shakespeare I, iii, 81; Brother Joseph, F.S.C., "Donne's Valediction: Forbidding
Mourning," The Explicator, XVI (1958), item 43. For "melt" as the volatilization of
pneuma in the lover see *The Golden Tract* (n. 75 above): "melted with the ardour of
love." This is analogous to a Petrarchan topos: "Ite, caldi sospiri, al freddo core; /
rompete il ghiaccio . . ." (Son. CLII). Dante "melts" at Beatrice's accusation: 'lo gel
che m'era intorno al cor ristretto, / spirito e acqua fessi e con angoscia / della bocca e
delli occhi uscì del petto." *Purg.* XXX, 97-99. The poetic terminology was thought to
have "scientific" foundation. The "melting" in the human soul comes about by the
warming of vital spirits in the heart which seek issue through the eyes, mouth, etc.
of the body. For an example of the literary use of this theme from the Aristotelian
physiology in the Renaissance see, among many, Castiglione, *The Book of the Courtier*
IV, 65, where the beauty of the lady "by warming [the lover's] heart, arouses and
melts certain dormant and congealed powers in his soul which . . . well up around his
heart, and send forth through the eyes the spirits . . ." trans. C. S. Singleton (New York,
1959), p. 350. An example of an imperative "melt," addressed to the heart by the lover
in a religious context, is provided by Lorenzo de'Medici: "Liquefatti come cera, / o cor

mio tristo e maligno. / Poiché muor . . . / Gesù tuo . . ." *Scritti scelti*, ed. E. Bigi (Torino, 1955), p. 116. In a similar vein, see Donne's *Sermons* V, 314: "Therefore *David* who was metall tried seven times in the fire, and desired to be such gold as might be laid up in Gods treasury, might consider, that in transmutation of metals, it is not enough to come to a calcination, or a liquefaction . . . nor to an Ablution, to sever drosse from pure, nor to a Transmutation, to make it a better metall, but there must be a Fixion. . . . Therefore he saw that he needed not only a liquefaction, a melting into teares. . . ." We have already seen that the alchemists associated liquefaction with death (above, n. 75 and n. 72), and that the literal meaning of "melt" is to drive off the volatile spirit. Thus, the "pneumatic dispersion" may be expressed by the word "melt" on every level of meaning in the poem.

78. Basil Valentine, *The Pratica* (Waite, I, 350). The point of having gold beaten to gold-leaf is so that it will react more readily with the Stone. The phrase "like gold to ayery thinnesse beate" may also have some allegorical force. John of San Gimignano suggests that "patience" is like gold because it endures no breach under the hammer of adversity, but submits in order to be "dilated" to charity. *Summa de exemplis* (Venice, 1577) f. 101ᵛ. Donne uses analogous alchemical imagery in the *Sermons* III, 148-9; VIII, 119-20. For a discussion of the principles of ductility and for the "pneumatic" reasons why gold is the most ductile of all metals, see Albertus, *Mineralium* II, ii (Borgnet V, 756). According to Taylor (p. 11), "The alchemists are never tired of reminding us" that gold engenders gold. Cf. Taylor, p. 36.

79. Aristotle *de Gen. et Corrupt.* I, quoted by Albertus, *Mineralium III*, ii, I (Borgnet V, 76). Cf. Thomas Aquinas *ad loc.* in an edition of Donne's time, discussing the stammering metals: "qui una litera prolata, aliam distincte non proferunt." *In lib. de Gener. et Corrupt.* (Venice, 1584), p. 24.

80. For the remarks of Lacinio see *The New Pearl of Great Price*, tr. A. E. Waite (London, 1894), p. 133. See also p. 331 for "tempestuous conditions." Our quote is from Thomas Norton, *The Ordinal of Alchemy* (Waite II, 148). Basil Valentine remarks that "too much rain spoils the fruit" (*loc. cit.*, p. 336). Tears enter into the allegory of the *Golden Tract* (Waite I, 47): "[she] covered him with overflowering tears, until he was quite flooded. . . ."

81. *The Sophic Hydrolith or, Water Stone of the Wise* (Waite I, 110).

82. "A philosophic fire never described by any philosopher but only whispered by the adept on his death bed is a tremendous secret." Lynn Thorndike (describing a work [ca. 1605] by Joachim Tanckins) *A History of Magic and Experimental Science* (New York, 1958) VIII, 106.

83. W. A. Murray, "Donne's Gold-Leaf and his Compasses," *MLN*, LXXIII, 5 (May, 1958), p. 329. Murray's argument may be supported by the venerable but legendary tradition that Origen believed the glorified body would be perfectly spherical in shape (*Dict. Théol. Cath.* s.v. "Origénisme," *cit.*) it would therefore be a living symbol of gold. The association of gold and the glorified body with two lovers is reinforced by Aristophanes' whimsical comparison of the body of the Hermaphrodite to a sphere in Plato's *Symposium*.

84. Murray remarked on the "integral" relationship of center and circumference and reproduced a text in support which will serve admirably to illustrate our point: "In puncto enim non minus circulus existit, ac in ipso cyclo. Iam quanto maior est cyclus respectu puncti? Et tamen utrique integri sunt. Sicut ergo fieri potest, ut circini pes immobilis circulum ducat, alter autem mobilis spatiosam peripheriam: sic aequale ac simile incrementum est magnitudinis hominis respectu coeli. Similiter etiam in decremento a coelo versus hominem veluti radii ab ambitu in punctum suum redeuntes."

The so-called Arabic *Theology of Aristotle* explains that since God is the point upon which all of nature depends (cf. Dante, *Par.* XIV, 1-3 and *Par.* XXVIII, 41: "Da quel punto / depende il cielo et tutta la natura," echoing Aristotle *Metaphysics* 30, 7) we can never stray from him: "Auch wir bestehen fest nur durch den ersten Schaffer; an ihn hängen wir uns, zu ihm sehnen wir uns, ihm neigen wir uns zu und kehren zu ihm zurück, wenn wir auch von ihm fern und weit ab sind. Denn unser Gang und unsere Heimkehr geht nur zu ihm, gleichwie die Linien (Radien) des *Kreises,* wenn sie auch fern und weit ab sind, zum Mittelpunkt gehen." *Theologie des Aristoteles* ed. & trans. F. Dietrich (Leipzig, 1883), p. 133. The first chapter of Poulet's book (see above, n. 3) deals fully with this theme of the mystics. Donne's innovation on the theme is to place his beloved at the center to which all radii must return.

85. See above, note 70. Since *pneuma* was believed to be the constituent of the fifth essence, then it also had to be the constituent of the heavenly bodies. This homologous composition was what accounted for their similar movement, according to Costa ben Luca, quoted by Albertus (above, note 57).

86. For the figures concerning exaltations and domiciles, see the table provided by Boll-Bezold, p. 59 and cf. Garin (quoting the Arabs), p. 545 for confirmation. Sexes were assigned to all of the planets, the higher planets were considered to be male and the lower female, except that Mercury was hermaphrodite. See Festugière I, 97.

87. Thorndike traces two separate theories concerning Mercury and the "tincture" —one was that earthly mercury had to be combined with a small measure of gold and silver in order to produce Heavenly Mercury, the other was that mercury alone would suffice (*Hist. of Magic etc.* III, 58 ff., 88 ff. and Index, s.v. Mercury). A typical example of the production of tincture from mercury is given by Paracelsus, who distinguishes two different kinds of mercury: "Take Philosophers' Mercury, prepared and purified to its supreme degree. Dissolve this with its wife, that is to say, with quick mercury, so that the woman may dissolve the man, and the man may fix the woman. Then, just as the husband loves his wife and she her husband, the Philosophers' Mercury purses the quick mercury with the most supreme love . . . [so that] . . . they have no difference. . . . For this reason, the woman is united to the man in such a way that she dissolves the man, and he *fixes* her and renders her *constant in every consideration* as a consequence" (Waite I, 85-6).

88. Mazzeo, p. 105, n. 5.

89. Quoted from the *Turba Exercitationum* I by Atwood, p. 72. She quotes Geber as saying "All is made of Mercury" (p. 77), a saying which is echoed by Arnold of Villanova (Thorndike III, 76).

90. For the generic principle of "circulations," reflux condensation, etc., see Taylor, pp. 118 f. and 142 ff. The spherical container might also be a limbeck. Mazzeo says (p. 110): "In 'spiritual alchemy' the tortuous curvings of the retort tube was analogous to the hard path traveled by the soul in the process of its purification." For the use of the term "refinement," Professor Chambers has referred me to Benedictus Figulus, *A Golden and Blessed Casket of Nature's Marvels:* "A refined spirit cannot appear except in a body suitable to its nature . . ." tr. Waite (London, 1893), p. 42.

91. Albertus says that "animalia mutant voces et sunt in motu tempore coitus et exclamant se invicem," and quotes Aristotle (*De hist. animal.* 5, 14 [544b 22 ff.]) in support: *Quaest. de animalibus V, 3 Opera Omnia* ed. B. Geyer *et al.* (Westphalia, 1955), XII, 155. Thus, the *strepitus* of coitus is bestial.

92. Albertus also describes the role of the *spiritus spumosus* in coitus (*Ibid.,* p. 273) and describes the debilitating effects of a lack of moderation. Leone Ebreo (*op. cit.,* pp. 80-1) speaks of the relationship between the earth (female) and "il suo

maschio" (the heavens) in sexual and alchemical terms. One line in particular is reminiscent of Donne's "makes no show / To move, but doth, if the "other doe": "Ella [i.e., the earth], se ben è quieta, si muove pur un poco per il movimento del maschio."

93. A resumé of a typical form of the *Timaeus* analogy is given by Festugière: (I, 92), where the head is said to be equivalent to the heavens and the "ventre" to the earth. It is because of this analogy that Renaissance theoreticians of love distinguished between rational and carnal love with the terms "celestial" and "terrestrial."

94. *Courtier* IV, 64 (Singleton, p. 349 f.).

95. *Midrash Rabbah*, trans. Rabbinowitz (London, 1939), p. 187 (Deuteronomy II, 10). Pico takes issue with Ficino's interpretation of the kiss of Agathon in the *Convivium* and suggests that the real significance is the ecstatic *binsica* (*binšîqah*), or "death by the kiss." Castiglione's remarks paraphrase the long passage in the *Commento . . . sopra una Canzona de Amore . . . composta la . . . Girolamo Benivieni* III, stanza quarta (in G. Pico della Mirandola, *De Hom. dig., Heptaplus*, etc., ed. Garin, Ediz. naz. dei class. I [Firenze, 1942], p. 557 f.).

96. For the kiss as the recapitulation of a whole life, see Guarini, *Il Pastor fido* II, 1: "la mia vita, chiusa / in così breve spazio, / non era che un bacio," quoted by N. Perella, "Fate in the *Pastor fido*," *Romanic Review* XLIX, 4 (Dec. 1958), p. 262 and note. Professor Perella is preparing a monograph on the subject of the kiss. Giambattista Marino's *Baci* (*La Lira* II, iv) provides an example of scientific and sensual virtuosity on the subject. Echoing Guarini, he gives a scientific basis to the ecstasy of the kiss: "*spiriti* rugiadosi, *sensi* d'amor *vitali,* che 'n breve *giro* il viver mio chiudete" (italics mine). Another verse echoes Castiglione's (and Donne's) conceit: "e più d'un' alma in una bocca asconde!" Again, he recalls the ecstasy in a purely erotic sense: "quel bacio, che mi priva di vita mi raviva." Finally, he combines sigh, whisper, smile and kiss: "un sol bacio beve sospir, parole e riso." (*Marino e i marinisti*, ed. Ferrero. La Lett. ital.: storia e testi, vol. 37 [Milano, 1954], 352-5). In another poem, Donne refers to the ecstatic kiss of rational love as a banality, which he rejects in favor of the epistolary ecstasy popularized by Ficino (Cf. Merritt Hughes, *op. cit.*): "Sir, more than kisses, letters mingle Soules . . ." (*Verse epistle: To Sir Henry Wotton*).

MILLER, "Donne's 'A Nocturnall upon S. Lucies Day' and the Nocturns of Matins"

1. All quotations from Donne's poems are from the edition of Sir Herbert Grierson, 2 vols. (Oxford University Press, 1912), except for the two "Anniversaries," which are quoted from the edition of Frank Manley (Johns Hopkins University Press, 1963).

2. There has been much inconclusive speculation about when the poem was written and whether it concerns Lucy, Countess of Bedford, or Donne's wife. For a summary see Theodore Redpath, *The Songs and Sonets of John Donne* (London, 1956), p. 71—to which should be added Louis Martz's *Poetry of Meditation* (Yale University Press, 1954), pp. 214-215, and Doniphan Louthan's *The Poetry of John Donne* (New York, 1951), pp. 140-148.

3. K. W. Gransden (*John Donne*, London, 1954) calls it "Donne's finest metaphysical treatment of permanent division, permanent separation, permanent loneliness" (p. 79). See also Hansruedi Faerber's *Das Paradoxe in der Dichtung von John Donne* (Rüschlikon-Zürich, 1950), p. 38.

4. *Interpretations*, ed. John Wain (London, 1955), p. 52. He discusses the dual movement in the diction and metrics of the poem, but especially in its imagery: "But the terms of his description of destruction anticipate the re-creation. Night is always followed by day, even the longest night of the year must be followed by the day; winter presages spring. Each of these things has the two qualities: present annihilation,

future life" (p. 51).

5. *John Donne's Lyrics: The Eloquence of Action* (University of Minnesota Press, 1962), p. 179.

6. Redpath, p. 74.

7. Martz, p. 214.

8. The *OED* cites Donne's "Nocturnall" for the meaning "nightpiece," but it gives no other example; and it gives one example (1670) of "nocturnal" with the meaning "night service, a nocturn." The aesthetic meaning of "nocturn," as in music, seems to be an outgrowth of romanticism, not found before the nineteenth century. In Donne's lifetime Bartholomaeus Gavantus noted: "Sunt autem apud Auctores haec synonima pro eodem, Nocturnum, Vigiliae Nocturnae, & Matutinum" (*Thesaurus Sacrorum Rituum* . . . 5 vols. [Venice, 1791] III, 104). Volume III of Gavantus's massive collection, originally printed in Venice in 1627, is devoted entirely to the divine office ("Complectens omnia Gavanti Commentaria in Rubricas Brevarii Romani"). Reprinted, supplemented, and commented upon, the *Thesaurus* was a standard work on the office for more than 150 years (I quote, perforce, from the 1791 edition). Gavantus himself gathered together the opinions of the most notable writers on the office, such as Amalarius (died c. 837), Hugh of St. Victor (1096-1141), Guglielmus Durandus (1237-1296), and Cesar Baronius (1538-1607). Two of these, Hugh and Baronius, Donne himself cites in his prose (see Mary Paton Ramsay's *Les Doctrines Médiévales chez Donne* [Oxford, 1924] pp. 273, 294). Amalarius's works on the office were published in 1568 at Cologne (see *La Grande Encyclopédie* [Paris, n.d.] XV, 108) and there were at least three more editions of them between 1610 and 1624 (*British Museum General Catalogue of Printed Books* [London, 1961]). Durandus's *Rationale divinorum officiorum* was reprinted at least 40 times between 1459 and 1500 (*Encyclopaedia Britannica*, 1961), and at least ten times between 1504 and 1614 (*British Museum General Catalogue*).

9. Helen Gardner ed., *John Donne: the Divine Poems* (Oxford, 1952), p. xxviii.

10. Gardner, pp. 57-58. Miss Gardner adds: "Any Breviary Donne used would be a Roman one, since the Sarum Use fell into desuetude after the Reformation." But even granting this, there was no one "Roman Breviary" in the sixteenth century. Apart from the special breviaries of the papal chapel and the religious orders, the simplified breviary by Cardinal Quignonez enjoyed great popularity from its first publication in 1536 until 1568, when it was abolished and superseded by the Tridentine Breviary issued by St. Pius V. And in 1602 this too was revised by a commission including St. Robert Bellarmine (with whose works Donne was thoroughly familiar), Baronius, and Gavantus. See Joseph Maugère, *Il Brevario Romano Commentato*, tr. Nivardo Bossi (Savona, 1892), pp. 14-16. Fortunately, many features of the office, like those cited by Miss Gardner, remained relatively stable amidst these complicated revisions.

11. Gardner, pp. 59-60. Perhaps it should be added that some of the passages Miss Gardner cites from the office of the Blessed Virgin are also found in the Common of the Mass of the Blessed Virgin.

12. The association of the "Nocturnall" with the office of Advent and hence with "La Corona," for which the date 1607 is a "highly probable conjecture" (Gardner, pp. 55-56) provides additional support for Martz's suggestion of 1606 for the "Nocturnall."

13. Gavantus, III, 104.

14. Martz, pp. 223-228.

15. There is another resemblance between the two "Anniversaries" and the "Nocturnall": the "her" of the "Nocturnall" remains unidentified, just as Elizabeth Drury

is never named in the "Anniversaries" but is always called simply "Shee." In fact, since Elizabeth Drury was buried on 17 December 1610 (see Martz, p. 353) one may wonder why she has not been suggested as a candidate for the "Nocturnall," assigned by Donne to December 13.

16. *OED*, Nocturn 1.

17. Gavantus (III, 105) cites Amalarius on this point, and he might have added Hugh of St. Victor (*Patrologia latina*, ed. J. P. Migne [Paris, 1879], CLXXVII, 342).

18. Many days had only three, but double feasts (like St. Lucy's) regularly had nine. In 1521 St. Lucy's feast was only a semidouble, but in the Tridentine Breviary St. Pius V raised it to the rank of double (Gavantus, III, 258). I have not been able to obtain an earlier edition of the Tridentine Breviary than one printed at Paris in 1854.

19. Gavantus, III, 105. In a homily assigned to matins (lesson 5, 2nd nocturn, Common of Virgins in the Tridentine Breviary), St. Ambrose describes the upward flight of a virgin soul ("nubes, area, Angelos, sideraque transgrediens") and points out why it is especially fitting that the virgins should be compared to the angels: " . . . quoniam quae non nubunt, neque nubentur, erunt sicut Angeli Dei in coelo. Nemo ergo miretur, si Angelis comparentur, quae Angelorum Domino copulantur."

20. Gavantus (III, 105) cites Hugh of St. Victor, who stresses this point (*Patrologia latina*, CLXXVII, 342, 414, 874).

21. Some authorities insisted that matins and lauds together constitute only one canonical hour. The question was disputed on the basis of whether there is better scriptural justification for eight or for seven hours (Gavantus, III, 2). The other six (prime, terce, sext, nones, vespers, and compline) are spaced throughout the day until nightfall. Though he is thinking of the hours of light, Donne does mention the "seaven houres" of St. Lucy's day in the "Nocturnall" (line 2).

22. Who himself translated the "Office of the Holy Crosse."

23. Donne's "Epitaph on Himselfe" follows (with some ironic reversals) the cycle of death and resurrection: the "wormeaten carkases" are finally "enabled . . . to scale / Heaven."

24. From the Tridentine Breviary, but the same lessons appear in the Hereford Breviary (ed. W. H. Frere and L. E. C. Brown, Henry Bradshaw Society, 3 vols. [London, 1904-1915]), which agrees, in these lessons and most of the other features I mention, with the breviaries of York and Sarum (see Frere and Brown, *Hereford Breviary*, III, x, xxiii).

25. Gavantus, III, 29.

26. Gavantus (III, 140), citing Amalarius.

27. Gavantus, III, 140.

28. *Interpretations*, ed. John Wain, p. 57. A few details of Mr. Sleight's analysis should be corrected by consulting Helen Gardner's *The Metaphysical Poets* (Penguin, 1957), p. 69.

29. When she talks down the pagan judge before whom she is arraigned, he tells her, with a malicious pun, that "cessabunt verba, cum ventum erit ad verbera." She replies that God will provide words for those who live chastely. He counters by threatening to have her carried off to a brothel so that the Holy Spirit will depart from the violated temple. She has a good answer for this, too.

30. The Quignonez Breviary early in the sixteenth century and the Colbertine Breviary late in the seventeenth were radical attempts to restore the readings from scripture.

31. *The Two Liturgies, A.D. 1549, and A.D. 1552*, ed. Joseph Ketley, Parker Society (Cambridge University Press, 1854), p. 17.

32. But in the *Book of Common Prayer* of 1559, in Elizabeth's Latin Prayer Book

(1560), and in the New Calendar (1561), the readings from Genesis are shortened and returned to the period between Septuagesima Sunday and the fourth sunday of Lent. Lucy's name reappears in the New Calendar, which also changes the reading from Isaias on her day from chapter 32 to chapter 39. See *Liturgies and Occasional Forms of Prayer . . .* , ed. William K. Clay, Parker Society (Cambridge University Press), 1856.

33. See p. 83, above.

34. Dom Ernest Graf, O.S.B., *The Church's Daily Prayer* (London, 1938), p. 38.

PETERSON, "John Donne's *Holy Sonnets* and the Anglican Doctrine of Contrition"

1. Louis L. Martz, *The Poetry of Meditation* (New Haven: Yale University Press, 1954); Helen Gardner, *John Donne: The Divine Poems* (Oxford: Clarendon Press, 1952).

2. All quotations from the *Holy Sonnets* are from Miss Gardner's edition.

3. Miss Gardner's conclusions concerning her classifications of the *Holy Sonnets* are as follows: (1) Of the first group of twelve: "I suggest that it is impossible when one reads these twelve sonnets in the order in which they were printed in the first edition, and as they appear in the two groups of manuscripts which have the higher authority, to resist the conclusion that they were intended to be read as a consecutive set of twelve, made up of two contrasted sets of six." (2) Of the four sonnets interpolated in the edition of 1635: "Read together, as I have printed them, they are seen to be, if not so obviously a sequence, at least four sonnets on a single subject. They are all penitential and are linked by their common emphasis on sin and tears for sin. They also handle, in the manner of a meditation, a traditional subject for meditation." (3) Of the Westmoreland sonnets: They "are entirely unconnected with each other" and "really deserve to be called 'separate ejaculations' . . . they are also quite distinct in their inspiration from the sixteen which precede them in the manuscript. They owe nothing in either subject or treatment to the tradition of formal meditation. The first is highly personal, on the death of Donne's wife; the second is a prayer to Christ for unity in his Church; the third is again purely personal, but is analytic and not devotional" (xli-xlii).

4. *RES*, New Series, V (January 1954), 74-83.

5. *The Sermons of John Donne*, ed. Evelyn M. Simpson and George R. Potter (Berkeley: University of California Press, 1953), VI, 113.

6. *Catholic Encyclopedia*, "Contrition."

7. *The Sermons of John Donne*, I, 203-04.

8. See Richard Hooker, *The Works of Richard Hooker* (Oxford: Clarendon Press, 1865), II, 239-40.

9. Gardner, xvi.

10. *The Works of Richard Hooker*, II, 240.

11. *The Sermons of John Donne*, VI, 106.

12. Miss Gardner observes that "meditation, designed to deepen religious fear, needs to be followed by a meditation to awaken love" (Introduction, xlii), but she does not develop the point in any way that suggests she is aware of the disciplines of contrition that I have been discussing.

13. Donne's conjecture as to whether or not the souls of the dead perceive intuitively is also relevant to the subject of contrition, specifically, to the question of assurance. Contrition is a matter of inner conviction, achieved only with the aid of grace, and, consequently, supra-rational. It cannot, therefore, be perceived through the senses, but only intuitively, a mode of knowing possessed only by God, angelic substances, and, perhaps, by the souls of the dead. The point that Donne makes im-

plicitly is this: although his sorrow may appear outwardly to be proper, the only real evidence is the feelings of his own heart; thus only God, angels, and perhaps the souls of the dead can know whether his assurance is justified.

14. Gardner, xli.

15. To maintain that the sonnet is inspired by the desire to fulfill the obligations of contrition does not contradict Miss Gardner's excellent explication of the poem. See Appendix C in her edition, pp. 121-27.

16. *Caelica*, CIX, *Poems and Dramas of Fulke Greville*, ed. Geoffrey Bullough (New York: Oxford University Press, 1945), I, 152-53.

17. Hooker describes the effects of over-scrupulosity: "Now there are . . . others, who doubting not of God's mercy toward all that perfectly repent, remain notwithstanding scrupulous and troubled with continual fear, lest defects in their own repentance be a bar against them. These cast themselves first into very great, and peradventure needless agonies, through misconstruction of things spoken about proportioning our griefs to our sins, for which they never think they have wept and mourned enough. . . . Yet do what they can, they are still fearful, least herein also they do not that which they ought and might." *Works*, II, 323.

18. The distinction between sorrow motivated by fear and sorrow motivated by love is familiar in Renaissance literature. Fulke Greville in *Caelica*, XCVII, confronts the same parodox that has confounded Donne and clearly states the proper resolution:

> Thy power and mercy neuer comprehended,
> Rest lively imag'd in my Conscience wounded;
> Mercy to grace, and power to feare extended,
> Both infinite, and I in both confounded;
>   Lord, I haue sinn'd and mine iniquity,
>   Deserues this hell, yet Lord deliver me.
> If from this depth of sinne, this hellish graue,
> And fatall absence from my Sauiours glory,
> I could implore his mercy, who can saue,
> And for my sinnes, not paines of sinne, be sorry:
>   Lord, from this horror of iniquity,
>   And hellish graue, thou wouldst deliuer me.   (St. 2-3)

Shakespeare also observes the distinction in *Measure for Measure*, II, iv, 30-37. Vincentio, masquerading as a friar, is anxious to see that Juliet has made full repentance. Juliet assures him that she has, but he is not satisfied; he wants assurance that her sorrow has been properly motivated:

>   . . . but lest you do repent,
> As that the sin hath brought you to this shame,
> Which sorrow is always toward ourselves, not heaven,
> Showing we would not spare heaven as we love it,
> But as we stand in fear—

At this point Juliet interrupts to assure him that her sorrow is proper:

> I do repent me, as it is an evil,
> And take the shame with joy.

Whereupon, the Duke is satisfied: "There rest."

GRENANDER, "Holy Sonnets VIII and XVII: John Donne"

1. *The Donne Tradition* (Cambridge: Harvard Univ. Press, 1930), p. 47.
2. *John Donne: The Divine Poems* (Oxford: Clarendon Press, 1952).
3. New Haven: Yale Univ. Press, 1954.
4. "The Religious Thought of Donne in Relation to Medieval and Later Traditions," *Studies in Shakespeare, Milton and Donne* (New York: Macmillan, 1925), p. 227.
5. Basic to the poem is the scholastic epistemological theory of the immediate and intuitive insight of angels, which yet is inferior to God's apprehension of the intellect and will. See Grierson's note on "The Dreame," *Poems of John Donne*, II, 34-35.
6. "Dropsy" I take to mean here "an insatiable thirst or craving"—see *OED*— not the "disease" Mrs. Joan Bennett identifies with it in her *Four Metaphysical Poets* (Cambridge: Cambridge Univ. Press, 1953), p. 36.
7. Milton Allan Rugoff, in his *Donne's Imagery: A Study in Creative Sources* (New York: Corporate Press, 1939), pp. 86-87, has noted other Holy Sonnets in which "religious devotion becomes a sexual relationship": Nos. XIX, XVIII, XIV, and XIII. Joan Bennett, pp. 26-27, makes a similar point; as do Williamson, pp. 50-51; Martz, pp. 215-216; and George Reuben Potter, "John Donne's Discovery of Himself," *University of California Publications in English*, IV (Berkeley: Univ. of California Press, 1934), 5.

CHAMBERS, "Goodfriday, 1613. Riding Westward: The Poem and the Tradition"

1. Donne's use of this figure is a comparison of the heliotrope to the soul, one following the sun, the other following the Son of God. See *The Sermons of John Donne*, ed. Potter and Simpson (Berkeley, 1953-), IV, 310 (hereafter referred to as *Sermons*).
2. Contarini, *De elementis* (Paris, 1548), fol. 26^v, as paraphrased by Lynn Thorndike, *History of Magic and Experimental Science*, V (New York, 1941), 553; Peacham, *The Compleat Gentleman*, VIII (London, 1622), p. 67; Donne, "Hymn to God my God, in my Sickness" (cf. Drake, *The World Encompassed*, ed. W. S. W. Vaux [London, 1854], pp. 72-4).
3. See M. A. Haworth, "The *Translatio Studii* in the Carolingean Renaissance," *Class. Bull.*, XXVI (1950), 52-3, and R. C. Cochrane, "Bishop Berkeley and the Progress of Arts and Learning: Notes on a Literary Convention," *HLQ*, XVII (1954), 229-249. Donne (*Sermons*, VIII, 224) applies the *translatio* to religion.
4. *Paradiso*, VI. 1-3 (tr. Lawrence Binyon). In preparing this essay, I have been endebted to Mr. John Freccero, Dept. of Romance Languages, The Johns Hopkins University, specifically for first calling this passage in Dante to my attention and for the reference to William of Conches in note 11 below.
5. Benvenuto, *Comentum*, ed. L. Lacaita (Florence, 1887), IV, 418; *Dante con l'espositione de Christoforo Landino et d'Alessandro Vellutello* (Venice, 1596), p. 301^r.
6. Ed. C. Giannini (Pisa, 1858-62), III, 158-9.
7. *The Garden of Cyrus*, IV, ed. John Carter (Cambridge, 1958), pp. 96-7.
8. *Ibid.*, pp. 106-7.
9. *Timaeus*, 44d, tr. R. G. Bury (Loeb).
10. Those who have studied the history of microcosmic thought claim that it is found in the pre-Socratics, but the evidence is necessarily fragmentary, and in any case there is nothing quite like this before Plato. See George P. Conger, *Theories of Macrocosm and Microcosm in the History of Philosophy* (New York, 1922) and

Rudolf Allers, "Microcosmos from Anaximandros to Paracelsus," *Traditio*, II (1944), 319-407. Hereafter I occasionally group references together at the end of paragraphs.

11. Plutarch, *De vir. mor.*, III (and see *De animae procreatione in Timaeo*, especially chapter XXIV); Philo, *Quis rer. div.*, XLVIII, tr. F. H. Colson, *Works*, IV, 399 (Loeb); *Corpus hermeticum*, X. 11 in *Hermetica*, ed. and tr. Walter Scott (Oxford, 1924), I, 195; Plotinus, *Enneads*, II.ii.2, tr. Stephen MacKenna, rev. B. S. Page (New York, n.d.), p. 90 (and see II.iii.5; IV.iii.12; IV.iv.36); Proclus, *In Platonis Timaeum commentaria*, 235 f., ed. Ernest Diehl (Leipzig, 1904), II, 310; *Platonis Timaeus commentatore Chalcidio*, XCV and CCIII, ed. Ioh. Wrobel (Leipzig, 1876), pp. 167 and 244; William of Conches, quoted by J. M. Parent, *La Doctrine de la création dans l'école de Chartres* (Paris and Ottawa, 1938), p. 163; "Ein Timaeoskommentar in Sigtuna," ed. Toni Schmid, *Classica et Mediaevalla*, X (1949), 249; Ficino, *Divini Platoni opera omnia* (Frankfurt, 1602), p. 1036.

12. Macrobius, *Saturnalia*, VII.ix (the *Commentary on the Dream of Scipio*, I.vi.47 says that the eastward movement of the planets is needed to counteract the swift motion of the sphere above; this view also proves to be common in later times; see, e.g., Isidore of Seville, *Etymologiae*, III.xxxiv); Boethius, *op. cit.*, III, met. ix (see also III, met. xi); Pseudo-Aquinas is printed in Aquinas, *Opera omnia* (New York, 1948-1950 [=Parma, 1864]), XXIV, 82; Dionysius, *Opera omnia* (Montreuil, 1896-1935), XXVI, 376; pseudo-Johannes Scotus is quoted by E. T. Silk, "Pseudo-Johannes Scotus, Adalbold of Utrecht, and the Early Commentaries on Boethius," *Medieval and Renaissance Studies*, III (1954), 29, from his edition in *Papers and Monographs of the American Academy in Rome*, IX (1935).

13. Aristotle, *op. cit.*, 434a, ed. W. D. Ross (Oxford, 1951), pp. 82-3. Ignoring the problem of ὥσπερ σφαίρα for the moment, an almost literal translation would be this: Sometimes this desire conquers and moves that one, but sometimes that one [conquers and moves] this one, whenever there is incontinence. W. S. Hett, working from a text which reads νικᾷ δ' ἐνίοτε καὶ τὴν βούλησιν . . . translates "In fact it [appetence] sometimes conquers and moves the will. But when one appetence controls another, as one celestial sphere controls another, is the occasion when incontinence occurs" (Loeb). Sophonia, *Commentaria in Aristotelem Graeca*, XXIII, pars I (Berlin, 1883), 145; Simplicius, *Ibid.*, XI (1882), 310; Themistius, *Ibid.*, V, pars III (1889), 121. I am aware that my translation is awkward; so is the Greek:

ποτὲ μὲν ἡ ἄλογος τὴν λογικήν, ποτὲ δὲ τοὔμπαλιν, κινεῖ δὲ ἡ κρατοῦσα
τὴν κρατουμένην οὐ παύουσα τῆς ὁρμῆς ἀλλὰ συμπεριάγουσα ἑαυτῇ,
ὥσπερ ἐπὶ τῆς σφαίρας τῆς οὐρανίας ἡ τῶν ἀπλανῶν τὴν πλανήτων
οὐχ ἵστησιν, ἄλλα κινουμένη ἰδίαν κίνησιν ὅμως ἑαυτῇ συμπεριάγει.

14. Averroes, *Commentarium magnum in Aristotelis De anima libros*, ed. F. Stuart Crawford (Cambrdige, Mass., 1953), p. 530; Moerbeke's translation of Themistius is edited by G. Verbeke, *Corpus latinum commentariorum in Aristotelem graecorum*, I (Louvain and Paris, 1957); Moerbeke's translation of Aristotle is printed in Aquinas, *Opera omnia*, XX, 138; Aquinas, *Ibid.*, XX, 139 (see also, *De motibus corporum caelestium*, *Opera*, XXIV, 218); Albertus, *Physicorum libri VIII*, VIII.i.9 and *De anima*, III.iv.9 in *Opera omnia* (Lyons, 1651), II, 323 and III, 180; Suarez, *De anima*, V.x.4 and V.x.7 in *Opera omnia*, III (Paris, 1861), 778, 779; *Commentarii Collegii Conimbricensis Societatis Iesu in tres libros De anima Aristotelis*, 3rd ed. (Cologne, 1600), pp. 527, 537, 545.

15. *The Sphere of Sacrobosco and its Commentators*, ed. Lynn Thorndike (Chicago, 1949), pp. 86, 215, 302, 378.

16. Moses Maimonides, *Guide for the Perplexed,* I.lxxii, tr. F. Friedländer, 2nd ed. (New York, 1956), pp. 118-9; Alain, *PL,* CCX.866 (for the *De planctu* passage, see column 443); Vincent *op. cit.,* III.29 (Douay, 1624), col. 180; Duns Scotus, *Quaestiones in libros Physicorum Aristotelis,* VIII.vii in *Opera omnia,* III (Paris, 1891), 441; Geminiano, *Summa de exemplis,* I.xxxiii (Antwerp, 1630), p. 42ᵛ; Bonaventura, *Collationes in hexaemeron,* VI.19 in *Obras de San Buenventura,* ed. Leon Amoros, *et al.,* III, 2nd ed. (Madrid, 1957), 310 (and see also XVI.7, XXII.40). This paragraph represents no more than a selection of medieval material; a few other examples may be mentioned here. Origen writes that there are stars placed within the heaven of our heart (*PG,* XII.47; see also col. 449). Pseudo-Dionysius has an important passage on the spiral movement of the soul (*De div. nom.,* IV.ix). The author of the *Mundi constitutio* knows that man is a microcosm but is uncertain whether he is a small world because composed of the four elements "aut sphaerico motu" (*PL,* XC.907). Ibn Gabirol thinks that the orbit of the particular soul follows that of the universal world (*Fons vitae,* III 58, ed. Baeumker, *Beiträge z. Ges. d. Phil. d. Mittelalters,* Band I, Heft, 2-4 [Münster, 1895], p. 209). St. Hildegard has a long passage on the spheres (*PL,* CXCVII. 814) as does Godefridus of St. Victor (*Microcosmus,* XXXVI, ed. Delhaye [Lille, 1951], p. 58). John of Salisbury has a brief discussion of the "same" and the "other" (*PL,* CXCIX.952).

17. Ficino, *op. cit.,* XV.9 (Paris, 1559), p. 269ᵛ; the passage quoted from Pico is *Heptaplus,* IV.1, ed. Garin (Florence, 1942), p. 270 (the *In astrologiam* passage is III.4); Agrippa, *De occulta philosophia,* II.28 (Lyons, ?1531), p. 249; *The Hermetical and Alchemical Writings of . . . Paracelsus,* tr. Waite (London, 1894), I, 173 (see also I, 122, note; I, 53, note; II, 285); Bruno "To the Principles of the Universe," tr. Sidney Greenberg, *The Infinite in Giordano Bruno* (New York, 1950), p. 88; Kepler, *Harmonices mundi libri V,* V.10 in *Opera omnia,* ed. Frisch, V. (Frankfurt, 1874), 326 (see also IV.1 [pp. 220-1] for a reference to Timaean spheres). A few other examples from the Renaissance are worth noting. Nicolas of Cusa compares the motive force of heavenly bodies to intellect, the motive force in man (*De visione Dei,* XXIV; see also *De docta ignorantia,* II.x). Leone Ebreo has a lengthy discussion of the microcosm and a brief one of the spheres (*Dialoghi d'amore,* ed. Caramella [Bari, 1929], p. 93). Francesco Giorgio uses the analogy as one part of an extremely detailed system of correspondences (*De harmonia mundi totius,* I.vi.22 [Venice, 1525], p. 116ʳ). Scaliger finds it profitable to argue about the heavenly motions by first stating what human motions are like (*De subtilitate,* LXIX [Frankfurt, 1576], I, 258). See further Southwell, *Complete Poems,* ed. Grosart (1872), p. 28; John Davies of Hereford, *Complete Works,* ed. Grosart (1878), "The Muses Sacrifice," p. 28; Sylvester's *Dubartas His Divine Weekes & Workes,* I.iv (London, 1608), p. 111; Daniel, "Musophilus," 517-8; Chapman, *Hero and Leander,* III.238-9; Fludd, *Philosophia Moysaica,* quoted by A. E. Waite, *The Secret Tradition in Alchemy* (London, 1926), p. 13; *Works of Giles and Phineas Fletcher,* ed. Boas (Cambridge, 1908), II, 247; Joseph Beaumont, *The Minor Poems,* ed. Robinson (Boston, 1914), p. 388; Traherne, *Centuries, Poems, and Thanksgivings,* ed. Margoliouth (Oxford, 1958), II, 203.

18. Hall, *Occasional Meditations* (London, 1633), pp. 3-4 and *Meditations and Vows,* III.i in *Works,* ed. Wynter (Oxford, 1863), VII, 487; Pope, *Essay on Man,* III. 313-6; Wordsworth, *The Prelude* (1850), VIII.430-2.

19. My text is from *The Divine Poems,* ed. Helen Gardner (Oxford, 1952).

20. The classical texts have been collected and discussed by A. O. Lovejoy and George Boas, *A Documentary History of Primitivism* (Baltimore, 1935), pp. 290-314.

21. Plutarch, *De Iside et Osiride,* XXXII; Proclus, *In Platonis Timaeum commentaria,*

12d (*ed. cit.*, I, 75). Lucan, like the Egyptians, seems to think that the left is south (*Phar.*, III.247-8). The Greeks also looked upon the west as dangerous ground: "All beyond that bourne [Hercules' Pillars] cannot be approached either by the wise or the unwise. I shall not pursue it; else may I be deemed a fool" (Pindar, *Olym.*, iii.43-5).

22. *De divinitate*, II.39.

23. *Odyssey*, IX.236; *Annales*, II.5.

24. *Iliad*, XII.237-40; Plato, *Laws*, VII (760d); Aristotle, *De caelo*, II.ii. In the *Timaeus* (36c), Plato says that motion from east to west is to the right, and in the *Epinomis* (987b)—if, of course, that work is truly Plato's—says just the opposite. The meaning of the phrase ἐπὶ δέξια has been much argued over, however; see Alice F. Braumlick, "'To the Right' in Homer and Attic Greek," *Amer. Jour. of Phil.*, LVII (1936), 245-60.

25. Aristotle, *De caelo*, II.ii. Aristotle's position on the top and bottom of the world is later followed by the middle ages (e.g., Bede, *PL*, XC.209-10 and Aquinas, *Opera*, XIX, 85).

26. *Stobaei hermetica*, XXIV (*ed. cit.*, I, 503); Chalcidius, XCIII (*ed. cit.*, pp. 164-5). Cf. also Leone Ebreo, p. 86 for the world as a stretched-out man.

27. *Die Fragmente der grieschischen Historiker*, ed. Jacoby, IIIA (Leiden, 1940), 153-4 (the source is Plutarch's *Quaest. Rom.*, LXXVIII); Dionysius, *Ant. Rom.*, II.v.5.

28. Livy, I.xviii.6-8; Servius on *Aen.*, II.693.

29. *Hist. nat.*, II.55 (see also VI.24).

30. *PL*, CXI.261.

31. Gregory, *PL*, LXXVI.808-9 says merely that the four directions may be understood as the four virtues, but Bonaventura, *Collationes in hexaemeron*, VI.14-8 calls for a parcelling out of the virtues, temperance to the east, prudence to the south, etc.

32. Origen, *PG*, XII.665; Augustine, *PL*, XXXVI.68-9. And see: Gregory, *PL*, LXXVI.26; *Allegoriae in universam Sacram Scripturam*, *PL*, CXII.860; *Glossa ordinaria*, *PL*, CXIII.1254; Rupert of Deutz, *PL*, CLXVIII.231; Alain de Lille, *PL*, CCX.133, 706.

33. *Anglo-Saxon Poetic Records*, ed. Krapp and Dobbie, I (New York, 1931), 11; *Paradise Lost*, V.755-60; Spenser, *F.Q.*, II.ii.19; Beaumont, *The Minor Poems*, p. 181 (italics mine).

34. Gregory, *PL*, LXXVI.436 and LXXIX.516; *Allegoriae in universam Sacram Scripturam*, *PL*, CXII.869; Garnerus of St. Victor, *PL*, CXCIII.56-9; Alain de Lille, *PL*, CCX.715-6, 857.

35. *Religious Art in France of the Thirteenth Century* (New York, 1958), pp. 5-6. See also Rabanus Maurus, *PL*, CVIII.1154; *Glossa ordinaria*, *PL*, CXIII.1015.

36. Origen, *PG*, XII.981-2; Jerome, *PL*, XXV.1458. See Cyril of Jerusalem, *PG*, XXXIII.1073; Gregory, *PL*, LXXVI.167; Haymo of Halberstadt, *PL*, CXVII.240; Hugh of St. Cher, *Opera omnia in universam Vetus, & Novum Testamentum* (Venice, 1703), V, 217ᵛ.

37. Beaumont, *Minor Poems*, p. 135.

38. Lactantius, *PL*, VI.307-8; Eucherius, *PL*, L. 740-2; Rabanus Maurus, *PL*, CXI. 260-1; Hugh of St. Victor, *PL*, CLXXVI.640-2 (see also cols. 678 and 684); Durandus, *Rat. div.*, IV.24 (Lyons, 1578), pp. 117ʳ-8ʳ.

39. Pico, *De hominis dignitate*, ed. Garin (Florence, 1942), p. 128 (the translation is by E. L. Forbes, printed in *The Renaissance Philosophy of Man*, ed. Cassirer [Chicago, 1948], p. 236); Paracelsus, *op. cit.*, I, 218, note; Donne, *Sermons*, IX 70. See also Andrewes, XCVI *Sermons*, 4th ed. (London, 1641), p. 509.

40. "Who sees God's face must die": Aquinas (*S. T.*, Part I, Q. xii, Art. 4) argues that a vision of self-existent being (Donne's "self-life") is granted only to those to

whom God unites himself; Donne believes that a vision of God's essence is impossible: "only in heaven shall God proceed to this . . . manifestation, this revelation of himself" (Sermons, VIII, 232); "no man can see God in this world, and live, but no man can see God in the next world, and dye" (Sermons, IV, 168); "no man ever saw God and liv'd; and yet, I shall not live till I see God; and when I have seen him I shall never die" (Fifty Sermons [London, 1649], XIV.117). Relevant texts on Nature as God's lieutenant would be: Alain de Lille, De planctu naturae; Chaucer Parliament of Foules; Hooker, Ecclesiastical Polity, I.iii.4; Davies, "The Immortality of the Soul," V.vi; Browne, Religio Medici, I.xvi. On the antipodes, see Armand Rainaud, Le continent austral (Paris, 1893). The blood is "ordinarily received to be sedes animae, the seat and residence of the soul," says Donne, (Sermons, IV, 294), a statement with which Burton would have agreed (Anatomy, I.i.4). Christ's blood was not, however, the seat of his soul, for—according to Donne—the shedding of his blood did not cause his death; rather, Christ had to give up his soul voluntarily, and his divine soul remained with him in the bloodless grave; see Biathanatos (New York, 1930), pp. 189-91; Sermons, II, 208-9; III, 103, 106; IV, 104, 332; VI, 155; IX, 348. Christ's blood transforms dust into dirt because dust is dry while dirt is moist (OED).

41. Sermons, II, 170. Cf. Sermons, III, 308: "I see those hands stretched out, that stretched out the heavens, and those feet racked, to which they that racked them are foot-stooles; I heare him, from whom his nearest friends fled, pray for his enemies, and him, whom his Father forsooke, not forsake his brethren; I see him that cloathes this body with his creatures, or else it would wither, and cloathes this soule with his Righteousnesse, or else it would perish, hang naked upon the Crosse."

42. Sermons, II, 199.

CHAMBERS, "The Meaning of 'The Temple' in Donne's La Corona"

1. An Exposition of the Dominical Epistles and Gospels . . . The winter part . . . (London, 1611), p. 119.

2. See, e.g., J. F. Stedman, My Sunday Missal (New York, 1956), p. 100.

3. Helen Gardner, John Donne: The Divine Poems (Oxford, 1952), p. xxii; Louis L. Martz, The Poetry of Meditation (New Haven, 1954), pp. 107-12. My citations from La Corona are from Miss Gardner's edition.

4. PG, XIII, 1850.

5. Life of Christ, I.7, in The Whole Works of . . . Jeremy Taylor (London, 1835), I, 81.

6. PL, CLVII, 815.

7. Religio Medici, II.5; ed. J. J. Denounain (Cambridge, 1956), p. 85.

8. Augustine, PL, XXXIII, 342; Ambrose, PL, XV, 1657; Bede, PL, CXCIV, 64-66. This interpretation is so common that it has not seemed profitable to list all occurrences separately. The references to come on later points should be consulted on this one as well.

9. Cf. Donne, LXXX Sermons (London, 1640), ii, 19: "Immanuel est verbum infans, saies the Father [Bernard]; He is the ancient of daies, and yet in minority; he is the Word it selfe, and yet speechlesse; he that is All, that all the Prophets spoke of, cannot speake . . . He is Puer sapiens, but a child, and yet wiser then the elders, wiser in the Cradle, then they are in the Chaire."

10. Biblia cum glossa ordinaria . . . et interlineari (Strassburg, 1481?).

11. Ambrose, PL, XV, 1657; see also Bede, PL, XCII, 348-49; Smaragdus, PL, CII, 78; Glossa interlinearis in Biblia cum glossa ordinaria . . . et interlineari (Strassburg, 1481?); Haymon, PL, CXVIII, 122; Wernerus, PL, CLVII, 813-14; Isaac de Stella, PL, CXCIV, 1713; Dionysius Cartusianus, Opera Omnia (Montreuil, 1900), XI, 437.

12. *Biblia latina cum postillis Nicolai de Lyra* . . . (Nuremburg, 1497); Dionysius, XI, 435; "Graecus" as paraphrased by Aquinas, *Catena Aurea* (Turin, 1938), II, 45; Epiphanius, *PG*, XLI, 458; Latimer, *Sermons and Remains*, ed. G. E. Corrie for the W. F. Parker Society (Cambridge, 1848), p. 158. See also Cyril of Alexandria, *PG*, LXXII, 510.

13. Origen, *PG*, XIII, 1848; Chrysostom, *PG*, LIX, 130; Taylor, I, 80. See also Ambrose, *PL*, XV, 1657; Hugh of St. Cher, *Postillae* . . . (Venice, 1732), VI, 148.

14. *LXXX Sermons*, xl, 395. Cf. also lxxvi, 766: "The first words that are recorded in the Scriptures, to have been spoken by our Saviour, are those which he spoke to his father and mother, then when they had lost him at Jerusalem, *How is it that you sought me? knew yee not that I must be about my Fathers businesse?* . . . He lets them [his parents] know, that, if not the band of nature, nor the reverentiall respect due to parents, then, no respect in the world should hold him from a diligent proceeding in that worke which he came for, the advancing the kingdome of God in the salvation of mankinde." See also xliii, 425 and *L. Sermons* (London, 1649), xi, 85.

15. Augustine, *PL*, XXXIII, 342; Hall, *Contemplations upon . . . the New Testament*, II.i, in *The Works of Joseph Hall* (Oxford, 1837), II, 301.

16. Ambrose, *PL*, XV, 1657; *Glossa*, *PL*, CXIV, 251; Haymon, *PL*, CXVIII, 122-23; Radulphus Ardens, *PL*, CLV, 1738; Wernerus, *PL*, CLVII, 816; Hugh of St. Cher, VI, 147; Hall, II, 300.

17. *PL*, CLXV, 364.

18. Ambrose, *PL*, XVI, 827, 1474 and XVII, 1211; Leporius, *PL*, XXXI, 1225-26; Alain de Lille, *PL*, CCX, 803. Further documentation for the points covered in this note and in the following one may be found in R. E. Kaske, "*Gigas* the Giant in *Piers Plowman*," *JEGP*, LVI (1957), 177-85.

19. Augustine, *PL*, XXXVI, 161 and XXXIX, 1662-63; Cassiodorus, *PL*, LXX, 137; *Glossa*, *PL*, CXIII, 870; Peter Lombard, *PL*, CXCI, 205.

20. *L Sermons*, XI, 93. The Vulgate reading—"in sole posuit tabernaculum suum"— leads to an interpretation of "sun" as the Virgin (see notes 18 and 19 and Kaske for documentation), but Donne follows the later Protestant reading which identifies the sun with the bridegroom and hence with Christ. See *LXXX Sermons*, lxviii, 688: "This is *Tabernaculum Solis*, Here in the Christian Church, God hath set a Tabernacle for the Sunne"; and xlv, 450: ". . . when as this Sun *exultavit ut Gigas ad currendam viam.*" See xlvii, 470, for another occurrence of the *Gigas* image.

LOVE, "The Argument of Donne's *First Anniversary*"

1. Louis L. Martz, *The Poetry of Meditation* (New Haven, Conn.: Yale University Press, 1954).

2. John Donne, *The Anniversaries*, ed. Frank Manley (Baltimore: Johns Hopkins Press, 1963).

3. George Williamson, "The Design of Donne's *Anniversaries*," *Modern Philology*, LX (1963), 183-91.

4. Martz, p. 221.

5. *Ibid.*, p. 222.

6. William Empson, *Some Versions of Pastoral* (London 1935), p. 84.

7. Martz, p. 229.

8. *Ibid.*, p. 231.

9. *Ibid.*, p. 229.

10. *Ibid.*, p. 233.

11. "Fabula est quae neque veras neque veri similes continet res . . . ," *Ad. C.*
herennium de ratione dicendi I. viii. 13. See also Cicero *De inventione* I. xix. 27.

12. See *Ad herennium* III. ix. 17-x. 17 and, for the general principle involved, Milton's
elaborations of Ramus in *The Art of Logic*, II, xvii, in *Works*, Vol. XI (New York,
1935), pp. 482-85.

13. Cicero, I. xv. 20; Quintilian *Institutio oratoria* IV. v. 1-12.

14. Thomas Wilson, *The Arte of Rhetorique* (1553), ed. R. H. Bowers (facsimile ed.;
Gainesville, Fla., 1962), pp. 19-20. Wilson's concept of the proposition as "a pithie
sentence, comprehendyng in a smale roume, the some of the whole matter," does
not seem to have direct classical authority, but cf. Quintilian, III. ix. 1 ff. and IV. lv.
1-9, and Cicero *De oratore* II. lxxxi. 331.

15. *The First Anniversary*, l. 330.

16. *Ibid.*, l. 433.

17. Williamson, p. 189.

18. *Ibid.*

19. In Donne, p. 13.

20. Particularly evident in ll. 156-89.

MAHONY, "The *Anniversaries:* Donne's Rhetorical Approach to Evil"

1. In *Rhetoric*, I, 3, Aristotle's clearcut distinctions between the three types of
orations (deliberative, forensic, and epideictic) tend to render them mutually exclusive.
In light of the New Rhetoric, one is becoming increasingly aware of the confluence of
many Aristotelian rhetorical categories. See Wilbur Howell, "Renaissance Rhetoric and
Modern Rhetoric: A Study in Change," in *The Rhetorical Idiom*, ed. D. C. Bryant
(Ithaca, 1958), pp. 53-70, and *New Rhetorics*, ed. Martin Steinmann (New York, 1967).

2. Clearly, the full titles of the companion poems are expository or, at best, argumentative in an epideictic rather than a deliberative or forensic way: (1) *The First
Anniuersarie. An Anatomy of the World. Wherein, by Occasion of the Vntimely Death
of Mistris Elizabeth Drvry the Frailty and the Decay of This Whole World Is Represented.*
(2) *The Second Anniuersarie. Of the Progres of the Soule. Wherein: by Occasion of
the Religious Death of Mistris Elizabeth Drvry the Incommodities of the Soule in This
Life and Her Exaltation in the Next, Are Contemplated.* I suspect that these titles
(henceforth to be abbreviated *FA* and *SA* respectively) served as a will-o'-the-wisp
distracting critics away from the deliberative nature of the poems. Hence, in the enlightening *The Enduring Monument* (Chapel Hill, 1962), O. B. Hardison nevertheless
makes the following restrictive judgment: "Epideictic theory offers a perspective
within which the *Anniversaries* can be read without distortion" (p. 186).

3. In "The Design of Donne's *Anniversaries*" (*MP*, LX [1963], 183-91), George
Williamson has offered many fine comments on the *Anniversaries* and their relationship
to the Pythagorean tradition and to Donne's earlier "Metempsychosis." But I contend
that Williamson has not succeeded in discarding the meditative structure which Louis
Martz found in the *Anniversaries* (*The Poetry of Meditation*, rev. ed. [New Haven,
1962], pp. 211-48). Furthermore, as my paper will show, Williamson has overlooked
certain rhetorical insights that such a meditative pattern could afford.

I have been greatly aided by Frank Manley's edition, *John Donne: The Anniversaries* (Baltimore, 1963), the basis for all my textual references to the *Anniversaries*
in this paper. Manley's insights, though often deeply acute and penetrating, remain
half-realized and not fully elaborated and synthesized in terms of the poems' rhetorical
context. Of especial note is his perception of the heroine as both the realization of wisdom and the means to the realization of wisdom (see pp. 19-20 and 41-43).

4. See Harold Love's "The Argument of Donne's *First Anniversary*," *MP*, LXIV (1966), 127, 129-30. I may add that the companion poems present a somewhat divisive conception of the heroine with respect to her two defining notes: a moral exemplar and a World Soul. If she is the source of moral force for man, yet he is not asked to make any symbolic identification with her as World Soul; in this sense she is defective (*FA*, 61-62), she was afflicted by primal "Corruption." Thus the over-all direction in both poems is a spiritual flight from earth to heaven.

5. In referring to the various sections of the *Anniversaries* as the meditations, eulogies, and morals, I am following Martz's widely accepted nomenclature and out-line. See Martz, esp. pp. 222-23, 237.

6. Donne described his heroine as "the Idea of a Woman." See *Ben Jonson*, ed. C. H. Herford and Percy Simpson (Oxford, 1925), I, 133.

7. The *Essays in Divinity*, incidentally, serve to bring out some of the deeper meaning in this passage. As Evelyn Simpson asserts in her edition (*Essays in Divinity* [Oxford, 1952], p. 136), Prayer I in the first part of the *Essays* is the key to its second part, which deals with Exodus. In Prayer I, Donne sees Exodus as history, allegory (the deliverance of the Church "through the Red Sea of Christ's blood"), and as the deliver-ance of his own soul from the bondage of corruption. Donne's association of *FA* with the Song of Moses is intended to indicate that the purpose of his poem is to maintain people in goodness and to free them from the bondage of forgetfulness and sin. This reminder of Exodus is actually repeated in the beginning of *SA*. Here, though, the Biblical Red Sea and the Red Sea of Christ's blood undergo a Metaphysical transforma-tion; they flow from the head and trunk of a beheaded man, the personification of a world spiritually dead (*SA*, 9-16, 21-22). Donne capitalized "Red" presumably with the Exodus and Christ references in mind (*SA*, 10).

8. Briefly, Donne addresses a new spiritual world which tends to be somewhat rhetorically externalized from himself in *FA*, and which tends to be more fused with himself in *SA*. In the first poem, the poet as narrator (l. 59) predominantly uses a communal first person plural pronominal form (ll. 60, 61, etc.); throughout the morals, he addresses his "hearers" singly as "thou" (ll. 183, 184, etc.) and as "you" at the poem's conclusion. In *SA*, though the poet as narrator in the first person singular is stressed from the very opening line, there are many uses of the first person plural form, and most outstandingly in lines 370 and 448. In *SA*'s meditations, Donne directly talks to his own soul (ll. 45, 57, 85, etc.), which is nearly imperceptibly blended with the soul of his audience (ll. 115-16 and 183-84).

9. *John Donne: The Anniversaries*, p. 41.

10. As the later Donne said, there are various types of spectacles: "Young men mend not their sight by using old mens Spectacles; and yet we looke upon Nature, but with *Aristotles* Spectacles, and upon the body of man, but with *Galens*, and upon the frame of the world, but with Ptolemies Spectacles"—*The Sermons of John Donne*, ed. George Potter and Evelyn Simpson (Berkeley, 1953-62), VII, 260. Hereafter, references to this edition will be indicated parenthetically by volume and page number.

11. See Manley, pp. 175-76, who uses this passage as a gloss on *SA*, 27-32.

12. The following are further references to the capital importance of memory as a means of salvation: "The art of *salvation* . . . but that" (*Sermons*, II, 73); "Here then . . . to him" (II, 235); "And therefore . . . for them" (II, 237).

QUINN, "Donne's *Anniversaries* as Celebration"

1. "Notes on the Art of Poetry," in *A Garland for Dylan Thomas*, ed. Oscar Williams (New York, 1963), p. 152.

2. All quotations are from *The Anniversaries*, ed. Frank Manley (Baltimore, 1963).

3. The traditional definition of celebration which structures this essay is drawn from Josef Pieper's *In Tune with the World, a Theory of Festivity*, tr. R. and C. Winston (New York, 1965).

4. All quotations are from *The Sermons of John Donne*, ed. G. Potter and E. Simpson, 10 Vols. (Berkeley, 1952-1963). On commemoration, see also IX, 240 and X, 190.

5. "Donne's Christian Eloquence," *ELH*, 27 (Dec. 1960), 283.

6. Pedro Lain Entralgo presents the relevant views of Augustine in *La espera y la esperanza* (Madrid, 1957), pp. 48-61.

7. *Devotions upon Emergent Occasions* (Ann Arbor, 1959), pp. 107-108.

8. On the various senses of "world," cf. VI, 323-327, where Donne distinguishes *mundus magnus, mundus homines, mundus mali*, and *mundus sancti.*

9. For a more elaborate development of the paradox, see V. 292-293. Cf. the similar view of Pieper: "It is significant that according to Greek myth all great festivals had their origins in the celebration of funeral rites. And historians of religion have repeatedly pointed out that the ancient Roman festivals must not be considered simply as days of rejoicing . . . A festival becomes true festivity only when man affirms the goodness of his existence by offering the response of joy. Can it be that this goodness is never revealed to us so brightly and powerfully as by the sudden shock of loss and death?" *In Tune with the World*, p. 22.

10. O. B. Hardison, *The Enduring Monument* (Chapel Hill, 1962). My debts to this important study are extensive; however it does not seem to me that the framework of Renaissance literary theory, especially in its rhetorical aspects, is sufficient to bear the weight and breadth of Donne's poems. For an admirable critical summary of recent scholarship on the *Anniversaries* see Harold Love, "The Argument of Donne's First Anniversary," *MP*, 64 (Nov. 1966), 125-131. Obviously, I concur in his emphasis (vs that of Martz) on the eulogistic parts of the poem, as well as his point that Donne sees the death of Elizabeth not only as cause but also as consequence of the death of the world.

11. Pieper, *In Tune with the World*, pp. 17-24.

12. *Enarrationes in Psalmos*, CXLI, 18 quoted in *An Augustine Synthesis*, arranged by Erich Przywara (New York, 1958), pp. 1-2.

13. See I, 386, where the song of Moses is related to holiday, commemoration, and praise. On the song of Deborah, see IV, 179-180, and 187.

SICHERMAN, "Donne's Timeless *Anniversaries*"

1. T. S. Eliot, "Tradition and the Individual Talent," *Selected Essays, 1917-1932* (New York 1932), 4.

2. These are the main critical and scholarly works from which, as the body of this essay makes evident, I have benefited: Marjorie Hope Nicolson, *The Breaking of the Circle* (Evanston, Ill. 1950; rev. ed., New York 1960), Ch. 3; Louis L. Martz, *The Poetry of Meditation* (New Haven 1954), Ch. 6; Ralph Maud, "Donne's *First Anniversary*," *Boston University Studies in English*, II (1956), 218-25; Patrick Cruttwell, *The Shakespearean Moment* (New York 1960), Ch. 3; O. B. Hardison, Jr., *The Enduring Monument* (Chapel Hill 1962), Ch. 7; Frank Manley's edition of the *Anniversaries* (Baltimore 1963); George Williamson, "The Design of Donne's *Anniversaries*," Ch. 9 of his *Milton and Others* (Chicago and London 1965); Rosalie L. Colie, *Paradoxia Epidemica* (Princeton 1966), Ch. 13; Harold Love, "The Argument of Donne's *First Anniversary*," *Modern Philology*, LXIV (1966), 125-31. Conversations with Kathleen Ferguson, Cornell 1968, have helped immeasurably in putting Elizabeth Drury in her place. I must also acknowledge my debt to Sheldon S. Cohen and Bertram A. Levy, whose patience I tax annually.

3. Donne, *The Second Anniversarie: of The Progres of the Soule*, title-page, p. 87 in Manley's edition. All quotations of the *Anniversaries* are from that edition, cited in

n. 2; *u* and *v* have been normalized. Further references will be included in the body of this essay, *PS* standing for the second poem and *AW* for the first (subtitled "An Anatomy of the World").

4. Donne, Holy Sonnet XIV (10 in this edition), quoted from Helen Gardner's edition of *The Divine Poems* (Oxford 1952), 11.

5. Dennis Quinn insists, to the contrary, that the *Anniversaries* "are pre-eminently public poems" and that "Donne's main purpose in recalling Elizabeth is to cause the reader to remember himself": "Donne's *Anniversaries* as Celebration," *Studies in English Literature*, IX (1969), 99. My view, which seems equally if oppositely guilty of extremism, does however include a recognition of the public aspect of the poem and of its address to all souls as well as to Donne's own.

6. See Louis L. Martz, *The Poetry of Meditation*, 229-33.

7. These topics are included in Donne's "A Funerall Elegie," ll. 75, 86 (in Manley's edition of the *Anniversaries*, p. 84) and in Joseph Hall's "To the Praise of the Dead, and the Anatomy," l. 46 (in Manley's edition, p. 66). Manley remarks that Elizabeth's death was "a very great shock to her parents" (p. 3). See also another poem commemorating a young girl: "Elegie on Mrs Boulstred," ll. 49 ff. and 69 ff. in *The Poems of John Donne*, ed. Herbert J. C. Grierson, 2 vols. (Oxford 1912), I, 283-4.

8. See W. Milgate's edition of *The Satires, Epigrams, and Verse Letters* (Oxford 1967), in particular certain of the letters to the countesses of Bedford and Huntingdon. The latter is "a new starre," a "miracle," Astraea, "Elixarlike," the source of "all vertues"; Donne claims to be her "Recorder . . . or . . . Speaker" or "Prophet" (pp. 86-8). The Countess of Bedford's body thinks, for she has a "through-shine front"; she incorporates "both rich Indies," is *"Balsamum"* or "Balme"; until she rises the day is "but a grave," and her rising produces a "new world" with "new creatures"; because "verse embalmes vertue," Donne wishes to "show future time / What you were" (pp. 101, 95, 91, 92, 99). In a prose letter Donne tells *"the worthiest Lady M^{rs}* Bridget White"* that her "going away hath made *London* a dead carkasse. A Tearm and a Court do a little spice and embalme it, and keep it from putrefaction, but the soul went away in you": *Letters to Severall Persons of Honor*, ed. Charles Edmund Merrill, Jr. (New York 1910), 1-2; the letter was probably written a year or two before the *Anniversaries* (Merrill, p. 274). See also "A Feaver" and Helen Gardner's note in her edition: *The Elegies and the Songs and Sonnets* (Oxford 1965), 187.

9. "To the Countesse of Bedford," ed. Milgate, 93. It may be that the conventional metaphors in the *Anniversaries*, easy and superficially suitable, account for some of the confusions in the poems, diverting Donne's profounder explorations at times into the shallower channels of polite (if charnel) expression.

10. The phrase is of course Crashaw's (whose "shee" is *"not* impossible") in "Wishes. To his (supposed) Mistresse," in *The Poems, English, Latin, and Greek*, ed. L. C. Martin, 2nd ed. (Oxford 1957), 195. Eric LaGuardia thinks "shee" is not merely impossible but "outrageous"; although he regards the "rhetoric generated by this shee-idee" as resulting in "gaudy imprecision," he perceives correctly that "shee" functions as "a muse of relationship," "a deity of symbolic wholeness," "a goddess of analogy," and he argues that Donne in the "Anatomy" "is inquiring into the nature of poetic trope": *Diogenes*, LXII (1968), 59-60.

11. I am adopting the structural analysis (and the terminology) suggested by Louis L. Martz; see *The Poetry of Meditation*, 221-3, 236-9. Martz's account of the structure has been much criticized (for example, by Hardison, Williamson, and Love, all cited in n. 2 above) but not I think successfully demolished.

12. Dennis Quinn notes the traditional connection between memory and self-knowledge (*SEL*, IX, 98-9).

13. Donne probably meant to discriminate between the corrupt world without and the paradise within, which is compact of her virtue; and, furthermore, to imply that we exist in both, the one being our trial and the other our comfort. Hardison notes that the "Anatomy" is based on the metaphor of the Christian's second birth through baptism: "Since the Christian after conversion usually lived on in the world of mortals, he was said to 'live in the world but not of it,' and this is exactly how Elizabeth's mourners respond to her death. Although they live 'in' the old secular world that they occupied before her death, they are 'of' the new world" (*The Enduring Monument*, p. 176). But there is a gap between Donne's probable intellectual intention and his achieved emotional statement: the theory of the new world gives way to the feeling of despair.

14. The joke about "that first mariage" echoes the lines Donne wrote ten years before the "Anatomy" in his "Poêma Satyricon," "The Progresse of the Soule": "Man all at once was there by woman slaine, / And one by one we'are here slaine o'er againe / By them" (stanza x, ll. 91-3, in *The Satires*, ed. Milgate, p. 30).

15. Harold Love observes that Donne advances "two visions of Elizabeth Drury . . . in the poem—animating spirit and vulnerable body," and that "it is from the periodic collision of these images that a good part of the fascination of the poem derives" ("The Argument of Donne's *First Anniversary*," *MP*, LXIV, 131, 127). Unfortunately he uses this perception more to rationalize than to explain the "Anatomy."

16. The metaphor still serves to justify Donne's writing "The Progres" (see *PS*, ll. 39-40). It is a necessary inconsistency: Donne cannot both write the poem and follow his own advice to "forget this world" (*PS*, l. 61). Even so, in the second poem the metaphor has weakened to become the negative power of preventing putrefaction, and such metaphors cease entirely once Donne bids adieu to the manner of the "Anatomy" in his last full echo of the "morals" of the first poem (*PS*, ll. 81-4).

17. The second section of "The Progres" also has a "moral" (ll. 147-56), but it no longer has the formula, "Shee, shee is gone; shee is gone; when thou knowest this . . . thou knowest" (*PS*, ll. 81-3), which is present in every section of the "Anatomy."

18. *PS*, ll. 85-185. The concentration of command is actually even stronger, as "thinke" occurs only in the "meditations" of sections II and III—twenty-one times in section II (ll. 85-121), twelve times in section III (ll. 157-85): thirty-three times in sixty-six lines.

19. The suggestion that *PS*, l. 22, contains an "implication of maggots" is made by Manley in his commentary on that line, p. 175. Compare the later image likening man on earth to a worm feeding on the carcass-world (ll. 55-6).

20. There are still occasional lapses: any "decay" in "Gods Image . . . / Within her heart . . . / Was her first Parents fault, and not her own" (ll. 456-8). The suggestion of decay is inconsistent with her perfection.

21. I take note of but dismiss Miss Nicolson's fancy that Donne is here writing an allegorical account of the reign of Queen Elizabeth. No doubt conventional praises of the Queen helped fix the ideals Donne invokes, but that does not make these lines praise of that Queen. See *The Breaking of the Circle*, rev. ed. (New York 1960), 96-106. Marius Bewley also insists that "she" is Queen Elizabeth and offers yet wilder readings to support his theory that the *Anniversaries* partake "of the nature of a sinister private joke"; see "Religious Cynicism in Donne's Poetry," *Kenyon Review*, XIV (1952), 628-33. I cannot agree, either, with Richard E. Hughes' identification of "she" as St. Lucy: "The Woman in Donne's 'Anniversaries,'" *ELH*, XXXIV (1967), 307-26.

STANWOOD, "'Essentiall Joye' in Donne's *Anniversaries*"

1. "Ben Jonson's Conversations with William Drummond of Hawthornden," quoted in Ben Jonson, *Works*, ed. C. H. Herford and Percy Simpson, I (Oxford, 1925), 133. Donne commented in his letter "To Sir G.F.," written about 1612, that "it became me to say, not what I was sure was just truth, but the best that I could conceive" (quoted in *The Life and Letters of John Donne*, ed. Edmund Gosse [London, 1899], I, 306). Cf. T. S. Eliot's passing remark that the *Anniversaries* are "the finest of Donne's long poems," in "The Devotional Poets of the Seventeenth Century," *The Listener*, 3 (March 26, 1930), 552.

2. See Rosalie L. Colie, *Paradoxia Epidemica: The Renaissance Tradition of Paradox* (Princeton, N.J., 1966), pp. 428-429. I am indebted to Miss Colie's discussion of Donne's *Anniversaries*, and also to A. F. Bellette, "Form and Vision in Four Metaphysical Poets" (unpubl. diss., The University of British Columbia, 1968), esp. pp. 62-63. See as well Dennis Quinn, "Donne's *Anniversaries* as Celebration," *SEL*, 9 (Winter, 1969), 97-105, and especially Carol M. Sicherman, "Donne's Timeless *Anniversaries*," *UTQ*, 39 (January, 1970), 127-143. Marjorie Hope Nicolson's important study, *The Breaking of the Circle* (rev. ed., New York, 1960), Ch. 3, "The Death of a World," is nevertheless misleading. But the ambitious work by Richard E. Hughes is notably tenuous. His *The Progress of the Soul: The Interior Career of John Donne* (New York, 1968), esp. Ch. 4, "The Anniversaries," relies on slight historical and textual evidence for an archetypal or mythic explanation of the poem.

3. See P. Gregory Stevens, *The Life of Grace*, Foundations of Catholic Theology Series (Englewood Cliffs, N.J., 1963), p. 108. Cf. E. Towers, "Sanctifying Grace," in *The Teaching of the Catholic Church* (2nd ed., London, 1952), Ch. 16. Cf. also *OED*, II.6, esp. b., for its definition of "grace."

4. See *The Poetry of Meditation* (rev. ed., New Haven, Conn., 1962), p. 330, and Appendix 2, "The Dating and Significance of Donne's *Anniversaries*," a reply to Nicholson and others who have organized Donne into too careful a shape. Martz himself, whose description of the *Anniversaries* seems at times too formalistic and rigid, recognizes that "the central point of both poems lies in the assertion that religious virtue is the greatest of all human values . . . [that Donne] is celebrating the values of 'interior peace'" (p. 356).

5. O. B. Hardison, Jr., *The Enduring Monument: A Study of the Idea of Praise in Renaissance Literary Theory and Practice* (Chapel Hill, N.C., 1962), p. 186.

6. See Harold Love, "The Argument of Donne's *First Anniversary*," *MP*, 64 (1966), 125-131. He argues that Elizabeth Drury's death is cause as well as consequence of the innate corruption of the natural world, "that the death of Elizabeth has been caused by the death of the world" (p. 127).

Quotations from Donne's *Anniversaries* are from the edition by Frank Manley, *John Donne: The Anniversaries* (Baltimore, 1963). The only exception I take is typographical: I prefer to give *j* for *i* and *v* for *u*, the reverse of Manley's practice.

7. *Essays in Divinity*, ed. Evelyn M. Simpson (Oxford, 1952), p. 92.

8. "Hymne to God my God, in my sicknesse" is the notable exception. Donne thinks of himself and the poem he is writing as simultaneous offerings.

9. Ben Jonson's ode "To the immortall memorie, and friendship of that noble paire, Sir Lucius Cary, and Sir H. Morison" (from *Under-Wood*, 1640) also plays on *fall* and attempts to disclose a model life which has the perfection of the sphere:

> Alas, but *Morison* fell young:
> Hee never fell, thou fall'st, my tongue.
> Hee stood, a Souldier to the last right end,

A perfect Patriot, and a noble friend,
But most, a vertuous Sonne.
All Offices were done
By him, so ample, full, and round,
In weight, in measure, number, sound,
As though his age imperfect might appeare,
His life was of Humanitie the Spheare.

(ll. 43-52)

(Jonson, *Works*, ed. Herford and Simpson, VIII [1947], lxx.244).

10. *The Satires, Epigrams and Verse Letters*, ed. W. Milgate (Oxford, 1967), p. 13.

11. See the Commentary to his edition of *The Anniversaries*, p. 194.

12. See Robert W. Gleason, S.J., *Grace* (London, 1962), p. 3; of special interest is Appendix 4, "Grace and Philosophy."

13. Psalm 95, "Venite, exultemus Domino," stands traditionally at the beginning of the Office of Matins (or Morning Prayer in the *Book of Common Prayer*).

14. See Manley's edition of *The Anniversaries*, p. 200, which cites Ezekiel 33.1-7, and passages from Donne's sermons. The first of these, which is quoted above, occurs at the conclusion of a Lincoln's Inn Sermon (preached about 1621), in *Sermons of John Donne*, ed. George R. Potter and Evelyn M. Simpson, III Berkeley, 1957), 133. Donne preached the second of his Prebend sermons at St. Paul's on January 29, 1626, and Simpson and Potter call attention in their introduction (*Sermons*, VII [1954], 3-4) to close connections between this sermon and a number of lines of *The Second Anniversary*. The passage quoted appears near the end of the sermon (p. 69); *Venite benedicti* are the first words of Matt. 25.34.

15. Donne may indirectly be referring to the Sacrament of the Eucharist in *The Progres*, ll. 45-47. He has just looked forward to "Gods great Venite," but his "insatiate soule" must meanwhile serve its thirst "with Gods safe-sealing Bowle." See Manley's note, p. 177, which recognizes the commonplace equation of sacraments to seals. But Manley does not suggest which sacrament; the reference to Apoc. 7.3-4 is not very helpful when Donne seems more obviously to have the Eucharist in mind.

LABRANCHE, "'Blanda Elegeia': The Background to Donne's 'Elegies'"

1. E. R. Curtius, *European Literature and the Latin Middle Ages*, tr. W. R. Trask (New York, 1953), p. 187.

2. See Robert E. Hallowell, *Ronsard and the Conventional Roman Elegy* (Illinois Studies in Language and Literature, 37, 1954), especially pp. 41-7 and part 3.

3. *L'Inspiration personnelle et l'esprit du temps chez les Poètes métaphysiques anglais*, 3 vols. (1960).

4. *The Poems of John Donne*, edited by H. J. C. Grierson, 2 vols. (Oxford, 1912), II, 60-3. All quotations of Donne are taken from this edition.

5. Grierson, II, 61, 76. This title is not found until 1635.

6. *Review of English Studies*, 20 (1944), 224-7. See also W. Milgate in *N.&Q.*, 195 (1950), 246-7.

7. Grierson, II, 101-2. For the background in satire see Edmund Gosse, *The Life and Letters of John Donne*, 2 vols. (1899), I, chapter 2. For a recent consideration of the line of Petrarchan wit behind Donne, see D. L. Guss, 'Donne's Conceit and Petrarchan Wit', *P.M.L.A.*, 78 (1963), 308-14.

8. F. W. Weitzmann, 'Notes on the Elizabethan Elegie', *P.M.L.A.*, 50 (1935), 435-43.

9. George Williamson, *Seventeenth Century Contexts* (Chicago, 1961), chapter 5;

Alvin Kernan, *The Cankered Muse* (New Haven, 1959), chapters 1-3.

10. *Les Poètes métaphysiques*, III, 191, 326-8.

11. Georg Luck, *The Latin Love Elegy* (1959), chapters 2-3; H. H. Hudson, *The Epigram in the English Renaissance* (Princeton, 1947), chapter 1.

12. Ben Jonson's Poems: A Study of the Plain Style (Stanford, 1962).

13. L. P. Wilkinson, *Ovid Recalled* (Cambridge, 1955), pp. 8-10; Hermann Fränkel, *Ovid: A Poet between Two Worlds* (Berkeley, 1945), p. 6 and notes; W. A. Edward, *The Suasoriae of Seneca the Elder* (Cambridge, 1928).

14. F. Arnaldi, 'La "Retorica" nella Poesia di Ovidio', in *Ovidiana*, ed. N. I. Herescu (Paris, 1958), pp. 25-6. The phrase is originally applied to Horace, 'il simpatico shizofrenico di Orazio'.

15. Ellrodt, III, 297 ff.; *Ad Herennium*, edited by H. Caplan (Loeb Classical Library, 1954), pp. 405-9.

16. For example, *Heroides*, 2.31-44.

17. See A. A. Day, *The Origins of the Latin Love-Elegy* (Oxford, 1938), chapters 2-3.

18. The close association between love-epistle and elegy can be traced, in an age closer to Donne's, in the French poets of the 16th century, especially Clément Marot, whose poems reflect an epistolary style joined to the casuistry of courtly love. (See V.-L. Saulnier, *Les Elégies de Clément Marot* (Paris, 1952), chapter 3.)

19. This observation applies also to *Under-woods*, XVIII and XIX. For the controversy on authorship, see *The Works of Ben Jonson*, ed. Herford and Simpson, (Oxford, 1925-52), XI, 66-70; Evelyn Simpson, 'Jonson and Donne: A Problem of Authorship', *Review of English Studies*, 15 (1939), 274-82; J. B. Leishman, *The Monarch of Wit* (5th ed. 1962), pp. 66-9. The last book appears to give the authoritative discussion of Donne's *Elegies*.

20. Herford and Simpson, XI, 70.

21. For example, III, 3, 4, 10, 13 in Marlowe, translating Ovid 3.3, 4, IIa, 14. Citations are from *The Works of Christopher Marlowe*, edited by C. F. Tucker Brooke (Oxford, 1910) and the Loeb Ovid (1921).

22. Anthony Caputi, *John Marston, Satirist* (Cornell, 1961), chapters 1 and 2; Ellrodt, III, 289 ff.

23. K. Quinn, *The Catullan Revolution* (Melbourne, 1959), especially pp. 81 ff.; Luck, chapter 3.

24. See T. F. Higham, 'Ovid: Some Aspects of His Character and Aims', *Classical Review*, 48 (1934), 105-16; A. G. Lee, 'Tenerorum Lusor Amorum', *Critical Essays on Roman Literature*, edited by J. P. Sullivan (1962).

25. *Ovid*, p. 11.

26. *Ovid*, p. 21.

27. See Luck, chapter 10.

28. Ellrodt, III, 49.

29. *Baroque Lyric Poetry* (New Haven, 1961), pp. 121-37.

30. See the essay by Harold Jenkins in *Shakespeare Survey 8* (1955), 40-51.

31. For a discussion of the role of self-consciousness in the lyric, see Bruno Snell, *The Discovery of the Mind* (New York, 1960), chapter 3.

32. See A. L. Wheeler, 'Propertius as Præceptor Amoris', *Classical Philology*, 5 (1910), 28-40; *ibid.*, 440-50, and 6 (1911), 56-77.

33. See Higham, p. 114.

34. F. O. Copley, 'Emotional Conflict and its Significance in the Lesbia-Poems of Catullus', *American Journal of Philology*, 70 (1947), 22-40.

35. *Donne the Craftsman* (Paris, 1928), pp. 47 ff.

36. Grierson, I, 288.

37. *Ovid*, p. 29.

38. For example, 'Womans constancy', 'Aire and Angels', 'Breake of day', 'Twicknam garden', 'Loves Alchymie', 'The Apparition', 'The broken heart', 'The Will', 'A Ieat Ring sent'.

39. *I, III, IV, VI, VII, XI, XII, XV, XVI.*

40. Ovid, 1.6; 3.11 and 14; Propertius, 1.8, 15, 18; 2.5, 6, 8a, 13a, 18a, 19, 30, 32 and so forth (I use the Loeb numbering).

41. *Ovid*, p. 30.

42. *Review of English Studies*, 7 (1931), 69-71. In the following I use the Loeb translation of Ovid.

43. Fränkel, p. 32. See A. W. Allen, '"Sincerity" and the Roman Elegists', *Classical Philology*, 45 (1950), 145-57; H. Bardon, 'Ovide et le Baroque', in *Ovidiana*, ed. Herescu.

44. Compare the similar rhetorical structure of *Amores*, I.II. 45-8; *Heroides*, 12. 77-9.

45. Arnold Stein, *John Donne's Lyrics: The Eloquence of Action* (Minneapolis, 1962), p. 151; Ellrodt, I, 82-164.

46. The loci are *Amores*, I.I; 3.1 and 15; Jonson, ed. Herford and Simpson, VII, 108.

ANDREASEN, "Theme and Structure in Donne's *Satyres*"

1. *English Literature in the Sixteenth Century Excluding Drama* (Oxford, 1954), pp. 469-470.

2. *The Cankered Muse* (New Haven, 1959), pp. 117-118.

3. Mary Claire Randolph has stressed the dramatic qualities of classical satire in her article "The Structural Design of Formal Verse Satire," *PQ*, XXI (1942), 368-384.

4. *The Poems of John Donne*, ed. H.J.C. Grierson (Oxford, 1912); all references to Donne's poetry herein are to this edition.

5. In observing Grierson's editorial notes at the bottom of the pages of the text, the reader will note that the satires were not always placed in this order in all the manuscript editions which circulated in Donne's time; but this is the order used in the most reliable ones.

6. There may be a further implication in the accusation that the fop is like a Puritan. As the OED indicates, the title "Puritan" was considered wonderfully ironic by the right wing of the church, and the religious controversialists who set forth its position in the seventies and eighties maintained that it really meant impure or filthy.

7. John Peter, *Complaint and Satire in Early English Literature* (Oxford, 1956), p. 135.

8. This satire in particular looks forward to Donne's later meditative and devotional verse and prose. The connection between satire and devotional literature is, surprising as it seems, rather close. Both are highly dependent on the process of visualization; both have action or a change of attitude as their final goal; and both move from misery to consolation.

9. Donne probably began writing them about 1593, when he was twenty years old; for a detailed discussion of the problems of dating them, see Grierson, vol. II, pp. 100-105.

10. *Donne's Poetry and Modern Criticism* (Chicago, 1950), passim.

SLOAN, "The Persona as Rhetor: An Interpretation of Donne's *Satyre III*"

1. See Don Geiger, *The Sound, Sense, and Performance of Literature* (Chicago,

1963), Ch. vi.

2. Critics, in search of a way to put fascination with Donne's biography into a clear, literary perspective, were drawn to dramatic analyses of Donne's poetry, such as Leonard Unger's excellent analyses of some poems in *Songs and Sonets* as monologues and soliloquies, involving a "speaker"—not necessarily Donne himself—and a "situation," either general or particular (Leonard Unger, *Donne's Poetry and Modern Criticism,* Chicago, 1950). Currently it has become popular to regard Donne, that great "frequenter of Playes" and "visiter of Ladyes," as speaking from behind a mask —a *persona,* the term frequently used by modern critics for "character" or "speaker" —as he stages amorous pursuits, turmoils, and frustrations.

3. N. J. C. Andreasen, "Theme and Structure in Donne's *Satyres,"* *Studies in English Literature,* III (Winter 1963), 59-75.

4. Thomas Wilson, *The Arte of Rhetorique* (1553), fol. 16. In all quotes from Wilson and other Renaissance rhetoricians I have modernized the long *s.* Though I shall call mainly upon Wilson in this analysis, I do not mean to suggest influential relationships between his rhetoric and this poem. To a great extent, Wilson was representative of rhetoric in this period: moreover, his treatment of partitioning is the fullest to be found in rhetoric books of the period. However, I have also turned to other sources available to Donne: *De Inventione,* esp. i. 20-109; *De Oratore,* esp. i-ii; *De Partitione Oratoria,* esp. viii. 28; *Rhetorica ad Herrenium,* esp. iii; *Institutio Oratoria,* esp. iii-iv; Dudley Fenner, *The Artes of Logic and Rhetorike* (Middleburg, 1584); Abraham Fraunce, *The Lawiers Logike,* 1588; and Roland MacIlmaine, *The Logike of the Most Excellent Philosopher P. Ramvs Martyr,* 1581.

5. Wilson, fol. 34^v.

6. Wilson, fol. 55^v.

7. The text of the poem is from *The Poems of John Donne,* ed. Herbert J. C. Grierson, I (London, 1912), 154-158. Again, I have modernized the long *s.*

8. Wilson, fol. 66^v.

9. Wilson, fol. 71^v.

10. Wilson, fol. 62.

11. Fraunce (note 4, above), fol. 114.

12. *Ibid.*

13. The earliest date possible for *Satyre III* is 1593. Grierson places its composition sometime between 1594 and 1597 (II, 103).

14. It is illuminating to read the last lines of this poem, in which Donne compares Elizabeth-Power to a stream, in light of the following lines from *Satyre V* (ll. 28-30):

> Greatest and fairest Empresse, know you this?
> Alas, no more then Thames calme head
>   doth know
> Whose meades her armes drowne, or
>   whose corne o'rflow:

Though when two poems are brought together one must serve only to illuminate rather than to explain the other, it is perhaps also significant that a few years after he wrote *Satyre III,* Donne was at work on his most ambitious satire, *Progresse of the Soule,* in which he planned to trace the passage of the soul of heresy from Eve's apple to Queen Elizabeth. The illumination which this affords is to serve as a reminder that it was not until after the first decade of the seventeenth century, so crucial in the turbulent religious history of Donne the man, that Donne the poet could reveal an appreciation of Elizabeth as head of both state and church. In *Satyres III* and *V,* his *personae* speak of Elizabeth as the "calme head" of a stream; as applied in the satires, the image works two ways: in *III*, she is part of the natural order but only as head of *state* and, as such, her bounds must be known and kept; in *V*, she is, even as head of state, insensitive to and unaffected by the corruption in her own court.

15. Throughout the poem the surgeon can be seen concealing his knife. For example, concealment accounts for the relatively greater length of the "Graius" example, in which it lends both pungency and irony to the "shee" that "dwels with us," to the "*God*fathers," to the "fashions" that capture the hearts of young men, and above all to "tender" as the scornful opposite of "courage" and "valour," virtues that are part of the true subject of the poem. Also, as noted earlier, it illuminates the meaning of "easie wayes and neare / To follow" (ll. 14-15).

16. For an analysis of Donne's pulpit *personae*, see Joan Webber, *Contrary Music: The Prose Style of John Donne* (Madison, 1963), pp. 115-122. Although she is referring specifically to prose style, Miss Webber has put her finger on the source of some of our difficulties with the *personae* in Donne's poetry: "It was not possible in the late Renaissance for a man to think of himself as a unique and lonely romantic figure. An abundant egotism and individualism still willingly involved in tradition is *part* of what creates the now-you-see-it-now-you-don't character of the baroque; you are almost never really sure which is the actor or writer, and which his mask" (p. 116). As Miss Webber demonstrates, our best view is to see the *persona* in terms of the rhetorical requirements of the discourse.

17. For a rhetorical analysis of the structure of Marvell's ode, see John M. Wallace, "Marvell's Horatian Ode," *PMLA*, LXXVIII (March 1962), 33-45. Wallace differentiates the rhetoric from the poetry in Marvell's ode by associating "the rhetoric with the formal [i.e., structural] intention of the ode (to persuade readers of Cromwell's vocation) and the poetry with the verbal detail by which a simple intention is sustained within a complex variety of ideas and feelings. . . . The ode is a fine poem not because it moves in so orderly a manner and has a clear 'intention,' but because Marvell's invention, disposition, and diction—in short, his imagination—are employed so freely and richly within the limitations of a formal pattern" (p. 44). Such a criterion proves the poetical excellence of Donne's poem, too.

18. See *Coleridge on the Seventeenth Century*, ed. Roberta Florence Brinkley (Durham, N. C., 1955), p. 654. Concerning *Satyre III*, Coleridge said, "If you would teach a scholar in the highest form how to *read*, take Donne, and of Donne this satire. When he has learnt to read Donne, with all the force and meaning which are involved in the words, then send him to Milton, and he will stalk on like a master *enjoying* his walk" (p. 521). Such advice is no less meaningful for the modern student of interpretation. That Coleridge read Donne aloud to his friends has been reported by one of his contemporaries, who upon hearing Coleridge read Donne's satirical *Progresse of the Soule* found "somewhat unaccountable" Coleridge's "fit of enthusiasm for Donne's poetry" —Donne's poem sounded like wild and drunken ravings to ears nicely attuned to romantic harmonies (p. 529).

19. Even Donne's poetic masterpieces, the two *Anniversaries*, which in the past were brilliantly analyzed for their meditative structures (Louis L. Martz, *The Poetry of Meditation*, New Haven, 1954), have recently been viewed for the ways in which they satisfy Donne's contemporaries' expectations for epideictic, or demonstrative, oratory (O. B. Hardison, Jr., *The Enduring Monument* [Chapel Hill, 1962], Ch. vii).

NOVARR, "Donne's 'Epithalamion Made at Lincoln's Inn': Context and Date"
   1. *The Poems of John Donne* (Oxford, 1912), II. lxxxi, n. 2.

2. Ibid., p. 99.

3. *The Poems of John Donne* (Oxford, 1933), 'Note on the Text and Canon', p. 1.

4. *The Poems of John Donne* (1912), ii. 91; *The Divine Poems* (Oxford, 1952), p. lxxix.

5. 'John Donne and Lincoln's Inne, 1591-1594', *T.L.S.*, 16 Oct. 1930, p. 833, and 23 Oct. 1930, p. 861.

6. 'The Date of Donne's Travels' in *A Garland for John Donne*, ed. Theodore Spencer (Cambridge, Mass., 1931), pp. 121-51. Mr. Sparrow thinks there is a 'strong probability' that Donne left London before Christmas (p. 133), but he settles on 1595-6 (p. 134) to reconcile his date with Grierson's suggestion that indications in the Satires and Elegies make it probable that Donne was in London during 1594 and 1595 (*The Poems of John Donne* (1933), p. xvi).

7. Mr. Bald's evidence is based on an action in Chancery which Donne brought in 1598 against one Christopher Danby, a gentleman of Yorkshire (P.R.O., C. 3, 266/93). It was presented in a paper, 'Donne's Travels', read before the English VI group of the Modern Language Association in New York on 29 Dec. 1948. I am indebted to Mr. Bald for sending me his manuscript and permitting me to quote from it.

8. *The Divine Poems*, pp. lxiv-lxv.

9. Cited by A. Wigfall Green in *The Inns of Court and Early English Drama* (New Haven, 1931), p. 113. Browne's words 'please ourselves in private' do not imply that his masque was performed exclusively for the members of the Inner Temple. Many guests had been invited to the performance. See J. Bruce Williamson, *The History of the Temple, London* (London, 2nd edn., 1925), p. 314.

10. Green, p. 12. Williamson says (p. 174) that the Inner Temple records for 1561-2 refer to sums laid out for 'maskes, playes, disquysinges or other like' (*sic*).

11. W. P. Baildon, ed., *The Records of the Honorable Society of Lincoln's Inn. The Black Books* (London, 1897-1902), i. 4. Hereafter these volumes are referred to as *Black Books*.

12. Ibid., p. 18. It is difficult to generalize about the frequency and the occasions of revelling because of the nature of the records in the *Black Books*. These are mainly concerned with promulgations, appointments, fines, and accounts; customary procedures can only be inferred. An entry of 5 Nov. 1566 refers to All Saints and Candlemas as 'the two principall festes' (p. 353). In 1614, All Saints, Candlemas, and Ascension weeks are called 'graund weekes' and Trinity Sunday is called a 'graund day', but only when Midsummer Day is not in term. If Midsummer Day fell in Trinity Term, it, rather than Trinity Sunday, was celebrated as a grand day (ii. 166). In 1622 reference is made to 'the 4 festivall Graund Dayes' (ii. 235).

13. Ibid., i. 291 (*anno* 1549).

14. i. 306 (*anno* 1553).

15. ii. xxviii, 131 (*anno* 1610).

16. ii. 16; also i. 295; ii. 22, 43, 91, 102, &c.

17. ii. 115.

18. i. 313, 316, 321, 324.

19. i. 273 (*anno* 1546).

20. i. 329.

21. 'The Maner of Rejoysings at Mariages and Weddings', bk. i, chap. xxvi.

22. The Latin epithalamion of Secundus is a real bedding ballad which starts at the wedding couch, describes in detail similar to that of Carew's 'The Rapture' the amorous combat, and ends with a stanza of hope that the marriage may be fruitful.

23. See Robert H. Case, *English Epithalamies* (London, 1896), p. xxi, and Cortlandt

Van Winkle, *Spenser's Epithalamion* (New York, 1926), pp. 6-7, 19.

24. See Van Winkle's edition of the *Epithalamion* and also James A. S. McPeek, 'The Major Sources of Spenser's *Epithalamion*', *J.E.G.P.*, xxxv (1936), 183-213.

25. Grierson says that Donne comes nearer to Spenser in the epithalamia than in any other kind of poem (*The Poems*, ii. 91), and Professor Osgood thinks that Donne here imitates Spenser's metre and design (*The Works of Edmund Spenser, Variorum Edition; The Minor Poems*, ii (Baltimore, 1947), 659).

26. See Sir Henry Ellis's revision and enlargement of John Brand's *Observations on the Popular Antiquities of Great Britain* (London, 1877), i. 298-308.

27. Cited in Brand, i. 318. The reference is to Dekker's third day's triumph, 'Candle-light, or The Nocturnall Tryumph'.

28. See *Malone Society Collections III* (Oxford, 1954), pp. xxiii, 36.

29. Robert Withington, *English Pageantry*, i (Cambridge, Mass., 1918), 44-47.

30. Brand, i. 326-8.

31. i. 310.

32. i. 311, 314-15, 330 ff.

33. See the statement by Horace Howard Furness, ed., *A Midsummer Nights Dreame*, vol. x of *Variorum Shakespeare* (Philadelphia, 1895), p. v.

34. Williamson, p. 119, n. 3.

35. For the conjunction of Midsummer with St. John's Day, see Brand, i. 298-305.

36. For example, at Lincoln's Inn, the appointed Stewards of Christmas were fined in 1586 and in 1587 (*Black Books*, ii. 5, 9). At the Inner Temple it was customary to reappoint annually for several years the same persons to Christmas offices, and the same persons were repeatedly fined for not appearing (Williamson, pp. 442-3, 209).

37. *Black Books*, ii. 1, 5.

38. During Donne's residence at Lincoln's Inn, the custom of keeping Christmas in all its ancient grand ceremonial seems to have been largely discontinued. In 1597 some sort of 'shew' was presented (ibid., p. 55), but with reference to the omission of a solemn Christmas in 1595 Baildon notes: 'This custom of keeping solemn or grand Christmas seems to have been given up' (ibid., p. 44).

It is possible that Donne spent Christmas 1594 frolicking at Gray's Inn, for this was the year that the gentlemen of Gray's kept up their merriment from 20 December until Shrove Tuesday (Green, pp. 73, 99). To be sure, the gentlemen of Gray's had invited only the gentlemen of the Inner Temple to join their festivities, but gentlemen at the other Inns may have been attracted by the noise and have tried to participate.

39. Sir Richard Baker's description of Donne at Lincoln's Inn, in *A Chronicle of the Kings of England* (London, 1643), p. 156.

STAPLETON, "The Theme of Virtue in Donne's Verse Epistles"

1. The dating of Donne's *Letters to Severall Personages* (which for convenience I refer to as his verse epistles) has in many cases not been established. In this article, I have accepted Professor R. C. Bald's assignment of one group of epistles to the earlier part of the decade 1590-1600 ("Donne's Early Verse Letters," *Huntington Library Quarterly*, XV (1952), 283-89). Otherwise, I have usually been guided by the dates suggested by Professor Herbert J. C. Grierson in the notes of his edition, *The Poems of John Donne*, 2 vols. (Oxford, 1912). All citations from Donne's poems in my text will be from this edition.

2. Grierson, II, 140-1.

3. Quoted from Donald M. Frame, *Montaigne's Discovery of Man* (New York, 1955), pp. 35-36, a study particularly valuable for its reappraisal of Montaigne's stoicism.

4. *Letters to Severall Persons of Honor,* ed. Charles E. Merrill, Jr. (New York, 1910), p. 84.

5. *The Dialogues of Plato,* trans. by Benjamin Jowett, 3d ed., 5 vols. (New York, 1892), I, 150-51.

6. *Ibid.,* pp. 172-3.

7. *Laws* XII, 694; *ibid.* V, 335.

8. *Biathanatos,* Reproduced fr. First Edition, with a Bibliographical Note by J. William Hebel (New York, 1930), p. 58.

9. Noted by Mary Paton Ramsay, *Les Doctrines médiévales chez Donne* (London, 1917), p. 295. Mrs. Evelyn Simpson, *A Study of the Prose Works of John Donne,* 2nd ed. (Oxford, 1948), states that "Donne's knowledge of Greek authors was confined to those whom he knew in Latin translations" (p. 54). She adds that in *Pseudo-Martyr,* Donne uses a Latin translation of Plato by Serranus.

10. Among other references to Paracelsus, Grierson cites two important parallels in his notes (II, 154-55). See also W. A. Murray, "Donne and Paracelsus," *Rev. Eng. Studies,* XXV (1949), 115-23, a detailed analysis of Paracelsian elements in two of the *Songs and Sonnets,* "Love's Alchymie" and "A Nocturnall upon S. Lucies Day"; A. Rugoff, *Donne's Imagery* (New York, 1939), *passim*; Professor Marjorie H. Nicolson, *The Breaking of the Circle* (Evanston, 1950), pp. 15-16, 83; Charles M. Coffin, *John Donne and the New Philosophy* (New York, 1937), pp. 20, 173.

Donne owned a copy of Paracelsus's *Chirurgia Magia,* which was one of the first books sold after his death. See Geoffrey Keynes, *A Bibliography of John Donne,* 2nd ed. (Cambridge, 1932), Appendix III, 319 (p. 178). Further information may be obtained when the list of Donne's books in the Middle Temple has been added to the forthcoming edition of Keynes's *Bibliography.* Professor R. C. Bald discovered the location of these books; a brief preliminary description is given by John Sparrow, "Donne's Books in the Middle Temple," *T.L.S.,* July 29 and August 5, 1955. It will be of interest to see whether he owned a copy of the works of Leonicenus, the disciple of Ficino with whom Paracelsus had studied at Ferrara.

11. *Biathanatos,* p. 216.

12. *Letters to Severall Persons of Honor,* pp. 84-85.

13. John Donne, *Divine Poems,* ed. with introd. and commentary by Helen Gardner (Oxford, 1952).

14. *Hermetic and Alchemical Writings of . . . Paracelsus,* trans. by Arthur E. Waite, 2 vols. (London, 1894), I, 131 n. Note that in the second of these two passages the plural, "virtues," represents an old word in the alchemists' and physicians' vocabulary and does not carry all the strength of *virtus* or life-force in the singular.

15. Waite, I, 21 and 21n.

16. "Concerning the Nature of Things," Book IV. Waite, I, 135.

17. Paul Kristeller, *The Classics and Renaissance Thought* (Cambridge, 1955), p. 62. Cf. Professor Kristeller's *The Philosophy of Marsilio Ficino* (New York, 1943), esp. pp. 42-43, 114-15 and ch. XV. See also Professor Felix Gilbert, "On Machiavelli's Idea of *Virtu,*" *Renaissance News,* IV (1951), 43-4.

18. *Letters to Severall Persons of Honor,* p. 101.

19. (New Haven, 1954), Appendix 2.

20. *The Breaking of the Circle,* pp. 73-88.

21. *All's Well That Ends Well,* II. iii. 146-47.

MURRAY, "What Was the Soul of the Apple?"

1. *Works,* ed. Masson (London, 1897), x. 100: 'Massy diamonds compose the very

substance of his *Metempsychosis,* thoughts and descriptions which have the fervent and gloomy sublimity of Ezekiel or Aeschylus.'

2. H. J. C. Grierson, *Donne's Poems* (Oxford, 1912), ii. 218 ff.

3. Philo Judaeus, *c.* 20 B.C.-post A.D. 40, Alexandrian philosopher and chief exponent of Hellenistic Judaism. The translation I have used in this article is that of the Loeb Classical Library, and the commentary to which I am chiefly indebted is that of H. A. Wolfson (Cambridge, Mass., 1948).

4. Philo is a well-established part of the Christian tradition, having influenced Origen, and St. Jerome, whose *Onomasticon* even appears in the same volume as *Quaestiones in Genesim,* and *Liber Antiquitatum* (of ps.-Philo), to which I refer below. *Onomasticon* concerns itself with the allegorical interpretation of Hebrew names, e.g. *Cain* is 'possession'.

5. E. Gosse, *Life and Letters of John Donne* (London, 1899), i. 177.

6. Philo was a fashionable interest in Britain as well as on the Continent. James VI possessed an edition, or rather a French translation; see J. Craigie, *Poems of James VI of Scotland* (Edinburgh, 1955), p. xix.

7. See Grierson, ii. pp. xviii ff., for the main discussion of this poem.

8. M. M. Mahood, *Poetry and Humanism* (London, 1950), p. 106.

9. Jonson, *Works,* ed. Herford and Simpson, i. (Oxford, 1925), 136.

10. Gosse, i. 138.

11. Grierson, ii, p. xx.

12. Ps.-Philo, *Philonis Iudaei Antiquitatum Biblicarum Liber,* ed. Budaeus (1527), p. 1: 'Initio mundi Adam genuit tres filios et unam filiam, *Cain, Noaba, Abel,* et *Seth*: et vixit Adam, postquam genuit Seth, annos DCC, et genuit filios duodecim et filias octo: et haec sunt nomina virorum, Aeliliseel, Suris, Aelamiel, Brabal, Naat, Harama, Zasam, Maathal, et Anath: et hae filiae eius, Phua, Iectas, Arebica, *Siphatecia,* Sabaasin'; and below: 'Cain autem habitavit in terra tremens secundum quod constituit ei Deus, postquam interfecit fratrem suum: et nomen mulieris eius *Themech....*'

If we accept Moaba, in Donne's poem, as a slight error for Noaba, six out of the seven names used are to be found in this short passage of ps.-Philo, and the name Siphatecia is given in its correct order, as that of Adam's fifth daughter. This is a high degree of correspondence for lists of this kind, and is, I think, conclusive proof that Donne had as his source notes or reasonably accurate recollections of the *Liber Antiquitatum,* the ascription of which in his day was acceptable enough.

Examination of the Pseudepigrapha of the Old Testament has shown no forms like these except Cain, Abel, and Seth. Grierson (ii. 224) misses the name Themech in his note. L. Ginzberg, *The Legends of the Jews* (Philadelphia, 1938, 1946-7), v. 145, n. 42, remarks: 'The fictitious names frequently found in this pseudepigraphic work and in ps.-Philo (particularly the names of the women of ancient times) are entirely unknown in the old rabbinic literature, and are only found in the writings of the Arabic period, when the Jews became more familiar with the Christian and Mohammedan pseudepigraphic writings.' 'Adam's oldest daughter, whose name has been transmitted in no less than twenty-two forms. . . .' In such circumstances the degree of correspondence between ps.-Philo and the poem is sufficient to direct our attention to the Philonic opus as a whole, from which I suppose Donne to have derived the concept of the soul of the apple.

13. *Works,* i. 121. The same idea is also found in a passage in *Quaestiones in Genesim,* and is borrowed by an author of whom Donne was very fond, 'the divine Francis George'. The expression 'sens moral' is used as a translation of Philo's term. (See *L'Harmonie du Monde, . . . Premièrement composé en Latin par Francois Georges*

Vénitien, et depuis traduict et illustré par Guy Le Fèvre de la Boderie (Paris, 1579), p. 583.)

14. *Works,* iii. 235. The last sentence describes the type-episode of *Metempsychosis.*

15. Wolfson, *Philo,* i. 99.

16. E. Panofsky, *Albrecht Dürer* (London, 1948), ii. 234 and fig. 179. 'Adam holds the cross because the tree which was to furnish its wood had grown from a sapling of the Tree of Life (or, according to another, less original tradition, the Tree of Knowledge) planted on Adam's grave by Seth.' The iconography of Bosch represents another arrangement of these elements, closer to the imagery of the poem. I do not suggest any connexion among the three, except that of using common material.

17. J. Combe, *Hieronymus Bosch* (Paris, 1946), p. 68. The fruit in this picture, or something very like it, appears in an engraving of Dürer, *The Four Witches* (Panofsky, ii. fig. 97), about the iconography of which there has been much dispute. The similarity with Bosch may be held to settle the matter.

18. W. Fränger, *The Millenium of Hieronymus Bosch* (London, 1952), *passim.* I do not regard Fränger's case for the *Millenium* as an Adamite 'altar-piece' as proved beyond doubt, but the Eden associations are obvious enough.

19. Donne, *The Divine Poems* (Oxford, 1952), p. 135.

20. See Fränger, p. 8; Combe, p. 18 and p. 57, n. 42.

21. Wolfson, i. 431-2. The whole discussion of free will in Philo, and in Plato, is relevant to the *Metempsychosis.*

22. Gosse, i. 197. The various Biblical references to the mandrake are also relevant. It is interesting that, about this time, the American mandrake was added to the drugs used in childbirth.

23. Cf. *An Epithalamion on the Lady Elizabeth,* stanza 1.

24. The swan is extensively used in Bosch, occurring in the form of swan-shaped boats, floating in air, and carrying men in armour. As a royal bird, it is perhaps a symbol of power.

25. Donne's position as Egerton's secretary placed him so close to the heart of affairs that he must have had opportunities of knowledge, and occasions of reflection about the Essex revolt. The connexion with the *Metempsychosis,* if there is one, seems to me to be entirely indirect and general, none the less.

THE POETRY OF JOHN DONNE:
A SELECTIVE BIBLIOGRAPHY OF MODERN CRITICISM

For a fully annotated and comprehensive bibliography of modern criticism of Donne's poetry and prose, the reader is advised to consult John R. Roberts, *John Donne: An Annotated Bibliography of Modern Criticism, 1912-1967* (Columbia: University of Missouri Press, 1973), which contains 1280 items. More recent studies are listed in the annual bibliography of the Modern Language Association (*PMLA*). The major editions of Donne's poetry (Grierson, Gardner, Milgate, Shawcross, etc.) contain important introductions, commentary, and notes.

COLLECTIONS OF MODERN CRITICISM

Bradbury, Malcolm and David Palmer, eds. *Metaphysical Poetry*. Stratford-Upon-Avon Studies, 11. New York: St. Martin's Press, 1970.

Clements, A. L., ed. *John Donne's Poetry: Authoritative Texts, Criticism.* Norton Critical Editions. New York: W. W. Norton & Co., 1966.

Fiore, Peter A., ed. *Just So Much Honor: Essays Commemorating the Four-Hundredth Anniversary of the Birth of John Donne.* University Park and London: Pennsylvania State University Press, 1972.

Gardner, Helen, ed. *John Donne: A Collection of Critical Essays.* A Spectrum Book: Twentieth Century Views, S-TC-19. Englewood Cliffs, N.J.: Prentice-Hall, Inc., 1962.

Keast, William, ed. *Seventeenth Century English Poetry: Modern Essays on Criticism.* A Galaxy Book, 89. New York: Oxford University Press, 1962. Rev. ed., 1971.

Kermode, Frank, ed. *Discussions of John Donne.* Discussion of Literature. Boston: D. C. Heath & Co., 1962.

Kermode, Frank, ed. *The Metaphysical Poets: Key Essays on Metaphysical Poetry and the Major Metaphysical Poets.* With an introduction. Greenwich, Conn.: Fawcett, 1969.

Pepperdone, Margaret, ed. *That Subtile Wreath: Lectures Presented at the Quartercentenary Celebration of the Birth of John Donne.* Agnes Scott College, 1973.

Smith, A. J., ed. *John Donne: Essays in Celebration.* London: Methuen & Co. Ltd., 1972.

Spencer, Theodore, ed. *A Garland for John Donne, 1631-1931.* Cambridge: Harvard University Press; London: Humphrey Milford, Oxford University Press, 1931. Rpt.: Gloucester, Mass.: Peter Smith, 1958.

CRITICAL STUDIES

Alvarez, A. *The School of Donne.* London: Chatto and Windus Ltd., 1961.

Andreasen, N.J.C. *John Donne: Conservative Revolutionary.* Princeton: Princeton University Press, 1967.

Bald, R. C. *John Donne: A Life.* Ed. Wesley Milgate. London: Oxford University Press, 1970.

Bennett, Joan. *Four Metaphysical Poets: Donne, Herbert, Vaughan, Crashaw.* Cambridge: University Press, 1934. 3rd ed. with a new chapter on Marvell and title change to *Five Metaphysical Poets*, 1964.

Bennett, Joan. "The Love Poetry of John Donne: A Reply to Mr. C. S. Lewis," in *Seventeenth Century Studies Presented to Sir Herbert Grierson,* pp. 85-104. Oxford, 1938. Rpt.: Keast (1962) and Clements (1966).

Bethell, S. L. "Gracián Tesauro and the Nature of Metaphysical Wit," *Northern Miscellany of Literary Criticism,* 1 (1953), 19-40.

Brooks, Cleanth. "The Language of Paradox," in *The Well Wrought Urn: Studies in the Structure of Poetry,* pp. 3-20. New York: Reynall & Hitchcock, 1947. Rpt.: Gardner (1962) and Kermode (1962).

Bush, Douglas. *English Literature in the Earlier Seventeenth Century, 1600-1660.* Oxford: The Clarendon Press, 1945. Rev. ed., 1962.

Coffin, Charles Monroe. *John Donne and the New Philosophy.* Morningside Heights, N.Y.: Columbia University Press, 1937. Rpt.: 1958.

Denonain, Jean-Jacques. *Thèmes et formes de la poésie "métaphysique": Étude d'un aspect de la littérature Anglaise au dix-septième siècle.* Publications de la Faculté des Lettres d'Alger, 18. Paris: Presses Universitaires de France, 1956.

Duncan, Joseph E. *The Revival of Metaphysical Poetry: the History of a Style, 1800 to the Present.* Minneapolis: University of Minnesota Press, 1959.

Eliot, T. S. "The Metaphysical Poets," *TLS,* 20 October 1921, pp. 669-70. Rpt.: *Selected Essays, 1917-1932,* 1932.

Ellrodt, Robert. *L'Inspiration personnelle et l'esprit du temps chez les poètes métaphysique anglais.* Paris: Jose Corti. 2 vols. in 3, 1960.

Empson, William. *Seven Types of Ambiguity.* London: Chatto & Windus Ltd., 1930. Rpt. in part: Gardner (1962).

Esch, Arno. *Englische Religiöse Lyrik des 17. Jahrhunderts: Studien zu Donne, Herbert, Crashaw, Vaughan.* Tübingen: Max Niemeyer, 1955.

Freeman, Rosemary. *English Emblem Books.* London: Chatto & Windus Ltd., 1948.

Gransden, K. W. *John Donne.* Men and Books Series. London: Longmans, Green and Co., Ltd., 1954.

Grant, Patrick. *The Transformations of Sin: Studies in Donne, Herbert, Vaughan, and Traherne.* Amherst: University of Massachusetts Press, 1974.

Guss, Donald L. *John Donne, Petrarchist: Italianate Conceits and Love Theory in The Songs and Sonets.* Detroit: Wayne State University Press, 1966.

Hughes, Richard E. *The Progress of the Soul: The Interior Career of John Donne.* New York: Morrow, 1969.

Hunt, Clay. *Donne's Poetry: Essays in Literary Analysis.* New Haven: Yale University Press; London: Geoffrey Cumberlege, Oxford University Press, 1954. Rpt. Hamden, Conn.: Archon Books, 1969.

Hunter, Jim. *The Metaphysical Poets.* Literature in Perspective. London: Evans Brothers Limited, 1965.

Kermode, Frank. *John Donne.* Writers and Their Works, No. 86. London: Longmans, Green and Co., Ltd., 1957.

Leavis, F. R. "The Line of Wit," in *Revaluations: Tradition & Development in English Poetry,* pp. 10-41. London: Chatto & Windus, Ltd., 1936.

Legouis, Pierre. *Donne the Craftsman: An Essay upon the Structure of the Songs and Sonnets.* Paris: Henri Didier; London: Humphrey Milford and Oxford University Press, 1928. Rpt.: Russell and Russell, 1962.

Leishman, J. B. *The Monarch of Wit: An Analytical and Comparative Study of the Poetry of John Donne.* London: Hutchinson University Library, 1951.

Lewalski, Barbara K. *Donne's Anniversaries and the Poetry of Praise: The Creation of a Symbolic Mode.* Princeton: Princeton University Press, 1973.

Lewis, C. S. "Donne and Love Poetry in the Seventeenth Century," in *Seventeenth-Century Studies Presented to Sir Herbert Grierson,* pp. 64-68. Oxford, 1938. Rpt.: Keast (1962) and Clements (1966).

Louthan, Doniphan. *The Poetry of John Donne: A Study in Explication.* New York: Bookman Associates, 1951.

Mahood, M. M. *Poetry and Humanism.* New Haven: Yale University Press, 1950. Rpt.: Port Washington, N.Y.: Kennikat Press, 1967.

Martz, Louis L. *The Poetry of Meditation: A Study in English Religious Literature of the Seventeenth Century.* Yale Studies in English, 125. New Haven: Yale University Press; London: Oxford University Press, 1954. Rev. ed.: 1962.

Martz, Louis L. *The Wit of Love: Donne, Carew, Crashaw, Marvell.* Ward Phillips Lects. in Eng. Lang. and Lit., 3. Notre Dame, Indiana: University of Notre Dame Press, 1969.

Mazzeo, J. A. "A Critique of Some Modern Theories of Metaphysical Poetry," *MP,* 50 (1952), 88-96. Rpt.: Keast (1962) and Kermode (1962).

Mazzeo, J. A. "Notes on John Donne's Alchemical Imagery," *Isis,* 48 (1957), 103-23. Rpt.: *Renaissance and Seventeenth-Century Studies* (1964).

Miner, Earl. *The Metaphysical Mode from Donne to Cowley.* Princeton: Princeton University Press, 1969.

Miner, Earl, ed. *Seventeenth Century Imagery: Essays on Uses of Figurative Language from Donne to Farquhar.* Berkeley and Los Angeles: University of California Press, 1971.

Nicolson, Marjorie Hope. *The Breaking of the Circle: Studies in the Effects of the "New Science" upon Seventeenth Century Poetry.* Evanston: Northwestern University Press, 1950.

Peterson, Douglas L. *The English Lyric from Wyatt to Donne: A History of the Plain and Eloquent Styles.* Princeton: Princeton University Press, 1967.

Praz, Mario. *John Donne.* Torino: S.A.I.E., 1958.

Rugoff, Milton Allan. *Donne's Imagery: A Study in Creative Sources.* New York: Corporate, 1939.

Sanders, Wilbur. *John Donne's Poetry.* London: Cambridge University Press, 1971.

Sharp, R. L. *From Donne to Dryden: The Revolt Against Metaphysical Poetry.* Chapel Hill: University of North Carolina Press, 1940.

Smith, A. J. *John Donne: the Songs and Sonets.* Studies in English Literature, No. 17. London: Edward Arnold; Great Neck, N.Y.: Barron's Educational Series, Inc., 1965.

Smith, A. J. "The Metaphysic of Love," *RES*, n.s. 9 (1958), 362-75. Rpt.: Kermode (1962).

Smith, A. J. "New Bearings in Donne: 'Aire and Angels'," *English*, 13 (1960), 49-53. Rpt.: Gardner (1962).

Smith, James. "On Metaphysical Poetry," *Scrutiny*, 2 (1933), 222-39. Rpt.: *Determinations*, ed. F. R. Leavis (1934).

Stein, Arnold. *John Donne's Lyrics: The Eloquence of Action.* Minneapolis: University of Minnesota Press, 1962.

Summers, Joseph H. *The Heirs of Donne and Jonson.* New York and London: Oxford University Press, 1970.

Tuve, Rosemond. *Elizabethan and Metaphysical Imagery: Renaissance Poetic and Twentieth-Century Critics.* Chicago: University of Chicago Press, 1947. Rpt.: 1961.

Wallerstein, Ruth. *Studies in Seventeenth-Century Poetic.* Madison: University of Wisconsin Press, 1950.

White, Helen C. *The Metaphysical Poets: A Study in Religious Experience.* New York: The Macmillan Co., 1936. Rpt.: Collier Books, 1962.

Williamson, George. *The Donne Tradition: A Study in English Poetry from Donne to the Death of Cowley.* Cambridge, Mass.: Harvard University Press; Oxford: University Press, 1930.

Williamson, George. *The Proper Wit of Poetry.* Chicago: University of Chicago Press; London: Faber and Faber, Ltd.; Toronto: University of Toronto Press, 1961.

Williamson, George. *Seventeenth Century Contexts.* London: Faber and Faber Ltd.; Chicago: University of Chicago Press, 1960.

Williamson, George. *Six Metaphysical Poets: A Reader's Guide.* New York: Farrar, Straus and Giroux, 1967.